SERIOUS PIG

ALSO BY JOHN THORNE

Outlaw Cook (1992)
Simple Cooking (1987)

SERIOUS PIG

AN AMERICAN COOK IN SEARCH OF HIS ROOTS

JOHN THORNE

with

MATT LEWIS THORNE

North Point Press
Farrar, Straus and Giroux
New York

Portions of this book have appeared, most in different form, in *Wigwag Magazine, Down East Magazine, The Maine Times, Chili Pepper Magazine*, the anthology of Maine writing, *The Portable Moose*, and in the authors' *Simple Cooking* food letters.

LIBRARY OF CONGRESS CATALOGING-IN-PUBLICATION DATA
Thorne, John.
    Serious pig : an American cook in search of his roots / John Thorne, with Matt Lewis Thorne.
    p.   cm.
    Includes bibliographical references and index.
    1. Cookery, American.   I. Thorne, Matt Lewis.   II. Title.
TX715.T48154   1996   641.5973—dc20   96-5564   CIP

We wish to express our gratitude to the following individuals for their generous permission to quote from letters they sent to us (or to other people) or to reprint essays they wrote for *Simple Cooking*: John H. Thorne, Sr., Dorothy Bangs, Bill (and Charmane) Bridges, Maida Heatter, Jeri Jarnagan, Augustus M. Kelley, Tim McTague, Hubert A. Templeton, and Ed Ward.

We also want to extend special thanks to Edward Behr, Bob Bowen, Karen Hess, Jim and Megan Gerritsen, Jeanne Lesem, John Logan, Doug and Patti Qua, Arnold and Bonnie Pearlman, and Jerry Soucy for their advice and support.

We have made a concerted effort to obtain permission to quote from copyrighted works. Grateful acknowledgment is made to the following:

Jim Harrison. Excerpts from *Just Before Dark*, by Jim Harrison. Copyright © 1991 by Jim Harrison. Reprinted by permission.

W. W. Norton & Company, Inc. Excerpt from *Cache Lake Country*, by John J. Rowlands. Copyright © 1947 by W. W. Norton & Company, Inc. Reprinted by permission.

Random House, Inc. Excerpt from *The New Orleans City Guide*, by The Federal Writers Project. Copyright © 1938 by the Mayor of New Orleans. Reprinted by permission.

Houghton Mifflin Company. Excerpt from *The Member of the Wedding*. Copyright © 1946 by Carson McCullers, © renewed 1974 by Floria V. Lasky. Reprinted by permission of Houghton Mifflin Co. All rights reserved.

Carlos Ashley, Jr., Esq. Excerpt from *That Spotted Sow and Other Texas Hill Country Ballads*, by Carlos Ashley, Sr. Copyright © 1975 by Carlos Ashley, Sr. Reprinted by permission.

Miriam Ungerer. Excerpt from *Good Cheap Food*, by Miriam Ungerer. Copyright © 1996 by Miriam Ungerer. Published by Ecco Press in 1996. Reprinted by permission.

Patrick McGrath. Excerpt from *The Grotesque*, by Patrick McGrath. Copyright © 1989 by Patrick McGrath. Reprinted by permission of Donadio and Ashworth, Inc.

Harvard University Press. Excerpt from *The Dictionary of American Regional English*, Vol. 1, edited by Frederic G. Cassidy, Cambridge, Mass.: Harvard University Press, copyright © 1985 by the President and Fellows of Harvard College. Reprinted by permission.

Elmore Leonard. Excerpt from *Swag*, by Elmore Leonard. Copyright © 1976 by Elmore Leonard. Used by permission of Dell Books, a division of Bantam Doubleday Dell Publishing Group.

Joan Nathan. Excerpt from *An American Folklife Cookbook*, by Joan Nathan. Copyright © 1984 by Joan Nathan Gerson. Reprinted by permission.

Allen Ginsberg. Seven lines from "A Supermarket in California" from *Collected Poems 1947–1980*. Copyright © 1955 by Allen Ginsberg. Copyright renewed. Reprinted by permission of HarperCollins Publishers, Inc.

Oxford University Press. Excerpt from *The Land of the Crooked Tree*, by U. P. Hedrick. Copyright © 1948 by Oxford University Press. Reprinted by permission.

For brother Peter,
longtime co-conspirator

Author's Note

The "I" that speaks from these pages is mine in every chapter of this book, except in those letters where the contributor is explicitly named —my father, Bill Bridges, Tim McTague—and in the one chapter, "Beyond Pie: Blueberry Bread-and-Butter Pudding," where it is Matt's. Even so, Matt has considered every word of every draft, reacting, suggesting, amending, and, hence, *reshaping*, what appears herein. As I noted in our first collaboration, *Outlaw Cook*, this means that the subjective self who speaks out of these pages is a larger, braver, much more interesting person than that which belongs to me alone.

Also, as in my two previous books, *Serious Pig* assembles a selection of essays written over the past several years, most of them originally published in our food letter, *Simple Cooking*. Those who read this book with pleasure might also be interested in subscribing to it. If so, we'd be delighted to send you the relevant information. Either write to us in care of North Point Press, 19 Union Square West, New York, NY 10003, or drop by the *Simple Cooking* home page on the World Wide Web at http://home.earthlink.net/~outlawcook/index.html.

CONTENTS

LIST OF RECIPES

SERIOUS PIG

HERE

The cottage—for that, despite its lack of quaintness, is what it is—lies tucked into the side of a hill, just below the road into town and above a small cove, where the water glistens through a stand of trees. The walls have been insulated, a modern bathroom has been installed, as has electric heat to help out the woodstove when winter pulls its worst. Still, without a doubt, it is a summer place.

You know this immediately. It has the air of vulnerability always present in the sort of Maine house that is too airy, too full of light to have been built for living in all year round. There are other hints, too, especially in the motley mix of splurge and meanness that is the one feature common to almost any summer house: the neatly painted wood floors and the real pine paneling on the one hand; on the other, salvaged from older houses, the conspicuously mismatched doors and window frames.

These have their charm. Not so the kitchen, which sits in an addition tacked onto the back of the house by a later owner when the cottage was remade into a year-round rental property. This room has its amenities—lots of space, good light, plenty of counters, a decent sink. Against these must be weighed walls covered by fiberboard embossed in fake pine, a dropped ceiling of greasy Styrofoam, cabinets crudely hammered out of cheap plywood and shellacked to a repellent gloss.

The floor is covered with a casually laid roll of linoleum that has begun to split in long, curling cracks where the addition meets the house, for that part of the room rises when the ground freezes and comes down when it thaws. The refrigerator, turned as low as the knob will go, still ices up lettuce in the vegetable bin. Two of the burners on the electric range will barely work—the other two, as with most electric ranges, work only too well.

Worst of all, this is a real Maine kitchen. The slapdash standards of construction actually reinforce its just-us-folks sense of coziness that is the vernacular Maine counterbalance to winter . . . and to cold. That was what flashed into my mind the moment I first stepped inside. I hardly noticed the fake paneling, the torn linoleum, the crummy ceiling. Instead, I had a sudden vision of the previous occupant—an Israeli boat designer, as it happened—pulling open the battered aluminum storm door (a plywood square already replaced the lower wind-shattered pane of glass) on a bitter January night, stamping his feet and blowing on his fingers as he tugged it shut against the ice-edged darkness pushing in behind. A shiver ran up my spine.

I had come back to Maine to live in a summer cottage, because for me a Maine summer cottage was home. I had chosen Castine because it was almost an island, on the tip of a peninsula, out of the relentless up-and-down traffic of the highways that now sunder most Maine sea-coast towns. At once patrician, historic, and picturesque, it was hardly free of summer folk—they came in droves. The difference was that most of them arrived by yacht. There were no motels on the outskirts of Castine, no fast-food places at its center. As full of traffic as it might be on a summer Sunday, you could walk the streets at nightfall from one dim streetlight to the next in total quiet, smelling the green sweat of the trees and watching the night float through the shoals of stars.

Sentimental? Well, right then I wanted to roll in sentimental. The first night I slept there I awoke at some early hour and heard an owl softly hooting as it flew by outside. The next morning I found roses blossoming in hedges all over town and wild swamp iris blooming in roadside gutters. I remember how purely happy I was those first few weeks, how often I kept thinking, Why have I waited so long?

I had first thought about what coming home might mean ten years before, when I moved into the upstairs apartment in my grandparents' house. I had come to keep an eye on my grandfather—my grandmother had died and he himself was failing—but it gave me the opportunity to return to the very place my mother brought me back to after I was born, to wait for my father to come back from the Second World War.

Instead, as it turned out, he made the army his career, and we went to *him*. I was four when my mother, my new baby brother, and I took the train to Texas. From there we went on to many other houses in many other places. Some of these I remember better than others, but not one of them gave me a lasting sense of home.

Consequently, just as children forced to grow up with strangers learn to read adults with preternatural care, so have I come to read houses. Childhood memories, when summoned, arrive in the form of snapshots, a catalogue of unconnected favorite parts: the sharp twist of a staircase, the glint of a bath knob, the bright compactness of a butler's pantry, the dim, moonface glow of a radio dial on a bedside table.

There were two exceptions. One was my grandparents' house: a two-storied, dark-green shingled monster with a wide front porch, a basement made of granite blocks, an enormous, empty attic, and a second floor that my grandparents had turned into two one-bedroom apartments, which, when family wasn't staying in one or the other, they rented out.

Thirty years later, the one my mother and I had lived in together was nearly unchanged, right down to the electrical fixtures. The walls were papered with the same bland flowery chintz; the woodwork was stained the same dark oak; the same double sink—the deep side for hand washing clothes—waited in the kitchen . . . as did the same secondhand Magic Chef stove that my mother, pregnant with me, had helped my grandfather carry up the stairs.

I had left when I was four, but flashes of memory came back to me as I settled in at thirty-five. Looking out the same bedroom window at the soft summer evening light on the roofs across the street, I become again the restless three-year-old who was sent to bed with the day still bright outside.

Even so, I remain astonished at the smallness of the place; it had been so large before. This sense of seeing everything through a reversed telescope never entirely went away, and sometimes I would lie down on the floor, just to make it fall back in place.

If I had a home at all, I thought, this was it. Instead, I had only returned for one last visit. It was my grandparents' house, not mine—as I would discover during the year of caretaking after my grandfather died, which he did just four years after I moved in. Soon after the estate was settled and the house sold, I came to Maine.

As some readers will already know, since, without my intending (or, until now, even noticing) this, it is the subject of the first chapter of each one of my three books—my grandparents had also owned a house there, a summer cottage, built at the edge of a cliff on an island in Casco Bay. When I was growing up, more summers than not, my father drove us—my mother, two brothers, a sister, and me—from wherever in the country we then lived to spend the summer there.

It was the one place in the world that I loved purely—by which I mean that it seemed to me so perfect that I craved it in all its parts. It haunts my memory the way certain childhood books do—the ones from which any random phrase can summon from deep memory a luminous wash that combines the sound of the parent's reading voice with the sight, feel, even smell of the actual page. This cottage is the place, were that possible, I would want to claim as home.

Except I can't. It's gone. When my grandfather died it went to an uncle, who renovated it out of recognition . . . or, rather, into something very much like the cottage I was now renting in Castine. Although even to write this fills me with bitter sadness, I don't blame my uncle (in any case, he is now also dead). He loved the cottage; his way of expressing that love was to fix it up. He rewired it, insulated it, installed a real bathroom, walled in the screened porch . . . and, somewhere along the line, he killed it. The last time I was there, it felt, it looked, like any other house.

A summer cottage, by definition, is only marginally a house and can never be a home; it is too long left empty for that. A proper home is drenched with the presence of the people who live in it even when they are away; enter it then and you feel an intruder, a violator of a private world. Go into a summer place left vacant for the winter and it leaps to welcome you with the impartial affection of a homeless dog. Pet me, it says, feed me; I'm yours.

Even the best-kept summer house has this hunger for affection, this hint of bone against the skin. A true summer cottage must be left empty three seasons of the year if it is to remain permeable to the one season we want to let inside. In summer, in cottage as in clothing, the thinner the membrane we drape around us, the greater the pleasure in inhabiting it. We want the lawn to roll right up to the front door stoop, the fresh air to pour in through wide-open windows, the rain to be just that close as it slides past us off the roof.

A home radiates a comforting certainty not only because of its solidity but because it is defined by a series of near-inalterable rules, which, in a summer house, are in constant violation. My mother also called the place "the camp," which gets it right. We went there to camp out, no matter the walls, roof, doors, and windows. Not only did outside and inside get pleasantly confused, so did public and private, adult and child—all familiar orderings rendered magically contingent. Each and every summer day, it seems—especially to a child—the world has the chance of being made over fresh and new.

In our cottage we went to bed, not to a bedroom, but out on the front porch, to crawl under thick quilts and listen to the waves rustle, to the wind toss through the trees. On stormy nights, we climbed up the narrow stair ladder by the fireplace to the attic and the old horsehair mattress laid out on its floor. There, we breathed mysteriously ancient air and shone our flashlights on the things that pushed out from the shadows: old boots, chamber pots, coffee cans full of nails, piles of gramophone records. The rain pattered on the shingles over our heads and ran splashing into the rain barrels set into the wall beside us. The next day, we washed our faces with it out of a basin in the side yard, drying ourselves with the morning sun.

Here was a world a child could understand: the rain water collected in a barrel; the drinking water was hauled up in a bucket from a well. When we were cold we made a fire in the fireplace, and for a long time, when it was dark, we lit candles and kerosene lanterns . . . and carried one with us to the outhouse. We brought big chunks of ice for the icebox up from the dock in a wheelbarrow. We dug clams and picked berries and roasted hot dogs on sticks over a fire at the shore.

This was a life, it goes without saying, that was far from self-sufficiency—but one very close to self-revelation. Here was a world made tangible to the senses, one whose flesh seemed as fragile as our own. It is a small thing, maybe, to lie snug and safe, listening to the cold wet night pawing at the wall beside your ear. An experience complexly sensuous and sad, it gives substance to our understanding of safety, warmth, and comfort. Today, only the summer cottage has walls thin enough for the outside to reach us at all.

This is why I came back as a young man to spend my summers on the island: to lie in bed and listen to rain fall on the roof. I came to have fires in the fireplace and to cook for myself in the tiny camp kitchen. Shake the home-ec associations out of "homemaking" and it almost describes my apparently paradoxical mission: to make a home in a house that could never really be one.

This, though, was the point. Just as some people feel most at home in a sailboat cabin or a hunting shack, what I needed was a house hungry for company—a hunger physically embodied in the fireplace. Built by my grandfather when my mother and her brothers were children out of enormous stones that they dragged up from the beach, it was a hulking monster that sat in the center of the cottage and dominated all its rooms.

Maine island summers are full of rainy days and chilly evenings, of time spent sitting, reading, talking, eating, playing cards or board games—all of it done in front of the fire. A fireplace generates a sense of companionship not only because it casts off heat but because it is a presence in the room. You feed a fire, you clean up after it, and always, you keep an eye on it. In an ordinary house, "inside" is defined by absence: a pervasive, padded silence, itself drowned out by the television or the CD player's unctuous purr. Reality is neutered, like an unsexed, declawed pet. In a house warmed by fire, "inside" has a living edge. It is not entirely subservient to you.

Fire making was also the end of a whole series of related activities which connected me to this place: finding driftwood, rowing it home, cutting it into lengths, splitting it into logs, and stacking them in the woodbox under the stairs. All in all, I spent more time feeding the house than I ever spent feeding myself, because feeding it was what excited and pleased me. Like a child giving a carrot to a horse, I adored being, for that moment, the sole conduit of its needs—not a visitor or an owner, but a friend.

So I expected, when I came back to Maine to live, to reacquaint myself with wood. What I hadn't expected was to be thrown back into a Maine kitchen. When we think about the particulars that define "place," we usually see this in terms of bonuses: Maine equals lobsters, blueberries, fiddleheads, and soft-shell clams. But just as the best wines can come from vines planted in hardscrabble hillside plots, so can the limits of a particular kitchen, the cook's own microclimate, do more to shape our cooking than any other thing. And Maine, like nowhere else, is a place of hardscrabble kitchens.

The camp cottage kitchen was one kind, the one in Castine another. The camp kitchen was dark, dank, and cramped. Eight feet square, it was illuminated by a solitary wall fixture set over the stove. Any cooking task away from the frying pan was done in shadow. The single tap spilled a weak flow of rainwater that always had to be rationed and could never be drunk, as its faint and slightly sweet smell of sun-baked algae warned. A bucket of well water sat, a dipper by its side, on a special shelf beside the door. The stove's burners spluttered weakly and coated the pots with soot.

I haven't been there for a decade and I can still smell the thin, sharp stink of the propane gas and the sour, weedy smell of damp plywood; feel the pitted, black-encrusted bottoms of the huge aluminum frying pans; hear the acidulous hiss of water droplets vaporizing on the giant kettle as it heated the dishwater. I can see the pig-shaped wooden cutting board; the huge green tin breadbox holding a half-empty, wax-paper packet of tired saltines; the kitchen shelf with its frilly-edged shelf paper and the row of soup cans on whose tops my mother had carefully written the year of purchase, since after one winter they all began to look the same.

Every year, the morning after my arrival, the pancakes would stick to the frying pan. The drip coffeepot refused to drip. The toast would burn on the toasting rack that fitted over a burner on the stove, and I would burn my fingers trying to get it off. This resistance to casual use brought back, bit by bit, forgotten skills. As I relearned the knack of washing dishes in a small basin of water, of striking kitchen matches against damp sandpaper, of baking my own bread in the willful oven, a self emerged from hibernation that I otherwise never experienced— one that knew its way around.

The Castine kitchen seemed much more ordinary, but that was because I hadn't learned to read it yet. The appliances were extra-large: the freezer section of the refrigerator took up one whole side; the stove had two ovens, one large, one small. The refrigerator spoke of distance—it was a long drive to the nearest supermarket, and farther still to the nearest good one.

What the stove spoke of, however, was weather. It would be months before I discovered this, but that Castine place was a house besieged by cold. Not only was it a cottage, but it was nestled low into the side of a wooded hill, where the winter sun could barely touch it. The kitchen, stuck to the far end of the house, had three outside walls. The winter cold pushed right through them. No amount of heat would drive it out; the best I could hope for, I learned, was to pin it to the floor. When I sat at the kitchen table, I could reach down and touch it, a foot-deep layer of frigid air gnawing quietly at my feet.

The Castine cottage had a tiny Irish Waterford woodstove in the living room. I took this to be the equivalent of a fireplace. I imagined myself lolling in its toasty warmth on winter mornings, frying up buckwheat pancakes and brewing coffee on its cooking plate. However, as the sole source of winter heat, the stove was at once too small to warm the house and far too hot to sit by. During the day, I seemed to be anywhere but in that room.

And how it ate up wood. I brought it in daily from the enormous, ice-locked woodpile, armloads full, and stacked it on the floor to thaw. All through the dead of winter I fed the stove, as if it were a baby, every two hours, day and night. I put my bed beside it to stay warm and to make less onerous the nighttime feedings: midnight, two, four, six, and eight.

Wood: the whole place had a permanent smoky tang. Little wonder that, the summer after, I was inspired to dig my parents' meat smoker from their barn and take it home. I set it up on the cottage deck and, for the first time in my life, began to turn out serious barbecue. A further permutation would be the building of (and subsequent struggle to master) an outdoor wood-fired bread oven.

But I lived all winter in that summer cottage in front of the double-barreled electric stove. Each morning, first thing, I used the small oven to roast a fresh batch of coffee beans; when I came back from the walk into town, I made a batch of sausage and biscuits in it to eat while I was going through the mail. The small oven was also the perfect place for baking beans, the larger one for making a skillet of griddle corn-bread. There was never such a situation for baking in my life and never such persuasive motivation. By the next summer I was turning out fresh raspberry cake and green pea pie.

Even as a teenager, I could feel the summer cottage of my youth slowly but steadily sloughing off its past as a snake does its skin. Electricity came up the road; electric lights and the refrigerator followed soon after. As islanders phased out their iceboxes, the ice boat stopped coming. With electricity, kerosene lamps became at once an affectation and a hazard. And few Maine towns now permit outhouses in any but the most temporarily inhabited hunting camps; the island cottage now has indoor plumbing.

All this is fine. It isn't that I can't bear how things change—it's that I can't bear to be the one who does the changing. If, at forty-four, I found myself a year-round tenant in someone else's summer cottage, it was because I'm gun-shy of owning property. For years and years I thought of myself as someone who yearned to own his own place. But when I had the chance to buy the cottage in Castine at the end of my tenure there, I turned it down. Matt and I moved to Steuben instead.

Like everyone else, I cling to the things I own, but I have learned to tremble at the idea of possessing place—to live in a summer cottage is to be constantly reminded of its vulnerability. Every texture, every timbre—the smell of sun-soaked shingles or of coffee percolating up through attic floorboards—reminds us that however often we may be allowed to experience these things, we can also never hope to own them. To try to is to risk losing everything about them that we love.

To buy the cottage would have meant becoming a home owner. It would have meant doing what the owners did the moment I moved out: ripping out the kitchen ceiling, floors, and walls; installing modular cabinetry complete with dishwasher; taking the woodstove out of the living room and putting in forced-air oil heat instead.

The essential difference between the local and the summer person, between the owner and the renter, then, is this: the latter is always conscious of his or her good fortune in being there at all. The local person sees the same things but is distanced from their poignancy; he is as unlikely to surrender to their sheer delight as to lie in bed and marvel at the beauty of his wife. It is there, he is not exactly insensible to it, but affection—if it is expressed at all—is conveyed through the deprecation that possession inevitably brings. *Yeah, yeah, but you should have seen her when.* Or, more dourly: *Yeah, yeah, but you don't have to live with her.*

Our culture doesn't permit our imagination the luxury of perceiving —even appreciating—the fact that houses also have a life. It is a realization possible only for people who have stayed in the same one all their lives, and they experience it subconsciously—that is, as a strong but inarticulate resistance to change.

Those of us who move into such a house find its aura almost impossible to save. The truth is, you can't move into someone else's place; instead, you inherit the mess that is their leavings. These things, everything in you rightly says, *have* to be fixed up. Then one thing leads to another—and there you are. The only alternative is to somehow leave what is not well enough alone.

Doing that is why, I think, each of my Maine kitchens has left its mark on me. They have given my cooking a certain shape that, when I moved on, it would both never assume again . . . and never quite escape. *Vulnerability to place:* what else is "here" about? If you don't change a place into you, it will, after its fashion, change you into it. And you may get the better of the exchange in ways you don't expect.

I moved into the cottage in Castine in June of 1987. Summer went, and for the first time in my life, I stayed. I was so happy about that that I immediately started thinking, once again, *This* must be the place. As I now know, it wasn't. All that the feeling of welcome meant was that this place had remained just enough of a summer cottage to take a stranger in.

But that was all right. A few months later still, when it was me coming out of the cold into that winter kitchen, I started to hear what the room had tried to tell me from the first. *Go throw some logs on the fire and get the coffee started,* it was saying . . . *stay awhile.*

CASTINE, MAINE, JULY–OCTOBER 1987
STEUBEN, MAINE, JUNE 1994

GREEN-PEA PIE

I first came across this pie in Camille Glenn's *Heritage of Southern Cooking,* and I think I would have been drawn to it even without her introductory evocation:

> If I were asked to name the greatest fresh vegetable dish in the whole wide world, it would have to be Fresh Green Pea Pie . . . It has succulence, flavor, freshness, elegance, and charm—and one doesn't meet it every day.

The notion of combining a rich short crust with the clean sweet taste of green peas moved directly from the page to my mouth, in that way that signals—even if you're just idly leafing through a cookbook—the first encounter with a recipe that is going to be hanging around in your kitchen for a while.

Fresh green-pea pie may seem like a strange dish to make itself at home in a Maine kitchen (how truly *Southern* it is, I just don't know— I've never seen it mentioned in any other cookbook). But when I set out to make it, I discovered that my subconscious had been busy adapting the recipe to accommodate—and resolve—two of my culinary preoccupations.

The first of these had been an obsession for several years: how to make a chicken pot pie in which the chicken is actually moist and succulent and the crust not soggy. Green-pea pie offered a solution. Make a pie seasoned with a hint of onion and lots of little bits of crisped chicken fat—what Jewish cooks call *gribenes,* the poultry variant of cracklings—and cook the chicken separately.

This proposition also addressed my second concern, which may not be a central one in your household but certainly was in mine: what to do with those large chunks of chicken fat that you pull out of the bird's cavity before poaching or roasting it. For a long time my answer was to bundle them in plastic wrap and toss them into the freezer, where they had a tendency to accumulate.

Since peas and onions (or, better, shallots) are about the only things worth putting in a chicken pie besides the chicken meat, it's no surprise that they make a terrific pie by themselves. And frozen peas do it best. This is because the baking period is just the time they need to heat up to perfection. If you use fresh peas—which ordinarily I prefer, even if they're old and mealy (as, in supermarkets, they always are)—they have to be precooked before they go into the pie, and so come out of it overcooked. Perhaps fresh baby peas straight from the garden would work . . . but these are too rare a treat to risk finding out.

Green-pea pie made itself so quickly at home because it took a few simple things I already had in my kitchen and did something special to them. If you think a pie of peas is a silly notion, cut a slice and watch the contents swirl out into an alluvial delta of sparkling emerald . . . taste the tender sweetness that melds so softly with those rich flakes of crust and unctuous little bits of chicken fat. From then on, you'll find reasons to make it often, chicken on the side or no. If your freezer isn't full of chicken-fat packs, a pea pie can also be seasoned with salt pork or with butter and a spritz of herb vinegar. However you make it, don't forget that it's a fine meal all by itself.

GREEN-PEA PIE
(SERVES 4 TO 6)

Your favorite pastry for a standard 9-inch 2-crust pie
Cooking oil
¼ cup chicken fat, cubed
3 or 4 shallots, minced
3 cups frozen tiny green peas
1 tablespoon minced tarragon or parsley
Salt and pepper to taste

Remember to prepare the pastry ahead of time so it has a chance to relax in the refrigerator for about half an hour before you roll it out. When it is time to make the pie, preheat the oven to 375°F. While it is heating, roll out the pastry for the pie, setting the bottom crust into the pie pan.

In a hot skillet made slick with a little cooking oil, render the chicken fat, scraping the bits as they crisp into a small bowl. When all the bits have been removed, add the minced shallots and sauté briefly until translucent. Put these in the bowl with the fat bits, along with about a tablespoon of the hot rendered chicken fat. Pour in the 3 cups of *un-*

defrosted peas and mix together well. Sprinkle with the minced herb and the salt and pepper.

Pour this mixture into the pie shell. Brush the edges with a little water and press on the top crust firmly, trimming away any excess dough and crimping the two crusts together with your fingers or a fork. Make slits in the top crust with the tip of a sharp paring knife so that steam can escape. Bake the pie until the crust is golden, about 35 minutes. Let it cool for 5 minutes or so before serving, but do serve it hot.

CASTINE, 1987

Maine Home Fried

1

Crossroad Farm in Jonesport, Maine, is down a dirt road leading off the eastern end of the loop that is state Route 187. The round trip from our house in Steuben is about fifty miles. Matt and I drove it this spring for fresh asparagus; we're back this fall for potatoes. Before it dips into the woods, the track runs past blueberry barrens where, the last time we drove through, hives of bees were stacked, surrounded by an electric fence to keep out honey-hungry bears. Now the bees are gone, the blueberries picked, and the plants a brilliant swathe of scarlet beneath the cool, faded blue of the October sky.

Briefly, the road gravel turns into rocks that seem the size of grapefruits. When we hit this stretch on our first visit, we wondered if Crossroad Farm ever had a repeat customer . . . or how many lost heart before they even got there. This would explain the sign that suddenly appears out of the trees to promise that the farm really is just ahead. Sure enough, the road evens out and the woods pull back to reveal a tranquil maze of small green plots burgeoning with vegetable life.

To complete the picture, add a large farm pond, a windmill, a funky Age of Aquarius farmhouse with a giant lilac tree at one corner, outbuildings overflowing with farm implements, and a pair of ancient Land Rovers, regal even in decay. The requisite farmhouse dogs, at once friendly and suspicious, bound up barking to case out the car and its occupants. Then they return to their sunbath in the middle of the road. Everyone else is away at work. If you want help, blow your horn.

Although Arnold and Bonnie Pearlman grow a wealth of organic salad and cooking greens, onions, squashes, strawberries, and other produce, they have a passion for potatoes and raise about seventy varieties. This may not be a world record for a farm, but it's more than any other place we know and plenty enough for us. The Pearlmans have a cold cellar that keeps many of these potatoes perfectly from harvest right through to the next summer.

On our spring asparagus runs, Bonnie also sold us small bags of Bellruss, Carola, Early Bangor, Early Gem, Red LaSoda, Desirée, and Yellow Finn, all in prime shape. Today she brings out a bag of German Butterballs, another of Green Mountain, and still another of a new, highly rated red potato, the Bison. On top of these she places as a gift two potatoes she wants us to try: a rare variety, Levitt's Pink, the flesh of which is a mottled, deep rose.

Crossroad Farm is unique only in the number of its varieties. All the different farmstands we visit—Silveridge Farm in Bucksport, Hay's Farm in Blue Hill, Darthia Farm in Gouldsboro, Fairview Farm in North Brooksville—grow potatoes and sell them to their neighbors at prices (unless they're buying by the fifty-pound sack) that are higher than the supermarket's. But there are still a lot of people in Maine who like potatoes enough to want to know exactly what they're buying. They don't want just boiling or baking potatoes; they want Irish Cobblers, Kennebecs, Shepodies, Katahdins, Yellow Finns, Green Mountains.

Not that these potatoes are necessarily obscure. The Kennebec, as you might guess from its name, is a standard Maine all-purpose potato; Irish Cobbler, a delicious, mealy white potato, is one of five seed potatoes sold nationwide in the Burpee seed catalogue. Even so, there is something touching about stopping at a small roadside farmstand, untended, with a coffee can left out on the table for you to put your money in, and finding a single, not-quite-full bag of potatoes for sale with IRISH COBBLERS scrawled on it in red crayon. The bags of tomatoes and green beans, the peppers, the broccoli, and the summer squash are not similarly identified; the only other vegetable the Maine farmer treats with equal respect is her dried beans; the only fruit, her apples.

At first glance, you might not think Maine's love for potatoes is reflected all that much in Maine eating. A potato-chip lover, I came here hoping to find a local mom-and-pop concern frying chips fresh all day from spuds picked from their own potato patch and selling them in grease-stained, brown paper bags out of their kitchen door . . . the way, for example, you can buy crabmeat in these parts. If there is such a place, we haven't found it.

There is a single world-class kettle-cooked Maine commercial chip-

—Maine Coast potato chips—but even in-state, these aren't all that easy to come by. Go into any 7-Eleven in Pennsylvania Dutch country and you'll find stacked on the snack racks more local brands of potato chips than you can easily count. Not so here, and while Maine Coast potato chips have that clean, salty-sweet, fresh-fried taste that separates the leaders from the pack, they lack the determinedly distinctive this-is-the-way-we've-always-done-it character of, say, the lard-fried chips produced by Dieffenbach's in Womelsdorf, PA.

Still, eating around, we found that if we order mashed potatoes in even the least pretentious of Maine eateries, chances were they would arrive hand-mashed, freshly made, and good. If this observation hasn't been confirmed by more rigorous testing, it's because we discovered at the same time that Maine is one of the best places in the nation to eat French fries. Even the ordinary ones are crisp and good, and the extraordinary ones can be something truly special.

Up in Frenchville, at the very top of the state, Rosette's Restaurant is said to serve up the *world's best* French fries. If they are, they have some competition. In the restaurant listings in the 1991 *Maine Times Summer Guide*, Winnie's Dairy Bar and Restaurant in Presque Isle boasts of just two specialties: lobster stew and homemade fries. And Doris's Café in Fort Kent deep-fries potato cubes into golden, crusty squares—potato eating lifted right into home-fry heaven.

All this called to us when we finally drove up to Aroostook County, and we even thought of making the run clear up to Frenchville to try the fries at Rosette's. But I was unexpectedly sandbagged in Presque Isle by Fat Man's Texas-Style Barbecue. After snacking on half a slab of ribs slathered with the Fat Man's own secret sweet and vinegary sauce, I felt no special urgency to drive another sixty miles for a French-fry tasting. But we did stop in Houlton at the Elm Tree Diner, which serves *four* different kinds of fries (not counting home fries): French, country, curly, and barbecue. We ate the curly and the country, and can especially recommend the former: wiggly strips of potato, peel and all, about the thickness of a McDonald's fry but twice as long, crisper, and, well, better.

I mention all this not only because I like fried potatoes but because, to understand the Maine way with potatoes, you have to forget about fancy cooking, signature dishes, regional specialties. Whenever a bunch of "Maine" potato recipes are assembled in a book, there's always the whiff of the county extension service to them. These recipes are meant, mostly, for out-of-state cooks, who, when it comes to potatoes—it is felt here in Maine—can't leave well enough alone.

Some Maine cooks can't either, but the best do. The potato, not bread or rice or pasta, is this state's starch of choice, the backbone of Maine cooking. Backbones should be solid not ornate, and solid is the word for the potato in Maine food. It bulks up chowders, comes to the table smothered with salt-pork-and-clam gravy, and gets mashed and made into doughnuts. But the real glow comes when potato talk turns to the frying pan.

French-fried potatoes are one thing, pan-fried potatoes another. One is restaurant food, the other—although every eating place here worth its salt has them on the menu, too—is something else. After all, they aren't called home fries for nothing. I ask Bonnie Pearlman, who grows those seventy varieties, how she cooks her potatoes. She shoots me a surprised, slightly wary glance and answers, "Well, mostly we fry them."

2

It was Noel Perrin who lodged the Green Mountain potato in my brain. In a chapter called "The Gourmet Potato Grower" in *Third Person Rural*, he reports on a series of tastings he held with friends and neighbors. The entries were the fifteen varieties of potatoes he grew that year on his Vermont farm. The preferred mode of testing? Frying. The ultimate winner? Green Mountain. After reading this, I began to notice how often that particular high-starch potato is mentioned when people talk about flavor.

The Green Mountain potato—Edward Behr further instructed me in "Potatoes," an essay in the summer 1991 issue of his food letter *The Art of Eating*—was introduced in 1885 by a Vermont breeder, O. H. Alexander. At the time, Aroostook, the state's largest and northernmost county, was already potato country, and potato farmers there were soon growing, essentially, only two varieties of potato: Irish Cobbler and Green Mountain.

The Irish Cobbler was an early producer that went to market in the summer, bringing needed cash until the massive fall harvest of the latter. As Charles Morrow Wilson wrote in *Aroostook: Our Last Frontier* (1937):

> There are 108 breeds of dogs in the United States. There are about the same number of varieties of potatoes. The great standby of Aroostook, and of most of New England, is the Green Mountain, a smooth-surfaced, brown-gray Vermont potato which has held dominance for three-quarters of a century. Next to the

Green Mountain comes the Cobbler, a round pinkish potato, earlier than the Green
Mountain, pink-blossomed (the Green Mountain's is a creamy white), comprising
from a fifth to a third of the Aroostook crop.

Such monocropping exacts its penalties. Even as Wilson was penning
that passage, both these potatoes were struck down by the ravages of
disease. Their reign was over. By the time chemical sprays were devised
to control the disease, Aroostook's large commercial farmers had
switched over to other varieties, and with these they have stayed.

Jim Gerritsen of Prairie Wood Farm told us that organic farmers still
find Green Mountain and Irish Cobbler potatoes almost impossible to
grow in Aroostook County. Even here in Washington County, the Pearlmans have trouble with them; Jim Gerritsen, situated between Houlton
and Presque Isle, doesn't even bother. And the one potato at Chris
Holmes's New Penny Farm in Presque Isle that isn't certified as organic
is his large-sized Green Mountain.

Still, this potato remains popular with Aroostook home gardeners and,
it seems, in one particular way with some commercial growers, too. We
read in the catalogue of Pinetree Garden, a Maine nursery that sells
Green Mountain seed potatoes (grown, as it happens, at Crossroad
Farm), that Aroostook potato growers, while they raise field after field
of Kennebecs and Superiors for the market, still put in a few rows of
Green Mountains for themselves. This is the reason for our trip to Aroostook, or "The County," as it's known here in Maine: to find out if this
is really so.

Or at least in part. Already, our experience with Maine potatoes has
drawn us to the feeling people here have for them, something as elusive
and yet as real as the tone in my father's voice when he talks about the
Kennebecs and Green Mountains he used to grow in his own garden.
Ed Behr quotes Eugene H. Grubb, potato expert and author of *The
Potato* (1912), who remarks that in Aroostook the potato

is the sole topic of conversation where two or more men are gathered together . . .
Houlton, Maine, the center of potato work, is the only place where I have been
talked to a standstill on the subject of potatoes.

So, we're also heading for The County in the hope of catching some
echo of that century-old conversation.

Past Calais, heading north, U.S. 1 plunges into dense woodlands of
spruce and birch. For almost a hundred miles, it seems as if we'll never

emerge. Just beyond Danforth, about a third of the way to Houlton, the highway climbs up the side of Peekaboo Mountain and runs for a few spectacular minutes above tree level. To the east the Chiputneticook Lakes sprawl out like a vast inland sea; to the west and north the landscape falls away in mile after mile of autumnal forest until it comes to rest at the edge of the mist-shrouded foothills of Mount Katahdin. No farmland in view. And none will be, either, for the next thirty miles.

Then the highway swings around Westford Hill and arrives at Hodgdon Corners. The woods recede and small fields appear. These become larger and larger until, finally, there is only farmland, a landscape of sky and field. On this October morning, the sky spreads all around us, above and beyond, as far as the eye can see, and the effect is surprisingly exhilarating, almost moving. Expressions like "room to breathe" and "a place where a man can stand up" suddenly take on weight. John Logan calls Aroostook Maine's big-sky country, and that's exactly right. This is the way we imagine Montana, the Dakotas, Saskatchewan.

John Logan is director of quality control at the Maine Potato Board, headquartered in Presque Isle. Some of the questions we want to ask him will have already been answered when we reach his office, because, as luck would have it, we've arrived in The County in the middle of the potato harvest. In fact, Jim Gerritsen, whose farm we had also planned to visit, has had to beg off; rain is threatening to arrive by the end of the week, and he's going to be out in the fields all day, getting in as many potatoes as he can.

By the time we reach Houlton, once the farthermost army post in the northern wilderness, now the county seat and first of several cities— Presque Isle, Caribou, Limestone, Fort Kent—built by potato money, U.S. 1 runs, as highways always do in serious farming country, as if laid across the map with a ruler. We have already begun to pass huge bulk trucks, built like railroad hopper cars, piled high with freshly harvested potatoes. Now we see the enormous, galvanized-steel-sided warehouses of the potato distributors and, more picturesquely, the farmers' own potato barns. Because these buildings must keep their contents moist and cool, they are really giant root cellars, built when possible into the side of a hill, but otherwise with their outside walls heaped up with dirt.

A silo full of wheat may inspire admiration for the farmer who grew it but not necessarily make you want to go out and bake a loaf of bread. Similarly, no visions of fries dance in our heads as we watch these bulk trucks roll by, and it's a relief when small roadside stands begin to appear. These often sit right in front of the farmhouse, selling that farmer's own crop of potatoes, bagged in ten-, twenty-, and fifty-pound sacks. Hand-lettered signs offer Irish Cobblers, Shepodies, and, again and again, Green Mountains. There's no doubt that the Green Mountain still lives in Aroostook County, and it can be had here for a song: the fifty-pound sack we eventually buy will cost us six dollars, or twelve cents a pound.

A little later we're sitting in John Logan's office, talking potatoes. He tells us that the Green Mountain's demise resulted from its susceptibility to an aphid-carried disease, net-necrosis, which, at the time, farmers were unable to control. They've since moved on to more productive as well as more disease-resistant varieties, such as Kennebec, Katahdin, and Maine's current potato king, the Superior.

He agrees that the Green Mountain does have an excellent flavor, but it's clear that his heart is where the action is today, not yesterday, in Maine potato production. We've already seen that the farm of every organic potato grower we've visited could be easily fitted onto one massive Aroostook field. John Logan's job is to advise these commercial growers, and they make money by supplying the potatoes most in demand. This means paying attention to the needs of commercial processors, potato-chip makers, and the large, bulk-buying supermarket chains.

At our local Shop'n Save, however, we've noticed a small but growing number of specialty potatoes—organic russets, "chef's" potatoes (a large, oblong white)—and the introduction of yellow-fleshed potatoes like Yukon Gold, whose packaging emphasizes their "buttery" taste. Is there any chance that this might foreshadow a trend?

Mr. Logan concedes that the yellow-fleshed potato—long a European favorite—may be finding a market here, but the fact remains that the very phrase "gourmet potato" in commercial parlance refers to size, not flavor or type. In short, there is no perceptible effort by commercial growers to offer consumers potatoes grown especially for flavor. There are still too few eaters who find that small distinction between good and great potato taste something worth seeking out . . . and paying for. Consequently, while the Maine Potato Board puts out many pamphlets and brochures, not one lists Maine growers of specialty eating potatoes, mail-order or otherwise.

Not that Mr. Logan is oblivious to potato flavor. Although more burly than heavy, he offers his girth as evidence of an interest in potatoes pursued outside working hours. The one time in our conversation when gears shift out of the informational into the personal is when we begin to talk about our efforts to perfect our pan-fried potatoes.

He smiles widely and leans back in his chair. He gestures with his arm. Yes, he says, you have to start with the right frying pan—a *cast-iron* frying pan, of course—and butter, plenty of good butter, not any kind of substitute. His own approach is to bake them first and then fry them. And the potato from his own garden he likes best prepared this way is the Alasclear, a newly developed Alaskan variety of the all-purpose oblong white.

We share with John Logan his enthusiasm for the Maine potato and the Maine cast-iron-pan-fried potato, but as we shall now see, we go our separate way as to specifics, regarding both potato and method.

3

My first winter in Maine, I bought a fifty-pound sack of Delta Golds from Hay's Farm and ended up giving away whole grocery bags full. I loved their taste and texture, but I was simply out of practice cooking potatoes. One year later, Matt had moved in with me, and we bought another fifty-pound bag, this time Kennebecs from Silveridge Farm. When we asked Bob Chasse what his Superiors tasted like, he presented us with a ten-pound bag of those and another of his Chieftains so that we could find out. We ate them all—Kennebecs, Superiors, Chieftains —by sometime in January, without giving away a single one.

On the cellar stairs this autumn sits a fifty-pound bag of yellow Carolas, another of Green Mountains, and assorted weights of several other varieties. We've been learning potatoes. We make different potato soups, a lot of chowders, scalloped potatoes with walnuts and Cheddar, mashed potatoes topped with sautéed scallions and mushrooms or greens. Our current day-to-day eating consists mostly of single-dish meals made of pasta, bread, rice, or potatoes, and vegetables, with little or no meat (which is mostly saved for special occasions). This means that we rarely use potatoes as a side dish. Instead, they are themselves the reason for the meal.

So, for a long time, home-fried potatoes—a side dish, it seemed to us, if ever there was one—played no role at all in our eating. Then I chanced to read the section on pan-fried potatoes in Haydn Pearson's *The Countryman's Cookbook*, written in 1946. He writes that when he was a boy their farmhouse kitchen had two large cast-iron spiders (or frying pans)* because his father

> liked fried potatoes for supper often. We varied them of course with chowders; we liked New Hampshire–style tomato soup with pilot bread. Sometimes we had moist gravy hash. But year in and year out, fried potatoes was a standard supper dish, and that's why a home needs two spiders.

The first thing, then, to learn about pan-fried potatoes is that they can make the meal. This was never a secret in Yankee cooking, where it was known as "necessity mess," "very poor man's dinner," or, more appealingly, "Scootin'-'Long-the-Shore."† But like many vegetable-intensive main-course dishes, it had the stigma of poverty to it and, like them, too, lost favor as meat became more affordable.

It might be time to look at them again. A plate of fried potatoes— eaten with a small bowl each of cottage cheese and homemade bread-and-butter pickles, or perhaps a salad of bitter greens and a piece or two of bacon on the side—makes a fine supper for two consenting adults, who know that pan-fried potatoes have, ounce for ounce, fewer calories than unbuttered bread, and that frying is a synonym not for damnation but for satisfaction.

This, of course, is true only if they are made right. What we are *not* talking about here, as Haydn Pearson puts it, is that

> insipid, mangled, tired-looking conglomeration that most people call fried pota-toes. The average cook takes any two- or three-day-old cooked potatoes that have been accumulating in the refrigerator, chops them into defenseless, spineless bits, and calls the result fried potatoes.

Unfortunately, this is the way most people—and especially most res-taurants, including Maine ones—make home fries, from leftover boiled potatoes. This is because the dish takes twice as long to make with raw potatoes. But such potatoes, while they are an acceptable side dish at

---

* Before cast-iron ranges replaced the hearth, frying pans often had spindly legs to lift them out of the ashes—and looked like huge black spiders squatting in the coals. Language in Maine changes more slowly than circumstances, and "spider" remained in use well into this century, long after the legs were gone.

† This last according to Mrs. Mae Bangs Twite, of Oak Bluffs on Martha's Vineyard (quoted in Imogene Wolcott's 1939 *The New England Yankee Cookbook*). She says it was a favorite working meal of Cape Cod fishermen, who made it while they were doing just that. Whenever her grandmother asked her "grandad" what he wanted for lunch, his inevitable response was "Well, Mother, make it Scootin'-'Long-the-Shore."

breakfast pushed up next to scrambled eggs and bacon, simply do not stand up as a main dish.

Neither should pan-fried potatoes be confused with French-fried potatoes: two different methods, two different ideas. This needs mentioning because more than a few people expect too much—or the wrong thing entirely—from a skillet of home fries. Like ambitious parents with a reluctant child, they keep pushing harder when they should ease up.

The pan-fried potato cannot be a French fry. Deep-fat frying is fast and furious. Intense heat encases the potato, cooking it through in minutes. The only potato that can cook this fast is the starchy, loose-fleshed baking potato—most familiarly, the russet. The hot fat immediately seals shut the potato's surface; the super-heated moisture vapor within each fry cooks and fluffs the interior as, expanding, it finally escapes . . . leaving behind a dry, flaky inside and a golden, crisp outside. This effect is enhanced by presoaking (or prefrying) the slices, which removes the starch.

The pan-fried potato is gently fried one side at a time in a small amount of grease. Pushing up the heat cooks the surfaces without reaching the interior, turning out a product that is burned, gummy, greasy, lousy. Most cooks try to overcome this problem by using precooked potatoes. Unfortunately, potato flavor is very evanescent. Pan-fried potatoes made from already cooked potatoes are, at best, a pale imitation of the real thing. Made from scratch, their inside is meltingly tender and flavorful; their outside is more than just crisp . . . it is brown and crunchy. There are no shortcuts to this effect. To achieve it, pan-fried potatoes must be cooked—please mark this down—*slowly*.

MAINE HOME FRIES

Potatoes
Fat
Salt
Fresh parsley, minced
Black pepper

THE POTATO. As it turns out, the Green Mountain makes an excellent pan-fried potato. Some suggest you soak it in cold water first to remove some of the starch. We feel this is a mistake. True, the unsoaked potato is more likely to stick to the pan, but strategic thrusts of a thin-edged metal spatula can take care of that. Left in place, the potato's starch caramelizes in the hot fat to create a dense, crunchy crust—a pan-fried potato that beats hollow almost any French fry we've ever eaten.

However, much to our surprise, good-flavored, waxy-textured potatoes also make fine pan fries. These take longer to cook and their crunchiness is not as spectacular, but they have more substance, both in the pan and in the mouth. The mealy texture of the Green Mountain allows so much water to evaporate that the pieces actually shrink while you cook them, and the resulting fry, like French bread, is largely crust. The pan-fried waxy potato, on the other hand, keeps its moisture. Frying it produces a crisp outside that enrobes a dense, molten-soft, and delicious interior. When pan-fried potatoes are to make a meal, a red-skinned Bliss, Norland, or Bison will give you more of one. Only the all-purpose Carola was a disappointment, without enough starch to give it crunch or the density to provide a really luscious interior.

THE PREPARATION. Choose your potatoes, and clean and peel them.* We find four medium potatoes (about 1½ pounds) make a meal for two or a side dish for four, and—more to the point—completely cover the bottom of a 12-inch skillet. The smaller the cubes, the faster they cook, but also the more they crowd the pan: we cut ours into half-inch dice.

THE PAN should be large and have a cover. Also, because the potatoes are to be cooked slowly over a low flame, it should have a heavy bottom to distribute the heat evenly. Cast iron is the traditional choice. As Robert P. Tristram Coffin wrote in 1944 in *Mainstays of Maine*, one of the few wrongs war ever righted was that it got aluminum out of the kitchen and back into airplane bodies.

THE FAT. Use no cooking *oil* except olive or peanut oil. Any *fat* that suits your taste is fine—goose, duck, or chicken fat are all excellent. So is rendered lard or salt pork or bacon fat or suet or, of course, butter. Only good (not great) olive oil or peanut oil enhances the taste of potatoes; other vegetable oils simply replace it with their own, and despite what the cookbooks say, there is no such thing as a tasteless oil. Butter is the beginner's best choice. It makes delicious fried potatoes, and it's a sure guide to correct temperature. Ignore cooks who warn you to mix the butter with oil to keep it from burning. The secret to perfect pan-fried potatoes is gentle cooking . . . slow enough so the butter *doesn't* burn.

---

* I'm not usually fond of pan fries cut from unpeeled potatoes, but one of the best batches I ever made was with whole, unpeeled, baby Red Bliss potatoes the size of pullet's eggs. I just fried them following the procedure outlined here, gently rolling them about as the cooking progressed, until they were blistery crisp all over.

THE COOKING. Put about two tablespoons of the chosen fat or oil in the pan. The bottom should be well oiled but not swimming with grease. We're not deep-frying, remember. The trick is to allow them to stick— just *that* much—to the bottom of the pan. No stick, no crust . . . which is why potatoes take forever to fry on a nonstick surface. To start, melt the fat slowly over a low-medium flame. After a while the surface of the fat will cover over with bubbles. These will begin to move, and a faint hiss can be heard. This is your cooking temperature. Don't be tempted to turn the flame up higher. (You'll feel the pull to do so, first when you put in the potatoes and there's no loud sizzle . . . and later when you want things to hurry along. Resist.)

Distribute the potato pieces evenly over the bottom of the pan. Sprinkle them with a generous pinch or two of salt. Now *cover them* and let them cook for twenty minutes. The only noise you should hear is that gentle, bubbling hiss. At the twenty-minute mark, lift off the cover (carefully, so that the moisture condensed on it doesn't spill back into the pan) and put it aside. Give the potatoes their first turn, patiently using a flexible-edged metal spatula to free any potato flesh that has stuck to the pan. Here, and in all the turns to follow, you'll find that your fingers are a necessary accessory tool.

Raise the flame just a little. Now turn the potatoes over with the spatula every ten minutes for the next half hour, for a total of four turns. The edges of the potatoes should be getting crisp. Raise the heat one more time—again, only just a little—and now turn them every five minutes for the next twenty minutes (four more turns).

Total cooking time is 1 hour and 10 minutes. Total number of turns, eight. Depending on the moisture content of the potatoes and the intensity and evenness with which your skillet radiates heat, the potatoes will be about done. Don't despair if they need more cooking, just keep turning. By the time the inside has melted into a buttery soft amalgam, the outer surface will have turned brown and crunchy—and will stay that way. During the last minutes of cooking, mix in the fresh parsley and grind some black pepper over them. Serve out onto warmed plates and eat at once. You'll find the meal worth the wait.

THE SOMETHING ELSE. Pan-fried potatoes are amenable to a host of simple adaptations, as long as you take care *when* the additional ingredients are added: put them in too early and they'll burn to a crisp before the potatoes are done. The following variations are exercises in dealing with that problem; good in themselves, they also provide a variety of useful strategies for working out your own improvisations. The first, sometimes topped with a handful of grated Cheddar, is the Maine camp standby. The rest, although from out of state, are all good, too.

Onions and salt pork or bacon. Dice a slice or two of salt pork or bacon and try it out in the skillet until it crisps up and gives off some fat. Remove and save the crispy bits. Calculating one small onion for each skillet of potatoes (more and you have a potato-onion stew), cut this into fine dice. Prepare and cook the potatoes as directed above. Add the diced raw onion at the end of the first twenty minutes of cooking. When the potatoes are done and the onion bits edged with brown, sprinkle on the reserved crunchy salt pork or bacon bits and serve at once.

Olive oil and garlic. Use one or two garlic cloves for each skillet of potatoes. Slightly flatten these with the side of a cleaver and let them steep in the cooking oil for an hour or so. Just before cooking, fish out the cloves and mince them fine. Add to the potatoes during their last five minutes of cooking, along with a generous amount of minced fresh parsley or a modest amount of minced rosemary or oregano. Use a spatula to mix this into the potatoes, finish cooking, and serve.

Anchovies and garlic. This classic Italian combination calls for frying the potatoes in olive oil to which a small amount of anchovy and garlic has been added. This hint of briny pungency enhances—rather than overpowers—the flavors of potato and olive oil. Calculate 2 tablespoons of olive oil, 2 anchovy fillets, and one or two garlic cloves for each skillet of potatoes. An hour or so before cooking, slightly flatten the garlic with the side of a cleaver and allow this and the anchovy fillets to steep in the cooking oil to flavor it. Just before cooking, remove them from the oil and mince them fine. When the potatoes are nearly done, stir in the garlic-anchovy mixture and a generous amount of chopped parsley or a more discreet amount of crushed dried oregano.

Cheese. Pan-fried potatoes and cheese is a dish that appears in many European cuisines, the recipe varying mostly as to the cheese. A soft, easy-to-melt, mellow cheese is preferable, such as a good Cheddar, Cantal, mozzarella, or Gruyère. Use at least 2 ounces of the cheese to each skillet of potatoes. Grate the cheese coarsely and sprinkle it over the top of the finished potatoes. Serve as soon as the cheese has melted and turned slightly crusty where it touches the surface of the pan. A grating of black pepper enhances this dish, as does a small pinch of an appropriate herb, minced—thyme or, very judiciously, a little fresh sage.

STEUBEN, 1991

A Note on Hash Browns

Hashed browns is the dish in which to use leftover boiled potatoes—
and since more and more Americans encounter these solely as greasy,
deep-fat-fried mucilaginous patties served as a breakfast item at fast-
food places, it's worth remembering what they are like when prepared
with interest and respect. Here is a recipe from Jessup Whitehead's
Hotel Meat Cooking (1921):

> Chop cold boiled potatoes quite fine and season with salt. Spread a spoonful of
> drippings or butter in an omelet pan or small frying pan and place the minced
> potatoes about an inch deep. Cook on top of the range like a cake, without stirring.
> Invert a plate that just fits the pan over the potatoes. Let them brown nicely and
> slowly, then turn over on to the plate. Push in the edge a little all around and
> serve on the same plate with the brown on top.

You might want to add a little freshly ground black pepper and possibly
even a little minced parsley. Many cooks like to fold the potatoes over
like an omelet and slide this onto the serving plate.

Speaking of omelets, Elizabeth David writes about one called an *omelet Brayaude*, made of potato cubes gently sautéed in the fat rendered
from a slice of salt pork. One of the finest dishes I ever made was an
inversion of this procedure—dropping two raw eggs into a smoking
skillet of almost finished hash browns, quickly salting and peppering
them, and folding the potatoes over the moment the whites began to set.
The fork cut through the crisp potato crust to release the still-runny egg
yolk, which moistened and enriched it.

Potato Buying Guide

Potatoes are usually divided into three categories. There are the "waxy"
or so-called new potatoes (Russian Banana, Desirée, Red Bliss), whose
dense, creamy texture is preferred for potato salads and roasting and
by some for gratins and pan-frying; the "floury" or "mealy" bakers (a
market dominated by russets but including, among others, the high-
starch Shepody, Butte, and Green Mountain), the usual choice for baking and mashing; and, in between, the all-purpose varieties (Kennebec,
Yukon Gold, Red Pontiac) that are generally thought to show their best
in stews, soups, chowders, and braises.

Our own experience has taught us that, at best, such categorizing
offers guidelines not rules. We prefer to get a potato, try it out in dif-

ferent roles, and see how it performs in them. It turned out that I loved the waxy Bintje in potato soup, relished the medium-starch Kennebec mashed more than any russet, and found baked red and yellow potatoes differently delicious.

Potato flavor is another elusive entity. Bonnie Pearlman told us that potato taste develops during cellaring; it takes time to produce distinctive nuances of flavor. New potatoes please with their delicacy and freshness, old potatoes with their special savor. Cobblers are a potato to eat young; Kennebecs get better as they age. Jim Gerritsen told me he raises over thirty different kinds of organic potato, trying to match "fantastic flavor" with good yield. Out of these, he might pick half a dozen or so to offer his mail-order customers. In 1991, these included a heritage variety, Russian Fingerling, and Butte, so new it was barely known in this country. Yet, for flavor, Yukon Gold is his own family's favorite. Our conclusion: go with growers committed to flavor and give them—and their particular varieties—the chance to prove their stuff.

NEW PENNY FARM (P.O. Box 448, Presque Isle, ME 04769 • 800–827–7551). Chris Holmes sells certified organic potatoes, Maine certified seed (and, in spring, fresh fiddleheads). He offers twelve potato varieties: Atlantic, Banana, Bel Rus, Bintje, Carola, Dark Red Norland, Green Mountain, Irish Cobbler, Kerry Blue, Kennebec, Spaulding Rose, and Yukon Gold. These are available as 10-pound, 4-potato-variety sampler packs for $27.50 in the following categories: (1) Maine, (2) low-starch, (3) medium-starch, (4) high-starch, (5) yellow, (6) red, and (7) your choice. Five pounds of a single potato cost $19.50; a single 20-pound selection is $34.50; all prices include shipping (a surcharge is added west of the Mississippi). His informative catalogue is free.

WOOD PRAIRIE FARM, RFD 1, Box 164Q, Bridgewater, ME 04735 • 800–829–9765 or 207–429–9765. Jim Gerritsen sells his more durable organic products (all are certified) by mail: rolled oats, maple syrup, grains, Jacob's cattle beans, Russian red-skinned garlic, Chantenay carrots, Lutz greenleaf beets, and flours and meals he grinds himself, including a cornmeal made from heirloom Indian Dandan corn. His potatoes include Yukon Gold (an all-purpose yellow), Russian Banana (a yellow fingerling), Butte (a russet high in Vitamin C and protein), Reddale (a bright red-skinned potato with white flesh), Elba (all-blue —blue skin and blue flesh—and good baked or boiled), and Caribé (a purple-skinned potato with bright, snow-white flesh). Prices start at $29.75 (postpaid) for a 10-pound, 3-potato-variety sampler pack—you choose the selection. His descriptive catalogue is free.

MAINE COAST POTATO CHIPS, Maine Coast Natural Foods Inc., P.O.

Box 851, York, ME 03909 • 207–363–6084. Surprisingly, many small-batch, kettle-fried chips are cooked in so-called flavorless (read less expensive, highly processed) oils that leave the chips with the same unpleasant flavor undertones you pick up in cheap baked goods. These chips stand out because small kettle batches of high-quality potatoes are fried in pure peanut oil—the best-tasting vegetable-oil frying medium for chips. Maine Coast Potato Chips are available by mail, minimum order one case of twelve bags for $22.08 (shipping included): natural (7 ounces), barbecue (6.5 ounces), and that Yankee favorite, salt and vinegar (6.5 ounces). Cases of mixed flavors are not available.

RONNIGER'S SEED POTATOES, Star Route, Moyie Springs, ID 83845. These folks offer the largest selection of organically grown seed potatoes in the U.S. Any serious potato lover will want their attractive, information-packed catalogue ($2), which contains—among other things—a clear and concise description of each variety. Ronniger's also sells ten varieties for eating (instead of planting), $16.50 for a 10-pound bag (postpaid): Anoka, Bake King, Caribé, Desirée, French Fingerling, German Butterball, Reddale, Red Gold, Yellow Finn, and Yukon Gold.

Knowing Beans

It was a singular experience that long acquaintance which I cultivated with beans, what with planting and hoeing, and harvesting, and threshing, and picking over, and selling them—that last was the hardest of all—I might add eating, for I did taste. I was determined to know beans.   —HENRY DAVID THOREAU, *Walden*

It is only a bit of hyperbole to say that only in Maine can you ever really get to know beans. Boston may still be described as "the home of the bean and the cod," but I lived near Boston for years before moving to the Pine Tree State, and so far as I could tell, that city is better described as "the home of the canned bean and the cod." It does go without saying that most of those canned beans come from the old Burnham and Morrill factory down in Portland, a majestic brick edifice dating back to 1913, where, once upon a time, neighbors would bring their casseroles to bake in the big brick ovens after production had shut down for the day.

B&M still bakes the beans in huge iron pots in those same brick ovens (most baked-bean processors "bake" the beans directly in the can), using the traditional New England seasonings of molasses, mustard, and salt pork. When these ovens are all fired up, they can take on twenty thousand pounds of beans. In the summer, with the windows open and the ventilating fans running, you can smell their hauntingly homey aroma miles away, as you speed past Portland on Interstate 495.

B&M baked beans are good beans—not too sweet and with a pleasing hint of char—but even as canned beans go, Maine does itself better. B&M makes its baked beans with little white pea beans—which are about as bland a bean as there is—and almost all of them are grown in Michigan. Trainloads of uncooked beans arrive from out of state, get baked and canned, and then most head right out of state on the same set of railroad tracks.

Conversely, the Kennebec Bean Company, in North Vassalboro, not only packages a range of Maine-grown beans but, under the "State of Maine" label, sells many of them canned, prepared to an old Maine lumber-camp formula, right down to the man-sized chunk of salt pork (the one in the B&M can is more the size of a thimble): soldier beans, Jacob's cattle beans, yellow eye, and red kidney beans.

This is how it should be. There is no "Maine" bean. In fact, a clever geographer might be able draw up a map that districted Maine by bean type. He might start by marking off southeast Maine as favoring the pea bean, farm-country Maine the soldier and the Jacob's cattle bean, lumber country the original Steuben yellow eye, the Bangor area the sulphur bean, and Down East (up the coast from Ellsworth) the marafax . . . and go on from there.

The marafax bean is big enough around here for the local Milbridge markets to hang out banners announcing the arrival of the new crop and to sell bags of them out of cardboard cartons heaped on the floor. Sweeny's, the town's biggest grocery, also offers them baked and hot the year round out of a giant serve-yourself electric beanpot. The marafax is a dense, chewy, strong-flavored bean, something like a cross between a kidney bean and a garbanzo; it cooks, but it doesn't cook soft. No mashing up a gravy with them. Whatever else you want to say about the marafax, it is a bean with personality.

Maine-favored beans all have at least one thing in common, and it's something they share with the people who eat them: aggressiveness of character. This is still a place where to be described as full of beans is to be complimented, and where to be thought of as not knowing beans is to be pretty much relegated to the level of sawdust sorter.

Even as a newcomer, you can't help but notice that a person's standing in a small Maine town is defined by his or her attitude toward a few commonly held but fiercely debated suppositions. One of these revolves around the making of beans. Not that it's the most important. That, so far as I can determine, is the cutting, storing, and burning of firewood. But beans come in nearly second.

Not only will you find that everyone in Maine has an opinion on these two subjects, but—to your surprise—*your* opinion on these matters is sought as well. This is not only because it is through such offhandedly elicited revelations—especially as they show a general lack of good

sense and occasional pockets of complete ignorance—that your neighbors take pleasure in your company. It is through such considering that
they show you where they stand, and where you stand with them.

This constant positioning is a way of defining attitude. It is Maine's
egalitarian solution to social situating—your position in the pecking
order being won or lost on the dexterity, that day, of your opinions. This
is about as much hierarchy as Maine can stand . . . as is evidenced,
for example, by front doors.

Even though almost every house in Maine has a front door, it is the
rare Mainer who acknowledges they exist. This is signaled in various
ways. In newer-built houses, the front door is left to float above the
ground without any connecting set of stairs. In older houses, it is often
conspicuously covered, year round, with an insulating layer of plastic.*

Even outsiders can read signs such as these. It takes a keener eye
to spot, through the sidelights of a seemingly functional entranceway,
the back of a chest of drawers. The oblivious stranger who knocks on
such a door is then discomfited by sounds of struggle, the groan of
shifting furniture, the creak of unoiled hinges, and, finally, a flushed
red face . . . the usual Mainer being too polite to bellow through what
is essentially a wall, "You fool, go around to the back!"

In the normal course of events, no matter the occasion, your neighbor
will naturally head for the kitchen door (and, more likely than not, walk
in without knocking). If a householder wanted to use his front door, a
decision would have to be made about who to and who not to let in by
it. A Mainer wouldn't want to do that to his neighbors, and would die
before he let his neighbors do it to him.

Small Maine towns—and it should be noted that true Maine nowadays starts north of the Bath Bridge, the suburban sprawl below it having been ceded in all but name to New Hampshire—are still the habitat
of a collation of unregenerate individualists. It isn't surprising, then,
that they share an ethos that unites them even as it sets them apart—
a desire for a self-reliant life . . . or at least as self-reliant a life as
these times will allow.

Put in practical terms, what most Maine citizens crave in the deepest
part of their hearts is to own a small plot of land on which to cultivate
a woodlot and a few bean rows—just enough to sustain them and otherwise allow them to do as they damn well please. And whenever they

---

* So was our next-door neighbor's front door in Steuben for the first three years we were
here. However, he then decided to completely *obliterate* the door by pulling the entire
frame out of the wall and shingling over the resulting hole.

smell a woodfire burning or dig into a plate of baked beans, this yearning is palpably present.

Present, that is, but also poignant—because, as it happens, most Mainers do *not* own such a plot. Even those who do rarely shake off the seductions of modern life to go there and live free. For every independent spirit who lives on a back lot in a trailer, grows her beans, cuts her wood, and taps her maples for spending money, there are countless others who do those things every now and then—just to keep their hand in—and many more who claim they did it once and are going to do it again . . . sometime.

This is the importance of attitude. Attitude accommodates all these things. It is part chastisement and part perpetually deferred expectation. It is a way of holding on even as it is a way of letting go. Most of all, it keeps alive what would otherwise be only memory.

There is, for example, no self-sufficiency in Maine without a source of free heat, which, in a state as cold as this one, winter *and* summer, is no small feat. This explains why firewood is important, but not why it is made more important than it actually is—into a subject requiring a lifetime to master. As a newcomer, no matter how much you pick up—how proficient you become in cutting and splitting, how knowledgeable in getting the best heat out of even a trash wood like "popple"—there's bound to be a venial flaw somewhere in your knowledge.

This gives your neighbor the upper hand, and he will eventually show you he has it. He will do this casually, indirectly, even—no, *often*—helpfully. For all he really wants to do is to position himself north of you. He wants to say to himself, "I may be getting soft, but I'm not yet as soft green as this fellow." Even as he says this, he is also gratified that you intend to heat your house with wood. It means you might smell the same thing in the Maine air that he does. It means that maybe next year he can show you how to put in your beans.

Fifty years ago, if you went to a small town in rural Maine, you would most likely have found it to be a community of (more or less) subsistence farmers. And every Saturday you would have found a pot of beans simmering in each kitchen woodstove. Today, if you went to the same small town, you'd be lucky to find more than one or two houses in which that is true. But what you *would* find—if you bothered to wait to hear it—would be passionate conversation about baked beans.

Listening to this, to all the odds and ends of opinion that would come your way, you would begin to piece together not only how to make baked beans but the feel of that lost community—of the endeavor that joined it together and that joins it together still. For, in Maine, the making of baked beans has not yet become a recipe. It is a matter of catching onto the thread of argument.

That thread, as it turns out, is nearly everywhere there for the grasping. You could, if you wished, assemble a book—a small one, to be sure, but a book even so—of Maine writers opining on the subject of cooking beans. Such narratives appear not only in the obvious places —Kenneth Roberts's *Trending into Maine*, Nathan S. Lowrey's folklore study, "Tales of the Northern Maine Woods: The History and Traditions of the Maine Guide"—but sometimes out of nowhere.

In *The House That Jacob Built*, John Gould (who swears by Jacob's cattle beans) interrupts his account of rebuilding the family house after the original burned to the ground to devote an entire chapter to the subject. Carroll F. Terrell, in *Growing Up Kennebec*, a funny, no-holds-barred narrative of a Maine boyhood in the twenties, stops the action to provide a step-by-step description of his mother's recipe (she prefers yellow eyes). Walter Howe pauses in his comic narrative, *Frost You Say?*, to explain *his* method (he leans toward Kentucky Wonders).

Such an anthology would serve a good purpose. As with any Maine baked-bean maker, each of these authors is solidly convinced of his own method's inviolable truth. Encountered by itself, such absolute surety is dangerously persuasive. Mix the same recipe in with a baker's dozen similarly firmly believed-in but wildly diverging ones—where almost no bean-baking tenet is left unchallenged*—and the reader can set the book aside at last understanding that this is not truth speaking but competitiveness. No one is ever allowed the final word: because that would be the end of it. Without attitude, there would be no interest in the subject at all.

Instead, all these jostling opinions, fragments of opinions—not one giving the least bit of ground to the next—have only one purpose: to keep nudging the disputants gently back in the direction of the bean row. The only way to resolve the opinions into a dish—*your* dish—of baked beans is to go find your bean. The salt pork, the sweetenings, the flavorings—these are all good, but if you take them too seriously

---

* I know this sounds like hyperbole, but it's true. To give just one example: Carroll Terrell's mother presoaked her beans overnight with *five tablespoons of salt*. For the Yankee bean baker, this is not only unheard-of, it is a kind of destabilizing blasphemy, the equivalent of watching someone pour black coffee over his breakfast cereal. The effect is all the more devastating because Terrell delivers it without apology or even the slight verbal flinch that might otherwise have telegraphed the launching of the punch.

they lead away from the bean row, away from self-sufficiency and straight to perdition . . . which is to say, straight to *Boston* baked beans.

Now, there's more than a little truth to the accusation that Maine folk too much relish the taste of cheapness in dishes that, if a bit more expenditure was involved, might actually taste good. Here is the downside to this same dream of self-sufficiency: the grim satisfaction of keeping temptation at bay, especially any that might lead to fancy groceries. It's all too easy to extend this criticism to old-fashioned Maine baked beans, which to the uninitiated mouth taste mighty skimpy of flavoring—of molasses measured by the spoonful, of seasonings measured by the pinch.

However, this accusation would be wrong. Maine takes beans seriously because it still knows how to taste them. People here grow beans, shell beans, so they can eat some fresh from the vine and thresh out the rest to keep for baking. Once you've brought some beans in straight from the garden to plunge into boiling water . . . and then had them dissolve on your tongue into a mass of buttery sweetness—you are less inclined to smother that flavor in molasses—or worse, tomato catsup! Even when they are dried and need hours, not minutes, in the kettle— you still won't. All you will want is a pinch of mustard to add a hint of tang . . . a fat spoonful of molasses or brown sugar to round out the flavor . . . a chunk of salt pork to baste their unctuous softness with melting richness.

At this point you are at the verge of stepping over from the camp of the "sweets" to the camp of the "naturals"—or "unsweets." Today, the latter is less of a camp than a select club. Robert P. Tristram Coffin wrote that his mother had to bake two pots of beans every Saturday of her adult life, because his family was split down the middle on this issue. A century later, most people—even those who have spent their whole lives here—have never tasted a pot of old-time unsweet baked beans.

Whatever you want to make of this situation, I know from personal experience that force of will won't carry us back to the nether side of the line. My palate simply balked when I presented it with one of the unadorned old-time versions. Even so, I've now spent enough time with these Maine writers to know that it wasn't meanness that made Maine bean dishes seem almost without savor—it was knowing beans. So perhaps my resistance is just a sign that I have yet to find my bean.

I'm still looking. Because, if there's any secret to making authentic Maine baked beans, it's that you have to start looking in them for the taste of your own bean row. It doesn't matter if you never have or never will plant a bean seed in your life . . . the flavor will come with knowing why you might want to. When you start doing that, you might find you yourself are acquiring attitude about baked beans. You will opine, maybe, that the flavor of your yellow eye melds so smoothly with a good Barbados molasses that there is no better sweetener for any bean. Or else, having become partial to Jacob's cattle beans, you'll declare molasses fatuous and bland—those beans crying out for maple syrup. And you'll turn a deaf ear on your neighbor who claims, because of a taste for red kidneys, that beans can prosper only when rasped by the abrasive taste of genuine blackstrap.

This is why in Maine such things as top-notch molasses, Colman's mustard powder, and salt pork with a real streak of lean can still be found in tiny mom-and-pop groceries. It is why there are as many different kinds of beans for baking here as there are kinds of firewood for burning, each with its own fervent band of sectaries. It is also why there are people here who still grow their own Swedish browns or Vermont cranberries—because no store-bought bean will do.

That's what attitude leads to—it gets you to go out and find your bean. I hope it does—even, maybe, right to your own bean row. Then you should come around to the back door, draw a chair up to the kitchen table, and add your two cents' worth to the confabulation that's already going on.

MAINE BAKED BEANS

My father, a native Mainer, is a man who has found his bean. Even though encroaching age has meant that his own bean row is now a thing of the past, there is still pure pleasure in his voice when he describes the baked beans my mother made from their crop of Jacob's cattle beans. In fact, it was such a conversation that got me thinking about beans and, subsequently, testing the water for myself.

I have to admit, though, that the Jacob's cattle is not my bean. Even so, once I realized that—for me—its distinctly winy presence wanted something smokier and tangier than salt pork and molasses, I found them the perfect bean to mix with maple syrup, chunks of cob-smoked bacon, and a generous amount of tart apple-cider jelly.

Peace thus made with my father, I returned to the yellow eye, a smooth-tasting bean that melds well with the traditional flavorings, to work out a version of old-style baked beans. The recipe that we came up with, after much trial and error, is well within spitting distance of most other tolerably sweetened versions.

This, however, doesn't really tell the story. Here is a dish where the smallest changes can reflect much tasting . . . and thinking. Sometimes the perceived wisdom is correct, and sometimes, correct or not, the demands of your palate insist you override that wisdom. One abiding truth regarding Maine baked beans is that a taste for them separates those who eat them from the out-of-staters whose disdain for the dish is evidenced by their lack of interest in putting in the necessary work to get it right. If you want a sure formula, open a can.

Sometimes traditional instruction is right on the mark; at other times, though, it isn't. Mrs. Ivy Gandy's pithy observation in Marjorie Mosser's *Good Maine Food* (1940)—" 'Slow oven' indeed; and who ever heard of a fast oven *down in Maine!*"—holds as true for baked beans as any other Maine dish. Cooking beans in a steady 350°F oven rapidly reduces them to sludge. Having learned that lesson, the next time I reduced the temperature to 250°F and tasted regularly. After about half the recommended eight hours of cooking time, I noticed that the beans had melted to a full-flavored but delicate softness, floating like glistening pearls in an unctuous and just-starting-to-thicken sauce.

How much more wonderful they'll be, I gloated, after four *more* hours. But instead of continuing to ascend to a mythical perfection, the flavor and texture of the beans began to fall away—since these, as it happened, were new-crop dried beans, which cook much more quickly than those that have sat in the store (or cellar) for a year. However, so captured was I by that imperative for a full eight hours of cooking time that I simply refused to believe the evidence of my mouth.

It is dangerous to draw a moral from this, because the same kind of evidence initially betrayed me in the matter of salt. Traditional recipes call for a scant amount, but when, after about two hours of cooking, the liquid was still crying out for it, I gave in and added half a teaspoon —and almost ruined the batch. The next time I restrained myself—to discover that enough salt eventually leached from the salt pork to give the dish exactly the right amount of savor.

I also discovered that half a cup of molasses was to my still-learning palate the right amount to bring out the most flavor from a pound of beans without also making them noticeably sweet. However, since I also yearned for a little more molasses taste, I pointed it up with a little dark rum—which draws the mouth to the dry edge of that flavor instead of toward its ever-elusive sweetness.

Other alterations: Rather than the usual single large chunk of fat salt pork, I preferred to take as lean a piece as possible, cut into small pieces and mixed throughout the beans; I eliminated the traditional onion from both versions, to the mysterious improvement of each. Although the resultant flavors might be too bright and clearly enunciated for an old Yankee palate, this is a version of Maine baked beans where the taste of the beans does shine right through.

UP-NORTH BAKED BEANS
(SERVES 4 TO 6)

1 pound (2 cups) Jacob's cattle (or soldier) beans (acceptable
    substitute: red kidney beans)
¼ pound thick-sliced, country-style bacon (see note)
⅓ cup maple syrup
⅓ cup apple-cider jelly (see note)
1 teaspoon mustard powder
Salt and pepper to taste

Pick over and presoak the beans as directed on pages 293–94. The next day, put the beans and what remains of their soaking liquid into a large pot, adding more water if necessary to ensure that the beans are covered. Bring this to a simmer and, after 15 minutes, check every 5 minutes until a sharp breath will split the skin of a bean. Then drain the beans and return the cooking liquid to the pot. Keep this at a low simmer while preparing the beans for baking. Preheat the oven to 250°F. Cut the bacon into bite-sized pieces. Put the prepared beans into a 2-quart bean pot. Stir in the bacon pieces, maple syrup, and apple-cider jelly. Dissolve the mustard powder in a little water and mix this in well.

Add seasoning to taste—starting with 1 teaspoon salt and ½ teaspoon pepper, adding more as needed. Pour over just enough of the simmering bean liquid to be visible through the beans. Cover the pot and put it in the oven. Bake the beans for about 6 hours, tasting occasionally, noting texture and seasoning, and adding more of the remaining bean liquid—or else water—as necessary. When the beans are soft and succulent, stir them well, uncover, and bake a half hour more to thicken the liquid into sauce. Serve with coleslaw and brown bread.

COOK'S NOTE. Lawrence's Smoke Shop sells a particularly delicate cob-smoked bacon and other Vermont smokehouse favorites: Route 30, Newfane, VT 05345 • 802-365-7751.

The apple-cider jelly used in this recipe is made by boiling down pure apple cider until it is reduced to a thick, tart, intensely flavored spread. Our own source for it is Willis Wood, who sells it (and maple syrup) by mail—write for brochure to RR #2, Box 477, Springfield, VT 05156.

DOWN-EAST BAKED BEANS
(SERVES 4 TO 6)

1 pound (2 cups) Maine yellow-eye beans (acceptable substitutes:
    Great Northern or white navy beans)
¼ pound salt pork
½ cup dark, full-flavored molasses (see note)
2 tablespoons dark rum (see note)
1 teaspoon mustard powder
Salt and pepper to taste

Pick over and presoak the beans as directed on pages 293–94. The next day, put the beans and what remains of their soaking liquid into a large pot, adding more water if necessary to ensure that the beans are covered. Bring this to a simmer and, after 15 minutes, check every 5 minutes until a sharp breath will split the skin of a bean. Then drain the beans and return the cooking liquid to the pot. Keep this at a low simmer while preparing the beans for baking. (Maine cooks traditionally discard both the soaking and the parboiling liquid, adding fresh boiling water to the bean pot. We have come to believe that this serves no real purpose while wasting some good bean flavor.)

Preheat the oven to 250°F. Cut the salt pork into bite-sized pieces and pour boiling water over to cover well. Drain after several minutes, discarding the liquid. Mix the salt-pork pieces into the prepared beans and pour them together into a 2-quart bean pot. Stir in the molasses and rum. Dissolve the mustard powder in a bit of water and mix this in well. Add seasoning to taste—starting with about ½ teaspoon each of salt and pepper. Pour over just enough of the simmering bean liquid to be visible through the beans. Cover the pot and put it in the oven. Bake the beans for 5 hours, tasting occasionally, noting texture and seasoning, and adding more of the remaining bean liquid—or else water—as necessary. When the beans are soft and succulent, stir them well, uncover, and bake ½ hour more to thicken the liquid into sauce. Serve with coleslaw and brown bread.

COOK'S NOTE. Crosby's Gold Star brand Barbados molasses is so much to the Maine taste that many stores carry no other brand and some stock it by the gallon jug. As late as the early 1950s, Crosby's imported its molasses from Barbados in wooden barrels, which were sold directly to the trade. Housewives would bring a jug to the general store and have it filled straight from the barrel.

Because Crosby's is headquartered in Saint John, New Brunswick, it has never been much written about in narratives of Maine food. This is too bad, because theirs is an intensely perfumed, rich-tasting, deep-flavored molasses without any off-putting bitter or chemical edge, and ought to be more widely known. It's the only molasses that I've ever loved eating straight off a spoon, and it does marvelous things not only for baked beans but for gingerbread and molasses cookies. Substitute any good dark, unsulphured molasses. Crosby Molasses Company, P.O. Box 2240, Saint John, NB, Canada E2L 3V4 • 506–693–6515.

Hand in hand with a taste for dark Barbados molasses goes a taste for dark, full-flavored rums, and bottles of the same can be found sitting on the shelves of small-town agency stores Down East—bourbon-colored, aromatic, barrel-aged rums like Black Seal rum from Bermuda, Pusser's Original Royal Navy rum from the British Virgin Islands, and Appleton Estate rum from Jamaica. Substitute Meyer's or Bacardi Black Label.

BOSTON BROWN BREAD

As we suggest in the above two recipes, nothing better suits a meal of baked beans than a side dish of coleslaw and a few slices of Boston brown bread. This is certainly what we have with it ourselves. The coleslaw adds the requisite crisp, green, sweet-sour presence sometimes provided by a small dish of bread-and-butter pickles, while brown bread is so unquestioned an accompaniment that Yankee canneries like B&M and Friends sell cans of it right beside their beans. Indeed, it might be argued that brown bread—the last Yankee steamed, whole-grain loaf—has survived only because of its affinity to baked beans.

At first, theirs seems a strange alliance. Brown bread, a chocolate-colored, raisin-studded soda bread made of whole wheat, rye, and "in-jun" is just as soft, dense, and carbohydrate-heavy as baked beans themselves—and yet, somehow, the two manage to play off, even en-hance, each other's goodness. Partly, as with cake and frosting, it is the contrast between the smooth richness of the beans and the soft, crumbly texture of the whole-grain loaf; partly, it is the nutritional union of two incomplete parts of a protein now becoming a single whole. Beans baking in the oven, brown bread simmering on the stove—this reversal of the usual situation, where the pot is on the burner and the bread in the oven—actually points up our awareness that this is old-fashioned, out-of-the-ordinary farmhouse cooking: delicious, inexpensive, fuel-intensive food, devised to provide hours of warmth and continuing sustenance to hardworking, weather-battered bodies.

BOSTON BROWN BREAD
(MAKES 1 BROWN BREAD)

½ cup rye flour
½ cup cornmeal, preferably white flint (see note)
½ cup whole-wheat flour
1 teaspoon baking soda
½ teaspoon salt
6 tablespoons molasses (see recipe note above)
1 cup buttermilk
½ cup raisins or dried currants
Butter for greasing a 1-pound coffee can

About 2 hours before the beans will be ready, set a large kettle of water on the flame to boil. In a mixing bowl, stir together the rye flour, cornmeal, whole-wheat flour, baking soda, and salt until well mixed. Pour in the molasses and buttermilk, and work into a smooth batter. Fold in the raisins or—our own choice—dried currants. Carefully butter the inside of an empty, clean, 1-pound coffee can (a 14-ounce can will do). Pour in the batter and cover the can with a doubled piece of aluminum foil. Press this down so that it stretches tightly across the top and reaches partially down the sides, and secure it in place with a sturdy rubber band.

Put a small round wire rack (if available) on the bottom of a deep pot. Set the filled coffee can on this—or simply set it on the bottom of the pot. Pour boiling water around the can until it reaches a little more than halfway up the sides. Bring the water back up to a murmuring simmer, cover the pot, and gently steam the bread for 2 hours, or until a straw inserted in the middle of the bread comes out clean. Remove, set on a cake rack, and let cool until the beans are ready to serve, then unmold the bread and serve warm. Brown bread is traditionally cut with a string; we use dental floss. Serve buttered, alongside—or, as some prefer, *under*—the baked beans.

COOK'S NOTE. Apart from some small touches, this recipe is identical to most traditional Boston brown-bread recipes. The goodness of the bread depends not so much on skill as on a determination to use fresh, flavorful rye and whole-wheat flours, a rich, pungent molasses, and a superior stone-ground cornmeal. Our choice for that is the Rhode Island white flint cornmeal ground by Tim McTague at Gray's Grist Mill (see page 359).

CASTINE, 1988 / STEUBEN, 1994

A NOTE ON MAINE BEAN TYPES

JACOB'S CATTLE BEAN. Also known as the trout bean, coach dog bean, and dalmatian bean, the Jacob's cattle is a handsome, plump, pure white, kidney-shaped bean with the vivid maroon splashes that give it its name (the biblical patriarch's cattle were "ring-streaked, speckled, and spotted," Genesis 30:39).

In Maine, the Jacob's cattle bean is second only to the yellow eye as the favored baking bean. It is full-flavored, holds its shape under long cooking, and stands up well to plenty of seasoning. Bean farmer Doug Qua considers the Jacob's cattle bean the "filet mignon" of baked beans, and told us that "it would most likely be the most popular bean if yellow-eye people would only try it."

MARAFAX BEAN. As already noted, the Marafax is a dense, chewy bean with plenty of flavor that, like the garbanzo, can take all the cooking you care to throw at it. Its origins are mysterious. One food writer reports that a bean grower told him that it was introduced by the U.S. government during the Depression to help alleviate poverty. Maybe so, but I suspect this to be a sample of Maine humor, since, as it happens, the only place the bean is eaten is in one tiny area along the Maine coast, where the only viable crops are blueberries and granite boulders.

SOLDIER BEAN. A popular New England heirloom white kidney-shaped bean with a distinctive maroon marking on the eye that resembles an old-fashioned toy soldier. Also known as the Johnson bean, it is closest in flavor to a Maine yellow eye.

SULPHUR OR CHINA YELLOW BEAN. A thin-skinned, nearly round bean, this relatively unknown Maine heirloom bean has been raised by Yankee farmers for over 150 years, and may have been developed by the American Indian. The name comes from their tawny yellow color, but they cook white and have a distinctly unique flavor.

VERMONT CRANBERRY BEAN. This stunningly attractive bean has been grown in New England since the eighteenth century and remains popular today because it is hardy, reliable, and delicious, both as a dry cooking bean and as a shell bean eaten fresh from the pod. As a dried bean, however, it is a better soup bean than a baking bean, because it does not hold up well to long baking.

YELLOW EYE BEAN. Widely hailed as *the* Maine baking bean, this lumberjack favorite can be found in several strains, all of them developed from the mother of all yellow eyes (and, in the opinion of some old Mainers, still the best of the breed): the Steuben Yellow Eye Bean. This is one of the oldest of heirloom beans (it is mentioned in Fearing Burr's 1865 *Field and Garden Vegetables of America*) and is also known as the dot eye bean, molasses face bean, and yellow-eyed china bean. The Steuben yellow eye is a lovely bean, plump and oval, with a two-toned bean-pot coloring, glossy white with a large, caramel-colored eye. It has a larger eye and a more distinctive "bean" flavor than the more popular Maine Yellow Eye Bean, which is the baked bean of choice for church and grange suppers, because its clean, mild taste has wide appeal (hence, too, its large out-of-state following).

SOURCES FOR SEED BEANS

VERMONT BEAN SEED COMPANY (Garden Lane, Fair Haven, VT 05743 • 802–273–3400) specializes in beans. Among their heirloom and hard-to-find beans are Dutch brown beans and Aurora small white beans (which they call "the Cadillac of baking beans"). Maine favorites include: Vermont cranberry, Great Northern, Steuben and Maine yellow eye, Swedish brown, Jacob's cattle, etc.

JOHNNY'S SELECTED SEEDS (Foss Hill Road, Albion, ME 04910–9731 • 207–437–4301) offers a wide range of heirloom and other vegetable seeds, including Jacob's cattle, Vermont cranberry, soldier, sulphur, Maine yellow eye, etc.

SOURCES FOR COOKING BEANS

THE BEANERY, R.F.D. #1 • Box 430, Corinna, ME 04928 • 207–278–3572. Doug and Patti Qua grow and sell at very reasonable prices a wide range of high-quality and meticulously selected dry beans, including all the Maine varieties listed here and others such as black turtle, calypso, and French flageolet.

KENNEBEC BEAN CO., Main Street, N. Vassalboro, ME 04962 • 207–873–3473. "State-of-Maine" brand Jacob's cattle beans and other good beans are available by mail, both dried and prepared in cans.

FIRST FIND YOUR BEAN POT . . .

Shortly after "Knowing Beans" appeared in *Simple Cooking*, we got a letter from subscriber Jeri Jarnagan, who lives in Pacific Palisades, California:

> For some time now, I've wanted to make *authentic* New England Baked Beans baked in an *authentic* bean pot, properly colored *brown*. I nearly bought a three-quart pot from Cookin' Stuff in La Habra. At the last moment, the salesperson I had on the phone told me that the color choices were (1) black and (2) white with blue flowers. I expressed astonishment and told her I wanted neither. A non-brown bean pot was like an American flag with yellow and white stripes and stars in a green field. I don't pester you with many letters, but I do hope you'll be able to tell me where I can purchase the real thing. My mom is in her 80s, and I know if I could learn to make this excellent dish she would be in bean heaven. She loves even the canned stuff, most of which I can tell is not very good.

Matt inherited a bean pot from her grandmother which has a size number printed on it and is as authentic as all get-out, but it is a two-tone beige-and-brown. Were bean pots ever the all-over brown of the spot illustrations for baked beans that appear in old-time cookbooks? Yes, replied Karen Hess, the culinary historian, when we asked her. The original New England bean pot was glazed all over in a simple, rich brown. The beige-and-brown version is a (relatively) newfangled notion.

Karen also directed us to the following quote from Mary Lincoln's *Boston Cook Book* (1893), which shows that Yankees were just as particular about other aspects of their bean pots:

> Much of the excellence of baked beans depends upon the bean-pot. It should be earthen, with a narrow mouth and bulging sides. This shape is seldom found outside of New England, and is said to have been modelled after the Assyrian pots. In spite of slurs against "Boston Baked Beans" it is often remarked that strangers enjoy them as much as natives; and many a New England bean-pot has been carried to the extreme South and West, that people there might have "baked beans" in perfection. They afford a nutritious and cheap food for people who labor in the open air.

Our first trip was to the local hardware stores, most of which not only still carried a bean pot but offered a whole range of them, from small to extended-family size. The problem with them was that they had not been made in New England by people who knew beans. (At least one of models examined had come all the way from Taiwan.)

To our mind, a bean pot should have clean lines—even to severity —and a crispness to the color. It should be at once modest and a pleasure to look at. These pots, although well priced at twenty to thirty dollars, were without dignity. They were something you would hide away when not in use. This was not what we wanted in a bean pot, and we didn't think it was what Jeri Jarnagan wanted, either.

So we then turned to several of the individual potters in the area. Here we found a very different situation. We had thought that bean pots might be a rarity, which they weren't, but neither was there anything traditional about them. Priced at—or over—fifty dollars each, they were the products of artistic craft. Some were made with a saturated iron glaze, others were elaborately decorated with seagulls or blueberries, still others came in a variety of lustrous color combinations. These pots were often very attractive, but somehow, they didn't seem like *bean* pots.

When we talked to Dan Weaver at the Maine Kiln Works in Goulds-boro, he told us that the old-fashioned rich brown glaze with its hint of olive was known to potters as Albany slip and was until a few years back still widely used. Unfortunately, the mine that produced it closed down, and the glaze has since disappeared from the market.

While we talked, I was turning one of Dan's own bean pots over in my hands. He makes them in two styles, one with the small, traditional opening and another with a larger mouth that is more adaptable to regular casserole cooking. The one I held—in the traditional shape— was glazed in a rich, variegated brown. I realized what troubled me about it wasn't the color but its one-of-a-kindness. It seemed much too elegant an object to concern itself with beans.

I understood then what we were looking for, and it wasn't a bean pot glazed in Albany slip. It was a pot from the kind of Maine artisanal potteries that used to slip-cast bean pots in plaster molds by the hun-dredfold, each identical to the next, each possessing the same utilitarian dignity of an article of necessary use. Such potteries, of course, no longer exist, and we ended up purchasing a small, beige-colored, one-quart, single-handed bean pot thrown by Scott Curry at the Christian Ridge Pottery in South Paris.

A one-quart bean pot would have horrified thrifty Yankees—think of firing up the woodstove to heat a pot as small as that! But it's a fine size for a pot of baked beans for two. However, it called out to us because of its modesty. It had simple, clean lines, a quiet, pleasing color, and was a pleasure to hold. And apart from its size, there was nothing particularly self-dramatizingly *artistic* about it.

This, in our experience, made it unique. Today, most Maine potters feel—and probably rightly—that anyone willing to spend fifty dollars or more for a bean pot (ours, by the way, cost about half that, which may explain something) is meaning to stand apart from their neighbors, and wants their bean pot to stand apart as well.

In the old days, the situation was the same—except that it was use, not price, and certainly not saturated iron glaze, that caused a pot to stand out. In *The House That Jacob Built* (1948), Maine author John Gould tells of the Saturday night when the bottom fell out of the bean pot. He terms this a "terrible catastrophe"—and not just because at that moment his wife happened to be transporting the pot to the table, so that the kitchen floor was suddenly swimming with fragrant, steaming-hot baked beans and pottery shards . . . or even because of the very un-Saturday-night supper of fried eggs and bacon, thrown to-gether once the mess was scooped up and fed to the hens. No, the catastrophe was having to start all over again with "a brand, spanking new bean pot from the store, which was shiny and untarnished and wasn't worth a cent."

It was an aunt who made them a gift of the new pot, and the comment wasn't made out of ingratitude. In those days, you could still find the real thing at any Maine general store, and it was surely locally made, a bean pot with integrity. The problem was that it was a totally untem-pered bean pot. As Gould's aunt herself said as she handed it over, gesturing to their newborn baby boy: "By the time the lad gets big enough to eat beans, this one'll be fit to bake some in." And Gould goes on to observe:

> She knew what she was talking about. She knew the pores of a bean pot take on a mellowing that comes from weekly bakings. It takes barrels of beans, gallons of molasses, whole saltings of pork, bushels of onions, and months of blue moons to fire the quintessence into a good bean pot.

The more important a dish is to a family, the more important the pot that it is made in becomes. I resent using the pot we make our rice in—and there is nothing special about that pot at all—for making any-thing else but rice. It is "the rice pot," and using it to boil water, even, seems at best risky, at worst impious. Our bean pot does get used to make a slow-baked beef stew now and then, which it does perfectly and

does not seem to resent. But it is a mark against me as a bean cook
that I allow this, and I know it.

BEAN HOLE BEANS

In the lumber camps of the great Northern forests, in Maine as everywhere, the "luscious, potent, belly-filling" dried bean was king. It was
made into soup and, most famously, baked beans. As Robert E. Pike
wrote in *Tall Trees, Tough Men*:

> Pork and beans, baked in a bean hole, remain the logger's main dish. There's
> good reason for it, namely, that there is nothing better in God's sweet world, when
> it is cooked right. The ample mess of fat pork, dissolved by the heat, is neither
> fried nor boiled, but becomes amalgamated with the beans and when the whole
> is well cooked it is a food that can't be beat for succulency of flavor and savory
> richness of nutrition. Such baked beans have staying power that is possessed by
> no other food.

"Logging berries" appeared at all three meals at these camps, even when
a wider range of foods became available. As one old logger, Hubert
Templeton, recalled:

> When I started going into the woods in the 1930s, there were beans on the table
> every meal. Of course there was plenty of other good food, too. A typical breakfast
> would be coffee, oatmeal, ham or bacon, eggs, fresh baked biscuits, and beans. I
> always ate everything and topped it off with beans.

Choppers (the Maine woods term for lumberjack) insisted that these
beans be made to formula—nothing was dreaded more than a French
Canadian cook who insisted on using lard instead of salt pork—and
that, even when conventional ovens were available, they receive an intensive, flavor-enhancing, lengthy baking in a stone-lined pit known as
a bean hole. The pit would be filled with logs which were burned down
to charcoal. The bean pot—a cast-iron affair so large that it took two
men to lower it—was filled up with the prepared beans, eased in, and
covered over, first with canvas and then with enough dirt to make a
thick layer of insulation on top.*

---

* For more on the exact workings of a bean hole, see "Baked Beans, Maine Lumberjack
Style" in Imogene Wolcott's *New England Yankee Cookbook* and "Bean Hole Beans"
by Suellen Simpson and Margaret Welch in Issue 7 of *Salt*, Maine's version of the
Foxfire series.

At lunchtime, two cookees, or cook's assistants, would hoist out the pot, hang it between them on a pole, and—with the rest of the meal also dangling from it—set out for wherever the choppers were cutting that day, which could mean a hike of several miles. When they arrived, however cold the day, the beans would still be steaming hot—and they would be eaten fast to keep them that way. A slow eater might find the last few bites frozen to his plate.

Meanwhile, back at the camp, another fire would already be blazing in the pit in anticipation of supper. And so it went. The camp cook was the last to bed and the first to rise. The final thing he did before turning in, after getting the sourdough bubbling for the morning batch of flap-jacks, was to seal a final pot away in the bean hole to cook all night. And the first thing he did in the morning after he got the coffee boiling was to crack open the bean hole. Only then, when those two summoning aromas were mingling in the predawn air, would he begin to bellow, "Rouse up! Daylight in the swamp!"

It is generally believed that the loggers learned to make bean hole beans from the Indians; hunters and fishermen certainly learned how to make them from the loggers. In Maine, even today, still-functioning bean holes can be found outside vacation camps in the great Allagash wil-derness (and in many tamer regions as well).

We encountered bean hole beans at Dick's Restaurant in Ellsworth. When he was in the mood and the weather was right, Dick would fire up the bean hole in his back yard, bake a big pot of beans, and bring these in with him to the restaurant, where they would be served all day. We had ours as a side dish for breakfast, and our waitress told us that we weren't alone. What we discovered is that bean hole beans are dif-ferent from other baked beans the way brick-oven-baked bread is dif-ferent from other breads; the exposure to that long, intense heat results in beans cooked to total smoothness beneath a thick, flavorful, chewy crust.*

Unlike us, my father encountered bean hole beans on their native turf, deep in the Maine wilderness almost sixty years ago, as he recalls in the following tale.

---

* Bean hole beans also float in more sauce than ordinary baked beans. Since the pot can't be opened during cooking time to check for evaporation, the cook puts in an extra ration of water. Consequently, lumber camp cooks made sure there were platters of sliced bread on hand when the beans went out so that the choppers could swab down their plates.

Back in 1935, my brother, Gordon, took me on a canoe trip up the East Branch of the Penobscot River in Maine. I was fifteen at the time, and this was really an adventure for me—after about two weeks in the back country, we were eating only fresh fish, oatmeal, and boiled potatoes . . . and not necessarily in that order.

We also had a small kettle in which we brewed our "coffee." During the day we would wedge it in the bow of the canoe so it wouldn't spill, for we had left in all the old grounds. At mealtime, we would add water and a little fresh coffee, and boil it over the cooking fire. This did stretch out our meager coffee supply and gave us a hot beverage at meals. And because of it, even to this day, I can tolerate pretty poor coffee.

Getting back to bean hole beans . . . We arrived at a campground at the entrance to Matagamon Lake, which was served by a narrow dirt road from Patten. We pitched our tent in an open space next to a semi-permanent camper, a retired lumberjack who spent the whole summer at this spot. He was very friendly and invited us to come over and have supper with him, for he was cooking up a "mess" of beans. When we arrived later that day, he explained what he had done.

At the site of his camp he had already dug a pit about three feet deep and lined it with flat rocks, both on the bottom and laid up around the walls much the way a water well is constructed. He said he had made it the previous year, the only upkeep required being occasionally replacing a rock shattered by the heat.

In preparation for cooking the beans, he had first built a fire in the pit the previous night and fed it during the evening. In the morning, he had a deep bed of embers and the rock lining was well heated. He then proceeded to place a flat stone on the embers. On that he set a covered bean pot already filled with parboiled beans, to which he had added molasses and a chunk of salt pork.

He placed a large flat rock on top of the bean pot and filled the rest of the hole with smaller rocks, raking them from his campfire, where they had been heating for this purpose. He had a small piece of canvas to cover it (the filled pit was nearly to ground level), weighing it in place with a few more rocks and some dirt. This was completed at about seven in the morning. He then took off for an all-day fishing trip.

When we arrived at about five that evening, all he had to do was uncover the pit. He flipped off the canvas, raked away the small rocks, and used a stick to remove the larger, flat rock that covered the bean pot. Then, using a large rag as a potholder, he reached in and lifted out the bean pot . . . and uncovered a steaming batch of baked beans.

We were hungry and this was the first meal in many days we hadn't had to cook, so in all aspects it was good . . . The beans were well done and tasty. In fact, if it hadn't been for the small bean-sized pebble in my portion, it would have been perfect.

—JOHN H. THORNE, SR.

Crab Rolls &
Lobster Stew

1

Lobster stew, by any Maine reckoning, is best contemplated if one or the other of two circumstances hold: (1) you are, or are married to, a Maine lobsterman, or (2) you have plenty of extended family, access to a Maine summer cottage, and a lobsterman next door. These, at least, were the thoughts that came to me as I contemplated the beginning of a lobster stew recipe, submitted by Rena Bunker, in the Maine spiral-bound cookbook *More Favorite Recipes from Matinicus Island*:

> Break off claws and tails of about twenty lobsters. Place in a kettle and cover with boiling water. Let stand a few minutes and pick out meat . . .

This receipt, in the old-time manner, may leave certain aspects of the preparation unclear—are those lobsters *alive*?—but it is a crystal-clear example of our rule. No one but a resident of a Maine island, surrounded by lobstermen, could so off-handedly present a dish calling for twenty—twenty!—lobsters.

From her bread recipe, which produces a substantial number of loaves, and from the presence of several other recipe-submitting Bunkers in the same spiral-bound, we may guess that she daily faced the task of feeding a family of hearty eaters. Even so, there is no hint that Mrs. Bunker was running a hotel. Matinicus Island lies in the Gulf of Maine, of all that state's inhabited islands the one farthest out to sea.

It is right in the center of prime lobstering territory, the sort of place where the taking of the claws and tails from twenty lobsters to make a stew is not the stuff of tall tales but plain cooking.

One might also guess—without, I hope, edging into impertinence—that Mrs. Bunker is married to a lobsterman. These days, any other Maine cook, wherever situated, would at least pause and take a deep breath before ordering twenty lobsters. But I deduce this mostly because lobstermen generally don't care to eat lobster in its ideal form—simply steamed. The last task anyone who has hauled in those beasts all day wants at the end of it is to wrestle with the carcass of one for his supper. But dropping a sack of shorts* at the wife's feet as he passes through the kitchen on his way to the La-Z-Boy and the TV is another matter entirely.

My mother, in the days when we spent our summers on Long Island in Casco Bay, would make a lobster stew now and then, and she would take, if not twenty, at least eight or so lobsters to do it. The difference was that these were *picked-over* lobsters. At any summer family gathering on the island—usually signaled by the arrival of my grandfather and an uncle or two—we would go down the road to the Doughtys', home of our nearest lobsterman, and bring back a big brown paper bagful.

We had an outdoor fireplace—really a three-sided enclosure of un-cemented stones, on top of which a metal grill was precariously balanced. In this, a driftwood fire would be built. As it burned into charcoal, we would carry a huge aluminum pot down to the beach. One or two of the youngest children would fill this with dripping-wet sea-weed, pulled from the rocks so that it wouldn't be full of sand, while the rest of us dug for soft-shell clams.

The lobsters and clams would be steamed in the seaweed over the charcoal with plenty of fresh-shucked ears of corn while, in the kitchen, butter would be melting on the stove, rolls warming, and potato salad

---

* Shorts, of course, are lobsters below the legal size. No Maine lobsterman would *ever* bring home shorts for a stew, but his competitors might, and it's rumored that these scofflaws have some mighty ingenious ways of doing so. To reduce the risk of getting caught to practically nil, they sometimes even whip up the stew right on board; it can then be safely left to age on the small gas stove (otherwise kept for heating hot buttered rum) until it's time to come home. As Mike Brown writes in *The Great Lobster Chase* (the best book there is on Maine lobstermen and lobstering): "Lobster stew can be taken ashore very lawfully, although wardens rant and rave and curse knowing full well the source of the chunks in the stew."

mellowing. The large family table would be covered with newspaper—nothing makes a mess like lobster—and the feast would begin with the arrival of a huge bowl of steamed clams. Everybody would dig in.

My mother and her brothers had a rigorous approach to lobster eating, which, I'm ashamed to say, I never managed to absorb. It generally shuns instruments in favor of cleverly applied leverage: with a twist here and yank there, everything edible in the lobster is exposed. The rule was that every little morsel must be picked, poked, or sucked out of the legs and body before you could allow yourself the reward of that huge, tender chunk—"slab" might be a better word—of tail meat.

Those of us under twelve, spurred on by much encouragement, would start off strong. Although we immediately surrendered the roe and to-malley (the red and green stuff, respectively, in the lobster's body) to any taker, we devoured the claw meat and sucked enthusiastically on the legs. It was, I think, the richness of the tail meat that undid us, because at that point, unexpectedly, we began to fade. Our appetite would suddenly turn its attention to the potato salad—that unfinished piece of tail and the underpicked body already tacitly surrendered to Sunday's lobster stew.

These days, however, the uncles are scattered to the four winds (or rather, I suddenly realize, *I* have now become one, myself), and our family, when it gathers in the summer, prefers to pack up a potato salad and a container of fresh-baked brownies and head for a lobster pound that sells the beasts ready-boiled for consumption (and disposal) on the premises . . . or, best of all, just outside them, at a picnic bench on the wharf.

Living here on the Maine coast, Matt and I do occasionally eat lobster, but each time we set out to buy them, the thought of doing anything but steaming them seems a waste of opportunity. Lobster meat, picked still warm from the shell, dipped in melted butter, is one of life's rare, purely transcendental tastes, equal to a piece of perfectly ripe unpasteurized Brie spread on a Parisian sourdough baguette or Beluga caviar mounded on a sliver of hot buttery toast.

The only problem is that, because of this attitude, we don't have lobster as often as we'd like. I didn't understand this as a child, but it takes a certain amount of stamina to deal with a lobster. They are large and alive. (*How* large and alive was impressed on me again the last time I went to buy one. The lobsterman dropped the fiercely kicking two-pound monster into my hands and said, "Here. Hope you brought a bag.") Once you get them home, however safely ensconced in the bathtub with a pail of seawater poured over them, they lurk, hulking, in the back of the mind all day . . . an odd mixture of pathetic victim and rather frightening, stalk-eyed, decapod crustacean. With lobster stew, the pot is waiting when you come in and the deed is swiftly done.

Furthermore, this is the dish that is best designed to deal with all that lobster mess. The cracking, breaking, twisting, poking, picking, and scraping that with boiled lobster is done at the table can now be done with fingers and spoons on top of a pile of newspaper spread on the kitchen counter. The refuse can then be wrapped up and disposed of while the sun is up. As fond as I am of a boiled lobster dinner, I dread that late-night trek into the mosquito-infested woods, a flashlight in one hand, a lobster pot full of debris in the other. No wonder that neighbors with weaker moral fiber just toss the stuff into the ditch across the road from their house.

The other argument for lobster stew is economy. Outside the lobstering fraternity, no Mainer thinks lobster cheap. This is partly because of the waste—one pound of steak is a pound of steak; one pound of lobster is more shell than food—and partly because the essential unit with boiled lobster is one (at least) per person, period. This is why the eateries that serve a mostly local clientele, if they feature lobster at all, offer lobster stew. With it you get what you pay for, which is meat.

No discussion of lobster meat can ignore the subject of the lobster roll. These not only exist but can prove a terrible temptation. I can't drive across the "singing bridge" over Taunton Bay without feeling an urge to pull in at Stuffy's, a window-service eatery at the Sullivan side. One memorable summer day, I stopped for a lobster roll on the way into Ellsworth and, on the way back, for another, followed by a cone packed with Gifford's coffee ice cream. But this is only to say that good lobster rolls are relatively easy to come by along the Maine coast and good lobster stew is not. That's because tourists drive up and down the coast of Maine. The lobster roll really belongs in a discussion not of lobster stew but of—as we shall come to see—the crab roll.

Lobster stew is a dish built out of subtleties of understanding. To explain what I mean, let me annotate the basic and almost perfect recipe in Cora, Rose, and Bob Brown's vintage (1940) but enduringly vital culinary romp through the forty-eight states, *America Cooks*.

LOBSTER STEW

Cut up and fry cooked lobster meat in butter. Then turn into
scalding hot milk, season with butter, salt, pepper, and paprika.
Let stand awhile before serving, to bring out full flavor.

For the lobster-stew maker, there is an eloquence in this recipe. Its
brevity salutes the simplicity of the dish; everything it says is important,
and what it doesn't say is even more important. It names none of the
egregious unnecessaries that spoil many another recipe—the clam or,
worse, chicken broth, the celery or onion salt. It leaves up to the cook
the proportions of lobster to liquid; it puts butter into the category of
seasonings, not major ingredients. It directs you to sauté the lobster
meat before adding it to the broth, which both coaxes out its flavor and
releases a delicate rosy tint, which then suffuses through the dish. And
finally, it supplies the essential trick: keeping the cooking time short,
the aging time long. If you follow this recipe, you'll make a good lobster
stew.

The problem is, no one but a lobster-stew maker will know *how* to
follow it. Consider:

CUT UP AND FRY COOKED LOBSTER MEAT IN BUTTER. For Matt and
myself, I get one 2-pound lobster. Three cups of unsalted water are put
in our large stainless-steel steamer. This is brought to a boil and the
lobster is put into the steamer insert, still alive, upside down, its head
against the steam vents. The rule for cooking a lobster, no matter what
any cookbook says, is to do so until you're convinced that it's dead.
Once, following the persuasive advice of Helen Witty (in her admirable
Mrs. Witty's Home-Style Menu Cookbook), I steamed a 2-pounder for a
mere 12 minutes. That time passed far too quickly. I was convinced—
even though it was motionless and bright red—that the lobster was still
alive. I was a murderer returned to the scene of the crime too soon; if
it had moved, I think I would have screamed. I tore it to pieces in a
state of fear and loathing. Now I cook a lobster this size for 18 minutes.
It isn't overcooked . . . and I know it *is* cooked. Helen Witty is the
braver cook.

I confess all this because grasping the visceral connection between
lobster and eater is the first step to any understanding of lobster stew.
Not only is that crustacean one of the only creatures we still bring live
into the kitchen, it is one of the few carcasses we tackle in its entirety

at the table. And apart from suckling pig, it is the most impressive. With a boiled lobster dinner, each eater confronts his own beast and with it makes his separate peace.

In lobster stew, however, this role is assumed entirely by the cook. The more atavistic the encounter, the better, the more authentic, is the stew. The cook who elides this task into the simple and fast-acting equation—*lobster stew = carcass − meat*—is not the one to choose. The first secret of this dish is that you must pick the lobster as if you were right then eating it yourself. Everything you are tempted to lick, suck, or chew, you must somehow save, somehow get into the pot. That is as it should be: the measure of your appetite is the measure of your lobster stew.

Set the lobster in a shallow bowl to catch its juices. On another plate, put every bit of meat you can winkle out with fingers, pliers, pick, even—unless you are feeding strangers—mouth. Quickly it piles up: chunks of tail and claw meat, slips of leg meat, shreds of body meat, flaps from the tail flippers. But this is only the start. Inside the body is the greenish tomalley, or liver, and—if the lobster is a female—red lumps of roe. Remaining inside the shell are blobs of a congealed white substance that some say is the lobster's fat and others its blood. As much of this as possible is spooned into a saucer. Then the body carapace, the shell part of claws and tail, is put to simmer a bit in the water at the bottom of the steamer. Add to this the juices that have collected in the bowl.

Final prep: The meat should be picked over carefully, the eye alert for bits of shell. The tail meat should be pulled open, and the intestine, a long, dark, oozy thread, picked out. What lobsters feed on, you do not wish to know. Cut the larger hunks of meat from the tail and claw into bite-sized chunks, but large, not small, ones.

With all this good stuff, the dish needs little additional savor. Chop up a small onion and a sprig of parsley and wilt both in two tablespoons of butter, seasoned with a pinch of cayenne (not paprika) and a generous spoonful of the blood/fat/roe/tomalley mixture—the rest of this being covered and kept safe in the refrigerator. The lobster meat is then stirred in and heated up.

THEN TURN INTO SCALDING HOT MILK, SEASON WITH BUTTER, SALT, PEPPER, AND PAPRIKA. The butter and hot pepper have already been attended to. Milk was richer when the Browns were writing; the "ordinary" milk we now drink has much less cream than when—even in my own childhood—it used to rise in a thick clot at the bottle's neck.

Today, with all milk homogenized, who would see it? Today, with all customers diet-conscious, who would want it?* Well, me, for one, and certainly in my lobster stew. So, instead of modern milk, I mix two cups of non-ultra-pasteurized half & half and the strained liquor of the lobster bath in a small pot and heat it until it almost simmers. Turn in the sautéed lobster meat. Add salt to taste, but hold the pepper.

LET STAND AWHILE BEFORE SERVING, TO BRING OUT FULL FLAVOR. Aging is the other secret of a great lobster stew. The change is real— even miraculous. What before was good and simple now also possesses character and depth. It's as if, somehow, the tide rolled in, bringing with it the mysterious whispering of undersea flavors. Like the tide, it takes about six hours to happen, although you can start to taste the difference in one.

In the days of wood-fired cookstoves, Maine cooks simply shoved the pot to the back of the range and left it there. Once the lobster has been stirred in, I let the stew cool, lid off, to room temperature and put it, loosely covered, in the refrigerator. With the arrival of each new tide, the dish grows in subtle complexity. The ideal aging time is said to be two days, but a single day is about as long as we can bear to wait. To serve, I reheat it slowly over a low flame, while also warming up the tomalley mixture (remember it?) in the top of a double boiler. This is carefully spooned into the lobster stew just before it is brought to the table. Before you do so, taste again for salt and grind some black pepper over. Serve with, if anything, some freshly made chowder crackers (see page 64) or hot buttered toast.

2

The crab, in Maine, is the second-class crustacean. Unlike in Maryland, where the blue crab is king, there's no talk here of jimmies, sooks, peelers, softs, she-crabs, buckrams, or boilers. There are no shouts of joy when the soft-shell crab season arrives, no heaping platters of beer-

---

* My grandmother, when my brother Fred complained—back in the mid-sixties—that the milk didn't taste right, tried it herself, agreed, and called our local Quincy dairy (White Bros., now, like most good local dairies, defunct) to find out why. The man she got on the phone agreed: "Thin stuff, isn't it?" The dairy had, he explained, switched over to a leaner formula. But they would, at a slight premium, still deliver the old-fashioned—rich and creamy—original (equivalent of "classic" Coke). She had them bring it until the dairy was no more. With it went classic milk, home delivery, and the milkman's familiar morning clatter in the back hall.

battered busters at roadside joints. A whole cookbook could be—and has been—written about Chesapeake Bay crab cooking; Down East crab cookery is nothing to boast about, hardly even worth mentioning.

The reason usually given for this state of affairs is that the crab common to the Maine coast is the rock crab, which has a poor culinary reputation. Alan Davidson speaks for many when he opines in *North Atlantic Seafood*, "These crabs do not enjoy, or indeed deserve, the esteem which attaches to the blue crab." However, to my palate, the freshly picked meat of the rock crab—unlike that of the Maine shrimp, which I have never found anything but insipid—is delicately textured and deliciously sweet. The blue crab must really be something if it is markedly better than that.

So, I don't believe it's any fault of the Maine crab that there is no crab dish here that isn't done better somewhere else; in fact, there are no distinctly Maine *crab* dishes at all. There are only crab*meat* dishes, and only one of these is worth a page of prose. The single item this state has to put up against the Chesapeake Bay's crab cake and Charleston's she-crab soup is the humble crab roll. However, it's enough.

Lobster rolls are not exactly uncommon in Maine, but crab rolls are endemic; the former is summer-people food, the latter is for—and is priced for—everybody. Even in takeout places, a lobster roll costs about seven dollars, or it isn't as heaped up with lobster meat as it ought to be. A lot of places sell a very good crab roll for four dollars, sometimes less. Thus, even if the bakery roll is the one fate our two crustaceans have in common, it's the most likely destination for the crab, and the least likely for the lobster.

When I first moved to Maine, I was puzzled by how easy it was to buy picked crab and how utterly impossible to buy picked lobster. Puzzled because, as good as a crab roll can be, lobster rolls are better. But I won't, can't, pick a lobster to make one . . . it's just too much labor for too short—however ecstatic—a moment of pleasure. No, the homemade lobster roll is the product of leftover lobster—which means that these days, it's just one more traditional Maine lobster dish we rarely see.*

---

* An even simpler variant of the lobster roll is leftover lobster meat heated up in melted butter and served with a mess of warm biscuits or spooned onto hot buttered toast— which, because of its next-morning nature, at least one Maine lobsterman, Dana Holbrook, calls "lobster fried over cold." Mr. Holbrook described the dish to Sarah Leah Chase in *Saltwater Seasonings: Good Food from Coastal Maine*, see pages 139–43. That Maryland crab cookbook, by the way, is John Shields's *The Chesapeake Bay Crab Cookbook*, which, interestingly enough, has over a dozen recipes for crab cakes but not a single one for crab rolls. This just goes to show what they know in Maryland, and what they don't.

But—and this is the nub of the matter—if I won't pick a lobster for anything but lobster stew, neither will I or almost anyone else in Maine pick crab for any meal at all. Boiled lobster, whatever the work, yields a lot of meat; a boiled crab, near nothing. Anyone used to lobster can't *bear* to pick crab . . . except, of course, for money.

However, there was one time in my life when I did pick crabs. It was during the summers I spent alone at the family cottage. When I broached the subject of setting out my own lobster trap to knowledgeable year-round neighbors, I was told that, while catching lobsters strictly for my own consumption *might* be legal, it would certainly make me enemies. As far as crabs were concerned, though, I could help myself. So I did, using a line-operated trap off the side of a nearby dock. They were a fearsome catch as well as hard to pick, but I did it happily all summer, because these crabs were free.

What I am talking about here is how we give weight to what we eat— how we decide whether it's important or not, and, consequently, how respectfully we end up treating it. For a crab to have weight in Maine, you have to be hungry and the crab has to be free. Lobsters, which are never free, have almost too much weight to be thought about at all; mostly they pass by in refrigerator trucks, heading out of state. Plain boiled lobster and lobster stew are both Maine ways of easing them onto the table without turning the meal into some kind of state occasion.

For crabs to get weight enough to become pan fodder, they have to undergo considerable transformation. They, like lobsters, are scavengers, and they are attracted to the same kinds of bait. Because of this, a lot of them end up in lobster traps, to the annoyance of lobstermen, who consider them a kind of trash fish and mostly a nuisance. As Willan C. Roux writes in *What's Cooking Down East*: "Years ago, any lobsterman would give you a bucketful of crabs for the asking. Later they sold for a penny apiece." More recently still, they passed that bucket on to their wives, who boiled them up, cracked the shells, picked out the meat, and sold that for pin money.

I write this in the past tense because, these days, lobstermen do well enough for their wives to need do no picking—although, of course, some wives still have to, and some do anyway. Mostly, however, other women have taken on the job, buying their crabs from the local lobster pound, where, relatively speaking, they're still cheap. At the Winter Harbor lobster pound, for example, a wooden crate holding a hundred pounds of crabs—which, incidentally, is the only way they are sold—goes for thirty dollars. About 15 percent of blue crab is meat, so a crate of them yields fifteen pounds. Crabmeat retails for around seven dollars a pound. A meticulous picker can pick about three pounds, or twenty-one dollars' worth, in an hour, yielding a profit of fifteen dollars. This, in Maine, is not bad pay.

When I asked the women who picked crab why they didn't pick lobsters, too, they answered in ways that at first I took to be evasive but which I now understand were more indicative of helpless incredulity. Only a fool would pick lobsters for meat when there's a ready, easy market for them alive and kicking. The number of fools in Maine (as opposed to askers of fool questions) can be gauged by the fact that, while between May and November most coastal roads are generously seasoned with hand-lettered crabmeat signs, you'll never encounter one offering picked lobster. In fact, there aren't all that many signs offering *plain* lobsters, since lobstermen know you'll find your way to their door, regardless.

Again, this business of weight—which brings me to another, equally revealing way of stating the difference between lobster and crab here in Maine: the buying of one is an outside transaction, the other happens in the house. Lobstering is considered a variant of hunting/trapping and hence male work; crabs, the raw stuff of womanly craft. When my mother sent me to the Doughty family to buy lobsters, I would walk down to the dock with Mr. Doughty, who would row out to one of his holding traps to get them. If I came for crabmeat, I would be invited right into the warm and steamy Doughty kitchen.

Today, the kitchen is still the place to buy crabmeat, but while some of it is still picked entirely by women, in others it is the team effort of a semi-retired husband and wife. For instance, we buy ours from Walter Tibbetts, around the corner on Pigeon Hill Road, whose kitchen is as dauntingly clean as his containers are heaped with big chunks of leg meat. (He also takes his sign down when the day's picking is sold out, a rare courtesy—Mainers hate for potential customers to turn away, even if there's nothing on hand for them to buy.) When you stop to buy it, as often as not, he is sitting at the kitchen table over a tray of crabs, mallet in hand. His wife takes your money and hands you your crab, in neat-packed half-pound containers, out of the refrigerator.

Maine crabmeat is wonderful. Why is the cooking done with it so drab? The answer is, I think, that while in Maryland crab picking remains women's work, crabbing, which here is considered a no-talent occupation, has there been raised to a high (and, of course, pretty much all-male) art. In the Chesapeake Bay, crabs have absolutely perfect weight. Marylanders expect to get something good—really good—for their money when they eat crab, and very often, they do. The only Maine seafood that competes on *these* terms isn't crab or lobster at all but the soft-shell clam.

Down East, even picked crab lacks weight—and so it gets tossed into casseroles or cracker-crumb "pies" and stuffed with cheese into fish. It gets treated right only when it's put on a par with the lowly hot dog, which, even more than the burger, is native Maine's fast food of choice. Down at this level, crabmeat is the deluxe offering, and so finally gets some respect. Here, for example, is Sarah Leah Chase on the subject (again in *Saltwater Seasonings*):

> As would be expected, there are good crab rolls and bad crab rolls. Good crab rolls start on a base of a buttered and toasted hamburger or hot dog bun, which is then filled with an ample quarter-pound of fresh crabmeat bound lightly with good-quality mayonnaise and absolutely no additional celery or minced onion as fillers—an incredibly simple and pure affair. Bad crab rolls consist of inferior crabmeat further bastardized by celery and onions slopped lazily onto an unbuttered and untoasted bun.

This description requires little explication, but it does call for a small amount of dissent. The first caveat regards the roll. Although Sarah Leah Chase admits the use of hot-dog rolls, her bias is for the hamburger bun—which, in fact, is what she calls for in her actual recipe. But crab rolls are called crab rolls and not crab buns for a reason: a hamburger bun makes for too much bread. Crabmeat should be bursting out of the top of a crab roll, not dribbling out of the sides of a bun. The proper container for crabmeat is the sort of hot-dog roll that has sliced sides to allow for crisping on a griddle. Or, to put it exactly: the base of the perfect crab roll is a buttered and *grilled* New England-style hot-dog roll.

I also disagree with her regarding celery. Like her, I'm happy enough not finding it in the crab rolls served at roadside drive-ins; there, its presence is usually a signal of all she says it is. Still, as Maine cooks have long known, crab and celery have a natural affinity. Unlike the luscious, almost buttery taste of lobster, crabmeat has an edge to it that mayonnaise alone can only smother but a touch of celery somehow modulates . . . as does the acidic tang from a few drops of a Cajun *green* hot pepper sauce. Not an orthodox Down East crab roll formula maybe, but a good one.

REBEL ROLL
(MAKES 2 CRAB ROLLS)

¼ cup Cain's mayonnaise
2 tablespoons finely minced celery
2 or 3 drops green Louisiana hot pepper sauce
½ pound good Maine crabmeat
Salt and freshly ground pepper
Butter for grilling
2 Nissen or other New England-style hot-dog rolls

Mix together the mayonnaise, minced celery, and hot pepper sauce. Stir in the crabmeat and season very carefully with salt and pepper. Lightly butter the sides and bottoms of the rolls. Grill them until toasty brown on both sides and—for one last minute—on their bottoms. Split, heap to overflowing with the crabmeat mixture, and eat at once, with a handful of potato chips on the side.

We have other ways of giving Maine crabmeat good weight, but one is especially appropriate with which to end this piece: a very simple corn and crabmeat stew. Shuck and cut the kernels from 4 ears of sweet summer corn, being careful to scrape every bit of milk from the cobs. Melt a knob of butter in a cooking pot and season it with a little salt, a generous dash of hot pepper sauce, and black pepper. Mince a stalk of celery, a sprig or two of parsley, and a small yellow onion. Mix these in. When they have softened, add the corn, along with 2 cups of milk. The moment the corn is cooked, stir in half a pound of crabmeat, and remove the pot from the heat—let sit for a few minutes to let the flavors develop, while the chowder crackers are divided up and the bowls got down from the shelf. Serves 2.

STEUBEN, 1992

Homemade Chowder Crackers

We love these homemade crackers. They're crisp, crunchy, and tender, with a clean wheat taste. We bake a batch most of the time we make a chowder now, pushing the pot to the back of the stove to mellow out during their short baking and cooling time. Then the only problem is deciding whether to eat them straight or crumble them into the bowl. If a sourdough loaf is in the works, we knead up a little extra dough for these crackers as well, working in the shortening, developing the dough, and preparing the crackers as described below. However, even with commercial yeast, the long, slow rise gives these little nuggets a deliciously delicate tang.

There are three secrets to these crackers. The first is the daylong aging, which develops the nutty flavor of the flour. The second is letting the dough rest halfway through the rolling out, which relaxes the gluten, allowing it to be rolled out even thinner. (It may be possible to roll the dough too thin, but I've never managed it.) This makes a crisp cracker. The third secret is baking them on a dark metal cookie sheet. This kind of pan browns them perfectly.

CHOWDER CRACKERS
(MAKES ABOUT 4 DOZEN)

5 ounces (about 1 cup) unbleached flour (see note)
¼ teaspoon regular dry yeast
½ teaspoon salt
1 tablespoon fresh lard or vegetable shortening (see note)

THE EVENING BEFORE: Put the flour, yeast, salt, and lard in a mixing bowl. Stir in enough water (about 5 tablespoons) to work the mixture into a coherent mass. Knead this for about 15 minutes, until it forms a slightly resilient dough. It will have none of the pleasing elasticity of an ordinary yeast dough—working it is not unlike kneading putty. Put the dough into a small bowl and cover with plastic wrap. Poke a few slits in the plastic with a sharp knife and put the bowl in a cool, draft-free place—like the floor of a closet or the top of the cellar stairs, but not the refrigerator—to rise. Check the dough now and then to make sure it is not rising too fast.

THREE HOURS BEFORE: Punch the dough down and, with a rolling pin on a floured surface, roll it out into—more or less—a square, about a quarter inch thick. Cover with plastic wrap and let it rest where it is for about 30 minutes. Now roll it out to the thickness of a board of a hardcover book (or about ¹⁄₁₆ inch). Lay the dough on a cutting board and, with the tines of a fork, prick a close-set pattern of holes all over the dough.

Then carefully cut the dough into 1-inch squares with a sharp chef's knife and set these on an ungreased dark-metal cookie sheet. (Of course, you can cut the crackers into any size you want, even using a small round dough cutter to punch out authentic-looking oyster crackers.) The crackers can be placed close together on the sheet, but they shouldn't touch. Set the sheet in a warm, draft-free place to allow the crackers to rise for about 2 hours.

TO BAKE: Preheat the oven to 450°F. Put the cookie sheet on a rack in the middle of the oven and bake 8 minutes. At this point the bottoms of the crackers should be lightly browned. If so, remove the sheet from the oven, turn them all over, and bake another 6 minutes, or until lightly browned on both sides. Cool on a rack and serve warm.

COOK'S NOTES. These crackers don't keep. All-purpose flour is acceptable, but for best results use a hard-wheat bread flour. Homemade lard gives these crackers an especially nice flavor, but a good vegetable shortening does just fine.

STEUBEN, 1992

Fix Your Hash

The first time I ever made a hash I was twenty or so and spending the summer on Long Island in Casco Bay, Maine. Despite its name, the island was only a few miles long, and at least once a week I would walk from my end to the other, civilized, end, the location of the laundromat, the fire station, the snack bar, and, most important, the country store. The proprietor, old Everett Clarke, knew my family and gave me credit. Each summer I ran up a bill there, provisioning myself as best I could from their spartan shelves, knowing that at summer's end my grandfather was going to bail me out.

In those days at Clarke's you went to an ordinary refrigerator to get your milk and cream and to a home freezer with a lift-up top for cans of frozen orange juice and the square waxed boxes of frozen corn and frozen peas. A row of wooden produce crates along the floor of one wall held the fresh vegetables available that week: always potatoes, cucumbers, celery, iceberg lettuce, and apples; occasionally corn on the cob, plums, peaches, and local tomatoes. On the rare occasion when I bought a steak, Mr. Clarke himself went into the walk-in locker to cut it to order from a side of beef. On the counter where he did the trimming and packaging, a quarter-wheel of decent sharp Maine Cheddar sat under a glass bell.

After I made these rounds I would wander among the remaining shelves searching for any previously overlooked delicacy—say, Maine sardines packed in mustard sauce—and gathering up a few of the ones I had already come across: Moxie soda, Uneeda crackers, Habitant French Canadian pea soup. It was in this context that I picked up and considered my first can of pressed corned beef.

Recently I was surprised—pleased, I suppose—to discover that this can still be found on the supermarket shelf; even in 1963 it seemed part of a disappearing era. To start with, the stuff comes from South America—Brazil or Argentina, depending on the brand—conjuring up not so much exotic locales as slaughterhouses far from USDA inspectors. Then there is the strange shape of the can—a kind of truncated pyramid—immediately suggestive of primitive processing machinery.*

Since Mr. Clarke sold both hamburger and a cheap stew beef that possessed its own rugged authenticity (one of my uncles used to joke that he had once found an Indian arrowhead buried in a cut of it), I'm still not sure what drew me to purchase that first can or, once I'd tasted its contents, caused me to buy another. But I did. And there was never any doubt in my mind what to do with it: the stuff exists to be made into hash.

This essay is about pressed corned beef only to the extent that that substance served as my doorway into hash making; I haven't bought a can of it in years. But I retain fond feelings for it, and I understand why some people continue to buy it, the way some others, in this era of the microwave and fat-gram counting, buy Hormel canned chili, Underwood deviled ham, and Armour Vienna franks.

For those who can still feel that tug, a can of pressed corned beef is attached to our past by many interesting threads. The British call it bully beef (from the French *bouilli*), and in World Wars I and II it was to the Tommies what Spam was to the Yanks. Pressed corned beef is the food of early twentieth-century cookhouses in mining and lumber camps, oil rigs, and other male culinary outposts. It fueled polar explorations, sailing voyages, and hunting trips. Tom Stobart writes in his *Cook's Encyclopedia* that "on expeditions, I have depended on it for months on end."

These connections place its greasy toughness: this is the universe of

---

* Actually, that can was invented in America late in the last century by J. A. Wilson, and it revolutionized the meat-processing industry. Cheap cuts of beef were cooked in brine and saltpeter (to preserve the pinkness), then shredded to allow tight compacting. Not only did this process transform the toughest longhorn into edible meat, it resolved a problem that continues to afflict even the choicest canned unpressed beef: no matter how carefully prepared, it emerges from the can with the loose, mushy texture of dog food (still the bane of canned beef stew or, for that matter, of canned corned-beef hash). Wilson's compacting process presses the shreds into a "piece" of meat; the unique pyramidal design of the can allows it to slide out as a single chunk. *Voilà:* corned beef in a can. Until the advent of frozen dinners, a dusty tin of this could be found in the back of most American food cupboards. Not anymore. But if our local supermarket is any indication, it remains a choice commodity here in Maine.

blue-collar romance. Even the awkward mechanism of the can—the inadequate key, the stubborn, razor-edged metal strip that it is supposed to peel away—adds its own particular frisson (opening one once, I slashed all five fingers of one hand—and this the night before I had to shovel out the outhouse), with a compensatory sense of mastery and skill. Denser and tougher than Spam—and saltier and greasier, besides—so far as this can be said of anything out of a can, pressed corned beef is one mean chunk of meat.

I chose to make a hash with this stuff because (a) "hash" snaps to "corned beef" as firmly as a carpet tack to a magnet; (b) carrots, potatoes, and onions were pretty much the sum of my vegetable larder; (c) hash is one of those dishes that to taste is to know how to make; and (d) the stuff was too awful to be eaten except diluted in a mess of vegetables.

It was exactly for reasons like these that hash became America's standard cheap meal—the hamburger before the hamburger—from the Civil War well into our own century. The word worked its way into our language as a metaphor for any cheap grub, giving us "hash house," "hash slinger," and such spin-offs as "to make a hash of things," "to fix someone's hash," and—now lost, but my favorite—"to go back on your hash." This meant to back out of eating when you saw what had been put on your plate, a sign that you couldn't be trusted when things got tough.

Like the hamburger, too, a plate of hash spoke of the relative luxury of meat, the comfort of heat and grease. But where the hamburger is fried minced "steak," hash is just fried stew. There is no pretense about hash, which is one of the best things about it. In fact, I think a case could be made that the hamburger was able to shake itself free of its sissy Salisbury-steak image only when it insinuated itself into a bun.

Fast-food places today are part of our homage to the automobile. A Burger King has big glass windows so that we can look outside at the road and the cars and trucks that rumble past. The old-time hash house, on the contrary, was a windowless cave; outside were flies, clouds of dust, horses and their endless droppings, men pushing wheelbarrows, women lugging loads of laundry. You went inside to put all this at a distance—leaving your troubles behind with the daylight. Then, to sit down and eat a meal off a plate was the luxury; today, it is to own—or at least have access to—a fast car. So, fast food. A hamburger already *looked* like a car wheel: it left hash behind in the dust.

As a solitary rebel growing up on an army base in the 1950s, my images of outsider life were indelibly formed by books I got from the post library—male adventuring on the order of Jack London or, to be more honest, the tramp steamer pulps of Howard Pease. Even today, the word "hash" for me evokes the smell of hot grease, not the resinous reek of hemp. This difference between my contemporaries and me was spelled out when I spent part of the summer of 1969 with some college friends on their commune.

They had bought a secluded farm, were growing cucumbers to sell to a local pickle plant, and did the sorts of things that got the neighbors to "drive by" down a dead-end road just to gawk. For this left-leaning, bluegrass-playing, free-lovemaking, dope-smoking, organic-gardening crowd, I forked out a good part of my capital to buy an armload of those pyramidal tins and made a farm-table-sized canned corned-beef hash. It was received well enough—even hippie farming is appetite-making work—but also a bit bemusedly.

Commune cooking was already tending toward whole-grain semidemi-vegetarianism, and that meal stood out from the regular roster like a sore thumb. I soon moved on to other things. A duck hash was one of the earliest meals I ever made for Matt (the first was a homemade Cajun boudin), but for years and years, hash was no longer a regular part of my own culinary routine.

Here in Maine, however, hash has come back into my life. At first, it was something that we went out to eat. Breakfast is a meal most small-town Maine eateries do well, and often hash—along with blueberry pancakes, biscuits, and molasses doughnuts—is one of the featured items on the morning menu. As we began to sample it here and there, I noticed two variations. The first, most memorably eaten at Dysart's, a truckers' haven on Interstate 95 near Bangor, is hash made of very finely minced corned beef and potato, as delicately textured as a potato pancake.

This is in contrast, of course, to the familiar greasy, crusty slab of corned beef and potato cubes—itself nothing to sneer at if, as it can be here in Maine, it is made from the remains of the restaurant's Thursday night boiled dinner special. Last winter, we regularly braved zero-degree temperatures to drive to the nearby Cherryfield Inn, where, each Sunday morning, the cook cranked up the grill to deliver a mahogany-crusted hash topped with two perfectly poached eggs and served with hot biscuits on the side. The sheer elegance of this version, the fact that the meat it was made of came from a meal and not a can, drew me back in. I began, at first by the by, to read up on the subject. There proved to be more to it than I thought.

The hash that nineteenth-century hash houses slung on plates was simply a mince of cheap cooked meat, a low-end version of the classic French *hachis*. *The Larousse Gastronomique* contains dozens of recipes for this type of hash, all unfamiliar to American eaters. The hashes we know—corned- or roast-beef hash, red-flannel hash, salt-fish hash . . . all variations on a theme of small-cubed meat or fish, onion, and root vegetables like potato, carrot, and beet or turnip—are American and relatively recent. Printed mentions of corned-beef hash, for instance, start appearing only around 1900.

It is my belief that this hash—*our* hash—is the creation of Yankee cooks. I think this because of the voices of New England food writers when they turn to hash. They speak of eating it with longing, their instructions for making it are full of fine distinctions, and their indignation at the way others make it is real and rich. The Boston-based *Appledore Cook Book* (1872) is a collection of recipes, not culinary polemics, but when Maria Parloa comes to "meat hash," more than a page of advice and lament pours out of her—including a warning against heaping on the grease.

Unlike the old-style hash-house mince, these new-fangled hashes were neither greasy nor even all that meaty. Classic Yankee cooking was vegetable intensive, even if it did use meat fat as a means of heightening sensual pleasure. That Yankee culinary curmudgeon Haydn Pearson argued in book after book—but especially *The Countryman's Cookbook*—that red-flannel hash is not corned-beef hash made with the addition of beets (this, he says, is "calico" hash) but an authentic beet—i.e., *vegetable*—hash. He took nine beets, three potatoes, and one onion, cubed and fried them in a little bacon fat, then crumbled and tossed in the cooked bacon. "That," he wrote, "is a genuine New England red flannel hash. Unless you've eaten it, you've missed one of life's good foods. The blending of beets, potatoes, and onion with just a tantalizing whiff of bacon is superb."

This rural Yankee hash had no stigma of the leftover about it, and neither did the original corned-beef hash. In *Cooking American* (1957), Sidney Dean, a Yankee whose memory—and appetite—reached back into the last century, writes about his mother's New England boiled dinner:

> This dinner was a two- to three-day affair. We had corned beef hot, corned beef cold, and slices of the cold beef browned in butter: this last a pleasant hot supper dish served with quick biscuits just out of the oven and homemade preserve. We had the various vegetables hot the first day, then chopped to reappear as vegetable

hash . . . Finally, we had crisply browned corned beef hash itself, the best hash in the world if skillfully prepared.

Originally, *two* hashes were conjugated from a boiled dinner, a vegetable hash and a corned-beef hash. It was the first that cleaned the platter. "The next morning [after a boiled dinner], use what remains of the vegetables as a vegetable hash," wrote Mary Lincoln in her *Boston Cook Book*.

> Vegetable Hash. *Equal parts* of *cabbage*, *beets*, and *turnips*, and as much *potato* as there is of all the other vegetables. Chop all very fine; add a little *salt* and *pepper*; put *a spoonful of drippings* in the frying pan, and when hot add the hash, and cook very slowly until warmed through.

In contradistinction, a corned-beef hash was a fine mince of corned beef and freshly boiled potatoes. Some achieved this texture by running the ingredients through a meat grinder, but as Kenneth Roberts explained in *Trending into Maine* (1942), the ideal cook did it all by hand:

> Into a wooden hash bowl were put three cups of cold boiled potatoes and four cups of cold corned beef from which all gristle and fat had been removed. The hash-chopper was used on these until the meat and potatoes were in infinitesimal pieces . . . The important feature . . . was to make sure that the person who did the chopping shouldn't be too easily satisfied, but should lovingly labor until each piece of potato and each piece of corned beef was cut as small as possible.

This old-style hash is akin to a horseless buggy: its fine mince reaches back to hash-house hash; its near-equal blend of meat and potato connects it to the contemporary diner or lunch-counter hash. That you can still encounter it at places like Dysart's is a tribute to its ability to endure.

Wooden hash bowls and hash choppers are no longer stocked in Maine country stores. What they sell instead is *canned* corned-beef hash, which takes the vernacular-eatery style of greasy cubes of meat and potato and debases it into mush. At home—since not even Yankee cooks now want a four-day run from a boiled dinner—vegetable hash and corned-beef hash have been collapsed into a single dish: a fry of leftover meat, potato, carrot, onion—sometimes even cabbage.

This hash represents a culinary condensation: the melding and so simplifying of more complex traditional cookery to meet contemporary needs. The result can be good enough in its way, but it is, finally, just a dish of leftovers. I wanted a hash that called out to be eaten . . . which is to say, a hash made lean again with a survivor's cunning.

The foundation of a great hash remains a good piece of boiled beef. Our local grocer—Sweeny's Market in next-door Milbridge—prepares the classic New England version of corned beef, which is made without nitrites and so is gray instead of pink. We started our boiled-dinner-plus-hash experiments with it . . . and still would be if I hadn't sat down with John J. Pullen's *The Transcendental Boiled Dinner.*

If any single text could be designated the ultimate authority on that subject, it would be this one. Pullen, it turns out, lived up U.S. 1 from us somewhere between Machias and Calais. His is a classic Maine tongue-in-cheek narrative, where drollery at once masks strong affection for and points up strong opinion about a much made, much pondered, and much enjoyed Yankee dish.

Pullen not only drummed into our heads the single essential rule, *simmer*—"[The dish], properly prepared, is not boiled—boiling will ruin it"—and equally pungent injunctions—"He who puts an onion into a New England Boiled Dinner should have his ears cropped"—but a proposition that entirely changed our thinking: *not using corned beef at all.* Pullen adamantly advocates using a good cut of pot roast instead. He refuses to give his reasons (his basic pedagogic approach is "Just do what I say and don't ask stupid questions"), but it took only one try for us to come around. Even given a trustworthy source for minimally processed corned beef, the advantage of plain boiled beef lies in the flavor of the cooking liquid; the dish is worth making for it alone.

Our boiled dinner is simpler even than Pullen's classically proportioned model (we omit the turnips); what we were seeking, after all, was the basis of an ideal beef *hash.*

Boiled Beef

The cut Pullen recommends is a 3–4-pound piece of center-cut beef shin. We tried this and agree that the marrow does add a smoothness to the taste of the finished dish. But we are just as happy with an equal weight of beef chuck shoulder roast, which adds its own gelatinous richness and produces an even beefier-tasting broth. His method is to put the meat into a pot, cover it with fresh well water, add about a teaspoon of salt, bring it to a simmer, cook it for 4 minutes, then remove the meat to a plate and *pour the cooking liquid down the drain.* This seemed madness until we did it—and found even this brief cooking had encrusted the pot with scum which required a hard scouring to remove. This preliminary descumming will reward the cook with a perfectly cooked piece of meat floating in a limpid, full-flavored, clean-tasting broth.

The beef is returned to the scrubbed pot and covered again with fresh water, mixed with another generous teaspoon of salt. At this point, we part company with Mr. Pullen, starting with the contents of our *bouquet garni*:

A small sprig of fresh rosemary
A half tablespoon of black peppercorns
A teaspoon each of hot red pepper flakes and
Black mustard seed

This is wrapped up in cheesecloth and tied with a short length of string. The bundle is then lowered into the pot with the loose end of the string tied to its handle. With the help of a thermometer, a flame-tamer, and regular monitoring, we keep the liquid in the vicinity of 185°F and cook it for 6 hours, or until the meat almost collapses into mouth-melting tenderness. The pot is taken from the stove and the meat allowed to cool in the liquid for half an hour. It is then removed, and both broth and meat are divided in two—half for that night's boiled dinner, the other half for the next night's boiled beef hash.

Notice that there is no *pièce de résistance*, followed by a long run of leftovers. Boiled beef is as undimmed and delicious on the last night as it is on the first, and every meal makes the most of this. For example, dividing the broth before preparing the boiled dinner means that the reserved portion will have no tired or cabbagy overtones to muddy the flavor of the hash.

Boiled beef is to roast beef what an ox is to a wild steer: the one may possess all the drama, but the other, treated with respect, has sturdy nobility which gives character to the dishes made from it. That piece of chuck, simmered for hours in an aromatic liquor of its own making, is tender enough to be pulled into shreds with the fingers. We actually prefer to serve it this way in our boiled dinner.

That is assembled by simmering an appealing balance of potato, carrot, and cabbage—all cut into bite-size pieces—in its half the liquid, putting in the carrots 5 minutes after the potatoes, and the cabbage, along with some minced fresh parsley, 5 minutes after the carrots. The meat is returned to the pot just before serving, 15 minutes later. No further recipe is required; if you poach the beef as directed, the dish will be superb. And you are now prepared to make the hash.

MAINE BOILED BEEF HASH
(SERVES 4)

1 tablespoon rendered suet (or butter)
½ teaspoon ground hot red chile
1 teaspoon salt
4 all-purpose Maine potatoes, peeled
Reserved beef stock reduced to 1 cup
1 large onion, peeled
1 tablespoon butter
3 large carrots, peeled
1 garlic clove
1 sprig fresh leaf thyme
About 12 ounces of boiled beef
1 or 2 large sprigs fresh parsley
Black pepper to taste
¼ cup medium cream (optional)

In a large nonstick skillet (with a cover), melt the suet and season with the ground hot red chile and ½ teaspoon salt. Turn off the heat and let the flavors meld while you cut the potatoes into quarter-inch cubes (small, but not too small). Turn the heat under the skillet to medium-hot, add the cubed potatoes and ½ cup of the beef stock. Cover and let cook over medium heat while you cut up the onion into medium-size bits.

Melt the butter in a small skillet, add ¼ teaspoon of salt. Add the onion bits and cook these, stirring occasionally, while you cut the carrots into quarter-inch cubes. Mix these in with the potato cubes, stirring well with a spatula; then pour in another ¼ cup of the beef stock. Replace the cover.

Finely mince the clove of garlic with the fresh leaf thyme in a pinch of salt. Stir this in with the onion, along with a large spoonful of the beef stock. Now add this to the carrot and potato cubes, along with all the remaining beef stock.

Cube the boiled beef and mince the parsley. When the potatoes are firm but cooked and the carrots have lost their crunch, set the cover aside, stir in the onion-garlic mixture, the cubed beef, the parsley, and any remaining broth. Season with black pepper. Cook, stirring occasionally, until all the moisture has been absorbed.

Finally, press the hash down gently with the spatula into a single, firm cake, then turn up the heat to high. Dribble over the cream and cook for 5 minutes. Turn over an edge of the hash with the spatula to see if it's browning. If a brown, crusty layer has begun to form, turn over the rest of the hash to bring this crust up to the surface, re-form it into a cake, and continue to cook. Check after 5 minutes. Again, once a brown, crusty layer has formed, turn the hash over, re-form into a cake, and finish the cooking for another 5 minutes. This time, serve the hash out onto warmed plates, crusty side up.

COOK'S NOTE. This hash will not have a thick, crunchy hash-house crust—that requires plenty of hot fat—but it will be a hash with crisp-edged pieces and a delicious flavor. To make it with the minimal amount of fat called for here, a nonstick skillet must be used. The new generation of this cookware is designed to allow high-heat sautéing; however, we have done this with our old faithful 12-inch Wearever nonstick skillet for over a year without damaging the pan. The cream, by the way, serves the same purpose as the yolk of the traditional poached egg: lending a touch of unctuousness that points up the sense of richness. Those who feel it merely gilds the lily can leave it out.

Again, it is the intense flavor of the broth that lifts this hash into the realm of the extraordinary—although the resilient texture of the fresh-cooked vegetables adds to its sense of unexpected luxury. It is a dish that insists on being taken seriously and here, at least, retains something of its original hang-tough reputation, along with a not-unrelated Yankee economy of means. Such a hash can fill everyday life with a sense of quiet but tangible event, from the long poaching of the meat to the final climactic drama of the crust. The ingredients are friendly and familiar; the prep and cooking require only the kind of considering attention that is itself half anticipation. In this regard, a good hash is a provider of companionship, of a house full of aroma, and of hours enriched by agreeable expectation. Wrote Haydn Pearson, remembering:

> As a man comes through the woodshed with the milk pails on his arm, he inhales the smell and a smile lights his face. What better reward for a long day's work digging potatoes or picking apples?

STEUBEN, 1994

Spring Greens

One of my all-time favorite cookbooks is Pino Luongo's *A Tuscan in the Kitchen*. The food is good, simple, and full of character, as if it were made out of the stuff of someone's actual larder, and the recipes—because he gives no specific ingredient quantities—make you think and taste. The net effect is something that every cookbook should accomplish but only a few actually manage: you feel better about yourself as a cook after you put it down than you did before you picked it up.

I also like *A Tuscan in the Kitchen* because it has the feeling of a writer trying as much to remember something for himself as to explain it to his readers. Consequently, his prose has that richness of image that comes from letting the eye linger long enough on a scene for all its corners to be filled in.

Take mattresses, for example. The Luongo family slept on wool ones, and every spring they sent for the *materassai* to come air them out. This meant opening them, removing and fluffing up every piece of wool inside, and then putting it all back together again. It took the whole day, and so the *materassai* brought their lunch along: a flask of wine, a loaf of bread, a cold *frittata di pasta*, another flask that held a simple *condimento per insalata* (salad dressing) . . . and an empty salad bowl. The salad itself, "tiny field rugola, aromatic herbs, and wild spinach," would be quickly gathered from the fields around the house.

It all sounded very good, but what stuck in my mind after I turned the page was the confidence represented by that unfilled salad bowl. I don't mean by this the bringing of a little flask of dressing along to work each day, secure in the knowledge that the salad is waiting by the roadside. That kind of certitude I understand well enough.

Winter is long up here in Maine and seems longer still because I

grew up in places where the lilacs bloomed earlier than the end of May.
The first signs of green, of course, come much sooner—but still late
enough that my hunger to see them takes on a physical edge. Although
I'm not starved for Vitamin C, I want to put those first shoots into my
mouth and suck the spring right out of them.

The wild green that I, like everybody, most immediately recognize is
dandelion. It comes up early and comes up salad-ready. One early day
in May, as I cross the sun-warmed, southerly slope of the Castine cemetery, there they are, waiting for me—tiny bunches of tender, soft,
bright-green leaves.

Identification is no problem; they draw the eye right to them. The
difficulty comes when I've actually picked some and brought them home:
a salad of dandelion greens brings me close to gagging. The same is
true with other foraged greens and with the commercial ones closest to
them—cress, for example, or corn salad or chicory. It would be a different matter if I simply *disliked* greens, but I don't . . . It's just that in
eating them, I walk a tightrope between pleasure and actual physical
revulsion. It's like the edginess I get eating blood sausage or tripe
gumbo—there's something here that cuts a little too close to the bone.

A salad of buttery lettuces made piquant by a few bitter greens is
one thing; a whole plate of fresh-picked *weeds* is another—no matter
how charming their names. Here, then, is the conundrum that traveling
Tuscan salad bowl posed me: its confidence of appetite.

"Field salad" is a hot item in certain culinary circles these days. But
there has always existed in Maine—as in Tuscany—a deep-rooted native hunger for wild greens. I'm not the only one around here on the
lookout for dandelions, first of spring. Indeed, in Maine, a meal of dandelion greens has all the imperative of a moral duty. "Spring tonic," it
is called. As Hazel V. Hall remembers in *No, We Weren't Poor, We Just
Didn't Have Any Money*, it was the older children who were sent out
into the fields to pick them.

We would go armed with butcher knives and dish pans to gather the tender
morsels . . . After they were dug and carefully cleaned and washed we would
serve them in several different ways. For instance, we would put a big piece of
salt pork on to cook about one hour before we wanted to start the greens. Then
when the greens were all ready we would cook them in the broth of the pork and
water until done, with potatoes added for the last half hour of cooking. We always
served a mustard sauce on the pork . . . This was most certainly a feast for the
gods. Other times we would fry out several strips of bacon, mix a little vinegar,
sugar, salt, and raw onion in some of the fat to pour over the greens and stir until
wilted. On Saturday night we would make a salad of the little tender leaves by

mixing them with vinegar, salt, sugar, and pepper to go with the delicious, golden baked beans.

Dandelions were also salted down for winter eating.

> We would fill our jars full of [salted] greens and then wait a day or two and repeat this process as the greens had shrunk. Finally the day came when they were all filled. We would cover each jar with a plate with a good sized field rock on it and wait until winter to sample the wonderful flavor of salted greens.

Today, instead, a local firm over in Wilton puts up dandelions—and beet greens and fiddleheads—in cans under the "Belle of Maine" label. You have to have a strong sense of regional identity to want to buy a can of dandelion greens.

In my opinion, you also have to have real hunger to want to eat them at all. Rather than encouraging appetite, the rank, determined fecundity of the dandelion entirely dissuades it. All that bitter greenness—a field-ful of it makes no one hungry but a cow. Can anything besides plain ravenousness explain its culinary appeal?

The answer, I think, resides in the favorite way this place has of cooking it. Dandelion salads are not ignored, but Maine prose comes alive when the cook is instructed to take the greens—milkweed, cow-slip, "pusley" (purslane), dock, pigweed, but most often dandelion—heaps and heaps of them, toss them in a big cast-iron pot with a chunk of salt pork . . . and cook the bejesus out of them.

Hazel V. Hall sidesteps the actual cooking time, but Robert P. Tris-tram Coffin, never one to beat about the bush, states categorically in *Mainstays of Maine*:

> Dandelion-greens are to be boiled right up and down for three or four hours . . . [M]odern dietitians will blanch and hold the table until their knuckles show white. Let them . . . Let all the vitamins and salts go up in steam and out of the kettle. The dish is better off without such effete things.

Nor, if you cook your dandelions this way, will you be sorry. Coffin speaks rightly: "They are tender as butter and melt as fast . . . A man eats five plates of it, with a dash of vinegar on each mountain, and cries for more."* But that mountain isn't made of anything still identifiable

---

* Coffin wrote this in 1944, but his words are quoted with approval in Willan C. Roux's *What's Cooking Down East* a decade later—and they still hold true. Roux, like Hall, suggests throwing in a few peeled potatoes for the last half hour or so. "You'll want for nothing else at that sitting." No lie there.

as dandelion. It is dense, sinewy, slick with grease: a kind of green muscle, vegetable meat.

It takes a lot of greens to make a piece of meat, which is one reason we would rather let the cow do all the work . . . and then to eat the cow. What this meal does, for those without the cow, is face down this prolific aggressiveness with a determination equal to the dandelion's own. It is less a dish than a primal rite: devouring your enemy to incorporate his vigor. Put away five plates of boiled greens and you'll get your vitamins and mineral salts . . . and do your lawn a good turn, besides.

I don't have the rural roots that can regularly command this kind of appetite. Consequently, my way of coming to terms with the dandelion's essential otherness is much less strenuous, a compromise of sorts between the Tuscan and the Coffin method.

BACON AND DANDELION SANDWICH

Cut 2 thick slices from what food writers like to call a good, crusty loaf. Pick, clean, and pat dry a bunch of tender, young dandelion leaves (or some other astringent salad green). Fry up some country bacon. Brush the bread slices with hot bacon grease and assemble a sandwich of the dandelion and the bacon. Salt and pepper well and eat at once.

I claim nothing novel here: hot bacon fat and vinegar have long been used to dress a dandelion salad, the fat wilting as well as lubricating the greens. What is good about my method, however, is that the bread envelops all. It's the next best thing to eating whole the animal that ate the greens . . . an impression fostered by the sweetness of the fat and the soft, fleshy thickness of the bread.

This, I think, is the whole point. In that Tuscan meal, the bread is served on the side. But the olive oil provides the fat, and vinegar and salt the blood. A bowl of greens so dressed becomes—just like dandelions boiled with salt pork—entirely flesh.

CASTINE, 1990

The Call of the Wild Berry

On September 8, 1846, after a lengthy portage through wild country and a hard day of scrambling up over rock falls and past bear dens, Henry David Thoreau and a party of fellow climbers struck camp somewhere just below the summit of Mount Katahdin (or, in the more appealing spelling of the time, Ktaadn), Maine's highest and most majestic mountain.

As he relates in *The Maine Woods*, early the next morning, after a breakfast of hardtack, raw salt pork, and water, they began the final ascent. A combination of his own eagerness and the roughness of the terrain soon separated Thoreau from his companions, and he reached the top of the mountain first. Unfortunately, the summit was buried in a cloud bank, so he tarried there awhile, hoping for even a momentary break to reveal the vista of the lakes and endless forest that he knew was spread out far below.

However, as he waited, he began to wonder with growing anxiety why no one else was joining him. Should his friends have decided to start the descent without him, after all, he might find himself making the entire return trip to civilization alone. So, reluctantly, he finally abandoned his lofty perch to learn what had happened to them.

His party had been tarrying, he soon discovered,

> where I had left them, on the side of the peak, gathering the mountain cranberries, which filled every crevice between the rocks, together with the blueberries, which had a spicier flavor the higher up they grew, but were not the less agreeable to our palates.

Thoreau passes no judgment on his companions' moral fiber. All in all, it had been a hard trip, and such berry patches were one of its few rewards. Two days earlier, hacking their way through a dense thicket of yellow birch, spruce, fir, mountain ash, and moosewood—"the worst kind of traveling"—the party had found

> blueberries . . . distributed along our whole route; and in one place the bushes were drooping with the weight of the fruit, still fresh as ever . . . Such patches afforded a grateful repast, and served to bait the tired party forward. When any lagged behind, the cry of "blueberries" was most effectual in bringing them up.

Thoreau's party was neither the first nor the last to fall susceptible to the summoning power of the Maine berry. Nor is that berry always the blueberry, as it must—at least to outsiders—sometimes seem. Thoreau may have landed his hammer on the wrong nail when he commented that "when the country is settled, and roads are made, these cranberries will perhaps become an article of commerce . . ." but he does help establish this point: Maine is a place of many edible wild berries, and each of them, at one time or another, has received its share of praise.

William D. Williamson began his *History of the State of Maine: From Its First Discovery*, A.D. *1602, to The Separation*, A.D. *1820* with an extensive description of Maine's native minerals, plants, and animals, and he notes the abundance of black currants, wild gooseberries, wild plums, black and choke cherries, and, especially, brambles and hurtleberries.

> Of the *Bramble kind* we have seven species:—1 and 2, the *black* and *red Raspberry*; 3 and 4, the *upright* and *running Blackberry*, or *Dewberry*; 5, the *Brambleberry*; 6, the *Pigeon-berry*; and 7, the *Cloudberry*—all of which bear fruits succulent; and in most places they are abundant. The *pigeon-berry bush* is as tall as that of a blackberry, bears abundance of small purple berries, the chief food of pigeons. *Cloudberry* grows on the sides of mountains, or exposed and elevated grounds. The shrub bears a single berry on the top of the stem. In size and flavor it resembles a strawberry; having a greater though pleasant smartness, and making excellent preserves. Its colour is at first scarlet; turning, as it ripens, to a yellow. When eaten with sugar and cream, it is delicious, and so cooling as to abate fevers. The fruit lasts about a month.
>
> Of the *Hurtleberry* genus, there are four species:—1, the *Cranberry*; 2, the *Whortleberry*; 3, the *Blueberry*; and 4, the *Bilberry*—all of which are plentiful, nutritious and delectable to the taste. *Cranberries* grow about ponds and marshes. Great quantities are gathered every year on the Island Mount Desert and on the Cranberry Islands in that neighborhood. The berries, red and acid, containing many seeds, are borne by slender bushes 3 feet high, and give a most wholesome

and palatable zest to meats. Whortleberries are black; but bilberries, as well as blueberries, are blue, being the largest and sweetest of these three species.

"When eaten with sugar and cream, it is delicious, and so cooling as to abate fevers." Clearly, it was the cloudberry, an August berry that in Maine is also called the bakeapple and the heath mulberry, that excited William Williamson the most. It resembles a large golden blackberry growing out of a strawberry plant and has an unexpected lusciousness that can call exclamations out of not only nineteenth-century historians but the even drier texts of twentieth-century field guides. "Many consider this the most delicious of all far-northern berries," writes Lee Allen Peterson in his *Field Guide to Edible Wild Plants*. He then repeats himself, as if with a sigh, "delicious cold, with sugar and cream."

Good as these berries are, taste alone cannot explain their power over the Maine imagination. Berries grow in other places, too, and are probably just as tasty to those who pick them. To understand their importance here, you have to take a step backward—and look around.

Summer people tend to forget that winter, not summer, is Maine's essential season. It is winter—the dark, the wind, the snow, the endless, relentless, ever more intrusive cold—that defines the year-round inhabitant's character, by putting it to the ultimate test. Since the Maine temperament is enduringly Yankee in its sneaking delight in the mortification of the flesh for the good of the spirit, it is only fitting that Maine winters are endless and Maine summers are fleeting and capricious.

Those beautiful, hot, clear, color-drenched days of July with their cool, soft, star-filled nights—though these may seem the crowning perfection of this place—are to native Mainers the exception to the gloomier rule, to be enjoyed with caution and a certain diffidence. Their spirit, their lives, their houses are geared for winter, and it is best not to let the guard down too much.

There is more joy taken in a freak snow squall in June than in a week of unbroken sunshine. No matter that the flakes are all melted and gone in an instant, the next morning at the post office they will be the single topic of conversation, worried for portents, milked for humor, used as a fulcrum for remembering still worse summer weather back when.

The berry is the proper fruit to celebrate this spirit. Unlike the fat, sweet, unctuous fruits of other places—peaches, cherries, nectarines, melons, figs—the berry is small and tart. It thrives under hard conditions, in poor soil, in short seasons. The cranberry is associated with the bog, the blueberry with the barren, the cloudberry with the mountain heath, the raspberry and blackberry with waste ground. The berry insinuates itself where nothing else will grow (and with a vengeance—as anyone who has tried to root that invasive terror, the blackberry, out of their lawn will know).

Nor does it fall into your lap. The wild berry, if you want it, forces you to your knees . . . or worse. Rather than irritate, this trait calls forth a grudging admiration from a raw-knuckled tribe accustomed to spending the day picking over a pile of crab bodies, lugging a fresh crop of rocks out of the vegetable patch, hauling up lobster traps out of twenty feet of bay, or bent over a mud flat, digging bloodworms. This—to twist to a truer shape the state's egregiously humbug advertising slogan—is how life is supposed to be.

Listen, for instance, to the sheer relish in Robert P. Tristram Coffin's voice in *Mainstays of Maine* as he describes the haunts of the bramble:

> Raspberries grow in no such pleasant places as meadows. They get into skeletons of dead trees, into ravines, and around ledges . . . Blackberry bushes are spiked with steel, and they tear you apart. They are living barbed-wire entanglements. They band together and make thickets a rabbit cannot get through . . . You take them by side assault. Work gingerly up their flanks and snatch off a black cluster here and there . . . In no time you will be through and sitting on a ledge, picking the arrow-heads out of your person.

He doesn't bother to mention—perhaps because by the time he wrote those lines his own hide had toughened to leather—that while mosquitoes need blood to breed, they feed on berries. You can't truly appreciate the phrase "swarm of mosquitoes" until you've been surrounded by one in a berry patch on a muggy, lowering August afternoon.

The wild strawberry, which can be got without wading into bogs or reaching through briars—indeed, can often be picked right by the side of the road—costs what even in Maine is getting to be an expensive commodity: time. Pick-your-own strawberries are one thing, but the wild one is another; you can spend half an hour on your hands and knees and have just enough to cover the bottom of your plastic tub.

Blueberries are the exception to the rule. In some years, they are so much the exception that the rule can seem to no longer hold. In such summers, their amplitude is next to careless, the berries hanging, as Louise Dickinson Rich describes in *The Peninsula*, so thick on the low, dwarfed bushes that the earth seems to reflect the blue of the sky and the sea. In no time at all you can pick a whole milk-pan full. The foxes pick them, too, and the gulls and curlews. Sometimes during blueberry season the whole point seems to be covered with drifted snow as the great white flocks of gulls settle upon it to eat berries.

The blueberry is to other Maine berries what Mardi Gras is to Lent, except this is a Mardi Gras that arrives at summer's height. There are no parades, no floats, no dancing in the streets; this breaking of the fast is celebrated with a month of August awash with blueberry pie, blueberry-studded griddle cakes, blueberry bread-and-butter pudding. Hot kitchens get hotter as blueberry jam is boiled up in cauldron-sized pots.

The dizzy, celebrational edge to all this is that these berries are wild. This means, usually, free for the taking, even for those without land. Local fields are open to the casual picker.* Those too lazy to pick their own can buy them by the quart-sized container from the back of station wagons and pickup trucks. Like a midnight swim in a summer pond, there is a certain conspiratorial pleasure here—it is not the normal state of affairs, but there isn't anything demonstrably sinful about it either. It's just contrary to the usual expectations of rock-ribbed Maine life.

Of course, in some parts of the state the lowbush blueberry is now "wild" only by virtue of quotation marks. The picturesque blueberry barrens that stretch for miles in Hancock and Washington Counties are not natural but manmade constructs, and relatively recent ones. Only in the last few decades, with the discovery of selective weed killers that keep down the blueberry's natural competition, has it become profitable to fertilize the land and, year after year, produce what has to be called a crop . . . thus pushing Maine that much closer to the other forty-nine.

Predictably, Coffin is sniffy about the blueberry—"a big step down," he calls it (although he melts at the thought of blueberry pie). It's true that it doesn't have the panache of the raspberry or the subtle perfume of the strawberry. But its simple taste is as astonishingly bright and fresh as a dipper of cold well water. If summer has a flavor, it is blue-

---

* Although we live in prime blueberry country, while NO HUNTING signs abound, I've yet to see one warning NO BERRYING—except, of course, where the commercial people grow their blueberries. (Even then, all they put up is a sign, which some people choose not to see. So, occasionally, they put up another sign, this one with a skull and crossbones and the legend WARNING: BLUEBERRY PESTICIDE TESTING AREA, which does keep away the dimmer summer folk.)

berries eaten out of hand or, perhaps, in a cereal bowl (without the cereal, please), sugared a little and splashed with milk.

Less than a mile beyond our house, the dirt road we live on narrows until it is just wide enough, more or less, for two cars to pass. From there on, it wanders in and out of scraggly woods, skirting coves and crossing, finally, a long causeway to a small wooded island, where it eventually comes to an end. This road has no real shoulder. The verge crowds right up to it in a jumble of trees, shrubs, and wildly flourishing weeds. Here and there, smaller, rougher tracks head down to the shore and hidden summer cottages.

There are no boundary fences along its entire length. In part, this is because there is nothing here that is really worth protecting. This is land that can't be turned to the making of cash—or even into a decent lawn. It is strewn with boulders, clogged with storm-tumbled pine trees, scantily clad in lichen-covered acid soil.

For us, however, it is a wonderful place. On our regular walks, we keep our eyes and ears open not only for the occasional luminous encounter—the sighting of a moose or a bald eagle—but for the heart-stopping liquid trill of the hermit thrush at sunset, the velvet brown wings of the mourning cloak butterfly, the sun-baked sweet fern that fills the air with the scent of honey and eucalyptus.

Mostly, what we come upon are the wildflowers and the berries. There are so many of the former—wild rhododendron, wood lilies, swamp iris, sheep laurel, blue-eyed grass—that it would take a page to name them, and there are almost as many berries. Blueberries, blackberries, raspberries, lingonberries, bunchberries, partridgeberries, wild strawberries, and marsh cranberries grow everywhere along it, and they are yours for the picking.

I don't get the thrill out of picking berries that I used to, but I still do pick them. Sometimes it seems almost as if I *have* to—not because I want them but because it would be wrong to let them "go to waste." Once, climbing in the Blue Hills near Boston, I came across a place burgeoning with blueberries I knew no one was going to pick. I couldn't bear it. I returned the next day with a quart Tupperware container and filled it up, shamefacedly, as disapproving hikers went trooping past. To them, I was driven by greed to mess with nature's delicate balance. Not so. I was just responding to a different ethical imperative.

I started berrying when I was the next step up from infant, eating as many as I put into my pail. At that age, the berries are everything, a object of total concentration. I still get that feeling when I start: you see one, then a dozen, then a multitude (if never quite at the spot where you've chosen to get down on your hands and knees). By the time I was a teenager, after that first moment, my eye stayed only partly on the berries; what I came to love was how close berrying brings you to a patch of land.

When else, at the age of fifteen or fifty, do you spend all of a morning slowly crawling over one? The intentness is enough to shove out of mind the usual distracting thoughts, but not nearly enough to block out the quiet flow of peripheral sensation—impressions that are always there but are otherwise not let to reach the point of resonance. Hot sun, salt breeze, the coarse-textured granite under the knees, the taut, firm feel of the berries, the call of a solitary white-throated sparrow, piercing and melancholy, floating from a nearby grove of trees.

Berries, then, are a way of looking at your land. By "your land," of course, I don't necessarily mean owned property, just the place around. You would think that to live in a pretty place is reason enough to look, but as it turns out, it isn't. Looking is a learned art, not a natural habit. When you start looking at berries, the next thing that happens is that you find yourself looking *for* them. And then you find yourself seeing what you've never seen before.

It wasn't until I moved to Maine that I discovered that a lot of what I had previously taken to be trash fruit—bird berries—was edible, even good when made into preserves. Among such are the highbush cranberry, the Juneberry ("an excellent and far too neglected fruit," writes Peterson), the mountain ash with its brilliant orange clusters, and—despite its name—the chokecherry.

Up and down our driveway grows a nondescript shrubby tree. In the early fall this produces clusters of tiny blue-black berries which, when touched with frost, turn a soft red-tinged violet. As I was brought up to believe all such berries poisonous, it was a year or so before I even thought to look them up in our wild-food guide. But there they were: the wild-raisin berry.

Cautiously, I sampled one. The fruit was but a thin wrapping around a single, enormous seed, but it was sweet, with a faint, raisiny—or, more accurately, date-like—taste. I liked it, but what I liked even more was the sense, eating these berries, that I had been let in on a secret, brought a little closer to this place. Authentic rural hunger feeds identity as well as appetite—and it is this sense of connection as much as anything that fuels the urge to pick berries.

On a certain day each autumn, known only to themselves, two unfamiliar women slowly travel the length of our dirt road, stripping the verge of cranberries. By the end of the day they have filled a five-gallon bucket. When we lived in Castine, we discovered that every spray of elderberries—whole bushes worth—disappeared in the same way . . . whether to be made into jam or elderberry wine we never happened to discover. I'm slowly learning to understand such hunger, but I'll never completely share it. Too many things outside this small world compete for it; too many fears subvert it. This means that there will be many berries I won't ever meet—like the "sweet pear," a delicious berry that a neighbor occasionally encounters when he takes work raking blueberries.

Although her novel *The Shipping News* takes place in Newfoundland, E. Annie Proulx could well have been speaking of Maine when she set down this litany of summoning berries, so many of them outside my ken.

> On the headlands and in the bogs berries ripened in billions, wild currants, gooseberries, ground hurts, cranberries, marshberries, partridgeberries, squashberries, late wild strawberries, crowberries, cloudy bakeapples stiff above maroon leaves.
>
> "Let's go berrying this weekend," said the aunt. "Just over a ways was well-known berrying grounds when I was young. We'll make jam, after. Berrying is pleasure to all."

To all initiates, that is, of this hunger and its mysteries.

STEUBEN, 1995

STRAWBERRY SUNSHINE PRESERVES

A few weeks after I moved to Maine, I accompanied some friends to Silveridge Farm in Bucksport to pick strawberries. When you pick at a strawberry farm, containers fill quickly, no matter how many you also eat on the sly. It seemed I had barely begun when I had five full quarts and was on my way to a sixth. The obvious thing to do with all the berries that weren't going to fit in the shortcake was to turn them into strawberry jam.

As it happens, I love making preserves. Every summer I put up countless pints of blueberry jam and, depending on the appeal of the fruit that year, apricot, crabapple, Concord grape. Even so, there are some fruits whose evanescent freshness and flavor are so totally lost in the preserving process that I have always found it painful to make them into jam. Right away I think of raspberries: as soon as you bring them to a boil, the fragrance, the subtle flavor notes—the whole delicacy of the thing—is cooked away. With sweet cherries, too, it is all too easy to end up with a jam that has completely failed to capture that fruit's sharp, bright succulence.

Although many will disagree, I feel the same way about preserves made from strawberries, and I have never made (and almost never buy) ordinary strawberry jam. However, there is an old-fashioned way of preserving them in which small, perfect berries are stemmed, briefly boiled in sugar syrup, and set out in the sun in wide, shallow glass or enamel pans (preferably in a sunroom or greenhouse, but at least under glass). The ensuing gentle evaporation slowly thickens the syrup over a period of four to five days, producing bright red, flavorful berries immersed in fragrant syrup. Recipes for such "sun-kissed strawberries" can be found in many old preserving manuals and some new ones.

I adapted this method in two ways. The first was to eschew any cooking whatsoever; the second was to crush the strawberries so as to produce something more like a true jam. So, carefully discarding any soft, moldy, or bruised berries, I washed them, hulled them, set them in a bowl, and stirred in sugar in the same proportion I use in making regular preserves—for each pound of fruit adding three-quarters of a pound of sugar. I then mashed them up with a potato masher until the strawberries had yielded enough juice to turn the sugar into sludge. The result was very pulpy, with big chunks of berry. I mixed in a little fresh lemon juice to point up the flavor, scraped the mixture into a Pyrex baking dish (what I think of as a lasagna dish), covered this with cheesecloth* (held taut with a rubber band) to keep out insects, and set it out where it would get a full day's sun.

Maine is not the best place to perfect this process, and my notes immediately acquired an anxious edge—"hot and humid . . . the sun

---

* The first year I did this I used a sheet of glass, salvaged from a picture frame. To allow evaporation to take place, I used an epoxy-based glue to affix four dimes to the underside of the glass, spaced so that these would rest on the corners of the Pyrex dish. This did protect the mixture from unexpected showers, but moisture continually collected on the inner surface of the glass, which thus had to be gently lifted up every hour or so, so it could be poured off.

didn't appear until after noon"; "unexpected shower . . ."; "catastrophic weather conditions . . ." Still, at the end of the first day I was able to write that a thin but delicious strawberry-flavored syrup was floating above the pulp, with a thick sugar sludge at the bottom of the dish. By the end of the second day, the sludge had dissolved.

At sunset each night, I brought the pan in, covered it with plastic wrap, and kept it overnight in the refrigerator. If the next day was rainy, I just left it there. Otherwise, I stirred everything up and set it outside again. After two days, the thin syrup began to gel. Because the gel formed on the surface of the mixture, it slowed down evaporation unless I stirred it back in with a rubber spatula a few times a day.

By the fifth day, despite difficult weather, I had jam. It was not as thick as the commercial product but much denser than a syrup. Nor was it more intensely flavored than a good homemade boiled jam, but the taste of strawberry was at once fresher, more complex, and longer-lasting on the tongue . . . really splendid stuff. I put it into carefully cleaned half-pint jars. Two and a half pounds of fruit yielded four of them with about half a jar left over. I kept the jam refrigerated, and it wasn't until dead winter that I began to notice any deterioration in the flavor . . . at which point, of course, there was hardly any left.

The only real difficulty with this technique is deciding when to call it quits. The jam continues to thicken the longer it is left out, but the flavor begins to fade; a judicious balance must be struck each time. In subsequent years I've extended the method to such similar soft-fleshed fruits as peaches (fragrant and ripe but still firm to the touch, peeled, pitted, and cut into small chunks) and sweet cherries (stemmed, pitted, and cut into slivers). Same proportion of sugar to fruit, same tablespoon or so of lemon juice, same great results. My adventures with raspberries have been so complicated that they will require a separate narrative.

Is this method safe? Well, failproof preserving is only possible by strictly following USDA guidelines, and these say nothing about sun-cooked jams. Indeed, to the extent that any "preserving" is going on here, it comes not so much from sunshine but from the acidity of the strawberries and the ratio of sugar to fruit—high amounts of sugar retarding bacterial growth. I have prepared jam this way for years now without mishap, and when we consulted with two professional food writers with much experience in preserving, both cheerfully waved us on.

Helen Witty urged us to stress again that the fruit be sound (no soft spots, no signs of spoilage), the cheesecloth spotlessly clean, and the storage jars and lids boiled a few minutes (or put through the hot cycle in the dishwasher). Jeanne Lesem also suggested that freezing the finished jam instead of refrigerating it would prolong its fresh flavor and aroma without affecting its texture. So, if you have clean air, a sunny deck, and time on your hands this July, you might try a batch . . . it's the best strawberry jam *I've* ever had.

STEUBEN, 1994

Beyond Pie: Blueberry Bread-and-Butter Pudding

Matt Lewis Thorne

The season is only too brief when local fruit farmer Phyllis Shartner brings her small baskets of perfect strawberries, then raspberries, the bloom of freshness still on them, to sell at the Ellsworth farmers' market. All we want to do with our precious, fragrant hoard when we get it home is eat the berries straightaway with sugar and cream—or crush them gently, stir in a little sugar, and have them over vanilla ice cream. A few special times, we'll split and butter some biscuits hot from the oven, spoon the sweetened berries over them, and top each of these shortcakes with plain whipped cream. Those with their own berry patches may have more extensive repertoires, but we never get beyond taking our pleasure in the least complicated, most immediate ways.

It's different with blueberries. Good as they are eaten out of hand, they're even better cooked. And, up here, by midsummer they're everywhere. We can go out first thing in the morning and pick enough in a few minutes to dot our pancakes or add to a coffee cake. Quart containers filled to the brim with blueberries line the shelves of roadside stands and cover the tops of card tables set up at the ends of driveways.

Blueberry pie may be what most often comes to mind when imagining—or confronting—such bounty, and understandably so. But we're discovering that there are plenty of other things that cooks in blueberry country have devised to do with these berries between the time the first pie is put into the oven and the last jars of jam are stored away in the pantry. In fact, there's so much to explore that we've been happily occupied following just a single path—one we set out on thanks to a memory of John's.

His maternal grandmother, Irene Favorite—Nana—grew up in Gloucester and, as an adult, spent as many summers as she could (she was bedridden with arthritis for the last part of her life) in Maine, at the family cottage on Long Island. She was passionate about blueberries, and John remembers many a hot July afternoon spent in her kitchen, helping assemble the summer dessert she loved best—her blueberry bread-and-butter pudding.

Not surprisingly, a number of the "besides-pie" blueberry desserts bear close—or at least passing—resemblance to blueberry pie. Most of them involve a relatively generous portion of sugared berries being cooked en masse, either before or during baking, until their juices run together and they become a lovely, pie-filling-like proto-jam (this in contrast to proportionately fewer berries being folded into a batter and then exploding discretely throughout it as they bake, the way they do in a blueberry muffin). And just as a pie crust can underlie (in a tart), overlie (in a deep-dish pie), be layered, sandwiched, or spiraled with (in, say, a rolled pie), or, as it does most commonly, completely enclose this mass of berries, so can all sorts of other doughs. Such a dough can be baked by itself and later combined with the berries, or berries and dough can be baked—or steamed—together. Each partnership, each permutation, has its own distinctive effect and appeal, its own enthusiasts.

Naturally, the kinship to pie is more apparent when the dough emulates the shortness and presence of pastry—as does the rich biscuit paving on a cobbler. In a pandowdy, the same dough, rolled thinner, is baked for a while over the filling and then broken up and pushed down into the fruit for the last part of the baking. If the baking is uninterrupted and the finished dish inverted—à la tarte Tatin—for serving, it becomes a "plate cake." A not-quite-come-together shortbread dough goes to make both the crumbly topping of a crisp and the buttery underpinning of a kuchen. A blueberry shortcake—the berries sweetened with restraint and cooked just a few minutes, with no thought of thickening them; the shortcake itself, perhaps made with some good lard; the touch of fresh butter; the cold, thick cream—can heighten your awareness and appreciation of the separate components of blueberry pie, since with a shortcake the different parts are assembled only at the last minute, each at just the right temperature. Even the plump, yielding, less rich blueberry-and-dumpling pairings—the grunts, the slumps, the rolypolies—have their ties to the pie clan . . . looser, maybe, but still thought-provoking. (It's good to keep in mind that bakers regularly substitute one dough for another in all these dishes—and pinning down which name is used where for what dessert is a notoriously exasperating business.)

Of course, the most rudimentary crust is one of bread, and there is indeed a whole family of dishes built up out of blueberries and bread. In perhaps the most basic of these, sweetened stewed blueberries are ladled over hot buttered toast. Down East, this homely combination was often—is still!—eaten as a satisfying summer supper, with a glass of milk, a chunk of Cheddar, a scoop of cottage cheese, or a pitcher of cream alongside.

Starting out with the same ingredients that comprise this meal of blueberries over toast, Nana ended up in a very different place. In fact, when John first described her unbaked blueberry bread-and-butter pudding, it sounded like nothing so much as a sturdy, no-nonsense Yankee rendition of the English summer pudding.

I'd learned about summer pudding many years ago in Elizabeth David's *Summer Cooking*. There, she notes that "authentic recipes for it are rare," then proceeds to give this one:

> For four people stew 1 lb. of raspberries and ¼ lb. of red currants with about ¼ lb. of sugar. No water. Cook them only 2 or 3 minutes, and leave to cool. Line a round fairly deep dish (a soufflé dish does very well) with slices of one-day-old white bread with the crust removed. The bread should be of the thickness usual for sandwiches. The dish must be completely lined, bottom and sides, with no space through which the juice can escape. Fill up with the fruit, but reserve some of the juice. Cover the fruit with a complete layer of bread. On top put a plate which fits exactly inside the dish, and on the plate put a 2 or 3 lb. weight. Leave overnight in a very cold larder or refrigerator. When ready to serve turn the pudding out on to a dish . . . and pour over it the reserved juice. Thick fresh cream is usually served with summer pudding, but it is almost more delicious without.

By the time I finally came across some red currants for sale at New York's Union Square Greenmarket several years—and many British cookbooks*—later, I'd had my fill of reading about summer pudding and was ready to try my hand at actually making one. So I brought the currants, and some raspberries, home and then spent what felt like the rest of the day painstakingly assembling a model summer pudding— my first and, as it happened, my only. It was certainly delicious (how could anything made with those fruits and eaten with cream not be delicious?), but my most vivid memories of it are of pushing bits of bread into gaps in the casing and, after turning the pudding out, dribbling small spoonfuls of berry juice over spots of bread that had managed to remain dry and untinctured.

Nana didn't have the time or the temperament for a project like that—the intricately fitted pieces of bread, the search for the right-sized plate, the nervous unmolding. As John recalls, Nana cooked the blueberries for her pudding briefly and gently with sugar and a little water. Next, she took several slices of slightly stale, firm-textured bread— Arnold's Hearthstone was her favored loaf—and trimmed them of their crusts. She carefully buttered the bread and laid two of the slices side-by-side in the bottom of a smallish, loaf-shaped ceramic dish. Some of the stewed berries would now be tipped in. Nana alternated layers of bread and berries until the dish was nearly full, finishing with a top layer of berries. Then she set the dish in the icebox for the afternoon so that the bread could soak up all the berry juices. When the pudding was ready, Nana would simply spoon it out—moist, spongy, deeply purple—into waiting bowls. She liked to have hers with lightly whipped cream.

In addition to all the English references and recipes, I had also encountered, especially in the last ten years or so, numerous commentaries on and interpretations of summer pudding—some of them very lively and insightful—by American food writers (I think right away of Edna Lewis, Helen Witty, Richard Sax). Still, despite the freshness of thought and the Americanization of the ingredients (blueberries were often the featured fruit—or one of them), there was always the nod to England, if only implicitly in the unvarying roundness of the domed bowl or pudding basin or soufflé dish, in the snippets or triangles of bread, in the weight on the plate. I guess I'm only saying that they were always the same, recognizable summer pudding.

---

* Where, for instance, in her *English Food*, Jane Grigson opines that summer pudding should be served "with a great deal of cream; cream is essential for this very strong-flavoured pudding."

At least I hadn't ever read about one as fundamentally different as Nana's, one as simple and straightforward in conception and construction—or, for that matter, in the serving and eating of it. And because, for me, this pudding lived in John's story, I'd never thought to go looking for it in a book. So I almost didn't believe my eyes when I stumbled across a recipe for it—in, of all places, the cookbook I thought I knew better than any other, my mother's copy of the 1959 edition of *The Fannie Farmer Cookbook*. But there it was, in all its resolute Yankee practicality, right down to the loaf pan it was made in—and there was not a peep about summer pudding. In this edition it is described as "Maine Blueberry Pudding," but we were able to trace it back through the other Fannie Farmer volumes we have to its first appearance in the 1936 edition, where it is called simply "Blueberry Pudding" (and, where, bringing things even closer to Nana, a "glass bread dish" is specified).

The recipe calls for the buttered bread to be sprinkled with cinnamon, and later editions caution those using cultivated (as opposed to wild) berries to add lemon juice to improve the flavor. (I feel that the cinnamon is likewise best reserved for remedial purposes, although this sentiment is not shared by most Maine cooks.) It's true that the pudding is unmolded and sliced (and, through the decades, the "serve with" goes from thin cream to cream to heavy cream). But by the late fifties it's sliced right in the pan, and it's a short step from serving a slice to serving a spoonful. This was unmistakably the same pudding Nana made.

And, seeing it there on the page, I began to understand that, however I had first thought of it and whatever its connections might have been, this pudding was no longer a rendition or an interpretation of some other, faraway pudding. Somehow, it had come to stand on its own. It was what it was: the blueberry toast supper of summer puddings.*

Although neither Nana's pudding nor the blueberry toast supper ever saw the inside of an oven, all the various baked blueberry bread-and-butter puddings can be related to one or the other of these two elemental dishes. That is to say, there are some in which the ingredients lose much of their separate identities as they are transmuted into a single

---

* Since 1979, when Marion Cunningham took over the editorship of *The Fannie Farmer Cookbook*, "Maine Blueberry Pudding" has been replaced by a recipe, albeit nicely uncomplicated, for a traditional summer pudding.

whole, and there are others in which they retain these separate identities right up to the moment they are put into the mouth.

Many blueberry bread-and-butter puddings are as spongy and saturated with berry juices as Nana's. In *The New England Yankee Cookbook*, Imogene Wolcott describes her mother's version, which is put together almost exactly as Nana did hers. The slices of bread are trimmed and buttered and layered with berries (in this instance, the berries have been stewed with sugar only, no water). In Wolcott's mother's pudding, however, the melding of blueberries and bread is helped along by a quick turn (fifteen or twenty minutes) in a moderate oven. There is the same stay on the icebox shelf, though—for this pudding, too, is served "very cold with whipped cream."

In fact, the two puddings are so similar that they might once have been the same—the differences between them now a result of small inspiration or accident, the choice of one over the other a matter of fine-tuned discrimination. The baked pudding is a shade denser, more substantial, its flavor more concentrated; the unbaked one is fresher-tasting and lighter. Maybe it all comes down to whether you like the butter on the bread in your blueberry bread-and-butter pudding melted or not . . .

Indeed, why *did* Nana—and the cook whose recipe ended up in Fannie Farmer—butter the bread for an unbaked pudding? The English don't butter the bread for their summer puddings—not Elizabeth David or Jane Grigson or Alan Davidson or any of the others I consulted. (A few call for the pudding basin to be lightly buttered—as an aid to unmolding, I suppose.) But recipes for *baked* bread-and-butter puddings—plain or fruited—on both sides of the Atlantic often do specify, as does Wolcott's, that the bread be buttered. This may be another indication that Nana's was closer kin to these easily put together, thrifty puddings than it was to summer pudding.

(Curiously, many American food writers also butter the bread for their otherwise by-the-book summer puddings, and in wildly various ways— "very, very lightly," "lavishly," buttered sides in, buttered sides out, *both* sides buttered. How can we make sense of this? They, too, might be thinking of baked bread-and-butter puddings. Or the butter on the bread may be a reflection of the same tendency that has these writers eager to propose richer alternatives to the bread itself—challah, brioche, pound cake. Or maybe *all* these butterers are just making the jam sandwich of their dreams.)

One very likable oddball turned up in the "Penobscot County, Maine" chapter of *The Grass Roots Cookbook* (first published in 1977). There, Jean Anderson, with her characteristic attentiveness to detail, gives

Brownie Schrumpf's recipe for "Blueberry Fungi," a dessert of French-Canadian origin. This is a *super*saturated pudding—which makes us wonder if its name derives from the French word *fangeux*, meaning "muddy." Into a baking dish go two layers of buttered bread, each layer covered with a generous load of uncooked, sugared blueberries. A potato masher is then used to press down on the blueberries, crushing them. This pressing is repeated after the pudding has baked for about forty minutes. It's then returned to the oven for a final twenty minutes, "until the blueberries have a syrupy consistency and are bubbly." The fungi is cooled a bit before it is served "topped with gobs of sour cream."

The components of other, less soppy, blueberry bread-and-butter puddings remain distinguishable. Marjorie Mosser, in *Good Maine Food* (1940) dispenses with the preliminary stewing of the berries and the buttering and layering of the bread. Instead, she tosses bread cubes and uncooked berries with a mixture of butter and sugar, moistens the whole with water and a little lemon juice, and bakes it in a moderate oven for about half an hour. In other words, she nudges the pudding in the direction of a blueberry brown Betty, buttery and crisp at the edges— like the blueberry toast, but more of a piece.

In these three puddings—Wolcott's, Schrumpf's, and Mosser's—the stewed or oven-cooked blueberries replace the custard that binds the classic, and most familiar, bread-and-butter pudding. However, other puddings contain both berries *and* custard. Sometimes the sweetened mixture of eggs and milk or cream is simply poured over layers of berries and trimmed, buttered bread. The whole is set aside until the bread has absorbed almost all the liquid, then baked until the custard is set and the top layer of bread is a golden brown.

A recipe in Sheila Hibben's *American Regional Cookery* (1946) refines this procedure, moving the pudding closer to the blueberry toast side of the divide—and "Blueberry Toast," as it turns out, is the name given to this Massachusetts dish. Here, the slips of bread are first soaked separately in the egg-and-milk mixture. These pieces are used to cover over a baking dish filled with lightly cooked, sweetened berries, then it all goes into a hot oven until it is delicately browned on top. This pudding is dusted "generously with powdered sugar and lightly with cinnamon" and served with hard sauce.

June Platt pushes this method to its logical conclusion in one of the many blueberry recipes she offers in her *New England Cook Book* (1971). She fries up the egg-and-milk-dipped slices of bread in sizzling butter *before* they're positioned over the berries. Since the berries, too, are already cooked, the whole, sprinkled with cinnamon sugar as above, is simply passed under the broiler for a minute or two before serving. A pitcher of heavy cream accompanies the dish, which Platt calls "Blueberry Toast Dessert."

I had been keeping John apprised all along of what I'd been discovering about these puddings, but I have to say that it wasn't until I described June Platt's variation to him that I saw his eyes light up with something more than abstract interest—something like real appetite, in fact. Crisp, buttery, custardy toast sitting safe—and unsodden—above its blueberry sauce: this sounded good to him.

Because, truth to tell, one of the reasons the memory of Nana's pudding was so clear to him was that John, although he loved being party to his grandmother's happy anticipation, had himself *dreaded* this livid lump of a dessert. And I recalled that my own experience with summer pudding had been a one-time-only affair. That I had never noticed the recipe in my beloved Fannie Farmer was probably no accident either. After all, there are those who love slumps and those who love crisps, and so it goes with blueberry bread-and-butter pudding eaters. The two of us were of the same mind. We had come full circle, all the way back to the blueberry toast supper—but now it was transformed into a wonderful sort of upside-down blueberry French toast. Here, at last, was a blueberry bread-and-butter pudding that had us both wanting to try again.

BLUEBERRY TOAST DESSERT
(ADAPTED FROM *JUNE PLATT'S NEW ENGLAND COOK BOOK*)
(SERVES 4 TO 6)

6 thick slices good white bread
3 cups fresh wild blueberries (see note)
½ cup granulated sugar (or to taste)
½ tablespoon lemon juice (optional; see note)
1 egg
1 cup milk
Pinch of salt
1 to 2 tablespoons butter
Confectioners' sugar
⅛ teaspoon cinnamon or nutmeg

Trim the crusts from the bread and cut each piece into four squares. Pick over and wash the berries. Place these in a saucepan with the sugar and lemon juice if desired. Stir over medium heat until the sugar dissolves and the berries come to a boil. Reduce heat to low and simmer for 10 minutes. Pour into a shallow rectangular baking dish, approximately 6 by 10 inches (or any baking dish with a similar capacity).

Preheat the broiler. Whisk together the egg, milk, and salt. Melt the butter in a skillet. Dip the bread squares—both sides—into the egg-and-milk mixture. Over medium-high heat, fry them until golden brown on both sides. Transfer these to the baking dish, covering the blueberries neatly. (Some overlapping may be necessary.) Dust lightly with confectioners' sugar and cinnamon or nutmeg. Place the dish under the broiler just long enough for the sugar to melt and the toast to crisp up a little at the edges. Serve at once—accompanied, if you like, with a pitcher of heavy cream.

COOK'S NOTE. This dish is best made with fresh wild blueberries. If the berries are the large, cultivated variety, the lemon juice will point up their flavor. In our experience, frozen blueberries, even locally processed wild berries, have proved disappointing.

MAINE BLUEBERRY PUDDING
(ADAPTED FROM THE FANNIE FARMER COOKBOOK, 1959)
(SERVES 4 TO 6)

3 cups fresh wild blueberries (see note above)
¾ cup granulated sugar (or to taste)
½ tablespoon lemon juice (optional, see note above)
6 slices good white bread
1 to 2 tablespoons butter
⅛ teaspoon cinnamon (optional)

TO SERVE: Unsweetened heavy cream, plain or lightly whipped

Pick over and wash the berries. Place these in a saucepan with the sugar, lemon juice if desired, and ¼ cup of water. Stir over medium heat until the sugar dissolves and the berries come to a boil. Reduce heat to low and simmer for 10 minutes.

Trim the crusts from the bread. Two slices should fit neatly side-by-side in a loaf pan or a baking dish of similar shape and capacity (one quart or so). Butter the bread slices, sprinkle them, if you like, with the cinnamon, and then place them, two to a layer, in the pan or baking dish, covering each layer with an equal portion of the cooked berries.

Chill in the refrigerator for several hours. Serve by the slice or spoonful with the heavy cream.

VARIATION. Some cooks prefer to bake this pudding. To do this, butter the baking dish before proceeding as above. Bake the pudding for 15 to 20 minutes in a 350°F oven. Then serve it either hot, at room temperature, or chilled, accompanied with heavy cream, if you like.

STEUBEN, 1995

The Mushroom Hunt

It's hard to say exactly when autumn comes to Maine. Mostly it's a matter of the evidence piling up. The days are still warm but they've suddenly gotten short. Brown-eyed Susans depose the daisies, and Chinese mustard the buttercups. The flowers of the jewelweed drop away, leaving seed pods that explode when touched. The blackberries are in full fruit. Wild ducks start honking restlessly in the cove. Deer come crashing through the thickets to browse on windfall apples by the road.

It's early September. The woods still have that smoky smell that comes from trees baking all day in sunlight, but between their trunks now flickers a continual sift of leaves. This is when Matt comes home from her walk with her red-felt fedora filled with chanterelles (*Cantharellus cibarius*—Latin names are given here for accuracy's sake, not because I know them. I don't). Mushrooms can be found in all seasons, of course, some even in winter, but I connect them with that run of months from August through October, when summer smoothly segues into fall.

Some reasons for this are practical—we walk more in the woods now that the deerflies are gone and the mosquitoes waning—others are metaphorical. Mushrooms sport autumnal colors and have autumnal associations of—simultaneously—fruitfulness and decay. And then, autumn in Maine is hunting season, for deer, geese, duck, moose, and bear . . . and mushroomers think of themselves as hunters, even though they hunt with sticks instead of guns. Children, who like to admire their own dexterity and patience, may consider berry-picking hunting; for the rest of us, however, it's a chore. Gathering mushrooms is a very different kind of enterprise—which means that eating them is, too.

Mushrooms do appear in the vegetable section of the supermarket, but this, I think, is by default. Sautéed in garlicky butter and slid next to the steak, they can tug their forelock as humbly as any *pomme frite*. But toss them—without the steak—into a mass of pasta and watch them shoulder aside the other ingredients to seize center stage. A wild mushroom has authority no carrot would ever dare assert.

In part, mushrooms gain this power because they have a meatlike presence, sometimes almost to excess. The flesh of the beefsteak (also ox-tongue) fungus (*Fistulina hepatica*) is moist and sticky and marbled with fatlike veins; it also oozes bloody-colored juices when cut. And while one would never confuse a beefsteak tomato with its namesake, a well-cooked morsel of the fungus does in fact possess a meaty succulence . . . not like beef exactly, but easy to mistake for game.

The beefsteak fungus should not be confused with the beefsteak morel (*Gyromitra esculenta*), a "false" morel classified by Alexander H. Smith in *The Mushroom Hunter's Field Guide* as "dangerous, but edible and choice."* Such oxymoronic bravado reminds us that bosky flavor isn't the only connection here to hunting. Like wild animals, wild mushrooms can be fierce.

This brings us to the crux of things. All hunters put life at risk, but for mushroomers the moment of danger comes well after the quarry has been run to earth. The wild-boar hunter faces danger alone in the wilderness; the mushroom hunter brings it home to share around the table. Finding the mushroom is the initiation, but eating it is the test—which is why the eater, not the fungus, is the real trophy of the hunt.

So the mushroom hunter, though firm in his refusals to share his secret gathering places, is often generous with invitations to the feast. All the better if you think no mushroom is worth the risk of dying— it's the test of his self-confidence to convince you that there is no risk. You've never tasted any mushroom good as these, he says complacently, heaping your plate with *Amanita caesarea*—so named because they're fit for Caesar . . . if also close cousin to some rather terrifying kin. And should you, this once—sorry, can't imagine how I missed those veil warts—get a bit of *Amanita muscaria* in your portion ("Poisonings not usually fatal," writes the professor, "[though] the experience is one not

---

* The phrase is typical of Professor Smith, whose status as mycologist-guru to a generation of mushroomers can be explained not least by his sangfroid. On another page of his guide he observes that after consuming a large quantity of early morels (*Verpa bohemica*) "a definite lack of muscle coordination was noticed four to five hours later." Elsewhere he offhandedly notes the effects of ingesting the jack-o'-lantern fungus (*Clitocybe illudens*): "Nausea and vomiting are violent for a few hours, and then the patient recovers completely. The experience is very disagreeable while it lasts."

soon forgotten") . . . consider how peculiar, in civilized society, this whole situation is.

Hubris in mushroom hunters runs to all sizes. My kind is so modest it might seem not even to exist. Having only occasionally the patience to do a spore print and none for memorizing things like vital characteristics, I play it safe, finding just one or two mushrooms a season that are unequivocally (a) good to eat, (b) plentiful, and (c) easy to identify. When I lived near Boston, I brought home bunches of painted slippery caps (*Suillus pictus*) from the Blue Hills and, guided by a friend, picked cepes (*Boletus edulis*) in the heights that overlook U.S. 1 in Saugus. Before then, a teacher at a private school in the Berkshires, I would hurry out first thing in the morning to beat Gert, the school cook, to the puffballs on the lawn.

It should be noted, with wild mushrooms as with anything, that "edible" does not necessarily mean "tasty." The shaggy mane (*Coprinus comatus*) is a scrofulous-looking, deliquescent (i.e., "self-devouring") mushroom that comes up in huge clumps even on city lots (I once picked a meal's worth from the grass edging of a Boston post office). Most guides aver that it's not only edible but choice . . . at least if caught before self-digestion begins transforming it into a puddle of black slime. However, I find the intention is inherent in the flavor, each morsel attempting one last effort to consume itself even as I chew—a rather unnerving experience.

So there it is: the easiest mushrooms to identify aren't always plentiful or choice, and guidebooks sometimes disagree as to which of these are safe to eat. And even a mushroom as distinctive as the chanterelle has insidious mimics (including the jack-o'-lantern noted in the footnote). Once, after delivering a bagful to some friends, I felt a sudden loss of nerve and nearly snatched them back.

Hubris, yes, but not from appetite or an urge to show off before the neighbors. Mushrooms can just become something you want to get to know. Berries are collected by the handful, but chanterelles are gathered one by one. After you gently tug each free from its bed of moss, you stop and turn it over in your hands, absorbed by its muted golden color and delicately fluted veins, the chamois-like softness of its cap.

Its weight surprises you. Like a just-killed animal, a just-picked mushroom, however small, has an unanticipated heft. The thing you seek has so much *not* been there—not under those leaves, not by that tree trunk, not in that small hollow—that when you finally come upon it, you expect it to be as ethereal as a ghost.

But now, here it lies, solid in the hand. To know a mushroom, you have to hold it. When you do, you find that looking at it, touching it is not enough. You bring it up to your nose and smell . . . but even then what you *want* to do is take it in your mouth. The relationship is as visceral as that—and fear, however latent, is what makes it so. Your guests, having put their well-being into your keeping, may take no more notice of its flavor than of the broccoli or slices of roast lamb. But you will.

The simplest way to cook wild mushrooms is to brush them clean of dirt (never wash them, since they soak up water like a sponge) and then to sauté them in plenty of butter—or, even better, a mixture of equal parts butter and olive oil—with a little finely minced garlic and chopped fresh parsley thrown in toward the very end of cooking (seasoning it all, of course, with salt and freshly grated pepper).

The virtue of this approach—"recipe" is too presumptuous a word— is that it serves many purposes. If you have found several different kinds of edible mushrooms, they may all be cooked together into an intriguing (and hence intentional-seeming) mélange. This can then be offered— speared on toothpicks—as an appetizer, set beside or on top of a broiled steak, or heaped on a thick slice of toasted country bread. Served with a lightly dressed salad of bitter greens and washed down with a glass of beer or an earthy red—this is all you need to make a memorable meal.

CASTINE, 1990

Moosehead Gingerbread

Gingerbread is standard fare here in Maine, and local cooks have lots of opinions about making it. For example, the 1946 edition of *The Maine Rebekahs Cookbook* (a perennial Maine fund-raiser) has a whole chapter of gingerbreads, over three dozen recipes. Each is different, but—as in most kinships—it is really the similarities that count. The true flavoring agent in a Maine gingerbread is that old-fashioned, full-flavored Barbados molasses, and some recipes stop right there. When spice is added, ginger and cinnamon compete neck in neck for first place, with clove a distant and sometimes suspect ("if preferred," "use your own judgment") third.

These spices are added with caution, or at least with deliberation. For example, here—quoted in full—is a gingerbread recipe popular enough to have been submitted by three separate Rebekahs.

Gingerbread (for two)—¼ cup butter, ½ cup sugar, ¼ cup molasses, 1 cup flour, 1 egg, ½ cup boiling water (added last), ¼ teaspoon cinnamon, ¼ teaspoon ginger, ¼ teaspoon salt, 1 teaspoon soda.

As Maine goes, there is nothing mingy about such restrained spicing; there are plenty of recipes that add these flavorings by the quarter teaspoon, and not a few that call for an indeterminate "little," "some," or "pinch"—or simply say "spice" and give no measurement at all. Maine cooks tended to nurse the contents of their spice canisters through the decades.

The recipe for "Moosehead Gingerbread" that we encountered in *Maida Heatter's Book of Great Desserts* is something else again: a Maine gingerbread boldly flavored not only with generous amounts of the traditional molasses and sweet spices but also with coffee, mustard, black pepper—and brown sugar to heighten the molasses taste. Even the two Rebekah gingerbreads with pretensions to masculine heartiness—"He Man" and "Sportsmen's Delight"—seemed bloodless in comparison. It was like coming across a gathering of Maine woodsmen around a table at the local coffee shop and noticing, among all the unshaved faces, thick plaid wool shirt jackets, and Day-Glo–orange hunter caps, someone with a luxuriant white beard, leather vest, and cowboy hat. Who *is* this guy?

Not that it would have mattered much if the gingerbread wasn't good, but it was—better than good—and we wanted to know more about its unnamed creator. A laconic sentence—"This sharp and spicy gingerbread comes from an old-time fishing guide in Maine"—was the recipe's entire introduction, so we wrote to Maida and asked her if she would tell us the rest of the story. She replied:

> As for that gingerbread, we got the recipe over fifty years ago. My mother and father rented a summer house on Sugar Island in Moosehead Lake. We used to drive up from New York to the east coast of Moosehead, to the town of Lily Bay. Then we boarded a rowboat to get across the lake to the island. As clearly as I can remember the only other resident of the island was a fishing guide who was also the postmaster. He was a friendly man who loved to cook. He often brought us his gingerbread. He gave the recipe to my mother.

Moosehead Lake—Maine's largest and the source of the Kennebec —is away to the west of us, surrounded by mountains and evergreen forest. I say "away"—but the truth is that it's only about a hundred miles from here; the distance is mostly psychological. Even for people who spend their summers in the state, there is more than one Maine. I know of at least three (discounting the urbanized southern part of the state, which is now really a suburb of Boston): seacoast Maine, farm-country Maine, and deep-woods Maine.

I grew up spending my summers in the first of these places and Maida Heatter in the last of them. Our two summer worlds did have certain things in common. Islands in ocean bays, like cottages on remote island lakes, could be reached only by boat. Often the entrance to the nearby country store opened not on a road but on a dock. Supplies arrived by steamer; customers rowed over to get their mail and buy their groceries plus a big block of ice for the icebox, and rowed back home again.

Even so, the differences between seacoast and deep-woods Maine are profound. I discovered this myself, visiting a friend who owned some property up north of Skowhegan. I started noticing the difference the moment we left the power lines behind. It was then 1970, and I simply could not believe that there remained whole communities in Maine—with at least some year-round residents—that were still totally without electrification. Night fell, and as we drove through the gathering dusk, the faint glow that illuminated the windows of the houses we passed came from candles and kerosene lamps. Here was another country.

Deep-woods Maine is where moose and bear are common neighbors, not rare events, but most of all, it is a place of deep, green silence. Everything is so far away that distance takes on a palpable quality. The solitude of the deep woods is real in Maine the way winter is real: solid, implacable, potentially dangerous. Summer softens it—rounds the edges of the quiet, sweetens the sense of farness—but never entirely erases it. It gives things, for all the slow pace of summer life, an intensity; some deep part of the self wakes up and pays heed.

Lily Bay no longer has a postmaster—or, for that matter, a post office. But at the foot of the lake is Greenville, the area's major town, and I wrote the postmaster there to inquire if there was still anyone around who might remember the Heatter family's neighbor and friend. In due time, we received the following reply.

> Your letter about a guide-cook-postmaster was put in my mailbox by John Webber, Postmaster here at Greenville. The person about whom you inquired was William (Bill) Merservey, a descendant of the original settlers in the region, who owned and operated Camp Greenleaf on Sugar Island. Bill was about average height and in his later years got to be quite heavy. He was a fine, friendly fellow, very generous (you might even say a soft touch for anyone who needed a loan). I never knew him to get excited or angry. Bill was a hunting and fishing guide before he acquired Camp Greenleaf and, like any Moosehead Lake guide, was an excellent cook.
>
> —Respectfully,
> H. A. Templeton

Hubert Templeton worked in the lumber camps as a youth, and even though in ill health (he was to die in the fall of 1993), he still enjoyed spinning a yarn, offering us a glimpse into a culinary world that is now almost entirely lost—the deep-woods cooking of Maine guides and lumbermen.

Henry David Thoreau traveled widely in this area in the mid-1800s. As you can read in *The Maine Woods*, he visited Greenville and canoed across Moosehead Lake past Lily Bay, eating the cooking of hunting

guides and lumber-camp cooks and describing those meals in detail.
He would have immediately recognized the Maine woods of Bill Mer-
servey and Hubert Templeton, and much of the cooking. Male comfort
food is little susceptible to culinary fashion, camp cooking being as
much a tradition as a skill.

Logs were then still floated out downriver, and like hunting camps,
lumber camps were often established far from roads and other amenities
of civilization. The loggers lived and ate in a single log cabin, even
sleeping together in the same massive, bough-mattressed bed. Supplies
were lashed onto sleds and dragged to the camp by teams of oxen over
temporary trails that often ran on top of (and sometimes broke through
into) frozen lakes and streams.

The camp cook kept his flour and salt pork and salt cod in barrels,
his molasses in kegs, and his pantry supplies in a chest called a wangan
(or wanigan), the Maine woods equivalent of the ranch cook's chuck
box, but bowed in at the base so it would fit snugly into the bottom of
a canoe or bateau. His supply list was short—coffee and tea, flour, dried
beans, oatmeal, and dried fruit*—and his equipment sparse. Griddle
cakes were fried and flipped over the fire in a light, long-handled skillet;
beans were baked in a bean hole and bread baked in a Dutch oven
stuck into the fire and heaped with live coals.

The camp cooks who managed to cosset the appetites of ravenously
hungry men despite a perpetual diet of salt pork, biscuits, and black
coffee (or even blacker tea) became North Woods legends—like Tom
Cozzie, whose doughnuts were so light they could float the full length
of the Connecticut River without sinking. Such cooks made the morning
brew strong enough to get drunk on, served up baked beans of great
density and flavor, and produced biscuits and flapjacks of surprising
tenderness and delicacy. Thoreau, eating at a rough lumber camp near
Quakish Lake, found the biscuits "white as snow-balls, but without
butter . . . Such delicate puffballs seemed a singular diet for backwoodsmen." With them, he drank "tea without milk, sweetened with
molasses."

Just as whalers used to dip their ship's biscuits into boiling vats of
whale blubber, choppers rubbed their sourdough biscuits in pan grease

---

* This, for the most part, meant dried apples. The humble prune was a rare treat,
enjoyed both stewed and baked in pies. Writes Robert E. Pike in *Tall Trees, Tough
Men*: "As a French-Canadian cook, I think it was Joe Buckshot, once remarked, 'For
me, I'll take the prune. It makes even better apple pie than the peach.' "

and soaked them with molasses. Butter remained an occasional luxury; a deep-woods cook could rarely count on having any to mix into a gingerbread batter. What he used was salt pork, lard, or bacon drippings—or any other clean-tasting meat fat. As John J. Rowlands wrote in *Cache Lake Country: Life in the North Woods*:

> I almost forgot to say that I always keep a quart can with a top that clinches on for my bacon fat. That is important, for fat is mighty good to fry fish in, to make biscuits, and for many other things. I keep every drip, for it is nourishing food in the woods, and you can't make good flapjacks without it.

When Matt began to make Moosehead gingerbread with such fats—including the rendered suet from our New England boiled dinner—the missing piece of the puzzle called up by that aggressive flavoring fell into place. The combination of meat fat and generous spicing was a revelation, producing a sharp-edged, spicy cake with a savory, mouth-coating richness. The pungent flavorings "explain" the meat fat by placing it in the realm of the savory sweet, as they do in another old Yankee treat, mincemeat.

We once had a slice of mincemeat pie at the former Dick's Restaurant in Ellsworth in which a lard crust was filled with what was literally minced meat: chopped-up pot roast sweetened, seasoned with raisins and pie spices, and moistened with a little cream. It was a piece of pie to have as much *for* dinner as after it, and like nothing you would ever be offered in today's cooking world, where cheese is no longer an unquestioned accompaniment to your piece of apple pie.

Similarly, that touch of meat fat lifts Moosehead gingerbread off the genteel dessert plate and sets it down in a place where hard work, deep solitude, and clean, icy air make the appetite hungry for large flavors. This is a gingerbread to eat for breakfast beside the campfire, or to slide onto a plate of bean hole beans. We suggest you try Moosehead, just once substituting, say, bacon or pork drippings (or rendered chicken fat, a favorite of ours) for half the butter. Then you'll get all the taste of Maine outdoors cooking—the essential baking trinity of ginger, cinnamon, and clove, the baked-bean flavorings of mustard, molasses, and black pepper, the splash of campfire coffee—with the necessary hint of wood smoke to round it all off.

MOOSEHEAD GINGERBREAD
(ADAPTED FROM *MAIDA HEATTER'S BOOK OF GREAT DESSERTS*)
(SERVES 4 TO 6)

1 cup (scooped and leveled off) unbleached all-purpose flour
1 teaspoon baking soda
¼ teaspoon salt
¾ teaspoon powdered ginger
½ teaspoon powdered cinnamon
¼ teaspoon powdered cloves
¼ teaspoon powdered mustard
¼ teaspoon finely ground black pepper
2 tablespoons softened butter
2 tablespoons bacon drippings, rendered chicken fat, or the like
¼ cup firmly packed dark brown sugar
½ cup Barbados or other full-flavored unsulphured molasses
1 large egg, lightly beaten
½ cup strong, hot coffee

TO SERVE: Applesauce and/or unsweetened whipped cream

Preheat oven to 375°F. (If using a glass, dark metal, or other heat-retentive pan, set to 350°F instead and watch that the gingerbread doesn't overbake.)

Butter a 9 × 5-inch loaf pan.

Shake the dry ingredients (first 8 ingredients listed) through a sieve into a bowl and stir to mix thoroughly. In a separate bowl, cream the butter and fat with the brown sugar, add the molasses, and stir vigorously to blend. Stir in the egg. Add the dry ingredients all at once and stir slowly and firmly until fully incorporated. Pour the hot coffee over this mixture and again stir patiently to blend. The batter should be smooth and somewhat thin.

Scrape into the buttered loaf pan with a rubber spatula. Bake for about 35 minutes, or until the cake feels done to the finger (or tests done with a straw). Cool slightly in the pan, then serve warm with applesauce or unsweetened whipped cream.

The above recipe reflects our adaptation of Maida Heatter's original recipe. Specifically, we halved the ingredient amounts and we baked the resulting batter in a loaf pan, rather than a shallow baking dish. We experimented with different savory cooking fats in place of half the butter. In place of the instant coffee she calls for, we used ½ cup of freshly brewed dark-roast coffee (decaf is fine), made double-strength —that is, using 2 coffee scoops of ground coffee for each ¾ cup of water. (We measure the molasses and then the coffee in the same cup; the hot coffee dissolves the remaining film of molasses.) Most different, perhaps, is the way we mixed the batter, which is the "by hand" (as opposed to electric mixer) method we've worked out for making our regular gingerbread.

Steuben, 1994

Dinner at Duffy's

1

Duffy's Restaurant is easy to miss. It lies about seven miles east out of Bucksport on U.S. 1—the stretch that locals call the Ellsworth Road—tucked into the middle of a long, slow curve. Just before it appears on the left, your eye is drawn in the opposite direction as the sudden immensity of Toddy Pond flashes into view for a few seconds through a break in the pine woods. Even if you turn your head back fast enough to catch it, there's nothing much about Duffy's to hold your attention, especially if, as is often the case, a tractor-trailer has pulled up in the driveway directly in front of the restaurant, completely hiding it from view. Otherwise, what you see first is a line of green-painted posts topped with lightbulbs ensconced in up-ended jam jars. These border the driveway that climbs up to a small rambling cottage, painted white with green trim, its window boxes filled in season with bright red geraniums.

When we lived in Castine, I drove past Duffy's often and, strange as it now seems, at first took it for a roadhouse. This was partly because of the neon Miller's sign that glowed in the front window, partly because it had the slightly seclusive, clubby air of such places, and partly because the vehicles out front were that mix of Detroit behemoths with beat-up, rusted-out bodies and noisy but still potent V-8 engines and pinstriped, high-sprung, Japanese-built pickups with oversized tires and extra-long beds that is driven by male blue-collar Maine. I realized, however, passing by very early one bright fall morning, that the parking lot was fuller than I'd ever seen it. That crowd was there for breakfast, not booze. All of a sudden Duffy's seemed to exude the aroma of fried eggs, flapjacks, and hot coffee.

You don't have to live in Maine long to learn to tell the difference between the cheap-eat–type places aimed at the summer and leaf-peeper trade and those that mainly solicit business from their neighbors. Both are housed in nondescript buildings and advertise plain home cooking, but one makes a conspicuous effort to dress up Down East and the other, just as conspicuously, doesn't. If you want to eat with the locals, don't pull up at a joint, however down-home or just plain dumpy, draped with buoys and fronted with huge plywood cutouts of boiled lobsters. Especially avoid places with outdoor wood-fired lobster steamers smoking away or with names like Pop's Chowder House, Lucky's Lobster Land, Fisherman's Inn, or The Clamdigger.

Stop instead at the places without any tourist trappings. Their boardings, if there are any, should promise nothing more exciting than LIVER AND ONIONS TODAY, $4.95, MACARONI AND CHEESE, BREAKFAST SPECIAL: FRIED TRIPE, or—both outside Priscilla's Drive-In, also on Route 1 east of Bucksport—WICKED HOT CHILI and PRISCILLA MAKES THE PIES. Above all, they should bear homey, emphatically ordinary names without one hint of Vacationland: Just Barb's, Tall Barney's, Finally Mine, Hazel's Place, Gram's Place, Mary's Place, Rollie's Cafe, and, as I now saw, Duffy's.

This gradual realization about Duffy's made me curious about it but didn't necessarily make me want to eat there. For that kind of casual eating there were nearer and more amusing places, like the London double-decker bus parked on the side of state Route 174 just east of Penobscot, where a local character sold good fish and chips wrapped up in newspaper and sprinkled with malt vinegar, "just like the home country." But then Matt happened to come across an article in a past issue of *The New Yorker*. It was by Sue Hubbell and recounted a visit to Duffy's in a piece called "A Reporter at Large: The Great American Pie Expedition."

The article records—with an occasional recipe—pies the author encountered on trips here and there in the United States. On one of these excursions, she dropped in at Duffy's. She describes two of their several pies: the graham cracker and the blueberry. Graham cracker pie is a custard pie with a graham cracker crust and more graham crackers crumbled over the top. It is the kind of pie a Maine pie baker might make after hearing a report of—but not ever tasting or seeing—a New York cheesecake.

Sue Hubbell found that one good enough for those who like that kind of thing—the Maine sweet tooth is very sweet indeed—but what she really loved was Duffy's blueberry pie, the best blueberry pie she had had on the whole trip.

> The crust had been pinched up into extreme points, and was delicious. The local blueberries were delicious, too, and their flavor was enhanced by the generous addition of cinnamon.

Inflammatory text for two pie lovers. We bumped Duffy's to the top of our eating-out list. Consequently, in early August of 1990, at the height of the blueberry season, we finally turned up the driveway.

At the time, you stepped onto a small enclosed porch and then into what felt like someone's house, or rather, for it's almost the same thing, into a house that had been turned into a restaurant. Even though it has become a public place, it still signals "home" with the proportion of its rooms, the size and placement of its doors and windows. In the summer, with these all opened to catch the breeze, the smell of fried clams in the air, the random groups of casual eaters happily absorbed in their dinners, there was something immediately comforting and friendly about Duffy's. It was like a cabin in a Maine motor court: clean, cheerful, and individual, but also impersonal enough so that you don't feel an intruder in some stranger's home.

The food on the menu was equally unthreatening, a mixture of home cooking and old-fashioned fast food: pork chops with applesauce and baked ham with pineapple on the one hand, and cheeseburgers, clam rolls, and a variety of sandwich fillings heaped on "home-baked" bread on the other. We settled into a table by an open window, checked out the specials on the board, and ended up ordering what we usually order in a Maine restaurant: fried seafood—on this night, clams—French fries, onion rings, coleslaw, and a couple of beers.

The menu also offered a little history. Duffy's was originally called Laura & Sadie's after its first two owners, the grandmother and great-aunt of Lauralee Gilley, who now ran the place with her husband, Richard. Laura and Sadie opened it in the 1940s, operating it as a seasonal place for several years and then selling out to a Cape Cod man, William Tinney. He was the one who renamed it Duffy's, built it up into a year-round establishment, and ran it successfully until just that year, 1990, when Lauralee and Richard Gilley bought him out and brought the place back into the family.

Duffy's is, indeed, by any definition, a family restaurant. Not only were there families eating on every side of us, but Lauralee Gilley herself took our order, her husband was cooking in the kitchen, and her son Chad was busing the tables. Later we overheard them giggling together about the family of raccoons that came to beg for handouts at the kitchen door.

As mentioned earlier, there was something equally homelike about the place itself. Real pine paneling mingled cheerfully with fake pine wallboard; linen dish towels from Scotland decorated one corner, a vague gesture in the direction of the British Isles. The glass that topped the smaller tables (there are also some larger, oilcloth-covered, family-size ones) was mazed with cracks that have, from all evidence, been there for decades.

When, later, I asked Lauralee Gilley about this, she said that her grandfather, who had made them, used plain window glass, not anticipating the effect of years of stress—plates piled with food pressing down from above, the wooden tabletop sagging away underneath. They all cracked, but none actually broke. And—as the old Maine saw has it— if it ain't broke, there's no point fixing it. The crazed glass was so much a part of the decor now, she told me, that if they tried to replace it the customers would protest.

Finally, the atmosphere here was also "family" in a way that other places—however low-key and unpretentious—can't quite manage. The very presence of professional waitresses, shiny red vinyl booths, and uniform, Formica-covered tables signals the ultimate indifference of an entirely public place. They may also be comfortable spots, but they aren't as vulnerable to your opinion. Duffy's works hard to solicit your approval. Lauralee Gilley treats you with the anxious friendliness of someone whose new neighbors happen to have just stepped through the kitchen door. She wants you to be happy here.

Of course, roughly speaking, many of her customers *are* neighbors, and even the ones who are total strangers are still—or so it seemed on that evening and those that followed—neighborly. They are people, whether seasonal or year-round residents, young or old, poor or reasonably affluent, who firmly associate themselves with the old, unfussy Maine, a place where people like to think of themselves as making do, and making do well, with what they have.

Maine is still full of such restaurants, most of them geared, as Duffy's is, to serving a local clientele, one that swells in the summer but remains pretty much the same sort of folk. As Lauralee Gilley told the local paper—*The Ellsworth American*—when they wrote her up:

We have a family oriented atmosphere. We cater to the natives. We're always
pleased to see the tourists come, but it's the locals who keep you in business.

Such people recognize this place as theirs by its resolute lack of
pretension, or whatever the opposite is of "putting on airs." Others are
kept away by the simple expedient of the resulting invisibility—as Duffy's was, for so long, invisible to me. The first thing to notice about
these eateries, then, is how unnoticeable they are.

Restaurants of all classes, except at the very top and the very bottom,
are designed to demand attention. Jasper's, The Hilltop House, The
Mex, China Hill, Jordan's, Maidee's, The Wok . . . I can name most of
the restaurants we regularly pass on our shopping trip to Ellsworth, even
though we rarely stop at any of them. They do everything they can to
stamp their names into your brain as you drive by. But the places I'm
talking about seem to shyly duck their heads. In fact, one of them,
Dick's, in Ellsworth, was in demeanor so retiring that a hand-lettered
sign sat in one of the windows to say they were open. Otherwise, walking
by, you couldn't really tell.

Duffy's also has a sign that hangs, large and conspicuous, right beside
the restaurant door.

> WELCOME TO DUFFY'S—
> WE HERE AT DUFFY'S ARE A
> NATIVE ORIENTED RESTAURANT.
> WE AREN'T FUSSY,
> AND WE'RE CERTAINLY NOT FANCY . . .
> IF YOU ARE,
> ELLSWORTH IS 12 MILES EAST,
> AND
> BUCKSPORT IS 7 MILES WEST.
> YOURS TRULY,
> DUFFY

It was put there by the previous owner; it may express Maine sentiment,
but posting it required Massachusetts nerve. Nevertheless, it's appreciated. T-shirts with the text printed on them are a popular item. It's a
sign that—we've since discovered—has become legend with Maine folk
up and down this part of the coast.

2

Lauralee Gilley brought us our suppers. Fried seafood is often good in Maine eating places, and as we've written, so are French fries. The clams were sweet and fresh and fried whole, soft, succulent bellies and all, the way they are when eaters aren't put off by a clam's former life as a functioning bivalve. The beer was cold; the onion rings were great. The blueberry pie was awful.

Strangely, at first I found its badness difficult to admit. This was partly because much of what had preceded this piece of pie had been so good, but mostly it was because the people around us were so plainly enjoying theirs—the couple at the next table even making loud exclamations of delight. I had gotten this far in the meal feeling a companionable kinship with my fellow eaters; then, unexpectedly, my dessert exposed me as an interloper.

I knew that if those around me could have right then read my thoughts, they would have found them not only contrary to their own experience but personally offensive. I was being too fussy. One bad piece of pie, of course, may mean nothing more than the luck of the draw. But you learn to recognize the difference between accidentally bad and chronically bad pie—and we had already encountered plenty of the latter at places boasting about their "home" baking. Now, eating this one, I finally began wondering what was going on.

Everyone—outside the food world at least—knows that cooking that is better than you're prepared for can be as off-putting as cooking that is worse. Goodness in a meal is as much a matter of familiarity as it is of good taste, and familiarity is the specialty of places like Duffy's. Their pie was "good" because it was packed with real Maine blueberries and because it had been baked right there in the restaurant kitchen.

That it had so much cinnamon in it that you couldn't taste the fruit didn't matter, nor did the fact that the crust was so tough that I needed a knife to saw through it. Topped with vanilla ice cream, it offered generous, mouth-filling, familiar flavors and the soothing if teeth-aching richness of sweet and fat. The pie was "good" because to the right eater there was something comforting in the fact that it wasn't all *that* good.

When we had come into Duffy's we'd read the sign outside and were amused by it, but didn't particularly pause to think if it applied to ourselves. Us? Fussy? We were casually dressed; we didn't expect or want to find linen on the tables or stuffed lobster on the menu. But we also hadn't considered the fact that, for those who regularly eat at places like Duffy's, a certain imperfection in the food actually enhances rather than detracts from its flavor. The tangible anticipation on the faces of these customers as they came through the door was prompted as much by the welcoming signals sent out by the place itself as by any good smells of cooking issuing from the kitchen.

This communication, tacit though it is, establishes immediate complicity—which is why even mentioning that piece of pie seems a betrayal of trust. Treating Duffy's in the language of a restaurant review is as meaningless and, really, as tactless as sending your neighbor a critique of her cooking the day after she's had you over for supper. To do the place justice, you need to call on the talents of an E. Annie Proulx or a Carolyn Chute, not a Gael Greene or Mimi Sheraton. The writer's task is to flesh out the story of those fracture lines in the glass-topped tables, not to complain that the mashed potatoes arrived at the table cold or that the pieces of fried chicken weren't cooked all through.

At the very least, you have to get the signal. And as best as I can decipher it, it breaks down into three complementary tones that I'm going to name particularity, generosity, and—the dominant of the triad—frugality. By "particularity" I mean simply what someone in Maine means when they say they're particular about something—that they don't like spices in their baked beans and do like buttermilk in their doughnuts. Maine people pride themselves on drinking Moxie instead of Coke and eating Jacob's cattle beans and cold-cellaring a hundred pounds of potatoes every fall. Unlike being fussy, being particular is a way of being thrifty without being mean.

Generosity is another of those ways. Whatever else you want to say about dinner at Duffy's, the portions are ample. They bring a whole small loaf of bread to you, even if you're eating alone, and they heap so many French fries on your plate that they spill off onto the table. Supper offerings like roast stuffed chicken with cranberry sauce speak of Sunday dinner, but they're priced only a little above a lunch at McDonald's.

Within these guidelines, there is much to like at Duffy's. The menu has a distinctly but completely unself-conscious regional feel, in the sense that "Italian pasta"—shells filled with meat sauce and cheese—served with a side of coleslaw is as much a Maine dish as the two kinds of chowder, fish and clam, that the menu also offers. (The fact that the fish chowder costs more than the clam chowder is another clue that this isn't a tourist place.) The vegetables, apart from the coleslaw, are—to the Maine taste—all out of a can, and include such favorites as boiled onions, pickled beets, and applesauce. The coleslaw is homemade and sprightly. The baked beans come from an old family recipe, and the seasons are marked with dishes like strawberry shortcake and apple crisp. Instead of generic fried "fish," Duffy's serves you a generous portion of good haddock. The mashed potatoes are the real thing. At breakfast you can get an omelet filled with genuine Cheddar cheese or a plate of flapjacks: three big ones, crisp and brown without and fluffy and light within.

Despite all this, the cooking at Duffy's, like its tables, is shot through with fracture lines. Those flapjacks arrive at the table with a single-serving plastic container of Kraft syrup, a dull-flavored corn-syrup blend without a drop of the real maple stuff mixed in. The baked beans come with a slice of insipid ham cut from a daisy roll. The fried haddock is served with prepackaged Kraft tartar sauce. And when we moved up the coast and went to eat at Chase's, in Winter Harbor, we were served mini-loaves of "home-baked" bread identical to those brought to our table at Duffy's. Obviously the same supplier of frozen bread dough, laced with dough conditioner, visits them both. All this in a place where local people still produce maple syrup, smoke and cure country hams, and raise organic vegetables, lamb, beef, and free-range chickens.

Duffy's customers know these things and many know their taste, but they also know that, today, none of them comes cheap. Things like maple syrup that were once free or near to it are now costly and hence not used. Maine vernacular restaurants zig and zag on this issue—many serve real butter with their biscuits and real cream with their coffee—but while frugality and generosity are familiar constants, these places are now gun-shy about being thought too particular. If it's at all obtrusive, their customers are "agin" it.

Hence the absence of lobster on the menu. Native Mainers—including lobstermen themselves—are, at best, ambivalent about the beast, symbol of the occupation army of out-of-staters, and they rarely, if ever, eat it. "Too expensive," they say, capturing in that tart phrase the fissure that cuts the state in two: the old Maine on one side, the rest of us on the other. Tourist boosters in the state government got the lobster on our license plate; public outcry got a law passed allowing objecting citizens to paint it out.

Duffy's customers aren't necessarily poor, but they do differentiate themselves from the newcomers who wear Eddie Bauer outfits, have their hair cut by a hair stylist and not a barber, and eat lunch at Blue Hill's Left Bank Café by an unease about money. This unease means that the signal that Duffy's—and the many restaurants like Duffy's—

sends out has a certain dissonance to it, a sharp edge that, if you're not careful, can cut. It usually isn't conspicuous, but it's always there. You catch it in the tone of voice, the posture, the self-conscious restraint, the hint of bitterness, resentment even, masked by politeness and pride.

Like the people in any poor state, Mainers are in a fix regarding cash: they don't make much of it and they don't like what it does to people, but more and more, lack of it is crimping their lives. Maine people, in our experience, work hard—very hard—but at jobs that make sense to them and in ways that feel right, neither of which has much to do with intensifying cash flow.

Once, when our old Honda Civic started running on three cylinders, I took it to Bim's Garage, located on a country road in Penobscot. Bim came out, discussed my problem, took the car into the garage, fiddled around in the engine, and discovered that one of the spark plugs wasn't firing. He was going to get me a new one, when he remembered he had an "almost new" one in the garage attic that would do just as well. He went up the ladder, spent ten minutes rooting around through cans and boxes, found it, and installed it. All this took almost an hour. Bim charged me five dollars, giving me the spark plug for free, since it was used.

Again, the signal that this is the real Maine; again, the three familiar tones. The thrift: not throwing a good thing away; the generosity: not charging for it; the particularity: his determination to work at his own speed, in his own way. At a city gas station, the attendant would have put in a new plug and charged me twenty dollars. He also would have taken about fifteen minutes to do it. Bim engaged me in a long conversation which wasn't finished when the car was, being interrupted by both his trip up attic and two lengthy telephone calls. My payment was just enough to buy Bim breakfast someplace, with enough left over for the tip.

3

Breakfast is a good meal to go out for in Maine. The local eating places take it seriously, as do the local eaters. Not only are portions generous, but they include real corned-beef hash, blueberry pancakes, baking-powder biscuits, even genuine bean hole beans. However, the reason I pictured Bim spending his fiver on it is that—apart from tourists and summer people—the breakfasters at these places are predominantly men.

When we moved to Steuben, we occasionally went out to breakfast at the Donut Hole in Winter Harbor, a Maine seacoast town next to Schoodic Point. The place is little more than a lobsterman's shack, set down by the water in the center of town. Winter Harbor is big enough to have two places that compete for the breakfast crowd; Chase's, a real restaurant replete with booths and all, is just down the road. We'd eaten there but found that it was where the town movers and shakers went for breakfast, and the place was always noisy with business talk. The Donut Hole, although also lively, was more laid back. It was the *other* place in town, where people went not to do business but to get away from it.

Chase's also made an aggressive effort to snare the passing tourist on the way to Acadia National Park. It looks like a restaurant, with a restaurant's custom sign and big picture windows overlooking the road. By contrast, the Donut Hole, with its shabby plywood signboard and equally shabby, windowless front withdrew into itself in the now familiar manner of an eatery that plays host primarily to a native clientele.

Inside, the place is homey, cheery, and bright. Most of the windows face south, looking out over the harbor; on sunny mornings, the dining room is filled with light. There is room for only six or eight tables plus a short counter with stools. This means the place can fill up quickly, and our usual habit was to join the multitude of other takeout customers, buy some doughnuts, take these with a thermos of coffee out to Grindstone Point, and eat breakfast watching the waves roll in.

However, one autumn morning, we came in late enough—just after eight—to claim a table. Already a whole rescue team, out all night searching for (and finding) a couple lost at sea, had been in and eaten the entire morning's supply of sticky buns. Still, there was plenty to eat. Through the open door of the kitchen, we could see that Annie, who— except during the hectic summer season—handled the morning shift alone, had set a plate piled with popovers to keep warm on the range. Fresh-fried doughnuts—molasses, plain, chocolate, and cinnamon-sugar (on some days, there may be applesauce, whole-wheat, or squash)—were stacked in the doughnut jars. Grace, the owner, who handles the lunch shift, would be arriving an hour later with her station wagon full of pies.

We got a table by a window and settled in. Most of the other tables were occupied by local men who had already finished eating. They were nursing a last cup of coffee and conversing among themselves—and, intermittently, with Annie, either as she came out with a handful of plates or shouting in to her as she worked.

Even more than at Duffy's, the division here between kitchen and dining room, customer and server, is intentionally vague. In back of the counter hang several rows of coffee mugs, some sporting names, belonging to individual customers. When they come in, they grab their cup and go over to the coffee machine to fill it, calling their breakfast order into the kitchen.

We once watched three trucks pull into the Donut Hole's parking lot and fifteen men climb out to join the crowd inside a place not much larger than our living room. The resulting atmosphere is cramped, steamy, and, without being exactly convivial, friendly. Maine men, although usually polite, rarely come across as social animals; entering a room full of them has a fascinating, slightly edgy feel to it, like straying into a crowd of friendly black bears.

Anywhere you drive in Maine in the early part of the day, you find these gatherings; breakfast is the male social hour. People who work outside get up early (one morning we got a misdialed wake-up call from a lobsterman at 5 a.m.). Of course, lobstermen, except on stormy days, don't take their coffee breaks ashore, but construction workers, carpenters, linemen, and road crews—to name a few we've identified by their outfits or their trucks—do.

The smaller the town, the stronger the sense of community. Everyone in the room knows everyone else . . . everyone else, that is, except you. In Steuben, this gathering place is the Rusty Anchor, an old monster highway maintenance garage converted into an eating place by a local fisherman, which has vernacular Maine written all over its weather-beaten façade. And it's never busier than around nine in the morning, when the front of the place is lined with cars.

Regulars fill a special breakfast room called the Coffee Nook. If you happen in, there's a sudden hush while they size you up. After that, you are generally ignored, although conversational sallies are lobbed like softballs from one table to another, some right past your head. Whatever their content, the message is: You've intruded into a private place.

I once asked our UPS driver what he thought of the Rusty Anchor, since I'd noticed he ate lunch there every day. After he drove away, I realized that only thirty seconds of his description had been devoted to food. Clearly, what mattered most to him was that he was accepted as a member of the club.

This sense of clubbiness is emphasized by design. In other parts of the country, the resolute disinclination of these eateries to connect to the outside world would signal a roadhouse or saloon. Earlier, when I at first mistook Duffy's for one, I revealed how new I was to Maine, no matter the many summers I had already spent here.

Outside of big cities like Portland, this state is distinguished by the *absence* of drinking places. Maine took Prohibition seriously and in many ways is still markedly dry. Only recently has it begun to phase out the state-run liquor stores (or, in less densely populated areas, the designated "agency" groceries or drugstores) that controlled and limited the sale of hard liquor. Once you get away from the tourist trail, few restaurants offer mixed drinks, and a surprising number don't even offer beer. The traditional Maine beverage in a restaurant, whatever the meal, is a cup of weak coffee.*

Still, my reading was not altogether wrong. Such eating places offer a moment of rest and comfort from the pressures of the outside world. Like the traditional British pub—"pub" being short for "public house"—they are modeled on the room of the house in which customers will feel most at home. For Maine men, that room is a warm, friendly kitchen, especially if a woman is there on the other side of the counter to tease, cosset, and feed them.

Because everyone feels a little uncomfortable in the living room, home kitchens here are often divided into an eating and a cooking area, with a counter running between the two. The men, when they come in, wander over to one side only to get some coffee, banter a little with the cook, and check out what's on the stove. They then go sit down in the other part and get on with their talk.

So, too, at Duffy's and the Donut Hole. It is only a slight exaggeration to describe these places as possessing all the comfort of the home kitchen minus the discomfort (at least for some) of being in the company of their wives.

In other words, Maine is still a place where men are men and women get their traditional end of the stick. As already noted, in the early morning at the Donut Hole, except in summer, Annie ran the entire show—waitress, cashier, cook, and dishwasher. It wasn't unusual to find her frosting a sheet cake for lunch while simultaneously frying doughnuts, cooking a range of short-order breakfast dishes, and waiting on both the sit-down and takeout customers.

---

* Naturally, drinking does go on here, but it doesn't happen in bars . . . or, for that matter, all that much in homes. Instead, men hit the bottle—or, more usually, rip apart the six-pack—in hunting shacks, backlot sheds, gatherings of pickup trucks, and other all-male enclaves, kept secluded and separate from women.

Once when we were there, a woman came in to buy some doughnuts, took one look at the situation, and went back of the counter to pitch in. In a similar vein, I recently overheard another woman at the post office tell how she had been invited by an old friend to the Rusty Anchor for supper. The friend was late and the Rusty Anchor short a waitress, so she picked up a tray, even though she had already spent the day cutting fish. By the time her friend arrived she had to go home to wake her husband for his night-shift job. No wonder that more and more Maine women prefer to take the kids to Pizza Hut or Burger King, where teenagers do all the cooking and serving—that is, to places that remind them as little of their own kitchen as possible and where there is never any call to help out.

4

When powerline, telephone, or road crews have been busy on our road, predominant in the litter they leave behind, next to disposable plastic coffee cups, are empty boxes of single-serving pies. Eaten as mid-morning snacks, these show—so far as such casually gathered evidence can show anything—the enduring power of pie over candy bars, jelly doughnuts, or Little Debbie Swiss Devil Dogs, as Maine male comfort food. They epitomize a kind of home cooking that, we suspect, isn't cooked all that much at home anymore.

Pie is more than a mainstay on Maine menus: it's the Maine dessert. Mainers also like, and get, homey puddings—famously, Grape-Nut, but also bread and, sometimes, Indian. These are expected, but they're rarely featured. When a Maine restaurant boasts of its desserts, it's talking about its pies. The day we had the blueberry pie at Duffy's, we were offered a choice of six: banana cream, strawberry-rhubarb, pecan, apple, lemon meringue, and blueberry. Other days, different pies are on the list; the count, however, remains the same.

Still, Duffy's is a piker compared to Moody's, a diner on Route 1 in Waldoboro, midway up the coast, which may be Maine's most famous eating place, and is certainly its most famous diner. Moody's is a favorite with truckers and tourists, but whenever we've gone in, the majority of the customers were local. Mainers appreciate Moody's determination to be itself, neither a tourist attraction nor a self-consciously maintained antique. Visitors may see Moody's as Maine Past, but regulars see it as Maine Present—or at least that part of today's Maine that still holds on as firmly as it can to its roots.

The Moody family has fought hard to keep this connection alive, and few other Maine eating places speak so directly to traditional Maine taste. Moody's serves New England boiled dinner on Thursday, haddock with egg sauce on Friday, and baked beans on Saturday, with Indian pudding for dessert. Fish cakes, fried tripe, and liver and onions are all on the regular menu.

Moody's began as a lunch cart in the 1930s and, soon after, started adding: walls and a roof, a counter with stools, booths, bathrooms . . . until the place reached its current dimensions and ambience in 1948. (Some Mainers are resolute in their belief that neither they nor Moody's has ever left that year; it's not uncommon, settling into a vacated booth, to find that the previous diners have left behind a fifty-cent tip.) Even so, here, too, holding to frugality and generosity (the fish cake dinner —three fish cakes, fries, coleslaw—is still an astonishing $2.75) has meant a gradual eroding in particularity. The fault lines run as deeply here as they do at Duffy's. Order the beef simmered in onions and you get something almost inedible; order the fried tripe and you get something near transcendental. Until you taste, there's no way to tell. Each time you wander from the dishes you know they do well, you put yourself at risk.

Moody's is famous for its pies. Ask the waitress what she has on hand and she rattles them off: apple, custard, rhubarb, strawberry-rhubarb, squash, raspberry, raspberry cream cheese, lemon cream cheese, chocolate banana, peanut butter, walnut cream—a breathless listing that seems the realization of a pie lover's dream. These pies can be very good. The rhubarb on a late-spring visit had a filling of tangy-sweet fruit bound up in a simple, delicious egg custard and a crust prepared with a delicate hand.

But Moody's pies no longer carry the signature of a single cook. This means that, if you order wrong, you can end up with a slice where the filling is uninspired and the crust quite ordinary, and sometimes even stale. In the summer, when the pies pour out of the kitchen, they're always fresh; in the winter, however, they aren't. Once, when we asked, we found that only one pie out of the dozen offered had been made that day. And our waitress was clearly offended at our asking, treating the question as a shocking breach of good manners. Here we were, caught out being fussy again.

In this regard, Moody's is the direct opposite of Dick's, a now-defunct breakfast and lunch place in Ellsworth. As already noted, it was hard to see (and was even more so in its original location on the second floor of another downtown building). I was coming into Ellsworth for over a year before I figured out it was still functioning as an eating place. Although it sits on the corner of a major downtown intersection, the plate-glass windows were covered with gauze curtains. From outside, the place looked dark, drab, and, to my unpracticed eye, out of business.

Inside, once again, the story was different. Dick's might have been a little down at the heels, with a peeling painted-tin ceiling, a linoleum floor missing several of its tiles, and battered, generic luncheonette tables and chairs. But the row of booths were painted a bright blue, the tops of the counter seats were a cheerful canary yellow, and the customers who sat on them engaged in familiar, comfortable banter with the waitresses and the short-order cook.

Here, too, we were drawn to Dick's because we came across a small ad in the local paper in which Dick modestly reported that "some people say our pies are the best in Ellsworth." He could also have noted that he served a generous, delicious breakfast, your plate heaped with scrambled eggs, home fries, and bacon, along with—if you remembered to ask—a homemade biscuit instead of toast, which arrives with real butter and (on some days) a little cup of homemade blueberry jam. And the pies were outstanding . . . good fillings encased in a real old-fashioned flaky crust.

Unlike Moody's or even Duffy's, the daily pie list at Dick's was short. There were usually no more than four listed on the board. Blueberry appeared only in season. Otherwise, you might find apple, custard, lemon sponge, chocolate cream, peach meringue, raspberry, strawberry-rhubarb, and, now and then, that very individual mincemeat described on page 109.

It's telling that Dick's was the only place in Maine where we encountered a true lard crust. Their pride in these pies was palpable, and they didn't mind telling you which ones were fresh. In fact, once she discovered our interest, our waitress volunteered the information as soon as we sat down, sometimes offering to cut us two slices from our choice right then and set them aside. Pie, as we learned to our cost, went fast at Dick's.

You're fussy in Maine, not only when your expectations run outside the realm of economy/generosity, but when you let your particularness clash headlong with that of the place in which you're eating. It helped, of course, that it was that same waitress, Ruby Wilde, who made the pies. She took over when Dick's wife retired from the job, and she kept at it for a while when Dick himself retired and sold the place.

Ruby was born in Nova Scotia, which meant that she learned to cook on the far side of the great pie divide. She was brought up to be particular about her pies, and so she didn't mind us being particular, too. Even so, she found it more entertaining than truly encouraging. We, all of us, knew that at this point in time good pie making is a personal idiosyncrasy, not the shared cultural value it once was.

The great pie divide. Sue Hubbell arrived at Duffy's just a year or so before we did and landed on one side of it; when we finally showed up, we found ourselves on the other. And we saw the transition take place right before our very eyes at Dick's, when Ruby eventually moved to Wisconsin.

Today, in Maine, the kind of particularity that makes a good pie has been all but forced out of existence, even if no one will admit that this is so. Maine towns are full of eating places that brag about their pies, and almost none of them are worth the eating.

My father, who was born here, remembers when Maine pies all had their signature—a real one. Proud cooks worked their initials into the crust with the tines of a fork. That way, at the grange supper, you would know whose pie you were eating, and consequently, the baker would get due praise (or at least no credit would mistakenly be given a competitor). This was a time when those three strands of Maine character—frugality, generosity, particularity—were braided into a tight skein. The only pie ingredients not homegrown were the flour, the sugar, and the pinch of salt. The shortening was freshly rendered lard; the filling was custard contributed by the cow and the hens or fruit contributed by the orchard, the berry patch, or the monster rhubarb plant in the corner of the garden.

A pie was economical, filling, and good; it also allowed the maker to show her skills in the light touch required to make a tender, flaky crust. Home bakers opted for lard or butter or a mixture of the two, striving to balance flavor and tenderness and flake. They also had their tricks. Robert P. Tristram Coffin's mother, once a pie was ready for the oven,

> calmly turned on the cold-water faucet and let the water run over the top crust. It came out of the oven with a top to it like French pastry, only more so.

Although few bakers use lard in Maine today and fewer still render their own, many still take advantage of the state's natural abundance of pie fillings—pie timber, they call it—from rhubarb in the spring right through to squash in the fall. Frugality is one strand that still holds true. So does generosity. Even now, a piece of pie in Maine costs, in the sort of places we're writing about, under two dollars, and it's cut widely, with, if you want, a spoonful of real whipped cream set on top at no extra charge.

But the cost is in the particularity. Maine pies are fast losing their individuality. To bite into one is to risk encountering an indifferently concocted filling and a generic—and often stale—vegetable-shortening crust. Particularity is always the most volatile aspect of Maine character. If frugality is the red light and generosity the green, then particularity is the yellow or "caution" light—and to an outsider's confusion, it means at once "slow down" and "speed up." With pies as with traffic lights, the wrong decision can get you into trouble—and an accusation of fussiness is the least of it.

Homemade blueberry pie! It isn't the gaping space between claim and reality that makes you think Maine cooking has gone seriously amiss; it's the determination not to notice it. The result is disturbingly like stumbling across a chronic family problem that everyone has decided to pretend does not exist. The husbands smack their lips. The wives, some of them, roll their eyes but mostly hold their peace. They, unlike their men, know the cost as well as the taste of a well-made piece of pie; the arrival of one at their table could well be treated less as an occasion than as a threat.

5

When we moved here to the Maine coast, we had a fantasy of finding the "perfect" Maine eating place. It would be small—a cottage, actually, just like Duffy's—and it would serve only a few good things—nothing fancy—fresh-dug, melt-in-your-mouth clams coated with cracker crumbs and fried up in hot, sweet fat. In a companion fryer, shoestring fries would be turning a golden brown. There would be a crisp coleslaw, hot-from-the-oven baking-powder biscuits, and, for dessert, a slice of homemade blueberry or green apple or raspberry rhubarb pie.

Instead, the best we have been able to do has been to piece this fantasy eatery together from fragments of the real places. The Bagaduce Lunch in North Brooksville, a tiny takeout shack at Bagaduce Falls, provides the location—the rush of the tidal flow through the narrows, the bright blue sky, and the deep green pines. Duffy's supplies the clams and the coleslaw; Chase's the fries and onion rings; Dick's the biscuits and the pie. The coffee we have to bring ourselves.

Ironically, the closest we have come to finding the perfect Maine restaurant was when we celebrated my birthday one spring at Le Domaine, a French auberge-style restaurant on Route 1 in Hancock. Here, at first glance, "fussy" might seem the operative word. The tables are draped with white linen and set with handsome china. A fire blazes in a huge, walk-in fireplace. There is a murmur of quiet conversation and the clink of wineglasses.

Still, even though the dining room at Le Domaine exudes relaxed elegance and the food is prepared and served with finesse, this is not "fancy" dining in the usual upscale Maine mode, where one is confronted with a huge *carte de restaurant* proffering prime rib, rack of lamb, and a lengthy parade of those cacophonous dishes that are today's symbol of gourmet opulence—such as lobster meat *and* sea scallops *and* asparagus tossed together in pasta and dressed with lemon cream sauce.

In contrast, Le Domaine's owner/chef, Nicole Purslow, because she *is* particular, courageously keeps her menu short and her cooking free of grandiosity, while charging enough to be able to select her ingredients with care. The night we went, there were only half a dozen entrées, four on the menu and two specials. From choices that included grilled salmon, rabbit with prunes, and a beef filet, we had sautéed sweetbreads, served with wild rice and fiddleheads. The sweetbreads were perfectly prepared; the salad greens were picked from Le Domaine's own garden; the crusty rolls tasted only of flour, yeast, and salt; the after-dinner coffee was strong and good. The meal, with wine, came to about a hundred dollars.

Like Duffy's, the road-front presence of Le Domaine is discreet, just visible enough to alert those who are looking for it without flagging the attention of those who aren't. Also, there are no lobsters on either the sign or the menu. Those who come to Le Domaine—or, at least, come twice—come for the cooking, for food they already know how to eat. In this, the customers and the cook understand and appreciate each other, and often know each other as well.

Sometime ago, say, when Duffy's was still Laura & Sadie's, this was the case at many plain Maine eateries. The food may not always have been as delicious, but at least it had the chance to be. It was built on real home cooking—the frying done in freshly rendered lard, the chickens taken from the henhouse, the vegetables either brought in from the garden or taken out of jars put up from it. As at Le Domaine today, the cook knew most of her ingredients personally. So did her customers. They knew the blueberries in the pie; they knew a good crust when they ate one. She knew they knew, and their pleasure pleased her. In

Maine, praise may be rarely spoken, but it is implicit in this kind of understanding.

Maine women know what their mothers did then and what they themselves do now. Many still keep kitchen gardens and put up for winter, but hardly any raise poultry or a family pig. When they have time, they pick wild berries and gather windfalls. Mostly, however, like everyone else, they buy their food at the supermarket.

That food, aisle after aisle of it, is cast—as it is everywhere—in the form of convenience, which is to say with contempt for those two pillars of old-fashioned Maine cooking: the taste of real food and the honest value of kitchen labor. Today, you must make a choice: you can have frugality and generosity or you can have particularity. Most cooks here choose the former, and even as they come to depend on the cheapness of out-of-state produce and meat, they get accustomed—or at least resign themselves—to its inferiority.

Maine cussedness may be a necessary luxury, but it is a luxury for all that, and it is the women who foot the bill. The men cling to familiar ways because they still find their identity in them; the women stay with them because they love their men. But it is at a growing cost to themselves, if not in effort, at least in pride . . . something that the men do their best to ignore. This means a growing distance between Maine men and Maine women, a distance that doesn't get discussed. And that, if you like, is Maine cussedness, too.

One evening in Moody's, while I was waiting for my order of franks and beans, a family squeezed into the booth across from me, and I overheard the grandmother tell her grandson that Moody's served the best food in Maine. The sad thing is that if Moody's limited its menu to dishes it could imbue with genuine Maine character and plenty of good taste— if, in other words, Moody's really became a kind of everyday Le Domaine—such a family would probably find the place too particular for them.

What she might have said, instead, is that Moody's serves the most comfortable food in Maine. In fact, that is the problem with Moody's— the place is like a favorite pair of old shoes: impossible to replace, too comfortable to stop wearing out. The laces, heels, and soles can be perpetually renewed, but the shoe leather is worn and cracked and splitting at the stress points. Pretty soon, this particular pair is going to fall apart, and when it does it will be replaced, most likely, by an Irving Big Stop—a gas station plus convenience store plus eatery, the Moody's of the new poor Maine.

Maine food is shot through with cracks because the identity of the people who make and eat it is similarly fissured, and parts keep breaking away. As late as fifteen years ago, Percy Moody raised all the vegetables and much of the meat for his diner at his nearby farm. Now there is no farm. The landmarks of the old Maine that haven't been entirely covered by the encroaching tide have become rugged little islands poking out of a vast, bland bay . . . and so—though they don't often care to notice this—has the consciousness of those who look out over it.

Like any holding action fighting inevitable defeat, there is a poignancy, even a pathos, to Down East cuisine. It is wounded and lives with its wounds like others in that situation, mostly making the best of it but sometimes giving way to hurt and anger or, worse, sheer denial that there is any problem there at all.

Living here in Maine, you come to respect this situation. You learn to look for places where the cook, out of conviction or habit, remains particular about some aspect of Maine food, or at least some aspect of a favorite Maine dish. The pie filling may be overthickened and flavorless, but it is still encased in a deftly made, hand-rolled crust; the doughnuts may no longer be fried in lard, but the batter is made fresh from a time-honored recipe, not some suppliers' mix; the seafood may be coated in a generic batter and not fresh-crushed cracker crumbs, but it was brought to the back door by a neighboring clammer or fisherman.

Hoping to find a place cooking only the old Maine foods in the old pure and simple ways is as much an outsider's fantasy as expecting to find a one-room schoolhouse with a schoolmarm still teaching readin', 'ritin', and 'rithmetic. Today, such an eatery could be opened only by someone from out of state, or at least someone possessing an out-of-state sense of appropriate aesthetics. And people would gather there for the same reason that they come to an art gallery for an opening or a bookstore for a poetry reading: to share an aesthetic experience—in this instance, the artful reproduction of neighborliness, the connection of shared taste.

However, the people who eat at Duffy's and the like are genuine, old-fashioned neighbors. Even if they don't happen to know each other personally, they're still cut from the same local cloth, still feel their fate is tied to the place in which they live. Few have the time these days to hang out at the hardware store; come winter, no circle of chairs rings a woodstove or cracker barrel at the IGA. As the grange dances and movie theaters and even church suppers fade away, these eateries have become the one remaining locus of casual public conviviality, where locals can share together the bittersweet feeling of common identity—of belonging.

Le Domaine versus Duffy's—here are the two halves of America's wounded cuisine: real food on the one hand and real neighbors on the other. There are writers on each side of this divide who try to claim both these elements: that gastronomy is a form of neighborliness; that the eats at Moody's give unalloyed gastronomic pleasure. No . . . it's the longing for the closure that's the real thing, the yearning for real food and real neighbors . . . *and* for a national cuisine that can give us, as it ought to, both.

Meanwhile, there's the A-1 Diner in Gardiner, an idiosyncratic eatery where the two halves of modern-day Maine, old and new, sit down, if separately, to dine. A classic 1946 Worcester diner lifted by a dizzyingly high framework of steel girders to the level of the sidewalk on the Cobbossee Creek Bridge, its interior is a symphony of mahogany woodwork, blue and black tiles, and nostalgia items, with a pleasantly funky, Down East flea-market feel that keeps it well this side of chic.

The menu board offers such exotica as halibut with aioli, black-bean chili, and Thai garlic soup, but there's also plenty of good plain Maine fare—flapjacks with real maple syrup, French fries with gravy, meat loaf, macaroni and cheese, a flawless fried tripe—all of it priced cheap. Desserts include hummingbird cake, fresh raspberries and cream, and gingerbread with lemon sauce. The coffee, in traditional Maine style, is weak, but made from freshly roasted beans, it's also good.

Two young guys cook this food; a vintage Maine waitress dishes it out. The last time we were there the booths were crowded with summer people and local yuppies immersed in happy conversation. For the duration of our lunch, however, an old Mainer sat on a counter stool, hunched over a cup of coffee, navigating the distances, a cigarette end smoldering between his fingers. It may not all add up to a marriage made in heaven—but this isn't heaven, just Vacationland, and you leave the A-1 feeling okay . . . about the place, the eats, the people, and, for a hopeful moment, the state of Maine.

Coda

This piece was four years in the writing. During that time, Dick's became the Riverside Café and the Donut Hole closed down for good. Meanwhile, the Gilleys have expanded Duffy's—tacking a large addition onto the front, which has erased the pleasing proportions of the original cottage; installing air conditioning, which has effectively eliminated its breezy, summery feel; and replacing the front porch with a handicap-access ramp and an entrance hall. *They have taken on a staff of waitresses and gotten rid of almost all the crazed-glass-topped tables, diminishing much of the restaurant's original feckless character. There is no longer any sense of stepping into someone's house. The last time we ate at Duffy's was a Saturday, and the news from a waitress that they had stopped serving baked beans on Maine's traditional baked-bean day set the dining room abuzz. We drove by this summer and saw, attached to a post right beside the road, a three-foot-high cutout of a bright red lobster. The only good news is, come Labor Day, they took it down.*

STEUBEN, 1991–1994

Clamdiggers and Downeast Country Stores

A more modest proposition than the general store, the authentic country store is essentially a rural grocery, meeting the needs of a small, mostly local population. Like the convenience store, its coolers are full of milk and soda, its racks stacked with bread and potato chips. However, unlike the convenience store, it abounds with evidence of unique necessities and cravings. Down East, this includes the likes of snack sticks of dried fish, rubber gloves for bloodworm digging, and little tubs of pickled periwinkles.

While it often takes a sharp eye to pick out these items from the wash of fast-food dreck that otherwise fills the aisles of today's country store, a visitor is immediately made aware of the other difference between it and the now endemic Mainways and 7-Elevens. Like fast-food places, the "convenience" store has been designed to serve customers quickly and then get rid of them; from the beginning, the country store has invited them to stick around. Both always have hot coffee on the hob, but only the country store provides a bench or some seats on which to sit and drink it.

In *Clamdiggers and Downeast Country Stores*, geographer Allan Lockyer takes a ramble up and down what happens to be our local stretch of U.S. 1 to visit the few surviving members of this tradition, country stores that still serve the small communities that lie between Ellsworth and Machias, Down East Maine's two county seats, and talks to local people about some of the ones that are no longer here. Many of these closed down in the past decade; several others have vanished from the scene between the time of his trip and the completion of his book. Reading it, you discover not only why so few survive, but—more interesting still—how problematic is every aspect of their business.

As the author writes: "Country stores are places where rural folks go for advice, information, and companionship." At the turn of the century, the small Down East town of Cherryfield had over a *dozen* such stores, all located in near proximity to each other. Why so many? Part of the reason is that before the era of self-service, customers expected to be personally waited on. The proprietor cut the meat, took the canned goods down from the shelf, and measured out and packaged up the flour, beans, crackers, and similar goods—a time-consuming process.

However, that process also served—and so was an integral part of— the store's larger function of knitting up a community out of isolated rural families, almost all of whom knew someone else in the area but almost none of whom were on familiar, let alone good, terms with everyone around. The greater the number of stores, the more complex the texture of this fabric, because the wider the possible elaboration of differences. Cherryfield has only two of those twelve stores left, but the presence today of even two or three active groceries in a small Maine town signals the same thing as a Masons' lodge, an Oddfellows' hall, or a Shriners' temple: a community with enough remaining identity to be able to exfoliate a little.

Often a country store was not in a town at all. Such businesses were hardly "stores" in the conventional sense—often the proprietor set up business in his front room and went on living in the rest of the place. But whether he did or not, the building itself was almost always a house. Even if it had been built from the ground up to be a store, the only immediate difference between it and the houses around was that it fronted directly onto the road. I can remember from my own childhood that going into one of these stores was like going into someone's home —the way it still is now when you stop at the place of people who sell eggs or crabmeat.

True country stores retain this homey feel. The proprietor may not officially reside there, but it is where he spends most of his waking hours. In a convenience store, you deal with a clerk; in a country store, you deal with a person. This difference is sometimes subtle but always real. For the clerk, being there is just a job; for the proprietor, it is a life—and successful country-store owners continue to make their in-store life real and rich. Even today, their stores become embodiments of their personalities, from the jokey signs on the wall to the store dog that steps on your foot, harder and harder, until you give it a bite of your Baby Ruth.

Outsiders come into a Yankee country store hoping to find there some taste of vanished country life—a cracker barrel, jars of put-up bread-and-butter pickles, bottles of sarsaparilla—or the sight of a woodstove ringed with battered chairs. There are places patently assembled to satisfy this need—and, not unexpectedly, profit from it—famously, the Orton family's Vermont Country Store, the very name of which is a registered trademark, whose various spin-off "country" enterprises have taken over Weston, Vermont, like a folksy plague.

The reality remains vernacular without time's soothing hand-rubbed veneer. Today's "folk" want an automated sweepstake ticket dispenser and racks of Stephen Segal movies. The characters who used to hang around the cracker barrel are there, but they have become transformed into what seems suspiciously like loiterers. One proprietor discovered, after purchasing the Hancock Grocery, that the men who hung out at the lunch counter for hours drinking coffee and talking kept away women customers, "who apparently felt uncomfortable walking past the counter occupied by unkempt men."

Other store owners confirmed this correlation. The more a store attracted a clientele of rough-hewn male bloodworm diggers and clammers, the higher the sales of beer and snack foods. But women stayed away—and it is women who buy the groceries, meat, and milk.

Further Downeast, I met a proprietor who was trying to change the perception people had of his store . . . In the past, it had catered to the local clammers and wormers. He said, "Oftentimes a car would pull up and the husband would come in while the wife would stay in the car. The women refused to cross the threshold."

It goes without saying that most visitors and summer people are no more enchanted by the same atmosphere. Nor, if they do squeeze past the group at the counter, will they find much to remark on in the store. Strangely, Lockyer has almost nothing to say about the actual food he encounters in these grocery stores, perhaps because it is now so ordinary as to be near invisible. The culinary history of the late twentieth century here in Maine is going to have to be decoded from the steamed hot dog, the one comestible almost every one of these stores flaunts on its store-front signage.

Not that you can't find distinctively native food sold there, but it, too, is often not to the common taste—like whole dried fish, called "strip fish," because it is eaten by pulling off strips. Even natives can have their problems with it:

> "People like to keep strip fish on the dashboards of their cars," I said to Lucille. I remembered riding to baseball games in the 1960s with a Steuben man who always had a dried fish on the dashboard of his pickup truck. He'd tear off a strip, chew, and talk at the same time. His truck stank of fish.
>
> "Yeah, some have maggots in them," Lucille added. "We had one woman who always waited for those. She'd wait 'til the fish had maggots in it before she'd buy it."
>
> "And she'd eat it?"
>
> "Yeah, and then she'd eat it! 'Call me when it gets like this, okay?' "

No, the defining characteristic of the country store lies not in its contents but in the sum of the individual exchanges between proprietor and customer: a nexus of personal connection. As these go, so goes the store . . . or, more to the point, as these have gone, so has the country store also gone. Today, this linkage is mostly accomplished in the vernacular eateries that continue to flourish or at the town post office, where folks arrive early and pretend to wait for their mail to be sorted, while passing on the town news and gossip.

Lockyer's trip Down East provides the framework of the book but only some of its contents; the narrative is also, in its way, a voyage of personal as well as public, sociological discovery. If there is a subtext to this book, it is the undertow of latent anger that native Mainers feel about the erosion of their lives by modern life—defined by them as increasing (and increasingly stupid and intrusive) regulations, the crushing weight of a cash (as opposed to a barter) economy, and, above all, *outsiders*.

Lockyer himself grew up here but does not really come from here; he is not a native and is not considered such, even if he isn't classed as a leaf-peeper or a summer person, either. He is a sympathizer, a "friend"—the sort of person to whom it is said, when this anger bursts out, "Of course, I don't mean *you* . . ." Which, of course, also means, "I *do* mean you."

Poignantly, this polarity often cuts across the counter of the country store. More and more, the proprietors are from away and their customers exclusively, stubbornly native. The true country store has always been a family business. Open from before dawn to after dusk, seven days a week, 365 days a year, and rarely producing income enough to hire full-time help, it requires family labor to work the shifts and do all the necessary chores (ordering, stocking, and, often, cooking).

Today, however, few Maine families still work this way. Either the children don't want the life or the parents don't wish it on them. So the stores are sold to out-of-staters, attracted by the romance of the country store but with little sense of its reality. Consequently, these stores now change owners as often as every other year and, with each of these exchanges, lose more of their essential character.

This situation is worsened by the fact that not only summer people but many Mainers now get their groceries at the huge, well-stocked megamarkets. Only the canniest proprietors can make a living from a country store, and they do this by turning to locals who receive an influx of ready cash but who haven't yet become middle-class consumers.

The limited tastes and needs of these clammers, worm diggers, urchin divers, and scallop draggers are transforming the country store into a rural version of the smoke shop or candy store—selling items like beer, smokes, snacks, and lottery cards that absorb a disproportionate amount of local income without returning anything to the community, whatever their necessity to local lives.

This book was written as an elegy and as an indictment. It succeeds at both. Even so, when you put it down, what remains in mind is how much victim we all are, hate it and fight it as we may, to history and to change. Like many other half-abandoned parts of this country, Down East Maine is a landscape as much haunted as inhabited, and the best part of this book is the way Alan Lockyer has of getting the folks here talking. When they do, the ghosts all come to life.

STEUBEN, 1994

Saltwater Seasonings
Good Food from Coastal Maine

I knew that *Saltwater Seasonings* was my kind of cookbook when, early on in its pages, Sarah Leah Chase settles down for a chat with lobsterman Dana Holbrook:

> I met Dana on the rocks of the cove where he anchors his lobsterboat, Shady Lady, as he was coming in at about 4 p.m. after a long day of fishing that had begun close to sunrise. He was in a gregarious mood and looking forward to unwinding in his shanty (defined by him as "the place where I put my boots on in the morning—my place of business") with an "attitude adjuster"—a crude but satisfying blend of diet Pepsi and vodka poured from a half-gallon jug into over-size plastic cups. I accepted the offer of an attitude adjuster of my own, and we began to talk.

Now, if you live in Maine, you know that shack. You might even have one in your own back yard. And, regardless, portraits of the state that conspicuously exclude such things don't feel right, however neatly they get the soft plume of fiddleheads in spring or the briny, pungent scent of lobsters on the boil.

This book gives you the shack *and* the fiddleheads *and* the lobsters —and mostly manages to get it all right. Consequently, its pages have a richness to them that I haven't found in any Maine cookbook since those two early Down East classics, Marjorie Mosser's 1939 *Good Maine Food* and Robert P. Tristram Coffin's 1945 *Mainstays of Maine*. This is because Sarah Leah Chase and Jonathan Chase—sister and brother—

bring to their book both the rich memories of childhood summers spent on Blue Hill Bay and the talents of their subsequent careers: hers as a successful cookbook author (*The Nantucket Open-House Cookbook*, among others) and his as a chef whose Blue Hill restaurant, Jonathan's, is known for its adventurous use of Down East foods.

To write *Saltwater Seasonings*, Sarah Leah Chase, its narrator and, mostly, its writer, started out by visiting her brother's wide-ranging personal network of suppliers—mussel growers, cheesemakers, organic farmers (and ranchers), beekeepers, brewers of hard cider, and the like (a similar source list, by the way, appears at the end of the book). As chapter follows chapter, she introduces all these people, both the producers of traditional Down East edibles—crabmeat pickers, clammers, blueberry growers, alewife smokers—and the newcomers who are bringing such seemingly recondite items to the Maine menu as farm pheasant, goat Cheddar, and cultured oysters.

Whether you're old Maine or new, earning a living as a food producer here is difficult work and the rewards are slow to come. Those who tough it out have personalities distinctive enough to be worth knowing, and this book lets us do so, introducing us to old-timers like seventy-nine-year-old Lawris Closson, winner of Jonathan Chase's pea-raising contest, or newcomers like farmer Stanley Joseph, who calls his Cape Rosier place the Funny Farm. This portraiture is enriched by Cary Hazlegrove's photography, which is equally adept at capturing lady's slippers blooming in the Maine woods and Laura Stevens guarding the pies at a Dirigo Grange supper.

My favorite photograph, however, shows a sight much more rarely seen: a scissors-wielding sardine packer hunched over a stack of fish, trays of filled cans piled up by her side. The Chases devote a whole chapter to Maine sardines, including a visit to the Port Clyde sardine-packing plant. What is admirable about *Saltwater Seasonings* is not only that the Chases recognize that this Rockland cannery is as much a part of today's Maine as Phyllis Schartner's lush orchards of antique apples in Thorndyke or Chip Davison's Great Eastern Mussel Farms in Tenants Harbor. They also find a way to balance these sometimes edgily coexisting presences in a single equation, by factoring out what old Maine and new Maine have in common—their shared hunger for a sense of place.

To write well about Maine food you have to know that, whether he be newcomer or native, the saltwater farmer sitting on his back stoop of an evening with a bowl of blueberries and sweet, rich milk is in a state of quiet communion with his cows, his blueberry barren, and the

deep silence of the surrounding night. That bowl of berries is less a
meal than a navigational instrument, pointing him true north.

This is the purpose of good Maine cooking, however tasty it may also
be. Those who think otherwise never see the forest for the trees and
even, I think, miss some of the most interesting of those. It's here especially that *Saltwater Seasonings* has its priorities right. Whether it
takes you into the kitchen to make raw cucumber relish, out onto the
mud flats to dig for clams, or over to the grange supper for a plate of
beans, a lot of necessary orienting takes place before the conversation
comes around to the actual eating.

Organically raised Black Angus cattle grazing in Freeport, blueberry
wine aging in French oak barrels in Gouldsboro, Atlantic salmon swimming in pens near Eastport—what we have going on here in Maine is
what you might almost call exciting culinary times. What's somewhat
surprising—but also extremely heartening—is how greatly these products have expanded the range of good Maine food without much inter-
fering with its simplicity.

This brings us around, finally, to the cooking. When it comes to
mainstays of Maine, the Chases know what's what and, even more ad-
mirably, aren't afraid to say so. Despite the terror that animal fat has
struck in the heart of the American population as a whole, Down East
cooks still treasure the chunk of salt pork that lubricates the yellow
eyes in the bean pot and mellows the chowder, and they still like to
slick the pancake griddle with a scrap of ham rind.

Even so, I had my suspicions that, when it came to actually *preparing*
Down East dishes, the Chases wouldn't be able to leave well enough
alone. Jonathan's, after all, is known for dishes like linguine with
smoked mussels and pesto, and grilled lamb with Gorgonzola walnut
butter—not plain Maine fare like codfish pudding or parsnip stew. I
needn't have worried. Here, too, they listened to the source:

> One of the first Mainers we interviewed for this book was a mussel diver from
> Jonesboro, who replied when queried on his favorite way of cooking his catch:
> "The less you do to 'em, the better they are." We have been guided by this advice
> time and time again.

Thus, the Chases usually are to be trusted—even emulated—when they
lay out the rules for constructing the perfect crab roll and lobster stew,
baking molasses cookies, or preparing that quintessential autumnal dish
of new-crop potatoes and a choice root vegetable (carrot, turnip, ruta-

baga), the two steamed separately and then mashed up together into a gloriously savory, buttery mass.

There's a lot of similar good Maine cooking in this book—blackstrap-molasses-cured ham baked with cider and mustard, strawberry short-cake with Bakewell Cream biscuits, Northeast Harbor scallop soup, lobster "fried over cold," roast spring chicken with fiddleheads, hermit bars with coffee icing, wild blueberry tea bread . . . the list goes on and on. And whether the dishes are old Maine or new, the authors usually add just enough polish to bring out their deep, honest shine. These are recipes that will teach old cooks new tricks, and new cooks what Maine cooking is all about.

Not that *Saltwater Seasonings* is a book without flaws. The most serious if subtlest of them is the authors' obvious identification with the new-comers. Native Mainers are sensitively and affectionately treated, but the book is still permeated with a feeling of "them versus us." This means that while two pages are devoted to the cooking of a "nouveau-Maine" chef like Sam Hayward, humble eateries like Dick's restaurant in Ellsworth are virtually ignored.

Even as their book was published, Dick's changed hands, and I'll bet more eaters already miss the award-worthy beans that Richard Anderson simmered in his own home bean hole (something the Chases seem never to have heard of) and the equally notable lard-crusted pies baked by his wife, Gail, than have ever missed the cuisine at Hayward's defunct Brunswick restaurants, 22 Lincoln and Side Door Café.

This is meant as no slur on Hayward. But each year more restaurants offering interesting upscale cooking appear in Maine, while the vernac-ular eateries that cater mostly to natives are falling fast into the cate-gory of endangered species, as is the old-fashioned Down East home kitchen . . . and the Chases spend too little time in either.

Less troubling if more flagrant is the problem of the prose. Sarah Leah Chase writes about the state not with Down East understatement but with summer-folk gush. This is tolerable if wearying when applied to landscape or food, but she can be so uncritically boosterish of places like Bartlett's Winery—makers of very pleasant but rarely exceptional fruit wines—as to sound less like a writer than a publicist. And when it's lavished on the physical charms of Des FitzGerald, owner of Duck-trap River Fish Farm, producer of quite superior smoked seafood—as it is for an entire half page—it becomes downright excruciating. Would that she had seasoned such paragraphs with the same moderation as her Down East dishes.

With a few of these, too, readers may quarrel. The Chases don't seem to be able to make a fresh fruit pie or crisp without spooning in the thickener—flour, cornstarch, tapioca. A fresh berry pie, especially, should spill its insides out of a double crust across the plate in a flood of brilliant, unsullied flavor and color. Similarly, the old Maine way to prepare clam chowder is to cut up the potatoes into maul-shaped wedges, so that the edges crumble off during cooking to thicken the broth, obviating any need for flour. And just like lobster stew (but unlike fish chowder), clam chowder requires a few hours' aging at the back of the stove to taste its best.

All of this is forgivable. Here at last is a Down East cookbook devoted equally to the many different eatables to be found on its rock-ribbed coastline and to the rock-ribbed characters who catch, raise, or grow them. *Saltwater Seasonings* has a rare understanding of Maine life and Maine people and an infectious love of good Maine food. It's pretty much the best Down East cookbook to come along in fifty years and, things being the way they are—mostly trending away from good Maine culinary sense—it may be the best we're going to get for some time to come.

STEUBEN, 1992

Maine Eats

Do Maine cooks cook good? There's no denying that they used to. Not a world-class cuisine, maybe, but Maine cooking offered an array of humble yet distinctive dishes that—for the rest of the country, at least—came to symbolize the Northeast. If there are no such books as *Mainstays of Massachusetts* or *Good Connecticut Food*, it's because Yankee cookbooks used to come in two flavors: New England . . . and Maine.

This is no longer so. For obvious reasons—such as: my mother lives over in Searsmont—I'm glad *I* don't have to spell out the current state of affairs; *Yankee* magazine already has done so in their 1983 collection of *Great New England Recipes and the Cooks Who Made Them Famous*. In this collection of the best of the best, you have to read over a hundred pages to get to the first Maine cook, who provides four recipes (five, if you count one for frosting), and then 150 more to reach the second. Score: in 320 pages, two cooks, ten recipes. By comparison, New Hampshire—a state about which the best you can say is that it is the home of red flannel hash—gets nine cooks, *eighty* recipes.

Unfortunately, a sober assessment of contemporary Maine cookbooks confirms the justice of such treatment. Most of the food that won Maine renown until well into this century has nearly vanished; the few dishes that survive do so more in name than in spirit. Of course, this doesn't mean that there are no good Maine cooks left—just that the few that remain are too overworked to write any cookbooks.

I'm defining "Maine food" as food that people in Maine eat and generally agree to designate as theirs. So, for example, while a lot of *fajitas* are eaten here these days, they're still thought of as exotic fare. Conversely, Jean Ann Pollard can *call* her collection of tofu recipes and such *The New Maine Cooking*, but no matter how many copies it sells,

it still isn't Maine food. Made in Maine, maybe; Maine food, no. And
although there's a lot of truth in Carolyn Chute's observation that the
Maine license plate ought to sport a box of Kraft's macaroni-and-cheese
dinner and not a steamed lobster, no one here refers to Kraft's macaroni
and cheese as any kind of Down East specialty—even if those boxes
outsell the crustaceans a hundred thousand to one. Finally, dishes that
other states might also claim, like fried clams, are ruled *in*. We don't
care what they do or say in other states.

The essence of traditional Maine cooking is caring enormously about
the good, simple food at hand. The food, at least, is still there. Unlike,
say, Boston supermarkets, Maine grocers stock a wide assortment of
native-grown beans, gallon jugs of pure maple syrup and Barbados molasses, good-quality cornmeal, and all kinds of salt fish. Maine shrimp,
clams, lobster, and fresh-picked crabmeat are available from trucks
parked in vacant lots up and down the coast. Last autumn, driving up
to Calais, we noticed heaped-up bags of potatoes, turnips, parsnips, and
swedes—hardly tourist bait—for sale at roadside stands.

However, good Maine ingredients alone don't automatically make a
Maine cookbook. New England's most noted chef, Jasper White, in *Jasper White's Cooking from New England*, writes with sensitive appreciation of good Maine ingredients, and we consult his cookbook often
when making Maine food. Still, it's not, by our manner of accounting,
truly a Maine cookbook—his recipes use Maine food, but they belong
to him. Good Maine cooking has always put the food before the cook.

Because of this, recipes have never served classic Maine fare all that
well; it is better defined by argument . . . or by poetry. The very best
Maine cookbook—Robert P. Tristram Coffin's *Mainstays of Maine*—
expertly wielded them both:

> My mother's best dishes were tied into the different seasons. Strawberries and
> cream were tied into the Milky Way of daisies sweeping uphill over the June
> meadows. Spare-ribs were tied into the evenings white with hoarfrost, into the
> November air, into the bare trees—the time when the current pig hung, pink as
> a cherub in heaven, for once in his life, all passion spent and all bristles gone,
> opened wide and braced apart with spruce stretchers like a canoe, all his inner
> secrets bared, head down from the beam in the woodshed, at utter, utter peace.

Note that phrase "my *mother's* best dishes." This book was published
in 1944, and even then things that had once seemed eternal were slipping through the fingers. World War II seems to mark this watershed.
If you turn to the other truly great Maine cookbook—Marjorie Mosser's
Good Maine Food, published just before the war, in 1939—you find a

book of recipes for such old-time, honest Maine dishes as "Low Mull," "Lumberman's Winter Porridge," "Haymaker's Switchel," and "Porcupine Liver," with hardly any nostalgic keening.

Marjorie Mosser was Kenneth Roberts's niece and, at that point of time, his secretary. Roberts, a popular historical novelist, had published an article on Maine cooking in *The Saturday Evening Post* (it would later become a chapter of his classic *Trending into Maine*), which generated a firestorm of culinary correspondence with other opinionated Mainers.

Mosser—with Roberts's encouragement and active assistance—built *Good Maine Food* using these letters as its foundation. This gave the book a pleasant, argumentative character—as if the reader were listening in on a conversation at the local country store. In Samuel P. Capen's letter on the perfect salt pork/salt fish dinner, to give just one instance, the casualness of his instruction—"Prepare a common egg sauce"— and the easiness of his reference to the doings of others—"My neighbor says that the only difference between her hash and your grandmother's is that she first sautés finely chopped onion until brown and mixes it into the hash before it is cooked . . ."—speaks of a living, breathing Maine cuisine.

Compare this with Willan C. Roux's *What's Cooking Down East*, first published in 1964. It's full of Maine character—and third on my list of the state's best cookbooks—but you pick up immediately on its distinctly bookish flavor. Where Coffin writes about himself, Roux quotes Coffin—*and* Kenneth Roberts *and* L. L. Bean. His pages have the sound of a man arguing with books, not his neighbors, and riffling through old recipe files.

Note, too, the page count: 132. The easy abundance of *Good Maine Food* (later editions topped 400 pages) is fast shrinking to a handful of exemplary familiars: chowder, lobster stew, steamed fiddleheads, blueberry pie. By 1972, the subject is a single dish. That is the year John J. Pullen wrote the last great Maine cookbook (even if he neglected to put his state's name into the title), *The Transcendental Boiled Dinner*—a humorous but passionately argued little masterpiece about "boiled" (simmered! simmered!) corned beef plus vegetables.

Now, if twenty years ago it took all the strength a man had to sustain the life of his boiled dinner, no surprise that today Moody's Diner in Waldoboro is famous simply for *serving* it. Only the impious will inquire if John J. Pullen would commend their version—compared, you have to ask, to what? The cookbook is a different matter. Diner buffs will want to snap up *What's Cooking at Moody's Diner* for Nancy Moody Genthner's reminiscences and Rod McCormick's fascinating architectural renderings of Moody's as it evolved over the past fifty years, but not for the boiled dinner recipe or for any other Maine dish. Those recipes are too perfunctory and too few. The book's real passion is for such dishes as "Turkey and Broccoli Quiche," "Crockpot Mock Lasagne," and "Carefree Casserole."

These are the dishes that began to flood into Maine the decade after the war. Men were leaving craft-oriented, income-incidental, home-centered work to find jobs in mills and factories; recipes were bringing time- and cash-conscious cooking into the kitchen. Just when men like R. P. Tristram Coffin, Willan Roux, and John J. Pullen were complaining that they weren't getting the food their mothers used to make, their wives were finding the kitchen transformed into a low-skill, low-pay, low-esteem workplace.

No Mainer can read the title of Kathleen Olsen LaCombe's self-published *It's Edible: My Maine Recipes* without smiling or nodding assent to the author's explanation: "When I was growing up in Cape Elizabeth, compliments . . . were not liberally handed out, and we had to settle for what we got." But that attitude is one thing when the non-complimenter is hoeing the garden or flailing out the beans, another when he has spent the day at the office.

By the time Kathleen Olson had grown up, Maine family life no longer revolved around the big cast-iron, wood-burning cookstove. Now, in winter, other rooms were being heated, and everyone went to work to pay the fuel bill. Who could complain if supper started with "Cold Carrot Soup," made with curry powder, frozen orange-juice concentrate, and three-quarters cup of non-dairy creamer—especially when the best encouragement a cook could hope for was "It's edible"?

You can see this trend accelerating a third of a century ago in the *Rockland Courier-Gazette*'s collections of Maine recipes—starting in 1963 with *Maine Coastal Cooking*, and followed by *All Maine Cooking* in 1967 and *Maine's Jubilee Cookbook* in 1969. All are worth having for such traditional dishes as "Penobscot Alewives," "New England Poverty Pie," "Grandmother's Pear Mincemeat," and "Town Meeting Hardtack." Still, the time- and money-savers have started to crowd in: "Lime-Grapefruit Salad" made with Fresca, or "Easy Chicken Casserole":

1 can chicken rice soup; 1 can cream of mushroom soup, 1 can Chinese noodles, 1 small can evaporated milk, 1 can chicken. Stir all together. Place in baking dish and cover with crushed potato chips. Bake in a 350°F oven until bubbling, about 25 minutes.

So what, if they taste good? you ask. Well, only that this kind of thing hasn't anything to do with Maine at all (and, in my opinion, not all that much more to do with cooking).

The major exception, and this despite the recipes for "Dump Bars" and "Throw-Together Chocolate Cake," comes in the baking sections. Maine women are different from Maine men, in both their pragmatism and their pride. Maine men, on cook's night out, head for the chowder pot or the bean hole; Maine women, when they find the time, take down the rolling pin. Baking is the cooking they do to please themselves and to compete against their neighbors, and it's the last thing they're willing to give up.

Good Maine Food has near a dozen chowder recipes and one for banana bread; the *Camden Connection Cookbook*, a spiral fund-raiser for the Camden Public Library, circa 1985, reverses that count: twelve recipes for banana bread and one for chowder. This isn't Maine cooking; it's Maine *women's* cooking.

That, I think, is an important distinction. In Barbara Pullen's 1982 collection of her mother's recipes, *New England Recipes from Nana's Kitchen*, the "main course" recipes are fitted into exactly eight pages; the rest of the book is nearly all desserts. Clearly, when her mother, Anna Coe Young, fired up the cookstove in her Calais farmhouse kitchen, it wasn't visions of pot roast or chowder but "Bangor Brownies" or "Gifford House Cookies" or "Carrie's Lemon Pie" that danced in her head . . . and that linger on in her daughter's memory.

Still—and I think here of those dozen banana breads—even the baking has changed. As such things go, making banana bread is not a skill- or time-intensive activity. The books recalling grandmother's or even mother's recipes are for collecting more than for making—or, in what amounts to the same thing, they are for making "when there's time."

The old Maine cooking was frugal with money; its dishes required no more than a short list of ingredients and a brief note on preparation, since they called for foods the cook already had on hand and on skills she already possessed. Now, even where a hot stove remains the focal point of communal life—as it still is in much of rural Maine—the cook is likely to be more frugal with time than money, drawing on dishes where the largesse lies in the ingredients, not in the effort of making.

So, for instance, in *Merrymeeting Merry Eating: A Collection of Recipes Gathered in Maine* (1988), a fund-raiser for the Regional Memorial Hospital in Brunswick, desserts run to mocha chocolate-chip cheesecake and black-bottom ice cream dessert (made with crushed Nabisco Mystic Mint cookies). There are pies, too, but the elaborateness of their fillings whisper of the store-bought crust: mocha-fudge mud, luscious pineapple cheese. Even "Pennellville Red Raspberry Pie" is dosed with black-currant liqueur. Easy and elegant is the promise; whatever the results, they are a far, far cry from the plain speaking of Nana's brownies and lemon pie.

Indeed, the only cookbooks I've laid hands on recently that reminded me—and poignantly—of authentic, old-style Maine cooking came from Newfoundland. The real Maine, it seems, has retreated farther up the Atlantic coast. Not that Newfoundland doesn't have a flavor all its own. People in Maine may still remember fatback and molasses, but not brewis, toutens, seal-flipper pie, or figgidy duff with molasses coady. But what these books have in common with the old Maine cooking is the unaffected simplicity of the dishes they record and the honesty of the ingredients out of which they are made.

In a new edition of *Mainstays of Maine* (see page 150), its publisher, Carroll F. Terrell, includes a reminiscence of Robert P. Tristram Coffin, whom he had as a professor at Bowdoin. Coffin was a hefty man with an equally hefty walrus mustache. When he lectured, he would twirl it: first one end, then the other, and the more excited he got, the faster he would twirl. Talking about food always made him *very* excited, and it would have been a sight to behold if one could only have pressed a copy of Len Margaret's *fish & brewis, toutens & tales* into his hands and shown him the recipe for cod roe dipped in breadcrumbs, milk, and beaten egg, and then fried in the drippings of salt-pork rashers . . . or the dandelion dinner made with those greens, salt beef, carrots, turnips, and potatoes.

He would have been just as excited perusing a copy of *Fat-Back and Molasses*, edited by the Reverend Ivan F. Jesperson. Among its homey recipes are ones for baked cod tongue (still sold here by roadside fish sellers), potato pork cakes, and five different fish chowders. Here at last are two books a good Maine cook needn't feel in the least abashed setting on the shelf beside *Mainstays of Maine* and *Good Maine Food*.

CASTINE, 1988 / STEUBEN, 1991

STILL IN PRINT

Down East Books (P.O. Box 679, Camden, ME 04843) offers many of the vernacular Maine cookbooks discussed here, including attractive paperback editions of Marjorie Mosser's *Good Maine Food* and Willan C. Roux's *What's Cooking Down in Maine* (retitled *What's Cooking Down East*). Their catalogue has current ordering information.

Northern Lights (493 College Avenue, Orono, ME 04473) has reissued Robert P. Tristram Coffin's *Mainstays of Maine* as *Maine Cooking: Old-Time Secrets* in paperback for $8.95. Allan Lockyer's *Clamdiggers and Downeast Country Stores* (see pages 134–38), also a paperback, is $14.95. Include $2 shipping per book.

Nancy Moody Genthner's *What's Cooking at Moody's Diner* is available from Dancing Bear Books (P.O. Box 4, W. Rockport, ME 04865) for $8.95 plus $2 shipping per book.

Len Margaret's *fish & brewis, toutens & tales* is published as Volume 7 of Canada's Atlantic Folklore/Folklife Series. Contact Breakwater Books (P.O. Box 2188, St. John's, Newfoundland A1C 6E6 • 709–722–6680) for U.S. price and shipping costs.

Barbara Pullen's *New England Recipes from Nana's Kitchen* is $6.95 plus 90¢ shipping from A.I.C.E., 23 University Drive, Augusta, ME 04330.

Merrymeeting Merry Eating is $15.95 plus $2 shipping from RMHA (58 Baribeau Drive, Brunswick, ME 04011).

Down East Chowder

It was a crisp blue morning in early June. I was standing at the edge
of a cliff that overlooked the island-dotted waters of Casco Bay. I was
on an island myself, the bay waters lapping the jumbled rocks below.
A tiny clapboard summer cottage stood waiting behind me, its gray paint
bleached and powdered by years of salt and sun, with tattered green
shades pulled tight down over its windows. It was 1967, the summer
before my last year of college.

My backpack, suitcase, and typewriter sat in the tall grass in front
of the cottage door. I had just lugged them over the hill from the main
island road. A rutted dirt track crossed it to the cottage, but the island
taxi refused to traverse it, and the driver, Mary Justice, had let me off
at the edge of the pavement to foot it on my own. I stood in the sun
cooling off and drinking it all in again, the bay glistening in the late-
morning sunlight, the seagulls coasting lazily overhead, the barn swallows swooping in and out of the two birdhouses stuck up on poles in
the small patch of lawn.

I went to college under a joint scholarship-loan program and I was
expected to work each summer, to provide a share of my college keep
myself. However, I had persuaded a surprisingly understanding dean
that writing a novel could be considered work—even without the prospect of it actually earning any money—and would therefore meet that
requirement. And my grandfather had offered me a grant of exactly one
hundred dollars. It was all I had to live on for the whole summer, but
I was confident it would be enough. Since the key to the cottage came
with the money, my only major expense would be food and cooking
supplies.

Spread one hundred dollars over three months and you are feeding yourself on a dollar a day. Even at the time, the sum was not munificent. But since I had spent three of the past seven years as a college dropout living on that amount or less on the Lower East Side, I was sure I would manage just fine. Here, after all, I could have a garden. Even better, as everyone knew, there was food all around for the gathering.

During my last two years in New York, I had purchased a copy of Euell Gibbons's guide to wild foods, *Stalking the Wild Asparagus*. Looking back, I can't say what possessed me to do this. No wild asparagus or any other even faintly edible plant grew within easy picking distance of East Ninth Street. I did spend one fall afternoon taking the interminable subway trip up to Van Cortlandt Park in the Bronx, where I wrestled a hoard of acorns away from the squirrels, since Gibbons assured me that they were truly delicious once the tannic acid had been boiled out of them (the acorns, that is, not the squirrels).

After winnowing out the wormy ones, I began to boil them, tasting periodically after the first few hours, to see if the tannic taste was fading. I ended up boiling them for two straight days. By then, the tannic acid was thoroughly steamed out of the acorns and into my kitchen walls, which would reek of it for months, and the boiled nuts—after I coated them in sugar, also Gibbons's suggestion—would ultimately be bestowed on a city friend, who ate some and was then violently sick.

This did not turn me against Euell Gibbons, who is a naturally engaging writer and easily persuades you to pass over current failures by igniting fresh enthusiasm for new pasturage. I brought the book with me to Maine, where, to my disappointment, it still proved of little use. Sometimes it was the book's fault—the chapter on mushrooms, for instance, had no illustrations, a real handicap for the novice mushroom hunter—and sometimes mine, since I soon discovered I had little more tolerance for salads of rank wild greens than I had for sugar-coated acorns. But I remained a convert to the idea that nature will feed you well if you will only allow it to do so.

Therefore, I took the boat into Portland and hunted down his just-published sequel, *Stalking the Blue-Eyed Scallop*. This time, the illustrations were copious and more exact, and I could already identify many of the seaside denizens whose culinary uses he detailed. So, even though the book was available only in hardcover and the purchase made a large dent in my hundred dollars, I bought it and carried it back to the island—and opened a new chapter in my life as cook.

In retrospect, I realize that there were two reasons why Euell Gibbons had such a powerful effect over my imagination at the time, one of them

easy to explain and the other not. The first was his persuasive ability
to make you think of roadside or seaside foraging as a viable and even
meritorious pastime, not a desperate rummaging only a short step up
from dumpster diving.

If our culture has any one shared prejudice, it is that money sanctifies
all things. This means that anything too common to be salable has no
value and hence no meaning. In late spring, Maine supermarkets offer
heaps of already slightly fetid fiddleheads, whereas anyone here can
walk into the woods and pick spanking fresh ones—just as they can
pick a pan's worth of tiny, tender dandelion greens in less than half an
hour from their own lawn, whereas those in the supermarket are always
huge, weedy, and tough.

Euell Gibbon exercised his power over me in no small part because
he spoke from a book that I had paid good money for and was thereby
automatically granted an authority that I might not have granted him
had I met him rooting in a field. I know this because I had once come
across an elderly couple busily digging up wild greens in a public park
on a pleasant spring morning. When they noticed that I was watching,
they stopped and explained what they were about, suggesting I take
some home to try for myself. Pigweed? I smiled, took a large handful,
thanked them, and, once out of sight, tossed it all behind some bushes
. . . and dismissed the two foragers as harmless cranks. Euell Gibbons
devotes a whole chapter to pigweed (also known more appetizingly as
lamb's quarters), and there, on the page, it suddenly gained dignity.*

The other reason for my attraction to Gibbons had to do with my need
for a father. I had a real father, but this was a time when our relationship
was undergoing a violent transition. Eventually, we would find a way to
respect and love each other again, but right then we were at complete
loggerheads, and I needed him for things that I was not able to ask for
and he was not able to give.

My father enjoyed fishing. I would go out with him in the rowboat
and we would both catch pollack and mackerel. But there was something
in their frantic fight for life when hauled in that was for me as galva-
nizing and distressing as an electric shock. I shrank from the act of
killing them and so, inwardly, from allowing any transmission of the

---

* It's perhaps worth noting that foraging for wild mushrooms is a dignified pursuit
because these are too scarce and fragile for commercial exploitation and so, in their
way, almost beyond price—ask any New Yorker trying to purchase fresh morels during
their short season. It is one thing to show up at the kitchen door of Lutèce with a basket
of these, quite another to offer a bunch of fresh wild mustard or pigweed.

ritual from my father to myself—and even this kind of simple line fishing is full of ritual—from choosing the bait and place to fish to cleaning the catch, filleting it, and learning what to do with it when you get it into the kitchen.

Looking back after thirty years, I think now I simply wasn't close enough to my father to let him draw me past my squeamishness before the act. In fact, it would probably be more honest to say that I used this squeamishness to reject the rapport that men established by the shared act of actual (or symbolic) killing that is an important element of masculine identity. Later, I would try to learn how to accomplish this from books, only to discover that a book can't be there when your hands are full of death.

Because of this, although I have no moral objection to hunting or fishing (although I do, like anyone, make moral distinctions between *kinds* of hunting and fishing), I'm simply not able to do it. This isn't because I'm on the side of the duck or the fish. I can still clearly remember my father showing me how to clean the fish on the shore, squatting on some rocks so that we could rinse the gutted fish in the seawater, and my fascinated delight watching crabs—ordinarily never to be seen—scuttling out from crevices under the water, drawn by the blood and the entrails. My confusion came about because I wasn't sure, in the closeness of that rowboat, in my fear of/anger at my father, whether I was metaphoric co-conspirator or prey.

With Euell Gibbons there was no such confusion. What he offered was an alternative, lesser, but still important substitute ritual. Foraging is inherently a solitary activity. It doesn't so much deny the experience of male bonding as avoid noticing it—and so provided me a different path across the metaphoric boundary into male adulthood.

At least, I can see that this was what foraging meant to me by the fact that my interest in it that summer soon paled when it came to plants. What was wonderful about the seashore was that it is a place where the line is most blurred between foraging and hunting or fishing. For, while not a shot is fired in the whole of *Stalking the Wild Asparagus* or *Stalking the Healthful Herbs*, no squirrels potted, possums treed, or rabbits snared, the very title of *Stalking the Blue-Eyed Scallop* tells us that we are in a different territory. While there are a few chapters on seaside plants and fruit (beach plums, bayberries, etc.), this is really a book about gathering and eating sentient beings: clams, mussels, oysters, and crabs. (Gibbons wrote before the current interest in insects as food, or this line might also have been blurred on land.)

My whole family had all dug clams together, and I found that, at his urging, I had no problem going out and gathering them for myself. Even something as lowly as a clam resists being caught—razor clams, in fact, are quite successful at it. When your fingers, groping through the wet sandy muck of a tidal flat, encounter a clam, they feel simultaneously a shudder of alarm and an attempt at futile retreat. By contrast, the savage quickness of crabs was frightening, but fear dampens empathy, and I learned to trap and cook them, too, without injury or remorse.

This, then, is where I drew the line between myself as eater and those that are eaten: at the level of the clam and the crab. I'm not sure about the value of drawing that line compared to other acts of "growing up" —of saying to some other being that my hunger had more weight than its life. Even so, I know it has an effect: it deepens and complicates one's sense of self and life.

Even in those days, clams were getting to be in short supply; the most reliable source was on Little Chebeague, a deserted island just a short row across the bay. I already went there regularly to replenish the supply of driftwood for the fireplace and to pick raspberries and blueberries. Now, at the urging of the chowder pot, I returned with buckets of steamers, as well . . . even, as I learned how to trap them (don't try to grab, but instead plunge your hands deep down into the muck beneath them), a small hoard of razor clams.

More boldly, since it meant going against both my own fears and the prejudices of the neighbors, I began pulling mussels from the rocks where they clustered on a nearby beach. The only competitors for these were seagulls, and I nervously awaited signs of some kind of poisoning after I ate the first batch. But I survived, and mussel chowders soon became almost as common in my kitchen as clam. I begged mackerel heads from the fisherman next door to bait a crab trap I found buried under the cottage. By the end of the summer I was feasting on platters of garlicky periwinkles.

That time lingers in my mind as "the chowder summer." It was the start of my long love affair with that dish. The fragrant aromas of clam juice and milk mingling together still evoke not only the dish itself but the whole experience: the driftwood that I had carried up from the beach and sawn myself, now crackling in the fireplace; the chowder full of clams I had just dug, cleaned, and prepared, and potatoes I had carried back the three miles from the store, heating in the big battered pot on the propane stove.

True, after the Down East custom, the herbs came from containers that seemed as old as I was, and inevitably a little grit always made it from clam to pot to mouth. But my appetite was young and stimulated by honest effort, and my pride in this concoction of my own doing— the simple pleasure of sitting down to a meal I had scavenged myself from the sea and land about—was boundless.

Chowder, my mother once said to me, is what you eat when you can't afford anything else. She was speaking from tribal memory—by the time of my own childhood, the back of the pantry shelf would more likely yield the makings of macaroni and cheese or a pot of baked beans. The span of time between my mother's childhood and my own may have seen a rise in expectations generally, but not in night-before-paycheck suppers. Still, thanks to this summer, I now knew what she meant.

The history of chowder is a history of such memories. Chowder is a product of circumstance as much as recipe, and its origins seem confusing or complex only when this is forgotten. It is not by nature a nostalgic dish: it has endured while so many other early-American dishes have not because the circumstances that begot it have also endured, and because chowder proved the happiest means of mastering them. It is a savory meal of what were long the humblest of ingredients, a dish that could be prepared in the simplest of kitchens—as of necessity these kitchens often were.

ORIGINS

To find the "norma" or original basis of chowder, we must go back to the venerable Mrs. Hannah Glasse, in whose culinary "Novum Organum," and under the heading of "A Cheshire Pork-Pye for Sea," to which she specially directs the attention of master-mariners, there will be found the real foundation of chowder.
—JESSUP WHITEHEAD, *Hotel Meat Cooking* (1907)

Every nation fronting a seacoast has a native fish stew whose origins reach far back into history—the *caldeirada* of Portugal, for instance, or the *'t Zootsje* of Belgium, or the *zuppa di pesce* of Italy. And nations with borders on two seas have more, as with Spain's *caldereta* on the Atlantic coast and *bulevesa* on the Mediterranean. France, of course, is no exception, and while its Mediterranean-based *bouillabaisse* is the most famous, there are many others, including the *cotriade* of Brittany and the *chaudrée* of Poitou.

The *Oxford English Dictionary* traces the word "chowder" to the fishing villages of Brittany, where *faire la chaudière* once meant "to supply a cauldron in which is cooked a mess of fish and biscuit with some

savory condiments, a hodgepodge contributed by the fishermen themselves, each of whom in return receives his share of the prepared dish."*
It then goes on to say that "Breton fishermen probably carried the custom to Newfoundland, long famous for its chowder, whence it spread to
Nova Scotia, New Brunswick, and New England."

When John Cabot arrived at Newfoundland in 1497, he discovered
that its coastal waters were teeming with cod. His enthusiastic reports
soon brought English fishing vessels across the Atlantic, and as the fleet
grew, the island began to be utilized as a fishing station. In 1610 an
official charter for permanent colonization was granted to John Guy, who
established a settlement on Conception Bay.

However, in 1662 the French occupied the nearby Placentia Bay area
and began raiding the English settlements. The result of this and similar
French–English skirmishing in Canada resulted in Queen Anne's War,
settled by the Treaty of Utrecht, which in 1713 recognized Great Britain's claims to Newfoundland but gave France the right to catch and
dry fish on the northern and western shores of the island, rights that
France retained until 1904.

Newfoundland, in other words, was for centuries the processing center
for much of the dried cod that became a staple part of the French and
British diet until this century—and it is indeed probably here, where
fresh cod was free and plentiful and everything else scarce and costly,
that chowder first came into its own.

It is probably a vain hope that food historians will uncover the testimony of someone present at the birth of chowder, but I've come across
a narrative that describes it while still in its swaddling clothes. The
famous British botanist-explorer, Joseph Banks, spent several months
in 1766—three years before he sailed with Cook—botanizing in Newfoundland. Although his diaries are almost entirely devoted to the flora
and fauna of the island, he also made occasional observations of the
life going on around him.

> After having said so much about Fishing it will not be improper to say a little
> about the Fish that they catch & of the Dish they make of it Calld Chowder which
> I believe is Peculiar to this Country tho here it is the Cheif food of the Poorer &
> when well made a Luxury that the rich Even in England at Least in my opinion
> might be fond of It is a Soup made with a small quantity of salt Pork cut into

---

* Others point out that the word "jowter" (sometimes spelled "chowder"), with a very
different derivation, is a venerable Devonshire and Cornish dialect expression for an
itinerant fish-hawker (especially a woman). Quite possibly, these women made a fish
stew of what remained of their stock, and it assumed their own name.

Small Slices a good deal of fish and Biscuit Boyled for about an hour unlikely as this mixture appears to be Palatable I have scarce met with any Body in this Country Who is not fond of it whatever it might be in England Here it is certainly the Best method of Dressing the Cod which is not near so firm here as in London whether or not that is owing to the art of the fishmongers I cannot pretend to say.

There was guarded commerce between the British and the French settlements; Banks paid the other a visit and described the contrasting ways that the British and French salted their catch (the French were by far the more meticulous). It seems a reasonable enough hypothesis to assume that so simple and commonsensical a dish might have here passed hands.

Certainly, even as Banks was paying his visit to Newfoundland (and whether he knew it or not), chowder was in the air back home. Hannah Glasse had followed up on her "pork-pie of the sea" (a layered dish of pork and potatoes, baked in a crust) with an authentic chowder recipe in the 1763 edition of *The Art of Cookery*. A year earlier in 1762, Tobias Smollett had written: "My head sings and simmers like a pot of chowder . . ." with some expectation that he would be understood.

However, if this was then the case, it is no longer: one looks in vain for the name or recipe in collections of British dishes. Chowder just did not catch on. Nor did it in France. The French, who are rarely reluctant to claim a dish as their own invention, make no great effort to set forth any proprietary rights. The phrase *faire la chaudière* no long exists in Brittany—indeed, the word *"chaudière"* now means "steam boiler" and is today far more likely to evoke associations of steam heat rattling the radiators than festivities *sur la plage*.

In other words, beyond a certain point nationality is more perplexing than helpful as an explanation of the origins of chowder. But think of its parentage in terms of *place* and all confusion falls away. Chowder is the natural child begotten in the great convergence of fishermen off the North American coast, where its parents somehow, somewhere, met and fell in love.

Nor was it one child or one set of parents. A vernacular dish like chowder is rarely the creation of a specific cook in an identifiable moment of inspiration but is, rather, simultaneously concocted by any number of cooks confronted with the same limited supplies and the same restricted cooking conditions. Chowder was the inevitable outcome of a sea cook's confrontation with salt pork, ship's biscuit, and a freshly caught cod.

Once you grasp what it must have been like to cook at sea in a fishing boat—at least before this century—you will come to wonder not how chowder came into existence but what else they ever found to eat. As Harry Morton wrote, discussing this subject in *The Wind Commands*:

Even in the twentieth century . . . Seligman found that cooking "in a small galley at sea is an experience so heart-breaking that no one who has not actually tried it can possibly understand."

SON OF A SEA COOK

Few can live altogether on ship puddings, dumplings, or the like, without being sensible of an oppression and uneasiness.   —JAMES LIND (1753)

Until this century, ship staples had remained much the same (except on the most luxuriously provisioned ships) for hundreds of years: a monotonous round of salt meat (salt pork and salt beef, although salt pork might really be salt fat and salt beef almost anything, hence its popular and sometimes literally descriptive name "salt horse"), fresh and salt fish, dried peas, oatmeal, hard cheese, hardtack or sea (or ship's) biscuit, sauerkraut, and, while they lasted, potatoes and onions.

Apart from the occasional irate, knife-wielding sailor, the most daunting challenges the sea cook confronted were spoilage and cramped facilities. Spoilage, especially, was notorious. Ship's chandlers (or suppliers) knew they dealt with customers who would be far, far away before they discovered the true nature and condition of their goods. Traditional preserving techniques were at best less than foolproof. Finally, rats and other vermin were relentless and many.

Ship's biscuit, hard rounds of flour and water paste baked into solid bricks, was famous for combining inedibility (in the eighteenth and nineteenth centuries, the lowest grade of flour was called "ship stuff") and infestation. When Joseph Banks sailed with Cook on the *Endeavor* in 1769, he turned a knowing naturalist's eye to the subject, finding the flavor of these biscuits dominated by

the quantity of Vermin that are in it, I have seen hundreds nay thousands shaken out of a single bisket. We in the Cabbin have however an easy remedy for this by baking it in an oven, not too hot, which makes them all walk off, but this cannot be allowd to the private people who must find the taste of these animals very disagreeable, as they every one taste as strong as mustard or rather spirits of hartshorn. They are of 5 kinds, 3 *Tenebrios*, 1 *Ptinus* and the *Phalangium cancroides*; this last is however scarce in the common bread but was vastly plentiful in white Deal bisket as long as we had any left.

Sailors less versed in scientific distinctions divided them into two general types: maggots and weevils. Maggots were called "bargemen" and could be gotten rid of by tapping the biscuit on the table until they crawled out or by putting a large dead fish on top of an open biscuit sack. The maggots would crawl out of the biscuits and into the fish, and the fish was then tossed back into the sea . . . the process being repeated until no more came out of the sack. Weevils were simply eaten.

Rats were sometimes caught, skinned, cleaned, spitted, grilled, and eaten by midshipmen—young boys (some as young as six) with large appetites, who were fed on the leavings of the more senior officers' mess and so rarely otherwise saw fresh meat. (Ordinary seamen were forbidden this activity because of the ever-present dangers of fire.) On a large ship, killing rats was full-time work; what was objectionable about them, unlike the smaller vermin, was not so much their presence as the spoilage they caused. Food was kept in barrels in the hold—prime targets for sharp, gnawing teeth (rats occasionally tunneled their way right through the side of the ship). The cook never knew, on opening any storage container, what he would find within.

On sailing ships, the position of cook was usually held by a seaman who had lost a leg or other body part—life on ship was full of hazards—but wanted to remain at sea. He had no culinary training, and even if he had, little of it would have been of use. The ship's galley was always primitively equipped, and too small and poorly lit for the number of men to be cooked for. Hazards ran from scalds and flying cutlery to even greater dangers: the galleys of American clippers were often on open deck (to lessen the danger of fire), and when these ships rounded the Horn, a high sea could send a huge wave crashing across it, sweeping away the stove, the meal, and the cook. Small wonder drunkenness was an occupational disease and most sea recipes called for little more than boiling.

In *Two Years Before the Mast*, Richard Henry Dana reported eating a dish "of biscuits pounded fine, salt beef cut into small pieces, and a few potatoes, all boiled up together and seasoned with pepper," which is nothing if it isn't a salt beef chowder. Seamen on American and British sailing ships often augmented their diet by catching fresh fish, but they considered salt fish as lowly poverty food and refused to eat it, no matter the extremely dubious origins of their salt meat.

For fishermen, however, the situation was different, and it was as fishermen that a sizable majority of the men who lived along the New England coast then earned their living. It is the diet of those fishermen that is responsible not only for the evolution of chowder as we know it but for the strong hold that haddock and cod had for so long on Yankee cooking.

Samuel Eliot Morison wrote in *The Maritime History of New England* that on the Gloucester and Marblehead fishing boats of the last century and on the Cape Cod boats of this one, the cooks were boys nine to twelve years old who were given that position until they learned the ropes. Even more than the peglegged sailors who took up the trade on the clipper ships, these boys had scant opportunity and less incentive to learn to cook well.

Provisions consisted mostly of caught fish, augmented by the usual run of molasses, salt pork, flour, ship's biscuit, water, and rum. The cabin in which they cooked was so full of smoke that—at least until the invention of the "Gloucester hood"—fishermen would hang chunks of choice halibut from the cabin beams and have it smoked to a turn by the time they returned to shore.

No one reading about life on Cape Cod during the last century will ever again wonder how it got its name. Cod fisheries were so vital to the economy of the entire state that Friday was popularly "fish day" for everyone—a matter of patriotism as much as religion. On the Cape, however, it was a rare day that was *not* fish day. Even Saturday, sacrosanct to baked beans, was not exempt, since the traditional accompaniment was not the frankfurter but the codfish cake. And if any of these remained on the table after supper, they appeared at Sunday breakfast.

Thoreau found salt cod stacked on the wharves of Provincetown, "looking like corded wood, maple, and yellow birch with the bark left on." The houses of that city, he wrote, were fronted with racks where the fish were spread out to dry,

> leaving only a narrow passage of two to three feet wide to the front door; so that instead of looking out onto a flower or grass plot, you looked onto so many square rods of cod turned the wrong side outwards.

These plots, he added, smelled least like flower gardens on a good summer drying day.

Furthermore, when he went to have breakfast at his Provincetown hotel, he was offered the choice of "hashed fish or [baked] beans." Returning the next summer, he discovered that this was still the only alternative proposed here, and the landlord was still ringing the changes on these two words. In the former dish there was a remarkable proportion of fish. As you travel inland the potato predominates. It chanced that I did not taste fresh fish of any kind on the Cape and I was assured that they were not so much used there as in the country. That is where they are cured, and where, sometimes, travellers are cured of eating them. No fresh meat was slaughtered in Provincetown, but the little that was used at the public houses was brought from Boston by the steamer.

This isn't to say that the inhabitants ate only salt fish or, for that matter, only cod. The Cape waters teemed with all sorts of edible fish, its shores with lobsters, clams, crabs, and oysters. Even so, the cod dominated their diet and, for Cape Cod cooks, necessity was the mother of invention when it came to cooking it. Out of their fireplaces and off their woodstoves came boiled cod, cod cakes, fish hash, Cape Cod turkey (stuffed cod), and such other, lesser-known dishes as "hog's back son of a sea cook," which was salt cod cooked with salt-pork scraps. Such cooks had no reason to wait for a chowder recipe to arrive from Brittany via Newfoundland. Instead, all they needed was the notion and the name.

This was even more true in the isolated fishing communities up and down the coastline of New England and maritime Canada. Although the immediate ancestors of their inhabitants of these villages may have come here from England, life on this side of the Atlantic was very different. In England, there had been centuries of interaction between fishing and farming communities. New World fishing villages, however, were far more insular and self-sufficient, with customs and habits regulated in conformity to shipboard life, and with a galley-oriented cuisine that had been built up from scratch out of salt pork, ship's biscuit, and fish.

Even so, this world, however hidebound and resistant to change, also evolved over time. And chowder, because it was a product of circumstance rather than some single cook's imagination, evolved with it. Chowder has never been a fixed entity, nor has it ever followed a set formula. What all true chowders possess is a set of common features that allow us to recognize a shared genealogy. If we lay out the historical recipes before us and ponder them as we would a collection of family portraits, we discover that—if we go far enough back into history— these visages become so fierce and iconoclastic that we would hardly allow them into our kitchens today.

A FAMILY TREE

A large pot of victuals was prepared. They called it Chouder. Chouder may be made of any good fish, but the ingredients of our mess were as follows: 1) salt pork, 2) flounder, 3) onions, 4) codfish, 5) biscuit.

—Philadelphia Weekly Magazine (1798)

Chowder . . . is made in the following manner: a fish is . . . skinned, cut up . . . and put into a kettle, under which is laid some rashers of salt pork or beef, and some broken pieces of biscuit; then the whole is covered with water, and boiled about ten minutes.   *—Naval Chronicles XXI* (1859)

To tell her how to make a chowder . . . a layer of fish, then one of pilot-bread, and potatoes and onions, another of fish, a little dash of lard, milk, pepper, and salt; a dish for a prince.   —CHARLES I. BUSHNELL (1859)

Like a series of fossils exposed in their original strata, this skeletal chronology reveals chowder's evolutionary thrust—ship's biscuit giving way to the common cracker and the ubiquitous potato; water, at least in part, yielding to milk; and the proportion of fish (and number of different kinds of fish) gradually diminishing—as did that resource itself.

Furthermore, as we flesh out the skeletons, exploring the cookbooks of the last century for chowder recipes, we find that it was as likely victim as beneficiary of the whims and preferences of contemporary tastes. Some recipes are barely recognizable as chowder at all. For example, consider the first chowder recipe to appear in this country (indeed, the first known chowder recipe to have been printed anywhere), published in *The Boston Evening Post* on September 23, 1751:

Directions for making a Chouder

First lay some Onions to keep the pork from burning,
Because in Chouder there can be no turning;
Then lay some Pork in Slices very thin,
Thus you in Chouder always must begin.
Next lay some Fish cut crossways very nice
Then season well with Pepper, Salt, and Spice;
Parsley, Sweet-Marjoram, Savory, and Thyme,
Then Biscuit next which must be soak'd some Time.

Thus your Foundation laid, you will be able
To raise a Chouder, high as Tower of Babel;
For by repeating o'er the Same again,
You may make a Chouder for a thousand men.
Last a Bottle of Claret, with Water eno' to smother 'em,
You'll have a Mess which some call Omnium gather 'em.

It's an interesting recipe. The seasonings show that Bostonian cooking still retained an Elizabethan inspiration; the chowder recipe that would be published in a few years in England in *The Arte of Cookery* would reflect the contemporary British taste, with seasonings limited to pepper and allspice. That the onions are put into the pot first reminds us that salt pork has not always been as fatty as the stuff we use now, pigs then not being force-fed with corn but mostly having to fend for themselves. The onions would liquefy and keep the pork from scorching on the bottom of the pot.

If you were to follow this recipe, bottle of claret and all, the result would be a huge, scarlet-colored, fish-flavored pudding. This is certainly what the early, ocean-born chowders resembled, not only because they were rib-sticking meals for men who needed the calories, but because they used a minimum of one of the most precious shipboard supplies: water. These layered chowders persisted in New England cooking right to the turn of this century, because they represented a high-calorie, inexpensive, and, for the time, easy-to-prepare meal.

This is important to note because, apart from such criteria, other chowders in early-American cookbooks are that by virtue of name alone. The first chowder recipe to be printed in an American cookbook, *American Cookery* (1796) by Amelia Simmons, called for poaching a bass, frying it up with salt pork and a dozen softened crackers, and serving it with potatoes, pickles, and applesauce. Lydia Maria Child, in *The American Frugal Housewife* (1832), gave a recipe for "Boston Fish Chowder" thickened with a whole bowl of flour and water. She then had the gall to suggest yet a further improvement: "A cup of tomato catchup is very excellent." A thousand Yankee mariners groaned and rolled over in their graves.

It isn't until we arrive at Daniel Webster's fish chowder, as dictated to General S. P. Lyman and transcribed in that soldier's memoirs, that we come across a recipe that might actually summon us into the kitchen. Having lived in the Massachusetts coastal community of Marshfield, Webster knew how fishermen made chowder, and his recipe is simple, direct, and to the point.* Indeed, in my opinion, it is the only nineteenth-century chowder worth making.†

DANIEL WEBSTER'S FISH CHOWDER (1842). First, fry a large bit of well-salted pork in the kettle over the fire. Fry it thoroughly. Second, pour in a sufficient quantity of water, and then put in the head and shoulders of a codfish, and a fine, well-dressed haddock, both recently caught. Third, put in three or four good Irish potatoes, for which none better can be found than at Marshfield, and boil them well together. An old fisherman generally puts in two or three onions. Fourth, when they are about done, throw in a few of the largest Boston crackers, and then apply the salt and pepper to suit the fancy. Such a dish, smoking hot, placed before you, after a long morning spent in exhilarating sport, will make you no longer envy the gods.

Here we see the beginnings of New England chowder as we now know it, although we should notice that it is still made without milk. This was probably also the case with the most famous chowder in American literature, described by Herman Melville in the opening pages of *Moby Dick*, although the near proximity of a cow has confused some commentators.‡ Read closely, however, and what you apprehend instead is a merger *crying out* to be made, with the author, as often happens, oblivious to the impetus of his own prose.

However, a warm savoury steam from the kitchen served to belie the apparently cheerless prospect before us. But when that smoking chowder came in, the mys-

* Unfortunately, Daniel Webster's fame set into circulation many other chowders with his name affixed to them. Some are bogus but inoffensive, but not the one printed without comment in the *American Heritage Cookbook*, which calls for half a bottle of mushroom catsup, a bottle of port, half a grated nutmeg, cloves, mace, allspice, a few lemon slices, and twenty-five oysters! This is a variant of a recipe attributed to a certain Commodore Stovens—an almost identical version appears in *Miss Leslie's New Cookery Book* (1857).

† Readers who object to my cavalier dismissal of a century of American chowder cookery should turn to Richard J. Hooker's *Book of Chowder*. He has not only searched out an enormous number of nineteenth-century chowder recipes but has, by his own account, intrepidly cooked his way through them . . . including the Commodore's.

‡ Richard J. Hooker, for one, who wrongly accuses Melville of inaccurate observation. Even into this century, Nantucket chowders were famously made without milk—as, on the smaller nearby island of Cuttyhunk (at least as of 1982), they are still. Martha's Vineyard resident Dorothy Bangs who will be formally introduced into this narrative shortly—remembers the Cuttyhunk postmistress, for one, making it just that way. "Oh, I imagine there are some folks on that island who prefer the milk, but tradition demands no milk—probably due to the fact that the boat arrives from the mainland only once a week in winter—and probably far less frequently many years ago. Try it some time— a quahog chowder with plenty of quahog juice and no milk—strong but good."

tery was delightfully explained. Oh, sweet friends! hearken to me. It was made of small juicy clams, scarcely bigger than hazel nuts, mixed with pounded ship biscuit, and salted pork cut up into little flakes; the whole enriched with butter, and plentifully seasoned with pepper and salt. Our appetites being sharpened by the frosty voyage, and in particular, Queequeg seeing his favorite fishy food before him, and the chowder being surpassingly excellent, we despatched it with great expedition; when leaning back a moment and bethinking me of Mrs. Hussey's clam and cod announcement, I thought I would try a little experiment. Stepping to the kitchen door, I uttered the word "cod" with great emphasis, and resumed my seat. In a few moments the savoury steam came forth again, but with a different flavour, and in good time a fine cod-chowder was placed before us. . . .

Fishiest of all places was the Try Pots which well deserved its name; for the pots were always boiling chowder. Chowder for breakfast, and chowder for dinner, and chowder for supper, till you began to look for fishbones coming through your clothes. The area before the house was paved with clam shells. Mrs. Hussey wore a polished necklace of codfish vertebrae; and Hosea Hussey had his account books bound in superior old shark-skin. There was a fishy flavour to the milk, too, which I could not at all account for, till one morning happening to take a stroll along the beach among some fishermen's boats, I saw Hosea's brindled cow feeding on fish remnants, and marching along the sand with each foot in a cod's decapitated head, looking very slipshod, I assure ye.

"Fishy flavour to the milk . . ." Perhaps it was some early reader of *Moby Dick* whose culinary imagination caught hold of that phrase to first connect the idea of milk and fish. However it happened, though, we can be sure that it was done with no undue haste. *The New England Cookbook* (1905), an anthology of recipes culled from famous food writers of the time (probably without their permission), offers two fish chowders—one with and one without milk (it is the latter that is termed "New England Chowder")—and a clam chowder that calls for forty-five clams and a quart of sliced potatoes, to which is added, at the end of the three-hour cooking time, a *teacup* of milk.

So, it was not until the close of the last century that we arrive at what we now consider the classic chowder, particularized in Mary Lincoln's *Boston Cook Book* (1884): "Fish, potatoes, and crackers are all distinct in the creamy liquid, instead of being a pasty mush, such as is often served." Alas, at this point another obfuscatory force begins to edge its way into native New England cookery: gentility. Mrs. Lincoln—and her epigone, Fannie Farmer—both consider the onion and salt-pork scraps too vulgar to serve to refined eaters and so fish them out of the pot.

The Abhorred Tomato

There is a terrible pink mixture (with tomatoes in it and herbs) called Manhattan
Clam Chowder, that is only a vegetable soup, and not to be confused with New
England Clam Chowder, nor spoken of in the same breath. Tomatoes and clams
have no more affinity than ice cream and horseradish.
                                    —ELEANOR EARLY, *A New England Sampler*

About chowder's regional variations, it is wise to be cautious. As various
mythologists have had it, Maine calls for lobster bodies as a base to
give chowder flavor; New Hampshire wavers between clam and fish, but
eschews all vegetables; Massachusetts allows potatoes and onions, but
eschews the tomato (Cape Cod further waxes vociferously in favor of
steamer over quahog); coastal Rhode Island rejects not only the new-
fangled tomato but the equally newfangled milk,* while Connecticut,
contaminated by its proximity to Manhattan, allows tomatoes, but retains
some grace by otherwise fixing its chowders in the traditional New England manner.

All this is very fine, but a lengthy, exasperating, and finally disillu-
sioning tour of any number of New England cookbooks has convinced
me that a local name affixed to a chowder recipe is usually not tradition
speaking but the recipe writer's conceit. Indeed, if there is *any* regional
theme that unites New England chowder commentators, it is a delight
in heaping abuse on the poor tomato.

Tomato-hating may seem a paltry thing on which to erect the
foundations of regional difference, but the truth is that nowadays most
such distinctions *are* paltry things, and the topic "tomatoes and
clams" has become a mainstay of Yankee identity, or at least the
curmudgeonly, self-congratulatory kind. Among the innumerable instances of such tomato-baiting, my own favorite is a poem by Christopher La Farge, circa 1939, entitled "Rhode Island Clambake"
(incontradistinction, I suppose, to the notoriously tomato-intensive

---

* The food writer Edward Behr, in an essay on "The Coast of Maine," notes: "Some
tradition-minded Rhode Islanders continue to make chowder without [milk]. At least
one humble Rhode Island restaurant [offers] a pitcher of milk on the side." Perhaps
this tolerant, Roger Williams-ish notion of individual adjustment is *another* characteristic of Rhode Island chowders. A recipe for "Rhode Island Fish Chowder" in *The White
House Cookbook* (1915), an old-fashioned layered chowder which, indeed, *is* made without milk, ends with the suggestion: "Serve sliced lemon, pickles, and stewed tomatoes
with it, that guests may add if they like."

Manhattan clambake), each stanza of which concludes with some variation of:

> And bellow like a wounded moose
> If any says Tomato-juice!

All this flies in the face of a simple truth: the tomato and the clam
are fine flavor mates. This is evidenced not only by "Clamato," a clam-
and-tomato-juice concoction drunk all over New England, but by the
classic pairing of the two in such Italian dishes as clams in red sauce.
In fact, I suspect that the so-called Manhattan clam chowder is nothing
other than a New World variation of the very similar Neapolitan *zuppa
de vongole*. Many New York fish restaurants are owned and run by
Italians, and it is quite probable that an enterprising chef (or menu
writer) redesignated as a chowder the house clam soup, to make it more
appealing to the non-Italian clientele. At least, I can find no reference
to the recipe prior to the 1930s.

However, there *is* a chowder that does contain tomatoes and does
possess a Manhattan heritage. Pierre Blot, a Frenchman who wrote a
cookbook in this country, was a keen and amused observer of American
culinary custom. In his *Hand-Book of Practical Cookery* (1869), he gives
a chowder recipe made by "the most experienced chowdermen of the
Harlem River." In the mode of chowders of that time, it is a layered
affair, made of salt pork, clams, potatoes, onions, and—significantly—
tomatoes.

By the turn of the century, when encroaching pollution had robbed
Harlem River clams of their appeal, Coney Island chowder became so
much an integral part of boardwalk life there that the summer hotels
were called "chowder mills." Coney Island chowders were similarly
made with tomatoes, and while I have yet to track down an authentic
recipe for one, I doubt that it would prove much different from the many
New England chowders that were being made with tomatoes at the same
time.

Because, all bluster aside, some Yankee cooks were putting tomatoes
in their chowders from the middle of the last century, when *The American Matron*, a cookbook published in Boston in 1851, offered a recipe
calling for both milk and fresh tomatoes. By 1884, Maria Parloa, in
First Principles of Household Management and Cookery, gives her novice
cooks a recipe for a "tomato chowder," straight and plain, without any
seafood presence at all.

What are we to make of this? There is a possible clue in the 1915 edition of *The White House Cook Book*, which contains a recipe for clam chowder purporting to have originated in that old Massachusetts sea town New Bedford (and there are many nice touches in the recipe to support that claim). The instructions conclude (italics are mine):

> Just before it is taken up, thicken it with a cup of powdered crackers, and add a quart of fresh milk. If too rich, add more water. No seasoning is needed but good black pepper. *With the addition of six sliced tomatoes, or half a can of the canned ones, this is the best recipe of this kind, and is served in many of our best restaurants.*

During the final half of the last century, the tomato played a culinary role much like the chile pepper plays today, providing spice and novelty in what was already a cuisine tending toward the bland and homogenized. As early as 1842, farm journals were identifying themselves with what can only be called a craze. The *Cultivator* proclaimed that everyone except those determined to remain "nobodies" was learning to eat it; the *Connecticut Farmer's Gazette* pointed out that whereas only a few years ago prejudice ran against it, the tomato was now "decidedly popular with the friends of good eating and justly ranked among the choice products of the garden." Andrew F. Smith, who recently chronicled this revolution in taste in *The Tomato in America*, captures the tenor of the times:

> Philadelphia's *Farmer's Cabinet* decreed that no farmer should be without tomatoes. The farmer's family, it said, "will soon want their tomatoes, —once, — twice, —three times a day, —morning, noon, and evening!" Henry Ward Beecher, editor of the *Indiana Farmer*, announced that whoever did not love tomatoes was an object of pity. By the mid-1840s tomatoes were cultivated the length and breadth of the country, in almost every garden from Boston to New Orleans, and . . . from July to October . . . [were] sold in larger quantities than any other vegetable. As a British visitor observed in the early 1850s, tomatoes had become the "sine qua non of American existence."

Furthermore, as canning became an increasingly viable way of preserving vegetables, it was soon discovered that, because their high acidity resisted bacterial contamination, the tomato was an ideal canning vegetable. Smith reports that as the nineteenth century neared its end, more tomatoes were canned than any other fruit or vegetable.

> By 1884 a single canning factory, J. H. Butterfoss in Hunterdon County, New Jersey, produced 340,000 cans of tomatoes and 43,000 gallons of catsup. In 1885

more than two million cases containing twenty-four cans each were produced nationally.

That number grew with ever-increasing velocity each succeeding year of the rest of the century. Tomatoes, fresh and canned, were the thing, and there is plenty of evidence to suggest that trend-conscious cooks in southern New England were as eager as were cooks anywhere else in the country to add tomatoes to chowder . . . just as, in the middle of this century, they were equally eager to make them with heavy cream and white wine.

In most of New England, the militant preference for a tomato-less chowder is a relatively recent invented tradition. As Sandra Oliver wryly observes in a footnote in *Saltwater Foodways*, the line through Connecticut that separates the two chowder styles probably parallels the one that divides an equally vociferous interregional rift: the one between New York Yankee and Boston Red Sox fans.

However, if there was one place left mostly untouched by the great tomato craze it was Down East Maine. In 1855, a decade after the rest of the country was consuming them as if there were no tomorrow, the *Maine Farmer* was reporting that folks here were just beginning to acknowledge that they might be edible. Tomatoes, after all, have a pretty short season here. In our own tree-surrounded plot, we're lucky to get two or three weeks of ripe ones before the first October frost blasts the entire patch. Others, of course, do better—we have ripe tomatoes at our local farmers' market from late August on, but still not quite long enough to think of them as a culinary given, the way they are in most parts south.

Milk is more of a newcomer to chowder than the tomato, but it enhanced rather than changed what was an established taste. Cows have always been an accepted part of the Down East landscape; refrigeration and modern dairy farming have just regularized the milk supply, allowing it to become as unremarkable an ingredient today as salt pork and the common cracker were a hundred years before.

What it boils down to, though, is this: things are done the way they are here not because of any scorn for the tomato but because the very word "chowder" is simply and unreflectively evocative of a liquid elixir built on a foundation of salt pork, onion, and potato, aswim with seafood in a broth tempered with milk and thickened with a handful of crackers. And there's no reason in the world to want that to change.

Building a Chowder

The chowder-builder and the poet must alike be born, each to his "art unteachable, untaught."
                                             —*The Knickerbocker* (1840)

Chowder—This popular dish is made in a hundred different ways, but the result is about the same.   —PIERRE BLOT, *Hand-Book of Practical Cookery* (1869)

"Building a chowder" is a phrase that comes from the time when chowders were constructed upon a foundation of salt pork and onion, alternating layers of fish with layers of potatoes and crackers until enough had been assembled to feed an army. Outside the home kitchen, and sometimes in it, this building has often been claimed by men. Like barbecue and chili, chowder is one of those dishes that has acclimated itself well to an atmosphere of tobacco smoke and beer fumes, punctuated with profanity. A hundred years ago, "chowder and marching societies" functioned much as barbecue and chili cookoffs do today: as an excuse for men to get together, argue, party, and cook and eat to bursting their favorite food.

If chowder has been edged out of contention in this century, it is because seacoast life no longer provides the most compelling models of masculine behavior. But like its current replacements, chowder is a democratic dish, not only because it is cheap to make and evocative of the galley—a blue-collar cooking preserve if ever there was one—but because, ideally, one learns how to make it not from a recipe but from a communal pooling of experience and opinion.

There is a recipe here, too, of course, but it is to the made dish what a written sea chantey is to an actual performance. There, listening to various singers' interpretations of a song, one discovers that the words are not set in stone. Traditional ballads and chanteys are remembered differently by different singers. Sometimes that difference is a matter of word order; sometimes whole new stanzas are introduced and familiar ones deleted.

Paradoxically, in an oral culture—even a microculture like a communal fishermen's shanty—where the repository of such things as songs or recipes lies in shared memory, each participating member plays a much more important role than we as individuals do in our print-based culture. There, everyone consults his or her own memory and experience to confirm what is being said or done; an audience is not a passive but an active entity—remembering, abetting, appreciating, correcting.

This participation can be but is not necessarily overt. Often, the larger controversies have long been hammered out, and the interaction lies simply in perceiving and considering the behavior of the cook. You or I might go from house to house in a New England fishing village, tasting the chowder in each, and think them all the same. But to the inhabitants the differences, if not large, would be measurable and, more than that, meaningful. This, in a community where the same food may be eaten almost every night, is what continually revivifies a dish.

During my summers on Casco Bay, I lived in near proximity to lobstering families where this was still the case, but I was too shy, diffident, uncomprehending, to find a way to participate. Because of this, I would have to wait for years to experience chowder as colloquy. Narratives that capture such culinary interplay are rare, since the people who sustain chowder's oral traditions—fishermen, coastal boatmen, clammers, and such—are rarely writers and sometimes barely literate. I consider myself very fortunate to have come across just two, in the course of some twenty-five years of actively reading about chowder.

The author of the first of them, Augustus M. Kelley (who writes under the pen name "Theophrastus"), has spent most of his life among the fishermen and lobstermen of Little Compton, Rhode Island. His tract on chowder making, published as an appendix to the November 1985 issue of his newsletter, *Dwarf Conifer Notes*, is extremely opinionated, idiosyncratic, and rich with chowder lore. Some of it will be quoted later on, but what to me is most interesting and original about the piece is the important place he gives to the men—Tom Morissey, Marcus Wilcox, Lawrence Grinnell—who taught him chowder making, and the spirit of male camaraderie out of which the lessons came.

Significantly, he is unable to give an actual recipe for his chowder, preferring to take several pages to talk the reader through the act of building it—the nearest prose equivalent to how he learned this art himself—which concludes with the following instructive passage:

It may be objected that I have given no real receipt for chowder, either fish or clam. The foregoing remarks . . . are the result of years of thought and practice and I feel give a good cook all he or she needs to know to make a good chowder. Perhaps the following sketch can help. Many, many years ago—back in the 30's—one night I was peeling potatoes or doing something in preparation for an attempt at a chowder—when I heard someone breaking through the bushes around the kitchen window. "Who's there?" I cried. "What are you doing?" was the response. "Trying to make a chowder," I replied. "Do you want to make a better chowder?" he said. "Yes, of course," said I. "Put in more clams!" Lawrence Grinnell's words have been engraved in my heart ever since; he was a fisherman and lobsterman and a good friend.

The only way I can imagine the exhortation—"Put in more clams!"—truly helping the novice chowder maker would be if he or she also bears in mind how Theophrastus received it—not from a cookbook but as a gnomic utterance spoken out of the bushes of his back yard. It is this that transformed it from a tip into a talisman. The strong convictions Theophrastus holds on the subject come from lived experience, and his outrage at the treatment chowder receives in most cookbooks is directly analogous to the way those who personally knew someone respond to a biographical portrait assembled entirely from written sources.*

Of course, the oral tradition of chowder building is hardly limited to men. The second narrative, and perhaps the one that has had more influence on my own chowder making than any other, is a copy of a letter written in 1982 to Anthony Spinazzola, then the restaurant reviewer for *The Boston Globe*, by Dorothy (Mrs. Stuart A.) Bangs, in response to a piece he had written about clam chowder.

Although she spends two full pages describing in fine detail what she calls

> a real old-fashioned clam chowder, the kind made down here on Martha's Vineyard by the old folks and their families—and the kind made up in Nova Scotia where my mother came from . . .

she, too, never provides a recipe. Reading the letter, you soon understand why. For Dorothy Bangs, to talk about chowder is to engage in a kind of call and response. She needs to know things like what kind of clam you have and whom you are expecting for dinner:

> We prefer whole milk. But if I were serving for company I might use some light cream also. A lot depends on how much clam juice is available. If the chowder is from soft-shell or sea clams, then one can use more clam juice for flavor—thus the cream would be more desirable. But if one is using quahogs, then the juice is very, very strong and one uses less—and the whole milk is adequate.

When I began making chowder, I started accumulating recipes and soon had scores of them: "Rhode Island Fish Chowder," "Rockport Fish

---

* Years earlier still, when he was very little, it occurred to Theophrastus to ask Grinnell what fishermen ate in the winter. "Johnnycakes and chowder" was the reply. It's surely no accident that his two pieces of culinary writing concern these subjects alone.

Chowder," "Cape Ann Fish Chowder," "New England Fish Chowder." To their builders, I'm sure, each of these chowders was different; on paper, however, they all read the same.

This is because all a chowder recipe contains is the generally shared assumption regarding the *outline* of the dish. To make an authentic chowder, I had to internalize this assumption and then, switching over to the interrogatory mode, learn to build it in response to the particular situation and out of whatever likely timber came my way.

I realized that this had begun to happen to me when, soon after I received this letter, I came across a pile of lobster bodies at a giveaway price at a Boston fish store (there had been a rush on tail and claw meat) and a chowder immediately shaped itself in my mind. I bought a couple of pounds, steamed and picked them, and used the steaming water for the broth. Pretty soon after, a delicious chowder was pushed to the back of the stove to age a bit before supper. Most chowder recipes are similar; it's the chowders that are different. They never turn out the same at all.

Traditional Down East chowder is built out of what might be called the chowder trinity: salt pork, milk broth, and ship's biscuit and/or potatoes. Since the cook must give full attention to their particular qualities and uses, I have devoted a short section to each. There, so as not to have to repeat the same details in all the chowder recipes that follow, I have spelled out the necessary advice in *italics*. Please consult these passages before you begin cooking.

Salt Pork

The deciding factor as to whether a chowder belongs in a Down East kitchen is the presence of salt pork, not the absence of tomato. Historically, salt pork has pride of place over all chowder ingredients, including fish. (Take out the fish and you have salt-pork chowder, a tasty traditional dish.) Away from the sea, the staple diet of New England was based on Indian corn and salt pork—and the presence of both is still central to real Yankee cooking. Salt pork is as necessary to chowder as it is to baked beans, and it appears in countless other regional dishes right down to apple pie.

Like butter, salt pork adds a touch of richness, but it also provides the savor and substance of meat. It was the freedom to eat as much meat as a man could produce that separated the freeholder from the tenant farmer, the freeman from the bondsman. Even the small amount that went to give a chowder its rich edge was hard won, but all the more satisfying for being so.

Today the salt pork we buy is made from fatty chunks unmarketable in any other way, but when chowder was king, practically every rural and small-town Yankee household had a pork barrel in the cellar or cold house. The brine was a secret concoction of salt and flavorings, and the pieces of pork that floated beneath the stone cover had come straight from a pig, often the family pig. At slaughtering time, almost the whole of it went into the barrel, except the innards, any choice fresh cuts that might be cooked and eaten straightaway, and the head (which was boiled, picked, and transformed into "cheese").

Sometimes, after brining, the hams would be further cured in a smokehouse, but this does not seem to be as much a Maine tradition as it is elsewhere in the country. Once, when visiting some friends at their farm in the Hudson Valley, I was shown one that had been built as part of the original farm, clearly designed for smoking large amounts of meat. This is something I've never encountered in Maine.

Here, instead, the vernacular tradition is one of smoked fish. Not only do several world-class fish-smoking businesses make their home in Maine—Duck Trap Fish Farm in Lincolnville and Horton's in Waterboro—but people still fill their own back-yard smokehouses with racks of alewives. Plastic tubs of smoked mussels appear in the smallest groceries, and vacuum-sealed packets of applewood-smoked fish jerky are sold over gas-station counters. On the other hand, pork sparerib is a braised dish and true barbecue an unknown.

Why so? One tentative answer might be drawn from what we have already seen: Down East Yankee cooking was spun out of its maritime heritage and shaped by the limitations of a short growing season and what was often hardscrabble land. Maine is a place of determined but not luxuriously successful farmers; cooking did not so much depend on pigs as on the pig.

Salt pork is a misleading name. While it is possible to dry-cure pork in raw salt, the universal New England cure was in a brine, and the meat thus prepared has much in common with corned beef and what in both England and the American South is called pickled pork (see page 292). The following recipe, simple as it is, will improve your chowders and baked beans and give you a better sense of why a taste for salt pork endures in New England.

SALT PORK

Note that this brine cure is meant to flavor the meat, not preserve it. Freeze what you don't use. Since no nitrates or nitrites are called for, the meat will turn gray after the cure. This does not affect its flavor or indicate spoilage.

2 quarts of water
1½ cups pure salt (sea salt or fine kosher salt)
¼ cup brown or white sugar
2 tablespoons juniper berries (optional)
8 whole cloves (optional)
3 bay leaves (optional)
6 sprigs of fresh thyme (optional)
4 pounds of pork (fresh ham, fat back, belly, Boston butt, etc.)

Bring the water to a boil in a nonreactive (stainless steel or enamel) cooking pot. Stir in the salt and sugar until both have dissolved. Boil for 2 minutes. Remove from the heat and let cool. (This is the traditional Down East brine, but more flavor can be added to the pork by putting any or all of the optional flavorings into a stainless-steel teaball or tying them in a small square of cheesecloth and submerging them into the boiling brine. Let cool with the brine and then remove before combining with the meat.)

Bone the meat, if necessary. Cut it into chunks or leave whole as you please. Put the meat in a large glass or stoneware crock or bowl. Pour the cooled brine over it; the meat should be completely covered. To keep the meat from floating to the surface, weigh it down with a plate (or a plastic bag filled with additional brine and tied shut). If the pork lifts the plate, weigh it down with a clean stone or other weight. Cover the crock loosely with plastic wrap or its own cover.

Set in the refrigerator and let the pork steep in the brine for 3 days if the meat is cut into small chunks, or for as long as 6 to 8 days if it is all in one large piece. (If you find the pork too salty to your taste, next time parboil it briefly before using and reduce the curing time.) Remove the cured pork from the brine, rinse it with fresh water, pat dry, and either use or freeze it for future use. Do not reuse the brine.

The building of a chowder commences with the dicing of the salt pork, calculating about one ounce per eater. Cut away (but reserve) the rind and, with a sharp knife, cut the pork, which should have a good mix of fat and lean, into small dice, since the tiny bits of pork are today really more seasoning than ingredient. (If, as is now sometimes the case, the scraps are to be removed and discarded, the pork should be cut in strips.) In a large pot, over medium-low heat, gently try out the pork until it is translucent. ("Try out" is the old Yankee term for rendering fat; whale blubber was rendered in huge cauldrons called trypots, hence The Trypot Inn.) If salt pork is not to your taste, substitute lean diced bacon or—a distant third choice—butter.

The Milk Broth

The essential liquid in any chowder is that exuded and/or flavored by the seafood itself. This broth is so specific to the particular chowder, however, that it can't be generally discussed—except to advise the cook to be cautious of any purported "all-purpose" bouillon. A good chowder should taste mostly of itself, a flavor that is only muddied by bottled clam juice, dehydrated fish stock, or juice or commercial chowder base.

Many other liquids have found their way into chowders over the years, primarily alcoholic (from claret and champagne to cider and beer), but Down East chowder makers are usually content with a fish or clam broth mixed with milk or cream, both of which deserve some further comment.

As we've seen, milk began edging its way into chowders in the early nineteenth century and—thanks to the advent of pasteurization and universal refrigeration—has now become a staple ingredient. However, the electric refrigerator reached many Maine summer cottages only relatively recently, allowing a taste to develop for chowders made with evaporated milk. There remain deep-woods and island chowders around that call for it still.

I suspect the current use of cream in chowder is less a result of the universal culinary law of never leaving well enough alone as of the general decline in the quality of American milk. Unfortunately, anything made with large quantities of the bland, thick substance we call heavy cream will lose, not gain, in flavor, and those wanting more creaminess in their chowder than today's milk provides should, I think, instead look to mastering the "thick-thin" cutting of potatoes, described on page 181, which thickens a chowder without any sacrifice to flavor.

There is no special trick to adding milk to a fish chowder, but with a clam chowder it is important to have it hot to keep the chowder from curdling. Once, in the Shop 'n Save in Ellsworth, I overheard a veteran chowder maker confiding to a friend: "No one knows how to make chowder anymore. You've got to heat the milk separately on the stove and only stir it in just before you serve. Keeps the chowder from curdling—

always does, otherwise." My own method is to add the clams after the milk has been added to the chowder.

The Ship's Biscuit

The original ship's biscuit was an unleavened flatbread. It was made of whole-wheat flour from which only the coarsest bran had been sifted (captain's biscuits were made of more refined flour), worked with water into a stiff dough, rolled flat and baked, then stored in lofts over the baking ovens until they had completely dried out into rusks.

Such ship's (or soldier's) biscuit* was common fare wherever fresh baked bread was beyond a cook's means, and during the last century, much ingenuity was devoted to its improvement. Gradually, the cracker was transformed from a concoction molded out of the dregs of the baker's flour bin into something approaching luxury: puffy, crisp, salt-flecked, flavorful, and, thanks to the cracker tin, vermin free.

Sailors, of course, took great delight in the improved patent biscuit, a pleasure that was reflected in a whole little cuisine that grew up around them, and which flourished even into this century on sailboats, where galley accommodations almost universally remained dauntingly Spartan. As Rex Clements wrote in *A Gipsy of the Horn* (1924):

> We soon grew to like the food, rough though it was, and eked out our scanty fare by concocting various dishes beloved of apprentices. The chief constituent of them was sea-biscuit broken into pieces and baked with small morsels of beef or pork and called "cracker-hash"; sea-biscuits soaked into a pulp with water and sugar, and known as "dogs-body"; or—most delectable of all—sea-biscuits pounded up fine in a canvas bag, by the simple process of hammering it on the forebitts with an iron belaying pin, and then mixed into a thick stodgy cake with fat, sugar or molasses, and baked in a bully beef tin. This was "dandyfunk" and the most esteemed delicacy on our bill of fare.

This cracker cookery left its mark, too, on the Yankee shore kitchen. Out of it came cracker-crumb-based griddle cakes, crab cakes, and plenty of different cracker puddings, along with the popular bedtime snack of common crackers soaked in milk. Turn-of-the-century chowder recipes are replete with references to crackers that are now mostly memories: white browns, butter crackers, Boston or Common crackers, Cross or Montpelier crackers, and pilot bread.

* The American baking-powder biscuit takes its name from the ship's biscuit, of which it is a much improved (except when crumbled into chowder), fresh-baked approximation.

Probably the most intimidating of these was the Cross cracker, named for its inventor, Charles Cross. A hard, dry, bland cracker, an inch thick and as wide as the rim of a coffee cup, it *had* to be softened to be eaten, either by crumbling it into a chowder or by setting it in whole to sop up the liquid, and then serving it on the side to be broken into bite-sized pieces with the spoon.

The Common cracker (as it was called in Boston), or Boston cracker (as it was called everywhere else, at least outside of New England), was, in comparison, a delicacy; the size of a silver dollar and half as thick as a Cross cracker, it was best split, toasted, and buttered but, in a pinch, could be eaten out of hand. It was—and is—durable, homey, and good.

Ironically, the cracker's Golden Age peaked with the introduction of the deliberately upscale Ritz cracker in the 1930s, when the luxury of the patent cracker suddenly found itself enclosed in quotation marks. Just as the popularity of the bicycle paved the way for its own super-cession by the automobile by bringing into existence the sort of factory that could manufacture them (and, thanks to the lobbying of cyclists, the macadam road), so did the mechanization of cracker production open the door to Wonder Bread. As puffy, practically staleproof loaves filled the grocer's shelves, the cracker had no other choice but to go in the direction of the Cheez-It.

Even so, traditional common crackers are still made in New England,* both by the Orton family in Vermont and by G. H. Bent in Massachusetts. Although our own recipe for chowder crackers appears on page 64, and it pleases us very much, I'm no more immune than the next guy to the charm of the true common cracker, with its aura of the old-time cracker barrel and its sturdy, last-century character.

As it happens, when I was a child, every summer that we came back to visit my grandparents, our first stop was just across the town line in Milton at the rickety old wood-framed Bent bakery, then already more than a century old. There, a small factory store sold broken and day-old crackers and cookies at wholesale prices, and my mother would load the car with sacks of delicacies that were simply unobtainable in Fort Bliss, Texas, or Fort Leavenworth, Kansas.

The business was founded in 1801 by one Josiah Bent, whose "strictly

---

* Other old-fashioned bread-substitute crackers on the market include the saltine or soda cracker, the oyster cracker, Nabisco's Uneeda and Crown Pilot crackers, and the O.T.C. or Original Trenton Cracker, a lovable, simple, delicious sourdough hardball the size of a large marble, which dates back to 1848.

hand-made" cold-water crackers were a local specialty. They were about the size of a common cracker but with an even thinner, more brittle crust. (According to company legend, Bent coined the name "cracker" after the loud, crackling sound they made as they cooled. A nice story, but the word "cracker" was already in use a century before.)

The Pierotti family, who bought the business in 1944, has continued to make common crackers from the traditional Bent recipe, in which the dough is allowed to ferment overnight. This produces a tender, clean-tasting cracker as honest and satisfying as a good crust of bread, but with its own wafery cracker character. And they have recently brought back the original saltwater and pilot crackers as well.*

The ship's biscuit had a central role in truly old-fashioned chowders, where it provided the single source of carbohydrate. As the potato edged in, it was first used in tandem with the ingredient it was to mostly supplant. But gradually the crackers were pushed offstage and—even at chowder places—into little cellophane packets. Today, it is a rare Down East cook who still crumbles crackers into the broth. Mostly, they are floated across the top—a kind of Yankee crouton.

Still, you can improve any chowder with a trick my mother taught me: crumble a few common crackers in your fist or under a rolling pin and sauté these in the fat with the onion, before pouring in the broth. Then split and toast a few more—or, even better, fry them until golden in melted butter in a small skillet—to float on top of the chowder at the point of serving.

The Potato

Although a native to the Americas, the potato was introduced Down East by European settlers, and long after chowder was already flourishing. So the potato, too, had its moment of newfangledness—indeed, it might be argued that its arrival ushered chowder into the modern age, since it was its presence that turned chowder from a near-pudding into a stew.

The potato would make itself completely at home soon enough, even in the rock-ridged coastal communities of Maine. There is a lovely pas-

---

* Although G. H. Bent now makes its crackers in Scarborough, Maine, mail orders should still be directed to the old cracker factory at 7 Pleasant Street, Milton, MA 02186 • 617–698–5945. Also available by mail order is a well-regarded line of traditional common crackers produced at Orton's Vermont Country Store: P.O. Box 3000, Manchester Center, VT 05255 • 802–362–2400.

sage concerning potatoes in Sarah Orne Jewett's *Country of the Pointed Firs* (1899), which captures the feeling of a time when making chowder was as natural as breathing. In it, the narrator arrives with her landlady and friend, Mrs. Todd, at the house of the latter's mother, who is to prepare chowder for company. She takes a look at the haddock the two are bearing and remarks:

> "I expect you might have chose a somewhat larger fish, but I'll try an' make do. I shall have to have a few extra potatoes, but there's a field full out there, an' the hoe's leanin' against the well-house, in 'mongst the climbin'-beans."

This good-humored request is directed at the daughter, but the narrator takes it on herself,

> and straying out presently, I found the hoe by the well-house and an old split basket at the woodshed door, and also found my way down to the field where there was a great square patch of rough, weedy potato-tops and tall ragweed. One corner was already dug, and I chose a fat-looking hill where the tops were well withered. There is all the pleasure that one can have in gold-digging in finding one's hopes satisfied in the riches of a good hill of potatoes. I longed to go on; but it did not seem frugal to dig any longer after my basket was full, and at last I took my hoe by the middle and lifted the basket to go back up the hill. I was sure that Mrs. Blackett must be waiting impatiently to slice the potatoes into the chowder, layer by layer, with the fish.

The ideal chowder potato is neither the large mealy russet (which, in a chowder, dissolves into mush) nor the waxy-fleshed new potato (which refuses to interact with a chowder at all) but the plain, white, "all-purpose" potato, which holds its shape just until it reaches the mouth, where it crumbles into a soft-textured, flavorful mass. Green Mountain is an ideal chowder potato and so is Yukon Gold; Superior and Kennebec, the usual "all-purpose" Maine potatoes, do just fine.

Calculate one medium or large all-purpose potato per eater, with one or two more for the pot. Peel the potatoes, take a paring knife, and— this being an essential but too little known trick—slice them into bite-size pieces with the shape of an ax head. As Dorothy Bangs puts it:

> Now about the potatoes. I cut mine "thick-thin." I learned to do it this way from a very dear lady, the postmistress of Cuttyhunk Island. With potatoes cut thick-thin, one cuts small slices around the outside of the potato so that each slice has a thin side and a thick side—like little wedges.

Cut "thick-thin," bits of the edge break away to meld into the liquid as the potatoes simmer in the pot, creating a uniquely creamy body.

That—and the crumbled ship's biscuits mentioned above—are the only thickeners a chowder ever needs.

The Other Ingredients

"That was just what I was wantin'," said the hostess. "I gave a sigh when you spoke o' chowder, knowin' my onions was out."
—SARAH ORNE JEWETT, *Country of the Pointed Firs*

Chowder makers will rightly argue that the onion is as important as salt pork or common crackers or potatoes in making a proper chowder. But as the quotation from Sarah Orne Jewett suggests, the worry here is not in finding the right onion so much as in finding yourself without *any* onion . . . as, for that matter, without any salt or black pepper. Given a well-stocked larder, most cooks who give a sigh when you speak of chowder are thinking of that final ingredient—the one that might lift the dish up out of the ordinary, if only they knew its name.

There are many of these, of course, but all are best left to the imagination of the particular cook. A sprig of thyme minced along with the parsley, a whisper of garlic, a dash of hot red pepper, each can be a true enhancement. But after thirty years of chowder making, what keeps the activity fresh for me is the challenge of keeping it simple and getting it right. However, there is one nearly forgotten ingredient worth recalling when you reach for your kettle. It went into the first chowder and until recently was added to every subsequent one without a thought.

[It is] the odor of smoke . . . when you start a fire in the shipmate stove with bits of driftwood. Neither spruce bough nor birch twig has the delicious spicy odor of smoke from a fire made of fragments of an old, brine-soaked lobster trap found cast up on the shore.   —SAMUEL ELIOT MORISON, *Spring Tides*

FISH CHOWDER

A codfish of sixty pounds, caught in the bay, had been dissolved into the rich liquid of a chowder.   —NATHANIEL HAWTHORNE

Cod and bass make the best chowder. Clams and black fish tolerable good.
—MRS. A. L. WEBSTER, *The Improved Housewife* (1847)

Have ready a sufficient quantity of sea-bass, black fish, tutaug, porgie, haddock, or fresh cod.   —ELIZA LESLIE, *Directions for Cookery* (1848)

Say "chowder" today and most people immediately think of clams, but this is a relatively recent phenomenon. Historically, as we've already seen, chowder meant fish chowder, and fish chowder meant cod. It is only as the supply of these fish has radically diminished that we cooks have been urged to expand our horizons and try the "lesser" species that used to be consigned to the cat-food industry.

This is all to the good. Almost any saltwater fish with firm white flesh makes good chowder: blackfish, cusk, dogfish, grouper, monkfish, ocean perch, pollack, rock fish, sea bass, tilefish, and on and on. None of these fish, of course, make the *same* chowder. So, we ourselves have come to almost prefer pollack to cod as a chowder fish, while cusk— often recommended in fish guides (and by our own fishmonger)—has proven a disappointment.

Although the general recommendation is for a saltwater fish with firm white flesh and a mild taste, it's a rare angler who can land fish to spec. Thus, the first rule of chowder making is to adapt to circumstance, and a deft hand can produce sumptuous results from mako shark, kingfish, sheepshead, eel, or bluefish—out of which last, a New Bedford diarist noted in 1878, came "the boss chowder of the season." Freshwater fishermen boast of chowders made from perch and walleyed pike and Gulf Coast fishermen of chowders made from red snapper, redfish, and pompano. The first two recipes below lay out the master strategy for fish chowder. Learn them and you can tackle any chowder challenge you set your mind to.

Fish Chowder #1 (Whole Fish)
(serves 4)

A 3-pound chowder fish, cut into fillets, trimmings (head and fish rack [skeleton]) reserved
1 or 2 bay leaves
10 whole black peppercorns
Several sprigs fresh parsley, leaves minced and stems reserved
¼ cup diced salt pork (rind removed and reserved), or to taste
Salt
1 large onion, chopped
4 to 6 potatoes, cut "thick-thin"
3 cups milk
Black pepper to taste
8 common crackers
2 tablespoons unsalted butter

If you buy the fish at the fishmonger's, have him or her remove and reserve the head (minus the gills and scales) and skeleton (rack) and slice the rest into fillets (see Cook's Note below). Have the scraps wrapped up separately from the meat. If the fish is your own catch, clean and fillet it as you usually do, reserving the edible scraps separately.

When you begin preparing the chowder, put the scraps into a kettle with a quart of cold water, the bay leaves, the peppercorns, the parsley stems, and the reserved salt-pork rind (if used), and a teaspoon of salt. Bring to a simmer, and cook for 20 minutes. Strain, discard the solids (if the fish head is large enough, it can be picked for meat), and return the court bouillon—as it now is—to the pot. Reduce, if necessary, to about 3 cups.

In a small skillet, fry up the diced salt pork until some fat is rendered and the pork begins to turn light brown. Add the chopped onion and sauté this mixture until the pork is crisp and the onion soft and amber-colored. Add all this to the court bouillon. Bring this back to a simmer and add the potatoes. Cook for 10 minutes and add the fish fillets. Continue cooking another 5 to 10 minutes, or until the potatoes are tender and the fish begins to flake. With a fork, gently flake the fish into bite-sized pieces.

Now pour in the milk. Taste for seasoning, adding the minced parsley, freshly ground black pepper, and, if necessary, salt. As soon as the milk is heated through, turn the flame as low as possible and let the chowder steep for a few minutes. Meanwhile, split the common crackers and place under the broiler to brown. Ladle the chowder into warmed bowls, float the toasted common crackers on top, and drop in a chunk of butter—about half a tablespoon for each bowl—to melt on the way to the table.

COOK'S NOTE. If a whole fish is not available, one or two fish heads can be used instead. In New England fish markets, cod heads are sometimes available; otherwise, ask the advice of the fishmonger. For instance, Sheryl and Mel London note in *A Seafood Celebration* that "grouper heads make superb fish stock and are the secret ingredient for many Caribbean fish chowders."

This is a very basic fish chowder. Some cooks add celery—or fresh celery leaf—(a plus with stronger-tasting fish like pollack). A dash of Tabasco sauce never hurts, either.

Fish Chowder #2 (fillets only)
(serves 4)

2 pounds chowder fish, cut into fillets
1 bay leaf
Salt
¼ cup diced salt pork (rind discarded), or to taste
1 large onion, chopped
4 to 6 potatoes, cut "thick-thin"
3 cups milk
Several sprigs fresh parsley, leaves minced
Black pepper to taste
8 common crackers
2 tablespoons unsalted butter

Put the fish fillets and the bay leaf with 3 cups of lightly salted water into the pot in which you plan to make the chowder. Bring to a simmer and cook about 7 minutes or until the flesh turns opaque and can be flaked with a fork. Remove the fish to a plate with a slotted spoon. Meanwhile, fry up the diced salt pork in a small skillet, until some fat is rendered and the pork begins to turn light brown. Add the chopped onion and sauté this mixture until the pork is crisp and the onion soft and amber-colored.

Add the onion-pork mixture and the wedges of potato to the broth in the pot and simmer over medium heat until the potatoes are tender (about 12 minutes). Meanwhile, flake the fish into bite-sized pieces with a fork. Remove the bay leaf from the broth and add the flaked fish, milk, and minced parsley. Bring back to a simmer. Taste for seasoning, adding freshly ground black pepper and more salt as necessary. As soon as the milk is heated through, turn the flame as low as possible and let it steep for a few minutes, while you split the common crackers and place under the broiler to brown. Ladle the chowder into warmed bowls, float the toasted common crackers on top, and drop in a chunk of butter—about half a tablespoon for each bowl—to melt on the way to the table.

Cook's Note. For improvements, see recipe above. Salt cod (see below) produces a good fish stock. Sometimes recipes for salt-cod dishes call for discarding the poaching liquid when the fish is to be used without it—freeze this instead and use it as a fish chowder base. Cookbooks often utilize clam juice—which is sold in bottles in New England—to add extra flavor to fish as well as clam chowders, but I find that this muddies rather than enhances the taste of the finished chowder.

FISH CHOWDER #3 (FINNAN HADDIE). There was a time when finnan haddie meant smoked haddock and nothing else. Now, usually, it is neither smoked nor haddock (but any generic white-fleshed fish, and chemically processed with a "smoke" flavor). Some fishmongers in Maine actually sell the authentic article flown in from Scotland; others sell a locally smoked pollack. Both make a truly excellent chowder. In the old days, when this fish was both salted and smoked, it had to be soaked to lessen the saltiness. This isn't necessary today, but if the fish smells too strong for your taste, give it a bath overnight in sweet milk. Then give the milk to the cat and follow the procedure outlined in "Fish Chowder #2." We follow the same course when we make a chowder out of any smoked seafood, such as smoked mussels or smoked clams.

FISH CHOWDER #4 (SALT COD). Even Down East, salt cod is nothing compared to what it was—a year-round staple, as important as flour and tea. Elsewhere in the country, some import groceries still sell salt cod by the piece, but most supermarkets, if they have it at all, offer it either in bite-sized pieces in a plastic bag or cut into fillets and packed (along with a few odd scraps to make up the weight) in the traditional small pine box.

Salt cod makes a good chowder, but not one so special that it ought to be sought out for the purpose, since the reconstituted flesh has neither the succulent texture nor the subtle flavor notes of the fresh fish. Salt cod is better used to make cod cakes or salt-cod hash, with the cooking water kept for a chowder base. However, in a pinch, to use it to make a chowder for four, put about a pound of the dried cod pieces (fillet is best) in a wide, flat bowl and soak for 24 hours in several changes of water, keeping the bowl in the refrigerator. The thicker the flesh, the longer the soaking. (The only way to really tell if it's completely desalted is to taste a little bit.) Put the soaked fish with a bay leaf into a pot with a quart of unsalted water. Gently poach—the water should be kept at just below a simmer—until the fish is tender and begins to flake. Then follow the procedure outlined in "Fish Chowder #2." This chowder especially benefits from a stalk or two of celery, diced and sautéed along with the onion.

FISH CHOWDER #5 (TROUT). Trout chowder is something I've never tasted, but it is so much the stuff of Maine legend that some word of it ought to be included here. Although the phrase hardly needs a gloss, John Gould put an entry for it in his *Maine Lingo: Boiled Owls, Bill-dads, & Wazzats*, just so he could wax poetic on the subject (a "boiled owl," by the by, is the very opposite of a trout chowder—a phrase

Mainers use to signal a desperate appetite, as in "I'm so hungry I could eat a . . ."):

> More than a few discerning palates have discovered that a Maine trout chowder exceeds the more publicized lobster stew in delicacy and delight. . . . Put together much as a coastal fish chowder, it is a specialty of guides who prepare it at noontime for angling sports. It is thus made over an open fire and enjoys this advantage, but it also uses tinned milk, because of wilderness distances and lack of refrigeration, and when properly brought off will have a resultant "body" that coastal chowders do not always obtain.

Coastal chowders, too, can taste of wood smoke and be thickened with evaporated milk. What makes trout chowder unique is the appetite worked up during a morning of wading a cold forest stream, the strong sense of connection between chowder and catch, and the shared comradeship of campfire cooking. This is the sort of chowder for which an exact recipe is superfluous. What one wants is the take on the thing that John J. Rowlands gives us in *Cache Lake Country*—and no surprise that it blithely breaks (as does the milkless chowder above) most of the rules of chowder cooking.

> TROUT CHOWDER. It didn't take me long to find out what the Chief had in mind, for he loves the kind of trout chowder I make and he has even saved a few potatoes that he bought on his last trip to the settlement. I like my chowder without any bones, so I get rid of all skin and bones, and start by frying several thick slices of salt pork with chopped onions until they are well browned. This is put in the pot with the fish and raw potatoes cut in chunks with just enough water to cover. Then I add a generous amount of evaporated milk, which to my mind is even better than fresh milk for a chowder and many other kinds of cooking. When the chowder is done after cooking slowly for about an hour it is golden brown and Hank and the Chief love the flavor of the fried pork and browned onion.

CLAM CHOWDER

> The chowder by the sand beach made
> Dipped by the hungry, steaming hot,
> With spoons of clam-shells from the pot.
> —JOHN GREENLEAF WHITTIER

A picnic would be incomplete without . . . a clam chowder, which may be considered one of the New England national dinners.   —*The Standard* (1882)

Was the original, the ur-chowder, made not with fish but with clams? Alan Davidson floats this suggestion in his magisterial *North American Seafood*:

> If any one occurrence can be singled out as the starting point, it could well be the meeting of early French settlers, br'..ging with them their *chaudières* or iron cooking pots, and the Canadian Micmac Indians, who were partial to clams but had a primitive batterie de cuisine.

Perhaps. There's no doubt that the Micmacs took to the *chaudière*, although they incised a birchbark pattern directly into the cast iron so that the pot would more resemble their native cookware, just as the French took to the hard-shell clam, transplanting it to Brittany, where it eventually spread down France's Atlantic coast (the soft-shell clam has not fared as well there).

On the other hand, there were fishermen chasing cod off the North American coast long before the Micmacs were teaching the Acadians how to dig and cook clams. Newfoundland is not famous for its great clam-drying facilities; nor was Cape Cod ever called Cape Clam. Well into the last century, it was the cod and the haddock that dominated life in the Canadian Maritime and New England coastal communities, and consequently it was cod and haddock that also dominated the cuisine. As long as these fish (and oysters) were there for the taking, clams had the status of a trash fish.

Of course, this doesn't mean that clam chowder was not eaten—we already know the contrary from that famous passage in *Moby Dick*—only that "clam" was not generally the word that came to mind when chowder was mentioned . . . or vice versa. When Thoreau visited Cape Cod, he devoted several pages to the life and fortune of the oyster and the oystermen, but only occasionally mentioned the clam—and then only to note the huge mounds of clam shells whose innards had been taken as bait or used by farmers to fatten their pigs with. Although clamming was a seaside occupation for centuries, the contents of the clam carts were sold as pig fodder.

Significantly, during his entire trip, he ate only one. Wandering along the shore, he came across a large sea clam, six inches in length, that had been washed up by a storm. He carried it with him until lunchtime, when he

> kindled a fire with a match and some paper, and cooked my clam on the embers for my dinner . . . When the clam was done, one valve held the meat and the other the liquor. Though it was very tough, I found it sweet and savory, and ate

the whole with a relish. Indeed, with the addition of a cracker or two, it would have been a bountiful dinner.

Soon after, though, he began to wonder about the folly of his impetuousness, a worry inflamed by an old oysterman with whom he spent that night, who told him that while sea clams were quite good to eat, a certain part had to be removed that was poisonous enough to "kill a cat." Thoreau then "began to feel the potency of the clam which I had eaten . . . and was made quite sick by it for a short time."

However, recovering nicely soon after, he joked that he had "weathered the Clam cape" and was later pleased to discover that the same had happened to the Pilgrims when they first landed in Provincetown Harbor—pleased because the experience connected him to them and because it proved that "man and the clam lay still at the same angle to one another."

It should be noted that even then, at least at the shore, this was not a common prejudice. The old oysterman laughed at Thoreau's fears and told him it was all in his mind, reflectively commenting, "They are good. . . . I wish I had some of them now." To which his wife chimed in, "They never hurt me." They may well have been putting him on about the poisonous part, since this is not true.* (Thoreau was perhaps at more danger of an upset stomach after the next morning's breakfast, a meal of eels, buttermilk cake, cold bread, green beans, doughnuts, and tea, most of which the oysterman's wife prepared in the fireplace while her husband, sitting beside her, seasoned it all with sprays of tobacco juice.)

Clam chowder increased in popularity as the nineteenth century progressed. I suspect that there is a direct correlation between this and the burgeoning American infatuation with the seashore. Already, taking the sea air was considered restorative—almost a moral duty (as time went on, even the Shakers were doing it)—and the novice beach stroller soon found he or she could pleasantly while away the morning digging steamers for a clambake or a chowder fest.

Previously, a chowder party—whether all male or no—was associ-

---

* However, what isn't poisonous isn't necessarily edible. Dorothy Bangs, noting that the chowders one usually encounters in restaurants are made of frozen minced sea clams, observes: "Did you ever purchase a package of these frozen minced clams? I guess the entire clam is ground just as it comes from the shell. In our family the clam is stripped of its long black membrane, the stomach emptied, and it is well washed. Have you ever opened a sea clam? Do it someday and see if you want everything you find ground up and put into your chowder."

ated with a fishing expedition. When Thoreau saw the waters off the head of the Cape dotted with tiny boats, he observed that back home in Concord

> it is only a few idle boys or loafers that go a-fishing on a rainy day; but there [on Cape Cod] it appeared as if every able-bodied man and helpful boy in the Bay had gone out on a pleasure excursion in their yachts, and all would at last land and have a chowder on the cape.

Clam chowder allowed the chowder party to widen its embrace. No boats were needed, or any skill with rod and line. Clams are fun to dig and easy to prepare.* Even more than lobster, the taste of clam was associated with the pleasures of the seaside visit, and clam chowder soon became *the* expected dish to try, just as that culinary extravaganza the clambake became *the* seaside event. Walt Whitman spoke for many others as well as himself when he proclaimed:

> The boatman and clam-diggers arose early and stopped for me,
> I tuck'd my trowser-ends in my boots and went and had a good time,
> You should have been with us that day round the chowder-kettle.

While chowder fanciers who like to think of clam chowder as *the* chowder may not have history in their corner, they do have something else, nicely summed up by the food historian Raymond Sokolov in *Why We Eat What We Eat*:

> I have yet to find a really close analogue to our clam chowder in a French cook-book, and I doubt that I will find one because the plainness of our New England chowder is its hallmark and its genius.

No one is more inexorable in this regard than Theophrastus, who insists that clam chowder wants *none* of the modest flavorings that contribute to the pleasure of a fish chowder:

> A "true" clam chowder has nothing in it but quahogs, salt pork, onions, potatoes, and milk—no pepper, no salt, nor any other spices or herbs, no water, nor anything else, and if properly made—paradoxically—has a spicy flavor as if all those forbidden additives had been doused into it . . . There is nothing else that tastes

---

* While all this remains true, amateur clammers should always seek local advice regarding possible pollution, red-tide closures, and licensing requirements before heading out onto the mud flats.

like [it]—the clams or quahogs carry the melody—with the onions, potatoes, and
salt pork providing a modest but essential back-up.

Most chowder makers, even native ones, are not quite all as purist as
this, but the purpose of the exhortation is well taken: to remind us that
any addition to a clam chowder should have but one purpose: to
heighten the essence of clam. For some cooks, the clam itself is sufficient to the task.

Which clam? Well, if a clam is edible, it can be made into chowder.*
Euell Gibbons mentions a host of them: the butter clam, the bean clam,
the razor clam, the surf clam, and so on. Down East, chowder makers
tend to stick to the steamer; on the Cape they begin to argue steamer
versus quahog (say it "KOE-HOG"). From then on, the farther you pro-
gress down shore toward New York and New Jersey, the more the quahog is favored. Each has its merits and demerits or, rather, its boosters
and detractors.

Let's look at the steamer first. It is the clam of classic Down East
cooking. As its name implies, it is *the* clam for steamed clams, as well
as for clambakes. This is because it opens easily when heated and can
therefore be cooked to perfection in its shell. Because its long neck
makes a meaty portion, it is also excellent battered and fried. I suspect
more clams are eaten Down East out of the fry pot than any other way
(and here the bellies are fried along with the necks—not always the
case elsewhere). Perhaps the strongest argument *against* using the
steamer in chowder is that there are so many other things you can do
with it. With the quahog, it's either chowder or the meat grinder (or,
more often than not, *both*).

The steamer's greatest demerit is, as its alternate designation "soft-
shell clam" implies, its fragility. As anyone who has wielded a clam
hoe will know, even the gentlest-seeming thrust can poke a tine right
through them. Besides being easy to damage, their inability to close up
tightly makes them more vulnerable to spoilage. If you don't dig them
yourself, it's important to purchase them from a reliable fishmonger who
will vouch for their freshness—and then to look them over carefully for
damage. Always discard any clams that are broken, open, or that smell
bad.

Quahog is the name of the largest size of the same hard-shell clam

* So, of course, can other shellfish—mussels, scallops, oysters, etc. None of them,
however—in my opinion—is suited to make as *good* a chowder, and so any such are
usually wasted in this endeavor.

that, when smaller, is called the cherrystone and, smaller still, the lit-
tleneck, both of which are often eaten raw. These are the clams with
which to make pasta with clam sauce or clam pizza. For chowder, quahogs must first be opened, by either the fishmonger (have him save the
liquid) or yourself (using a clam knife and following the instructions of
a seafood book like Mark Bittman's excellent *Fish: The Complete Guide
to Buying and Cooking*). The same cautions apply to buying quahogs
as steamers, but because the quahog is a tougher customer, it is also a
better keeper.

Which tastes better? Dorothy Bangs compares them so:

> One rarely finds a soft-shell clam chowder in a restaurant—you know—the kind
> that has the little clam, stomach and all, floating on the top. Oh! Such a gentle
> delicate flavor! Larger soft-shell clams can be used but the cook takes and sep-
> arates the stomachs from the clam, chops the body (rim) and adds the stomachs
> whole but separate. This type of chowder is usually found in homes that are
> accustomed to digging their own clams and giving them the meticulous loving
> care that is needed to remove all the sand.
>
> As for quahogs, they make a wonderful chowder . . . Quahog shells are very
> hard and shaped differently from the sea clam or soft-shell clam. Quite tricky to
> open, too. The quahog itself is much, much stronger in flavor than the other clams.
> Many people unaccustomed to its flavor would find it much too strong. I personally
> squeeze the stomachs out of each quahog. I don't like seeing those little black
> pieces floating around in the chowder. But I don't know anyone else who does
> this.

Thomas F. De Voe wrote of the soft-shell clam in *The Market Assistant*, a comprehensive description of the comestibles sold in the public
markets of four major Atlantic seaboard cities in the middle of the last
century, that its "taste is more rich and luscious" than that of the hard-
shell clam (he seems more impressed by this clam's ability to trap rats
at night in the city fish markets). However, that very "luscious"
quality—the large, velvety-textured, briny-tasting belly—puts off some
eaters, who are happier with the chewier, more compact texture of the
quahog, regardless of the stronger flavor.

One wiseacre has suggested that the best of all clam chowders contains a mixture of both. That's like saying the best French wine is a
mixture of Bordeaux and Burgundy. The steamer and the quahog both
make an excellent chowder: the chowder lover will try each and find
the one that—to appropriate Thoreau's phrase—lies at the proper angle
to himself.

Clam Chowder #1 (Soft-Shell Clams)
(serves 4)

Old-fashioned clam chowders dealt nervously with clams, some recipes even discarding most of them after the broth was made. One old recipe I consulted gives elaborate directions for cleaning out the bellies, much along the lines of the tedious and unnecessary "deveining" of shrimp. The real danger lies in overcooking, which will toughen the clams—the best clam chowder is made quickly and then allowed to sit for a bit for the flavor to develop.

36 live soft-shell clams (1 quart shucked)
¼ cup diced salt pork (rind removed)
1 large onion, chopped
3 or 4 potatoes, cut "thick-thin"
2 cups whole milk
Salt and black pepper to taste
8 common crackers, split
2 tablespoons unsalted butter divided into 4 pats

If you have dug the clams yourself, watch out for shells that have been punctured or broken by the clam hoe, discarding these and any clams that are not closed. Wash the rest well in seawater and bring them back covered with clean, wet seaweed. In the kitchen, whether the clams are dug or bought, rinse them off in cold running water, scrubbing each with a vegetable brush.

Toss the wet seaweed (if you have it) into a pot and add a few more tablespoons of water. If you have no seaweed, put in half a cup of water instead. Add the clams, cover the pot, and put over high heat. As soon as the water boils, reduce the heat to low and steam the clams until all have opened. Remove the pot from the heat at once. With a pair of tongs, transfer the clams to a bowl. When they are cool enough to handle, remove them from their shells. Toss out the seaweed (if any), combining any liquid remaining in the pot with the broth in the bowl. Strain this through a few layers of cheesecloth or a paper coffee filter, or just pour it off carefully, leaving the grit behind.

Pull off the black neck caps and discard. Detach the soft bellies from the necks and reserve separately. Chop the necks and the tough membrane into small pieces. Fry the salt pork in a large pot until it has rendered some fat and begun to brown. Add the chopped onion and continue to fry until the onion is soft and the pork crisp. (If the pork is lean or only a small amount is used, it may be necessary to add a little butter to keep the onion from burning.) Measure the amount of broth and add enough water (or bottled clam juice) to make a generous 2 cups. Add this to the pot with the salt pork and onion and bring to a simmer. Add the potatoes and cook until they are still firm but done. Stir the milk into the chowder and season to taste with salt and pepper. Heat to simmering again before adding the chopped clam meat and the clam bellies. Do not let the chowder boil. Let this continue to cook at the barest simmer for another 2 or 3 minutes. Remove from the heat.

Clam chowder is best if, at this point, it is aged for an hour or so, kept warm (but not hot) on the back of the stove (or in a warm oven). Just before serving, reheat the chowder until it begins to steam (remember that it may curdle if it even gets near boiling). Split and toast the crackers while the chowder reheats, then float these and a pat of butter in each bowl when the chowder is served.

COOK'S NOTES. Even here in Maine you can find steamers at the supermarket bundled up like a cut of meat on a extruded plastic tray sealed in plastic wrap. *Not* a good idea. Unlike a cut of meat, a clam should be *alive* when you purchase it, and you should keep it alive until you cook it. Don't buy any clams wrapped in plastic and don't wrap them up yourself in plastic when you get them home. Just put them in a bowl in the refrigerator and eat them as soon as possible.

Soft-shell clams also invariably contain grit. Some say that you should purge them by putting the live clams in a bucket of clean, cold seawater with a handful (about a third of a cup) of cornmeal and leaving them in it for a few hours. Supposedly the cornmeal irritates them and they spit it and the sand out. I've never tried this. A little care in pouring off the broth leaves almost all the sand behind. As my mother says, you have to eat a peck of dirt before you die. Better it should be sea sand.

CLAM CHOWDER #2 (QUAHOG)
(SERVES 4)

Although smaller hard-shell clams can be quickly steamed open, quahogs get too much cooked that way and should be shucked before the chowder is started. If you have the fishmonger do it, make sure he reserves all the juices.

24 quahogs
¼ cup diced salt pork (rind removed)
1 large onion, chopped
3 or 4 "all-purpose" potatoes, cut "thick-thin"

2 cups whole milk
Salt and black pepper to taste (see note)
8 common crackers, split
2 tablespoons unsalted butter, divided into 4 pats

If you are unfamiliar with the task, have your fishmonger (or a knowl-edgeable friend) open the quahogs, reserving all liquid. When you begin to make the chowder, separate the clam meat from the liquid. If the clams are large, cut them in half or into quarters. Measure the broth, adding additional water (or bottled clam juice) to make a generous 2 cups.

Fry the salt pork in a large pot until it has rendered some fat and begun to brown. Add the chopped onion and continue to fry until the onion is soft and the pork crisp. (If the pork is lean or only a small amount is used, it may be necessary to add a little butter to keep the onion from burning.) Add the clam broth to the pot and bring to a simmer. Add the potatoes and cook until they are still firm but done, about 12 to 15 minutes. Stir the milk into the chowder and season to taste with salt and pepper. Heat to simmering again and mix in the clams. Let this continue to cook at the barest simmer for another 5 minutes. Remove from the heat.

Clam chowder is best if, at this point, it is aged for an hour or so, kept warm (but not hot) on the back of the stove (or in a warm oven). Just before serving, reheat the chowder until it begins to steam (remember that it may curdle if it even gets near boiling). Split and toast the crackers while the chowder reheats, then float these and a pat of butter in each bowl when the chowder is served.

COOK'S NOTE. The same keeping notes regarding fresh clams in the recipe above apply here, too. Alternatively, many New England fish counters sell pint containers of chopped clam meat—usually from surf clams—a passable if not exciting substitute. One reason Theophrastus omits salt from his clam chowder is that he makes it with quahogs, whose liquor is quite briny. This and the presence of the salt pork require restrained seasoning.

CORN CHOWDER

It's corn chowder and this grand popcorn Yankee one-piece dinner or supper ought to be cooked in an iron pot right in the middle of the garden, with friends from all the surrounding gardens.   —*The Chicago Daily News* (1944)

In *The Countryman's Cookbook*, Haydn S. Pearson describes the making
of an egg chowder. Strips of salt pork are tried out in a large, hot skillet.
When some fat has been rendered, cut-up onions and potatoes are added
and fried until the potatoes are about half cooked. At that point, all this
is turned into a chowder pot. Milk is poured in and heated until just
steaming hot—but not quite simmering. When the potatoes begin to
break apart, eggs are broken in. The whites meld with the milk while
the yolks poach whole. Everything is then portioned out, with plenty of
common or pilot crackers served on the side.

There is something about the way that Pearson presents this "old
Maine receipt" (his phrase)—his narrative is only slightly more detailed
than my own account above—that to me is an example of what Sidney
Dean meant when he wrote in *Cooking American* that, to the true chowder maker, "what matters more than any principal ingredient is the
method of chowdering." Chowder, as we've been discovering, isn't just
something you make; it is something you *do*. No Yankee cook needs a
recipe to turn out a poached-egg (or, as some Mainers prefer, a hard-
cooked-egg) chowder; given the everyday contents of the family larder,
the whole thing simply falls together.

However, there is more going on here even than that. The act of
making something into a chowder gives it, as a meal, the right anticipatory *weight*. Offered "egg soup" for lunch, our heart sinks—unless
we're in a Chinese restaurant. Offered, instead, "egg stew," we suspect
false advertising. Eggs are not the stuff of stews. Nor are many of the
other featured ingredients of Yankee farmhouse chowders: parsnips, carrots, butter beans, and, famously, corn.

One of the things a chowder does, then, is take a completely ordinary
item of food and make it something more. In this regard, it is the opposite of a stew, which is usually a bottom-line treatment of a relatively
luxurious ingredient. This is why the phrase "beef chowder" has the
wrong ring to it, while "meatball chowder" is an easy gustatory imagining. Beef and chowder don't bat in the same conceptual league, but
meatballs and chowder do.*

It is for this reason that I haven't included in these pages any lobster
or oyster chowders. Such recipes exist. But I believe that, whether one
considers the matter historically or from the viewpoint of culinary logic,

---

* This isn't to say that you won't find any recipes for "beefsteak chowder." You will—
in *The Martha's Vineyard Cook Book*, for instance. But you probably won't feel any
impelling desire to try any. We can only make our way through the labyrinth of chowder
making's contradictory particulars by holding tight to the guiding thread of anticipation.

lobsters and oysters are the stuff of stews, not chowders. If someone offers me an oyster or lobster chowder, I know that what I am going to get is an oyster or lobster stew extended with a lot of potatoes.

Similarly, while there are several traditional Yankee chicken chowders, a well-made chicken soup easily surpasses any of them, not because of the luxuriousness of chicken but because of chicken *broth*. For the same reason, however good it might in theory be, there is no *need* for an onion chowder—onion soup is quite good enough. (Traditional Parisian onion soup, with its generous additions of bread and cheese—analogues of potato and salt pork—is French cuisine's chowder equivalent.)

This brings us to the queen of all farmhouse chowders and the third-brightest star in the chowder maker's constellation: corn chowder. In many ways, corn chowder is an anomaly among chowders. While you can find recipes—even relatively recent ones—that build a corn chowder up in exactly the same way, layer upon layer, that old-fashioned fish chowders were built, this is not the norm. If chowder making had never evolved as a Yankee culinary craft, corn chowder as most people now know it would still exist. It would just be called something like "farmhouse corn and potato soup" instead.

However, it wouldn't be corn chowder. Consider in this regard the following account of corn chowder making, from Ulysses P. Hedrick's memoir of farm life in Michigan at the end of the nineteenth century, *The Land of the Crooked Tree.*

The wife of a New England neighbor tantalized Mother by singing loud and often the praises of clam chowder. We could not get clams, fresh or canned, so Mother sometimes made oyster chowder by adding cut-up canned oysters to corn chowder, one of our commonest dishes. Corn chowder was served on our table quite as often as baked beans, boiled ham, or beef stew. In all but spring and early summer, corn chowder was a supper dish about once a week. The addition of oysters was a pleasing variation. Corn-chowder season began soon after roasting ears came, and, made from dried corn, lasted until next May.

It requires a half day to make a good corn chowder. Mother started her chowder in an iron kettle on the back of the stove while doing her dinner dishes. Fried salt pork for dinner preceded corn chowder for supper, slices of crisp fried pork being saved for chowder. The pork was cut in cubes and put with a small amount of pork drippings in the chowder kettle sitting on the back of the stove. Two or three onions and an equal quantity of potatoes were then diced and put to simmer with the pork; then, in a half hour, a quart or two of milk and an equal quantity of cooked corn, freshly cut from the cob, canned, or dried, were blended in, the whole to cook, but never boil, until supper. From the number of times Mother told someone to stir the chowder, this dish seemed to need a good deal of stirring.

The finishing touches were to salt and pepper, after which it was served piping hot.

Corn chowder was a meal in itself, served with hot bread, soda biscuit, or corn bread. Store crackers might be crumbled in the bowlful of chowder. Uncooked sauerkraut, coleslaw, or pickled beets were usually served with corn chowder, their tartness making a harmonious blend of flavors. The supper ended with pie.

How do we read this passage? There is that tantalizing aura of real Yankee clam chowder, just out of reach, to which this corn chowder, even if only a country cousin, could still claim kinship. There is that needed sense in a world of hard physical labor of something both substantial and good already simmering on the stove, the dish getting tastier as the worker gets hungrier, the two movements maintaining a marvelous anticipatory synchrony. Finally, there is the matter of adaptability. For a dish, especially a vegetable dish, to be part of the regular rhythm of the weekly menu, it has to be available in one form or another nearly all year round.

Consequently, Hedrick's observation that his mother always made corn chowder from *cooked* corn is significant and helpful. Delicious corn chowder can be made with kernels cut from leftover roasted ears, frozen corn, canned corn, or dried corn . . . in other words, with whatever corn you happen to have around. This, even on a farm, is almost never fresh-picked sweet corn. On the contrary, for about 150 years the corn at hand—in the city or the country, for at least ten months of the year—was canned corn.

Before canned corn, of course, there was parched or dried corn, and you can make a passable corn chowder out of that. However, having done so, I can attest that such a dish is less a chowder than a potato-studded corn gruel. (Parched corn is not a really a vegetable but—like barley or millet—a grain.) This experience—and the lack of any record of dried-corn chowders in old cookery books—makes me suspect that parched corn was pressed into service only after the invention of canned corn made this chowder a regularly expected meal. Then a cook who was snowed in and found the cupboard empty might turn to the sack of parched corn as a last resort.

Until relatively recently, there was nothing of the last resort about canned corn. It was my favorite vegetable as a child. Unlike canned peas or green beans or carrots, canned corn has a certain specialness. Tomatoes aside (since they are more a sauce than a vegetable, even when put up whole), canned corn is the best of all canned vegetables, not because it is all that comparable to the fresh article, but because it emerges from the can with some character and flavor. You can develop a taste for canned peas or green beans, but you can't escape feeling that there is something a bit debased about this, whereas there is no such smirch on canned corn. And there is nothing that canned corn does better than make corn chowder.

This is not the case with fresh sweet corn—at least when brought in straight from the garden. That does not need or want the chowder maker's skills to bring out its best. With a small sharp knife (or patent scraper), cut the kernels from the cobs. Then, using the back of the knife, scrape down the sides of each cob to remove as much additional pulp as possible. Break the scraped cobs in half and simmer for a few minutes in hot milk. Lift these out and stir in the corn scrapings, cook just until hot, season gently with salt and pepper, and serve at once with a piece of butter floated in each bowl. Salt pork, onion, and potato can only diminish what is one of late summer's finest dishes.

This, I believe, explains why for fifty years, from the first edition (1896) to the tenth (1946), the corn-chowder recipe in *The Fannie Farmer Cookbook* called simply for canned corn. Chowder returns to canned corn an essential quality that this vegetable has otherwise lost: its milkiness. Canned *creamed* corn attempts to do this, too, but it is to corn what condensed milk is to milk, somehow seeming more an imitation than an adaptation. When I used to make corn chowder from canned corn, I would always buy a small can of creamed corn to use as a thickener. But the corn itself came from the much larger can of Green Giant Niblets that I also added; the clean taste and crisp juicy texture of those kernels were that chowder's *raison d'être*.

Today, obviously, there are many ways of obtaining corn on the far side of milky, perfect freshness. The corn chowder maker can choose among canned corn, frozen corn (the Shoepeg variety makes a delicious chowder), and, best of all, the truck-garden corn-on-the-cob that starts arriving in supermarkets in late spring, first from Florida and then, as the warm weather works its way up the coast, from successive points north. Better to wait until the local corn comes into the farmers' market before feasting on boiled ears, and to use the supermarket corn instead, cobs and all, to turn out the following summer chowder.

SUMMER CORN CHOWDER
(SERVES 4)

4 large ears of sweet corn, shucked or 1½ cups (approximately)
    canned or frozen corn

1 teaspoon salt, or to taste
2 tablespoons unsalted butter, divided
¼ cup diced salt pork, rind removed
1 large onion, chopped
4 potatoes, cut "thick-thin"
2 cups whole milk
Black pepper to taste
Ground hot red pepper to taste
8 common crackers, split

With a small sharp knife (or patent scraper), cut the kernels from the cobs. Then, using the back of the knife, scrape down the sides of each cob to remove as much additional pulp as possible. Break the scraped cobs in half and simmer these in a pot with 3 cups of boiling water and 1 teaspoon salt for 20 minutes. If using canned or frozen corn, go directly to the next step, using 2½ cups of salted water to cook the potatoes.

Melt 1 tablespoon of the butter in a skillet over medium heat. Try out the diced salt pork until it begins to crisp at the edges and some of its fat is rendered. Add the onion and sauté until translucent. Do not brown.

Fish the cobs from the pot and discard. Turn the potatoes into the pot in their place and simmer these for 15 minutes, or until they are just tender. Add the contents of the skillet, the corn kernels and pulp, and the milk. Taste for seasoning, adding salt as necessary, and grind in plenty of black pepper. Sprinkle a little hot red pepper over and heat through, just long enough for the corn to cook, or about 5 minutes. At the same time, in the broiler or a toaster oven, lightly brown the tops of the split common crackers. Divide the chowder into 4 bowls, top each with a bit of the remaining butter, and float a share of the toasted crackers in each bowl. Serve at once.

COOK'S NOTES. Corn chowder is often made with heavy cream instead of milk, but I find such ultra-velvetizing cloying; the combination of the corn pulp and the potato thickening provides a delicate creaminess that is special in itself and evidence of the care and interest of the cook.

There are plenty of Yankee precedents for adding some diced fresh red tomato to this chowder for the color as well as the flavor. If you do, add it at the same time as the corn, since it, too, should be just cooked.

Finally, a very different but interesting corn chowder can be made by reducing the butter to a tablespoon and replacing the salt pork with 2 tablespoons of unrefined, cold-pressed corn oil, using this to gently sauté the onions (keep the heat low since this oil has a tendency to foam).

VARIATION: SUCCOTASH CHOWDER. Those with access to fresh shell beans (such as cranberry beans) can make a superb chowder by substituting 1½ cups of these for the potatoes and cooking them until just tender in the salted cob water. Otherwise, proceed as directed above.

WINTER CORN CHOWDER
(SERVES 4)

This recipe has been fleshed out and adapted slightly from a description in Sylvia Thompson's The Kitchen Garden Cookbook, *where it is called "Maine Corn Chowder." I don't know about that, but the combination of bacon, corn, and Cheddar is a pleasing one, and this chowder makes a good hearty cold-weather meal.*

4 slices authentic smokehouse country bacon
1 large onion, chopped
1 teaspoon salt, or to taste
3 or 4 potatoes, cut "thick-thin"
1½ cups (approximately) canned or frozen corn
1 or 2 sprigs of parsley, minced
3 cups whole milk
Freshly ground black pepper
2 ounces tangy aged Vermont Cheddar, grated

Fry the bacon slices in a skillet until crisp. Remove and drain on paper toweling. Pour off all but 1 tablespoon of bacon fat. Add the onion and sauté until the pieces are translucent. Do not brown. Meanwhile, bring 1 cup of water to a boil in a pot. Season this with the teaspoon of salt and add the potatoes, gently cooking these for 15 minutes, or until just tender. Then stir in the sautéed onions, the canned or frozen corn, the minced parsley, and the milk. Taste for seasoning, adding salt as necessary and plenty of black pepper. Heat just long enough for the corn to cook, or about 5 minutes. Do not let it boil. Divide the chowder into 4 bowls, sprinkling each with some of the grated cheese. Finally, crumble over the reserved bacon and serve at once.

VARIATION. Substitute a chopped red bell pepper for the bacon. Sauté this and the chopped onion in a tablespoon or two of butter, and then proceed as above.

ENVOI

In the summer of 1994, I finally made it down to Boston to have dinner at Jasper White's eponymous restaurant on Commercial Street near the Boston wharf area. Jasper is also the author of what is probably the best book written in recent years about Yankee cooking, *Jasper White's Cooking from New England*. The book is full of genuine interest in New England foodways and respect for the region's ingredients. Even better, it challenges the cook by compelling example to reexamine old habits and reinfuse traditional Yankee dishes with vitality and fresh appeal.

The book had been a companion and an inspiration ever since I first laid hands on it, and I was looking forward to meeting Jasper himself and eating a meal he had prepared. There were five of us in the party, so I got to sample quite a bit of his cooking, and it was all very good. Afterward, recounting the events of the evening to others, I found it easiest to detail the restaurant's signature dishes—the grilled tuna salad with olives and capers, the seared duck foie gras with plums, the sesame crusted bluefish with stir-fried bok choy and Chinese noodles—since here simple description was all that was required of me. I would have found it much harder to explain why the one dish that actually dominated my private recollection was a straightforward lobster and corn chowder.

As it happened, this response was similar to that of another guest at our table, a professional chef himself. He told me during the course of the meal that Jasper's potato salad was the best he had ever eaten. How many chefs can astonish you with an honest, simple potato salad? How many even want to? Restaurant reviewers tend to emphasize a chef's personal creations, but eaters, I suspect, come away reflecting as much on what a cook has done to a dish that they already know. The new is always surprising . . . but the old made new is something akin to a miracle.

That's the way it was with this chowder. Words can make one dish sound Chinese and another Mexican, but the mouth takes in taste and texture and the interplay between them, and makes its own distinctions. An inspired chef makes you think with your mouth—without words, but still clearly and intensely—and my mouth could not stop pondering that chowder. It was rich but not cloying. There was a haunting note of smokiness to it, an undefinable freshness of flavor. I took mental notes; back home, I consulted the recipe for the dish as it appears in his book.

However, I gradually understood that I was going about the thing the wrong way. Jasper White had got me excited about his chowder not thanks to any secret ingredient or ingenious trick but because he cared to make it as good as possible. What made it stand out among all the chowders I have eaten in other restaurants was that, in those places, the cooks took chowder for granted. Jasper didn't.

So last year—after thirty years of making it—I started all over again with chowder. I looked at everything I did and what had become habitual I thought through once more. The result was a chowder that, if much improved, was no more like Jasper's now than my old chowder had been. That hint of smoke came from bacon, which is just right in a lobster and corn chowder but not what I want in the fish chowder I usually make. He uses cream; for the reasons already set forth above, I've decided to stick with milk.

This list goes on, but none of it matters. What Jasper did was challenge me to take my own chowder seriously again, to go the extra distance to get it right. I was so young when I first ate chowder that what I thought when that initial, cautious spoonful arrived in my mouth is now beyond recall. I was in my early twenties when I looked to chowder for a sense of self-sufficiency and found something near enough to make no matter. Now, in my early fifties, Jasper gave it back to me again, and I was filled with happiness that what I tasted affirmed chowder as something worth a lifetime, off and on, of contemplation as well as making.

> When the savory chowder was done, chocking the pot securely between two boxes on the cabin floor, so that it could not roll over, we helped ourselves and swapped yarns over it while the Spray made her own way through the darkness on the river.   —JOSHUA SLOCUM, *Sailing Alone Around the World* (1899)

BOSTON, 1982 / STEUBEN, 1995

THERE

I'm not sure of the exact count, but it would be a fair statement to say that I haven't spent more than a month of days in Louisiana, and I haven't been back for a visit in over a decade. Furthermore, I might never have gone there at all if a friend of mine, on his way back to California after a stay in Florida, hadn't decided to take a detour to New Orleans. His car broke down there and by the time it was fixed he was hooked. He ended up staying twelve years.

People say that New Orleans—actually, southern Louisiana—is another country, but as I discovered when I first came down for a visit, that doesn't really capture the experience. New Orleans doesn't hold a candle to Paris in any way but one, but that one is what makes it loom so large in the imagination. The Big Easy is part of the U.S.A. To go there is to enter an alternate reality, a world where the French added an enduring note to American vernacular culture. In New Orleans, *there* is still *here*, still familiar—but, at the same time somehow, subversively different.

For example, fast food is there, but it tastes good. Neighborhood places are just a little funkier, a little livelier, and a little more accommodating to the truly strange. The food seems somehow just naturally good, without—once you get a step away from the tourist places—any tang of self-congratulation. People there like to hang out—talk and dance and eat and drink—and do it in a way that suggests that this isn't something they're going to regret or swear off or think better of the next morning . . . The next morning they may even be right where they are now.

I came down to visit that friend twice and made a third trip to see another friend—and that's the sum of my Louisiana experience.

"There," then, doesn't just mean there-Louisiana, it means there-the-other-place . . . the woman you fell in love with but didn't marry, never see anymore but haven't in the least gotten over and never will.

The two experiences are very much the same. In 1987, when it became clear that I was going to have to move—I was living in my grandfather's house and he had died and the place had to be sold to clear the estate—I decided to make a clean break from Massachusetts and go somewhere else. I could have gone to New Orleans. I was still drawn to the place, and it was just then experiencing the height of the Cajun food craze. Instead, I moved here to Maine. Why?

There are some obvious answers. My friend and I had had a falling out. I had just met Matt, who was tied up with some business she couldn't immediately leave. She could come visit me regularly in Maine, which was only a few hours' drive from Boston, but not in New Orleans, which meant complicated and expensive flying time. But I think the truth is that I didn't go there because I was afraid that, if I did, the place would break my heart.

Even during my short visits, I could see that the "here" in Louisiana, like everywhere else, is fast slipping away. It's slipping away in Maine, too—if this book is about nothing else, it's about that—but with Maine I had a better sense of balance between expectation and reality. A Cajun cook can put garlic salt in a dish and still taste the real garlic she grew up on—but the newcomer can't. Maine, I know—even the out-of-season, off-Route-1 Maine I live in—leaves a tinny taste in the mouth of the expectant newcomer; to me, it still tastes real enough. When push came to shove, however, Louisiana didn't.

In any case, it turns out, most of us don't live there—there-the-other-place—either. As cooks, we have to figure out how to make do with what we've gleaned from the occasional visit, the not-altogether-helpful cookbooks, rumor, and the rare illuminating aside. And that is what is traced throughout this section: a gradual, personal assimilation of a cuisine.

No other regional American culinary style outside of Maine Yankee has affected my cooking more than Cajun/Creole, which is why I have written so much about it. This has nothing to do with the few days that I spent there. Or, rather, they are somehow both responsible and beside the point. The explanation falls within that indecipherable realm that we call "mutual recognition." All I know about this cooking may have come from cookbooks, but what sorted out truth from fiction in those cookbooks was a sense of connection already felt as real within myself.

The pieces that follow flesh out that connection. I don't know if it's possible to spell it out. If I had to, I would say that Cajun cooking connects to Maine cooking in this one way: both are cultures that spun their cooking out of a tight grip on a few culturally defining necessities. In Down East Maine, as we have seen, that is fresh seafood, preserved meat, dried beans, cornmeal, molasses, and root vegetables—especially the potato. In southern Louisiana, it is salted meat, fresh seafood, corn- meal, dried beans, cane syrup, rice, and seasoning greens. The cards may have different patterns on the back, but I felt immediately, when I saw the game, that I could sit in for a hand.

Still, I'm poignantly aware of the distance between what I do and what happens there. In "Bayou Odyssey," the first piece in this section, I write about the culinary borderline that separates Cajuns—or at least unregenerate Cajuns—from most other Americans. The Cajuns them- selves encapsulate that difference in their boast—which often takes the form of jokes—that they eat anything.

As it happens, that isn't even nearly true. As anthropologist C. Paige Gutierrez notes in *Cajun Foodways*:

> In the early 1980s some Cajuns in St. Martin Parish expressed revulsion at the alleged food habits of their new Vietnamese neighbors, who were rumored to eat cats, dogs, seagulls, shrimp heads, and rotten fish.

Cajuns don't eat horse—which the French still occasionally do—and they don't eat octopus, which is good and right out there for the taking. Even so, there is a border, and many Cajuns—especially male Cajuns— still live on the other side of it. Furthermore, the actual line of that border can be surprisingly fine. It isn't simply a matter of who eats 'gator or turtle. Consider frogs. You and I might eat frogs' legs in a French restaurant, but we don't catch, prepare, and cook them at home. A Cajun will do that—and what's more, a Cajun will pick the body for meat.

This brings us to the one ingredient that Cajuns think of as the essential, perhaps defining, ingredient of their cooking: the crawfish. They love it not only because it is abundant and, often, free but because it is a fierce little rascal and off-putting to strangers. Mudbugs scare the tourists alive and they scare them dead, boiled, and served up whole. This is so much the case that most of us think of crawfish as somehow localized in Louisiana bayous.

As we shall see in the chapter on crawfish *étouffée*, this isn't even nearly true. What is, is that most of us just don't want to eat them anymore. The taste for mudbug went the same way as the taste for squirrel, coon, and possum, other former American favorites that today we are more likely to feed than feed on. Our local Agway sells Havahart traps to catch and remove those cute but pesky critters from your property and, in another aisle, bags of small-animal feed to attract them *to* it. Either way, we consider them part of "nature" and ourselves not; the distinction is whether we want nature to come right up to the front door of the house or to stop at the other side of the electric fence.

Cajuns, many of them, don't have that luxury. They are still in the middle of it. That's why, on the one hand, they can jokingly refer to themselves as coonasses and, on the other, when confronted with a fat raccoon, see a straight-out competitor—and a tasty meal. Crawfish are also predators; there's nothing a mudbug likes better than tender young rice shoots. There is, then, in rural Louisiana, a visceral satisfaction in feasting on crawfish that comes from pure survival.

This is the kind of eating that, paradoxically, is energized by intimacy, like the *boucherie*, the feast held on pig-slaughtering day, and as much as anything, it explains the Cajun culinary ethos . . . and why you can sit there, enjoy the food, and still not get what is going on. The one time I joined Cajuns at a crawfish boil—beer in iced pitchers, crawfish heaped on giant platters, ears of corn that were boiled in the same pot, newspapers covering the table—it was this very same visceral satisfaction, the feeling of "What do you think about *that*, my little friend," that I recognized the line and on which side, mostly, I belong. This is why there aren't any crawfish recipes in this book.

That, then, is what *there* boils down to: I may cook Cajun now and then, but I never for one second think this makes me Cajun. As far as the authenticity of the food itself, however, I feel a little differently. If you make an effort to know where a dish is coming from, you have a good chance of getting it right enough . . . especially if you accept from the outset that you aren't ever going to get it perfect. Texas writer Ed Ward, introducing his own boiled crawfish recipe, hit the note exactly when he wrote:

> The first thing anybody learns about Cajun cooking is that no matter how you make something, it's wrong. You might have learned your recipe from a wrinkled-up 87-year-old lady back in the swamp who only spoke French, but the next Cajun you meet will check out what you're doing and say, "I'm sure that's gonna taste good, but that ain't how you make it." Smile, and ask how it's supposed to be done. Write it down. It'll be good, but the next Cajun you meet . . .

Bayou Odyssey

But if you wish once again to find the lost gate of Eden, if you wish to gain the promised land, if you wish to see in this rude, practical America of ours an "earthly paradise," where life is good, because Nature has invested it with everything that is delicious and fairest . . . seek the Teche country. Thither, more than a century ago, when the cruel order of the English dispersed them from their homes, Andry and the exiled Acadians took their mournful way. Thither they went, threading the swamps and wandering up the beautiful Atchafalaya.
—EDWARD KING, *The Great South* (1875)

En route to a Cajun fish-fry place in Henderson, Louisiana. The car has worked its way north from St. Martinville and Catahoula onto a road running along the top of a levee, one side of which slopes steeply down to a narrow bayou and the other to the western fringe of the great Atchafalaya swamp, Louisiana's Everglades, a seemingly endless expanse of murky, tree-studded waters.

Up here on the levee, for the first time, we get some sense of the spread of the country, a breath of fresh air. Southwestern Louisiana is relentlessly flat; the vegetation crowds in around you tightly. Driving along the narrow country roads, we travel less through a landscape than down an endless, damp, green tunnel, emerging only to pass through what seems the exact same small town or past featureless fields of rice and sugarcane. Bayou country is not so picturesque as it is claustral: despite the road map's assurances, for the past few hours we've felt trapped in a cunningly wrought vegetative maze.

Not that there aren't, for this stranger at least, exotic sightings. Cattle egrets skip along in the wake of massive Brahmin bulls. Herons, hunting frogs in roadside ditches, stand poised in motionless intensity. Twisted stumps of dead cypress grieve in a tiny desert that only yesterday was a lake. Stately mansions line the Bayou Teche, and a few towns, such as Jeanerette, still possess the architecture and sleepy feel of an earlier South.

Notwithstanding these moments of postcard prettiness, the general impression is one of guarded inwardness. Neither the land nor the people who inhabit it are interested in being too quickly known. Away from the highway's perpetual touristic Mardi Gras, the real character of the place takes hold. Houses are comfortably ramshackle, the yards littered with dead cars and empty propane tanks. A brand-new toilet, awaiting installation, stands proudly dead center in a front lawn.

This lack of concern is even more apparent out in the wetlands, where cabins pay homage to nothing but strict utility: random battens hold tar to spartan framing, the ground outside littered with the outspill of preoccupied and unself-conscious lives.

This is a people who are still a part of their landscape . . . who do not regard it, as tourists and summer people do, as outside themselves, something to stand back from and observe. They know it in the familiar and unreflective way that we, say, know that one special room in the house—study, bedroom, workshop—where no one else is allowed to enter, whose apparent chaos and confusion is merely an extension of ourselves.

The stranger who, by accidental navigation, stumbles upon such a place feels, like any unwitting intruder, embarrassed and confused. This is true of almost any rural area indifferent to outsiders, but it is especially true of Cajun country, populated as it is by a people who as late as 1933 were considered the nation's last unassimilated minority.

This is due less, maybe, to what seem the obvious reasons—the still strong cultural identity, the French dialect whose idiom is almost wholly their own—than to the very nature of a place that fights all human change. For the wetlands—the swamp and marsh that make up most of this land—offer its inhabitants a paradoxical gift: they can live well there only if they are content to live poor. Survival is almost always possible; prosperity, almost never.

The road that runs along the levee is narrow, and we pull over to the side to let past an oversized pickup coming the other way, driven by a tanned and shirtless Cajun youth, who amiably salutes us with his can of beer. The rear of his cab is fitted with a gun rack loaded with rifles; an aluminum pirogue—an alligator-shaped, shallow-draft swamp craft —is pushed onto the truck bed behind.

He's not alone. The shoulder of the levee is dotted with similar trucks, whose occupants have already slid their pirogues down its grassy side and slipped off into the Atchafalaya. Although not all Cajuns these days are raised in intimate familiarity with the wetlands, almost all are at least related to someone who is, and reaping the bounty of this place is still an integral part of their everyday life.

This is a land, after all, where even the stagnant, oil-slicked water of a roadside drainage canal can yield enough crawfish for supper. Catfish are easy to catch in the bayous. The brackish channels that crisscross the marshland by the Gulf shore can be dredged for oysters. As many crabs as you care to take can be trapped with a simple folding net. And wild game abounds, as the endless procession of roadkill on Louisiana's highways depressingly testifies: rabbit, squirrel, raccoon, opossum, deer, alligator, armadillo. In season, the wetlands are flush with ducks and geese, quail, woodcock, pheasant, and snipe.

The only string attached to this bounty is that none of it is guaranteed. For this is both a vulnerable and an injured land. It is most palpably vulnerable to weather, especially the hurricanes that sweep across it with terrifying violence and destruction, reshaping the very terrain. Cajuns tend to date their history in terms of hurricanes, rather than in terms of presidents or world events. Hurricanes have far more effect on their lives.

However, subtler natural fluctuations make themselves felt, too. One year there are more crawfish than anyone knows what to do with; the next year there are hardly enough to seem fair. The same flood tides that occasionally sweep seawater into the marshes, giving the oysters a succulent saltiness, also bring the oyster drill and the schools of drumfish that can wipe out an oyster reef overnight.

Cajuns have traditionally dealt with such uncertainties by hedging their bets. Jacks-of-all-trades, they trapped a little, oystered a little, and shrimped a little, and kept the larder full in the meantime with judicious use of the crawfish net and crab trap. They learned to make the most of anything the land had to offer, boasting that they would eat whatever failed to eat them first, and they have the recipes—braised bear steak, alligator sauce piquante—to prove it. When worst came to worst, they went without.

This self-sufficient aspect of the Cajun cook is reminiscent of pioneer cooking of the last century, but with one notable difference: the Cajuns are still cooking this way. Unlike most settler families, who wanted as much as possible to cook the way they had back East—and did so again as soon as they could—the Cajuns absorbed their new landscape into their cuisine with a remarkably unprejudiced appetite.

In this regard, Cajuns represent something unique, a people still living with a foot on either side of the boundary that runs between wilderness and civilization—the mythical line our forefathers drew to separate the savages from themselves. But Cajuns wove themselves into oneness with the land they settled, even while holding claim to an undisputed settler heritage . . . at once hunters and gatherers *and* farmers and tradesmen.

Cajuns, then, are a kind of an inverse Gypsy, another people who pass through our world as through a dream, taking what they want—or can—without being touched by it in any deep place. Unlike the Gypsies, however, Cajuns have their country . . . and it is we—up until now—who have passed by them.

This fact—that Cajuns dwell at the very edge of things—means that we see them as near-magical beings—the way we do Gypsies or, for that matter, Indians. Certainly, Cajuns are able to make us view their cooking as though under an enchantment. Because, when it comes right down to it, that cooking is nothing much. It has none of the suave complexity of flavor and technique displayed by Creole cuisine, its sophisticated city cousin. Cajun dishes depend on the quantity and quality of their ingredients, since they are made in the simplest of ways . . . and by cooks who, while they are often subtle and skilled, have an almost fatal weakness for every culinary shortcut they find glittering on the grocery shelf.

But when the spell is there, none of this matters. Cajuns themselves are the real flavor of Cajun cooking. They are one of the most enthusiastic groups of eaters we have left in this country, and they—men and women both—cook with a zest and passion that leaves the rest of us looking on in admiration and with no little amount of longing.

Most of all, we envy the way they can slip through the fragrant and mysterious jungle that is their cooking, where among the dense thickets of fragrant herbs wild things are caught and cooked in smoking cauldrons of dark-brown roux. It is a place that has taught them to take nothing for granted, and they are always seeing familiar things freshly anew. A gumbo made one way today will not be made that way tomorrow, because a neighbor has come by with a basket of crabs, or because there is some *chaurice* to use or a chicken to kill, or simply because the cook is practicing an entirely different spell.

This magic place is slowly shrinking. The land has been injured by man's meddling—directly, through pollution and flood control, and indirectly, through overfishing and the introduction of foreign flora and fauna which have upset delicate balances in the wetlands' fragile ecology. Cajuns are part perpetrator and part victim in this, but the net result has made the survival of their culture more questionable . . . if only because with each year civilization swallows up that much more of it, even as we are learning to admire the Cajun's way of life.

Pat's, the restaurant in Henderson that we've been driving to, illustrates some of the ambiguity of the Cajun encounter with modernity. Out in the middle of nowhere, it is no casual fish-fry place but huge, well-appointed, and frigidly air-conditioned. Even so, its menu swims with Cajun dishes—those with crawfish alone are enough to boggle the mind: crawfish gumbo, crawfish bisque, crawfish *étouffée*, crawfish au gratin, fried crawfish, boiled crawfish, crawfish pie . . . variations that are also played to the tune of shrimp and oyster. I take a taster's platter with a little of everything and settle back with a cold beer to watch the sun set down behind the Atchafalaya. The bayou that has run beside us along the levee flows right outside the picture window. Down below, some kids are hauling a catfish—a big fat one—out of it to join the others that already lie on the deck.

BOSTON, 1986

First You Make
a Roux . . .

Shrimps are much eaten here [in New Orleans]; also a dish called gumbo. This last is made of every eatable substance, and especially of those shrimps which can be caught at any time.   —*The American Pioneer* (1805)

"Gumbo, *j'aime le mieux,*" Mr. Vinet continued. "For a good gumbo, you have to cook your food for at least four hours. First you start with a roux . . ."
                    —JOAN NATHAN, *An American Folklife Cookbook*

Gumbo is the queen of Cajun cuisine, and the heart of gumbo is roux. This is a very touching and revealing thing. It means that the dearest thing to a Cajun cook—more than any other thing, more than crawfish or blue crab or oysters or shrimp or even rice—is a simple amalgam of flour and fat. The two are gently cooked until the raw taste of the flour is gone and the starch is broken down enough to absorb liquid without lumping. It is the first—and easiest—lesson in French sauce making.

Of course, there are some differences. The French make their roux most often with butter and sometimes with the flavorful fat skimmed out of a marmite. The Cajuns prefer lard for flavor or—more recently—vegetable oil for economy. They also claim the French don't cook roux the way *they* do, to a burnished mahogany . . . but, of course, long, careful cooking has always been the way to make a good brown sauce.

What the French don't do, however, is *care* as much about their roux as Cajuns do. So few French cooks possess any of the sense that Cajuns have of what a roux can be made to do, or of its fine gradations of texture, odor, and color, running from creamy pale to the smoky-flavored near-coal-black (but not burned) roux that Paul Prudhomme claims is essential to perfect gumbo.

Even so—a whole cuisine based on brown sauce! A cuisine in miniature maybe, but still a cuisine. It's as if a small group of poor English settlers had been abandoned somewhere in the Antipodes with nothing of their shared literature but a few remembered ballads. Their culture would then grow out of this handful of songs, incantations that—at first—spoke only of their origins among all the new, exotic experiences that would now be called home.

Then, gradually, each would be lovingly disassembled, like a treasured old hunting piece, and every part, as necessary, forged anew— the words carefully reforged, realigned, and once again made true. The original meaning would eventually be rubbed transparent, so that its possessors could use the poem as the familiar verbal frame to capture an entirely different life. So it is with Cajuns and roux. It is something more than a recipe they know by heart—it has become the culinary locution by which they apprehend their world.

"Cajun" is a corruption of "Acadian," the name for the French people who inhabited Canada's Maritime Provinces before the British forcibly evicted them in 1771. Their eventual gathering in the bayous of southern Louisiana happened over a wide stretch of time and was the last stop on what for many was a long and desperate odyssey. A substantial number were shipped to the French sugar and slave colony of Saint-Domingue, where they were housed in slave quarters and put to work building fortifications from which the French overseers would futilely resist the slave rebellion that would soon transform Saint-Domingue into the republic of Haiti.

Very likely, it was there that Cajuns acquired their taste for *gumbo* (from the Bantu *achinggûmbo*, meaning okra, but also [perhaps because of okra's mucilaginous qualities] a mélange or stew of greens) and possibly also for the fiery pepper pod, since that has always been a favored component of West Indies black cooking. (The famous tabasco pepper that launched a Louisiana industry had its origins much later in a gift to Edmund McIlhenny in 1848 from a friend who brought some pepper seeds back with him from the Mexican War. McIlhenny did not raise them commercially for another twenty years.)

However, the swamps and marshes of southern Louisiana certainly contributed the bounty of seafood that gumbo conjures in the mind— the crawfish, crabs, oysters, turtles. And the local Choctaw Indians provided *gumbo filé*, dried and powdered sassafras leaf, an alternative thickening agent that gives gumbo its own special texture. Some Cajun cooks use *gumbo filé* in preference to okra; others choose it when okra is out of season or unavailable; still others add them both.

There were, of course, black slaves in Louisiana, too, but they did not have the immediate influence on Cajun cooking that they had on the cuisine of the wealthier Creoles, who could afford to own them. Indeed, plantation owners were worried about the effect the Cajuns might have on their slaves and did their best to restrict contact between the two. As Frederick Law Olmsted explained in 1861 in *A Journey in the Seaboard Slave States*:

> Because . . . the slaves seeing them living in apparent comfort, without much property and without steady labor, could not help thinking it was not necessary for men to work so hard as they themselves were obliged to; that if they were free they would not need to work.

Still, despite the fact that plantation owners lost no opportunity to denigrate their new neighbors, Olmsted found that this had no effect on the opinions of their slaves, who respected the Cajuns as living as they themselves wished to—poor, perhaps, but independent and self-sufficient.

This, too, is part of the meaning of the central presence of roux in Cajun cooking: that Cajun cooking is poor cooking. Until very recently, the most prized possession of a Cajun cook was her cast-iron gumbo pot, often handed down from mother to daughter. If there was—as was often the case—more than one daughter, the situation was more complicated. As is explained in *Gumbo Ya Ya*, a collection of Louisiana folkways:

> Before a new one could be used it must be "broken in." First the pot was washed thoroughly, then red brick-dust rubbed in. After another washing, the inside was smeared thickly with pork fat and the pot placed on the fire to "season." Then the pot was ready for the cooking of the red beans and the black-eyed peas. These were always cooked with a thick slice of ham or salt pork.

All Cajun cuisine has evolved from this pot, from the simple crawfish boils and the multiplicity of gumbos to all the jambalayas and bisques and *étouffées*. Cajuns call this "pot cooking," a way not only to feed a lot of people for a little money but feed them well. Cajun cuisine is a paradox, for the Cajuns love to eat and are prodigally generous with what is bountiful—but are just as parsimonious with what is not. A

Cajun recipe for crawfish bisque thinks nothing of starting off with a call for "twenty pounds of live crawfish" and then in the next breath asking for six tablespoons of margarine. And of the thirteen ingredients in the recipe, only four might not be supplied by the bayou or family garden: salt, flour, pepper, and that oleo.

It is the roux that pulls these dishes together, that gives them coherence and grace. Especially gumbo, because gumbo contains within itelf the entire history of the Cajun diaspora. The roux itself grounds that dish to the France from which the Cajuns originally came. Then, its making was still *au courant*; the first written documentation of its use is that of La Varenne in 1750. To this is added the portion of salt pork or *tasso*, *andouille*, or *chaurice*—the cured pork products so beloved of French Canadiens. Next the okra and hot peppers from Saint-Domingue are stirred in, and then, finally, from this new, best home, *la bonne Louisiane*, the generous portions of seafood and fresh pot greens and aromatics—the celery, garlic, bell pepper, green onions. No wonder that the pot is left to simmer and remember for a good long time.

So for a Cajun roux making is, before anything else, an initiation. He or she establishes a right to cook Cajun by persuasive mastery of it, not only in making it, but in being able to defend it, since with Cajun, as with all orally transmitted cuisines, method is defined by a tension between received tradition and the experience of each individual cook.

Take a Cajun cook and put him or her someplace devoid of familiar things—your kitchen, say—and out of a roux and what was found in your cupboard, your refrigerator, a gumbo would be started. Because, you see, you can make a gumbo out of almost anything. And to make a gumbo, first you make a roux . . .

CAJUN ROUX

Cajuns agree to disagree about almost every element of roux making right to whether to stir it with a whisk or a wooden spoon. Some make it on the stove, some in the oven, and some (hélas) in the microwave. Finally, some prefer equal amounts of fat and flour and others vary those proportions slightly one way or the other. Lard is the traditional fat of choice and, to the most finicky Cajun tongues, still the best-flavored one, although vegetable oil—specifically Wesson oil—is now favored for reasons of economy. Chicken or duck fat, or beef suet, is also a good choice. But because the roux should be cooked to a rich brown, butter cannot be used for a Cajun roux unless it is clarified first, to prevent the possibility of its scorching.

1 cup fat
1 cup all-purpose flour

Heat the fat in a heavy cooking pot or a large cast-iron skillet. When the fat is hot, add the flour all at once, stirring or whisking quickly to combine it with the fat, smoothing out any persistent lumps with the back of a wooden spoon. Lower the flame and cook, stirring or whisking constantly. The roux will bubble and cast off a fine white foam and, after about 15 minutes, begin to caramelize. It takes about 45 minutes to reach a rich butterscotch color and almost an hour to turn deep mahogany—and become true Cajun roux.

It's important not to hurry the process and to be careful that the stirring or whisking turns over the entire mixture. If any small black flecks appear, the roux is ruined. That batch must be discarded and the process repeated with new ingredients. (If not, the roux, even if the burned bits are removed, will retain a bitter, scorched taste.)

When the roux has the desired color, the cooking can be stopped by adding chopped vegetables—a familiar step in gumbo making. If, however, a large amount of roux is being made, some to be reserved for other use, the pan should be removed from the stove and the roux continuously stirred until it begins to cool. Transferred to a container, it can be refrigerated for a week or frozen for up to half a year.

When stirring and handling the roux, remember that it is quite hot —far hotter than boiling water. If splattered, it can stick tenaciously and cause serious burns. Always use a slightly larger pan than necessary to protect against this happening.

The fat will separate out of a refrigerated roux. Stir it briefly to re-combine the ingredients before spooning it out. (Frozen roux can be scooped directly into a lightly greased cooking pot.)

Any liquid to be combined with a dark roux must be at least at room temperature (never cold) or the roux will separate. If it does, whisk it until it recombines.

In any of the recipes in this book that call for it, feel free to adapt the roux, reducing the amount to lessen the calories or substituting olive oil instead of plain vegetable oil for the lard. But those without the patience to make a real roux should experiment with *filé* powder or okra rather than with shortcuts. Only Cajun cooks have earned the right to abuse their patrimony with instant roux out of a microwave.

BOSTON, 1986

CREOLE/CAJUN MAIL-ORDER SOURCES

One of the great ironies of American cuisine is that Cajun cooking, which remains even today determinedly self-sufficient, has spawned such an enormous amount of meretricious seasoning mixes, barbecue sauces, and other such nonsense. The only ingredient *essential* to Cajun cooking which are not available in local supermarkets, apart possibly from *gumbo filé*, is an abundance of extremely fresh, extremely cheap —or better still, free—seafood, a problem no mail-order source is likely to remedy.

This isn't to say, however, that it's not fun to occasionally turn out a batch of red beans and rice with Camellia-brand red beans and Konriko rice, or to have some real *andouille* to toss into your gumbo. For the groceries, turn to The Louisiana General Store (620 Decatur Street, New Orleans, LA 70130, 800–237–4841). They carry a wide assortment of such ingredients as *filé* powder, crab boil, Creole mustard, and a great bunch of Louisiana hot sauces—plus plenty of Louisiana cookbooks and some Cajun and zydeco music to help you stir that roux.

For the meat, you can turn to K-Paul's Louisiana Mail Order (501 Elysian Fields, P.O. Box 770034, New Orleans, LA 70177–0034 • 800–4KPAULS) for *andouille* and *tasso* or to Comeaux's Grocery (1000 Lamar St., Lafayette, LA 70501 • 800 737 2666) for *andouille, tasso,* and three kinds of *boudin.* Comeaux's prices are quite reasonable; their *boudin*—especially—is good.

Out of the Gumbo Pot

Gumbos are New Orleans specialties, and there's a curious lack of uniformity about the ingredients which distinguish the various styles.

—Chicago Daily News (1947)

Black Creole cooks may have invented the gumbo pot, but Cajun cuisine evolved out of it. Consequently, even more than in Creole cooking, Cajun dishes are all bound together in a tissue of tight-knit family connections. It's a rare Cajun dish that doesn't exhibit some shared trait or other that immediately links it to another family member—as Cajun *boudin blanc*, for example, is clear kin to dirty rice, and oyster dressing to bread pudding. Even as regional cuisines go, Cajun cooking can be enclosed within a pretty small compass.

Still, the fact that gumbo is kissing cousin to many other Cajun dishes does not mean that it is made with any kind of monotonous uniformity. Cajuns are too independent-minded to conform to culinary rules, even ones they themselves insist are inviolable. As William Faulkner Rushton observed in *The Cajuns* of one such cook:

> When Ruth Fontenot sets out to cook a gumbo, all the pots and pans and spices in her kitchen sit up and take notice. None is certain which one or ones will be used this time around, for both the recipe and the size of the serving will vary from day to day, depending on Ruth's mood and assessment of the tastes of her dinner guests.

It's no insult to gumbo to adapt it to new circumstances; this is what the dish is all about. The recipes that follow illustrate both these points: the different ways that Cajuns imagine the dish and the various uses it can be put to when it is made far from home . . . that is, away from both an endless supply of inexpensive seafood and the boundless Cajun appetite for salt-cured meats. These are not, then, strictly as-made-in-bayou-country versions; anyone interested in such recipes would be well advised to turn to *The Picayune's Creole Cook Book* (see pages 270–74) or Richard and Rima Collin's modernized adaptations in *The New Orleans Cookbook*.

Even when improvising a gumbo, however, there are certain things to keep in mind. For instance, most Cajun gumbos are thickened, if not by a roux, at least by okra or *filé* powder, and almost always include that trinity of Cajun flavorings: bell pepper, green onion (scallion), and celery. Usually, both black and red pepper (cayenne) are used as seasoning. Tomatoes and garlic are also familiar regulars, as is plenty of chopped parsley. Indeed, fresh herbs are an important presence in gumbo—one difficult to represent in a recipe, since Cajun cooks simply use freely what they have at hand. When this is written out in a long list of quarter and half teaspoons, it looks ridiculously fussy and formulaic.

A roux of flour and fat, bell pepper, scallion, parsley, celery, garlic . . . it is these simple things, not chopped ham or two or three different kinds of seafood, that are most characteristic of contemporary Cajun gumbos—at least the ones not made from cookbooks. The point cannot be made too often (although these pages may come close to doing so) that the truly authentic gumbo is the one made simply from a cabbage and the leftover carcass of last night's roast duck, if that is what happens to be at hand, rather than the one assembled at the supermarket from a lengthy shopping list.

CHICKEN-ANDOUILLE GUMBO
(SERVES 6)

Andouille *is a Cajun cured-pork sausage flavored with vinegar and garlic and seasoned with hot pepper. This can be ordered from several Louisiana mail-order sources (see page 219), or garlic sausage or kielbasa may be substituted, adding a fresh hot pepper (seeded and diced) to the ingredients (stir it into the gumbo at the same time as the bell pepper).*

1 large fryer, cut into pieces
Salt, black pepper, and cayenne
½ cup lard or chicken fat
½ cup all-purpose flour
4 medium onions, chopped

1 green pepper, seeded and chopped
2 stalks of celery, minced (including leaf)
1 pound *andouille*, sliced thin
1 bunch (6 to 8) scallions, minced
2 or 3 cloves garlic, minced
Several sprigs fresh parsley
1 sprig fresh tarragon (optional)
1 tablespoon *filé* powder
Hot boiled rice

Season the chicken with salt and pepper. Heat the fat in a heavy pot and sauté the chicken until the skin is crisp and begins to brown. Remove the chicken and set on paper toweling. Make a roux with the flour and the fat remaining in the pot (see pages 217–18). When the roux is nicely brown, add the chopped onion, green pepper, and celery. Cover and simmer until the onions are translucent, stirring occasionally. Then add the chicken pieces and the sliced *andouille*. Cover and simmer 15 minutes, stirring occasionally. Meanwhile, bring 4 cups of water to a simmer in a kettle.

Pour the steaming water into the pot and stir in the scallions, garlic, parsley, and (if used) tarragon. Turn up the heat and bring the mixture almost to a boil. When the pot "shimmers," turn the heat down low and cook the gumbo for about 1½ hours, or until the chicken is tender enough to slip from the bone. As you prefer, either remove the pieces, debone them, and return the meat to the pot, or serve the pieces entire. Before serving, sprinkle the *filé* powder over the surface of the gumbo and gently stir in. Remove from the heat and let rest 5 minutes. Then ladle into deep soup bowls over hot boiled rice.

LENTEN SHRIMP & EGG GUMBO
(SERVES 4 TO 6)

Since this gumbo is a Lenten specialty, hard-boiled eggs are used instead of the more usual smoked sausage or cooked ham. The subtle flavor combination of egg and shrimp makes a delicately delicious gumbo, as is also the case when crabmeat is used instead of shrimp (and added at the same point in the recipe).

⅓ cup lard or cooking oil
⅓ cup all-purpose flour
3 medium onions
1 green pepper, seeded and chopped

2 or 3 celery stalks, minced (save leaves)
1 pound raw, unpeeled medium or large shrimp
6 sprigs parsley, minced (save stems)
2 bay leaves
Salt, black pepper, and cayenne
3 cloves garlic, minced
4 to 6 hard-boiled eggs
Hot boiled rice

Heat oil or lard in a heavy iron cooking pot and sprinkle in flour. Stir to make a dark brown roux (see pages 217–18). Finely chop 2 of the onions and cut the third one into quarters. Add the chopped onion, green pepper, and celery to the finished roux. Cook, stirring occasionally, until vegetables are soft. Meanwhile, peel the shrimp. Place the shells on a square of cheesecloth with the celery leaves, parsley stems, quartered onion, and bay leaves. Tie securely into a bundle. Bring to a boil and simmer 20 minutes. Discard the cheesecloth and its contents and slowly whisk the shrimp stock into the roux. Season to taste with salt and both peppers. Add shrimp, garlic, and minced parsley and simmer 5 minutes.

Peel the hard-boiled eggs. Cut these in quarters and add to the gumbo. Taste for seasoning, then cover and let sit for 5 minutes. Ladle into individual bowls over hot rice, distributing the eggs fairly. The egg should be broken into the gumbo as it is eaten.

BEEF-RIB & OKRA GUMBO
(SERVES 6)

This recipe is an example of the non-roux approach to gumbo making. Here, okra is used as a thickener. My problem with okra is not so much its ropiness as its aggressive blandness. But a generous amount of seasoning—including plenty of cayenne pepper—can bring it to life.

1 pound okra
¼ cup olive oil
3 pounds beef short ribs
3 medium onions, chopped
2 medium red bell peppers, seeded and chopped
3 cloves garlic, minced
1 cup crushed tomatoes
Salt, black pepper, and cayenne
1 bunch (6 to 8) scallions

Several sprigs parsley, minced
Hot boiled rice

Stem the okra pods and cut them into ½-inch pieces. Heat the oil in a heavy oven pot. Sear the ribs, 2 or 3 at a time, in the hot oil until brown on all sides. Add the onion, red pepper, garlic, crushed tomatoes, and okra pieces. Season to taste with salt, pepper, and cayenne. Stir well and reduce heat to a simmer. Cover and cook for 2 hours, stirring occasionally and adding water only if needed to keep the mixture moist. (If the flame is kept low enough, the ingredients should produce enough liquid for the gumbo.)

When the meat is fork tender, remove it and cut it into bite-size pieces, discarding the bones and any blocks of fat. Return the meat to the pot, add the scallions and parsley, and simmer for another 15 minutes. Serve in deep bowls over hot boiled rice.

BOSTON, 1986

Crawfish *Etouffée . . .*
and Others

As native Louisianan Glen Pitre points out in *The Crawfish Book*, the crawfish is indigenous to every state in the Union except Alaska and Hawaii. Where there is mud there are likely to be mudbugs, whether the place be a pond, a drainage ditch, or a rain-wet field of corn or sugarcane. Euell Gibbons boasted that he once caught five hundred of them one afternoon in a lake within the city limits of Seattle. In other words, when the crawfish was considered prime eating all across the country—it was *found* all across the country.

> From the bottomlands of Kentucky to the hills of Arkansas to the plains of Kansas, many pioneers undoubtedly forged the America we know today with the muscle and sinew that came from eating crawdads. After all, wasn't it on account of mudbugs that Nebraskans were once called "bug eaters"? Crawfish, which are numerous in times of flood, no doubt often saved from starvation those who'd watched their crops and livestock wash away . . .
>
> They also teased the palates of the wealthy. Sold in markets of Atlantic seaboard cities at least by 1817, by the late 1800s crawfish were enough in demand in New York that dealers extended the season by importing them first from the Potomac River, then from Lake Michigan, and finally the St. Lawrence River, chasing spring as it moved north.

Today, outside the South, as that appetite has all but vanished, so—to all intents and purposes—has the crawfish. Consequently, to notice that crawfish are plentiful and cheap in Cajun country is, paradoxically, almost to get the cart before the horse. Even if we live next to a stream or drainage ditch that is crawling with them, there are good reasons why we are oblivious of their presence. There currently exists no moral imperative urging us to go out and catch them—they endanger nobody's crops, the effort required to catch them eats up time that we can put to better use—or, truth to tell, any gastronomic imperative, either. Crawfish need to be both cheap (or free) and masterfully prepared to be worth eating. Otherwise, they are like lobster without its peerless briny tang—really, without much taste at all . . . which is why Cajuns are so fond of preparing them in so many different, highly seasoned ways.

Hovering somewhere here is a culinary law: a regional cuisine sustains itself out of necessity, but necessity, unless truly dire, is not all deprivation. It has its rewards—rewards that are far from secret but, even so, not all that easy for others to appropriate. It is easy enough, if you have the money, to order a crate of crawfish delivered via Federal Express; it is something again to get anything out of them once they arrive. Crawfish is famously *the* Cajun food, not because they trap and cook them in such casual quantity, but because, doing so for generations, they have come to know them in a way we never can.

With this in mind, consider the following short passage from Christopher Hallowell's *People of the Bayou* and you'll see why unthinking attempts to translate Cajun cuisine outside its native haunts are doomed to fail.

> Like those of many Cajun women, her eyes beamed while her tongue wagged on the subject of cooking. "Now, you go to the best restaurant about here and you won't find *étouffée* that's worth half the money they charge for it. That's 'cause they don't use the fat. They say it's too oily, but those people aren't real crawfish lovers. If you don't like the fat, you don't really like crawfish."

Crawfish *étouffée*, a delicacy many consider the best crawfish dish of them all, is not difficult to make. And at first glance, it seems modest in its requirements—usually only a pound or two of tail meat and a cup of the fat. Crawfish fat is not really fat at all but the greenish, viscous material that is the creature's liver and pancreas—what lobster eaters fondly know as tomally, that greenish, curdy stuff that tastes of essence of mud flat distilled into a custard.

In Louisiana, at crawfish feasts, they suck on crawfish heads to draw out the stuff—they call it crawfish fat (same taste, too, only more murky than briny). If the crawfish is the essence of Cajun cooking, crawfish fat, the essence of crawfish, is its *quintessence*. The only thing is, to get that cup of crawfish fat you need ten pounds of crawfish.

You also need them alive and kicking, because the "fat" is fluid only when taken from a living crawfish; cooked, it has more the texture of (sea-green) poached egg white. As Hallowell describes the process, you wrench the tail from the thorax and scoop the precious globules into a waiting bowl, all the while evading the thrashing creature's pincers. This is a fierce business—and even if you had the stomach for it, you probably wouldn't trust a cookbook to direct you in doing it. Consequently, recipes for the dish are almost always bowdlerized—removing all *crise de conscience*, along with what makes that dish truly great.

Thus humbled, what the non-Cajun cook must do is put unrealistic expectations to one side and accept the smaller but realizable rewards that come of disentangling the *étouffée* from the crawfish. Traditionally, an *étouffée*—often helpfully spelled "A-2-fay" on Cajun menus—was a way of braising meat or seafood—crab, shrimp, chicken, rabbit, even smoked duck—in a roux-thickened gumbo of familiar flavorings, but without the liquid. In fact, if you prepare the chicken and *andouille* gumbo as given on page 221 but omit the water (and *filé* powder), you have a very good chicken-*andouille étouffée*. (The beef-rib and okra dish on page 223, although I learned it as a gumbo, probably *is* an *étouffée*.)

In the same way, if you—again—omit the water (and the *filé*) from that same gumbo and add a (1 pound) can of whole tomatoes and a (1 pound) can of Ro-Tel stewed tomatoes (but not the can liquid), maybe a few lemon slices, and certainly a bit more hot pepper, you have a Cajun chicken-*andouille* sauce piquante. Sauce piquante was originally used to braise and tenderize game (armadillo, turtle, squirrel, 'gator, etc.), since the spicy sauce is a good match for the gamy taste. But Cajuns like the general effect of sauce piquante, and it has crept into more general use, especially in dishes using chicken.

Recently, Cajun *étouffée* recipes have been omitting the roux for convenience's sake, and so, apart from the fact that they are less spicily flavored and served *on* rice and not made *with* it, they very much resemble Cajun jambalayas. Because of the French word *jambon*, meaning ham, many cooks have come to believe that a jambalaya must contain ham. But as Karen Hess convincingly argues in *The Carolina Rice Kitchen*, the word derives from the Provençal *jambalaia*, a ragoût of rice and chicken. The defining characteristic of the dish is the use of rice instead of roux to thicken the stew, but you will recognize in the seasonings and flavorings the familiar lineaments of the Cajun gumbo pot.

CRABMEAT *ETOUFFÉE*
(SERVES 4)

½ stick (2 ounces) unsalted butter
2 tablespoons flour
1 large onion, chopped
2 stalks celery, minced (including leaf)
1 red bell pepper, seeded and cut fine
1 bunch (6 to 8) scallions, minced (including some green)
1 clove garlic, minced
1 pound fresh lump crab meat
Tabasco sauce
Salt and black pepper
Several sprigs parsley, minced
Hot boiled rice

Melt the butter in a large, heavy pot over medium heat. Add the flour and, stirring gently, cook for 15 minutes, to make a lightly colored roux. Stir in the onion and sauté until translucent, about 5 minutes. Then add the celery, red pepper, scallions, and garlic, cooking these until soft. Add the crabmeat and stir to distribute. Pour in 1 cup of water and, stirring and tasting, season with Tabasco sauce, salt, and black pepper. Finally, stir in the parsley, reduce the heat, and simmer for 10 minutes. Serve at once over hot rice.

CHICKEN JAMBALAYA
(SERVES 6)

Tasso is spicy-flavored cured pork, available, as is Creole smoked sausage, from various Louisiana suppliers (see page 219). Otherwise, substitute a spicy cured ham for the one and a cured smoked sausage like kielbasa for the other. One or two cups of canned crushed tomatoes are a tasty addition to this dish.

2 tablespoons lard or chicken fat
1 large frying chicken, cut into pieces
¼ pound diced *tasso* (or ham)
½ pound Creole smoked sausage (or other smoked sausage), sliced
3 medium onions, chopped
2 cloves garlic, minced
1 bunch (6 to 8) scallions, minced (including green)
3 celery stalks, minced (including leaf)

1 green bell pepper, chopped
Several sprigs parsley, minced
1½ cups uncooked rice
½ teaspoon dried oregano
1 teaspoon fresh (or ¼ teaspoon dried) thyme
Tabasco
Salt and black pepper

In a large, heavy pot, melt the fat over medium heat. Brown the chicken pieces in batches, turning them often so they do not stick. Remove the chicken and reserve. Add the *tasso* (or ham) and smoked Creole sausage (or other smoked sausage), and onions. Sauté, stirring constantly, until the onion is soft. Then stir in the garlic, scallions, celery, green bell pepper, and parsley. When this is well mixed, pour in the rice, and stir this mixture for a few moments, giving the rice time to absorb some of the fat and flavoring. Finally, add 1½ cups of water, return the chicken pieces, and stir in the oregano and thyme, seasoning to taste with Tabasco sauce, salt, and black pepper. Bring the mixture just to a simmer, cover, and turn the heat very low. Let simmer for 30 minutes, stirring occasionally. Then uncover the pot, raise the heat slightly, and, stirring gently, cook another ten minutes to dry out the rice. Serve at once.

PORK AND BURNT-SUGAR JAMBALAYA
(SERVES 6)

This recipe is adapted from one given by Mrs. Mordello Hebert in the spiral-bound Louisiana Lagniappe.

2 tablespoons lard or vegetable oil
2 teaspoons sugar
3 pounds meaty pork ribs
1 medium onion, chopped
1 green bell pepper, chopped
1 clove garlic, minced
1 cup uncooked rice
Salt, black pepper, and cayenne
1 bunch (6 to 8) scallions, chopped
Several sprigs parsley, chopped

Heat the lard or oil in a large, heavy pot. When the oil is hot, sprinkle in the sugar and brown it, stirring the while. Cut the pork ribs into pieces and carefully put these into the hot oil. Sauté these, turning them often, until they are brown on all sides. Stir in the onion, green pepper, and garlic, and cook these until the onion is translucent.

Add the rice and stir well, letting it absorb some of the oil and juices in the pot. Then pour in 3 cups of water and bring it to a faint simmer. Season with salt, black pepper, and cayenne. Cover and let cook over a low flame until the rice is done, about 15 minutes. Stir in the chopped scallion and parsley, and cook another 10 minutes over the same low heat. Adjust seasoning, if necessary, and serve at once.

BOSTON, 1986

La Cuisine Créole

The secret lies in this: She does not stint her table—trust a good Creole mother for that, for the well-supplied table is an ancient, traditional heritage of her race, from which she will not depart—but she manages most carefully, buying her supplies of sugar and molasses and rice, grits and flour when these are "down in the market"; putting up her dainty jellies, marmalades and domestic wines when fruits are "going begging," as the term runs, because the market is so overstocked. . . . As the months wane, and a new season dawns, the good Creole housekeeper, even of unlimited means, far from trusting entirely to the servants to do the marketing, makes it her duty to take a leisurely stroll through the French Market . . . and she takes her own mental notes, and knows just what to order when her cook comes for the daily interview. Again, many of the most famous housekeepers do their own marketing entirely . . . followed by some faithful old domestic who may still adhere to the fortunes of the family.

—*The Picayune's Creole Cook Book* (1901)

A prescription for a grand cuisine: Take a vigorous people, give them an empire, let them get accustomed to the spoils, and then take it all away again . . . bit by bit. Palates accustomed to good things will fight—hard, then harder still—to keep them, or to find replacements. Luxuries now rationed will become distilled. The ultimate cuisine may not be as luxurious as it was in its "glory," but it will be more inspired, more various, and more complexly realized. Roman cooking was lavish; Italian cooking is great.

Creole cuisine—or, more strictly speaking, New Orleans Creole cuisine, as distinguished from the various Creole cuisines of the Caribbean—is just such a case. For a time the dominant culture in a wealthy and prosperous area, it freely appropriated culinary elements from the many peoples that it had absorbed . . . only to find, during its decline and fall, that these things had become essential to its own sense of identity. And, despite the Spanish, English, Italian, and, especially, African influences, this was a cuisine that resolutely spoke French, called its dishes by French names, and, most important, cooked them with a regard to Gallic concerns and prejudices.

The Creoles, of course, are not the only French in Louisiana; the Acadians—the Cajuns—are there, too. Creole and Cajun cooking have much in common, which is not surprising. What is interesting is the subtle but distinct manner in which they stand apart. The common explanation for this difference is that the Creoles were wealthier than the Cajuns, more cultured, more attuned to culinary finesse.

This is so and also not so. The Creoles, many of them, struggled to keep up an appearance of gentility that their means were increasingly unable to support, while the Cajuns, though long poor in coin, had the advantage of the naturally abundant culinary resources of the Louisiana bayous. If you discount the cooking of the true Creole elite and the elaborate preparations of Creole restaurants and consider only *la cuisine Créole à l'usage des petits ménages*, you'll find the Cajun cook as artful in the kitchen as any of her Creole sisters.

What, then, is the difference? Well, there is more to a cuisine than the taste of its dishes: the imagination has its hunger, too. People who eat the same food may still conceive it in very disparate contexts and taste it accordingly. The Creoles themselves, explaining their cuisine, claim for it those strange (to us) French bedfellows, sensuality and economy, a combination equally characteristic of Cajun cooking. But while the Cajuns eat and smack their lips and think themselves fine fellows for making a feast out of what the servants of the plantation house up the road toss to the pigs, Creoles taste and then sigh for a past when such meals were an act of virtue as much as of necessity. The Creole cook must create the illusion that while things change, nothing has changed; for the Cajun, it is enough that today is today, and today is good.

In short, the Cajun culinary world is one drenched in bright Louisiana sunlight, boisterous, noisy, and, despite its French accent, extraordinarily American; Creole culture, while it lasted, was self-consciously crepuscular—eternally waning, nostalgically clinging to an image of itself as not only forever French but remaining, in some mystical if vestigial way, part of France itself.

There was a time when these characterizations could be reversed. Then it was the Acadians who clung to their memories of Cape Breton and to their own sense of being an exiled people, while the Creoles prospered famously. Although the colony of *la Nouvelle Orléans*—founded in 1718 in what has been described as "a small, verminous swamp"—got off to a rough start, by 1743 the entourage of the Marquis de Vaudreuil-Cavagnal, French governor of New Orleans, was able to pattern its existence after the court of Versailles, even to importing its own chefs from France.

Control of the territory passed temporarily into Spanish hands in 1762 and later, permanently, into American ones (purchased in 1803, Louisiana became a state in 1812), but the territory continued to prosper and to welcome French immigrants. Planters fleeing the slave revolts of Saint-Domingue, aristocracy fleeing the Revolution in France . . . the French Creoles continued to grow and flourish until, by 1860, New Orleans had become the fourth-largest city in the United States, the second-largest port, and a powerful economic center.

The Cajuns escaped the great engine of American assimilation until quite recently because of their poverty and relative inaccessibility; the Creoles encountered it early and forcefully. The importance of New Orleans to post–Civil War America—economically, militarily, strategically—meant that it would become an increasingly Anglicized city, with outsiders taking control of its financial and political reins. By the end of the century, the French Creoles found themselves becoming what their Anglo neighbors mockingly called a "red-beans-and-rice aristocracy"—too poor to paint and too proud to whitewash.

Gentility in reduced circumstances, regret and nostalgia, the nursed sense of chances lost—this is the resentment of all colonials, abandoned by *histoire* and *patrie*. For the French Creoles, history had ground to a halt. Their "France" became the France that they could least afford to keep up connections with, which is why, in New Orleans, France remains forever in *la Belle Epoque*.

For a time at least, their black Creole servants abetted in this withdrawal, for they, too, found themselves strangers in a strange land. Although the circumstances that caused this were almost diametrically different, the result was much the same—both groups came to find that the dominant Anglo culture kept their own sense of identity from successfully taking root.

As we shall see elsewhere in this section in the exploration of *gombo zhèbes*, for French and black Creole alike, this feeling of unrootedness was more than a metaphor: it was an actual feeling of physical deprivation. All of us (except, of course, native Indians) are transplants to these shores, but our larger American culture has a different, much more dominating relationship to landscape. We have no problem getting our herbs out of a jar (or plucking them from a single pampered plant), because we feel no special connection to the soil that nurtures and sustains us. Our love for "the land" is metaphoric and abstract.

On the other hand, for all their urbanity, the French remain a surprisingly land-rooted people. One reason they resisted Freudian psychology for so long is that they saw it as a symptom of, not a cure for, modernity, which French psychiatric theory believed to be caused by an increasingly attenuated connection to the countryside. Even as late as 1965, when traditional rural France had all but vanished, French psychiatrists still viewed urban life as pathological. Abandoning "organic and alive" rural settings in favor of "artificial" city life was considered an act that subjected the mental health of such *transplantés* to the gravest of risks.

The Americanization of France, which the French now confront with a mixture of fascination and horror, began with the French Creoles, who found that just as their financial base was eroded by American ambition and American money, their culture was being steadily undermined by American mores. Like any dominant culture, we ignored what we failed to comprehend and distorted what we chose to assimilate, transforming the Creoles' subtle sensuality into a freewheeling permissiveness that today as much characterizes Creole restaurant cooking as it does the honky-tonk dives of Bourbon Street.

French cooking is an amazing thing, for even at its most authentically extravagant, it strives to waste nothing, and this became a point of honor for Creole cooks. But the creative tension thus brought into play is so alien to our own culinary experience that I know of no French cookbook in English that makes a real effort to explain it . . . except *The Picayune's Creole Cook Book*. There you'll find both precept and example— for instance, a whole chapter, written with obvious gusto, devoted to the uses to which Creole cooks put *bouilli*, that tired remnant of the stockpot . . . a piece of dense, chewy, and nearly savorless boiled beef.

Certainly, however, their Anglo neighbors never saw the pleasure the Creoles took in eating as an integral part of this concept of husbandry, or good use. Although they might enjoy the meal, they failed to grasp the import of an underlying, scrupulous frugality that, in the minds of their Creole hosts, anchored the feasting—even at its most luxurious— to a larger and ultimately more sober vision of reality.

This, too, such meals said, can be accomplished by diligence in the pursuit of virtue. American virtue, however, does not talk this way. At bottom, we believe our obligations are not of this world; however much we love our land, we still do not believe that our flesh is made of it. Caretakers rather than lovers, we may make carnality, for a time, a virtue, but we do not go to it for instruction as to how we should live our lives.

Consequently, we understand the frugality of the Creole housewife wrongly—or, rather, we see no difference between her careful economy and our own, except that she, being French, somehow manages to be the better cook . . . a matter of lessons, or some innate gift.

This is the tragedy of Creole cuisine. So long as their culture remained vital, its decay only refined the Creoles' culinary instincts, inspiring cooks to rework their dishes to take advantage of what ingredients remained abundant, while judiciously limiting those that were not. But, meanwhile, the convictions of the dominant culture ate into the fabric of their own belief, their sense of connection to the landscape fading as they gradually half-assumed their neighbors' opinions of themselves.

New Orleans is still unlike other American cities; its citizens have an open, happy love of food that, in this country, is almost unique. But, influences apart, Creole culture exists now almost only in name. Franco-American culture is completely Cajunized, and all things Creole are opportunistically marketed as similarly upbeat and accessible. The same forces that eviscerated the old French Market now merchandise "Creole Classic Gourmet Bar-B-Q Sauces."

Of course, you can still step into Antoine's, at 713 St. Louis Street, and find in its elegantly sepulchral ambience and untranslated, unexplained French menu a sense of *temps perdu*, the romance of the old Creole arrogance and splendor. The waiters see you only if you inherited your table; the dishes they bring are made from the original recipes that set the standard for New Orleans restaurant cuisine. When Antoine's opened, Creole cuisine was already looking for its mausoleum; no surprise, then, that a hundred and fifty years later the atmosphere is still the same. This is a place where, more and more, only ghosts and tourists come to dine.

CASTINE, 1990

New Orleans Remembered
Bill Bridges

When we devoted an entire issue of Simple Cooking *to New Orleans Creole cooking, we asked our subscriber and Texas correspondent, Bill Bridges, a former* Life *photographer and author of* The Great American Chili Book, *to share some of his memories of the place and the food, back when . . .*

In the late 1930s the Depression was waning, and my father was doing well running two movie houses in New Orleans. One was on Baronne Street and the other on St. Charles, both about a block or so away from the French Quarter. My mother wanted me to finish school in Houston, but we spent the summer vacations with my father in an apartment on Canal Street, almost at the cemetery, and I usually rode the streetcar into town. The summer before I was to enter high school, my father gave me a make-work job filing in an empty office upstairs over the Baronne Street theater. It was hot, humid, boring work (air conditioning was the exception in those days), and I spent a lot of time trying to catch a breeze and looking out the window at a lunch place across the street.

On Friday mornings they would start frying shrimp right after they opened, dumping basket after basket of it as it came out of the fryer into a bin behind the front window. By noon, the bin would be full—a golden mass of fried shrimp, two or three feet deep by about the six-foot width of the window glass. The summer sun on the window kept them hot. Office workers on their lunch breaks crowded into a line that began outside the door for heaping plates of shrimp dipped out of the window bin as fast as they filed in. Beyond that were nickel bottles of Dixie beer, opened and sweating on the counter. The shrimp and beer would be carried to one-arm chairs along the wall and in the back. By one o'clock, the crowds and shrimp would be gone . . . nothing left but a greasy smear on the front window.

In summer in New Orleans, it rained every afternoon at four o'clock. You could almost set your watch by it. In a quarter of an hour it was over, but rather than cool things off, the rain just made it muggier. Out on the steaming streets, it was a cooling sight to see men in white uniforms on three-wheel bikes, pedaling behind white boxes mounted between the front wheels. The boxes, lined with dry ice, contained Elmer's Gold Bricks—little cubes of chocolate laced with chopped pecans, wrapped in gold tinfoil. These weren't ice-cream bars, mind you, just chocolate bars. The coolers kept the Gold Bricks from melting in the heat.

Gold Bricks couldn't have weighed more than an ounce or so, and cost at least a whole nickel, a lot of money in those days. Five cents would buy a quarter-pound Power House or Three Musketeers, and a penny would buy a Tootsie Roll. But pricy as they were, the little chilled Gold Bricks were very popular. Besides, in that heat, any chocolate bar that took more than two quick bites to eat would have ended up a gooey mess.

On Saturdays, at quitting time, men in cotton seersucker or Palm Beach suits and Panama hats or straw boaters boarded the streetcars for home. Some were carrying little cardboard pastry boxes with something nice for the family weekend. These boxes, from places like Maison Blanche, were neatly tied with a string, and they were held that way— by the string—away from the body, to keep the contents cool. Other men carried home oyster loaves for Saturday supper. These were long French loaves, split and buttered, filled with fried oysters and wrapped in white butcher paper. Unlike the pastry boxes, these were carried under the arm, to hold the heat in.

On weekends, we would sometimes drive out to Lake Pontchartrain, where, besides the fancier seafood places built on piles out over the water where it was cooler, the shore was dotted with outdoor eateries serving fresh-boiled lake shrimp in the shell. These places had a huge pot for boiling the shrimp, a beer cooler, and some chairs and wooden tables spread with newspapers. A basket of shrimp—boiled with lemon and spices—was dumped in the middle of the table, and everyone fell to. The only other necessities, besides the beer, were a bottle of hot sauce and perhaps a cracker or two. At the finish, the shells were rolled up in the newspaper and deposited in handy trashcans, and the table was ready for the next round.

The best lunch I ever had in New Orleans came later, when I was taking pictures for *The Saturday Evening Post*. I was in town with Vincent Price, who was there on a one-day art-buying trip for Sears, Roebuck, which then had big plans to sell art to so-called Middle Americans on the time payment plan. The art dealer was anxious to keep Price out of the reach of other dealers, and when we broke for lunch he quickly offered to have sandwiches sent in.

The gastronome Price balked at this—we were in New Orleans, after all!—so we were taken to a small nearby place in the French Quarter where, I guess, he hoped they wouldn't be looking for us. It was called Buster's and it didn't look like much. But the dealer and Buster were old buddies. We were led to a big round farmhouse table in the back and given a cold Dixie beer, and Buster started bringing it on. There was okra gumbo, red beans and rice with sausage, and pork and sweet potatoes and black-eyed peas and greens and cornbread, and I don't know what-all. But all good—better than good—spread out on the table until there wasn't room for a bottle of Tabasco. We ate and drank and joked with Buster until the dealer called us back to task. Price and I —both on expense accounts—vied for the check, which turned out to be something like nine dollars for the three of us.

After Price had left town, I stayed on, unable to tear myself away. I was taken to breakfast at the old Brennan's by a young couple who were living on the premises where the Preservation Hall Jazz Band performed. We each had Brennan's special of "Oysters Three Ways"—Rockefeller, Bienville, and Casino, as I remember—plus a few pitchers of Ramos Fizzes, and the check came to over fifty dollars, an astronomic tab for those days, especially for *breakfast*. So that made up and more for Buster's, and I couldn't put it on my expense account.

PALESTINE, TEXAS

Oysters & Herbs:
A Creole Medley

Everyone who has visited New Orleans in winter has noted the exceptionally palatable oysters that are sold in every restaurant and by the numerous small vendors on almost every other corner or so throughout the lower section of the city. In the cafés, the hotels, the oyster saloons, they are served in every conceivable style known to epicures and caterers.

—*The Picayune's Creole Cook Book* (1901)

When fertile land lies about in abundance and human labor is cheap, appetite has a unique opportunity to test its limits. To imagine Creole cuisine at its height, you must first grant yourself the luxury of a talented cook working full-time in your kitchen, markets with a profusion of fresh meat, game, vegetables, and fruit—most of it extremely cheap—and time enough to take your leisure in consuming the several daily meals produced by the one from the other.

The 1901 edition of *The Picayune's Creole Cook Book* contains a week's worth of suggested "economical" menus, "showing how a family of six may live comfortably and with variety on from a dollar to a dollar and a half a day." Just glance over Monday's menu: breakfast includes sliced oranges, hominy with milk, broiled beefsteak, batter cakes, and *café au lait*. Lunch features a simple meal of *saucisses à la Créole*, but supper embraces a vegetable soup, baked red snapper, roast beef, tomato sauce, boiled rice, potatoes *à la Maître d'Hôtel*, butterbeans, lettuce salad, apple dumplings *à la Créole*, cheese, and *café noir*. Little wonder, then, that when the 1991 edition tried to re-create one of these menus its editor discovered that "not only did [making] it take us from early morning to late at night, [but] the grocery bill was over $125.00 and we had excluded several items."

The *Picayune*'s original editors would have thrown up their hands in horror at this whole exercise. They had put together these menus with due consideration of the Creole larder and appetite at the turn of the century. If we wish to understand their inherent economy, we must reimagine what a good Creole cook would do when confronted with *our* larder . . . and *our* appetite . . . *today*.

To begin with, such a cook would consider her recipes less as unique individuals than as members of a particular, familiar Creole family. Most cooks today judge a new recipe, as they would a new friend, with regard to its own special merits and attractiveness. But it is sometimes more helpful when trying to understand a traditional cuisine to look at its dishes the same way that those who made them did, with a longer view in mind.

The old Creole family names, however aristocratic-sounding—Rouquette, De Pouilly, Fallier, Seignouret, Marigny, Dupuy—represented mercantile, professional, and artisanal families as well as genuine former nobility. The complex network of relationships the Creoles established through intermarriage not only bound them together but gave them each a distinguished ancestor to point to and, from that, a distinct and lively sense of pride in their past. Creole cuisine is exactly the same: a network of interrelated ingredients of relatively narrow lineage, also with a distinguished member somewhere to add luster to the tribe.

Take the oyster. It alone might stand as the signature ingredient in Creole cuisine, as the crawfish stands for Cajun cooking. Think of New Orleans food, and whatever else comes to mind, there will be oyster gumbo, oysters Rockefeller or Bienville or Roffignac, oyster pie, and the ubiquitous (and delicious) oyster loaf.

Oysters are what they are in Creole cooking because they were not only delicious but also abundant and next to free. However, just as the Creole aristocracy has had to tuck in some flounce over the years, so, too, have its oyster dishes. And if this is the case in New Orleans, where oysters are still relatively cheap, you can be sure that a Creole cook, visiting your market with your food budget in hand, would not come home with a bushel of them.

Even so, the dishes she (or he) would make with the pint or so that *were* brought home could be easily traced to their place on that old New Orleans family recipe tree. And most likely, it would be found that this branch was the one long affiliated with another, humbler, but equally venerable clan—that familiar set of Creole seasonings: scallions, garlic, celery, thyme, parsley, bay leaf, and cayenne.

Once you buy the oysters and chop up the herbs, you need only add milk to have an oyster stew, rice and egg to have an oyster stuffing, or pasta and olive oil to make up a dish of Creole oysters and spaghetti. And so it goes. Put the mixture into a pie tin, cover it with biscuit dough, and you have Creole oyster pie . . . put it on toast, bake it in the oven, and you have Creole coddled oysters . . . add some *filé* powder and Creole sausage and you're on your way to an oyster gumbo. You're also on your way to something more.

During one visit to New Orleans, I had eaten a chicken-liver po'boy at Ye Olde College Inn on South Carrollton Street, which made a specialty of it. The friend who took me there said that you take that chicken-liver po'boy and spin out of it a whole kosher Creole cuisine —shellfish being *tref*—but it isn't hard to imagine *any* Creole cook denied or simply not caring for oysters making the same connection. After all, substitute chicken livers for oysters in oyster dressing, omit the egg, and you already have dirty rice. Here in Maine, where crabmeat is almost as cheap as it is easy to come by, I use it instead of oysters to make a "Creole" crabmeat omelet, "Creole" crabmeat and spaghetti, and a great "Creole" crabmeat stew.

This is just how *The Picayune's Creole Cook Book* set out to teach us to cook—to make us understand the importance, more than of oysters or even Creole herbs, of family connection. Get to be friends with the brother and you are several steps along toward getting close to the sister. Creole cuisine is one big family, and as with any family, this way or that, it all finally comes together. This is why, if you can find an old Creole cook with a well-stocked larder, even now it wouldn't cost her $125 to put together one of those old Picayune menus . . . or take her all day and night to get it on the table, either.

Basic Prep

Creole cooks use the chive-green ends as well as the onion flesh of scallions (which they call "shallots"), but do discard any fronds that are wilted or soggy. These, celery (including leaf), and sweet pepper should be coarsely chopped.

All fresh herbs should be stemmed and minced (but bay leaf is left whole). If possible, choose the cleaner-tasting flat-leafed Italian parsley. Garlic should be roughly chopped and then minced with the parsley to ensure even distribution through the dish.

Oysters and their liquor have more flavor when they are freshly shucked. (A pint contains about two dozen.)

Finally, although these recipes, following the Creole originals, call for cayenne pepper, our own preference is for a less hot, fuller-flavored New Mexican ground dried chile pepper like Chimayo (*not* "chili powder"). Tabasco sauce, of course, may be used instead.

Feel free to alter proportions and substitute ingredients, whether these be herbs, aromatics, or another choice for the main ingredient itself. For example, the oyster omelet and stuffing would each be delicious made with shrimp; crab could nicely replace the bivalve in the oyster stew.

CREOLE OYSTER STEW
(SERVES 2 TO 4)

1 bunch (6 to 8) scallions, finely chopped
1 large stalk celery, coarsely chopped, with leafy top reserved
Several sprigs parsley, finely chopped
1 sprig fresh thyme, minced
4 cups milk
1 bay leaf
2 tablespoons unsalted butter
1 clove garlic, minced
1 pint oysters, with liquor
Salt, pepper, and cayenne
Oyster or common crackers
Tabasco sauce

Prepare the scallions, celery, parsley, and thyme as described in Basic Prep, mincing the parsley and celery leaf together. In a small saucepan, heat the milk with the bay leaf. Lower the flame to keep this steaming but do not let boil. Meanwhile, melt the butter in a large saucepan. Stir in the scallions, celery, and thyme. When these have softened, add the parsley-celery leaf mixture and the minced garlic. Once this is hot, strain off the liquor from the oysters and pour this (about ½ cup) into the pan along with the heated milk, discarding the bay leaf. Season with salt, pepper, and cayenne and let simmer until the celery is quite soft. Finally, add the oysters, cooking them gently for 4 to 5 minutes, until their edges curl. *Do not let boil.* Divide evenly between warmed bowls and serve with oyster or common crackers and Tabasco sauce.

Oysters and Spaghetti
(SERVES 2)

2 tablespoons unsalted butter
2 tablespoons olive oil
3 or 4 scallions, finely chopped
1 small green bell pepper, seeded, cored, and chopped
1 small sprig thyme, minced
3 or 4 sprigs parsley, minced
2 cloves garlic, minced
½ pint oysters, liquor reserved
salt, pepper, and cayenne
8 to 12 ounces of spaghetti

Preheat oven to 200°F. Melt the butter in a large, heavy, ovenproof saucepan over low heat. Mix in the olive oil and sauté the chopped scallions and green bell pepper and thyme. When the scallion and pepper bits have softened, stir in the minced parsley and garlic. Chop the oysters and add them and their liquor to the mixture. Heat for a few minutes, stirring gently, and season to taste with salt, pepper, and a little cayenne. Then cover and remove from the heat while preparing the pasta.

Cook the pasta in salted water in your usual manner, but remove and drain it just before it is *al dente*. Stir it gently but thoroughly into the herb-oyster mixture, re-cover the pot, and set in the warm oven for 5 minutes. Toss again and serve in two heated shallow bowls.

Oyster Omelet
(SERVES 2)

½ pint oysters in their liquor
4 eggs
Salt, pepper, and cayenne
2 tablespoons sweet butter
3 or 4 scallions, finely chopped
1 small red bell pepper, seeded, cored, and chopped
1 small stalk celery, finely chopped
1 sprig thyme, minced
1 bay leaf
3 or 4 sprigs parsley

2 cloves garlic
Hot buttered toast

Preheat the oven broiler. Strain off and reserve the liquor from the oysters and cut these into pieces. Beat the eggs with 2 tablespoons of the oyster liquor, and season lightly with salt, pepper, and a touch of cayenne.

Melt a scant tablespoon of the butter in a medium sauté pan and add the scallions, red bell pepper, celery, thyme, and bay leaf. When the scallions and celery are soft and translucent, stir in the minced parsley and garlic. Season again as above. Add the chopped oysters and cook these, gently stirring, for a few minutes. Then transfer all of this to a small bowl, discarding the bay leaf.

Wipe the pan with a paper towel, turn heat to medium-high, and add the remaining butter, spreading it about the pan as it melts. As soon as it stops bubbling, pour in the beaten eggs, shaking the pan gently as you do so. When a skin of egg has formed, distribute the oyster mixture evenly over the surface. Cook until all the egg has set, quickly finishing it by holding it under the broiler for 15 to 30 seconds. Do not let the egg turn leathery. Cut in half and serve at once, with lots of buttered toast.

OYSTER DRESSING
(SERVES 3 OR 4)

My single best eating experience in New Orleans happened on my last trip. It was at Eddie's Restaurant—"Home of New Orleans Cooking"— an unobtrusive, windowless place in a poor section of town. There I spooned down a spectacular gumbo—better than any I was to sample out on the bayous—and the best pork chop I ever ate in my life (thick, succulent, and sweetly tender, a mouth-ravishing coat of garlic and greens baked on top). With it came a side of Eddie's famous oyster dressing—a savory bread stuffing studded with bits of bivalve and green onion, so rich and full of flavor it would make any roast turkey filled with it weep in jealous rage. The following version, which substitutes rice for New Orleans French bread, has never drawn sobs from a turkey, no doubt because we prefer to have it as a simple supper all by itself.

3 tablespoons unsalted butter
1 bunch (6 to 8) scallions, finely chopped
2 stalks celery, chopped, with leaves reserved
1 sprig thyme, minced

1 or 2 cloves garlic, minced
1 or 2 small fresh sage leaf, minced
Several sprigs parsley, minced with reserved celery leaves
4 cups cooked rice
1 pint oysters, chopped, with liquor
½ teaspoon salt
¼ teaspoon black pepper
Cayenne pepper to taste
2 eggs, lightly beaten
Tabasco sauce
Lemon wedges

Preheat the oven to 350°F. Melt the butter in a medium skillet and sauté the scallions, celery, thyme, garlic, and sage until the first two begin to soften. Then stir in the minced parsley and celery leaf, the rice, and the chopped oysters with all their liquor. Season with the salt and black and cayenne peppers. Remove from the heat and stir in the beaten eggs. Mix well. The mixture should be damp but not wet.

Turn into a greased ovenproof casserole and bake in a preheated oven for 20 to 25 minutes, until the eggs have set and the dish is piping hot. Remove from the oven and let sit 5 minutes to cool and to allow any surface liquid to be reabsorbed. Serve with the Tabasco bottle and lemon wedges. This will feed 6 as a side dish or up to 4 as a light meal with a salad of tossed greens. (It may also be used, unbaked, to stuff a 10-pound turkey.)

CREOLE OYSTER PIE
(SERVES 3 OR 4)

½ cup flour
½ teaspoon double-acting baking powder
¼ teaspoon salt
1 tablespoon lard (or vegetable shortening)
¼ cup sour cream
4 slices lean bacon
1 bunch (6 to 8) scallions, finely chopped
1 pint oysters
2 or 3 sprigs parsley, minced
Fresh lemon juice to taste
Salt, pepper, and cayenne

THE BISCUIT TOPPING. Sift the flour, baking powder, and salt together twice. Cut the chilled lard or shortening into the mixture and then, with your fingers, work the flour and fat together to a crumbly consistency. Work in the sour cream to form a coherent dough and briefly knead this with lightly floured hands until the texture is smooth and it can be gathered into a compact ball. Cover this with plastic wrap and set it aside to rest.

THE FILLING. Chop the bacon into small pieces and sauté these in a small skillet until the fat is rendered. Stir in the scallion bits. Cook until the scallions are soft. Do not let them brown. Cut the drained oysters in half. Then put them in a mixing bowl and toss with the bacon-scallion mixture, the minced parsley, and a spritz or two of lemon juice. Season to taste with salt, black pepper, and cayenne.

THE PIE. Preheat the oven to 400°F. Butter an 8-inch pie pan and spread the oyster filling evenly inside it. Unwrap the biscuit dough and place it on a lightly floured board and, with flour-dusted hands or pastry roller, gently pat or roll out the dough into an 8-inch circle. Cover the pie, fitting the edges of the pastry snugly into the pie plate. Use a small, sharp knife to cut several neat vents in the top of the crust. Bake the pie in the preheated oven for 20 to 25 minutes, until the topping has risen and turned golden brown and the contents are bubbling. Serve in shallow bowls, as you would a chicken pot pie.

CASTINE, 1990

A NOTE ON OYSTERS ROCKEFELLER

Oysters Rockefeller is a dish in which fact is so entangled with fiction that it might be best to begin with a simple, tentative proposition. In 1899 or thereabouts, Jules Alciatore, proprietor of Antoine's restaurant in New Orleans and son of its founder, served his customers a baked oyster dish with a rich herb-and-butter topping that became an immediate and lasting success.

At the time, Creole restaurateurs were not so self-conscious regarding the burden of their heritage. Otherwise, M. Alciatore might have called his creation *Huîtres à la Louisiane* or, perhaps, "Oysters Tchoupitoulas." Instead, he saw the names he gave his dishes as a means of providing his place with a little furbishing. There was already a Toast Rothschild, a Tomato Frappée Julius Caesar, a Terrapin St. Anthony. Why not a . . . a . . . a . . . *Huîtres en Coquille, Rockefellow*!

Legend (and correct spelling) were to follow. The recipe appears everywhere and yet it remains a "sacred family secret." This is how it should be. When restaurateurs pretend to provide recipes for a trademark dish, they usually mean to muddy the waters. Better by far that other palates should attempt to decode it and that M. Alciatore should speak out only when these replications infuriated him—most notably the ones made with spinach.

Certainly, the refusal to divulge the "secret" sold as many servings as the taste, and eventually Roy, son of Jules, would sit down, flashbulbs popping, to commemorate the millionth order by selfishly eating it himself. For a long time thereafter, ordinary diners would receive a little card on which was stamped the number beyond that million reached by their own plate.

Did Jules Alciatore actually create the dish? Some claim that his stroke of genius was in transferring a garnish from snails that no one wanted to the oysters that everyone did. Theories such as this spring from writers who are not familiar with Creole cooking. It takes only a look at *The Picayune's Creole Cook Book* to see that Oysters Rockefeller is an elaborated (i.e., restaurant) version of "Oysters Broiled in Their Shells." There's no need to drag *beurre à la bourgignonne* into it.

The real "secret" to Oysters Rockefeller is the freshness of the herbs and their balance, which taste, not recipe, holds constant. Since it always bears repeating, let's say it again: A great restaurant dish is what it is because of the pride of the chef who makes it . . . day in, day out, all day long. Polish, polish, polish—no wonder it shines; no wonder, no matter how carefully you follow the directions, you don't get it exactly right.

The following recipe is fleshed out from one that Louis P. De Gouy said he received directly from M. Alciatore himself. It sounds right and, if so, reveals how imitation shows loss of nerve by loss of restraint. Most versions of Oysters Rockefeller inter that bivalve under what looks like a dense green lawn. This one dispenses with the bunches of spinach and/or watercress (and also the bacon, the garlic, and the grated cheese). Rich with butter and bright with herbs, it's still a dressing that knows you came to eat the surf, not the turf.

OYSTERS ROCKEFELLER
(SERVES 4 TO 6)

4 sprigs Italian parsley
4 scallions (including green)
Handful of fresh celery leaves
6 or more fresh tarragon leaves
6 or more fresh chervil leaves
½ cup dried homemade bread crumbs
12 tablespoons (1½ sticks) unsalted butter
Salt and pepper
Tabasco sauce
2 tablespoons Herbsaint (optional)
Rock or kosher salt
24 oysters on the half shell (liquor reserved)

Mince together the Italian parsley, scallions, celery leaves, tarragon, and chervil as finely as patience permits. Scrape the resulting herbal paste into a mortar with the bread crumbs and butter, and work these into a smooth (but still-textured) paste. Obviously this whole process can be done instead in a blender or food processor fitted with its steel blade. Season to taste with salt, pepper, and Tabasco, plus, if desired, the Herbsaint (about which, see the note below).

Preheat broiler. Spread enough of the coarse salt in a large baking pan to keep the oyster shells from tipping over. Dampen the salt slightly. Embed the shells, open side up, in the salt and put an oyster in each, along with some of its liquor. Spoon an equal amount of the prepared herb butter onto each of the oysters.

Put the pan on the middle shelf of the oven and broil the oysters until their edges have curled and the topping is bubbling hot, about 4 to 5 minutes. Serve and eat at once.

COOK'S NOTE. Herbsaint is a New Orleans herbal liqueur created in 1934 by J. Marion Legendre, following a wormwood-free formula his father had learned in southern France. Any anise-flavored liqueur (Pernod, for example) can be substituted, or it can simply be omitted from the recipe.

CASTINE, 1990

Gombo Zhèbes

At all events any person who has remained in [New Orleans] for a season must
have become familiar with the nature of *"gombo filé," "gombo févi,"* and *"gombo
aux herbes,"* or as our colored cook calls it, *"gombo zhèbes"*—for she belongs to
the older generation of Creole *cuisinières*, and speaks the patois in its primitive
purity, without using a single "r." Her daughter, who has been to school, would
pronounce it *gombo zhairbes:*—the modern patois is becoming more and more
Frenchified, and will soon be altogether forgotten.

—LAFCADIO HEARN, *Gombo Zhèbes* (1885)

Jadin loin, gombo gâté.—Garden far, gumbo spoiled.

—CREOLE PROVERB (*Gombo Zhèbes*)

Some dishes attract by what they are *not* as much as by what they
are. *Gombo zhèbes* is like that. Granted that no gumbo is ever—at least
in *la belle Louisiane*—made quite the same as the next, even by the
same cook in the same gumbo pot, *gombo zhèbes* is still unique. As
Richard and Rima Collin say in *The New Orleans Cook Book*, it's the
gumbo that breaks all the rules.

There are three basic rules-of-thumb by which a gumbo can be identified, and the most important of these is the appearance of okra.
"Gumbo," in fact, comes from the Bantu word for that vegetable, the
thick mucilaginous texture of which gives a Creole gumbo its characteristic translucent, glittering physiognomy.

New Orleans cuisine speaks French but was originally made in most
Creole kitchens by black cooks, who gave it some unique grammatical
constructions and a defining accentuated lilt. They also brought to it
some distinctly African ingredients and dishes, among these, respectively, okra and gumbo.

However, these black *cuisinières* discovered that okra wasn't as regularly available in not-quite-tropical New Orleans as in the West Indies or, for that matter, West Africa. What *was* to be had, though, was powdered sassafras leaf, used by the Indians as a similar thickening agent. Hence, *gombo filé*, named after the fine mesh of filigree formed when it is stirred into the stew. It is really a kind of instant gumbo powder, and for generations, the Choctaw squaws who sold it (and other herbs) from baskets spread out on the sidewalk were a fixture at the entryway to the old New Orleans French Market.

So, *gombo févi** (as it was originally called) or *gombo filé*, okra or okra-esque: this is the rule and all Creole gumbos follow it—all, that is, but one. A true *gombo zhèbes* isn't made with either. And as for the other two rules of gumbo making, it ignores them, too. It isn't made with the famous mahogany roux, the long-cooked fat-and-flour thickener that is the base of all other Cajun and Creole gumbos. Nor does it contain the usual combination of fish and flesh, "in which crabs seem to struggle with fragments of many stewed meats" (Lafcadio Hearn, writing in 1885), that has always been the dish's trademark.

Gombo zhèbes is seasoned with salt pork or ham, but fundamentally, as Evan Jones notes in *American Food: The Gastronomic Story*, it's just a great big mess o' greens. If I've insisted on retaining the original black Creole name, it's because that's the one it was given by the conjure-women in those old New Orleans kitchens as they summoned it up out of African memory. It wasn't *gombo aux herbes* or even *gombo z'hairbes* but *gombo zhèbes* that cast its spell on those first French Creole eaters.

The enchantment lingers on. Although the okra- and *filé*-based gumbos multiply with each new Creole (and Cajun) cookbook, *gombo zhèbes*, while remaining a solitary presence, is nevertheless saluted in these same books as the "queen of gumbos." Traditionally served on Good Friday, it holds a wealth of rich and nostalgic association.

Leon E. Soniat, Jr., recalls in *La Bouche Creole* setting out just after daybreak with his mother and grandmother to walk to the French Market.

> When we got to the vegetable stands, where we bought the ingredients for the *gumbo z'herbes*, there would be the vegetable men or hawkers and their cries of "Get your greens, lady, get your twelve greens, get your fifteen greens, get your seven greens"—the number changed as we passed by each of the different stands.

* Why *févi* is a mystery to me. Maybe the bright-green okra pods reminded the French Creoles of fava beans (*fèves*). Although the term appears in all the early Creole cookbooks, its use has since fallen away—but the classification still holds.

Legend had it that for every green that was put into the gumbo, a new friend would be made during the succeeding year. And Memere and Mamete, being warmhearted and gregarious people, would put in as many greens as they possibly could.

Although winters in New Orleans are rarely severe, they—like those of France—are drab, damp, and uncomfortable. In the North, raging storms and subzero temperatures create a distinct season that marks all activities and meals with its presence. In mild Louisiana, on the other hand, winter's effect is less noticed but more insidious; gradually, quietly, it weakens the flesh and saps the spirit. It should come as no surprise, then, that each new fresh herb was greeted by the black Creole cooks as it emerged with the warmth and relief due the return of a long-lost friend.

Gombo zhèbes breaks all the rules not out of orneriness but because it's what the Creoles call a *potage maigre*, a gumbo scrimped up catch-as-catch-can from the season's first greens, to soothe the body and restore the heart. It was kept plain—unencumbered with roux and seafood and *filé*—because the prescription worked.

The New Orleans French, urbane as they may have been, retained, like their black servants (and unlike their Anglo-Saxon neighbors), a native respect for the revitalizing powers of herbs and greens. As the anonymous author of *French Home Life* (1873) observed of their compatriots back home:

> The wise employment of herbs and of tisanes is universal. It belongs to no province and to no department in particular; it is everywhere throughout the land. No salad is complete without its *fourniture*, which consists of chervil, pimpernel, tarragon, and chives, all daintily chopped up, so that their subtle perfumes shall pervade the leaves of Romaine or of lettuce. Scarcely a sauce is possible without its "bouquet" which results from the distillation in it of a little bunch of parsley, thyme, and laurel . . . As for tisanes, their name is legion.

France remains a country of herbalist shops, herb-based liqueurs, and recipes for herb infusions that reputedly serve as general restoratives and, of course, spring tonics. The French housewife who fills her teapot with dried linden flowers to brew a soothing tisane does not much distinguish between its gustative and calmative effect; for her, the two are the same.

Likewise, the French Creoles' respect for their black cooks' herbal lore was an awe in which culinary and medicinal aspects were inextricably mingled. A dish was all the more delicious if its ingredients also had connotations of goodness and health, and no dish was more replete with such resonance than *gombo zhèbes*.

Our own word "herb" carries traces of this jointure, but they are mostly inarticulate. Few of us now remember that mint was once considered to have digestive properties, or thyme analgesic ones. The word itself has consequently shrunk, today more evocative of powdered flavorings than the essence of all things vegetative. In French, however, *herbes* embraces a larger, leafier, and more complex designation, right down to the grass on the lawn. The closest we come to it in English is "greens."

Compared to most American markets, French ones are awash with all manner of green leaf, sweetly fresh and giving each moment of the season its own identifying taste. At one time, the New Orleans French Market was full of them, too: chervil, cress, corn salad, chicory, mustard greens, roquette, sorrel, spinach dock, any number of lettuces . . . the venders could easily make up their bundles of seven, twelve, fifteen greens without resorting to the carrot tops or Brussels sprouts that pad out more recent recipes.

Consequently, while it isn't inaccurate to think of *gombo zhèbes* as "greens and pot likker" with a French name, it also isn't quite right. Unfair as it may be to that familiar Southern dish when made by skilled and loving hands, its image remains one of collard and beet greens boiled for hours in a slick of grease.

However, to become the queen of gumbos, *gombo zhèbes* had to be born a Creole princess. You could do worse than to think of it as such: delicate, supple, mysterious—a simmered salad of fresh spring greens, sweet and pungent, made savory with country ham, garlic, scallions, and hot red pepper . . . served on rice.

Si moin té gagnin moussa, moin té mangé gombo.—To make the gumbo, you must first get hold of the rice.   —CREOLE PROVERB (*Gombo Zhèbes*)

GREEN GUMBO
(SERVES 4)

Although gombo zhèbes *is traditionally a Lenten dish, gardeners will like it best in early summer, when there's an abundance of fresh greens at hand, to be either picked or weeded from the garden. The dish makes excellent use of the green leafy tops of radishes, beets, and turnips. A possible version for four is suggested below in italics. There's little point in contracting the dish any further, but it can be easily expanded. Choose a bunch of greens per person, remembering that these cook down—as a main course, a pound of spinach is not too much for a single eater—and adjust the rest of the ingredients proportionally to taste.*

THE GREENS: Choose a bunch per person from *spinach, romaine, escarole, watercress*, arugula, chicory, endive, radish tops, beet greens, broccoli rabe, young dandelions, etc.

THE HERBS: Choose a *bay leaf*, a good handful of *leaf parsley*, and, as you will, fresh *thyme, sorrel*, oregano, marjoram, sage, tarragon, etc.

THE AROMATICS: *2 cloves fresh garlic, 1 medium sweet bell pepper (green or red), 4 to 6 scallions* (and/or chives, shallots, onions), *1 small crumbled hot red pepper pod* (or dash of Tabasco), etc.

PLUS: *2 tablespoons olive oil, 1 to 2 teaspoons wine vinegar or lemon juice, 4 ounces or more country-cured ham, and 1 cup uncooked white rice.*

Cook the rice in a small covered pot. When done, keep it in a warm spot on the stove. Clean, stem, and mince the fresh herbs (leave the bay leaf whole). Mince the garlic. Seed, core, and dice the sweet pepper. Trim and finely chop the scallions (including their green tops). Cut the country ham into slivers. Heat the olive oil in a skillet. When hot, add the ham, scallions, and sweet pepper. When these have cooked for a few minutes, add the minced herbs, the bay leaf, and the crumbled hot pepper. Cook, stirring, over medium-low heat for another few minutes, until all the herbs have wilted. Now mix in the garlic and remove from the heat.

Pick over the greens, discarding stems and any damaged portions. Tear larger-leaved greens like romaine into pieces. Wash carefully, using, if necessary, several changes of water. Put a cup of unsalted water in a large pot and bring to a boil. Add the greens, cover, and, when steam returns, lower heat. Cook until wilted and tender, about 6 to 10 minutes, forking them over occasionally. Do not let the pot boil dry.

Mix the contents of the skillet into the greens in the large pot and cook together briefly until everything is hot and well blended. Taste for seasoning, adding the wine vinegar or lemon juice, along with salt and freshly milled pepper. Discard the bay leaf. Serve in bowls over the rice. This makes a fine light meal by itself, with a crusty loaf and some sweet butter, but it is also good company to such seafood dishes as boiled shrimp or crab, steamed clams, or fried fish.

Bouki fait gombo, lapin mangé li.—Billy Goat makes the gombo; but Rabbit eats it.
                                    —CREOLE PROVERB (*Gombo Zhèbes*)

CASTINE, 1990

GOMBO ZHÈBES

Gombo Zhèbes, as I discovered researching this dish, is also the title of a book by Lafcadio Hearn—a collection of black Creole proverbs. Many of them are about food, and they are often simultaneously funny and wise. Here are some of the best.

Bon chien pas janmain trappé bon zo.—A good dog never gets a good bone.

Bondié baille nouèsett pou ça qui pas ni dent.—The good Lord gives nuts to people who have no teeth.

Ça qui tine poélon qui cone so prix lagresse.—It's the one who holds the skillet who knows the cost of lard.

C'est bon khé crâbe qui lacause li pas tini tête.—It's because of his good heart that the crab has no head.

C'est couteau qui connaite ça qui dans coeur geomon.—It's the knife that knows the heart of the pumpkin.

C'est cuiller qui allé lacail gamelle; gamelle pas jamain allé lacail cuiller.—Spoon goes to bowl's house; bowl never goes to spoon's house.

Lapin dit: Boué toutt, mangé toutt, pas dit doutt.—Rabbit says: Drink everything, eat everything, but don't tell everything.

Manger yon fois pas ka rìser dents.—A taste won't wear out the teeth.

Napas éna fromaze qui napas trouve so macathia.—There's no piece of cheese but that can find its crust of bread.

Poule pas ka vanté bouillon yo.—Chickens don't brag about their own soup.

Quiquefois wou plante zharicots rouze; zharicots blancs qui poussé.—Sometimes you sow red beans and white beans come up.

Si zannoli té bon viann, li sè pas ka drivé lassous baïe.—If lizard were good to eat, you'd never find him under the tub.

Vie cannari ka fé bon bouillon.—It's the old pot that makes the good soup.

Zaffaire ça qui sotte, chien mangé diné yo.—Dogs make their dinner upon what belongs to fools.

Cajun Dirty Rice

The three basic methods of cooking rice are the Chinese, the Indian, and the Creole; that is to say the glutinous, the dry, and the greasy.
—H. PEARL ADAM, *Kitchen Ranging*

Dirty rice is one of those dishes that seem always to have been hanging out in Louisiana bayou kitchens. If you haven't met up with it yet, it's essentially a rice dish concocted from those constant companions of Cajun cooking—scallions, green bell pepper, celery, garlic, and parsley—all minced and fried together with various bits of offal and then mixed in with cooked rice.

I offer this portrait with some hesitation. While it is adequate enough in its way, you can't really understand dirty rice without some grasp of the freewheeling Cajun attitude toward "plain" rice. I came face to face with this myself recently when, wanting to include our shelf of Louisiana Creole/Cajun cookbooks in some rice cooking research I was doing at the time, I pulled down Chef Paul Prudhomme's anthology of his family's very down-home Cajun cooking, *The Prudhomme Family Cookbook*.

I located "rice, basic cooked" in the index and looked it up—only to find a recipe with about ten ingredients. Rice, yes, but also butter, onion, celery, bell pepper, scallions, garlic, and cayenne, to name the most prominent. This seeming anomaly is not commented on; neither is the fact that the mixture is set in a loaf pan, covered with foil, and baked for over an hour in the oven. This is not your ordinary way of making rice.

Obviously, at least in the Prudhomme family, to make rice is to be already nine-tenths of the way to dirty rice. More interesting, though, is the fact that there is no recipe for that dish in the whole book. Instead,

Malcolm and Versie Prudhomme offer *"Riz à la Graisse"*—"Greasy Rice"—which is that "basic" cooked rice fried up in bacon fat, with the bacon crumbled up and served on top. Reading this, I realized I couldn't recall ever seeing the Cajun French for "dirty rice"—even in Cajun cookbooks . . . which made me suspect that it is a relatively recent addition to the Cajun cooking repertoire.

Not that it hasn't always been around. On the contrary: slide dirty rice one way and you have Cajun *boudin blanc*, which is essentially dirty rice made with the fresh pork offal from the family pig slaughtering and stuffed into the intestines of the same pig (about which see my first book, *Simple Cooking*). In fact, the older Cajun recipes for dirty rice call for the meat and vegetables to be run through a meat grinder together before they're cooked . . . just as if you were making a sausage filling.

Slide dirty rice another way and you have what is pretty much a chicken-liver jambalaya. Slide it again and you have rice dressing. C. Paige Gutierrez, who has been observing Cajun eating and cooking since 1976, doesn't mention dirty rice in her *Cajun Foodways* at all. She does, however, write about rice dressing, which she describes as the "classic accompaniment" to roast meat and poultry, a side dish that always appears next to the Sunday or holiday meal.

> Rice dressing consists of cooked rice that has been combined with "dressing mix" shortly before serving. Dressing mix is made from ground pork and/or ground beef; ground pork, beef, and/or chicken liver (other organ meats such as beef or pork hearts or chicken gizzards may be added); and ground seasoning vegetables. These are cooked together, with water and perhaps a roux, for hours, until the meat is very tender and the blood from the organ meat has produced a medium-thick gravy. Shortly before serving time, the cook folds the dressing mix into the cooked rice. The resulting dish is light brown, with pieces of meat and seasoning vegetables throughout. It is moist, but not runny, and can be eaten with a fork.*

About twenty years ago, as family *boucheries* declined and a lot of Cajuns became more accustomed to buying their *boudin* at the grocery, rice dressing began to lighten up a little. Without all the pork innards at hand, it became greasy rice plus a touch of meat and offal . . . and so dirty rice was born.

Cajun cooks often use plain hamburger (sometimes plus pig liver),

---

* Sound familiar? Substitute eggs and oysters for at least some of the organ meat and you have oyster dressing (see page 244).

but I think the best way to make it is with the innards of a chicken. In my bachelor cooking days, I used to let the giblet packages accumulate in the freezer until there were enough (one packet per serving was my measure). Now we buy our chickens fresh from a local farm and celebrate the monthly pickup day with a big batch of dirty rice made from the giblets, carcass pickings, and some surprisingly large, incredibly handsome, fresh-tasting livers.

Because our dirty rice has gradually shaped itself to fit our needs and tastes, it has become an interpretation rather than a true reproduction of the dish. For instance, most Cajun recipes call for the seasoning vegetables to be diced extra small; some Cajun cooks even crank the whole mixture through a meat grinder. Because our dirty rice is a meal, not a side dish, we cut the vegetables into small bite-sized pieces. Also, in Louisiana scallions and parsley are stirred in at the very last minute as a potently freshening garnish—a little too potent, as it turns out, for us. Be that as it may, our version lives up to Terry Thompson's definition in *Cajun-Creole Cooking*:

> It is filling, it is cooked in one big pot, it will feed a lot of people for a little money and, most important, it is delicious . . . Even if you despise chicken livers and gizzards, you will love Dirty Rice.

OUR DIRTY RICE
(SERVES UP TO 4 AS A MEAL, UP TO 6 AS A SIDE DISH)

Meaty carcass of a roast or poached chicken
Uncooked heart, gizzard, neck, and liver from same chicken

2 or 3 large stalks celery
1 green bell pepper, seeded and cored
1 red bell pepper, seeded and cored
1 bunch (6 to 8) scallions
1 or 2 cloves garlic
1 sprig thyme
Celery leaves from stalks
3 or 4 sprigs parsley
1½ cups raw long-grain rice
2 tablespoons olive oil
½ teaspoon powdered chile
Salt and freshly ground black pepper

Pick away as many slivers of meat and bits of other edible debris as possible from the carcass. If any pieces are large, cut to bite size. Put the heart, neck, and gizzard (reserving the chicken liver) into a pot holding a quart of lightly salted water. Bring to a boil and simmer until the giblets are tender and the neck meat starts falling away from the bone, about 45 minutes. Remove from the heat.

Meanwhile, prepare the vegetables, cutting the celery, bell peppers, and scallions into smallish, bite-sized pieces. Include the green part of the scallion that isn't wilted or damaged. Mince the garlic and thyme together as finely as possible and then the celery leaves and parsley, this time more coarsely. Have all this ready in separate piles.

Remove the giblets from the broth. In another (or the same cleaned) pot, start the rice cooking, using the giblet broth instead of water. Measure it as you do ordinarily (about 2 cups of liquid for every cup of rice) but do not salt. Reserve the excess broth. (There should be at least ½ cup. If not, reserve that amount and add a compensatory amount of plain water to the rice.) The rice should be checked from time to time and removed from the heat when done.

Heat the olive oil in a large pot. When hot, sprinkle in the powdered chile and an equal amount of salt. Set in the reserved raw chicken liver and cook over medium high heat, turning frequently, 3 or 4 minutes, until crusty on the outside. The liver should not be cooked through. Remove with a spatula and set on a cutting board.

Immediately lower the heat to medium-low and add the celery to the hot oil. Stir well and cover. After the celery has cooked for 5 minutes, add the pieces of bell pepper. Stir, cover again, and let this cook 5 more minutes. Now add the scallion bits. Stir, cover, and let cook 5 more minutes.

Chop the giblets fine. Discard the fat attached to the neck and then pick away all the bits of meat, discarding the bone. Add the mixed meat bits and chopped giblets to the carcass meat. Slice the liver into bite-sized pieces. Finally, stir the parsley and celery leaves into the pot, along with the reserved meat slivers, chopped giblets, liver, and broth. Turn in the cooked rice, mix well, and taste for seasoning, adding more salt and plenty of freshly ground black pepper to taste. Cover and let the flavors mingle and the dish heat through over a very low flame for a few minutes before serving.

STEUBEN, 1993

LOUISIANA RICE

C. C. Robin, a Frenchman who traveled in Louisiana at the time of the Louisiana Purchase, noted in astonishment the Creole appetite for rice:

> Its consumption in this country is prodigious . . . It is seen on all the tables of the Creoles instead of bread. Boiled rice and cornbread replace wheat completely.

However, until recently, when mechanization brought down the cost of rice to its current bargain-basement price, Cajuns grew their own small family crops and hand-milled it in a wooden mortar and pestle—the erratic nature of the crop and the tedious work of hulling it combining to make it a relatively rare and treasured dish. C. Paige Gutierrez observes that

> for some families as recently as the 1930s . . . grits, not rice, was the staple accompaniment for many Cajun dishes. Many members of the younger generations, however, have never eaten grits with gumbo, and few Cajuns express regret over the demise of that combination.

Today, rice is grown commercially in Cajun country, rice that is arguably the best this country produces. This rice comes from two strains, the first of which, Della, is a cross between basmati and American long-grain rice. It is marketed variously as Texmati, Louisiana popcorn rice, and wild pecan rice (the "pecan" color of the last is due to a special milling process), and it does indeed have both popcorn and pecan flavor notes. The other, Jasmine, which was introduced in 1989, possesses a unique floral fragrance, sweet taste, and a distinctly tender, slightly sticky texture. After tasting samples from over a dozen different growers, our personal favorites are listed below.

Della

ELLIS STANSEL'S RICE, P.O. Box 206, Gueydan, LA 70542 • 318–536–6140. We've eaten hundreds of pounds of Ellis Stansel's Louisiana popcorn rice and think it the best American rice we've tasted, with a superlative texture and an elegantly balanced flavor. Mr. Stansel is now deceased, but his family continues to do business in the same personal way, so call them—or write—for prices and shipping. We pay $18.47 for a 10-pound bag, shipped to Maine.

GUILLORY'S LOUISIANA POPCORN RICE, Route 3, Box 55, Welsh, LA 70591 • 318–734–4440. Paul and Anne Guillory's delicious Louisiana rice has the most distinctly "popcorn" taste of the varieties we sampled. They sell it (white or brown) in 2-pound ($3.50) and 5-pound ($7.00) bags. Order by mail or phone.

Jasmine

LOWELL FARMS, 311 Avenue A, El Campo, TX 77437 • 409–543–4950. The organic Jasmine rice Linda and Lowell G. Raun, Jr., grow on their farm over the Texas border in El Campo is also something special. The grains are almost uniformly perfect, the aroma has delicate floral notes, and the rice cooks dry and slightly sticky—a classic "rice bowl" rice. The Rauns have two price lists: one for Texans and one for the rest of us. Out-of-state, six 2-pound bags are $20.00; a 25-pound sack is $27.25, shipping included with both.

Coffee & Dessert

One of the small mysteries of New Orleans cuisine is when—and *why*—the Creoles began to appreciate the presence of chicory in their coffee. This is usually explained away as an old Creole custom, but such evidence as I have been able to unearth indicates that, if it is a tradition, it's a relatively recent one.

Chicory and endive are different names for the same family of plants, which explains why the Belgian endive is sometimes confusingly named as the source of roast chicory. This, however, is made from Magdeburg chicory, a plant that produces long, fat, parsnip-shaped roots. These are sliced, kiln-dried, and roasted to a deep brown. When these chips are put through a grinder, the result does resemble ground coffee beans, both in appearance and, to a more limited extent, aroma.

The use of roast chicory root as a coffee extender was first observed in Sicily in 1769. Soon after, it was adopted in Germany and, to a lesser extent, elsewhere in Europe. (At one point, its use as an adulterant in coffee became so endemic in England that it was forbidden. But chicory lovers complained loudly, and the law was soon amended to require proper labeling instead.)

Governor James Bowdoin of Massachusetts introduced the drink to the United States in 1785. By 1865, Fearing Burr, in *Field and Garden Vegetables of America*, not only describes three varieties of large- (or turnip-) rooted chicory, but encourages growers to plant them, noting: "It is an article of considerable commercial importance, and large quantities are annually imported from the south of Europe to different seaports in the United States." After explaining the process of raising and processing the root, Burr goes on to comment on its use:

After being roasted and ground, Chiccory is mixed with coffee in various proportions, and thus forms a pleasant beverage; or, if used alone, will be found a
tolerable substitute for genuine coffee.

Well, maybe. I suspect that these two passages tell us more about
the quality and price of coffee beans at that time than they do about
the pleasures of drinking roasted chicory. As a hot beverage it isn't at
all unpleasant. The slightly fruity flavor is complexly bitter and sweet,
and it is still used (by Celestial Seasonings, for one, in their Morning
Thunder blend) to give body, color, and flavor to herbal teas. However,
as a coffee substitute it has two strikes against it. It doesn't taste much
like coffee and it doesn't contain any caffeine. But these lacks matter
less if the coffee you drink doesn't have all that much coffee flavor to
begin with . . . and has more than enough caffeine to spare.

Almost all the world's coffee comes from two varieties of coffee plants,
Coffea robusta and *Coffea arabica*. Coffees with a distinct "coffee" taste
(whatever their other overtones) come from the *arabica* variety. But since
the *robusta* variety is hardier, more productive, and easier to grow, it,
not *arabica*, produces most of the world's supply of coffee beans . . .
and all of its cheapest ones.

Doesn't all coffee taste like coffee? Yes, it does . . . but a cup brewed
from *robusta* beans tastes like *instant* coffee—that is, coffee with something missing. Almost all instant coffee is 100 percent *robusta*, and that
as much as the instantizing is why it tastes the way it does. In such a
brew, roast chicory not only adds a fruity, acidic tang but also serves
the same purpose as the "tone" button on a cheap radio—it inserts a
false but still satisfying mellifluous depth.

No one in their right mind would add chicory to *arabica* coffee, but
forced—by problems of supply or personal means—to drink a *robusta*
brew, one might do worse than to roast the beans black as the devil and
throw in a scoop of chicory to round the flavor out. This dilution also
helps with digestion, since *robusta* beans are naturally high in caffeine
and more are used when making a dark-roast brew.

However, the most important aspect of dark-roasted, chicory-flavored
coffee may be that it allows the impression of a conscious choice. It is
the preferred choice of the poor but proud, who can justly claim to like
what poverty forces them to choose. Louisiana had its first taste of this
method during the Civil War, when the Northern blockade cut off regular coffee shipments. Even so, if one can trust the evidence of later
cookbooks and visitors, there was no lingering affection for it. Mark
Twain, for example, despite his many visits to New Orleans, seems to

have first met up with (and thoroughly detested) coffee with chicory in Germany.

Nor does any mention of it appear in the early Creole cookbooks, including *La Cuisine Créole* and *The Picayune's Creole Cook Book*, which devotes considerable space to the art of making a good cup of coffee. It wasn't until the Depression leveled what Creole fortunes remained that "Creole coffee" became coffee with chicory . . . that old Louisiana custom.

If you like your coffee dark-roasted, try adding one part chicory to three or four parts ground bean, brewing it strong, and diluting the result with plenty of scalding milk . . . and having it for breakfast. Although Louisiana chicory-flavored coffee blends are available, I recommend purchasing the two ingredients separately and combining them yourself just before brewing.*

CAJUN CAFÉ AU LAIT
(SERVES 4)

A cup of coffee is the center of Cajun social life; the coffeepot is the first thing filled in the morning and the last thing emptied at night. Cajuns love their coffee strong and thick—Peter Feibleman wrote in American Cooking: Creole and Acadian *that it "makes even Creole coffee look limpid"—and drink it either black or, in more leisurely moments, in this rich version of café au lait. Traditionally this was made by filling a teaspoon with* la cuite, *or thickened cane syrup, and dipping that into a small bowl of powdered pecans. This confection was then dissolved into a cup of hot café au lait.*

2 cups hot dark-roast New Orleans coffee with chicory
2 cups hot milk
2 tablespoons white sugar
1 tablespoon light brown sugar

Prepare the coffee, using by preference a drip pot or a filter system, and a proportion of ¼ cup ground coffee to each cup of water.† Keep

---

* Roast chicory is available at the time of writing for $2.45 a pound (plus shipping) from: Community Kitchens, P.O. Box 2311, Baton Rouge, LA 70821–2311 • 800–535–9901.

† This is slightly weaker than the true *café au lait*, which is usually made with a double strength proportion of ¼ cup ground coffee for each ¾ of water. But most readers will find our proportions strong enough, especially in a paper-filter-type brewing system.

this hot. Heat the milk to steaming, but do not let it boil. Have it ready on the stove. Combine the white and brown sugars and 1 tablespoon of water in a heavy 2-quart saucepan, over medium heat. Let the sugar caramelize, using a wooden spoon to gently scrape back into the syrup any froth that hardens on the sides of the pan. When the sugar turns a delicate hazelnut color, remove the pan from the heat and stir in the hot milk slowly, being careful not to let the bubbling syrup splatter or foam. Then stir until the mixture is well blended.

To serve, place the caramel-flavored milk, still steaming, in one pre-heated pitcher and the hot coffee in another. Pouring from both pitchers at once, fill each cup with an equal measure of milk and coffee.

Oreilles de Cochon
(makes 16)

These crunchy Cajun treats (the translation, of course, is "pig's ears") are best the moment they're cool enough to eat. An excellent cane syrup is available by mail order from Community Kitchens (see page 263). The Cajun substitute for cane syrup is a mixture of half molasses and half dark corn syrup. I prefer to use maple syrup instead.

For the pastry
2 cups all-purpose flour
1½ teaspoons double-acting baking powder
½ teaspoon salt
2 eggs
6 tablespoons butter, melted and cooled
Lard or vegetable shortening for deep frying

For the topping
1½ cup cane syrup
1 cup toasted, chopped pecans (see note)

Sift the flour, baking powder, and salt into a bowl. Stir well to mix. In a large mixing bowl, beat the eggs until frothy. Blend in the cooled melted butter and then work in the flour, half a cup at a time, until a soft dough forms. Divide the dough into 16 pieces and quickly shape each of these into a ball. Roll the balls out, one at a time, on a lightly floured surface into as thin a round as possible, about 6 inches in diameter. Stack these at the side of the pastry board, letting each round overlap the next enough so that it can be easily lifted off to be fried.

Melt the shortening in a large pot to a depth of about 2 inches. Heat to 360°F. When it is hot, fry the *oreilles de cochon* one at a time. Slip each round into the hot fat, and as soon as it rises to the surface, form the pig's ear by piercing it in the center with a long-handled, two-tined serving fork and twisting it about a quarter turn, to create the ear ridges. Then flip an edge of the dough over itself to form the ear flap. Finally, turn the pastry over so it can brown lightly on the other side. Remove it to a paper towel while you make the rest. (If you're nervous forming the ears in the hot fat, this can be done on the pastry board just before you put the dough into the pot.)

When they are all made, heat the cane syrup in a saucepan and stir over low heat until the syrup thickens to the soft-ball stage, about 238°F (a few drops poured in cold water form a soft ball). Add the toasted, chopped pecans, cook for 2 more minutes, and then dribble an equal portion of this mixture over each ear. Serve the *oreilles de cochon* warm or at room temperature with *café au lait*. (In a tightly sealed tin, these will keep for one or two days.)

COOK'S NOTE. To toast the nuts, spread pecan halves or large broken pieces in a single layer on a baking sheet and put into a preheated 350°F oven. Bake for 10 minutes, or until the nuts are lightly browned and begin to smell toasted. Remove to a cutting board and, when they are cool, chop them small.

BOSTON, 1985 / CASTINE, 1990

Two Creole Classics

WHY CRABS ARE BOILED ALIVE
And for why you not have of crab? Because one must dem boil 'live? It is all vat is of most beast to tell so. How you make for dem kill so you not dem boil? You not can cut dem de head off, for dat dey have not of head. You not can break to dem de back, for dat dey not be only all back. You not can dem bleed until dey die, for dat dey not have blood. You not can stick to dem troo de brain, for dat dey be de same like you—dey not have of brain.
—Lafcadio Hearn (New Orleans *Item*, October 5, 1879)

One sure indication of the vitality of the legend of New Orleans Creole-style cooking is the continued interest in old Creole cookbooks and the willingness of various publishers to keep them in print—a situation that any region outside the South has reason to envy. Now there are two books to swell this list. From Pelican Publishing, of Gretna, Louisiana, comes *Lafcadio Hearn's Creole Cook Book*, a reissue of their 1967 version of that author's anonymously published *La Cuisine Créole*, and from *The Times Picayune*, a new, sesquicentennial edition of *The Picayune's Creole Cook Book*.

The first of these is an attractive edition containing facsimiles of the original pages interleaved with some of the woodcuts and short pieces Hearn produced for the New Orleans *Item* and seasoned throughout with many of the Creole proverbs he assiduously collected. Even as Creole cookbooks go—and they are, all told, a bunch of pretty unusual characters—*La Cuisine Créole* is the true *gombo zhèbes*, which is to say, both authentic *and* an anomaly. In this it is like its author himself. Although generally considered an American writer, Lafcadio Hearn was born on Leukas, an island in the Ionian Sea, of Irish and Greek parents. Educated in England, he came to America in 1869 at the age of nineteen, first settling in Cincinnati, where he learned the newspaper trade while living in the public library.

Eight years later, fleeing both public censure and the black wife who was the cause of it, he arrived in New Orleans and spent there the ten happiest of his American years. Always restless, however, he moved on, sailing first to the Caribbean and then to Japan, where he married, took on native ways, did his best writing . . . and died prematurely at fifty-four of overwork, struggling ceaselessly to provide for his extended family. His last words were *"Ah, byöki no tamé"*—Ah, on account of illness—a sigh of relief as much as any epitaph.

The more you learn about Hearn, the more truth you find in Malcolm Cowley's observation that "no American author of the 19th century had a stranger life." Many of his devoted readers—and he still has them, though his literary stock is not what it was—know of his anonymously published cookbook, but few will be aware that it was born in part from a conviction that his experience at feeding himself on pennies a day might be parlayed into a profitable restaurant.

Despite Hearn's perpetual indigence, he managed to find a partner, scrape together the necessary money, and actually open one, albeit on a shabby back street far from the French Quarter. Advertisements in the *Item* (the local newspaper for which he wrote a column) and on printed handbills announced:

THE 5-CENT RESTAURANT
160 DRYADES

This is the cheapest eating house in the South. It is neat, orderly and respectable as any other in New Orleans. You can get a good meal for a couple of nickels. All dishes 5 cents. Everything half the price of the markets.

Before it opened, Hearn renamed the place The Hard Times, no doubt feeling he had failed to underscore its attractions enough. The new name was unappetizing but prophetic: the place failed three weeks after opening, his partner fleeing with the cashbox and the cook.

The only thing worse than Hearn's luck was his eyesight—he risked his life every time he crossed the street. Hearn had a flawless ear for the rhythms of everyday New Orleans, but his nearsightedness (and equally notorious shyness) meant that he was a better listener than interrogator, using his acute intuition to fill in the gaps in his understanding.

This is the technique that produced the short, shrewd, colorful impressions of city life that he wrote for the *Item*, but it posed some potential problems for the fledgling food writer. Take an early (1880) piece on gumbo for the *Item* called "Attention! Azim!" What he makes of that dish is such a jumble—including mistaking gumbo *filé* for powdered okra—that the resulting recipe is impossible to follow . . . as is admitted by the lamely concluding offer: "If Azim needs further information, he must inform us, and we shall send him to a first class Creole cook, with whom he can converse at leisure."

In other words, the worst way to approach this book is as some kind of authoritative treatise on Creole cuisine. There are too many recipes in it that were diligently but not always accurately copied from other cookbooks or diligently but not-quite-comprehendingly gleaned from Creole cooks (although this time around he does get gumbo right).

This is only to say, however, that the value of the book lies elsewhere. For Hearn *was* an appreciative eater and, at least when it came to simple dishes, a good cook. Writing about what personally interests him, he conveys a dish with lively clarity, as witness his instructions for broiling a chicken:

> Clean it as usual and split it down the back, break the breast-bone with a stroke of the potato beetle, spread it out flat and lay it on the gridiron over clear coals; put the inside of the chicken to the fire first. Put a tin cover over it, let it broil quickly until nearly done, then turn it and finish without the cover. When nicely browned take it on a dish, season it with salt and pepper, and butter it freely; turn it once or twice in the butter and serve it hot.

Read the book as the culinary journal of a nearsighted, bookish, delicately constituted, and often nearly starving genius and its pages spring to life.

We soon learn to recognize the dishes he cooked for himself on the gas ring in his rented room. Some are clearly destined for the menu of The Hard Times—"Cheap White Soup," "Louisiana Hard Times Cake," and "Pumpkin with Salt Meat" ("Better than many things with more reputation"). There is also such bachelor fare as an "Omelet for One Person" and "Veal Hash for Breakfast," as well as the oddball recipes, like "Cucumber Pickles in Whisky," that always seem part of a single man's culinary repertoire.

More interesting still are dishes he was served when he ate *en famille* with prosperous friends, causing him to seek out from their black Creole cooks the making of "*Soupe et Bouilli*," "Jambalaya of Fowls and Rice," "Cod au Beurre Roux," or "Crab Gombo, with Okra." From them, too, may have come the delicate culinary touches given to many of the vegetable and seafood dishes and such purely French-inspired fare as "Eggs with Browned Butter and Vinegar" and "Tripe with Mushrooms," and the simple, good recipe for French mustard.

Hearn may have been weak on exact detail, but he is a master of color. Although the book is, mostly, a collection of recipes, as you read through it images accumulate, some delightful, others shocking—as in the casual cruelty of "Take six nice fat crabs, wash them, and while alive chop off their claws." This is an instruction as true to its time as the "antique" feel of the list of ingredients in the recipe for "Boston Caramels": "one pint bowl of bakers' chocolate grated, two bowls of yellow sugar, one bowl of New Orleans molasses . . ."

But what the accretion of these images best captures is the shimmer of New Orleans itself—its summer heat, its abundance of wild game (canvas-back duck, teal, wild goose and turkey, Carolina rice birds, partridge, quail, etc.), its seafood, its French Market with the vegetables and herbs, its saloons with their absinthe drinks and their *pousse cafés*. And, of course, its restaurants. Hearn had already separately published a New Orleans guidebook, in which he conveyed their ambience; here, he concentrates on his favorite dishes and his favorite good times:

> At large dinners in New Orleans a great deal of wine is served, and you will be expected to drink with your raw oysters, a light white wine; with soup and hors d'œuvre, sherry or Madeira; with fish and entrées, a heavy white wine; with relevés and entremets, a good claret followed by a *Ponche Romaine*, which is the turning point of the feast, or rest; after which will be served with the roast, champagne; game and salad, fine claret or burgundy; and with dessert, café noir and liqueurs.

Note these last words. Hearn gives some good dessert recipes, but there's no doubt that what the end of the meal meant to him was the coffee and the liqueur, not the sweet. The most famous passage in the book is his evocative account of the serving of a grand brûlé. The fin-de-siècle prose may no longer be to our taste, but it still evokes the *luxe* and *nostalgie* of period New Orleans.

> The crowning of a grand dinner is a brûlé. It is the pièce de résistance, the grandest pousse café of all. After the coffee has been served, the lights are turned down or extinguished, brûlé is brought in and placed in the center of the table upon a pedestal surrounded by flowers. A match is lighted, and after allowing the sulphur to burn entirely off is applied to the brandy, and as it burns it sheds its weird light upon the faces of the company, making them appear like ghouls in striking contrast to the gay surroundings. The stillness that follows gives an opportunity for thoughts that break out in ripples of laughter which pave the way for the exhilaration that ensues.

If Lafcadio Hearn's *La Cuisine Créole* had appeared during the 1884 Cotton Centennial Exposition in New Orleans, when but for printing delays it would have, it might have earned that hard-pressed author a decent amount of royalties from souvenir sales—and the book itself indisputable title as the first in English on Creole cooking. This palm it must now share with *The Creole Cookery Book*, a recipe collection assembled by the Christian Woman's Exchange, also published in 1885.

This dual publication marked the auspicious beginnings of a rewarding colloquy in Creole cookbooks between worthy anthologies of "*la cuisine Créole à l'usage des petits ménages*," as goes the subtitle of one of the first, Célestine Eustis's *Cooking in Old Créole Days* (1904), and such idiosyncratic personal records as Natalie V. Scott's *Mirations and Miracles of Mandy* (1924). The best of them all combines elements of them both in a single volume, producing one of this country's true culinary treasures, *The Picayune's Creole Cook Book*, the first edition of which was published in 1900.

If the book itself will soon mark its centenary, *The Times-Picayune* celebrated its 150th year in 1987 by releasing a new edition of its cookbook. The intent, at least, was notable: to take the text of the second (and best) edition; edit, correct, and annotate it; add a few other Creole favorites published in later editions; and then retest all the recipes, adding modern measures, substitutions, and advice as necessary to make the book accessible again to the home cook. And so we have *The Picayune's Creole Cook Book—Sesquicentennial Edition*, published locally by *The Times-Picayune* itself, and then nationally by Random House.

At first, this might seem like wonderful news. The second (1901) edition of *The Picayune's Creole Cook Book* is among the finest cookbooks America has produced. Although it is no longer easy to cook from, its humane culinary philosophy, its candid enjoyment of good eating, its wise opinions about cooking, and its imaginative use of Louisiana's native bounty combine into one of those savory Creole concoctions in which there seems no end to the variety of delicious morsels, no possibility of discerning every taste in the rich amalgam of herbs and seasonings, and no worry of ever hearing the serving spoon scrape the bottom of the pot.

A pretty heady dish this, especially when you add the book's generous lagniappe—its many vignettes of local color. Some are as simple as the root-beer recipe that calls for ten gallons of Mississippi River water. Others are as lengthy as the extended tour, month by month, of the produce flowing into the French Market . . . or the evocative description of the old black women crying *"Belle cala! Tout chaud!"* through the Sunday-morning streets of the French Quarter, selling from the cloth-covered bowls balanced on their heads the crisp, hot rice cakes that, with a cup of steaming *café au lait*, were the start of many a Creole family's Sabbath.

All this charm, however, would be nothing if it were not for the underlying simplicity of its purpose: to teach this century's increasingly Americanized young Creole cooks the traditional French ways of turning little into much. The need of the editors to both explain these methods and make them seem appealing shows how much was already fading out of the commonly shared understanding. The urge to make faith explicit comes with the threat of its demise.

In this stated purpose, it is not unlike another great American cook-book published about this time (1883), *Mrs. Lincoln's Boston Cook Book* (the book that inspired Fannie Farmer). Both books gave instruction to young, bourgeois housewives who could no longer depend on their moth-ers' experience as a guide to managing the house—or expect to find trained servant girls to perform the cooking and cleaning for them.

Despite their personal flavor, both can be seen as textbooks; the dif-ference is in their approach. Mrs. Lincoln begins her book with a lec-ture: "[Cooking] must be based upon scientific principles of hygiene and what the French call the minor moralities of the household." The *Picayune* begins *its* cookbook with instructions on how to brew a good pot of coffee. Why? Because to be able to do this was one of the first prerequisites of Creole social life.

Where Mrs. Lincoln opens class with an admonitory shake of the pointer and an appeal to principle, the *Picayune* bids everyone pull up a chair and have a cup of coffee before getting down to making the pot-au-feu. For the one, cooking has already been relegated to its modern place as a mere activity, another household task; for the other, it remains as well a sensual experience, a communal sharing of pleasure and tradition.

The Picayune's Creole Cook Book mentions a host of foods that do not appear in *Mrs. Lincoln's Boston Cook Book*, even though many of them were still then being eaten, if more and more ashamedly, in New England. This is the difference between Yankee and Creole frugality: a distrust of sensuality versus its enlistment to the cause.

The Puritan ethos could not stamp out pleasure but did make it snobbishly fussy—turning up its nose at what it was not compelled to desire. No one would know from Mrs. Lincoln the pleasure humble Yankee eaters took from their vegetables. Her book has no mention of the following, all found in the *Picayune*: butter beans, curled kale, broccoli, Brussels sprouts, ccpcs, chervil, chives, collard greens, cress, endive, kohlrabi, leeks, lentils, hot peppers, rocket, shallots, and sorrel. Nor does she much touch on herbs, whereas the *Picayune* is fragrant with them, listing twenty-seven, from anise to wormwood.

However, as time has passed, *The Picayune's Creole Cook Book* has become harder for the home cook to navigate with any certainty and the aficionado of Creole cooking to read with absolute trust. The original authorial voice, though both knowledgeable and charming, has the anonymous quality of all editorial writing, and the book thus misses, as such compilations tend to do, the guiding sensibility of a single palate, a problem compounded by the fact that no indication is ever given of the provenance of any particular recipe.

Thus, in revising it, *The Times-Picayune* had the splendid opportunity to at least attempt to discover who the original editors were and where they got their recipes—and especially to distinguish which of these were truly made by Creole cooks and not taken from French cookbooks that had made their way into Creole households and then copied into this one to give it tone. In other words, the best possible choice would have been to find an editor for the project with impeccable Creole credentials, a strong sense of New Orleans history and Creole cuisine, and a generous measure of intellectual curiosity about the book and the people who put it together.

Instead, *The Times-Picayune* put the project into the hands of Marcelle Bienvenu. Although the jacket blurb claims that she "collaborated with the editors of the Time-Life American Cooking Series on . . . *Acadian and Creole Cooking*," in that book itself she is credited as the local consultant for the photographer—"a public information assistant at LSU" hired to get him through doors. Since then, she has been in the restaurant business and even produced a food column for *The Times-Picayune* called "Cooking Creole."

Unfortunately, being born into a French Creole family and having written about and cooked Creole dishes all one's life doesn't automatically bestow an intuitive understanding of that cuisine's French Louisiana roots, let alone a working, factual knowledge of it. For instance, she confesses that she spent an entire week attempting to track down "Maunsell White, which for a short time we believed to be a wine"— this, although the *Picayune* clearly states that it is a pepper-based bottled sauce. Then there is her bland observation that the French Market "no longer exists as it was known in the early 1900s. It has been replaced by hundreds of supermarkets." "Overthrown," "deposed," "subverted" . . . yes. But *replaced*?

That she knew next to nothing about the cookbook itself is evident from the "two-hour crying jag" she went into when she realized it had "more than a thousand recipes!" Of course, one can but sympathize. If only she had resigned forthwith, everything might have turned out for the better. Instead, it seems, she and *The Times-Picayune* agreed that many of those thousand recipes would have to go, keeping only those that (my italics) "*I felt* were indicative of the Creole cuisine at the turn of the century, as well as those *I think* are Creole classics and favorites."

Obviously, the original editors' opinion mattered little, since one of the first to get the ax was "Rabbit Soup," described by *them* as a "famous Creole soup." As one turns the pages, noting what gets in and what gets left out, Bienvenu's actual criteria become clear: (1) Do we already have one? and (2) Is it "quaint"? "Winter Okra Soup" goes, though different from "Okra Soup," because one such soup is enough. A sausage of boiled beef, *Saucisse de Bouilli*, gets dumped despite its fascinating combination of French economy and extravagance (boiled beef and truffles!) and Creole seasonings (garlic, allspice, cayenne)— because, one supposes, the editor looked at it with confusion: Who would ever make *this*?

Yes, well, still . . . lop, lop, lop, and what do we have left? Not, admittedly, something quite as bad as *The Picayune's Greatest Creole Hits*. But with so much historical legitimacy lost on the cutting-room floor, what remains is not much more than an anthology of Creole recipes—something less than the original edition, even if the majority of the recipes were culled from it. (Among the dishes taken from later ones is "Oysters Rockefeller," without noting that the recipe for herb-and-butter-topped oysters broiled in their shells that appears in the original edition shows that Jules Alciatore's creation was hardly cut from whole cloth.)

This shabby treatment of a culinary classic might be understandable (though still not excusable) if the pruning and the many hours of recipe testing by Food Innovisions [sic], Inc., had produced accessible versions of even a selected number of recipes. Instead, a system of sporadic annotation was decided on, which, while occasionally helpful, all too often falls into the category of insipid ejaculation—"Steamed or boiled potatoes are delicious!"—or confession of failure, such as this coy note appended to the cake section: "After testing, only a few of these recipes were found to be workable. Good luck!" Thanks a lot.

The moral here, if there is one, is that in modern America, you aren't born with roots—you have to work hard to grow your own. Until *The Picayune's Creole Cook Book* finds an editor who understands that, the cook—Creole or otherwise—is still best advised to seek out the inexpensive facsimile reproduction available from Dover Publications. Despite its old-fashioned double columns and tiny print, it's still quite readable and, best of all, in its original version remains forever innocent of the fact that later editors will find it "charming, entertaining, and educational" . . . and treat it accordingly.

CASTINE, 1990

. . . AND A NOTE ON THE CAJUN SPIRAL-BOUND

Happily, true down-home Cajun cooking can be found in abundance in the locally published spiral-bound cookbooks which still flourish in Louisiana and which—unlike most of their genre—are often well worth seeking out. However, they must be approached with caution. For if we are still without anything like a definitive Cajun cookbook, the major reason for this may be the one inadvertently revealed by Trent Angers in *Acadia Profile's Cajun Cooking*. When he went out into the community to gather recipes, he discovered that his subjects "seemed a bit surprised that anyone could be so naïve as to think that a real Cajun cook would have recipes in written form."

So Angers himself watched what they did and wrote down the basic structure of the dish in recipe form. The rest—the magic touches that made each dish different from the way it was made the day before and marked it as the distinct creation of a particular cook—was devalued as too personal and too insubstantial for print, depending as it did both on whim and what was in the larder that day.

Consequently, in that cookbook and in the many like it, any given recipe is—at best—the simple tune that a Cajun is humming in the back of her mind when she starts cooking. But you won't pull the actual riffs out of that recipe any more than you can work up Clifton Chenier's way with *"Jolie Blonde"* from sheet music. If you want to cook Cajun, such cookbooks are only a starting point. You have to go out and taste the cooking to get a feel for the beat—and then try to figure out how to work that harmony into your own gumbo pot.

The value of these cookbooks, then, does not lie in their individual recipes. Only if you are willing to search out the relationship of one dish to another and to compare different versions of the same dish from book to book can you hope to learn something of what Cajun cuisine is all about. Consequently, you will need at least a few of them, and you will want them to be as authentic as possible.

To begin with, look for mention of dishes you've never heard of and ingredients that in another context might completely put you off. When it comes to vernacular cookbooks, the rule is, the more unself-conscious the better—wherever that may lead. The acid test of a true Cajun cook-book is the sense it conveys of omnivorous intimacy with the local flora and fauna (such as *Louisiana Lagniappe*'s armadillo sauce piquante or *La Cuisine Cajun*'s blackbird gumbo).* Even if you can't or won't do this kind of cooking, it helps guarantee that these recipes spring from the vernacular tradition of that area and not from some food editor's head.

How to get hold of these books is another question. The next best thing to an afternoon searching through the souvenir shops in the French Quarter is spending some time with *Best of the Best from Louisiana*, an anthology edited by Gwen McKee and Barbara Moseley. It is comprised entirely of recipes taken from vernacular spiral-bounds. Not only is the source of each recipe clearly identified, but a section at the end of the book briefly describes each of the books excerpted—about fifty or so —with the information needed to order them. It is an attractively pro-duced sampling of Louisiana's cuisine, a complex and not at all homogeneous mixture of Creole, Cajun, Italian, and black and white Southern cooking.

Among the spiral-bounds *not* sampled in that compilation, however, is one of my own favorites: *Acadia Profile's Cajun Cooking*, edited by Trent Angers and Sue McDonough (Angers Publishing Corp., P.O. Box 52247, Lafayette, LA 70505). Two other excellent sources for these cookbooks have already been mentioned: Pelican Publishing (1101

---

* Nevertheless, I've yet to encounter in any of them a recipe for nutria gumbo. Nutria are water rodents with garish, Velveeta-colored fangs, introduced into southern Loui-siana as a fur-ranching animal around 1940. They have since run rampant, becoming a serious danger to the marsh ecology. Cajuns trap and skin them—there is a strong European market for their pelts—and although they don't as readily admit this, they eat them. Nutria, according to one aficionado, makes a "thoroughly rich and mysterious gumbo." There are drawbacks, even so. Reporting on the failed effort of Louisiana market researchers to drum up an interest in nutria meat, the Baton Rouge *State Times* (January 18, 1982) noted that "nobody wants to eat nutria because, at heart, nobody wants to eat a big, ugly, overgrown rat."

Monroe Street, Gretna, LA 70053), which has a long list of contemporary and reissued vintage Louisiana cookbooks, and The Louisiana General Store (see page 219), whose catalogue has several pages of vernacular Cajun and Creole cookbooks.

THE CAJUN/CREOLE FILMS OF LES BLANK

Les Blank is an independent filmmaker (*Burden of Dreams; Garlic Is as Good as Ten Mothers*) who has carried on a career-long love affair with Louisiana music, grittily and yet tenderly captured in such films as *Hot Pepper*, *Piano Players Rarely Ever Play Together*, *Zydeco*, and *Les Blues De Balfa*. This affection has spilled over into four more movies about Louisiana bayou life—black and white, Creole and Cajun.

The first, *Dry Wood*, follows around the zydeco musicians "Bois Sec" Ardoin, his sons, and Canray Fontenot, while the second, *Spend It All*, hangs out with the Balfa Brothers, Nathan Abshire, and Marc Savoy. While one is about black Creoles and the other about French Cajuns, the lives of both are very much the same. Each group of musicians does a lot of playing at dances, eating places, and parties, including some of their own. And in both films, as we come along to these various road joints, barbecues, pig killings, and gumbos to watch and listen, we find ourselves drawn into the circle of family and friends.

There is no narration in either film. Like any newcomer, we're left to make out for ourselves who's related to whom, what's going on, and why. But as we do so, we feel these people become our neighbors—and want some of them, at least, to become our friends. Les Blank accomplishes this intimacy by letting his camera linger on his subjects as they have their say. He holds these shots long after you would expect him to cut away, giving us time not only to hear and see but also to feel.

These two movies were made in the 1970s. How much has changed and how much remains the same can be seen in two more-recent films Blank released in 1990. The first of them, *Yum, Yum, Yum!*, is a light-hearted exploration of the current Creole/Cajun culinary scene. Although it has a cameo appearance by Paul Prudhomme (and some remarkable shots of his chefs at work in the kitchen of his New Orleans restaurant, K Paul's Louisiana Kitchen), the emphasis is on true bayou cooking.

In fact, perhaps its funniest moment comes when three rural Cajun cooks, having just assembled a "goo court bouillon" (a fish stew of goujon, a local variety of catfish) and cooked it over an outdoor wood fire, are asked by an off-screen Les Blank if they've ever heard of Paul Prudhomme. Looks of total bafflement: not one has. In fact, none of the three has ever read a cookbook. When Blank asks how they learned to cook, they answer in unison: "Just watchin'."

Again, Blank's camera tarries on the doings long enough for us to take it all in—Queen Ida Guillory working up an okra *étouffée* with shrimp, Margaret Chenier making dirty rice, Marc Savoy preparing a roux—and even get some feel for the cooking style itself. My favorite passage is the interview with Margaret Chenier, who explains how she won over her husband, Clifton Chenier, to her own way of making biscuits, while in the background we hear a recording of Clifton's "*J'aime pain du maïs*," in which he sings about just how good those biscuits are. As she goes on, you realize other reasons why Clifton might have been won over. That Margaret is some lady.

The fourth and last film, *Marc and Ann*, returns to Marc Savoy, Cajun musician, accordion maker, and mentor to a whole younger generation of Cajun musicians. The couple, first seen in *Spend It All*, are shown here still struggling to preserve their lives and culture from encroaching cultural homogenization . . . and Cajun media saturation.

Once, when Marc Savoy was asked if he regretted that the Cajuns had ever been discovered, he replied, "I'm even sorrier the Cajuns have discovered themselves," warning that their culture is in danger of dying of "acute cuteness." However, there is nothing cute about these movies. Even in as easygoing an effort as *Yum, Yum, Yum!*, Blank manages to show that the wildness of bayou good times is a corollary of the hardness of bayou life—the pain remains in the lyrics even as it is transformed by the driving lilt of the tune. Similarly, a feast of boiled crawfish starts with a long shot of the amphibious equivalent of a lobster boat rolling across a flooded rice field as its driver yanks up trap after trap and dumps his fiercely squirming, claw-clicking catch into the waiting plastic tubs.

Videotapes of these and other Les Blank movies are available from Flower Films, 10341 San Pablo Ave., El Cerrito, CA 94530, 415–525–0942. Their catalogue is $1.00.

CASTINE, 1990

Rice & Beans
The Itinerary of a Dish

People who were raised on this basic food develop a craving for it that persists no matter to what dizzying heights they rise in business and commerce. All the way from South America to the Mason-Dixon Line, variations of rice and beans are a way of life. —MIRIAM UNGERER, *Good Cheap Food*

Being from New England, I didn't encounter my first plate of rice and beans until I was an adult. It was love at first bite. Even though no winter ever goes by without our setting the bean pot in the oven and filling the house with the heady, mustardy, salt-pork-and-molasses odor of baked beans, it is an event in our lives, not a Saturday-night regular. This is not true with rice and beans. They are as aromatic and flavorful as baked beans, but almost always lighter, more digestible, and, frankly, more interesting. A Haitian or Jamaican or black New Orleans Creole cook can take up the same basic ingredients—rice, dried beans, some seasonings, and maybe a bit of pot meat—and, a few hours later, set down on the table before you a dish at once recognizable and transformed.

The result: the more you know about rice and beans, the more the dish inspires you as a cook and delights you as an eater. I had only to try them once to recognize the start of a lifelong romance. My first pot of rice and beans came off the stove when I was living out my starving-writer days in a tenement on the Lower East Side, and they are still coming off my stove in these sadder and wiser days as a responsible citizen.

Until I tasted rice and beans, my impression of Southern cooking reflected the opinion of one James Creecy, who lamented of nineteenth-century Mississippi, "I have never fallen in with any cooking so villainous," or that of a medical man of the same century who succinctly laid out the variations in Southern fare. "Fat bacon and pork, fat bacon and pork only, and that continually morning, noon, and night, for all classes, sexes, ages, and conditions," he lamented. "Hog's lard is the very oil that moves the machinery of life, and they would as soon think of dispensing with tea, coffee, [or] tobacco . . . as with the essence of hog."

Essence of hog! The Southern-white vernacular diet traditionally has been laden with pork dishes and fried breads. "Hog and hominy," as one scholar put it. You must turn to Southern black cooking to find the inspired herb and vegetable dishes that have come to be numbered among the region's specialties. Drawing both on native African traditions and foods brought with them (although not necessarily *by* them) to this continent, black slaves soon managed to provide for themselves (when they were allowed to) a varied and nutritional diet, especially when compared to the fat-laden, vitamin-hungry eating of poor Southern whites.

It is true that black cooks utilized the same meats, but traditional black cooking is based on different cuts, different amounts, and a very different approach. Slave owners kept the best parts of the pig for themselves, leaving the slaves to deal with the fatback, the innards, and the offal. This challenge to the ingenuity of the black cook produced a cuisine that combined sound nutrition with highly flavored and imaginative dishes.

Their cuisine is based on the combination of starch—for over a century, only fortunate black cooks had rice—and legumes, with greens. It was only as rice became universally cheap and universally available that it pushed out corn mush and pounded tropical roots to produce the signature dish—whether the hoppin' John of the Carolinas, Creole red beans and rice, or the *feijoada* of Brazil—of a common cooking tradition whose elements can be identified in the cuisines of the Caribbean, the American South, and those parts of Latin America—especially Brazil —where a slave culture existed.

Of course, an inventive bean cookery is part and parcel of all Latin American culinary traditions, since the true bean (as opposed to the lentil and the fava) originated there. But dishes that combine beans with rice are relatively rare, because rice itself is a recent introduction. Consequently, almost all strictly Latin recipes call for *"arroz con . . ."* ("rice with") and not *"arroz y . . ."* ("rice and"), rice being an addition to and not an integral part of the dish.*

It is this judicious balancing of rice and beans that makes the dish so memorably fine. While most rice and bean dishes are no strangers to "essence of hog," the amount (and type) of fat used is completely under the control of the cook. The combination of rice, beans, fat, and seasonings produces a dish that is endlessly variable, economical, highly nutritious, and digestible. Rice and beans combine to make an almost perfect protein (entirely completed when the traditional side of cornbread is served).

It is this, I think, that makes rice and beans seem so easy on the digestive tract. I know, despite the many portions I have consumed in my researches, that I still look forward to the next. Few dishes offer so much for so little, and fewer still have wended their way through our history to the present moment remaining as redolent as this dish is of its culinary heritage, or so aware of its origins.

THE HEARTH AND THE COOKING POT

The start of any story of black cooking in the Americas is on a plantation, whether growing sugarcane in Dominica, cotton in Georgia, or rice in the Carolinas. Wherever it was, the story was pretty much the same. At sundown the slaves left off work to return to their cabins, some made better than others, but the best with no more than a planked floor, windows without glass, and a large hearth. This might be fully four feet across, the fireplace itself most often made of mud, clay, and sticks, and thus only partially fireproof. As Benny Dillard, a former slave, remembered:

> De fireplaces was a heap bigger dan dey has now, for all de cookin' was done in open fireplaces den. 'Taters and cornpone was roasted in de ashes and most of de other victuals was biled in de big old pots what swing on cranes over de coals. Dey had long-handled fryin' pans and heavy iron skillets wid big, thick, tight-fittin' lids, and ovens of all sizes to bake in. All of dem things was used right dar

* An exception of the sort that proves the rule is Nicaragua's *gallo pinto*, a delicious version of red beans and rice (the *gallo pinto* is itself a small red kidney bean much like the Louisiana red bean) where the rice and beans are cooked separately and then fried together—some say the longer the better—in onion-flavored lard.

in de fireplace. Dere never was no better tastin' somepin t' eat dan cooked in dem old cook things in open fireplaces.

With luck, embers would still be smoldering in the ashes, for otherwise restarting a fire, rubbing flint rocks over cotton lint until a spark caught, was a time-costly business. Slaves, especially when they cooked for themselves, were adept at saving time: they could pluck, dissect, and fry a chicken in less than half an hour . . . when there was a chicken to cook.

Those who were allowed their own garden plots raised chickens and ate them when they quit laying eggs, either pan-frying them or wrapping them in cabbage leaves to roast under a heap of hot coals on the hearth floor. Squirrel, raccoon, rabbit, or catfish might be on the menu or, if other skills were put to use, one of de massa's turkeys or suckling pigs. (Whole pigs might be commandeered also, but presented more of a problem to the acquirer. "You have to catch him by the snoot so he won't squeal, and clomp him tight while you knife him," remembered Richard Carruthers of Texas, a former slave.)

Usually, however, the meal would be much simpler fare, such as cornmeal and fat cooked up together in a skillet. But surprisingly often, the exhausted black women coming in from the fields found the strength to put up a meal from the humblest and scantiest provisions that was tasty, nutritious, and filling, and that to a remarkable extent reflected their African birthright.

The food historian Karen Hess, in her ground-breaking study of the African influences on rice growing and cooking in the Carolinas, *The Carolina Rice Kitchen* (see pages 409–10), has shown that rice culture already existed in Africa at the time of the slave trade, and that—on the Carolina rice plantations—slaves from that part of Africa were especially valued. Indeed, it might be argued that wetland rice cultivation in America was almost entirely a black contribution, albeit an unwilling one.*

The slave population in the South in general, however disparate its African origins, still shared common culinary roots. As with the cuisine of all poor people, the central food in most of Africa is starch, called "fufu," made from various root vegetables by pounding these into a paste

* The contents of this essay were issued as a tiny culinary pamphlet long before the publication of *The Carolina Rice Kitchen*, and in that book Karen Hess often takes issue with it. Indeed, whenever she castigates "certain white writers," chances are she means me. The following text, while it still does not carry her imprimatur, has substantially benefited from that critique.

and cooking them in water to produce a thick porridge. In the parts of Africa where rice is not grown, fufu is made of yams, cassava, plantain, or cocoyams; in the American South, except in Carolina plantation country, these vegetables were most often supplanted by cornmeal.

The protein complement was made up with the generous addition of beans—whether kidney beans, cowpeas, black-eyed peas, lima beans, or pigeon peas. Vitamins came from salads and stewed greens, including the nutrition-rich "pot-likker," and fat came from the weekly ration of fatback. Finally, and also in the African tradition, this largely bland fare was picked up by the addition of herbs and spices, and particularly with hot peppers.

The Portuguese introduced hot peppers to Africa around 1500, where they enchanted not only native Africans but native African birds—who gradually spread the seeds throughout the continent. Hot pepper is now an integral part of African cuisine, so much so that it is said that the fondness of a wife for her husband can be read in the hotness of her spices. One of the secrets of the black cook is a deft but bravura hand with it.

Most blacks during slave days ate beans without rice. Rice was an important cash crop and was common fare for slaves only on the rice plantations that produced it. There exist many soul bean dishes that call for no rice at all. Most likely, the combination of rice and beans began in the West Indies and spread through those islands' amazing polyglot patchwork of cultures, and only then to the United States. Very probably, the logical start for any investigation of the roots of this dish should start in the Caribbean, not the American South.

The danger there is that the romantic dazzle of calypso and reggae rhythms, the torchlit nights and brilliant days, the aquamarine waters lapping glistening beaches, might all conspire to make us forget that the cooking these islands share is the legacy of slaves who created in the privacy of their huts over the warmth of a small fire an elaborate cuisine that preserved a sense of self and provided a convivial center of life.

Look, then, across the darkening fields, silent except for the occasional call of a whippoorwill, to that solitary sharecropper's cabin. In the window can be seen the spluttering blue flame of a battered kerosene stove. In front of it, bent over a few meticulously kept pots and pans, a black woman, who has worked all day with a short hoe beside her husband, begins the evening meal. Such are the memories, the rich web of evocative associations still called forth in the South by hoppin' John. Evan Jones defines soul food in his *American Food* as "the application of culinary genius to overlooked odds and ends and leftovers," and amplifies that definition with these words from soul-food restaurant proprietress Princess Pamela Strobel:

> Soul food, black folk cooking is compassion food . . . still close enough to honest-to-God hunger to impart to food a savor deep enough for joy and solace.

THE DEEP SOUTH & THE COWPEA

Their chief sustenance is a porridge of cowpeas, and the greatest luxury with which they are acquainted is a stew of bacon and peas, with red pepper, which they call hopping John
—FREDERICK LAW OLMSTED, *A Journey in the Seaboard Slave States* (1866)

As a food for man, the cowpea should be to the South, what the White, Soup, Navy, or Boston bean is to the North, East, and West: and it may be prepared in a sufficient number of ways to suit the most fastidious palate.
—GEORGE WASHINGTON CARVER (1903)

Cowpeas were not the only beans that blacks grew in their gardens, but for most Southerners, black and white, they are the bean with the strongest association of place. As Mrs. T. J. Woodward wrote:

> South Carolinians . . . who have been away from home a long time . . . always long for something called Hopping John, with an accent on the John. This substantial dish is as characteristic of South Carolina as are baked beans of Massachusetts. It is made with what are known in the South as cowpeas. It may be impossible to secure these in the North.

The cowpea comes in many variations and appears under many names. It is called the Tonkin pea, the Jerusalem pea, the whippoorwill pea, the marble pea, and, most often, the cornfield pea. This last is usually now shortened to field pea, because it was often planted in the borders of the cornfields, beans and corn having as natural an affinity in the garden as on the plate. Close relations include the black-eyed pea, the brown-eyed pea, and the cream pea.

Although all are of the same family, each variety has its own appearance and flavor, and cooks in this or that corner of the South insist that *their* pea is not interchangeable with any of the others, a preference so steeped with conviction that it can seem near-visceral. However, today, outside those corners, the black-eyed pea seems to have generally replaced the cowpea as the common denominator in Southern dried-pea recipes. Certainly, whether canned, frozen, or dried, it is the most likely of the group to be found on the grocer's shelf elsewhere in the country.

The basic Southern recipe for cowpeas is to boil them until tender in water with a chunk of pork (whether salt, pickled, or fresh; lean or fat) until done, seasoning to taste. If it is possible to distinguish between black and white versions of so simple a dish, it is in the matter of emphasis: for all but the poorest white cook, boiled peas is categorized as a side dish; for black cooks, even if it is prepared as a side dish, it remains at heart something more . . . and may still be made with a little more side meat, and the side meat might more likely be hog jowl, hog maw, or tail.

Another distinction—which, given today's growing taste for hot pepper, is fast fading—is the use of cayenne versus black pepper. As already noted, Southern blacks are used to having a patch of fiery peppers in their garden. Black pepper, however, as Karen Hess notes, is store food, and relatively expensive store food at that. An informant told her that in one black community there were those "who had never seen black pepper"—and this "as recently as the memory of a man born in 1914."

Of course, all black cooking is no more highly seasoned and heaped with side meat than all white cooking is universally bland, but cultural patterns are a matter of historical record. Although these are the two mighty rivers whose confluence is Southern cooking, their sources are distinct . . . however much they have now come to mingle. And today, most Southerners, no matter their color, hold hoppin' John to be the best and most beloved of all the dishes in which cowpeas play a part . . . perhaps even the most beloved dish of all.

Hoppin' John

The one most astonishing thing about hoppin' John is the endurance of its rigorous simplicity. As Karen Hess notes, "receipts for hoppin' John have remained remarkably traditional for as long as they have been printed." Cowpeas or black-eyed peas are cooked with fat pork, to which raw rice is added at the proper time. Seasoning is restricted to salt and black or red pepper. Elaborations are few and slight: some cooks add an onion, others a bit of fresh herb.

To understand the great and poignant imaginative power that has held this dish true to its origins through the centuries, we must first face the fact that when one talks of the foods that slaves "brought with them from Africa," we are allowing ourselves to elide a painful reality. The only thing that Africans brought with them was their memories. If they were fortunate enough to have been taken along with other members of their own community and to stay with them (which rarely happened)— there was also the possibility of reestablishing out of these memories some truncated resemblance of former rituals and customs. But of physical possessions, they had *none*.

Even in the best of circumstances, the Atlantic crossing had devastating effects on all aboard, evidenced not only by persistent slave attempts at suicide but by the surprisingly high mortality rate of slave-ship *crews*. As to the slaves themselves, perpetually shackled, penned in fetid, hot, and near-airless holds, and vulnerable to the unfettered run of contagious disease, terror, and despair, their mental as well as physical health deteriorated at a rate alarming even to the slavers— who, after all, could profit from their human cargo only if it was delivered, at the very least, alive.

One of the few possible ways of easily ameliorating the slaves' lot, apart from drugging them with alcohol and tobacco, was to feed them tolerable meals. These, in good weather, were served on deck in the fresh air, and the slavers soon learned to try to make them as palatable as possible by concocting out of shipboard rations some faint simulacrum of native fare.

As early as 1707, the Royal African Company—the British slavery syndicate—was directing its ships when loading slaves in Africa to also take on the following cargo to sustain them: "fifty chests of corn, forty pounds of malaguetta pepper, twenty gallons of palm oil, two bushels of salt, and twenty gallons of rum for each hundred slaves."

As much as possible, slave traders attempted to augment this basic diet with foods associated with such different groups of Africans as they might carry: yams for the Ibos, for example, and rice and corn for slaves from the Gold and Windward Coasts. They also obtained plantains, coconuts, and other foods capable of easy purchase and storage, and all this apart from large stores of flour, ship's biscuit, and beans (plus huge amounts of rum, tobacco, and the cheapest kind of clay smoking pipes) that had been on-loaded before the departure from England.

The slaves were fed twice a day. Alexander Falconbridge, a British surgeon hired to keep the slaves alive on these crossings, described this event in his harrowing narrative of that experience, *An Account of the Slave Trade on the Coast of Africa*, published in 1788:

The diet of the negroes, while on board, consists chiefly of horse-beans, boiled to the consistence of a pulp; boiled yams and rice, and sometimes a small quantity of beef or pork. The latter are frequently taken from the provisions laid in for the sailors. They sometimes make use of a sauce, comprised of palm-oil, mixed with flour, water and [hot] pepper, which the sailors called *slabber-sauce.*

However, the hollowness of such self-serving "humanitarianism" can be seen in the slavers' obtuseness regarding the essential component of this diet: the beans. Horse (or fava) beans were large, coarse-textured beans that in England (as the name implies) were used primarily as fodder. They were nothing at all like the African cowpea or black-eyed pea, and so far as the slaves were concerned, to be forced to eat them exacerbated rather than alleviated the nightmare. As Falconbridge observed:

Unless [the Africans] were narrowly watched, when fed upon deck, they will throw them overboard, or in each other's faces when they quarrel.

To the slavers' mind, beans were beans, and it was easier and cheaper to obtain them in England, especially as they had to be purchased in such quantity (the slave ship *Norman,* planning to carry three hundred slaves, set sail from London in 1714 with well over a thousand pounds of them). However, to their captives, a people who had lost everything, the eventual acquisition of their own native peas would have a sweetness that still reverberates down the centuries. This sweetness is reflected in the peas themselves: black-eyed peas especially are uniquely delicate and delicious, in a way quite different from any other dried peas (fresh, their only competition is the English—sweet green—pea). No wonder they provide the foundation for black Creole cuisine . . . and the prime ingredient for its essential dish: hoppin' John.

Every indication points to hoppin' John coming to the American South from the Caribbean Islands, since at least some etymologists believe that "hoppin' John" is a corruption of *pois à pigeon* (especially if the *à* is elided in the Creole manner to make *pois pigeon* [pwaah-peejon]).* Pigeon peas were another bean brought from Africa to the Americas. Although widely prolific in the West Indies, they have not flourished in this country, and cowpeas have more or less supplanted them.

Cut off from the source of its name and gentrified into "hopping

* Karen Hess, again in *The Carolina Rice Kitchen,* makes a case for a more complex derivation, tracing "hoppin' " from the Hindi word for cooked rice and "John" from the Malay for pulses.

John," hoppin' John became a meaningless phrase, and folk etymologies evolved to supply the necessary "explanations," as did, for example, Harriet Ross Colquitt in *The Savannah Cookbook* (1933):

> As children, it was our custom, when word went round we were to have hoppin' John for dinner, to gather in the dining room and as the dish was brought forth to hop around the table before sitting down to the feast.

It eventually wended its way into the *American Heritage Cookbook*, where, bereft of the ingenuousness of young Harriet, it becomes a condescending platitude:

> The name [hoppin' John] may have derived from the custom that children must hop once around the table before the dish is served or may have been the sobriquet of a lively waiter.

Or . . . well, others still tell of a certain John who came "a-hoppin' " when his wife took the dish from the stove; still others of an otherwise obscure South Carolina custom of inviting a guest to eat by saying, "Hop in, John."

In all probability, hoppin' John—name and dish—was brought to this country by slaves transported from the rice plantations in the West Indies to those in Louisiana and South Carolina, especially the Gullah country in back of Charleston. From there it gradually spread throughout the South, ultimately to win from blacks and whites alike a partisan loyalty equal only to that held by grits and barbecue.

However, most hoppin' John recipes are identical except for tiny variations—one cook using bay leaf, another thyme—so rather than repeat them all I have composed the following master recipe, which allows for individual taste in the matter of seasoning and explains the traditional options that a Carolina cook might elect in order to give the dish her personal signature.

Hoppin' John, like almost all rice-and-bean dishes, is considered lucky, especially when served on New Year's Day. "Eat poor that day, eat rich the rest of the year" is both the explanation and the hope . . . but the experience is one of reaffirming one's roots. Finally, vegetarians will want to note that in New Orleans, on Fridays and during Lent, butter or vegetable oil was substituted for all meat and fat. A hoppin' John made with olive oil and a generous pinch of hot pepper is a very good dish. Be sure to read the recipe through carefully, to chart your own course, before you begin to cook.

HOPPIN' JOHN

1 cup black-eyed peas or cowpeas prepared for cooking as directed on pages 293–94; a small chunk of lean slab bacon, sliced thick, *or* a cracked ham or beef bone (George Washington Carver recommends the latter, saying, "It adds much to the flavor") *or* a small chunk of salt pork, sliced and simmered in ample water for 15 minutes to reduce the salt; 1 onion, chopped; 1 cup raw rice; 1 hot red pepper, fresh or dried, seeded and diced, *or* Tabasco sauce to taste; and (all, some, or one of the following, as you choose) 1 clove of garlic, minced; 1 bay leaf; minced fresh parsley; a little thyme. Season well with salt and pepper.

Bring 5 cups of water to a boil. Add the beans, with the bay leaf, if using, and let them simmer for about 45 minutes. (If you are using a cracked pork or beef bone, add it now also, and ignore all bacon/salt pork instructions, frying up the onion in a bit of melted fat or oil and adding it when you add the rice.) While the beans are cooking, prepare the bacon/salt pork by frying it until the pieces are crisp. Either reserve these until the end of cooking (to lend a touch of crispness) or put them into the beans when the rice is added. Fry the onion in the fat once the pork has been removed until it is translucent but not brown. Either way, reserve the fat.

At the end of 45 minutes, taste the beans for doneness; your tongue should be able to mash them against the roof of the mouth. If they are soft but not mushy, they are done just right. Eyeball the remaining liquid in the pot—there should be at least 2½ cups. If not, add more water. Pour in the rice and mix in all the other seasonings, the bacon/salt pork bits (unless holding them for the end), and all—or as much as you want of—the cooking fat. Stir the mixture well and bring the liquid up to a simmer. Let cook for another 20 minutes. Then turn off the heat and let the hoppin' John rest for 10 minutes. Taste. The beans should be just a little more tender, the rice perfectly cooked. Crumble over the reserved bacon or sprinkle over the crisp salt-pork bits, if any, and serve. Pass around a platter of cornbread and a salad of fresh greens or a bowl of cooked ones. This is a meal that will feed 4 very well indeed.

RED BEANS & NEW ORLEANS

Red beans are to New Orleans what the white bean is to Boston and the cowpea
is to South Carolina.   —FEDERAL WRITERS PROJECT, *New Orleans City Guide*

The Creoles hold that the boys and girls who are raised on beans and rice and
beef will be among the strongest and sturdiest people
                                                    —*The Picayune's Creole Cook Book*

As A. J. Liebling once happily observed, "The Mediterranean, Caribbean, and Gulf of Mexico form a homogeneous, although interrupted
sea"—a sea that connects New Orleans as much to Marseilles as to
Port-au-Prince. And it was the French influence on the black Creole
cook that transformed hoppin' John into red beans and rice.

> Quartee beans and quartee rice,
> And a little *lagniappe* to make it nice.
> —NEW ORLEANS STREET VENDER'S CRY

A "quartee" was half a nickel's worth, and the lagniappe—a familiar
Creole term meaning a little something extra for free—was the pot seasonings. It is the addition of the *potager*—such French pot seasonings
as carrots, onion, parsley, celery, garlic, and so forth—that as much
differentiates the dish from hoppin' John as the substitution of red beans
for black-eyed peas.

Jambalaya au congri, the Louisiana name for hoppin' John, appears
in early Creole cookbooks made, as it is elsewhere in the South, with
rice, cowpeas, onion, and salt pork. The Creoles decided, however, that
they liked the flavor of red beans better than cowpeas, and over the
years the identity of *jambalaya au congri* was absorbed by *haricots
rouges au riz*. The nature of this merger becomes clear when you consider one of the earliest published recipes for red beans and rice, as it
appears in the 1902 edition of *The Picayune's Creole Cook Book*:

HARICOTS ROUGES AU RIZ

1 quart of dried red beans; 1 carrot; 1 onion; 1 bay leaf; 1 Tbsp.
butter; 1 lb. ham or salt meat; and salt and pepper to taste. Wash
the beans and soak them overnight, or at least five or six hours, in
fresh, cold water. When ready to cook, drain off this water and put
the beans in a pot of cold water, covering with at least two quarts,

for beans must cook thoroughly. Let the water heat slowly. Then add the ham or salt pork, the bay leaf, butter, onion and carrot, minced fine. Boil the beans at least two hours, or until tender enough to mash easily under pressure. When tender, remove from the pot, put the salt meat or ham on top of the dish, and serve hot as a vegetable, with boiled rice as an entrée, with Veal Sauté, Daube à la Mode, Grillades à la Sauce, etc.

Notice that the dish—as made then—is not necessarily even eaten with rice . . . quite unlike *jambalaya au congri*. However, as the years passed, Creole cooks took the method of making hoppin' John (and the legends that surrounded the dish) and prepared it instead with the ingredients in the recipe above, coming up with a composite dish that can bring the best out of both.

Red beans and rice are to New Orleans eaters, whether black or white, what chili is to Texans, so central a part of their culinary identity that Louis Armstrong used to close his letters with "Red beans and ricely yours." It was traditionally made on Monday with the bone of Sunday's ham, along with any remaining scraps of the meat or fat. Paul Prudhomme explains in *The Prudhomme Family Cookbook*:

> Red beans and rice is the traditional Monday meal in New Orleans. Monday was always washday and the family cook, or the lady of the house, could put on a pot of beans to cook and then get on with her washing while the beans simmered for hours with little or no attention. When the washing was done, the beans were ready to eat.

The dish's homey origins have been obscured by the fame it has enjoyed as a New Orleans restaurant dish, especially, thanks to the effusions of Calvin Trillin in *American Fried*, the version made by Buster Holmes at his restaurant at 721 Burgundy Street in the French Quarter.

When Buster Holmes moved to that location from his original hole-in-the-wall lunch counter on Dumaine Street in 1960, he sold a plate of his red beans and rice for twenty-six cents. When I tried them in the early 1980s, a heaping plateful was still under two dollars and had a richness that I then ascribed to a generous amount of ham fat, but which, if his cookbook can be believed, might well have been ham fat *and* a large dollop of margarine, added at the very last minute. (He also used smoked ham hocks for the meat, a little minced green bell pepper, and plenty of garlic.)

Buster Holmes—the restaurant—has had a varied history since then, and the last time I ate there the red beans and rice were not what they had been. Fortunately, however, excellent versions can be had in eateries all over the city, from the funky milieu of Eddie's on Law Street or Mandich's on St. Claude Avenue to the slick ambience of Copeland's. This is as it should be—red beans and rice is the heart and soul of southern Louisiana cooking.

Red Beans & Rice

As with hoppin' John, rather than reproducing a dozen or so very similar recipes, I've composed a master recipe, explaining the options so that the individual cook can fine-tune the results to taste. This explanation must begin with a few introductory words about the major ingredients.

First, the bean. Because I happen to detest kidney beans, for years I convinced myself that a special red bean was grown in Louisiana— the fabled *haricot rouge*—that New Orleans cooks kept to themselves and used to turn out red beans and rice. How else, I asked, could the dish be so *good*? However, I have since been forced to face the fact that "red bean" is just the literal translation of the French for kidney bean, and the phrase has become accepted New Orleans usage. But while there's no getting around that, a smaller, more delicately flavored kidney bean *is* grown in Louisiana for making this dish, and it is available—by the sackful, if you wish—from suppliers of Creole and Cajun foods.

Next, there is the matter of the ham bone. One camp, probably today the majority, insists that it is impossible to make a good batch of red beans and rice without one. The ham bone, cracked so that all the marrow will meld into the sauce, gives the beans a rich and unctuous coating, so much so that it "seems to drain them of starch, and produces a silky food that is more like an incredibly tender meat than a vegetable." Or so writes Peter S. Feibleman.

The minority, however, still opts for pickled pork. This New Orleans staple is cured in vinegar, herbs, spices, and hot pepper, producing a spicy, tangy meat that those who prefer it say is more in tune with the other seasonings in red beans and rice, while the ham bone, though good, makes it taste, as one New Orleans native told me, "just like a goddamn bowl of pea soup." Of course, recipes exist that call for *both* pickled pork and the ham bone, but this, I'm afraid, is a case of wanting to be everyone's friend and ending up no one's.

Pickled pork will definitely give your red beans and rice a distinctive flavor and, if you use a lean cut of pork, can help reduce the amount of fat. While it is generally unobtainable outside Louisiana, it isn't all that difficult to make. The following recipe makes enough for a couple of pots of red beans and rice. Note that this curing is for flavoring purposes only: keep the meat refrigerated.

PICKLED PORK

½ cup mustard seed; 1 tablespoon celery seed; 1 dried hot red pepper *or* 2 tablespoons powdered chile *or* 2 tablespoons Tabasco sauce; 1 quart distilled white vinegar; 1 bay leaf; 1 tablespoon pure salt; 12 whole peppercorns; 6 cloves of garlic, peeled and crushed flat with the side of a knife blade; and 1½ pounds fresh boneless pork butt, cut into 2-inch cubes, *or* 2–2½ pounds fresh country-style spare ribs, cut into individual ribs.

Combine all ingredients except the pork in a nonreactive (stainless steel or enameled cast-iron) pot and bring to a boil. Simmer for 3 minutes and let cool to room temperature. Place pork in a deep crock or bowl and cover with the pickling liquid, stirring with a wooden spoon to ensure that all air bubbles have been released. Set a small plate that fits inside the crock over the meat to press everything below the surface of the liquid. Cover lightly with plastic wrap and leave to cure in the refrigerator for at least 3 days, stirring occasionally. Use within 2 weeks.

There is also a school that prefers spicy Louisiana sausages to the ham bone or pickled pork, but the usual method is to add these as well rather than employ them as a replacement. Richard and Rima Collin's *The New Orleans Cook Book* gives recipes for making these sausages. They can also be ordered by mail or—most easily—replaced with Spanish *chorizo* or smoked kielbasa.

Finally, there is the controversy over whether the red beans and the rice should be cooked together. As noted above, *The Picayune's Creole Cook Book*—at least so far as *jambalaya au congri* is concerned—strictly directs that they be cooked separately. In part, this decision is an aesthetic one; there is something immediately visually appealing in the contrast between the still-white, still-fluffy rice and the smooth, dark gravy dotted with red beans, when the two are combined at the last possible moment. However, the starch that the cooking rice releases is an excellent sauce thickener, and those who like their red beans and rice with lots of liquid may well prefer to let the rice cook with the beans for the last half hour or so in the pot.

(Possibly one reason New Orleans citizens have come to object so strenuously to mixing the rice and the beans is that it prevents them from slipping some extra pods of garlic into the rice pot. Calvin Trillin reports that a child raised on Buster Holmes's rice [which—he claims —tests out at about 8 percent garlic by volume] refused to eat some ordinary rice served him on a trip away from the Big Easy, complaining that it tasted funny.)

Red beans and rice is again similar to chili in that fanatics have recently begun attempting to make names for themselves by transforming this relatively simple dish into a "gourmet masterpiece," producing recipes for it that look as though the chef's creativity was held in check only by the limitations of the kitchen spice shelf. On principle, I have rejected from consideration any additions such as catsup, flour, Worcestershire sauce, sugar, beef broth, vinegar, paprika, and more than two herbs (not counting garlic and/or parsley) as being more enthusiastic than truly productive. The real issue is more subtle. As the *New Orleans City Guide* cautions:

> Remember that there is a difference between one bay leaf and two bay leaves; and the difference between one clove of garlic and two cloves of garlic is enough to disorganize a happy home.

Cooking the Beans

The cooking of dried beans is simplicity itself, but it is no exact science. This is particularly the case with the amount of water to use and the length of cooking time. These both depend on the size of the bean, its age, and such other variables as the hardness of the cooking water. There's no way around it: well-cooked beans require attentive care.

First things first. All beans must be carefully picked over and washed before anything is done with them, because, likely as not, you'll find an inconspicuous pebble nestled among them, all malice aforethought. Inspect them, rinse them thoroughly in a colander, set them in a bowl, and cover them with about 3 inches of water, discarding any beans that float to the surface.

This traditional presoaking of the beans has come under fire recently, and the conventional wisdom may soon be that this is a total waste of effort. Even so, we continue to do it. Watching the beans plump up during the course of the day enriches our pleasure in our bean dishes.

There is another, more practical reason. The no-soak, straight-into-the-bean-pot method presumes that the beans are all of the same age and dryness, which, in most instances, they may very well be. But if they're not, the result—at least with some bean varieties—will be a pot of beans with some surprisingly underdone individuals. Our rule of thumb is to soak the beans until they have *all* plumped up—a span of time that will differ from bean to bean and year to year.

On the other hand, we are now persuaded that periodically discarding the soaking liquid in the hope of leaching out the complex sugars that are said to cause flatulence is a lost cause. Common sense argues that Mother Nature would not have been doing her job if it were that easy to soak essential nutrients from what is, after all, a *seed*. Paradoxically, the best way to deal with the problem seems to be to eat more beans: in this way, the digestive system learns how to deal with them. We now always cook our beans in their soaking liquid.

Some small beans—lentils, split peas, small cowpeas—don't need to be soaked; check the packaging for details. Immerse those that do require it in good spring water and let them completely rehydrate in their own good time. Don't hustle things along by parboiling them; this will just turn them into mush. Unless experience has taught us otherwise, we usually soak our beans for 6 to 8 hours.

Depending on age, beans will absorb (after soaking) three to four times their weight in water while they cook. There's no set rule and every chart is different. Keep an eye on them now and then while they cook and add water as needed, making sure there's enough for the gravy. Don't ever let them cook dry or turn into mush. As an old Mexican cook told James Michener in *Iberia*:

> My garbanzos are soaked for two days in cold salt water. They are cooked slowly, and when they are sure of themselves, I throw in some salty ham, three different kinds of hot sausage, some potatoes and cabbage, and let them stew for eight hours.

Cook your beans until they are sure of themselves.

Red Beans & Rice: Master Recipe

1 pound (about 2 cups) red kidney beans, prepared for cooking as
    instructed above;
One ham bone with plenty of meat and fat still clinging to it,
    sawed in half or cracked (a firm, well-placed blow or two with a
    hammer will do the trick), *or* half the amount of pickled pork in
    the recipe given above *or* (worst option) ¼–½ pound lean salt

pork, cubed and boiled in ample water for 10 minutes to reduce
saltiness, then strained

1 pound smoked Creole sausages *or* the same amount of some other
spicy, garlicky cured sausage, like *chorizo* or kielbasa (optional
but recommended)

2 medium onions, coarsely chopped

1 small bunch flat-leafed parsley, minced

1 bunch (6 to 8) scallions, finely minced, including the green tops,
½ cup of which reserve, uncooked (Note: scallions are called
"shallots" in New Orleans, but scallions are what is wanted)

2 large bell peppers, one red, one green, both cored, seeded, and
chopped (optional but recommended)

2 medium carrots, peeled and finely diced

2 celery stalks, finely diced (optional but recommended)

4 cloves of garlic, minced (amount optional)

Generous pinch of dried thyme (or a sprig of fresh, to be fished out
at the finish of cooking)

1 or 2 bay leaves (to be left whole and also removed at the end of
cooking)

At least 1 small hot red pepper, cored, seeded, and chopped fine,
either fresh or dried, *or* a generous hand with the Tabasco
bottle

Salt and pepper to taste (go carefully with the salt if using the bone
and scrap meat from a country ham or the salt pork).

Sufficient rice to feed all eaters. This recipe makes enough to serve
8; if you are feeding fewer, you may want to make only enough
rice for that number, separating and freezing a portion of
the bean mixture before the rice is added. Calculate from
¼–½ cup raw rice for each eater, cooking it in your usual
manner.

Put the prepared beans in a large, heavy pot with a cover. Pour over 2
quarts of good water (if your tap water is notably hard, use an inexpensive half-gallon container of uncarbonated spring water). Bring the water
to a boil and let the beans cook in the roiling water for at least 10
minutes. Then lower the flame to bring the pot down to a simmer and
cook the beans for 1 hour. Add all the ingredients except the rice.
Bring the cooking liquid back to a simmer and taste for seasoning.
The beans should be done in another 1½ hours. Check the amount of
liquid occasionally, adding more water if necessary to keep the beans
swimming. As they begin to soften, mash some of them against the side

of the pot and stir this pulp into the liquid to make a thick, creamy sauce.

When the end of the cooking hoves into sight—the beans are soft and savory, the sauce thick and richly flavored—cook the rice. Let it sit covered for 5 minutes on the stove after it is done to dry out a little, then fluff it up with a fork and put it into the bowls first, covering it with a generous amount of the red beans and their gravy. Serve and pass around the following:

TOPPINGS. The matter of what to put on the beans at the table is strictly personal. Mandatory are the reserved minced scallion tops (remember them?), but other options (not all recommended) include: vinegar, hot sauce, sweet relish, catsup, cane syrup, chopped raw onion, and/or hot peppers marinated in vinegar. One informant told me that her great-grandfather kept hot pepper plants in his garden right by the kitchen door, so that he could pop more peppers into the vinegar jar whenever its potency started to flag. Hot pepper sauce is a necessity; so, to my mind, is a crisp onion salad, made as follows:

ONION SALAD
(SERVES 4)

1 large red onion
¼ cup olive oil
1 tablespoon wine vinegar
Salt and pepper to taste

Cut the onion into rings, slicing as thinly as possible. Separate them into a large bowl and steep in cold water for a few hours, changing the water several times. Then drain well, pat dry with paper towels, and return to the empty bowl. Pour over the olive oil and wine vinegar, seasoning to taste with salt and black pepper. Let marinate, stirring occasionally, while the beans finish cooking, and serve as a topping when they are done.

The following red bean and rice recipe, kindly given to me by a native New Orleans cook, is different enough from the usual versions to be presented separately. It is very similar to hoppin' John and may trace its lineage back to the recipe for that dish submitted by "Uncle John" of South Carolina to Célestine Eustis, who gives it in *Cooking in Old Créole Days*.

CLAIRE CLARK'S RED BEANS AND RICE

2 pounds red kidney beans, prepared for cooking as directed for
    cooking on pages 293–94
3 or 4 bay leaves
10 to 12 slices of bacon
2 medium onions, chopped
10 cloves garlic, minced
2 pounds smoked pork sausage
Ham bone or ham pieces (optional)
Salt and pepper to taste
Tabasco sauce
Cooked rice for the number of people eating the meal (this recipe
    will serve at least a dozen)

Cover the beans with at least 3 inches of water (about 1 gallon for this amount of beans) and add the bay leaves. Bring the water to a boil. Let the beans boil for 10 minutes and then reduce the temperature until they are simmering gently. Cut the bacon into 2-inch pieces and fry them in a pan until translucent. Do not brown. Add these to the beans and use the fat that remains in the pan to cook the chopped onion. When the onion bits are soft and browning at the edges, stir in the minced garlic. Cut the sausage into chunks and add these to the pan. As soon as they are heated through, add the whole sausage-garlic-onion mixture to the bean pot, along with the optional ham bone/ham pieces.

Taste for seasoning and cook at a simmer, stirring occasionally, for 2 more hours, adding water if the beans begin to get dry. Flavor the pot with plenty of Tabasco sauce toward the end of the cooking time, grind over some more black pepper, and serve on cooked rice with any of the toppings mentioned above.

Butter Beans & Rice

No survey of New Orleans bean cookery can ignore the Creole way with butter beans. Butter beans are reputedly of the same stock as limas, but anyone who has tasted them both will know this can't be true. There is a sullen inhospitality to the lima bean, as if it resents being food and wills itself to remain a solid, sour bullet no matter the culinary attentions lavished on it. Not so with the butter bean, which is amenable to digestion and yields a melt-in-the-mouth texture and luscious flavor that does call up thoughts of its namesake, even if, as in the recipe below, none of it has been added.

BUTTER BEANS AND RICE
(SERVES AT LEAST 8)

1 pound dried butter beans, prepared for cooking as directed on
    pages 293–94
1 onion, chopped
1 carrot, chopped
3 cloves garlic, minced
1 pound Creole smoked sausage or smoked kielbasa or garlic
    sausage, cut into 1-inch chunks
Hot pepper sauce to taste
1 large bay leaf
Generous pinch of dried thyme (or a sprig of the fresh herb)
Salt and black pepper to taste
Cooked rice for the number of people eating the meal

Put the beans into a large, heavy pot and add enough water to cover (about 2 quarts). Bring the water to a boil. Let the beans boil for 10 minutes and then reduce the temperature until they are simmering gently. After an hour, add the rest of the ingredients. Return to a quiet simmer and cook until the beans are tender but not mushy and a thick gravy has formed. Rima and Richard Collin in *The New Orleans Cook Book* suggest that you then mellow the dish by removing them from the heat and uncovering the pot for 15 minutes. Then re-cover and let them steep in their own juices for 2 hours, gently reheating the pot just before serving time (adding a little more water if necessary). This produces the tenderest possible butter bean.

ALL MIXED UP AND BORN
ON THE ISLANDS

"All mixed up and born on the islands"—this Caribbean definition of a Creole, a native born of mixed racial heritage, is also the best definition of island Creole cooking. The West Indies kitchen has inherited an eclectic mélange of cooking ingredients and techniques from Europe, Africa, and Asia and has honed them into a disciplined cuisine out of the need to adapt to the limiting factors shared by all the islands: the hot, humid climate, the restricted amount of growing space, and the universal poverty.

Island cooking, regardless of whether the place was originally Dutch, English, Spanish, or French, shares related and often interchangeable strategies for coping with the rarity and expense of fresh dairy products, meat, and cooking fuel and for making a varied and palatable diet based mostly on seafood, greens, and root and starchy vegetables like cassava, taro, plantain, squash, and yam. The islands also share a passion for the familiar flavor combinations of their African heritage, seasonings rich with herbs and the pungency of hot peppers. There is no other area in the Western Hemisphere more dominated by the culinary instincts of native black cooks.

Indeed, it is impossible to overemphasize the influence of slave culture on Caribbean life. While no one knows for sure how many of the fifteen million slaves brought to the Americas between 1518 and 1865 stayed on the islands, it is known that during the height of the slave trade, two million Africans went to the British West Indies alone. The logistics of feeding such a huge slave population were too staggering for plantation owners to depend on imported food, and they were unwilling to devote much of their limited field space to food crops. Consequently, slaves were assigned yards for growing their own food by their living quarters or, as in Jamaica, given provision grounds, "palinkas," in the nearby hills.

The slaves became fiercely attached to these small plots, and this experience of independence allowed them to develop a culture far less influenced by their white masters than was the case in the American South. The Jamaican blacks, for instance, turned their small pieces of land to such productive advantage that they were able not only to feed themselves but to produce enough surplus to control 20 percent of the cash circulating on the island. In their small plots they grew yams, plantains, and pigeon peas, planted fruit trees and coconut palms, and raised chickens and pigs. When abolition came, the slaves quit the plantations entirely (thus effecting the influx of Asians, who brought with them the island's third culinary force), determined to escape share-cropping by eking out a living from these same tiny bits of land.

In different variations, this pattern repeated itself throughout the islands, so that today much of West Indian life revolves around large households, independent and firmly attached to whatever small plot they may own, no matter how poor its soil may be. On all but Puerto Rico, the majority of island inhabitants are black. Most homes are still rickety structures with galvanized metal roofs, the kitchen usually a hut separated from the main dwelling to keep cooking heat out of the house. In the poorest homes, the kitchen is entirely out in the open, and the cooking is done in small pots hung over braziers or open pits, with boards nailed between trees serving as counters.

The staples of the Caribbean are those of a poor people. Like the cooking of the American South, West Indian cooking depends for interest on pork fat (or palm oil) and herbs and spices in the preparation of a narrow, if exotic, array of carbohydrates. And because beans flourish on all and rice on several of the islands, this is also a culture of rice-and-bean dishes. On Jamaica, the dish is known as rice and peas. Jamaicans, as do many West Indians, call dried beans "peas"—namely kidney beans, which are so common they have taken the generic term as their own. The most famous Jamaican rice-and-bean dish, called "The Watchman," is made with red beans, rice, and coconut.

Haiti also makes a red-bean-and-rice dish, *riz et pois colles*, which is such common fare that it is also called *le plat national*. On Trinidad, "rice and peas" means rice and pigeon peas, also called Congo or goongoo peas. Rice and pigeon peas is familiar fare in Jamaica and elsewhere on the islands, too, including Puerto Rico, where it is called *arroz con gandules*. Pigeon peas, by the way, are rumored to have a slight narcotic effect, which may explain the stupor that can befall an overavid eater. *Gandules*, sometimes prepared from the fresh pea and other times from reconstituted dried ones, can be found in cans under this name in the Latin section of supermarkets.

In Cuba, the specialty is black beans, and the famous Cuban rice-and-bean dish is *moros y cristianos*, or "Moors and Christians." While Cuba follows Mexican usage and calls its beans *frijoles*, Puerto Ricans tend to call them *habichuelas*, which explains the diplomatic but confusing tact with which Spanish-labeled bean cans and packages call pink beans *habichuelas rosadas*, but red beans *frijoles colorados*.

I'm sure the list goes on. In what I still think is the best book on the subject, *Caribbean Cooking*, Elisabeth Lambert Ortiz apologizes because she has yet to visit Bequia or Barbuda. Bequia? Barbuda? For an armchair traveler such as myself, whose closest contact with those troubled but enchanted islands has been "Reggae Bloodline" on the radio and the writings of V. S. Naipaul, Derek Walcott, and Jamaica Kincaid, her admission shames me, not her. There are more than seven thousand islands in the West Indies, and not even all thirty of the most populated are represented here. But there can be a surfeit even of rice and beans, and the generous sampling that follows may help explain, at least, the passion for the dish that runs through the entire Caribbean.

Jamaica

Of all the islands, Jamaica is the most in love with the hot red pepper, where aficionados of that fiery chile argue the relative merits of the Scotch bonnet and the country pepper with the intensity of Frenchmen comparing two *deuxième* growths from the Médoc. Connoisseurs of hot pepper sauce should seek out the different hot sauces now being imported from Jamaica—and elsewhere in the West Indies—including (to name just a few) Doc's Special Jamaica Hellfire, Island Treasure Papaya Pepper Sauce, Island Heat, and Pickapeppa Hot Red Pepper Sauce (not to be confused with Pickapeppa Hot Sauce itself, a not-so-fiery condiment similar to A.1. steak sauce).*

A necessity for making authentic Jamaican rice and peas is coconut milk, which Jamaicans make by laboriously grating and squeezing the coconut meat by hand. Don't confuse coconut milk with either the loose liquid in the coconut, called coconut water, or with the sugar-rich coconut "creme" used to make piña coladas. To make coconut milk, you need either a whole coconut or unsweetened, desiccated coconut meat, which can be found in natural food stores.†

COCONUT MILK
(MAKES 3 TO 4 CUPS)

1 large coconut or 1 pound desiccated coconut flakes
2 cups of water or milk

---

* The best mail-order source we know for exotic island pepper sauces and condiments is Tim and Wendy Edison's *Mo Hotta, Mo Betta* (P.O. Box 4136, San Luis Obispo, CA 93403 • 800–462–3220). As they say on the inside front cover: "If you can't stand the heat, get out of this catalogue!" This catalogue—which always announces its arrival in our mailbox with a dramatic burst of color—offers lots of other neat things, too, including authentic Jamaican jerk seasonings, ground Jamaican Scotch-bonnet hot pepper ("If it were any more authentic, it would be illegal"), and rare whole dried chiles from around the world.

† Thanks to the recent surge of interest in Caribbean and Pacific rim cooking, many supermarkets now carry canned coconut milk, offering the cook a third option that was not available when I wrote this in 1981.

If using the desiccated coconut flakes, skip down to the next paragraph. If using a fresh coconut, with a hammer and a thick nail pierce two of its three eyes and drain the coconut water out into a large bowl. Set the coconut onto a firm surface, eyes down, and whack at it judiciously with the hammer until it has broken into several pieces. Carefully (for yourself, not for the coconut) pry out the coconut meat with a sharp knife or, better, a screwdriver. The brown rind on the meat does not need to be removed. If you have a food processor, you can grate the coconut into flakes—after precutting it into 1-inch chunks—using the steel blade (*not* the grating disk). Otherwise, grate the meat by hand.

Mix this grated coconut meat with the reserved coconut water in its bowl. Stir into this 2 cups of boiling water or, for a richer flavor, 2 cups of ordinary milk, heated to scalding. Let this mixture sit until it is cool enough to put your hand into and then, being careful not to lose any liquid, strain it through a double fold of cheesecloth (or a clean dish towel) held over another bowl. When the liquid stops flowing, twist and squeeze the cloth to extract as much fluid from the flakes as possible. Unless otherwise directed in the recipe that calls for this ingredient (as, for instance, the one directly below), discard the squeezed flakes, reserving the milk. Store the milk in the refrigerator, where it will keep for 2 weeks.

Jamaican rice and peas is always made with coconut milk, but beyond that essential ingredient, as Linda Wolfe notes in *The Cooking of the Caribbean Islands,*

> every cook is on her own; the variations in recipes are endless. Some call for adding sweet peppers and tomatoes, some for bacon, some for beef soup or stewing beef, some for onions or chives or hot peppers, some for any combination of these.

The following is just to get the flame turned up under the pot.

THE WATCHMAN (RICE AND PEAS)
(SERVES 4 TO 6)

1 cup red kidney beans, prepared for cooking as directed on pages 293–94
1 cup raw beef, cut into small cubes, or 6 to 8 slices lean bacon
2 tablespoons cooking oil (if using beef)
1 medium onion, chopped
1 hot red pepper, seeded, stemmed, and minced

1 or 2 tomatoes, chopped

2 cups of coconut milk from above recipe, plus the squeezed
coconut meat

2 cups raw rice

1½ teaspoons salt and ½ teaspoon black pepper

Simmer the beans in 7 to 8 cups of unsalted water until almost tender, about 1½ hours.

During the final half hour of the bean cooking time, sauté the beef cubes in cooking oil until the beef begins to brown and then add the onion and cook it until golden. If using bacon, fry the bacon pieces until crisp, remove from fat, and then fry onion pieces until translucent. In both instances, reserve at least some of the fat with the onion and meat.

When the beans are almost done, check the amount of liquid in the pot. There must be more than enough to cook the rice, or at least 6 cups. Add more liquid, if necessary, and then add the meat, onion, fat, hot pepper, tomato, coconut milk, reserved coconut meat, and the raw rice. Add the salt and pepper, adjusting seasoning to taste. Cook until the rice is tender. Let the dish sit off the heat for 10 minutes before serving.

RICE AND PEAS (VEGETARIAN)

Follow the basic preparations and instructions in the recipe directly above, but omit the meat and the tomatoes, substituting instead ½ teaspoon of dried thyme. Prepare the dish in the same way, frying the onion in 2 tablespoons of coconut or vegetable oil and adding the fried onion, the coconut meat and milk, hot pepper, and thyme at the same time as the rice.

VARIATIONS: Omit the thyme and add instead ¼ cup sultana raisins. Both this and the Watchman can be made with pigeon peas instead, using two 15-ounce cans, drained, and 5 cups of water. Mix all the ingredients together and cook until the rice is done.

Trinidad

PEAS AND RICE
(SERVES 6 TO 8)

1 pound smoked ham hocks
1 pound lean stewing beef, cut into ½-inch cubes
2 cloves garlic, crushed
1 teaspoon powdered clove
Salt and pepper to taste
2 tablespoons cooking oil
1 large onion, chopped
1 red or green bell pepper, seeded and chopped
1 fresh hot green or red pepper, seeded and chopped
2 tomatoes, roughly chopped
2 cups raw rice
2 15-ounce cans pigeon peas
Hot mango chutney

Cut the meat from the ham hocks and mix with the cubes of beef in a bowl. Stir in the garlic and clove, and salt to taste. Heat the oil in a heavy iron pot and sauté the onion and chopped sweet and hot pepper until the vegetables are soft. Add the meat mixture and sauté until all sides of the meat are seared. Put in the tomatoes along with 1 cup of water and simmer, covered, until the meat is tender, about 45 minutes. Measure the liquid left in the pot and add enough additional water to measure 4½ cups. Add the rice and pigeon peas, taste for seasoning, and cook another 20 minutes, or until the rice is tender and most of the liquid has been absorbed. Serve with hot mango chutney.

RICE & T'INGS
(SERVES 6 TO 8)

1 cup red kidney beans, prepared for cooking as directed on pages 293–94
1 bay leaf
2 cups raw rice
¼ cup palm or other cooking oil
1 cup chopped baked ham

3 or 4 scallions, chopped, including green
Salt and pepper to taste

Cook the beans in 6 cups of unsalted water with the bay leaf until they are tender. When the beans are nearly done, cook the rice separately in 5 cups of salted water. Drain the beans, discarding the bay leaf. Heat the cooking oil in a large skillet and stir in the ham and scallions. When the scallions are soft—about 5 minutes—stir in the rice and beans, mix well, season to taste, and serve when very hot.

Barbados

RED BEANS AND RICE
(SERVES 6 TO 8)

3 tablespoons palm or other cooking oil
1 pound stewing pork, cut into 1-inch pieces
1 clove garlic, crushed
1 cup red kidney beans, prepared for cooking as directed on pages 293–94
4 pieces pickled pig tail, each 1-inch long, or 4 pieces pickled pig hocks
1 cup coconut milk, prepared as directed on pages 301–2
Salt and pepper to taste
2 cups raw rice

Heat the cooking oil in a large skillet. Add the pork and crushed garlic clove to the hot oil and stir until the pork pieces are seared on all sides. Remove from the heat and discard the garlic. Heat 6 cups of water in a large iron pot. When the water boils, pour in the kidney beans and cook at a boil for 10 minutes, then reduce to a simmer and cook for 1 hour. Add the pork, pig tail or hock pieces, and coconut milk, season to taste with salt and pepper, and continue to cook until the beans are almost done. Cook the rice separately and serve with the beans.

Haiti

RIZ ET POIS COLLES (PLAT NATIONAL)
(SERVES 6 TO 8)

1 cup red kidney beans, prepared for cooking as directed on pages
    293–94
2 tablespoons lard or cooking oil
¼ pound salt pork, cut in small dice and parboiled 10 minutes to
    reduce saltiness
1 medium onion, minced
2 cups raw rice
4 scallions (including the green), minced
¼ cup minced fresh parsley
Salt
Hot pepper sauce to taste

Bring 2 quarts of water to a boil and add the beans. Boil for 10 minutes
and then reduce to a simmer. Cook for 1½ hours, or until the beans
are almost done. Drain them, reserving the liquid. In a large skillet,
melt the lard and sauté the salt pork and onion pieces until the latter
are translucent, then stir in the beans, rice, scallions, and parsley.
Measure the reserved bean liquid and add more water if necessary to
make 1 quart. Stir this, bit by bit, into the rice and bean mixture and
season to taste with the salt and hot pepper sauce. When it begins to
simmer, cook, stirring occasionally, until the rice is done, being careful
not to let the skillet boil dry.

BLACK BEANS AND RICE
(SERVES 6 TO 8)

½ cup olive oil
2 large onions, chopped
2 cloves of garlic, minced
1 green bell pepper, chopped
1 pound black beans, prepared for cooking as directed on pages
    293–94
1 bay leaf
Pinch each of oregano and thyme

3 tablespoons cane or rice vinegar
Salt and black pepper to taste
2 cups raw rice
1 4-ounce jar pimiento pieces, drained

Heat the oil in a large pot and add the onions, garlic, and bell pepper. When these have softened and the onion is translucent, add 2 quarts of water, the black beans, and the herbs. Bring this mixture to a boil for 10 minutes and then simmer until the beans are almost done, about 1½ hours. Then add the vinegar and salt and pepper to taste. Stir in the rice, adding more liquid if needed. When the beans and vinegar have cooked 15 minutes, stir in the minced pimientos and cook until the rice is done.

Cuba

MOROS Y CRISTIANOS* #1 (Vegetarian)
(SERVES 6 TO 8)

1 onion, chopped
1 carrot, cubed
1 stalk of celery, minced
1 head of garlic, broken into cloves, peeled, and minced
¼ cup olive oil
1 pound black beans, prepared for cooking as directed on pages
   293–94
1 bay leaf
1 teaspoon crushed hot pepper flakes
Juice of 1 orange
Salt and pepper to taste
2 cups raw rice

---

* This dish originated in Cuba when that country was still a possession of Spain, from where it spread to Mexico, parts of South America, and, later still, to Miami. It also went back to Spain—where many Spaniards have come to think of it as indigenous. It was out of such confusion that *The Horizon Cookbook* says the name of the dish recalled "centuries of coexistence between Moors and Christian Spaniards." As Wolfgang Pauli noted in another context, this isn't even wrong. The name, of course, comes from the contrast of the black beans and the white rice, *moro* being a Spanish colloquialism for blacks, as in the now rare English word "blackamoor."

TO GARNISH
Fried or sliced hard-boiled eggs
Thinly sliced rings of onion
Minced parsley
Orange wedges

In a large cooking pot with a cover, sauté the onion, carrot, celery, and garlic in the olive oil until the onion is soft. Then add the beans and the bay leaf and pour over them a generous 2 quarts of water. Bring to a boil and cook for 10 minutes, reduce the heat, and gently simmer, partially covered, until the beans are nearly tender, about 1 hour. Remove and discard the bay leaf, stir in the hot pepper and orange juice, and season with salt and pepper. When the beans are done, let sit covered off the heat while the rice cooks. Serve over the rice, garnished with the eggs, onion rings, and parsley, and with the orange wedges served on the side.

MOROS Y CRISTIANOS #2
(SERVES 6 TO 8)

1 pound black beans, prepared for cooking as directed on pages 293–94
Large, meaty ham bone, or 2 pounds ham butt, cubed, or ¼ pound salt pork, cubed and simmered in ample water for 15 minutes to reduce the salt, and then fried until brown
3 cloves garlic, minced
1 bay leaf
Generous pinch dried thyme
Several sprigs fresh parsley, minced
¼ cup olive oil
1 large onion, chopped
1 green bell pepper, seeded, cored, and chopped
2 tomatoes, coarsely chopped
1½ tablespoons cane or wine vinegar
1 teaspoon crushed hot pepper flakes
Salt and pepper to taste
2 cups raw rice

TO GARNISH
Chopped hard-boiled eggs
Thinly sliced onion rings

Olive oil
Lime wedges

Place the beans in a large pot with the meat, garlic, bay leaf, thyme, and parsley. Cover with a generous 2 quarts of water and bring to a boil. Cook for 10 minutes and then lower to a simmer and continue cooking until the beans are tender, about 1½ hours.

When the beans are almost ready, heat the olive oil in a large skillet and sauté the onion and green bell pepper until the onion is soft. Add the tomatoes, vinegar, and hot red pepper, and simmer until the mixture has blended and thickened, about 10 minutes. Strain and discard any remaining liquid from the beans, pour in the sauce to replace it, and put over a very low flame. Season to taste with salt and pepper. Prepare the rice in a separate pot. When it is tender and dry, turn it onto a platter, top it with the black beans and the garnishes, and serve.

Virgin Islands

BLACK BEANS AND RICE WITH RUM
(SERVES 6)

1 pound black beans, prepared for cooking as directed on pages
   293–94
2 onions, coarsely chopped
2 cloves garlic, minced
2 stalks celery, diced
2 carrots, cubed
1 bay leaf
Pinch of dried oregano
¼ cup minced parsley
Salt and pepper to taste
4 tablespoons butter
¼ cup dark rum
Enough rice to serve all eaters, prepared separately
1 pint sour cream
Lime slices

Boil 2 quarts of water and add all the ingredients except the butter, rum, sour cream, and lime. Boil for 10 minutes and then reduce heat and simmer for 1 hour, or until beans are almost done. Remove the bay leaf, add salt and pepper to taste, stir in the butter and half the rum, make sure at least 2 cups of liquid are left, and then pour the mixture into a large casserole. Stir well, cover, and bake in a preheated 350°F oven until the beans are completely tender, or about ½ hour.

Meanwhile, cook the rice. Remove the casserole from the oven, pour over the remaining rum, and serve over the cooked rice, allowing diners to help themselves to the sour cream and lime slices.

Puerto Rico

RED BEANS AND RICE
(SERVES 4 TO 6)

1 cup red kidney beans, prepared for cooking as directed on pages 293–94
¼ cup *achiote*-flavored lard*
1 large onion, chopped
1 4-ounce jar pimiento pieces, drained
½ pound baked ham, cut into cubes, or same weight of any cured Latin sausage, cut into 1-inch pieces
2 tomatoes, coarsely chopped
Salt and pepper to taste
2 cups raw rice

Put the beans in a large pot with a generous quart of water and bring to a boil. Cook at this rate for 10 minutes, then lower the heat and gently simmer until almost tender, about 1½ hours. At that point, melt the lard in a large frying pan and sauté the onion until tender and golden. Add the pimiento, meat, tomatoes, and salt and pepper to taste, and cook until the sauce has thickened, about 10 minutes. Measure the bean water and add more to return the amount to the original generous quart. Add the raw rice and the sauce to the beans, season to taste with salt and pepper, and simmer about 20 minutes, or until the rice is done.

---

* *Achiote*—sometimes *achote*—seeds impart a delicate flavor and orange color to cooking lard; jars of *manteca de achiote* are available in the Latin section of supermarkets.

MARIA LANDA'S *ARROZ CON GANDULES*
(SERVES 6)

Gandules *(pigeon peas) are popular in Puerto Rico, and the above dish is often made with them instead of beans. The following one, given to me by a native Puerto Rican cook, is traditionally served at Christmas and other festive occasions.* Sofrito *(as opposed to the Spanish sauce of the same name) is a mixture of lard and seasonings;* recaito *is sofrito minus the lard. Look for the Merenge brand ("Esto si es sofrito") in the Latin section of supermarkets, or substitute* sofrito *and omit the oil.*

1 15-ounce can *gandules* (prepared from dried, not fresh, pigeon peas), liquid reserved
1 4-ounce jar chopped pimientos
2 tomatoes, coarsely chopped
1 clove garlic, minced
Generous pinch dried oregano
1 heaping tablespoon *recaito*
2½ tablespoons corn oil
3 cups raw rice
Salt and pepper to taste

Preheat oven to 300°F. Put pigeon peas, pimientos with their liquid, tomatoes, garlic, oregano, and *recaito* into a large ovenproof pot. To the can with the reserved pigeon pea liquid add enough water to fill and pour this into the pot. Heat on top of the stove until the mixture simmers, stirring well. When the mixture has simmered 15 minutes, add the oil. Simmer another 15 minutes and add the rice. Add 7 cups of water to the pot and salt and pepper to taste. Bring to a simmer, stir one last time, and then cover the pot and place it in the oven. Five minutes later, remove the pot and, with your largest cooking spoon, fold the mixture over. Return the pot to the oven and repeat this procedure twice more at 5-minute intervals. After the last one, replace the lid with a loose piece of foil. Continue to cook, checking regularly, until the rice is done, which should take another 5 to 10 minutes.

Africa

How close are African rice-and-bean dishes to those made in the New World? Not surprisingly, very close indeed, especially to their Caribbean cousins, where both climate and culture closely approximate that of their points of origin, as can be seen in this Kenyan dish, adapted from *The Africa News Cookbook.*

MAHARAGWE (SPICED RED BEANS AND RICE)
(SERVES 4 TO 6)

1 cup red kidney beans, prepared for cooking as directed on pages 293–94
2 tablespoons peanut oil
2 medium onions, chopped
2 tomatoes, coarsely chopped
2 teaspoons turmeric
½ tablespoon crushed hot pepper flakes
1 cup coconut milk (or more to taste), prepared as directed on pages 301–2
Salt to taste
4 to 6 cups boiled rice

Cover the prepared beans with water and simmer about 1½ hours, or until they are tender. Heat the oil in a medium skillet. Add the onions and sauté until golden brown. Stir the rest of the ingredients into the pot and simmer just until the tomatoes are cooked. Serve over the rice.

Brazil

It would be impossible to list all the ingredients that go into a *Feijoada*, but the standard items are beans, sausages of different varieties, jerked beef, cured meats, bacon, tongue, and the ear, foot, and tail of a pig.

—*Dictionario do Folclore Brasileiro*

Brazil did not begin importing slaves until well toward the end of the eighteenth century, but blacks were soon to make their impression on Brazilian cooking, the slave owners of that country—like their counterparts elsewhere—being quick to appreciate their brilliance in the kitchen. Indeed, the Brazilian national dish, *feijoada completa*, is a comprehensive display of the skills of the black cook. While *feijoas*, or black beans, had long been a staple of Brazil, no record exists of a *feijoada* before the nineteenth century; and the list of ingredients of any version is full of staples of traditional black cooking, right down to the *farofa*, or toasted cassava meal.

Feijoada, or at least *feijoada completa*, which can be roughly translated as *"feijoada,* the whole hog," is to rice and beans what *cassoulet de Castelnaudary* is to baked beans. These two masterpieces have much in common, being complexly delicious, expensive to prepare, open to violent argument as to their making, and renowned for the difficulties they pose to the digestive system. The result is that it is impossible to face a *feijoada completa* without an unholy combination of sweet anticipation and trepidation bordering almost on fear. Rufus Gunn, in his novel *Something for Sergio,* sets the scene perfectly:

> The *feijoada* was completissimo: I had never seen one with so many ingredients. To the beans had been added smoked sausage, tongue, salt pork, oxtail, jerked beef, and these were only the readily identifiable ingredients in the rich mush of vegetables and spices . . . Mama sprinkled mandioca flour over each plate, turning to the Corcovado Christ with some unspoken words on her lips. It came as something of a shock when I realised that her prayers were directed not at the New Testament deity but at little twin-headed red devils I had not noticed between the flowers. We mixed our drinks now, changing to chilled beer to accompany this richest and most incongruous of national dishes for a *pais tropical.* I thought I heard Mama tell me between pulses of the loudspeakers that with *feijoada* the more it stewed the better; this one had only cooked overnight—it would have been better if it had been simmering for a week. It was the opposite in *Carnaval* where the LESS the better! The less you WORE, she meant!

The rich mélange of flavors and textures that make each bite an excitement have a composite effect that gives a depth never before imagined to the word "indigestible," especially because it is compounded by the profound stupor that inevitably follows after. *Brasíleiros* traditionally eat the meal for Saturday lunch, leaving the rest of the afternoon free to sleep it off. Heitor Villa-Lobos composed a four-part fugue in honor of *feijoada,* each part representing one basic element of the dish. One is tempted to suspect that the piece, entitled "Fugue without End," was never finished because somnolence overcame the composer before he could gather together the completing measures.

No slur is meant here on the cook. Instead, it is a tribute (of sorts) to *cachaça,* or Brazilian white lightning, the sugarcane rum downed continuously during the meal—"an aid to digestion," as Margarette de Andrade dryly puts it in *Brazilian Cookery.* The multitude of meats is sliced and arranged on platters, the beans poured into a giant tureen, the rice heaped on another platter, and everyone digs in, helping themselves to the toppings—fried collard greens, toasted cassava meal, a pungent lime-and-hot-pepper sauce, and slices of ripe orange. Clearing the palate of grease as necessary with an orange slice, the eater plows on, intermittently "aiding his digestion" (in reality, blasting clear his gullet) with another tot of rum.

After a few such rounds, this eater found himself involuntarily pounding on the table with a clenched fist, gasping for air. It's all, I'm sure, a matter of acculturation, but the fact remains that I have neither the budget, the ability, nor the constitution to guide you through the making of a *feijoada completa*. For that, turn to the extensive presentation in Andrade's *Brazilian Cookery* or in Barbara Karoff's *South American Cooking*. The following recipes essay something more manageable and still maintain a whiff of the original experience.

FEIJOADA INCOMPLETA
(SERVES 8 GENEROUSLY)

2 pounds black beans, prepared for cooking as directed on pages 293–94
2 pig's feet, well scrubbed and cut into quarters
¼ pound lean bacon in the slab
3 ounces beef jerky strips
3 pounds smoked pork butt (fully cooked)
3 tablespoons bacon drippings or lard
4 onions, chopped
3 or 4 tomatoes, roughly chopped
3 cloves garlic, minced
1 bay leaf
1 teaspoon crushed hot pepper flakes
1 strip fresh orange peel
1 pound *linguiça, chorizo,* or smoked kielbasa
1 pound hot Italian sausages
Salt to taste
Brazilian rice and the toppings given below

Bring 8 quarts of water to a boil and add the beans. Let boil for 10 minutes. Add the pig's feet, the slab of bacon, and the beef jerky. When the pot returns to a boil, turn the heat down to a gentle simmer and cook for 50 minutes. Then add the smoked pork butt and let the bean pot simmer a second hour.

Meanwhile, heat the bacon drippings or lard in a large frying pan. Add the chopped onions, tomatoes, and garlic, stirring together to make a sauce. When that thickens (in about 10 minutes), add the bay leaf, the hot pepper, and the orange peel. Let this simmer another 10 minutes and remove from the heat.

Cut each of the different sausages into 2-inch pieces. Add these and the sauce to the beans at the end of their second hour of cooking. Salt to taste and remove ¼ cup of the bean liquid for the hot pepper and lime sauce (see below). Cook the meat-and-bean mixture for another hour, and then remove the meat.

Slice the pork butt and the slab bacon and place this on a platter with the beef jerky and sausage pieces. Pour the beans, which should have a thick, soup-like consistency, into a large tureen. Let each guest ladle a generous helping of the beans over cooked rice (recipe on the next page) and add the toppings to taste. Don't forget the rum and plenty of orange slices.

FAROFA

This is traditionally made from toasted cassava meal. The following makes a reasonable substitute.

¼ pound butter
1 small onion, chopped
1 pound uncooked Cream of Wheat
Salt to taste

Melt the butter in a large skillet and fry the onion until the pieces are golden brown. Stir in the Cream of Wheat and cook over low heat, stirring constantly, until the cereal grains are golden. Sprinkle some of this over each helping of *feijoada*.

MOLHO DE PIMENTA E LIMAO
(PEPPER AND LIME SAUCE)

2 tomatoes, roughly chopped
1 teaspoon crushed hot pepper flakes
¼ cup fresh lime juice
½ cup olive oil
1 red onion, chopped
2 or 3 sprigs fresh parsley, minced
1 clove garlic, minced

¼ cup reserved bean liquid from the *feijoada*
Salt and pepper

Mix ingredients well, season to taste, and serve.

BRAZILIAN RICE

3 tablespoons bacon drippings
1 medium onion, chopped
2 cloves garlic, crushed
2 cups long-grain rice
Salt to taste

Melt the bacon drippings in a heavy pot with a lid. Add the onion and cook until golden brown. Add the garlic and rice. Stirring constantly, cook the rice until it begins to brown. Pour in 4½ cups of water, season with salt, bring to a boil, reduce heat, cover, and cook the rice until done, about 20 minutes.

CHOPPED GREENS

3 pounds collards, chard, or a similar green, well washed and
    patted dry with paper towels
¼ pound lean salt pork, cut into small cubes

Shred the greens with a sharp knife. Fry the salt pork in a large skillet and remove and reserve the cubes. When the *feijoada* is ready, reheat the pork fat and cook the greens until wilted. Turn out onto a separate platter, topping with the crisply fried salt-pork bits.

Now hopping-john was F. Jasmine's favorite food. She had always warned them to wave a plate of rice and peas before her nose when she was in her coffin, to make certain there was no mistake; for if a breath of life was left in her, she would sit up and eat, but if she smelled the hopping-john, and did not stir, then they could just nail down the coffin and be certain she was truly dead.
    —CARSON MCCULLERS, *A Member of the Wedding*

BOSTON, 1981 / STEUBEN, 1995

EVERYWHERE

Once, long before I ever wrote about food, I had a dream about a supermarket. I was in my early thirties and planning a trip down South to visit a friend who had moved to South Carolina. This was the dream's starting point—me stepping off a Greyhound bus onto the dawn-lit streets of a Southern town. As early as it was, the day was already steamy, and since no one was there to meet me, I decided to find a café where I could get in out of the heat and have some breakfast and a cup of coffee.

However, as I glanced around the courthouse square, the only building I saw with any sign of life was one of those half-pint supermarkets, the downtown variety that you can still find in places where there isn't enough native income to support a shopping mall. With no better option at hand, I headed into this one.

As I poked around, I began to notice that nothing on the shelves looked familiar. Well, that's not right: the *items* were the same; it was the brand names, the packages, that were different. A salt container emblazoned with a huge red cross . . . even after fifteen years, I can remember standing there, staring in puzzlement, searching for the Morton girl with her umbrella.

And so it went, aisle after aisle, product after product—cans of soup and tomatoes, bags of sugar, boxes of breakfast cereal, jars of fruit juice—all had unknown faces. It made me uneasily—but not unpleasantly—excited; it was like being a kid again, when to visit a supermarket was to overdose on wonder.

The dreams that stick with you are the ones that want to tell you something—something that you often not only lack words for but can't even see. This dream was layered with meaning—but it was only much later that I managed to break beneath its surface.

I never made it to South Carolina, but soon after that, I did get down to Florida. Since I was staying—and cooking—with friends, I saw the insides of all the local supermarkets, and unlike in my dream, I found little of wonder in them at all. There were, of course, products aimed at local tastes—Goo Goo clusters, Moon Pies, Cheerwine, RC Cola—but you had to look for them, and when you found them, they rarely proved that special.

For instance, this seemed an ideal time to stock up on some good stone-ground cornmeal. But everywhere I went I kept coming across the exact same brand, and although it was Southern it was clearly mass-produced and mass-marketed. There was nothing remotely local about it at all. I bought some anyway, along with a can of Steen's cane syrup. Still, I felt like a Georgian coming back from a trip to Vermont with such generic Yankee stuff as King Arthur flour and a bottle of Camp brand maple syrup.

My dream, it seems, was trying to tell me something else. I was so caught up in the strangeness of the merchandise that I failed to register how at home I felt in the store itself. Master a supermarket in Maine or Massachusetts and you'll feel completely at ease in one in Florida or Louisiana—or, for that matter, anywhere in the country. You take your cart and turn to your right into the produce section. If you push it around the store's perimeter, you pass the deli, the fish and meat counters, the dairy section, the frozen foods, ending up at the in-house bakery. To your left, the long aisles beckon, not always, one store to another, stocked in the same order, but always to the same plan: here the breakfast cereals, there the jars and cans of coffee, the domain of snacks.

Supermarkets are where we buy our food, and the experience of shopping in them has become so commonplace that we hardly think about it. When someone prompts us to do so, it's usually to scare us. These places, we're warned, cannily manipulate us to spend more than we intend, and on products for which we have no real need. Brand-name foods contain things we've never heard of and should think about twice before allowing into our house.

Why does all this go in one ear and out the other? Perhaps because these jeremiads seem beside the point. Those who utter them just don't understand why, on the whole, we so much *need* our supermarket visits. Or if—as can happen—this needing starts to fade, why they still affect us so strongly.

You go along and, with only the rare exception, anything you see you can pick up, look at, and, if you want, put in your cart. No wonder there is something calming, even sedating, about the place. This sense of weightlessness—of free-floating through a sea of desirable, obtainable objects—has become the norm; but not so long ago it was a novelty, and a pretty amazing one. Department stores, hardware stores, shoe stores, and, before supermarkets, grocery stores as well . . . there was always someone eager to wait on us (and simultaneously, it goes without saying, keep us under close observation). Shopping was as much about interacting with salespeople as it was about anything else. Dealing with clerks . . . it was one of those things that, like not being able to switch off the telephone, we never knew how much we longed to escape.

However, once we did, there was no looking back. Soon, what had begun with the supermarket exploded into the mall. Its exterior may be a lumbering, graceless warehouse, landscaped with asphalt, but the interior is a fantasy of community. Fountains splash, benches are laid out beside lushly planted gardens, store frontage is demarked by open, dazzlingly lit, inviting space. The crowds of people strolling amiably about, although most ostensibly there to shop, have also come to enjoy the experience of being in so welcoming a place. The supermarket, the mall—these are our realization of utopia . . . utopia, that is, as Teflon-coated public space.

Money is our culture's all-purpose solvent, and one of the things it dissolves best is social intercourse. Money speaks so that we don't have to. Supermarkets and malls are so shaped by this that it is as much a part of the background as year-round climate control.

At first, this may not ring true. These places expend an enormous effort to radiate a sense of personal attention. The supermarket chain we shop at puts up huge posters of grateful, smiling customers embracing employees who went the extra mile. There are signs everywhere announcing FOR YOUR CONVENIENCE, and BECAUSE YOU ASKED FOR IT.

However, all this is not to convey a truth but to fill a void. Such signage masks how little encounter there actually is, how empty this world is of real social connection; the most any of us interact with a store employee in a half hour's worth of shopping will probably be the brief exchange of banalities at the checkout counter.

In other words, when McDonald's tells us we deserve a break today, they mean something beyond relieving us of the onus of frying our own hamburgers. After all, the better the restaurant, the more stringent the need to be socially on your toes. You must dress to the nines, navigate a menu written in another language, and, especially, deal with lots of people. Hatcheck girl, headwaiter, waiter, wine steward, chef—they're all at your service, but it is a service that requires practiced social skills to get. At McDonald's, you can do it all by pointing.

Before the fast-food places, the eateries where you were served with minimal or even no such interaction—the automat, the cafeteria—were universally depressing, purveying the meanest of amenities to the materially—and, as often, psychically—impoverished. These places met a need, but at the cost of making you feel that you were only a step away from institutionalization . . . as Jane and Michael Stern— unwittingly—suggest in *Roadfood*, writing about Ann's Cafeteria in Boston.

> The interior is bathed in the greenish glow of overhead fluorescent lights. Tables, topped with boomerang-pattern Formica, are lined up in rows, like prison or school lunch; and the big ones down the center of the room, with six chairs each, are often shared by strangers. There are no waiters or waitresses or printed menus. When you enter Ann's you proceed to the back of the room to the service counter, behind which are posted at least a dozen menu boards on which movable white letters on a black background list everything the kitchen is currently producing.

Now, Burger Chef, Kentucky Fried Chicken, Pizza Hut combine comfort food, an uncomplicated menu, counter ordering, and an upbeat tempo in both decor and advertising to sweep all bad vibes away. Walk in and the spirit lightens, if only in homage to the days when we could be so readily beguiled.

Anyway, why should a lack of human connection work against quality or tastiness? So goes, at least, the argument of the upscale imitators now crowding on McDonald's heels. I recently visited one, sited in a prestigious suburban Boston shopping mall. It offered chicken to go, whole or in part, roasted on a giant assembly imported from France, with side orders that included real mashed potatoes, puréed winter squash, marinated green beans, espresso coffee, and tiramisù for dessert.

It's easy enough to savage such places—the supermarket, the mall, the fast-food outlet. Utopian fantasies brought to life, even when intentions are best, always have something of Frankenstein's monster about them —especially when new. For instance, there is nothing more barren, regimented, and seemingly soul-dead than a just-constructed housing tract. As time passes, though, and gardens grow, trees mature, fences, toolsheds, and other structures exfoliate—and, with them, each individual householder's idiosyncrasies—these places settle in. And, on the rare occasion when I've stumbled across an old A & P or Safeway, vintage 1952 or so, I've found that time has given them, too, a weathered charm.

In any case, like everyone else, there I am, silently guiding my cart down the aisles of the supermarket, tossing in objects of necessity and desire, feeling quite at home in this place that is no place. And this is where I touch bottom in my dream.

Stepping off an unmet bus into an unknown town, I felt—outside on the early-morning street—conspicuously a stranger. But as soon as I went inside the supermarket, I became that altogether ordinary personage: the customer. That the shelves were filled with unfamiliar brands may have reflected my feeling of alienation, but at the same time it lessened it. At a party, I'm the one poring over the bookcase—I deal better with strange books than I do with strange people. In a strange town, I know that my social abilities are at least commensurate with the demands of an unknown brand of baking soda.

Perhaps it's because I am so susceptible to the supermarket's cheerily comforting ambience that I am also so wary of it. If, despite liberated opinion and even positive experience, we remain slightly uneasy before realms in which our fantasies are allowed free rein—whether pornography or Nintendo or pseudonymous net surfing—it may be that such freedom not only prospers as social bonds weaken but actively conspires to replace them.

The dreamy weightlessness we feel, adrift at the mall or in the supermarket, is abetted by the alluring flood of images, most of them only tenuously linked to what they purport to describe. This assumes surreal proportions in the video rental store, where we take up, ponder, and are made excited by entirely empty boxes. But more perhaps than we want to admit, in the supermarket, too, the filling is often all but nugatory. Snack-food bags and frozen-dinner containers are, like video boxes, ways of parceling imaginary space.

Today, our eating is not embedded in a particular place but floats unmoored, roots dangling, in a clear but still, we hope, nutritious hydroponic broth. Virtual reality—you could find it at the supermarket long before it turned up on the computer. Indeed, the young Allen Ginsberg might have been sitting down in front of the one rather than stepping—as he did one night back in 1956, "in my hungry fatigue, and shopping for images"—into the flickering fluorescent brightness of the other.

There, as he relates in "A Supermarket in California," he encountered none other than America's bard and great enumerator, Walt Whitman, checking out the cuts of meat and eyeing the grocery boys. Ginsberg chases after him.

> We strode down the open corridors together in our solitary fancy tasting arti-chokes, possessing every frozen delicacy, and never passing the cashier.
> Where are we going, Walt Whitman? The doors close in an hour. Which way does your beard point tonight? . . .
> Will we walk all night through solitary streets? The trees add shade to shade, lights out in the houses, we'll both be lonely.

The question is rhetorical; Walt gives no reply. But we, today, know where his beard is pointing: to the time when supermarkets will never close—there to assuage our loneliness all twenty-four hours of the day.

STEUBEN, 1995

Serious Pig

1. DEFINING IT

Six miles of roast pig! and that in New York City alone: and roast pig in every other city, town, hamlet, and village in the Union. What association can there be between roast pig and independence?

—CAPTAIN FREDERICK MARRYAT (reporting on a Fourth of July celebration during a visit to America in the 1830s)

In the beginning was the rack. Made of green wood and called a *barbacòa*, it was used by the Amerinds of the Caribbean to smoke-cook meat over an outdoor fire. This was a process that slightly dried the flesh, giving it a firmer texture, a rich and delicious taste. Almost any flesh can be treated similarly; early travelers saw the method applied to venison, bear, fish, even pumpkin. According to one writer, barbecue was first used to make savory the most problematic of all meats—human flesh.

The early colonists, however, once they mastered the *barbacòa*, soon realized that its most spectacularly successful application was to pig. If barbecuing—the name of the implement having become the name of the process—made bear edible, it made pork remarkable.

Unlike good beef, which is best when least tampered with, pork is a little too sweet and flabby—one might almost say epicene—when cooked plain. Something more is needed to inflame the imagination: the year-long stay in the smokehouse that firms the texture and intensifies the flavor of the country ham; the coating of garlic and herb, the quick turn in the hot oven that produces the juicy, fat-seared roast loin of pork. Barbecue takes these good things and trumps them, every one:

all smoke and crust without, *all* melting succulence within, savor heightened with a rich rub of spice and flavorings.

The English language first took note of barbecue in 1661; by 1732, Alexander Pope was imploring, "Send me, Gods! a whole Hog barbecu'd." Once conjoined, the two words have since been difficult to separate. As an adjective, barbecue can be applied to anything on the grill; as a noun, it means one thing and one thing alone. In the South especially, but everywhere else, too, save deepest sheep or cattle country, the fortune of barbecue has always been tied to the fortune of the pig.

For centuries, that fortune has been good. In temperate climes, there is no better meat animal for the small producer. The pig is omnivorous, it gains weight quickly, it is practically entirely edible. In frontier areas, it could be let fend for itself in the woods or by the roadside, with the occasional carrot tendered to remind it to come home. Even when circumstances demanded the pig be penned, much of its feed was what would otherwise go to waste: whey from the dairy, cabbage leaves and turnip tops from the midden, and such detritus of the harvest as windfalls or sweet-potato vines.

All animals interest those who raise them, but of those that are eaten, the one that stirs the most emotion in the farmer is his pig. Theirs is an uneasy alliance, for the pig is halfhearted regarding domestication; it feels it could just as easily strike out on its own and often seizes the chance to do so. Such truculence angers the farmer, but also wins respect. Like himself, his pig is curious, stubborn, and independent. It relishes the same foods and tackles them with audible enjoyment; it turns beet red when angry.

Not that the pig is all that much like us. Human traits less make a beast a person than remind the person he is also a beast. The mirror the pig holds up to us never fails to agitate: it fascinates or disgusts, but leaves few indifferent. Some make favorite piglets into pets, feed them special treats, and allow them (when young) the run of the house. Others treat them with vicious disdain—feeding them the worst sort of slop and forcing them to wallow in their own filth—to thus make perfectly clear who is person and who pig . . . an important distinction, after all, considering what will happen next.

Relations between man and pig are slippery indeed, and death less resolves this than wraps it in permanent unease. Tomi Ungerer, in *Far Out Isn't Far Enough*—his account of time spent on a small homestead in rural Nova Scotia—noticed this among his neighbors.

Pig killing is always a great topic of conversation. Actually they say around here that it is bad luck to use the word "pig": the proper substitute is "Mister Dennis." My mother, when we killed Mr. Dennis, she locked herself in the house and played the harmonium.

Ungerer and his wife wanted to kill their pig by the old-fashioned method of "sticking," which produces the best-tasting meat. To do this, the pig must be hoisted up on a rope until it hangs upside down. Then its carotid artery is punctured by a sharp, single stab from a butcher's knife. With all blood cut off from the brain, the pig is immediately rendered unconscious, but its heart continues to pump until all the blood circulating through the body has been forced out of the wound.

This pig was a friend, raised as a pet, pampered on cranberries and green apples. These faced his slaughter alone, with nothing to guide them but an outdated Morton salt pamphlet, because the method unnerved their neighbors. They preferred to use a gun, thus easing their conscience while obtaining a pig no less dead but whose meat was flaccid with blood. So the Ungerers lured theirs into the barn, snared its rear feet in a noose, raised it squealing on a block and tackle, and made their stab.

Luckily, correctly: for only if done right the first time can the method be called humane. Soon they were scooping out and devouring the innards, then cleaning the intestines and making blood sausages, which they found "deliriously delicious." The meat was the best they "had ever tasted, whether fresh, salted, brined, or smoked"; the experience "cosmic . . . You, as butcher, are the only one who really knows, from the feeding, the sticking, down to the dish, what food *really* can be."

Note especially that word "deliriously"; its presence is no accident. In small-farm life, a pig slaughter brought about a dizzying moral inversion. The more provident the upbringing, the more urgent the gluttony: this food must not go to waste. No other animal possesses more parts that are edible, and a good proportion of those parts are immediately perishable. Especially without, but even with, refrigeration (offal must *always* be quickly consumed), there is much that has to be eaten at once, if it is to be eaten at all.

Naturally, the large pieces of meat—the hams, shoulders, and slabs of bacon—would be set to cure, and smaller pieces cut into chunks and salted or pickled in brine. But much of the meat was consumed fresh. As one English writer described it: "souse, griskins, blade-bones, thigh-bones, spare-ribs, chines, belly-pieces, cheeks, all coming into use one after the other." For many small farmers in America this was the one encounter with simple plenitude—"Pigs! Pigs! Pork! Pork! Pork!" enthused a nineteenth-century diary entry recording a first litter.

Nevertheless, for a frugal folk, no matter the justification, the gorgings attendant to the pig killing could not wholly escape the taint of guilt. For such, the whole thing took on the character of a devil's dance: the sticking, the bleeding, the spilling of the still-hot and reeking guts . . . and, directly thereafter, the endless devouring. Whose fault was it that they were compelled to bolt down those lengths of *boudin*, slabs of head cheese, platters of chitterlings, bowls of backbone stew? Mr. Dennis, *he* made them do it.

This is hunger lashing back at appetite: our terror that, despite our best efforts to the contrary, there will never be food enough to go around. It is behind the impulse to scold a child for seeking seconds and then rebuke it when it fails to clean its plate. Eat what you are given; leave the table a little hungry and there will be food tomorrow.

Against this rule of want has always stood the pig, mogul of appetite, lord of misrule, the king who must die. Indeed, by its very nature it is already condemned. Piggish, hoggish, pigheaded, hog-wild, or hogwash—each is a synonym for self-debasement and loss of all control. "Pig, n. (3) A person whose habits resemble a pig's: selfish, greedy, grasping, rapacious, gluttonous, filthy, grossly fat."

The pig is maligned not because it is dirty, not even because it is intelligent, but because it bears a dangerous gift. It is, despite itself, an accomplice, even though it is its own innocent self that is the crime. The cow does not understand the hunger for beef, or the sheep for mutton, but the pig . . . *mon semblable—mon frère* . . . gives us an all-too-knowing wink.

The glutton dies; his death sets off a delirium of gluttony. If the logic is that of a guilty executioner, the truth of the ritual lies somewhere else. It gives depth and dignity to the death of an intimate—a shape to the rage, confusion, and frenzy that accompanies the killing of a companion whose only crime is the great generosity of his being.

And what better funeral pyre for the late, great gourmand than a bed of slow-burning hickory coals, giving his mourners time enough to gather around, anoint his flesh with savory oils dripping from fragrant twigs of sage. The ensuing transformation turned grief into gladness, seasoned with a guilt that made the meat taste sweeter still. Thus, as pig passed into pleasure, so did barbecuists pass into pig.

———

Except, now, the pig has gone. He is no longer our neighbor, grunting in his pen by the kitchen door. In these new times, he has been pushed even farther from us than the cow or sheep, whom we can still occasionally encounter on a country drive, pushing their noses contentedly through the tall meadow grass. But the pig, reduced to a pathetic meat machine, is raised in factory barns under conditions so atrocious that the mind dares not seek him out but leaves him abandoned to his doom.

Not even appetite remembers him; there is a difference between the pig himself and the need *to* pig. Now that our gorging is continuous, his death has lost all meaning and his meat all flavor. It was, after all, always a flesh meant not for constant gobbling but for occasional feasting. His death was the great exception to hunger's iron rule.

This is why pork today is a meat of loose texture and almost no flavor at all, unless the flavor is bad. Most of it is simply not worth eating. It can—sometimes—be *made* delicious, but in itself it is without virtue. The store-bought hams are flabby, the badly cured bacon gluey and limp, the chops tough, tasteless, and greasy. We go on eating it because that once-powerful relationship still causes appetite to quiver, but it no longer takes note of what it eats.

Even in the South, where small producers raise pigs and know how good pork should taste, something strange has happened. In the Piggy Parks, the Pig Pits, the Porky's Places, the pigs that grace the signs are pink, pleasingly plump, clean-scrubbed, and innocent as babes—while the places themselves are greasy, slovenly, and unkempt.

I don't mean, of course, the slick roadhouses with their giant gas-heated smoke ovens, but the real McCoys, the small, authentic places that serve real pig out of a wood-fired pit. Their architecture is a taunt to genteel expectation; their kitchen hygiene a gesture of contempt at the county sanitation officer; their charred chunks of greasy meat, sopped in calorie-laden sauces, a sneer at every tenet of good nutrition; and their sticky Formica-topped tables and bare cement floors a smirk at any eater so foolish as to confuse good taste with tastes good.

A neighbor, upset at the good care the Ungerers gave their pig, warned them, "Clean pigs gain no weight, 'tis the Lord's truth." Now, instead, the barbecuist believes that clean pits give no flavor, and his customers believe it, too. The barbecue joint is hunger's pigpen, our last conspicuous display of licentious appetite. In the last century, when pigs roamed free and men thought them slovenly, barbecue had no gross aspect at all. Now that we have driven that animal from our moral landscape, we go to eat barbecue wearing its face ourselves.

Mr. Dennis, he dead. But his ghost won't leave us be.

2. MAKING IT

Barbecue—before I ever tasted it, I hungered for it. The first time I visited the South all I wanted was to find the best barbecue place in town and sit down to the real thing. Fort Lauderdale wasn't exactly prime barbecue territory, but thirty-eight miles away in Boca Raton I ate baby back ribs that were a revelation. They were like nothing I had ever made and called by that name, and I became obsessed with finding out how I could make them just like that at home.

At the time I knew next to nothing about authentic open-pit barbecue, but it was something I was willing to learn. However, doing that turned out to be much more difficult than I ever imagined. I had to get a lot of education first, and like any good schooling, the hardest lessons were the ones in which I was taught something about myself.

The word "barbecue" has long denoted two separable things: a specific kind of meat cooking and also the good-time atmosphere that is its boon companion. Barbecue is not only a kind of *making* but also a kind of *eating*—the sort of casual feast where you can have your fill of meat and drink, then wipe your hands on the tablecloth, lean back, and savor the tang of charcoal smoke and seared grease in the warm evening air.

Although I thought it was simply meat that I hungered for, my yearning for barbecue was so much under the spell of that second meaning that for the longest time I was unable to grasp the plain fact that authentic barbecue simply could not be made on my kitchen stove or, more important, on my outdoor grill.

In this I was not alone. Real barbecue is something so rarely made these days outside of commercial barbecue pits that, if the word weren't so fragrantly evocative, it would long ago have been relegated to the culinary sidelines, the sole possession of those few fans still willing to take it on.

But appetite won't let barbecue be. The same outdoor cook who would never even think to attach tandoori to the chicken on the grill to suggest an image of exotic spice and succulence would unhesitatingly call that same meat "barbecue"—because "barbecue" conjures up ambience, and it is this as much as grilling that gives the meat its flavor.

Barbecue the ambience can be had in any back yard; barbecue the rightly made meat in almost none. But once you've tasted the authentic article, you can't hear the word without your appetite craving to join them back together, which is why barbecue book after barbecue book keeps promising recipes for the real thing . . . and then producing the same old pot roast laminated with secret sauce.

I learned this lesson the hard way back in 1983, when I was again laid low by barbecue fever. A genuine barbecue joint—the Rainbow Rib Room—had opened up in Boston, and I was hot to supplement my weekly trips there with some rib turning of my own. However, I found myself seriously constrained by a dearth of literature on the subject.

Unlike chili, whose mysterious affinity with the temperament of old newspapermen had even then inspired a piquant outpouring of adoration (*chili con blarney*, one dispassionate critic summed up the literature), barbecue was still seeking its poet laureate. At the time, the only decent writing on the subject was "My Pig Beats Your Cow," an essay by Jim Villas that had just appeared in *Esquire*, but—alas—it was as weak in actual instruction as it was vigorous in invective.

Not that there weren't plenty of books around with the word "barbecue" in their titles, but these were almost universally about outdoor grilling. I had now visited enough bona fide barbecue joints to know that, whatever they might be up to, it wasn't *that*. "Barbecuing" might refer to the one or the other, but "barbecue" was just one thing: flesh slow-cooked over hardwood coals until it was dense, fragrant, savory— something that would collapse into a tangle of moist shreds when tugged at with a fork.

Then, one day, I happened past a Cambridge bookstore that had Jane Butel's *Finger Lickin' Rib Stickin' Great Tastin' Hot & Spicy Barbecue* displayed in the window. The sight stopped me dead in my tracks. Here was a book that took the real thing as its subject, that boasted "forty of the best recipes from barbecue chefs throughout the country." I was so euphoric with expectation that I rushed in, bought the book, and cracked it open as soon as I got on the subway.

In the store my eye had been caught by the text that prefaced her recipe for "James Beal's Barbecued Ribs," so I turned directly there. James Beal, a Dallas native who had removed to Seattle to run J. K.'s Wild Boar Soul BBQ Pit, cooked his ribs a minimum of *fourteen hours*. "Folks have been known to faint with anticipation," Jane Butel murmured enticingly into my ear, and her words alone made me feel pretty weak myself—this was exactly what I wanted so much to learn.

Now that I was actually perusing her recipe, however, I found myself brought up short. A quick computation of her cooking times revealed a discrepancy of over twelve hours. Whereas Mr. Beal took more than half a day to cook his ribs, Jane Butel accomplished the task in *less than two hours*. The emphasis of her recipe was the sauce, a concoction heavy in sugar and liquid smoke—as if it had been *that* that those customers were fainting for. Regarding the technique of that long, slow smoking of the ribs, she dropped nary a clue.

With heart now notching downward, I flipped the page over to her recipe for "Super Secret Baby Back Pork Ribs"—another of my fave raves. "When created in their original setting," she lilted, "the ribs were specially smoked, but this backyard version is just as irresistibly delicious." A frantic search through the rest of the book revealed only more of the same. As far as Jane Butel was concerned, the creators of "Alabama Smoky Barbecued Chicken," who prepared that delicacy in homemade barrel smokers, were simply wasting their time. "You can get the same effect with any covered grill." Yeah, sure. *Finger Lickin' Rib Stickin' Great Tastin' Hot & Spicy BUT NOT Barbecue.*

There is obviously a profound divide in cookbook land between barbecue expectation and barbecue reality. How could a knowledgeable food writer sink her teeth into significant ribs—*know* that the secret of their flavor and texture was all those hours over wood—and yet proffer one paltry simulacrum after another, instead of instructions for replicating the actual original?

The answer is simple: Jane Butel is cookbook author first and barbecue lover second. Authentic barbecue cannot be put into recipes, but barbecue sauces can. Consequently, in *any* book of recipes, sauce takes precedence over meat—so much so, in fact, that in the world of cookbooks sauce has *become* barbecue.

To learn to make real barbecue, the first step is to clear the mind of our unspoken but central culinary tenet—that all good cooking starts with learning the recipe. That notion has been so thoroughly drummed into our heads that we no longer think it an idea—we take it for plain fact. But any route to authentic barbecue first requires letting go of the parental hand of recipe to go *mano à mano* with the piece of meat.

No doubt about it, this is not easy. Long after my eating self had figured out that barbecue had nothing to do with recipes, my cooking self kept helplessly sifting through them, looking for answers that were never there. How would I know if the meat was burning? How would I know if the coals were hot enough—or *not* hot enough? How would I even know if it was done? To set the books aside was to face panic; to cling to them was to continue eating sauce-slopped, foil-steamed ribs.

That, in a nutshell, was my quandary: these books all gave me recipes for something else and told me to call *that* barbecue. I had eaten authentic barbecue, I had read enough to know something about the demanding, time-consuming way it *had* to be made, and yet I kept on making the other stuff. I just couldn't help it . . . appetite wouldn't let things be, and the cook in me couldn't make them different.

True barbecue, let me now explain, is meat slow-roasted over wood at a low enough temperature that it loses about a third of its weight in moisture during the cooking process. It is this partial jerking that gives barbecue its dense, tender texture and rich, concentrated flavor, the same gentle heat also providing the characteristically crisp and savory crust.

To accomplish this, the surface of the meat must be exposed to a slow but constant flow of smoky air, hot enough to sweat out the moisture, but never so hot as to turn it into steam. Too hot a fire boils the meat with its own juices, leaving it tough and dry; too low a fire won't cook the meat at all. Consequently, the ideal barbecuing temperature is only a little higher than that which the meat will register when completely done. Roast pork, which has an internal reading of about 165°F when done, should be barbecued within a temperature range of 180°F to 200°F; for beef, that range is lower still—170°F to 190°F.

At these low cooking temperatures, the smoke helps prevent bacterial spoilage before the meat is heated through. This purpose is also served by the salt and spices rubbed in before barbecuing and the sauce of vinegar and hot pepper mopped on during it. Each of these leaves its trace of flavor in the crust, although, despite what is often written, this does not actually penetrate into the meat.

It is because of the nature of the cooking process—slow *and* dry— that barbecue cannot be done on the usual barbecue grill. If closed, it steam-cooks the meat; if left open, it roasts it too quickly. Nor can true barbecue—by *any* contrivance—be made in or on a kitchen stove, because there you don't have the smooth, even flow of smoke.

However, you *can* cook barbecue on a simple rack suspended over a small fire; all you need is patience and a still day. This is how barbecue was first made, and all subsequent adaptations have had but a single purpose: to get more control over the flow of heat and smoke. This is the logic of the pit—a deep, stone-lined hole filled with hot coals. A grill is set into it near the top; the heat, protected from any draft, rises straight up and surrounds the meat. A piece of sheet metal, laid over the top, holds the smoke in.

The fanciest barbecue rig adds little to this arrangement but convenience, lifting the grill up to waist height so that the barbecuist no longer needs to squat to cook, hinges the lid so that it easily lifts out of the way when the meat needs turning or mopping, and adds a separate, connected firebox, so that the meat is subjected to less direct heat and cleaner smoke.

The barbecuing itself, once all this is understood, becomes self-explanatory: a constant play of adjustment that keeps the meat just at the edge of slowest roasting. The coals are kept no more than smoldering; if the meat starts to cook too quickly, it is cooled with mopping sauce and the fire beat down still more. The meat also must be turned on occasion to allow the crust to form evenly. Apart from dealing with the occasional grease flare-up, no more is required but to bring the meat to the table when it starts to fall off the bone.

Gradually I came to understand all this—only to discover in myself an unexpected reluctance to actually do it. Appetite could easily get me into the ring with a five-dollar cut of meat, but it had a much harder time persuading me to spend a day and night in the back yard wrestling with it. I might devote that kind of attention to a whole pig, but so far as the lesser cuts were concerned, the cook in me demurred: there are just easier ways to get good eating out of cheap meat.

Not that barbecue demands constant work—long periods can pass when there are no tasks at all to do—but it does demand your constant company. There is no way to predict when the meat will need mopping or the coals need stoking—except by being there.

My resistance wasn't laziness—what easier way is there to spend an afternoon than sipping beer and mopping meat—but an initial misreading of barbecue's invitation to revelry. I had skipped ahead too quickly to the part concerning eating, drinking, and being merry, and so I had missed out on half the party—it had begun long before I ever thought to arrive.

Barbecue comes from a place and time not only where any kind of meat was a rare and enviable commodity but also where, more often than not, its eating happened at a juncture of communal celebration. A chicken was slaughtered when the preacher came for dinner; a pig was roasted whole to signify an especially momentous event.

Community is built into the very nature of the barbecue pit. Not only does barbecue cook a lot of meat, but its many-tasked, time-consuming structure demands participation. "We can't cook all this meat alone," it says, delightfully inverting the usual sense of neighborly obligation. As in corn-husking or maple-sugaring, "Come help" also means "Come have fun."

The richness of association attached to barbecue begins with this sense of cooperative effort, a form of secular communion that we now seldom experience. Barbecue today comes closest to this when it is turned into a mock tribal rite—an excuse for friends to stay up all night around a fire, laughing and drinking together, and then on the morrow to return smelly and exhausted to their families, triumphantly bearing a feast. Given that the whole cloth of barbecue must be trimmed in some way to fit our smaller tables, it is far less demeaned by being turned into escapade than into recipe—but either way its original stature is reduced.

That this social core eluded me is not surprising: my first taste of barbecue, after all, was in a huge, windowless roadhouse with black smoke belching out the back. Although I sat in the midst of a pandemonium of meat hunger, each of us ate our ribs alone. It never occurred to me that their making might require any other effort than my own.

Not that a single person can't barbecue over a pit. Many still do—just as others still tap their maple trees for syrup. But for most of us, these things are a spectacular investment of scarce free time. Today meat is cheap, time dear. If we still want the authentic article, we must translate the process into more convenient terms—and accept the inevitable loss of poetry in its making.

For me, that meant the pit had to go. Ironically, it opened the door to real barbecue and then stood in it, blocking my way. I couldn't get myself to use it and I couldn't get its image out of my head. Consequently, I stumbled across my first homemade batch of the real thing by accident—setting out to smoke some spareribs in an electric fish smoker, I ended up, to my complete astonishment, with barbecue instead.

I had eaten store-bought smoked pork before and found it much like Canadian bacon—too quickly cooked to be anything but merely smoke-flavored. My own smoker, however, was so low-powered that at first it seemed unable to cook the ribs at all. But I wrapped the smoker in some additional insulation and gave it the day. What I took out had a strangely familiar appearance.

First, the surface of the ribs had the look of licked mahogany that comes from the slow melting away of surface fat. Then, when I ripped a rack apart, the meat came away cleanly from the bone, separating into long, moist shreds. Finally, and most important, that meat had barbecue's famous, unmistakable signature. Called the "smoke ring" in barbecue circles, it is an opalescent, deeply pink layer of meat just below the crust, very different from the grayish-pink color of undercooked pork. On barbecued pork shoulder, this ring can reach as far as an inch into the meat. On baby back ribs, it is barely an eighth of that—just enough to signal that this was the real thing.

When I sank my teeth into the juicy and finely textured meat, all those separate pieces of understanding fell together with an almost audible thud: the long cooking at low temperature and the slow but steady passage of hot dry air, full of rich-flavored hickory smoke given off by the pan of chips set on the smoker's tiny burner.

Although I didn't know it at the time, I had reinvented the "Cook-Shack," an electric-based cooker the shape of a restaurant-sized dishwasher that more and more barbecue joints are using—partly out of ignorance, partly out of laziness, and partly because, given local fire codes, they have no other choice. However, true barbecue lovers consider any such an out-and-out naked fraud.

In my own defense, I might point out that using a fish smoker to make barbecue isn't quite the same thing. After all, it must be used out-of-doors, it is so underpowered as to require a substantial amount of time to do the work, and it is susceptible to so many variables (ambient temperature, wind, thickness of a particular cut of meat) as to be beyond recipe (which is why in its instruction booklet its manufacturer doesn't even discuss making barbecue: all its smoked meat is brine-cured first). This much, at least, is authentic.

But even if the smoker does make real barbecue possible, it also completes the rupture of its dual meaning. There is nothing at all convivial about the meat smoker: only so much appetite can be whetted by smoke seeping slowly from a cardboard-wrapped metal box; only so much pride can be gleaned from a barbecue rig out of which, as W. Park Kerr sardonically notes, "an electric cord snakes its way to a socket just inside the garage door."

That's the price I've paid to find my ribs. They're good, more than good, but the experience goes no further than that. Their making asks so little of me: no basting, no turning, no keeping the coals alive—the smoker does it all. I can eat my barbecue, but I can no longer know it—all its mystery has fled. And there's no way at all to retrieve it— at least not until about nine months after the arrival of our first pig.

3. SAUCING IT

Barbecuists put secret ingredients into their sauces for the same reason that dogs leave their mark on trees, to claim a piece of territory as their own. The secret ingredient is not intended to make the sauce taste "better" but to mark it in such a way as to leave no doubt that it's unique. The praise it wants is not culinary exclamation but surrender: to make the taster swear that he or she has never tasted the like.

Barbecuing is only incidentally cooking, and barbecuists avoid, as much as possible, confusing the two. Barbecue is play—serious, mind-concentrating, important, risk-running, even exhausting . . . anything, in fact, except a chore. In real barbecue there's no washing up.

Consequently, where the serious *cook* would make a sauce from scratch, the serious *barbecuist* looks at that approach with skepticism. It is the wrong kind of seriousness, much too close to actual work.

This is because, for the cook, the very word "sauce" calls up such qualifiers as hollandaise, Périgord, béchamel, Béarnaise . . . while for the barbecuist, who very likely has never even tasted hollandaise, sauce is something that comes out of a bottle . . . slowly. It is thick and spicy and full of fruit or fire (or both)—Worcestershire sauce, chili sauce, A.1. steak sauce, catsup, Tabasco sauce. For the barbecuist, a brown sauce is not a sauce at all, it's gravy.

For the cook, at least the serious cook, this poses an insoluble problem. You can, if you feel the need, make your own catsup from scratch, but you cannot make it taste like *real* catsup. No matter what you do, it will still turn out tasting too fresh and healthy to fool even a child.

For the barbecuist, a sauce is a patent substance, an already made thing. It is individualized the same way a car is: by jacking up the suspension, adding oversized wheels, souping up the engine. A cook wants to re-create a sauce; a barbecuist wants to wrench it into a purely personal fit.

This is what ties sauce to barbecue. Indeed, otherwise there is no such thing as a "barbecue sauce"—because, strictly in terms of flavor, good barbecue needs no saucing at all. Knowing this is what separates the real barbecuist from the dilettante: where for the latter the sauce is everything, for the former it is only a florid signature attached to an already written poem.

In *A Bowl of Red*, Frank X. Tolbert describes a master barbecuist who attributed his success to a "secret devil's sauce."

He wouldn't tell anyone, not even his family, the formula, although some of the ingredients were obviously fresh chili pepper, Worcestershire sauce [he said he made his own], black pepper, and vinegar.

This is a sauce that, out of a bottle, would taste no better than any other good patent sauce. But served on a slab of beef ribs by a wizardly eighty-seven-year-old black man who has just spent the whole previous night (as Tolbert portrays him doing) pampering this meat as it crusts up over hickory coals—this same devil's brew outconjures any other sauce at all. It is context not content that gives it its genuine magic . . . which is why a lesser cook's potion—whatever the ingredients—contains only a wishful one.

In other words, a barbecue sauce is something you earn. Stay up the whole night communing with a smoldering fire, turn and baste each chunk of meat as it tells you to, and there will be nothing randomly inspirational about the sauce you concoct to set on the table with it. The more important this ritual is to you and the longer you perform it, the more certain you will be about what that meat wants—and that much more able to translate your certainty into an elixir of commanding potency.

No one would spend the time customizing a car if they didn't already take that vehicle seriously, weren't awed by its capacities for power and speed . . . and especially if some visceral aspect of the car's design didn't cry out to be liberated from suggestion into rampant display. Customizing may be anarchic but it's never accidental. No one should meddle with a sauce who doesn't feel a pulsating urgency to wrench the bottle out of the manufacturer's gutless hands and fill it with fire and life—with garlic . . . hot peppers . . . crushed raisins . . . dollops of Southern Comfort—because it *needs* to be sweeter, hotter, and far more puissant withal, or you wouldn't deign put it on your meat.

While a genuine barbecue sauce is very much one of a kind—however smoothly blended, it always has a rough, raw edge that bespeaks the essentially unrefined nature of the occasion—the taste of most commercial products is all in the label. However funky the packaging, what oozes out usually has the flat, sludgy taste that comes when a parsimonious amount of flavor is spread as far as possible through a whole lot of sauce.

More than a few barbecue joints bottle up their own sauces, and these can be very good. However, be careful. Because large food corporations have discovered that private-label barbecue sauces have special appeal, they attempt to disguise mass-production quality behind labels sporting barbecue-country addresses. One rule of thumb is that if the sauce isn't made near you, most likely it did not come out of a real restaurant kitchen, since it's unlikely that a small producer will find national distribution for its sauce. Another touchstone is the absence of any taste of smoke. Sauce laced with liquid smoke is to barbecue what meat tenderizer is to steak—a sign of priorities gone askew. Burning wood, not creosote-flavored water, is what is supposed to put the smoke into barbecue.

If you eat at a joint that sells its sauce over the counter and you like it, buy a couple of bottles. Collect them, taste them, compare them, and learn from them—but remember, they're *already* customized. Don't think you can add some hot pepper or a splash of bourbon to one of them and claim it as your own. That's just playing at the thing. To do it right, you have to go out and get your bottle of catsup, your jar of mustard, your can of RC Cola, your shaker of onion salt, and do the job yourself.

Meat Rubs and Mopping Sauces

A rub is a salt and/or spice mixture massaged into the meat before it is barbecued. Traditional rubs are based on salt and red and black pepper (salt helps wick moisture from the meat), and in barbecue country, it often goes no further. Kreutz Market in Lockhart, Texas, regularly rated among the state's top ten barbecue joints, serves smoked beef shoulder and sausage to devoted patrons, who eat it off butcher paper at knife-scored tables to which communal cleavers have been chained. Their rub formula is equal parts salt and black pepper, with ground red pepper stirred in to taste.

When Jim Auchmutey, an Atlanta-based reporter and food writer, asked Don Schmidt, one of the brothers who runs Kreutz Market, about barbecue sauce, he was told that all they offer is a hot pepper sauce:

> "I don't have anything against barbecue sauce," he said, "but we don't believe it's necessary. I wouldn't know how to make a barbecue sauce."

It should be noted, however, that Kreutz Market's specialty is barbecued beef, which needs less seasoning than pork. Pork rubs often contain chili powder, ground cumin, cinnamon, nutmeg, and things like lemon pepper, celery salt, and garlic powder.

My own rub for pork ribs started as a similar shake-on mix of salt, black pepper, dry mustard, nutmeg, and ground hot red chile pepper.

But it gradually evolved into the following paste, amalgamated in a small composite-stone Thai mortar.

HOME-GROWN PATENT RUB
[COATS 3 OR 4 RACKS BABY BACK RIBS]

1 teaspoon non-iodized salt
1 teaspoon ground hot red chile pepper
1 teaspoon whole peppercorns
1 teaspoon whole black mustard seeds
3 or 4 whole juniper berries
1 tablespoon peanut oil
1 tablespoon apple cider vinegar
1 tablespoon dark brown sugar
1 large clove garlic, crushed through a garlic press

Pound all this for a few minutes in a mortar (or pulse-process in a food processor) until the blend is a thick paste. Then thin it, if necessary, with a dribble of hot water until it is the consistency of bottled grainy mustard. Work the resulting rub evenly into the meat with the fingers and let it sit for about 30 minutes before putting it into the cooker. For beef ribs, omit the mustard seed and juniper berries.

Bastes or mopping sauces are applied to the meat as it cooks. As well as adding flavor, they cool the meat if it starts cooking too fast. Most mop sauces are essentially cider vinegar, or sometimes beer, flavored with salt, pepper, and spices, sometimes elaborated with such ingredients as meat stock, minced onion, garlic, and/or Worcestershire sauce. Because the basting mop returns meat juices and the tang of smoke to the sauce pot, the baste becomes increasingly tasty as the barbecuing proceeds—which is why some aver that the best table sauce of all is that last rich remnant of mopping sauce thickened out and sweetened a bit with some chile sauce or tomato catsup.

Since real barbecue is still a rare and exciting event for me, I've yet to bring myself to eat it doused with barbecue sauce, even one of my own concoction. Still, they fascinate me, especially because—as a vernacular foodstuff—their creators continue happily to reinvent the wheel. The following sauces illustrate not only some of the different regional styles but also their ageless appeal. The "Texas Chuckwagon BBQ Sauce" that Bob, Rose, and Cora Brown recorded in Texas three years before I was born is probably right now being created afresh in some San Antonio kitchen.*

MEMPHIS-STYLE BBQ SAUCE
(ADAPTED FROM *REAL BARBECUE* [1988], BY GREG JOHNSON AND VINCE STATEN)
(MAKES 3 CUPS)

1 cup tomato sauce
1 cup distilled vinegar
¼ cup Worcestershire sauce
1 tablespoon butter
½ small onion, minced
½ teaspoon black pepper
½ teaspoon cayenne pepper
1 teaspoon salt

Combine the ingredients in a saucepan with enough water (about ½ cup) to make a liquid sauce. Bring to a simmer over medium flame, reduce heat, and cook for 10 minutes. The authors note: "Used full strength, it's a typical table sauce. For a basting sauce, mix one cup of the recipe . . . with one cup of vinegar and one cup of water."

TARHEEL VINEGAR BBQ SAUCE
(ADAPTED FROM *REAL AMERICAN FOOD* [1986], BY JANE AND MICHAEL STERN)
(MAKES 2 CUPS)

½ cup (1 stick) butter
1 cup cider vinegar
1 large sour pickle, minced
2 tablespoons onion, minced
2 tablespoons Worcestershire sauce
1 tablespoon lemon juice
1 tablespoon brown sugar
Salt and pepper

* Those looking for further guidance regarding rubs, mops, and sauces could do worse than seek out *The Ultimate Barbecue Sauce Cookbook*, by Jim Auchmutey and Susan Puckett. These two Southerners know their way around a barbecue pit, and their observations are as astute as their recipes are authentic.

Combine the ingredients except the salt and pepper in a saucepan. Put over a low flame and heat just long enough for the butter to melt, stirring frequently. Add salt and pepper to taste. Use as a mop or table sauce. Makes 2 cups.

TEXAS RANCHHOUSE BBQ SAUCE

(ADAPTED FROM *AMERICA COOKS* [1940], BY CORA, ROSE, AND BOB BROWN)

(MAKES 2 CUPS)

½ cup (1 stick) butter
1 large onion, grated
2 cloves garlic, minced
1 cup distilled vinegar
½ cup tomato catsup
2 tablespoons Worcestershire sauce
2 bay leaves
Juice of 1 lemon
2 teaspoons dried mustard
2 tablespoons Texas chili powder
¼ teaspoon cayenne
1 teaspoon black pepper
1 teaspoon salt
¼ cup sugar

Melt the butter over low heat in a saucepan and stir in the grated onion. When it turns translucent, mix in the garlic, vinegar, 1 cup of water, catsup, Worcestershire sauce, bay leaves, and lemon juice. Let this simmer while mixing together in a small bowl the mustard and chili powder, cayenne, black pepper, salt, and sugar. Stir this into the sauce and continue to simmer for at least 10 minutes, removing and discarding the bay leaves before using. Makes about 2 cups of sauce, enough for 4 to 5 pounds of meat.

BAYOU RED WINE BBQ SAUCE

(ADAPTED FROM *LOUISIANA COOKERY* [1954], BY MARY LAND)

(MAKES 4 CUPS)

2 tablespoons wine vinegar
1 bottle (3 cups) red wine
½ cup olive oil
4 tablespoons onion, minced

1 clove garlic, minced
1 bay leaf
Pinch each thyme, rosemary, basil, salt, and black pepper

Make the sauce the day before barbecuing. Mix the ingredients well and refrigerate before using as a mopping sauce. This is especially good on duck and game.

FLORIDA CITRUS BBQ SAUCE
(ADAPTED FROM *HOW AMERICA EATS* [1960], BY CLEMENTINE PADDLEFORD)
(MAKES 3 QUARTS)

1 quart cider vinegar
1½ bottles catsup
⅓ cup A.1. sauce
¼ cup Worcestershire sauce
1 tablespoon black pepper
¼ cup (½ stick) butter
¼ cup sugar
1 or 2 cloves garlic, crushed
1 tablespoon Tabasco sauce
½ orange, juice and rind
½ grapefruit, juice and rind
1 small onion, minced
½ bay leaf
1 teaspoon oregano
Salt to taste

Combine the ingredients in a large pot and bring to a boil. Remove the sauce from the heat and let it sit overnight. Strain before using. (This sauce can be kept for several weeks in the refrigerator.)

CASTINE, 1990

COOKING WITH WOOD: AN UPDATE

When I originally wrote this piece, I gave directions for using a Luhr•Jensen Little Chief smoker for making real barbecue. However, in the years since then, things have changed—for both myself and the world at large. That this was the case for the world was brought home recently when, wandering through our local Wal-Mart, I came across a massive barbecue rig for sale, with smokestack, separate wood firebox, etc., priced at just under two hundred dollars. Next to it was a simpler electric meat smoker-cooker, very similar to the Little Chief but with a strong enough electric element so that the cooker does not need its original packaging as insulation. Clearly, if a taste for real barbecue has spread to Down East Maine, something is going on.

What all this means is that, when I originally asked the rhetorical question: "What would keep a man in the back yard all day cooking a five-dollar piece of meat?" I had foolishly overlooked the obvious answer: a five-hundred-dollar barbecue rig to play with. The Wal-Mart version is a discount knockoff of boy toys that can run over a thousand dollars—and the proliferation of barbecue cookoffs around the country is an indication of how much their owners want to show them off.

Although I have yet to acquire such a monster, when we moved up the coast from Castine I did leave our exhausted Little Chief behind. My brother had given us a non-electric barrel smoker-cooker as a wedding present, and I had ambitions to advance a little up the barbecue evolutionary chain and do some cooking over real wood heat. At first I tried commercial charcoal briquettes. These were not entirely satisfactory, since when used for the kind of lengthy cooking that real barbecue requires they tend to smother themselves in a thick cloak of ash, requiring that they be regularly raked over to keep the heat even.*

As it happened, I was operating my smoke-cooker within spitting range of a five-foot-high pile of split, seasoned firewood, and eventually the foolishness of the situation penetrated my brain. I took some logs and split them down a little further, built a tepee in the cooker's firebox, stuffed it with newspaper, and fired it up. Then, since we live in the middle of a pine woods, I set the barrel shell around the burning logs to contain the flames and put the two grill racks—crisscrossed—on top to catch any flying embers.

---

* Barbecuists are fond of pointing out that commercial briquets are mostly sawdust and pulverized coal—their actual charcoal content can be as little as 20 percent (call them charcoal-*flavored* briquets). Even so, they do the job, and they're cheap and convenient as well. So while I agree that real charcoal is preferable for grilling, if you can't produce your own, it's an extremely expensive barbecue fuel . . . and, let's face it, probably not all that much better for you. People talk about "natural" charcoal as if it were some kind of health food rather than a proven carcinogen. I personally think an occasional meal of smoked meat is worth the risk, and I'm not going to pretend I've lessened it any by joining with the pot to call the kettle black.

The logs were nicely aged oak and maple, and they quickly burst into flame. In about fifteen minutes, the cooker contained a roaring fire. Big, black, molten bubbles began bulging out of the sheet-metal sides, and for a horrifying moment I thought the whole unit was actually melting down. But no, it was just the black paint—heatproof but not *that* heatproof—beginning to disintegrate. The grills started to glow a bright red, and the plastic handles at the top of the metal tube (for lifting it on and off the firebox) deliquesced into sludge and oozed off their bolts, vaporizing as they slid down the white-hot metal.

I pulled on my leather welding gloves, lifted the whole assembly off the firebox, and let the logs burn themselves out. They did produce wonderful, all-natural, long-lasting charcoal . . . at which point I was able to put everything back and barbecue a couple of racks of baby back ribs to perfection. Still, my rig now looks less like a smoke-cooker than a chunk of detritus scrounged out of the rubble of a three-alarm fire. Thus I learned an important lesson about cooking with wood: it burns *hot*.

This leads me to a simple point that applies to all barbecue cooking, no matter what kind of equipment you use. IF YOU WANT TO COOK OVER WOOD, USE A SEPARATE FIRE PIT TO BURN THE WOOD DOWN TO CHARCOAL BEFORE INSERTING IT INTO YOUR COOKING RIG—HOWEVER SOPHISTICATED THAT COOKING RIG HAPPENS TO BE.

W. Park Kerr, writing in *The El Paso Chile Company's Burning Desires: Salsa, Smoke, & Sizzle*, inadvertently shows to what absurd lengths you have to go if you ignore this advice. Kerr barbecues in what is now the upscale barbecuist's choice: a pricier version of the unit I encountered in Wal-Mart—a cast-iron barbecue rig with a firebox, smoking chamber, and smokestack.

He burns his wood only in the rig's firebox, noting accurately that when he starts the fire it gives off " 'bad' smoke, which is thick and yellow, and which quickly makes foods too tongue-numbingly bitter to eat. Eventually there is 'good' smoke which is lighter, thinner, and whiter. This appears in about thirty minutes."

When the fire gets low, Kerr just chucks in a fresh log, which means his meat gets basted with a lot of that same thick, yellow, bitter smoke—i.e., creosote—while it burns down into charcoal. A long-cooking piece of meat like beef brisket can take only so much of this treatment, so he has had to develop a special technique for dealing with it. After a few hours of smoke cooking, he puts the cut in foil, douses it in beer, wraps it up, and finishes it off in his oven.

Kerr rationalizes his behavior by observing that "barbecue joints tend to use natural gas for heat, and only a few chips or chunks of wood for flavor, which lets them smoke brisket for all the many hours needed to be falling-apart luscious." Well, yes, sadly, more and more pits are doing just this, but—as we know—out of laziness, not necessity. And while many ace Texas barbecuists finish off a brisket by wrapping it in foil, they do so only after *twice as much* smoke cooking (sometimes much more than that)—and then they continue to cook it, wrapped in foil, in their pit.

This is because they not only use wood but know *how* to use it. The home barbecuist who starts with wood will want to finish with it, and that means keeping a separate fire pit to provide a continuous supply of charcoal to shovel into the cooker . . . whatever kind of cooker it may be. Get your taste of smoke from the discreet use of wood chips— or, as I now prefer to do, with small branches of green wood, cut from the tree (in my case, apple), trimmed of leaves, and snipped into usable lengths. I toss in a handful of these each time I add more coals.

STEUBEN, 1995

READING ABOUT IT

Although there are now some reputable mainstream cookbooks available that detail the making of authentic barbecue—notably *Smoke & Spice* by Bill Jamison and Cheryl Alters Jamison—such efforts, with their universal emphasis on recipes, recipes, recipes, lack the austerity of the true barbecuist where the essential interest lies in method. On the rare occasion that a practiced, dyed-in-the-wool barbecuist produces a book, it can be recognized at once by its thinness—evidencing lack of patience for techniques other than the author's own—and by the fact that often a whole chapter is devoted to selecting the right hardwood or cut of meat.

Unfortunately, a book like this is almost always self-published in an out-of-the-way location; by the time you find out about it, it's out of print. Consequently, I've obtained more of my education as a barbecuist from reading good barbecue guidebooks than from any cookbook or instruction manual. Serious seekers of commercial—or, as it usually is, *barely* commercial—barbecue observe a lot more than the contents of their paper plates.

For instance, the publication of a book on South Carolina geography recently caused enough of a stir in scholarly circles to merit a story in *The Wall Street Journal*. Its authors had used barbecue sauces as a theme for one of their regional maps, dividing the state by local preference for tomato-, catsup-, vinegar-and-pepper-, or mustard-based sauces.

This will come as no surprise to Allie Patricia Wall and Ron L. Layne, authors of *Hog Heaven*, on whose work (and map) the geographers based their own. Their book describes and rates over a hundred South Carolina barbecue joints, a narrative prefaced by a knowledgeable account of various methods of professional barbecuing (with designs!), an explanation of the different styles of saucing, and detailed instructions for building your own home pit.

Serious barbecuists, wherever they may live, will want this book, both for that prefatory material and for the authors' meticulous descriptions of the art of many different pit masters. At Sawgrass Jim's Bar-B-Q House in Spartanburg, to give just one example, the pitmaster uses a dry-cure cooking process that requires a double-chambered pit:

> The smaller compartment holds burning wood coals, which Mr. Howell obtains from green hickory. The smoke produced is drawn naturally through vents up and into the adjacent compartment, a large oven where the meat is hung or placed on metal racks. Thus, the smoke, not the flames, from the burning hickory cooks the meat—indirectly. To make this barbecue, Jimmy Howell places whole hogs in the closed pit . . . and smokes them for 10–11 hours at about 190°F to 195°F. Since the smoke can permeate the meat from all directions, no turning of the hogs is required. However, he does season the meat a little with dry spices while it is cooking.

Such passages will not only inspire South Carolina longings in home barbecuists but lend suggestions for more imaginative meat work of their own.

Of course, guides like these date quickly; nowadays, especially, barbecue joints are fading fast. However, for those seeking clues to the ethos and practical operation of a serious pit, this datedness can actually turn out to be a plus. This certainly applies to *Real Barbecue*, by Greg Johnson and Vince Staten, published as a trade paperback in 1988 and now out of print.

These two guys not only know barbecue but have figured out how to write it. (They're off to a great start with the sentence "The best thing to do with a book about barbecue is wipe your hands on it.") The ostensible purpose of *Real Barbecue* is to review and rate almost seven hundred barbecue joints around the country—to the extent that a par-

ticular part of the country has a joint worth rating. Some areas are
entirely out of luck (the only state on the West Coast to win a mention
is California); the nearest one to me here in Maine is a good seven-hour
trip—Bub's Bar-B-Que in Sutherland, Massachusetts. The authors make
the drive sound worth it.

Almost all real barbecue books are passionate about their subjects,
but what makes this one special is its depth of understanding. The
authors know that not just anyone is likely to go out and open a barbecue pit, and they're genuinely curious about the type who will. Consider the Cafe Tattoo in Baltimore, a barbecue joint that shares space
with a tattoo parlor called, not surprisingly, Tattoo Cafe. (If you're confused, just be sure to go in the front door.) The owner, a displaced
Arkansan, explains that his wife runs the tattoo parlor and was the one
who inspired him to get into barbecue: "If it weren't for her, I'd be sleeping in a cardboard box over some steam grate." Not the sort of confession
you'd expect from Jacques Pépin . . . but barbecue is another world.

It's a world, as they explain, where a pitman will spend all night in
his smokehouse to keep the temperature even, grow all the vegetables
for his sauce, and determine doneness by reaching into the pit and
laying his hand right on the piece of meat.

Such devotion is usually in inverse proportion to the effort spent on
interior decoration or, for that matter, cleanliness. In fact, among their
criteria for gauging the promise of an as yet untried joint (after you go
around back to see if there's a woodpile in view—stacks of wood out
front should be discounted as an advertising ploy, since no pitman is
going to lug logs to his pit from the front of the building) is the number
of dead flies on the windowsill and whether there's a sink for washing
up afterward right in the dining room.

They have a lot to say about the way these places cook the meat. Here's
Larry Sconyers (Sconyers' Bar-B-Que, Augusta, GA) on his own method:

> "It's the meat, not the sauce, that gives barbecue its flavor." He buys only hams,
> which are high on the hog, and cooks each one for at least twelve hours over
> wood coals. He has patented his cooking process: standing the hams on end so
> they can cook in their own juices . . . Sconyers cooks all his meats, chickens,
> ribs—everything—standing up. "It burns every single bit of the fat out of the
> meat." Sconyers serves up a chopped pork sandwich that will melt in your mouth
> if you try to savor the flavor too long . . .

Real Barbecue also offers some quality recipes for different regional
sauces—and such necessary eat-withs as "The Rib Joint Roadhouse's
Black Beans and Rice" and "Mama's Hot and Greasy Fried Pies."

There's also a comprehensive rating of mail-order sauces and information on how to get real barbecue FedEx-ed right to your own door.

Vogue magazine is not where you would turn first for evocative writing about authentic barbecue, generously seasoned with clearly described, practical detail. But when its food columnist, Jeffrey Steingarten, was invited to help judge the 1993 May World Championship Barbecue Cooking Contest in Memphis, he turned the occasion into a self-taught crash course on the subject. The result, "Going Whole Hog" (to be found in the September 1993 issue), is simply the best thing I've ever read on the competitive barbecue scene, awash with pointers gleaned directly from the pitmasters:

> Apple City cooks its loin and baby back ribs skinned and bone down for six to six and a half hours on a Ferris wheel that revolves in its menacing cooker with indirect heat from the sides and direct heat from underneath, both generated by Holland brand pure hickory briquettes . . . Right before every contest, Apple City cuts green applewood prunings to create an aromatic smoke in its cooker. The team believes that taking dry applewood and soaking it in water would remove its aroma; fully grown applewood logs contain too many harsh tars and resins.

Finally, there is Lolis Eric Elie's *Smokestack Lightning*, a back-roads odyssey through the Barbecue States in search of the ultimate mouthful of smoke. Elie is a New Orleans writer with a laid-back, gritty style that segues easily from the meditative to the sardonic, with occasional moments of plain wide-eyed delight. He is also very good—something not as easy as it might seem—at capturing the pleasure of eating meat.

> The hog is sitting up on its stomach, plenty of meat left, but many of the bones are showing from where it has already been tested and tasted. The meat along the loin is whiter and drier, like pork chops, and the meat along the hams and shoulders is darker and juicier. Quess's hog, without sauce, has a sweet flavor. It is too tender to slice, so I pull a few patches with a fork from this section and that, then eat them with my hands. I pick up a long juicy strand of dark meat and dip it into some Sauce Beautiful, Quess's product. It's a Memphis-style sauce, sweet, not real thick, with plenty of vinegar and black pepper.

He and his photographer sidekick, Frank Stewart—who has enhanced this project with some great sharp-edged, funky duotones—roam the South and Midwest from pit to pit, talking to the roughhewn characters who deliver the goods and checking out the other-side-of-the-tracks locations where they do it, all the while sampling the local specialties. These range from barbecued cow heads in Brownsville, Texas ("very rich, like brisket and other well-marbled cuts of meat, only more so . . . it's extremely tender"), to barbecued mutton in Owensville, Kentucky (of which Frank disapproves: "I don't like muttons. I didn't grow up around no muttons, and I don't see why we need to be encouraging the muttons by writing about them"), to barbecued pig "snoots" in East Saint Louis:

> The main thing that separates one snoot from another is the ratio of the hard parts to the soft crispy parts. If you can get enough crispy parts, then the crunchy parts are a nice change of pace. But if you find yourself biting around the whole snoot without getting a tooth in edgewise, it destroys the whole experience.

Did I mention that Elie is often very, very funny?

Road books, with their "here today, there tomorrow" pace, work best as a kind of verbal photography, presenting the reader with a stream of images, each one saturated with the feel of another, different place. Elie has a sensibility as absorbent as a pop-up sponge. He uses it to sop up all the fine details—the dish detergent bottle one barbecuist uses to dispense his sauce, the newspaper in which his snoots are wrapped to keep them crispy—and then wrings it out to give us the larger view— the creepy pervasiveness of chop suey joints in an increasingly decaying East Saint Louis; the buffet-style service and shared common tables at South Carolina barbecue places, which directly link them to the Baptist church socials out of which they only recently evolved.

Smokestack Lightning is the best book about barbecue I know. This is partly because Elie knows how to get beyond appetite without getting away from it—however interesting the talk, the taste of meat is always there somewhere in the reader's mouth. It's also because his book reminds us, like almost no other contemporary food writing, how much the craving for smoke-crusted, greasy meat remains a fundamental underpinning of the American culinary soul. But mostly it's because *Smokestack Lightning*—unlike, say, *Real Barbecue*—is a voyage of self-discovery. Elie doesn't wear this on his sleeve, but there's no doubt he's a different person at the end of this book than he was at its beginning, one with a much more complex—and very bittersweet—sense of roots. The reader gets into the back seat of their battered old Volvo—dubbed the Living Legend—hoping for a fun trip, and exits at the end of the road feeling privileged to have been asked along.

CASTINE, 1990 / STEUBEN, 1996

Cornbread Nation

1

"Jim, this is nice," I says. "I wouldn't want to be nowhere else but here. Pass me along another hunk of fish and some hot cornbread."
—MARK TWAIN, *The Adventures of Huckleberry Finn*

A traveler in Texas in the 1830s, riding up to a lonely cabin at the end of the day to ask the favor of a meal and shelter for the night, tells how the woman of the house, after bidding him welcome, would sing out to one of her children, "Run to the field and bring two or three ears of corn. I want to make some bread for the gentleman's supper!" These ears of corn would be shucked and the kernels cut from them, ground into meal, kneaded into dough, and baked into bread, as the traveler sat on the porch with the man of the house, watching the sun go down and telling the news of the world.

There is a discernible tone of condescending amusement in the traveler's account (he is A. A. Parker; his narrative *A Trip to the West and Texas* was published in 1834). He seems never to have recognized that to be presented with such a bread was both a courtesy and the sharing of what in these humble surroundings was a special culinary treat. There is not much better eating in the world than cornbread made of just-ground meal expertly baked in the fireplace. He only notes the wait entailed while all this is accomplished, and how primitive it seems: "I suppose this is the true method of living hand to mouth." And so it is. But the whole truth is far more complex—and far more interesting—than that.

"Corn—properly called 'maize'—is one of the first presents that Native Americans gave the original settlers of this country." This simple statement—a variation of which appears in countless narratives on American food—is so freighted with cultural bias that a book could be written picking it apart. We are a civilization beset with the idea of possession, and consequently one of claims and counterclaims, with the need to establish who first owned . . . invented . . . discovered what. Very often these records—and the kind of history they comprise—are beside the point. The Indians no more "gave" us corn than they "gave" us syphilis. These things, like much else we encounter when we go about the world, were themselves independent agents, catalysts of change.

Consider: in 1535—barely forty years after Columbus first set foot on this continent—the African explorer John Leo met people miles up the Niger River who had a large store of maize, "a round and white kind of pulse," which they called *manputo*—"Portuguese grain." Corn, once it was given access to the Old World, acted as if it had a will of its own. There was no owning or controlling it.

The word "maize" may today be considered the politically correct designation. But it is as arbitrary and Eurocentric as any other, because while it is the word that most European languages use, here in the Americas it was used by only one tribe of Caribbean Indians. In fact, there are as many Indian words for corn as there are Indian languages —more, since many of these languages are rich in corn words.

Thomas Hariot, in his account of a visit to Roanoke Island, Sir Walter Raleigh's ill-fated colony in North Carolina, wrote in 1588: "*Pagatowr*, a kinde of graine so called by the inhabitants, the same in the West Indies is called *Mayze* . . . Englishmen call it *Guinney wheate* or *Turkie wheate*." When Roger Williams compiled his *Key into the Language of America* (1643), which provided translations of the native Narragansett, he listed not only the term for corn—*weachim neash*—but those for boiled whole corn, parched corn, rotten corn, sweet corn, freshly ground meal, and parched meal, all of them different.

In England, the word "corn" meant grain or kernel (as in "John Barleycorn") and, by metonymy, is still used to designate a particular region's essential grain. However, the word carries with it a connotation of deeper import than "kernel of grain"—something more like "staff of life." All but the wealthiest English ate a diet based on grain—drunk as beer, supped as porridge, boiled as pudding, baked as bread. When the early settlers arrived in Virginia and Massachusetts, they found the Indians engaged in an activity that had immediate resonance with their own custom: these people also grew grain, and out of that grain they, too, made their daily bread.

As Sophie Coe observed in *America's First Cuisines*, the settlers were in a much better position to understand these foodways than we, since our cooking is no longer based on one fundamental carbohydrate so necessary to our eating that we are made humble by it—that, when a piece of bread falls to the floor, we kiss it to expiate the carelessness. In such a cuisine, the "daily bread" is the meal itself, not a pleasant but a dispensable accompaniment.

The phrase "Turkey wheat" comes from the French, for whom Turkey was at the time the generic origin of all things exotic. Similarly, "Guinea wheat" connects the grain to Guinea, on the west coast of Africa, which did the same service for the English (although it is possible that, as with the chile—"Guinea pepper"—British traders actually encountered corn there before they met with it here). In other words, foreign stuff. When the settlers came to call it corn, they were establishing the start of what would prove to be an enduring intimacy.

Before that, however, it was "Indian corn"—and "Indian meal" and "Indian bread." No other indigenous American foodstuff—the peanut, the potato, the chile pepper, the turkey—carries the same weight. In some instances, quite the opposite. The word "potato" is more likely to bring to mind the Irish or the Germans, the word "tomato" the whole Mediterranean, before either makes us think of the native cooking of this hemisphere. (The peanut, despite its host of associations with the American South, came to North America in the seventeenth century from Africa, where it had already taken a firm hold, rather than from Latin America. It was a "gift" of the slaves, not the Indians.)

Some food histories depict the Indians teaching the settlers—accustomed only to wheat breads—how to use this strange and much coarser meal. The truth is, however, that the settlers needed little such instruction. English cooking abounded in similar food. In fact, as late as 1904, Charles Roeder could describe the traditional basic fare of Lancashire and other counties in northern England as porridge made of oatmeal; havercake, an unleavened oat bread made of meal; bannock, a thick, unleavened oat bread, sometimes made of pease; and jannock (from which comes our own cornmeal johnnycake), a "thick, broad, unleavened oaten loaf, leavened later on, which was sometimes also made of barley or pease meal, and is of dark colour."

If we dig past the clichéd image of the giving Indian and the (temporarily) grateful settler, what we find just beneath is something more complicated: an occasion of mutual recognition and, at the same time, a collision of cultures. This, simplifying, we might call "grain versus corn." Old World grains—oats, millet, wheat, rye—required a careful, patient agriculture that reworked the same fields through the centuries. Those who owned the fields and the mills that ground what was grown in them owned the culture. Grain supports a feudal society of lords and serfs, a post-feudal society of landlords and tenant farmers.

A corn culture is more fluid. Corn is more adaptable as both a foodstuff and a crop. Skilled Indian agriculturalists could grow three crops of corn a year, and they could grow it almost anywhere they wanted—here one year and somewhere else the next. Unlike wheat (and similar grains), corn does not require plowed fields; it can be planted around the stumps of trees in freshly cleared plots.

Consequently, Indian culture itself was more fluid, not as hierarchical and not nearly as concerned with ideas of possession. As a Huron explained to a French *voyageur* at about the same time the Pilgrims arrived at Plymouth: "We are born free and united brothers, each as much a great lord as the other, while you are all the slaves of one sole man. I am the master of my body, I dispose of myself, I do what I wish, I am the first and last of my Nation . . . subject only to the Great Spirit."

It was for reasons such as these that Benjamin Franklin, a lifelong champion of Indian political ways and of their methods of persuasion, compromise, and consensus building, urged the Founding Fathers to draw on the example of the League of the Iroquois when framing the Constitution.

If the earliest colonists had had to depend on Old World grains to survive in the New World, they would all have perished. The land could not be transformed that quickly, certainly not by a people who were not, most of them, practiced farmers. Much has been made of the importance of corn in sustaining the original colonies, but little if anything about its immediate and subversive effect on the newborn American character. If there are no peasants in this country, it is because a peasant is wedded—as his family before him and after him—to a particular piece of land. In America, however, a man could take a bag of seed corn and an ax and head into the wilderness, to be there "as much a great lord as the other."

When Tom Paine served as secretary to the commissioners who negotiated for the American Revolutionaries with the Iroquois, he learned their language, and for the remainder of his political and writing career used them as models of how society should be organized. His radical reading of the rights of man was one of the earliest expressions of this evolving ethos, and although Paine himself did not understand this, that ethos was nurtured on Indian corn. Stephen Vincent Benét spoke truly in *Western Star*:

And they ate the white corn kernels, parched in the sun,
And they knew it not, but they'd not be English again.

2

Cornmeal made my bones.
—JOEL BARLOW (1793)

Cornbread Nation was populist, democratic, republican—printed in
all lower-case letters. It was a kind of agrarian radicalism, neither left
wing nor right, that proposed that this nation would work best if it was
a country of independent citizens, a majority of whom, whatever else
they might be—artisan or woodsman or merchant—were also small
landholders whose self-sufficiency would mean that they were beholden
to none. As equals among equals, they freely helped their neighbors
and accepted help from them, not out of obligation, but because it made
good sense.

At first this agrarian radicalism stood in opposition to the plantation,
to large landowners and tenant farming. But as the nation changed, it
found itself more threatened by the money economy created by the
Industrial Revolution. Now a man was held enslaved not to a piece of
land but to the necessity of sustaining a steady income. You are owned
if you are in debt, and it is hard—even impossible—to stay out of debt.
A money economy works by encouraging us to spend money faster than
we earn it—a simple mechanism, but one from which almost none
seems able to escape.

It should be remembered that the Civil War was a battle between an
agrarian and an industrial society—and that the industrial society won.
Ever since, the South has tarred the winners with the same brush: damn
Yankee. But there were many Yankees who were almost as opposed to
the money economy as they were to slavery, seeing the one as quite
similar to the other. For such as these, cornbread had the same importance as it had in the South—and for the same reasons. After all, one
of the most articulate expressions of independent self-sufficiency was
written by a Massachusetts man, sitting in his cabin on Walden Pond.
And he, too, was a cornbread maker.

Bread I at first made of pure Indian meal and salt, genuine hoe-cakes, which I
baked before my fire out of doors on a shingle or the end of a stick of timber
sawed off in building my house; but it was wont to get smoked and to have a
piny flavor. I tried flour also; but have at last found a mixture of rye and Indian

meal most convenient and agreeable. In cold weather it was no little amusement to bake several small loaves of this in succession, tending and turning them as carefully as an Egyptian his hatching eggs. They were a real cereal fruit which I ripened, and they had to my senses a fragrance like that of other noble fruits, which I kept in as long as possible by wrapping them in cloths.

All this is easy to romanticize. In reality, Cornbread Nation was made up of a restless population of poor whites and blacks who were constantly shifting about, seeking better situations than the marginal ones in which, despite their best efforts, they continued to find themselves. Often, they moved on every few years, generation after generation, never finding anyplace where they prospered long enough to sink in roots.

However, there is poverty and there is poverty. The very phrase "white trash" has an aura of impudence to it, of people unwilling to tug on their forelocks and slink into the background. American rural poverty has a defiant, don't-tread-on-me edge to it, the attitude of a people determined to get by without the help of other people's charity. Corn has always played a pivotal role in allowing them to do this.

In our own money economy, it is cash—not food—that is constantly in short supply; consequently it is hard for us to understand the sense of wealth that a good corn crop gave to a small landholder, or to appreciate the fine distinctions that made it the type of wealth it was. Sydney Poitier, in his autobiography, *This Life*, describes his childhood on Cat Island in the Bahamas, where his father fed them from a garden, fertilized with bat manure, where he grew tomatoes, string beans, sweet potatoes, yams, okra, peppers, and, above all, corn.

> Corn was the foundation of our diet—the center of almost every meal. It was roasted, toasted, baked, broiled, stewed, and ground into grits by a small hand-operated grinder, but first it had to be plucked, shucked, and dried in the sun until the kernels, hard as pebbles, could be easily rubbed from the cob. Grits and fish, roast corn and fish, grits with eggs, chicken and grits—cornmeal cereal and condensed milk. Whatever the time of day, whatever the meal, corn made its appearance.

However hard-won, such eating offered a largesse that transformed the experience of life for those who worked a small farm. Unlike wheat bread, a delicate cornbread can be made from the unripe—"green"—grain; that is, from the sweet pulp scraped from the kernels. It can also be prepared from ears that have gotten too tough to eat but are not yet dry enough to grind. As an Appalachian cook, Gladys Nichols, told a *Foxfire* magazine interviewer:

[We] shucked it and baked it in the oven. Then you would grate it off the cob, put you a little soda and salt and a little buttermilk in it, and bake it. That's called "roastin' ear bread."

Because corn is unique in being both vegetable and grain, it offers a wider range of culinary possibility than any other single food. In this regard, certainly, no grain—rice, millet, wheat, rye—can compare. Corn has bestowed on our cuisine not only countless wonderful dishes but a poetic food language of great beauty and vitality: hush puppies, pot dodgers, spoonbread, cornpone, Awendaw bread, cornmeal mush, hog and hominy, Indian pudding, spider cornbread, succotash, and on and on.

What corn gave the small landholder in the form of self-sufficiency it gave double in self-esteem. No wonder the power of the memories lingered on, especially among those who had tasted the freedom that it allowed. These people often came from rural backgrounds, where the reality of Cornbread Nation was most tangible. Its disappearance left a hole in their lives that somehow could never quite be closed.

3

The best corn bread we ever ate was from meal well-kneaded, with nothing but water and a little salt, and then made into lumps about the size and somewhat the shape of a man's foot, and raked in the embers just like potatoes to roast, and there allowed to remain and cook all night. Remember the three grand secrets about making good corn bread: Never grind your meal very fine, always have it fresh-ground, and never fear baking it too much.

—SOLON ROBINSON, *Facts for Farmers* (1866)

I've grown corn to eat green, and I've also ground dried corn into cornmeal, although the two acts were not connected. I did the latter when my mother gave me a hand-cranked grist mill and I wanted to see what it was like to bake cornbread out of fresh-ground cornmeal. Without a garden that year, I ordered a small sack of Rhode Island white flint corn kernels from miller Tim McTague.

These looked like tiny glass beads, and they ground up something like that, too. To turn them into meal was an arm-wrenching experience. The mill was bolted down to the kitchen counter, which, underneath its linoleum veneer, was an inch-thick piece of plywood. Even so, I was sure that I was going to rip a chunk right out of it before I was done. Enough cornmeal for one small cornbread was a half hour's grinding.

But it was lovely, fragrant stuff, and the resulting cornbread was delicious, possessing tiny flavor notes that are long gone by the time cornmeal arrives from the mill.

This was my one small taste of Cornbread Nation, and it was a chastening one. When Frederick Law Olmsted wrote an account of his travels through the antebellum Cotton States, he mentioned stopping for the night with a farm family in the Lake Charles area of Louisiana:

> On entering the house, we were met by two young boys, gentle and winning in manner, coming up of their own accord to offer us their hands. They were immediately set to work by their father at grinding corn, in the steel-mill, for supper. The task seemed their usual one, yet very much too severe for their strength, as they were slightly built, and not over ten years old. Taking hold at opposite sides of the winch, they ground away, outside the door, for more than an hour, constantly stopping to take breath, and spurred on by the voice of their papa, if the delay were long . . .
>
> When we asked to wash before supper, a shallow cake-pan was brought and set upon the window seat, and a mere rag offered us for towel. Upon the supper table, we found two wash-bowls, one filled with milk, and the other with molasses. We asked for water, which was given us in one battered tin cup. The dishes besides bacon and bread were fried eggs and sweet potatoes. The bowl of molasses stood in the center of the table, and we were pressed to partake of it, as the family did, by dipping in bits of bread.

No one who has spent time grinding cornmeal can read this passage without a pang. No grain is ever as good as it will be the moment it leaves the mill, but cornmeal clings closest to the field. Cornbread is not bread. Bread is a creation of the baker's art; no matter how good the taste of the wheat in it, it never takes you to the wheat field. Good cornbread, however, holds to its roots. It resists civilizing. And this means that—especially to anyone who grew up with wheat bread—it tastes of poverty. However cooked it is, the work that made it is still there, large and raw.

This explains a paradox often encountered in Southern cookbooks: on the one hand, tendentious insistence about how cornbread ought to be made and, on the other, the actual recipes—where this same advice is more often flaunted than obeyed. These days you aren't too likely to find anyone suggesting that you grind the meal yourself, eschew all leavening, and bake it overnight in the fireplace ashes. But there are echoes of this advice: *real* cornbread, we are told, must be made of coarse-ground, unbolted cornmeal and untainted by any hint of sugar, white flour, sweet milk, or fancy double-acting leavenings.

In other words, it ought to taste of self-sufficiency, and of the world that self-sufficiency once made. Make it like that, however, and it seems rude and coarse, not something to offer company. Which is why those civilizing things get brought in anyway. North or South makes no difference; cornbread isn't what it was. The closeness to the field is slip-sliding away.

Compare, for example, these two passages, one by a Maine store-keeper and the other by an Alabama herbalist:

I have sold a good many products I have been ashamed of—fine-ground corn meal, sulphur-dioxide molasses, packaged coffee—all things my grandmother would have turned her nose at clear back to here. In the back shed we had a meal chest—rye meal was in one end, and over the partition corn meal. Corn was harvested, traced, and hung on the big beams in the attic of the old farmhouse. One day grandmother would come down and opine the corn was dry enough to grind. Home from the old Holmes & Blanchard stone mill, the meal was coarse. We always had rye ground at the same time. And after the day at the mill, we had corn bread of such quality that my mouth drips as I recall it.
—R. E. GOULD, *Yankee Storekeeper* (1946)

When I was a boy we mostly ate cornmeal, not wheat flour. We grew the corn, used to have a little corn patch . . . We used to grow the white corn. We used the same corn for cornmeal that we fed to the chickens and the stock. About twice a month, we'd shell some corn and take it to the grist mill in Mackey or in Slackland. . . . The corn was ground between two big stones. The top stone would turn very slow, so the corn wouldn't get hot . . . You would tell the grist mill if you wanted it ground coarse or fine. Mother preferred it coarse . . . You sifted it at home to get the hulls out before you used it . . . Cornbread was around for every meal.   —A. L. TOMMIE BASS, *Plain Southern Eating* (1988)

It is hard to miss the note of sadness in these passages. Cornbread Nation . . . once it was a place; today it is only a dream—that tiny homestead in the hinterlands where you can raise what you need to eat and clothe yourself and so live free. Those huge Midwestern farms, with mile after mile of corn tassels fluttering in the summer breeze, emblematic though they may be of American prosperity, have nothing to do with it. So far as the farmers of such places are concerned, those lush fields might just as well be growing wheat.

What it comes down to is not so much wealth versus poverty as the distance between the cornfield and the cornbread. At farms like these it is very far indeed, which means that there is no longer any fierceness felt about good cornmeal—how it is ground and how often, and how it is to be made into bread. And if not here, who else will hold the course?

Tommie Bass tells how he came across a neighbor, a farmer, actually buying cornmeal at the store. Bass's distress is palpable:

> I said to him, "Mr. Burke," I said, "my goodness, man, what are you spending?" He said, "Tommie, we haven't time to go to the mill."

Recalling this conversation, he added—and the line might well serve as the epitaph to Cornbread Nation—"They don't even have their own cow, and they quit raising hogs!"

STEUBEN, 1994

THREE CORNBREADS

It was Matt who first taught me how to make cornbread—a real Southern cornbread—the batter of cornmeal, buttermilk, bacon fat, and egg poured into a smoking cast-iron skillet and baked in a hot oven. It cooked almost as fast as biscuits and it came out crisp and savory, better than anything I would ever have given cornmeal credit for. For years, when anyone came to interview me, this was what I would prepare. It was something that could be done—mixed, baked, eaten—while we were talking. Mostly I did it because I couldn't get over how good it was . . . or how much I liked making it.

I was especially drawn to its simplicity. Matt dictated the proportions and baking temperature to me, and I scribbled them on a yellow note slip that I taped to the refrigerator. (It moved with me, getting more stained and tattered, until Matt came to stay.) All I had to do was glance at it to know where I was. I also relished the drama: the oven-heated skillet; the sizzle as the fat went into the batter; the not knowing for sure, when I turned the finished cornbread out (especially from a cast-iron skillet), whether the crust would stay behind in the pan. (It did this only occasionally, but each occurrence was a memorable one.)

Making it was a liberating experience. It cast aside, once and for all, my prejudice that cornmeal was somehow second-class stuff, always needing something—cheese, garlic, hot peppers, even fresh corn kernels!—to make it good. Instead, this bread's simplicity taught me to care about the taste and provenance of its few ingredients—the cornmeal particularly, but also the buttermilk, the kind of fat, even the leavening. I discovered how tasteless most cornmeals are and, conversely, how truly wonderful a precious few. I realized how compromised commercial buttermilk can be. Absorbing such discriminations, the baker gradually learns to transform the humdrum into the exceptional.

There is also the matter of personal fit. We regularly make three different cornbreads. Each has its traditional roots, but we have modified these to conform to our own tastes and circumstances. The first of these, of course, is our version of the Southern skillet cornbread mentioned above. The second—baked in a pan—is the Yankee cornbread we both grew up with. A sweetened baking-powder bread, it is usually made of a blend of fine-ground yellow meal and flour, mixed with sugar, sweet milk, butter, and eggs. It is a moist cakelike cornbread, one to be eaten with butter and jam—although Matt fondly remembers her mother serving it for supper under creamed chipped beef.

The third bread—variously known as spider (an old term for a skillet, see page 23) or triple-layer or custard-filled cornbread—is as much at home in the North as the South and is everywhere treated as something special. This cornbread combines—in all sorts of permutations and with varying degrees of sweetness and richness—elements of both the other breads, but is distinguished by a surfeit of either sweet milk or buttermilk (or the two together) that forms a creamy custardlike layer in the center: cornbread on its way to spoonbread.

Whatever the origins of these cornbreads, however, we've diverged from both North and South in our strategies for making them.

THE CORNMEAL. For instance, although I was brought up believing that eggs should come in brown shells and cornmeal in bright corn yellow, after a decade of baking cornbread and trying different cornmeals, I have never yet tasted either a yellow or a blue cornmeal that comes close to the flavor of stone-ground, unbolted *white* cornmeal. Our favorites are the white flint ("jonnycake") meal ground by Tim McTague at Gray's Grist Mill (P.O. Box 422, Adamsville, RI 02801 • 508–636–6075) and by Richard Morgan at Morgan's Mills here in Maine (RR #2, Box 4602, Union, ME 04862 • 800–373–2756) and the white dent meal ground for John Taylor of Hoppin' John's (30 Pinckney St., Charleston, SC 29401 • 803–577–6404) at a small farm in North Georgia.

White flint produces a grittier meal that gives cornbread a coarser texture and a slightly more aggressive "field corn" taste, while white dent meal makes a softer-textured bread with the tender flavor notes of sweet corn. Both have to be tasted to be appreciated. Those seeking further cornmeal options should consult Joni Miller's superlative survey in *True Grits: The Southern Mail-Order Catalog.* All these meals contain the perishable germ and should be double-bagged and kept in the refrigerator (short-term) or the freezer (long-term).

THE BUTTERMILK. When we first moved to Maine, we found a local dairy that was producing an all-natural, unusually thick cultured buttermilk, with a clean, tangy taste. Every other buttermilk on the supermarket shelves was a cultured "product" containing such unwanted ingredients as modified food starch, carrageenan, and locust-bean gum. When this dairy was bought out in 1989, the buttermilk vanished and we were driven to experiment with things like yogurt or sour cream mixed with milk, none proving very satisfactory. We even considered mail-ordering an actual buttermilk culture, but discovered that we would have to purchase a fresh culture for each new batch.

Then, a few years ago, we came across a small home business that specializes in exotic cultures, most of them for fermenting soybean products like miso, shoyu, and tamari. However, they also offer two simple-to-make self-renewing dairy cultures—*viili* from Finland and *fil mjölk* from Sweden. Neither requires any special incubators, sterile jars, or complicated culturing—you just mix the starter in any room-temperature dairy product from skim milk to whipping cream, let it sit until thickened, and then refrigerate it. You make the next batch from the one before, with no diminution of taste or effectiveness.

As it turned out, the *viili* culture had a yogurt edge to it that I grew tired of, but the *fil mjölk* produced a thick soured milk with a smooth, delicate tanginess that not only worked wonderfully in cornbread but encouraged this non-yogurt-lover to lick the spoon. If you live in a place with good buttermilk, by all means use that. If not, write or call Gem Cultures (30301 Sherwood Road, Fort Bragg, CA 95437 • 707–964–2922) and ask for their free catalogue.

THE FAT. Skillet cornbread was traditionally made with lard. This slightly sweet, slightly porky-tasting fat is cornmeal's perfect flavor mate. Skillet cornbread was devised to take advantage of this fact, or, more specifically, of the magic touch lard gives to fried food—the crust of that cornbread being essentially *fried* to a crackling crispness.

However, even those who are willing to face down the howling pack of nutritional dogmatists who are currently bent on demonizing lard are going to find it almost as hard to get their hands on the real stuff. True, the hydrogenated bricks on the grocery shelf are composed out of what was once lard, but the act of providing it with eternal shelf life transforms it into something as dead-tasting as a spoonful of Crisco. (European peasants used to eat their dark bread spread with a thin coating of lard, seasoned with a pinch of salt. Try this with fresh lard and you'll at least see the point.)

One answer is to substitute bacon fat, which works very nicely;

another—if you have a source of fresh pork fat—is to render the lard yourself.* We, instead, order what is a generally excellent lard—pure white and creamy soft—in quart tubs from a Pennsylvania firm that takes its pork products seriously: John F. Martin & Sons, P.O. Box 137, Stevens, PA 17578–0137 • 800–597–2804. Their prices are quite reasonable—at the time of writing, two such tubs, which will last a home baker quite a while, cost about $3, plus shipping.

Those who prefer not to eat animal fat should use peanut oil instead—or, to intensify the corn taste, add unrefined, cold-pressed corn oil to the batter and bake the cornbread in a nonstick skillet, lightly coated with your usual cooking oil.

THE LEAVENING. Skillet cornbread, because it is made with buttermilk, is traditionally leavened with baking soda—sometimes with an admixture of baking powder—and pan cornbread most often with baking powder. However, neither of us much likes the somewhat soapy taste of baking soda or the slight bitterness of double-acting baking powder in unsweetened (or not very sweet) quick or griddle breads—biscuits and scones, pancakes, cornbreads, and the like. (Interestingly, it is often just these breads that are leavened with the heaviest hand. One recipe we came across—for "Perfect Old-Fashioned Corn Bread"—specified 2 tablespoons of baking powder to leaven a loaf the size of our pan cornbread; a more restrained but still whopping 1 tablespoon is common.)

So, over the years—by experimenting with formulas in older cookbooks and those of contemporary bakers who share this sensitivity— we've developed an approach to leavening these breads (sweetened breads are another matter) which gives us the freedom to use as little as possible to do the job well and allows the good taste of the other ingredients to come through clearly. This method turns out to be identical to that of many Celtic bakers: for every 4 ounces of flour or meal, we use 1 teaspoon of cream of tartar and ½ teaspoon of baking soda if the liquid ingredient is "sweet" and ½ teaspoon of each if it is sour.

---

* The simplest way we know to do this is to cut pure, fresh pork fat—preferably the leaf fat taken from around the kidneys—into small cubes, tie these in a Reynolds-brand oven bag, and lower this into a large pot of water brought to low simmer. Leave the bag for 2 hours, or until the fat has been completely rendered. Then use a pair of tongs to remove the bag and set it to cool in a bowl. When the contents are cool enough to handle but still warm enough to remain liquid, untie the bag and carefully pour them through a kitchen sieve to remove all debris, catching the lard in a spotlessly clean jar. Covered, this will keep for months in the refrigerator and almost indefinitely in the freezer.

ADDENDA. These breads are small—for two eaters who like their cornbread fresh out of the oven. Standard recipes generally yield loaves twice this size. Also, we weigh rather than measure our dry ingredients—but if you lightly spoon them into dry-measure cups and level the surface with a knife, you will come as close as you need to.

SKILLET CORNBREAD
(MAKES ONE 8-INCH CORNBREAD)

Because the method for baking this cornbread in a cast-iron skillet differs somewhat from the one utilizing a nonstick skillet, first-time bakers using a cast-iron skillet should first read through the seasoning and baking notes on pages 365–66. Note that the trick is to get the cast-iron skillet very hot before adding the batter. To accomplish this, we put it—with its fat or oil—into the oven when we first turn it on, so that they preheat together.

4 ounces (about 1 cup) stone-ground cornmeal
½ teaspoon cream of tartar
½ teaspoon baking soda
¼ to ½ teaspoon sea salt
1 large egg
¾ cup buttermilk
1 tablespoon lard, rendered bacon fat, or peanut oil

Preheat the oven to 425°F. Measure the dry ingredients into a bowl and give them a couple of turns with a whisk to mix them thoroughly and break up any lumps. Break the egg into a separate bowl and whisk gently. Add the buttermilk, whisking to blend.

Five minutes before you are ready to bake the cornbread, put the fat (or peanut oil) into an 8-inch ovenproof skillet (heavy-gauge aluminum with a nonstick surface or well-seasoned cast iron) and place it in the hot oven.

At about the 4-minute mark, add the egg and buttermilk mixture to the dry ingredients, whisking just to blend. A minute later—at the 5-minute mark—take the (HOT!) skillet from the oven and carefully swirl the almost-smoking fat around the bottom and up the sides, making sure to coat any rivets attaching the handle to the pan. If using a cast-iron skillet, immediately pour in the batter, using a circular motion so that the batter is spread evenly across the bottom of the pan. If using a nonstick skillet, pour the excess fat into the batter—it will sizzle—

and give it all a quick whisk. Then scrape the batter into the skillet with a rubber spatula.

Return the skillet to the oven and bake the cornbread for about 20 minutes, or until well set and golden brown. Remove from the oven and quickly invert onto a cutting board with a confident flip. Cut into wedges and serve.

COOK'S NOTES. The amount of salt will depend on the saltiness of the fat you use—and what the cornbread will be eaten with.

VARIATIONS. We make several other very tasty and quick three-grain skillet breads by replacing 2 ounces of the cornmeal with 1 ounce each (about ¼ cup each) of whole-wheat flour and another whole-grain flour—buckwheat, oat, barley, rye, brown rice. Each is good in its own way. We use peanut oil in these.

EATING NOTES. Our usual—and favorite—way to eat this bread is with cheese, as a light meal. We split it and strew the inside with grated or shaved cheese, close it back up, and wait a minute before eating for the cheese to melt. A good, sharp Vermont cheddar is wonderful, as is a pairing of fresh mozzarella and olivada. (The three-grain bread with buckwheat is delicious with Italian fontina.) Another terrific flavor match, this time combining the savory with a touch of sweet, is softened cream cheese spread with a thin layer of fiery jalapeño (or tart apple cider) jelly.

In the South, too, this cornbread is often put to savory use, eaten with (or dunked into) "fish stews, pilaus, gumbos, and greens," as John Taylor writes in *Hoppin' John's Lowcountry Cooking*, "with lots of the freshest butter you can get your hands on." He also notes, "My family reaches for the sorghum syrup when cornbread is served."

BAKING PAN CORNBREAD
(MAKES 1 SMALL LOAF)

2 ounces (about ½ cup) stone-ground cornmeal
2 ounces (about ½ cup) all-purpose unbleached flour
1 teaspoon cream of tartar
½ teaspoon baking soda
¼ teaspoon sea salt
2 tablespoons unsalted butter, softened
2 tablespoons granulated sugar
1 large egg, separated
½ cup milk

Preheat the oven to 425°F. Butter a medium (8½ × 4½ inch) loaf pan. Measure the dry ingredients into a bowl and give them a couple of turns with a whisk to mix them thoroughly and break up any lumps.

In another bowl, cream the softened butter with the sugar. Stir in the egg yolk. Separately, beat the egg white into soft peaks and hold at the ready.

Add the milk to the butter/sugar/yolk mixture, give it a stir or two, but don't try to blend it all smooth. Add the dry ingredients all at once and stir just to moisten. (This minimalist method helps ensure that the batter won't be overmixed.)

Fold in the beaten egg white and scrape the batter into the loaf pan with a rubber spatula. Place in the oven and bake for about 20 minutes, or until done (the sides will have pulled slightly away from the edges of the pan). Cut into pieces and serve immediately.

VARIATIONS. We like to substitute whole-wheat for the white flour and peanut oil for the butter. Since this variation makes perfect eating with butter and honey, we omit the sugar, simply stirring the egg yolk into the oil and proceeding from there.

EATING NOTES. This is the cornbread we bake to have with something sweet. We split and butter the pieces and spread them with jam or jelly (both raspberry and crabapple are great).

CUSTARD CORNBREAD
(MAKES ONE 8-INCH CORNBREAD)

3 ounces (about ¾ cup) stone-ground cornmeal
1 ounce (about ¼ cup) whole-wheat flour
½ teaspoon cream of tartar
½ teaspoon baking soda
¼ teaspoon sea salt
1 large egg
½ cup buttermilk
1 cup (in two additions) sweet milk
1 tablespoon unsalted butter

Preheat the oven to 375°F. Measure the dry ingredients into a bowl and give them a couple of turns with a whisk to mix them thoroughly and break up any lumps. In a separate bowl, whisk the egg gently. Add the buttermilk and ½ cup of the sweet milk, whisking to blend.

Five minutes before you are ready to bake the cornbread, put the butter into an 8-inch ovenproof skillet (a heavy-gauge aluminum with a nonstick surface works best) and place in the hot oven.

At about the 4-minute mark, add the egg and milk mixture to the dry ingredients, whisking just to blend. A minute later, take the (HOT!) skillet from the oven and carefully swirl the melted butter around the bottom and up the sides, making sure to coat any rivets attaching the handle to the pan. Pour the remaining butter into the waiting batter and give it all a quick whisk. Then scrape the batter into the hot skillet with a rubber spatula.

Dribble the remaining ½ cup of sweet milk over the surface of the batter (don't stir it in). Return the skillet to the oven and bake the cornbread for about 40 minutes, or until well set and nicely browned. Remove from the oven and invert onto a cutting board. Slice into wedges—once cut, a delicate line of custard will be visible—and serve at once with the golden underside still facing up. Prick this all over with a fork so that your butter (and whatever else—we love maple syrup) will soak right in.

VARIATIONS. For a more "refined" version, replace the whole-wheat flour with unbleached all-purpose white flour.

STEUBEN, 1994

THE CORNBREAD SKILLET

For years and years we made our cornbread in the same cast-iron skillet with which I had begun my cooking career back in 1963. However, over that time—since I refused to wash it—it had gradually gotten so encrusted with grease, inside and out, that its original outlines were actually obscured. Without our really noticing it, the pan had gone from cooking implement to artifact, and first gradually and then entirely, we were making our cornbread instead in an 8-inch nonstick Wearever skillet, which infallibly produces a very decent cornbread.

Writing "Cornbread Nation," we remembered how cornbread made in a cast-iron skillet, even if a somewhat tricky business, emerged with a nonpareil deeply crunchy crust. We realized we missed both that crust and, to be honest, the excitement. So we set out to buy a new 8-inch cast-iron skillet, season it, and get back to making cornbread in it.

We were happy to discover that cast-iron skillets are still as much a part of the local cooking culture as bean pots, easily available in hard-

ware stores. These were sold at what seemed like giveaway prices, compared to the high-tech cookware now offered at upscale kitchen shops;
the 8-inch pan we bought cost about $5.

Unlike the bean pots, these skillets are American made, well crafted,
and come in two styles. Those made by Lodge have a slightly textured
surface, while those made by Wagner, the other major cast-iron cookware producer, are machined absolutely smooth. Although my original
skillet had a smooth cooking surface, this time we opted for the other
kind. This seemed no more prone to stick and gives the cornbread crust
a pleasant nubbly texture.

Once you have a skillet, you need to season it. We did this with lard,
but either Crisco or plain vegetable oil can be used. As to the latter,
we recommend peanut oil (corn or safflower oil can leave a sticky res-
idue). Although the stated purpose of seasoning the pan is to build up
a nonstick layer on the inner surface, I'm not sure that this actually
happens. However, seasoning does condition the pan, and it removes
all the impurities—ash and metallic dust—left over from its casting.

To follow our method, you should first obtain a cheap, natural-bristle,
1-inch-wide paintbrush. Then scrub the skillet well with a non-sudsing
scouring pad and plenty of hot water. Dry it carefully and add half a
tablespoon of your chosen fat or oil. Brush this about the inside surface
of the skillet and put it into a preheated 250°F oven. After half an hour,
remove the pan and brush the fat or oil up around the skillet sides.
Return it to the oven.

Once the skillet has been in the oven for an hour, remove it and wipe
it clean of fat or oil with paper toweling. Then add another half tablespoon of fat or oil, wipe this about the interior surface with the brush,
and return the skillet to the hot oven. Again, remove it after half an
hour to rebrush the sides and after an hour to wipe it clean. Repeat
this whole sequence one more time, for a total of three hours. When
you wipe the pan clean for the last time, brush the pan with fat or oil
before putting it away—just enough to give it a light sheen. (There will
probably be enough fat or oil left on the bristles of the brush to do this.)
You can then either discard the brush or save it for further seasoning,
if this proves necessary.

Don't be discouraged if the batter sticks a bit the first few times. This
happened to us, too, when we started using our new cast-iron pan. At
first we thought it hadn't been seasoned enough, but by examining the
way it was sticking—only in the center of the pan—we determined that

the batter was absorbing the fat at the center of the pan and adhering to its surface before the heat of the pan crusted it over.

To correct this, we made absolutely sure we had preheated the skillet until it was *very* hot. So now we let the pan preheat with the oven *and* leave it in for five minutes at 425°F. If the pan is hot enough, the batter will sizzle loudly when you pour it into the pan (as will a few test drops of water). Then we add the batter, swirling it around the entire bottom of the pan instead of pouring it all into the center. By doing that—and by reserving the pan for this one purpose only—we've had complete success in turning out our cornbread ever since.

STEUBEN, 1995

THE EDUCATION OF A MILLER
Tim McTague

Our friend and subscriber Tim McTague is the miller at Gray's Grist Mill in Adamsville, Rhode Island, where he carries on a long tradition of grinding hard white flint corn into jonnycake meal. We could think of no better conclusion to a meditation on Cornbread Nation than to have him recall his apprenticeship there.

I have often tried to think back on my initial reactions to Gray's Mill. The intervening years have obscured the freshness of my first days working as a miller, but two powerful impressions endure in memory: that of John Allen Hart, the person who was to become my mentor as I struggled to learn the trade, and the physical entity of Gray's Mill itself.

I found the mill a very bony place. Not bony like a fish on a plate, but big-boned. Walking into the milling room was like walking unawares into the chest of a dinosaur. Bones overhead, bones around, and massive bones below. I could feel it breathing. My first chore was cleaning, and I approached it, like all my chores there in those initial days, with a touch of reticence, feeling my presence would bring change to something remarkable for lingering unchanged. But as I cleaned and learned the names of the bones and their fit, I also discovered that changes had already taken place. The mill might be a water-breathing beast, but it had had a pacemaker installed in the late forties.

I shouldn't overly personify the place, but I have come to feel that it has a life of its own and that the various people who have been millers pass through as curators as much as owners. Sometime between 1916, when he came to work for James L. Gray, and 1981, when I stuck my skinny neck through the door, John Hart made a conscious decision to keep the mill going—even if he had to use gasoline-run engines, even if he wasn't making any money doing it. I asked him once why he did it and he answered, "It doesn't make much sense to keep it going, but I've been at it so long it seems like hard work to stop."

Consequently, as water from the pond across the street became less reliable, he found himself installing tractors, Buick sedans, and finally a 1946 Dodge truck as power sources. John's father, Roland Hart, who also worked at the mill, would only grind using the old waterwheel and felt that John's use of all these engines was just another example of the younger generation going to hell in a handbasket.

At first John and I worked together in the early mornings. I would get to the mill at seven or a bit before. John would already be there, prepared to pass along anything he thought me worthy of knowing. Of course, I tried to be as unobtrusive as possible while at the same time absorbing everything I could from him. I was twenty-four at the time, and John was seventy-nine.

One of the most memorable visual treats of my life was when I first went with John behind the mill and watched him climb aboard the chassis of that 1946 Dodge truck. He started it up, put the clutch in, shifted it into second gear to get the stone turning, and then hit third gear—grinding speed. I remember thinking how important and what plain fun it was to see that. It's one of the treasures of my life, that memory . . . Smith & Hawken would have to hire Steven Spielberg to come up with something better.

Another visual treat was the tractor-powered sheller that we used for shelling flint corn. John had traded it for a mowing job and kept it in the front room of the mill, which had been grafted onto the original building at some point and otherwise served as a general storage area for items John held for the Old Stone Church rummage sales. He would back his tractor into the room through the big double doors, hook up the flat belt to the sheller, and away we'd go. It seemed just as fantastic and just as real as everything else I saw John do. We were alone in a room with a tractor powering this hundred-year-old machine that was stripping the kernels off corncobs.

The sheller, for all its primitive look, was mathematically precise and very sophisticated. Flywheels spun almost out of control right next to chainwheels that barely moved, while thousands of little kernels showered down a spout into a bag and the cobs rolled out the end of the machine to fall through a hole in the floor into the basement below. It was pure magic.

My first day on the job, I also learned to tie a miller's knot. We were packing twenty-five-pound bags of jonnycake meal for a local restaurant, the Common's Lunch in Little Compton. The knot is nothing more than a clove hitch with an extra turn, but it does a great job of closing bags of flour. We were turning a locally grown—and locally prized—obscure variety of corn into the freshest possible cornmeal, packing it up into paper bags, and tying them shut with plain cotton string. The fact that the cornmeal was ground by a two-hundred-year-old millstone linked up to a 1946 Dodge truck motor was icing on the cake to me. And who wouldn't love the lowly and yet classic jonnycake? So I was hooked.

In writing about it all, I realize how much I now miss the magic I experienced then, being introduced to all those new, wonderful things by John Hart. What was most impressive to my own hopelessly naïve mind was the integrity of it all. Even now, after almost ten years of typing countless miller's knots on literally tens of thousands of paper bags in an unheated little mill, I still sweep up the dust of the day's milling feeling as though I've done something good and done it well.

Sourdough Buckwheats

The cheery noise of bubbling pancake batter was as plainly heard as the singing teakettle every morning of the year in our house. I often lifted the cover of the batter crock to look at the bubbles, which reminded me of the eyes of animals.
—U. P. HEDRICK, *The Land of the Crooked Tree*

In *The Country Kitchen*, a memoir of life at the turn of the last century on a Michigan farm—and especially that farm's kitchen—Della Lutes recalls her father's increasing impatience one autumn, the buckwheat harvest in, for the start of the cold-weather regimen of buckwheat cakes every morning. Her mother, however, continued to ignore his mutterings, steadfastly refusing to admit that it had gotten cold enough to justify adding these to a breakfast menu that already consisted of fried eggs, ham, potatoes, and quick breads.

The problem with—or, as her father saw it, the glory of—buckwheat cakes is that once the batter is made, it is kept going day after day, with a little starter being reserved from each morning's batch to fire a fresh one that evening. Because the batter would become yeasty and unpleasant if a day was missed, her mother had thus to commit herself from then until spring to stand over a hot griddle every morning and turn out a continuous stream of buckwheat cakes while the rest of the family (plus the hired hand) ate their fill.

So she stalled. The frost came to the pumpkin and still no batter was set to bubbling. Then, one night when she was away tending to a sick neighbor, her father decided to take the matter into his own hands. He started the batter himself and tucked it away at the back of the kitchen stove.

Unfortunately, not being a cooking man, he misjudged the power of the yeast. During the night, the batter rose in a fury of gray froth and

flung itself over the sides of the bowl, leaving a huge mess on the stove
. . . and a mere smidgen of hungover batter in the pitcher. Della's mother
came down in the morning to find her husband with a mop in his hands
and a defiant and baffled expression on his face. Seeing her standing
there grasping for words, he exploded: "How many yeast cakes do you
put in the dang things?"

That question brings us directly to the heart of the matter of all buck-
wheat-cake making, and since Della's mother doesn't give the answer
—she simply orders her husband from the kitchen and, once he stalks
out, breaks down into helpless laughter—I will: *"Not one, Elijah, not
a single one . . ."* The answer wouldn't need giving if almost every
cookbook writer in the past fifty years didn't get it wrong—and in con-
sequence almost obliterate all that is worth tasting in a genuine buckwheat cake, by this same overenthusiastic adding of yeast cakes, or
their more modern equivalent, packages of dry yeast.

Make no mistake about it, buckwheat pancakes—or just plain "buckwheats" (the usage goes back at least to the 1830s, the flour even then
being used for hardly anything else)—positively bloom when the batter
is fermented overnight with a sourdough starter, mellowing and ripening
as it bubbles through the midnight hours. The flavor and aroma of *those*
cakes still waft from reminiscences of farm and pioneer life in the last
century. "It is hard for the American to rise from his winter breakfast
without his *buckwheat cakes*," wrote an English visitor in 1870. And
Harper's magazine acclaimed them in 1893 for their association with
"heat, sweets, aroma, and good cheer."

Alas, the pancake eater of today is likely to be baffled by this praise
when he or she is inspired by such prose to try the versions given in
most cookbooks. These are almost always travesties of the original—at
worst downright unpleasant-tasting and at best so overladen with ingredients that they are robbed of any real character. The pleasure of the
buckwheat is thus almost entirely restricted to the visual appeal of its
tiny black dots.

For instance, Marion Cunningham, in *The Breakfast Book*, offers a
recipe calling for ten ingredients (besides water), a list that is not only
twice as long as that in traditional recipes but includes such flavor
enhancers as sour cream and lemon juice—which, whatever their purpose, can't help suggesting that something must be wrong with the cake
if so many flavors are required for the frosting. Certainly no griddle-
proud cook would ever consider adding them to her regular flapjack
batter.

When I first became interested in buckwheat cakes, I took this ingredient overkill to represent some nervousness about the flavor of the
buckwheat itself—or at least its distinctly grassy undertone, a taste that
dominates the batter (although it is more subdued in the actual pancake). Puzzling over this matter, I decided to try some of the earliest
spartan farmhouse versions—those, as described above, that called for
little more than buckwheat and water—to see how palatable the stuff
actually was, and whether it was worth making pancakes out of it at all.

As I tried to figure out how those recipes actually worked, it became
clear what had happened. It was "Sourdough Jack" Mabee who, in his
little recipe pamphlet on sourdough cooking, provided the essential
clue:

> This marvelous old standby has been terribly mistreated in recent years. To make
> it more tasty and digestible it must be leavened with sourdough as it was back
> home on Grandma's vast old kitchen range.

Traditional buckwheats were made from a continuously freshened sourdough. Modern versions, however, are made not only with stronger-
tasting commercial yeasts but with enormous amounts of it. The
Cunningham recipe mentioned above, for instance, calls for an *entire
package* of dry yeast (enough to leaven three or so whole loaves of bread)
to activate a mere cup and a half of flour.

Its purpose, of course, is not only to make the recipe work without a
sourdough starter but to *guarantee* that it will work—and as quickly as
possible. For while she allows for giving the batter some extra time to
develop beyond the one or two hours it needs to rise, her recipe clearly
intends that the pancakes be made the morning the batter is put
together.

Unfortunately, that batter—if used without all the extra ingredients
—would produce pancakes tasting less of buckwheat than of a hard day
at the brewery. The reason for the addition of all those other flavors is
to muffle the flat, sour pungency of this overload of yeast.

Such recipes represent not a dislike of the taste of plain buckwheat
cakes but of the time and work entailed in making them properly. The
result, instead of keeping an old and honored recipe alive, is more like
summoning it from the grave—the shape is somewhat the same, but the
odor definitely different . . . and though the magic powder *seems* to have
given the batter back a simulacrum of life, it has not at all managed to
resurrect its soul.

The heart of real buckwheats, after all, is fragile, gentle, slow-beating, but indisputably alive . . . The cook fed the batter, cared for it, kept it safe and warm—and *it*, in return, mellowed into goodness what was, after all, a hardy but coarse-tasting grass otherwise grown for animal feed. It was that sense of necessary reciprocity, as much as anything else, that gave buckwheats the grasp they had on a century's worth of winter breakfasts.

As it turns out, the taste of a straight buckwheat pancake *is* a little vegetative. Those who persist may find that the flavor grows on them, if only because it proves a remarkable foil for the similar grassy tones in maple syrup. The two combine in a way that brings out the best of both—dipped in melted butter, a forkful of syrup-drenched buckwheat cake fills the mouth with a different but rich and woodsy sweetness it could well learn to love, especially in the company of some sage-seasoned country sausage.

Those not willing to go that distance, however, should try mixing the buckwheat flour in half-and-half proportion with unbleached white flour. Made into a batter sparked to life with some sourdough starter, left to ferment and mellow overnight, then sweetened in the morning with a little molasses, and baked on a griddle, the resulting soft, flannel-textured flapjack, with its delicate flavor and nutty, tangy aftertaste, is the pancake ethereal.

Truly, there is no other like it . . . and there's no improving on it either. The temptation to add milk and eggs ("to make it richer and better") impoverishes it instead. Even without those things, what has been done to the buckwheat pancake in the name of improvement is a pretty poignant illustration of the wisdom of leaving well enough alone.

Furthermore, make them as we direct below and you have the best of both worlds: old-fashioned flavor and new-fangled flexibility. In the morning, all you need do when you slide out of bed is to stir in the molasses and a pinch each of salt and baking soda (which helps balance out the sour, while adding its mite to the leavening)—and absolutely resist the temptation to add anything else . . . until the buckwheats come to table. Then, as Della Lutes explains, it's every man for himself.

In winter, breakfast took on new meaning, for then the fried mush, johnnycake, or ordinary plain bread gave way to buckwheat cakes. There were differences in taste regarding the lacing of these cakes. Some insisted that the only proper sauce was butter; others preferred sugar and thick cream; still others liked to pour over their cakes the hot brown fat from fried ham or pork. But the general preference was for butter and syrup. If maple syrup could be had, so much the better.

Sourdough Buckwheats

The Starter

[THE MORNING BEFORE]

(for 24 pancakes)		(for 36 pancakes)
6 tablespoons	warm (about 110°F) water	½ cup
3 tablespoons	unbleached white flour	¼ cup
3 tablespoons	buckwheat flour	¼ cup
¼ teaspoon	active dry yeast	¼ teaspoon

The morning before you plan to make the buckwheats, mix the starter ingredients in a small bowl. Cover loosely with a dish towel or plastic wrap. Place in a warm, draft-free location. Signs of activity should occur within a few hours. Check and stir occasionally.

The Batter

[THE EVENING BEFORE]

(for 24 pancakes)		(for 36 pancakes)
¾ cup	unbleached white flour	1 cup
¾ cup	buckwheat flour	1 cup
1½ cups	warm (about 110°F) water	2 cups
	Starter (as made above)	

Before going to bed, mix the flours together into a large mixing bowl. Whisk in the water gradually to make a smooth batter. Stir in the starter. Cover and place in a warm, draft-free location and leave to ferment overnight.

[THE FOLLOWING MORNING]

1½ tablespoon	unsulphured molasses	2 tablespoons
¼ teaspoon	salt	½ teaspoon
½ teaspoon	baking soda	½ teaspoon
	Fermented batter (as made above)	

The batter should be bubbling and fragrant. (If not, get out the oatmeal.) Mix in the molasses and salt. Dissolve the baking soda in a little water and stir it into the batter. Let the batter sit a few minutes while the griddle heats. Grease the griddle well (bacon fat is excellent), greasing again with every subsequent batch. Use a 2-tablespoon coffee measure to portion out the batter, one scoop per cake. Turn the pancakes as soon as the batter is set. Serve on warm plates with butter and maple syrup.

CASTINE, 1988

American Cheese

"What smelly feet you've got, Daddy," says Cleo. "Like a pair of old cheddars, aren't they, Mrs. Fledge?"
                                                    —PATRICK McGRATH, *The Grotesque*

In the Spring 1988 issue of *The Journal of Gastronomy*, Edward Behr describes a photograph of thirty or so cheeses that appears in Jean-Claude le Jaouen's *La Fabrication du fromage de chèvre fermier*:

> They are devoid of wrappings, except for chestnut leaves around a couple of *banons*, and they are rudely spotted and blotched with color, many of them hairy with blue mold.

This is not the sort of sighting you or I are likely to experience in any cheese store in this country, no matter how knowledgeable the monger. We customers are notoriously uncomfortable before moldy or—especially—*oozy* cheese. No difference if we "have traveled considerably and are well educated," Behr notes, for we "still consistently choose firm unripe cheeses over redolent ripe ones," even when given actual samples to taste and compare.

I thought about the implications of this passage recently when, still residing in Castine, I fell into conversation with one of the owners of the local store while we waited our turn at the post office. July not only brings summer people here to Castine but, tagging along after them, a scattering of gourmet groceries to the Tarratine Market. One of these—I told her I had noticed—was Craigston Camembert, a much acclaimed artisanal cheese made in Massachusetts.

Yes, she said, she had thought they might try carrying it. And so far they were impressed. The cheese arrived in a Styrofoam shipping carton that was so substantial she couldn't bear to throw it away. Furthermore, each order came with a little gift for the store—an apron with Craigston's attractive logo or an extra sample of the cheese for the help.

But what had most appealed to her—to everyone, it seemed, customers and store people alike—was the packaging. Each small, seven-ounce cheese comes wrapped in aluminum foil, fitted into a plastic container, and tied up with a bright red ribbon—over which a large, two-color label has been glued.

Tucked between the ribbon and the bottom of the container is a smartly designed brochure. It contains information about Craigston, recipes for using it ("crock cheese," "cannibal sandwich"), press reviews (". . . Craigston's mild, marvelous Camembert."—*New York* magazine) —and a personal note from Susan Hollander, owner of the Craigston Cheese Company, suggesting, among other things, that we give her a call ("We love talking about our cheese!"). Finally, attached to the top of the package is a smaller, equally smartly designed card that explains how the cheese is made, what it tastes like, and how and with what it should be served.

I examined all this at my leisure, for I ended up coming home with one to try for myself. I set it out, all velvety in its bright white flour coat, to warm up to room temperature and breathe a little—as suggested by the card—before reaching for the knife. The cheese's pull date was only a short time away, and as it lost its chill, the surface yielded softly to the touch. Inside, the texture proved smooth and rich, the flavor clean and decent. But it was also a flavor—as you might expect from all that packaging—overly anxious to make a good impression. It tasted like a cheese that had somewhere lost its nerve.

The poet Léon-Paul Fargue once inhaled a noseful of a French Camembert brought perfectly *à point* and murmured, "Ahhh . . . the feet of God." This is not something he would have said about Susan Hollander's Camembert, and had I taken up her invitation to telephone (508–468–7497), that's exactly how I would have put it: "Lovely cheese, Susan, but missing something between the toes."

About ten or so years ago the U.S. Customs Service blinked . . . and cheese importers managed for a time to bring into this country soft-ripened cheeses made with unpasteurized milk. It was by sheer luck that I stumbled across one of these at a cheese stall in Boston's Quincy Market.

Even so—though smart enough to know what I'd discovered—I hesitated. It didn't make sense that a cheese could be so expensive and look so . . . well . . . shabby. Whatever might be going on *inside* it, shouldn't the best cheese France has to offer stand up straight in freshly starched whites—not slouch like this one in smeary, off-color livery? Still . . .

"Taste, taste," the monger urged. Each bite coated the mouth like perfectly ripened butter. No wonder the edges sagged, the innards bulged out over the marble slab. This was a cheese that had clung to life just long enough for me to get it on my tongue—and for it to then expire there in a fragrant, deliquescent sigh.

Luscious, that Camembert—but also, honestly, unsettling. It was like tasting death and finding it good. Clifton Fadiman wrote that cheese is milk's leap toward immortality, which is witty but untrue. Velveeta is immortal, but it is not cheese; cheese is milk's leap toward a life of its own.

The life of some cheeses is brief but sunny: chèvres, farmer cheeses . . . they taste of nothing but freshness and youth. Other cheeses, like Parmesan, start life young and simple but grow old and wise; some very few, like Stilton, are to be eaten only after death. (Well, once upon a time, at least. Daniel Defoe, in his *Tour Through the Whole Island of Great Britain* (1724–26), said of the cheese that it is "brought to the table with the mites and maggots round it so thick, that they bring a spoon for you to eat the mites with.")

The majority of good cheeses, however, offer a choice: between those that live defying death and those that wait only to embrace it. This latter is what imbues a true French Camembert with its special character— that buttery perfume of anticipated corruption.

Craigston Camembert suggests no such thing. If anything, that packaging thrusts our expectation in exactly the opposite direction. Our cheese *might* die, it says . . . but would never be so vulgar as to stink.

Craigston is best described instead as a kind of *anti*-Camembert. It suggests no slow swoon toward putrefaction, but rather, at its finest moment, a delicate ripeness . . . as if picked from a tree like a peach. And why should it be otherwise? This is the only kind of ripeness that we—we Americans—can bear.

We are, after all, different from the French. We have not been brought up with uncles who smacked their lips over hung game, with grandparents who cured mold-covered sausages in their attic, or even with a mother who periodically soaked vile-smelling dried cod in the kitchen sink and then beat it with a stick, to thus transform it into a transcendental stew.

Instead, we have been conditioned from childhood to consider any manifestation of decay as spoilage, pure and simple. It does not signal an intensification of flavor to us; it signals rot. We see our food as we see ourselves at *every* age: vigorous, healthy, in our prime.

A few years ago, Paula Wolfert wrote a piece for the Living Section of *The New York Times* on brine-cured olives, in which she encouraged us to keep these not in the refrigerator but—well covered with olive oil— in a crock in the cupboard. Cold storage does not so much extend their lives as suspend them. Like good cheese, such olives are nothing if not allowed to live and breathe.

So this I did—and the result was all she said. But as time went on, I became more and more hesitant to thrust my fingers, or then even a spoon, into the harmless ropy scum that gradually came to surround them. First, I started rinsing each olive individually before I ate it. Then, one day, I caught myself letting the guests sample them before trying one myself. That was the day they went back into the refrigerator.*

I couldn't help it. Despite my efforts to the contrary, I'm part of a culture that avoids rot and makes a fetish of the fresh. We no longer want aged beef—but have no hesitation in eating it rare, even though undercooked beef is a potential source of tapeworm. We delight in pink roast lamb, despite the hazards of brucellosis, a most unpleasant bacterial disease. Sushi thrills us, though raw fish can be rife with parasites.

In other words, we shudder at imaginary risks and unknowingly run real ones—like every other culture in the world. What we think is our wisdom is really nothing more than our flavor.

Craigston Camembert is one of two really good American cheeses the local grocery carries; the other is a sharp Vermont Cheddar. With *this* cheese there is no foil, no ribbon, no brochures—just a whole plain wheel of it, kept right on top of the counter under a plastic dome. The Camembert is available only in the summer; the Cheddar is there the year round. You go in and order some, and they unceremoniously cut off a chunk and wrap it up for you in butcher's paper.

Sometimes the rind gets a little mold on it. They just wipe it away. No one worries. Cheddar, unlike Camembert, is a clean cheese. It is hard and yellow and smells sweetly, if ever so faintly, of cow and sum-

---

* I've gotten a little bolder in the five or so years since I wrote these lines. Preparing them for publication in this book I realized that I had in fact just taken a large tub of Kalamata olives from where it sits on the cellar stairs, opened it, and, without thinking much of it, literally *lifted* from the top of the brine its covering of mold, which had attained both the texture and the substance of a thick piece of felt.

mer pasturage. If you forget and leave it in the back of the refrigerator, it doesn't collapse into a puddle but hardens into a rock. You don't even have to worry about serving it at room temperature. Sliced thin as paper, it will warm up in the mouth.

Finally, and best of all, it has some tang, some bite. "Sharp" is the Yankee word, and sharp is perhaps the single character trait of which almost all Yankees approve. Soft and luscious may be a value appreciated in ice cream, but ice cream is a treat, the exception to the rule. Cheddar is workaday stuff, and with cheeses as with neighbors, what distinguishes mellowness from softness is a bit of edge or crust or bite. And should they—cheese, neighbor—prove to be *all* edge, *all* crust, *all* bite, well, that can be appreciated, too.

Because it is a cheese redolent of our particular virtues and forgiving of our flaws, our grocery can sell it without a label, let alone an explanation. We could not love a God whose feet smelled like ripe Camembert. Fortunately, we know they do not. They smell, if anything, like Cabot Vermont Cheddar, hunter's extra sharp, aged fourteen months, cut fresh from the wheel.

CASTINE, 1989

Burger Heaven

There is only one real hamburger. Start with a lump of ground fatty meat and press it flat. Fry it in stale grease, top it with a slice of gummy yellow cheese, scatter over it chopped raw onion and dill pickle, gob on catsup and mayonnaise, crown it with a flaccid lettuce leaf, clamp it in a doughy sesame-seed bun, and serve it floating on a sea of fries. The hamburger, the *real* hamburger, is trash.

When we're in the mood for that kind of trash, however, nothing else will do. Bite into one and succulent juices immediately start dribbling down the chin. The teeth sink into the yielding softness of the bun, break through the crisp resistance of the minced pickle, close around a satisfying mouthful of meat. Melted cheese coats the roof of the mouth; the sweet-sour tang of catsup, velvetized by mayo, smothers the taste buds in pleasure, lubricates the tongue.

This is good. Unfortunately, it is good in the exact same way that being drunk is good . . . not the thin enjoyment of a social drink or two but the bliss of being absolutely, car-keys-surrenderingly smashed. This is pleasure impossible to justify in the tongue of civilized discourse. So we tend not to discuss it at all, except—and only when compelled to —in the language of reform.

What in God's name got into me? This is a question impossible to answer. We sweetly mean each word when, facing the gastric aftermath—the stomach voicing its incredulous dismay and sweat still beading the forehead—we swear it all away. Too bad that intention has nothing to do with it. Maybe it would, if it were only the mouth that salivated at the thought of such a feasting, but this isn't so. Taste is merely the location of the pleasure. Its source, the origin of the bliss, lies somewhere else . . . somewhere that is primal, visceral, perhaps even feral, and certainly as deeply hostile to the orderings of good behavior as it is to those of good taste.

Consequently, nothing kills the excitement in this kind of eating quicker than when some culinary do-gooder wrestles it out of the gutter and claims to have redeemed it, as if somehow its louche character were an unhappy accident, instead of the reason we are drawn to it in the first place.

Such cooks think they are doing the world a favor by urging us to make our hamburgers with round steak instead of fatty chuck, to crank it twice through the grinder to give the meat some extra gloss, to work in wine or cream or fresh herbs, to replace the coating of processed cheese food with a slice of "decent" Cheddar or some other, even higher-toned cheese.

When I lived in Boston, the "Best Burger" awards were consistently bestowed on a clean-scrubbed, wholesome place right across the street from Harvard Yard—Bartley's Burger Cottage, which serves what it is pleased to call "the hamburger with a college education." It's a place well worth visiting for the onion rings, sliced thin as your fingernail and fried into a mass of crisp, golden filigree . . . but not for its burgers— even though, individually, they taste just fine.

No, the disappointment is cumulative. Every patty is made from a thick chunk of lean, juicy beef. It will actually be cooked rare if you think to ask for it that way. And you can have it topped with Cheddar or Swiss or blue cheese . . . even with Béarnaise sauce. They have as many different burgers as Howard Johnson used to have ice-cream flavors, and not one of them anything you'd be ashamed to make at home.

I know all this *sounds* good. The net effect isn't the realization of a burger lover's dream, however, but its domestication—the hamburger made virginally frolicsome. Eventually you come to understand that you don't want to eat a hamburger with a college education. You want one that flunked out of high school—or rather got *kicked* out, for bad attitude.

My own all-time favorite hamburger place was—and still may be (which is why I'm not giving more exact directions)—an authentically seedy drive-in out in the western part of Massachusetts, just a few miles south of Great Barrington. I was a teacher in a small private school, and the moment this drive-in opened in early June, a group of us young faculty members would pile into a car and head down U.S. 7 to celebrate the arrival of summer, the end of classes, and the enduring solace of grilled meat.

Part of the appeal then, admittedly, was the pretty college girls the owner managed to round up every year as counter help, but the hamburgers are what I remember now. The chef had to pry each one of them from the grill because he had spent the preceding time mashing it down with his spatula to squeeze out the grease. For another quarter, he would throw a handful of chopped onion to crisp along with it, and you could get single or double slices of Velveeta on the cheeseburger.

The fries were fat, crusty, and cut from real potatoes; the burgers themselves had the authentic flavor. That is, they were good but also anonymous, their taste evocative of all burgers past. Each bite teased forgotten synapses of memory into life . . . and as they began to fire at random, the mind began its slide down the greasy slope of memory into wordless reverie. Although we sat together in the car, each one of us ate alone, a solitary, silent figure, stroked by the Janus-faced comfort of appetite and satiety, reluctant to return to the present, pick up our cares, start up the engine, and go.

The American hamburger is road food. We've been eating them since at least 1912—but not at home, at least not if we go by cookbooks. As late as the 1950s, the dominant recipe for the ground-beef patty was the Salisbury or Hamburg steak: hamburger served on a china plate with gravy or tomato sauce poured over it, everyone pretending they were eating steak.

Such is the true parentage of the homemade burger and, for that matter, the gourmet burger. "If liked, moisten slightly with tomato juice . . . A slice of fat salt pork may be chopped with [the] beef to give additional flavor"; these tips come from the 1941 edition of Fannie Farmer in the recipe for "Hamburg Steak." The burger *we're* talking about didn't get in until the tenth edition, published in 1959.* There they're called, perversely, "hamburger buns," and no reader could fail to note the stiffness of body language behind a recipe that concludes: "For a more piquant flavor, dot the hamburgers with prepared mustard, chili sauce, or both."

If you tuned in *The CBS Evening News* on November 16, 1970, you heard Charles Kuralt, on the road, reporting on the hamburger. There was no doubt that he had actually been out there eating them . . . every one of his riffs had got that beat. "We've had grabba burgers, kinga burgers, lotta burgers, castle burgers, country burgers, bronco burgers.

---

* On the other hand, the *cheeseburger* did make the previous edition (1951), but there the recipe is wrong, too: "Make thin hamburg patties. Cook on one side. Put on toasted split buns. Sprinkle with salt and pepper. Put thin slice of cheese on each. Broil until cheese begins to melt."

Broadway burgers, broiled burgers, beefnut burgers, bell burgers, plus burgers. . . ."

The moral? Taste a real burger, taste exhaust fumes. Its flavor is that of the stand, the lunch counter, the joint. Who would intentionally make on their own stove a "grabba burger"? No one. And if they so inclined, they'd find that it couldn't be done. The general public is simply not *allowed* to get their hands on real hamburger meat. It would be too dangerous.

I know this because once one of the participants in those burger runs insisted on bringing along his German shepherd, Macho, a dog with a relentless appetite and no shyness in letting you know it. To get some uninterrupted eating time, we passed the hat around to buy him his own burger platter, which we decided—for reasons I no longer comprehend, since *he* certainly wouldn't have wanted it that way—should be served up raw.

We put in our order. The waitress hesitated—then shrugged and wrote it down. When she brought our tray over to the car, she silently handed in Macho's portion. The raw patty was as gray and full of fat as a chunk of tired breakfast sausage. In fact, the lean part looked as if it had been ground in as an afterthought, less substance than seasoning.

Appetite all but fled. We still ate, but we were shaken. We had been given a glimpse of what the less charitable find easy to sum up in a homily but what for most of us is just the other side of a truth we lack the courage to grasp entire—something to do with life and death, the nature of pleasure, the sadness after sex.

CASTINE, 1990

White Bread

A cold afternoon in late November, and I'm heading out of Bangor, crossing the Penobscot River on the "new new bridge" (the older "new bridge" being a little farther upriver). As I reach the far side, a familiar yeasty aroma fills the car. Memory is full of locked closets, their keys residing in particular smells or sounds. Happen onto one and—out of the blue—the lock is sprung. I once stood dumbstruck on a street in a small town in Germany because the effluent rising from a sewer grating flung me back into my six-year-old army-brat self, circa 1949, just moved to Fuchinobe, Japan.

A drunken second. Then, as always, it passes; words come. Even as they form the harmless phrase "someone's baking bread," the car is already turning onto its exit, just over the river, Route 15 down to Bucksport. There, never noticed before—but then, why would it be?— stands a Nissen bakery plant. A bright white cloud of steam floats lazily over its flat roof. They're busy inside turning out Nissen Butter Top, hot-dog rolls, hamburger buns, who knows what.

I drive on, south, homeward, outraged and ashamed that the smell of such bread could have such power over me. But there it is: it has. Baking, all loaves have the same good smell. And it is just because of that that the aroma conveys a poignant sense of loss. It makes me miss *bread.*

To lose something, though, you have to find it first. The year is 1960; Dad has piloted the Buick Roadmaster across France to Paris from our home in Germany. My Uncle Walter, stationed at the embassy there, has loaned us his apartment in the sixteenth arrondisement, right on the Seine. I'm seventeen, old enough to be allowed in daytime to wander by myself. The rest of the family will visit famous sites; my itinerary is different (and yet, I now realize, exactly the same): to give substance to the fact that I'm actually *here.*

It was Rimbaud, not cuisine, that interested me then. Even so, hunger eventually took me in hand. Too shy to step into a café, I eventually passed a *boulangerie*, its door, despite the wintry weather, propped open. The aroma drew me right up over the stoop. I'd had only two years of high-school French . . . but there was no doubt what this shop sold, or whether I could afford it out of the month's worth of allowance turned to francs.

I had been in bakeries before, mostly in Germany. The bread there was sour, pungent, dark. Some loaves were enormous, purchased by the kilo, your portion passed over in a crisp waxed-paper bag. Strange bread is what you expect to find in other countries; good bread, I was learning, too.

The *boulangerie*, however, was different from the *bakerei* . . . foreign in another way. The loaves stood casually on end behind the counter in a large wooden bin. Every single one of them was *white bread.* They were all completely familiar and utterly desirable. I had never seen such white bread before—shapely, taut, *tout nu.*

It was as if, in all innocence, I had stumbled into a brothel and—before I realized what was happening—found myself caught up in the first of its concupiscent pleasures: taking your pick. Every one of those unwrapped loaves enticed me. Rather than confusing me, it heightened my bliss. I knew the one I wanted the instant I saw it. Last out of the oven, its crust was deeply burnished, the sole a well-crisped brown. It crackled when the shop girl picked it up.

No bag was offered; the bread passed from her hand to mine. The crust—smooth, resilient, still slightly warm—for that moment that it connected us, aroused in my fingers a turbulent, completely un-expected sense of intimacy. It was as impersonal a contact as if she had asked me to hold her baby while she tied her shoe—but still somehow shockingly familiar. Blushing hotly, I paid her, took my loaf, and fled.

I ate as I walked. I had wanted a piece of cheese to eat with it, some wine to wash it down. But my moment of courage was all burned out. So, by itself, the bread became the meal.

Too many loaves now stand in the way for me to remember what it tasted like. I do know that I ate it with a sense of astonishment: "This is what bread tastes like." All white bread had had that flavor, but the taste had reached the mouth as a distant shout upon the ears, muddled and confused. Now here it was—clear, delicious, plain.

This taste, I have since learned, is that of unbleached white flour— salted, leavened, and baked. Such a loaf satisfies like no other food. Its very shape is meant to appease our hunger. A meal can be made of it three times a day and expectation will still not be exhausted.

It is, simply, appetite's body. The glowing warmth, the yielding, sensual firmness, the salt-and-sour scent . . . it begins to comfort the moment one takes it into one's hands. This is why, even though I don't remember the flavor of that first, revelatory loaf, I can still recall its *touch*.

Our national bread has nothing of this forthright corporality. Instead, it is a kind of cake, made with sugar, milk, and shortening, then frosted at the table with butter and jam. The qualities we like about it are also cakelike. It is light, tender, sweet, rich. We eat it in slices, and each slice melds to the tongue.

At its best, it can be quite good—it just doesn't like being touched. So we buy it wrapped in plastic, already sliced. Even at festive occasions, we do not pass the loaf around in open sensual enjoyment, hand to hand; instead, we put soft rolls in a napkin-covered basket, from which each eater takes a private piece.

Why is this? Because, I think, growing up, our sense of the paradigmatic romantic moment is the kiss: moist, soft, secret—the *real* contact hidden from view. We experience it in the hamburger, the peanut-butter-and-jelly sandwich, the chocolates in the sampler box: sweet and yielding on the outside, a swooning voluptuousness within. *This*, fantasy persuades us, is what love and eating are all about.

If a loaf of bread is the body we put to appetite, our appetite still has a teenage imagination, resisting the casual openness of true sensuality. Unlike cake, good bread has a body. It expects to be touched. Its pleasures are too real, too tactile, to be wasted in a plastic bag. It wants you to take it and slice it while holding it tight against your chest, or, even better, to pull it into pieces with your hands.

American bread has its place, of course—it provides the quintessential lobster roll, the only possible mop for a plate of barbecue, the butter-crisp crust of a grilled cheese sandwich. In short, where white bread is wanted to form a kiss, this bread does fine. But it has no body—and once you've held a loaf that does, no other bread will do.

This, then, is why that Nissen plant's aroma jerked me around—the smell still draws me even though I know its bread will push my hand away. Such a loaf only wants us to *want* to touch it. Its flaccid softness not only disappoints the fingers but makes them feel dirty, dirtying. Innocence, no matter how willful, can offer only so much. You can't give your body—or take another's—if you aren't yet able to fully acknowledge that you have one yourself.

CASTINE, 1989

The Toll House Cookie

When I was a kid, my absolute favorite cookie was the chocolate-chip cookie. In some ways, I suppose—at least in terms of durable attraction—it still is, but at age ten there was simply no competition. My mother liked them, too, but her taste was more catholic. The cookie jar might just as well be filled with brownies, peanut-butter cookies (my second favorite), sugar cookies, or *oatmeal* cookies.

I can remember coming home from school, catching the telltale scents of baking day, and rushing into the kitchen. There they were, spread out on the cooling racks, dozens of hot, brown-edged cookies, covered with dark, melty dots. Only, when I went to snatch one, I discovered that the dots weren't what I expected. My mother had made her own favorite, oatmeal cookies, the traitor cookie that looked like my favorite but tasted like . . . well, like porridge patties with raisin plops.

Hard to believe, but for my mother, while all these other cookies were old familiars from her childhood, the chocolate chipper was a novelty item, first encountered when she was a teenager in the late 1930s. In fact, although this won't appear on many calendars, the year 2000 will mark the seventieth anniversary of the fabled moment when Ruth Wakefield pulled the first batch of chocolate-chip cookies out of the oven at the Toll House Inn in Wakefield, Massachusetts.

If you know this legend, you know that no one was more surprised at this turn of events than Ruth herself. She had expected the chocolate to melt into the cookie. Instead, out came a crisp, buttery cookie shot through with molten nuggets. Lacking the advantage of hindsight, she christened it the "Chocolate Crunch Cookie."

In 1930, of course, there were no morsels or chips or nuggets; Ruth Wakefield had to break up a chocolate bar to get her bits—specifically, a bar of Nestlé's semisweet Yellow Label Chocolate. According to the official (i.e., Nestlé) account, the cookie became so popular with customers and neighbors that a sales rep finally came by to find out who exactly was buying all those chocolate bars. He discovered Ruth baking up a storm at the Toll House Inn . . . and struck a deal. Let's hope she drove a good Yankee bargain for herself, because Nestlé made out all right; by the cookie's fiftieth anniversary in 1980, the company was producing 350 million morsels a *day*.*

Nestlé's first move was to produce that bar scored into tiny squares, packaging it with a special tool to help break it up. By 1939, they finally landed the hammer directly on the nail and began cranking out the familiar already-formed morsels, in packages that still bear the color of the now-forgotten Yellow Label, and printed the recipe for "The Famous Toll House Cookie" on the back. An American classic was born.

My question, though, is: *why*? Why is the chocolate chip cookie *my* favorite cookie, *your* favorite cookie, nearly *everybody's* favorite cookie? Why have at least three separate entrepreneurs (not counting Ruth herself) make it the foundation of their cookie-chain empires? Why isn't it Famous Amos's Pecan Sandies, Mrs. Field's Benne Wafers, David's Gingersnaps?

Looking for the answer, I spent some time searching through a batch of early-twentieth-century New England cookbooks, the sort that might have roosted on top of Ruth Wakefield's Frigidaire. The amazing thing is how clearly we can now see the chocolate-chip cookie yearning, struggling, to be born. Here are Boston cookies with the familiar combination of brown and white sugar . . . here are chocolate walnut wafers, also very similar, but still not quite right . . . here are drop brownies, so close, so close . . . and so on.

The idea wasn't so much to get *chocolate* into the cookie as to get *intensity* into it. After a meal of roast beef and gravy, potatoes mashed with milk and butter, creamed onions, and hot rolls and butter, a slice of, say, pound cake comes as a bit of a letdown, something easy to refuse. So affronted home bakers brought out of the kitchen the triple layer cake covered with fudge frosting. No one was going to turn that down! And no one did . . . and mostly still can't.

To grasp what was going on, imagine a homemaker with a bowl of

---

* Ruth Wakefield continued to hope that the same bolt of lightning might strike her twice. Among her subsequent attempts was the "Toll House Ting-a-Ling," made with prunes, walnuts, ginger, chocolate chips, and cornflakes.

fudge frosting in one hand and a cookie in the other, trying to push the two together. Cookies don't take to being frosted; there's not enough *cookie* in a cookie to stand up to so much sweetness. If only you could bake a cookie with little lumps of fudge frosting all through it. You can't do that with frosting, of course, but you can with plain chocolate. *Voilà*, the cookie every home baker was waiting for, the cookie that was more than just another sweetened cracker, another teatime snack.

Like our national anthem, our national cookie demands more skill than many of us can muster. Cooks have always had trouble with the Toll House Cookie, and for good reason—it is really too rich for its own good. Although it evolved from a drop cookie and is still made like one, it is in truth closer to a refrigerator cookie—but without that cookie's ease of making. As Ruth Wakefield revised her Toll House cookbook, she kept pushing it in this direction, instructing that the dough be refrigerated overnight and the "drops" of dough be flattened by hand once they were put on the cookie sheet. Even so, as any cookie maker will know, there is no really foolproof method.

Interestingly, the many subsequent variations of the Toll House Cookie all seem bent on recapturing that initial experience of richness. The original recipe called for each cookie to be made with only half a teaspoon of dough; commercial versions such as David's and Mrs. Field's are much larger, demanding a proportional increase in the size of the chocolate chunks.* This meant, at first, a return to the old method of breaking bars up into genuine chunks, but recently Nestlé and other chocolate companies have bowed to the trend and begun producing mega-morsels.

This craving for richness piled upon richness is strictly an American one, and the chocolate-chip cookie, on the whole, has remained an unabashedly American taste. Unlike the hamburger, which has been an eager cross-cultural proselytizer, the Toll House Cookie has mostly stayed at home. European chocolate does not necessarily improve it; European *pâtissiers* are incapable of grasping its generous innocence.

This is because in Europe a cookie is generally considered a delicate thing: a tiny, subtle, bite-sized pastry meant to nestle at the edge of the teacup or even the brandy snifter. The blurb on the canisters of those Italian confections *amarettini di Saronno* recommends them as choice company for "fine wine and after-dinner liqueurs" . . . hardly something

---

* For instance, in her *Mrs. Fields Cookie Book*, directed to the home cook, Debbie Fields makes each cookie with a tablespoon of dough, or six times the original amount.

we'd want to pair up with a couple of chocolate chippers. *Their* best accompanying beverage is an icy glass of milk; their most appropriate milieu, the kitchen table.

Europeans, reminiscing about childhood treats, call up visions of nursery food or, perhaps, a slice of bread wrapped around a square of chocolate. Over there, dessert seems mostly an adult prerogative, and their cookies reflect this attitude. As much as they may call attention to themselves, such cookies have a certain *délicatesse*, as befits something baked to play the accompaniment to a tiny scoop of sorbet, a ripe pear, or a bowl of strawberries and Devonshire cream.

Mention the word "dessert" to an American, however, and what comes to mind? Memories of hot-fudge sundaes, coconut-frosted layer cakes, apple pie and ice cream, and Mother saying, "Clean your plate, dear— or no dessert." At the end of supper our appetite suddenly assumes a child's face. And what could be more of a kid pleaser than a handful of buttery crunchy cookies filled with chocolate chips?

The original chocolate-chip cookie recipe, of course, isn't the one printed on the back of the Nestlé package, since the Toll House Cookie predates the Toll House morsel. Here, for the record, is the recipe Ruth Graves Wakefield, Dietitian and Lecturer, first set down in *Toll House Tried and True Recipes* back in 1938.

Chocolate Crunch Cookies

Cream 1 cup of butter. Add ¾ cup each of brown and granulated sugar and 2 eggs beaten whole. Dissolve 1 teaspoon of baking soda in 1 teaspoon hot water and mix alternately with 2¼ cups flour sifted with 1 teaspoon salt.* Lastly, add 1 cup chopped nuts and 1 pound of Nestlé's Yellow Label Chocolate, semisweet, cut into pieces the size of a pea. Flavor with 1 teaspoon vanilla and drop by the half-teaspoonful onto a greased cookie sheet. Bake 10 to 12 minutes in a pre-heated 375°F oven. Makes 100 cookies.

CASTINE, 1990

* If this sentence seems a little confused, no wonder: Ruth Wakefield is directing us to alternately mix the flour-salt mixture and that little spoonful of baking-soda paste into the creamed butter and sugar. When she first created the recipe, this awkward approach was mandated by the coarse texture of baking soda. Since then, producers have learned to mill it fine enough so that it can be simply sifted into the flour with the salt. Amusingly, this posed later food writers with an unexpected problem: what to do with the now redundant teaspoon of water. Most dared not simply omit it, and so, decade after decade, you find chocolate-chip cookie recipes with a mysterious teaspoon of water separately stirred into the batter.

A Cup of Coffee

A cup of coffee and a cigarette. For twenty years I needed one in
each hand to start the morning—and I rarely came up with a better
idea for getting through it. A college dropout in the early sixties, I first
learned the art of lingering in the various coffeehouses that were then
still vital to Greenwich Village life. On a slow day I could nurse a
cappuccino for a couple of hours behind my copy of some literary mag,
inhaling an atmosphere dense with tobacco smoke, the aroma of coffee,
and soothing desultory chatter.

There were already at least two specialty coffee importers in the
Village—Schapira and McNulty's—but I wouldn't discover them for
years. Or perhaps I *did* discover them; it just never occurred to me to
go in. I hadn't yet learned that coffee might—perhaps even *ought* to—
taste good. I didn't like the actual flavor of cigarette tobacco, either,
but I did like smoking; coffee was the same. I loved their presence, the
way they were *there*, filling my inner and outer space. Most of all I loved
the way they got me buzzed.

Anyway, the times were gritty, hip, hard-up, and the style was cheap.
I smoked Disques Bleus, French cigarettes so harsh and rank they made
Camel smokers feel like sissies. (The Disque Bleu ad campaign at the
time pictured someone lighting one up in a theater line, and the half-
indignant, half-intrigued person behind him demanding, "What *are* you
smoking?!") In the same spirit, my coffee was a cheap, strong, oily brew
of no particular pedigree, purchased from a local *bodega* in an unlabeled
brown wax-paper bag. This stuff was roasted black as pitch; the burned
pungent aroma it released while brewing told me every morning that I
wasn't in Kansas anymore.

My first "gourmet" appliance was a Neapolitan coffee maker, what

Italians call a *machinetta*. This is made of two almost identical, can-shaped, tin-lined brass pots, one of which fits upside down on top of the other. To use it, you put some water in the bottom pot, scoop a measure of coffee into a perforated insert that slips inside, and finally tightly affix the second pot—the only one with a spout—on top. You heat the water in the bottom pot until it comes to a boil and then invert the whole assembly, allowing the boiling water to seep down through the grounds into the top pot, which is now, if you follow me, on the bottom.

As it turned out, mastery of this gizmo was beyond me. No matter how quickly I turned the damned thing over, no matter how firmly I twisted its parts together, water still gushed out at the seam. I retained it for purposes of display and returned to my small Mirro aluminum percolator. Coffee snobs detest this device, as well they might, for although ingenious in design, it overcooks its contents, giving them that sourish boiled flavor that most of us grew up believing was coffee's actual taste. Certainly it's a foolish thing to use with premium beans. No matter what goes into the basket, the same "coffee" pours out the spout. Still, for the percolator to become our country's emblematic coffee maker, it had to be doing something right.

It was. It brewed a whole pot quickly and efficiently; it distributed —like no other brewer—coffee aroma all through the house. Wake up and smell the coffee, it said—there was never any promise about taste. And it was a peculiarly, cheerfully, *animated* device. Where would "perky" and "perk up" be without their suggestion of the percolator's upbeat gurgle? In fact, until I wrote this piece I had always thought "percolation" meant the slowly accelerating rhythm that eases you toward wakefulness as you stand in front of the warm stove watching those darkening blips of water burst against the glass viewing knob, palpably becoming coffee. May Mr. Coffee, the current brewer-regnant, rule so well.

Even though I now hand-grind specialty beans to make my coffee and brew it in a biggin—a Creole drip pot—I really taste only the first few sips. That nod made to the lately acquired ritual of connoisseurship, I retreat into an earlier found, more satisfying place. The coffee grows cold, then sours in the mug . . . but that mug sits by my side all morning, as loyal as a pup. I go on drinking from it, oblivious to everything except my wish to make it last. These days it's all I allow myself.

Such companionship is why, in more impoverished circumstances, I used to blow my last bit of change for a pack of butts. It was why I would dodge the waitress's eye to keep from surrendering an empty cup.

To acquire a taste for coffee doesn't mean you have to learn to love its flavor—though, obviously, you can. What you *do* have to love, though, is the ritual.

And I mean all of it, from the way you take your coffee—straight black and scalding hot or modulated with cream and sugar—to the way you blow into it and wrap your hands around the cup, to the way you lift it to your mouth. This is our culture's way of allowing us to orchestrate a moment's worth of personal space. Whether you sigh and sink into a stupor at the counter with your cup untouched before you or drink its contents down in a flurry of agitated motions—for that instant everything has stopped. If someone happens to walk in as you pour yourself a cup, they know to hold their fire. "Stand back and let me have this," these gestures say. "I *need* it."

Home on the range: the break of day, the chuckwagon, the surly, sleepy cowboys, the coffeepot pushed up against the fire. You know this scene and you know you've never in your life wondered what variety of coffee boils in that very basic pot. It just has to be good . . . which is to say strong, hot, and tasting like coffee . . . or Cookie takes a bullet.

Those silent, irritable loners don't *want* Jamaican Blue Mountain, Kona, Tanzanian peaberry, or anything else that calls attention to itself. They aren't in the mood to be appreciative, to sort out flavor notes. The mouth is only the locus of this experience; its import lies somewhere else. Over a cup of java, by observing the gestures of their companions and being observed in turn, they mark out the boundaries of personal territory . . . and, so doing, cohere into a group.

This is, you'll notice, an inversion of the intimacy of the saloon, of hard-drinking, solitary men. Here the motion is toward sobriety, but the motivation is the same rueful inner soreness. It isn't by accident that AA members joke that the higher power watching over their meetings appears in the shape of a coffeepot. And *its* contents aren't brewed from gourmet beans, either.

This connection with hard liquor is, I think, why having coffee with your meal is not encouraged in fine restaurants. The flavors of wine and food can clash just as aggressively, but wine drinking and fine dining are complementary, not antithetical, rituals. Wine nurtures conviviality; coffee, like booze, creates an assembly in which every member remains apart. The last thing you get at dinner is either coffee or brandy. It is the start of the end, the signal for goodbyes.

Wine and coffee do, however, share a mysterious truth. Remove the alcohol from the one and, despite all that eloquent language about year, variety, and *terroir*, what you have left is a fancy kind of grape juice—

and with the same market value. Remove the caffeine from the other and it becomes the sort of bitter, roasted berry tonic that goes slowly stale on a back shelf of the health-food store.

In other words, coffee like wine is first of all a drug. After a certain point the language of connoisseurship is indistinguishable from the language of denial. Yes, gourmet beans make a great brew, but taking them too seriously is no different from drinking decaf—a way of admitting without saying it that you've lost your grip on whatever got you started drinking the stuff.

CASTINE, 1990

The Recipe Detective

Sometime in the mid-1970s, Gloria Pitzer was fired from her job as food editor at a local paper because she insisted on giving readers the recipes they wanted, not the recipes her editor felt they *ought* to want. Still convinced that she was right, she took in ironing until she had scraped up enough to purchase a mimeograph machine, and then she started sending out a food letter, *The Secret Recipe Report.* (Now called *Gloria Pitzer's Secret Recipes Quarterly*, it may well be the longest-lived food letter ever.* Ten years later she was making regular appearances on radio cooking talk shows all around the country and selling hundreds of thousands of copies of the cookbooks into which she was periodically gathering these "secret recipes," most famously her *Better Cookery Cookbook: Secret Recipes for Famous Foods from Famous Places.*†

This triumph was built on the brilliant intuition that a lot of home cooks were tired of the recipes offered in most cookbooks and newspaper food pages. These, usually, break down into two general categories: dishes that, on the one hand, require the cook to tackle new methods and new ingredients for ends that may or may not prove worth the effort

* Anyone interested in her food letter or her several books should send a stamped, self-addressed envelope to Secret Recipes, Box 237, Marysville, MI 48040 and request the free flyer with fifteen of her most popular recipes on one side and an order form on the other.

† Since Gloria Pitzer has revised and repackaged her work over the years—this book was known in an earlier incarnation as *The Best of the Recipe Detective*—it's important to note that the quotes that appear in this essay were taken from the September 1984 edition. I believe that subsequent editions have been abridged, with much of the autobiographical material discussed in this essay excised.

and, on the other, the all-too-familiar round of penny-scraping, time-cheating, fat-wary throw-togethers.

What Pitzer understood was that while this was what her readers may have said they wanted, it was secretly what they yearned to escape. Although they might be afraid to admit this, even to themselves, what would most excite them would be to learn how to make the food they most loved to eat: the fast food they bought at McDonald's or Kentucky Fried Chicken and the brand-name treats they brought home from the supermarket, stuff like Oreo cookies and Hostess Snowballs.

So Gloria Pitzer assumed both the title and the role of "Recipe Detective" and set out to decode these foods—at least to the point where she could replicate them in her own home kitchen. And she succeeded at this beyond her wildest dreams—sometimes to corporate fury and sometimes to its amused acquiescence.

It quickly became apparent that she had touched a public nerve. Her radio appearances—helped by her upbeat, unpretentious personality and unabashed enthusiasm—brought her thousands of letters. When she went on national television to teach Phil Donahue how to make Twinkies, she received over a million pieces of mail . . . an event that so traumatized her that she subsequently refused to appear on *Good Morning America* or in *People* magazine. (Nor did she return to the Phil Donahue show for another twelve years. But when she did in 1993, there were over 500,000 requests for a transcript—more than any other in the history of the show.)

Cookbooks offering homemade versions of popular restaurant and brand-name foods are nothing new. What made Gloria Pitzer different was both *what* she chose to replicate and *how* she chose to do it. For instance, Helen Witty and Elizabeth Schneider Colchie, in their award-winning *Better than Store Bought*, eschewed brand-name replication entirely, teaching their readers instead to make corn chips or tomato catsup in a healthier and more economical fashion. These authors shrink from any association with the shameful thrill of a mouthful of Pringles or raspberry-flavored marshmallow fluff.

In complete contrariety, Gloria Pitzer actively promotes what is vulgarly excessive about such things, instinctively grasping that it is the way junk food breaches culinary decorum that makes it so desirable in the first place. Consequently her versions are often worse for us than the originals and sometimes even more expensive to make.

You would search in vain in *Better than Store Bought* for a recipe for Cheez Whiz; Gloria Pitzer gives us *two*. She also explains what we surely would always have wanted to know if we ever believed anyone would tell us: how to make Lipton's instant cream of tomato soup, Eagle Brand condensed milk, General Foods "Suisse Mocha" instant coffee . . . and a host of other such familiars. Only Dream Whip has so far managed to stymie her, and that probably not for long.

How does the Recipe Detective go about deducing the secrets of these patent formulas? By trying, tasting, and—when these are available— perhaps casting a very casual glance at the ingredients list. Indeed, what to my mind makes Pitzer a true artist is her lack of interest in with what exactly a particular product is made. As she forthrightly puts it: "I do not know nor do I WANT to know what these companies put into their recipes." What she wants to replicate is less *it* than the experience of *eating* it.

So, to copy a 48-ounce jar of Hellmann's mayonnaise, she blends the expected ingredients—oil, eggs, lemon juice, vinegar, salt—with some that you might not expect—three-quarters of a cup each of sugar and evaporated milk and two sticks of margarine. Then, to offset the incredible greasy richness that this produces (did I mention the six egg yolks?), she ups the lemon juice and vinegar to a third of a cup each and the salt to four teaspoons.

A spoonful of this mixture explodes in the mouth like a culinary hand grenade. Salt! Sweet! Sour! Fat!—all hit the tastebuds simultaneously and with overwhelming intensity. This is cooking as an act of sensual violence. And while not all her recipes are like this, many are. Some go further.

Taken as a whole, this cooking is to ordinary fare as scarlet-covered romances are to ordinary life . . . normal caution cast aside for the pleasure of total surrender to the charming—and surely not *totally* unscrupulous—ravisher. Such food doesn't ask to be tasted; it compels the mouth to submit. The message: When pleasure forces itself on you, there's no blame in yielding. Relax and enjoy it.

Certainly, Gloria Pitzer herself treats the sweet-talking blandishments of her seducers as gospel truth. She writes with a straight face that the beef from which White Castle makes its hamburgers is "of such a high quality we can't possibly equal it with what we buy in our supermarkets." She spends months decoding Arthur Treacher's "secret" fish-fry batter and the Colonel's "secret" eleven herbs and spices.

It isn't, of course, that I don't think such secrets exist. I'm sure they do. I just don't think they have all that much influence on anyone's decision to buy Kentucky Fried Chicken. This may be why, when Pitzer and Colonel Sanders chatted together once on a radio program, he genially hinted that she look around the grocery store for a packaged mix that might contain eleven secret herbs and spices. Pitzer diligently did just that—to discover that the secret behind that finger-lickin' flavor was Good Seasons brand Italian salad dressing mix.

Another cook might have been dismayed—some secret!—but Pitzer was thrilled. Here, suddenly, reality was replicating fantasy, *her* fantasy. Her final recipe—for three pounds of fryer parts—mixes two packets of the salad seasoning into a blend of butter, corn oil, Crisco, milk, lemon juice, and sage-and-paprika-seasoned pancake mix.

Because it bombards us with pleasurable and irresistible stimuli, junk food offers an immediate comfort that ordinary food cannot . . . a comfort that few of us can resist all the time. But as it coddles, it also betrays, for like many seducers, it is not what it pretends to be. We know this, and we don't care. There is eating where the mouth is inquisitive, aggressive, alert, and appreciative, because it genuinely wants to get to know what it is devouring. Then, like an encounter between two strangers in a pickup bar, both looking for an easy one-night stand, there is eating that knows it had best not look too closely and just take it as it comes.

Such encounters have their flavor, but that comes from a willed confusion of fantasy and reality, of appearance and substance, reinforced by the ambience of the bar and smooth talk that is at once sincere and empty. In the world of food, these things arise from the aura that is woven around the brand name, associations that persistent advertising persuades us to equate with our own sense of pleasure. This is why economy-minded mothers serve cheaper, frozen fried chicken to their family in a carefully preserved Kentucky Fried Chicken bucket—it's the bucket, not the chicken (even less the herbs and spices), that provides the savor.

The sobriquet "recipe detective" might at first acquaintance sound like an attempt to become fast food's Philip Marlowe—a solitary seeker of truth stalking the mean streets of the Miracle Mile. In Pitzer's case, nothing could be further from the truth. The persona she projects in her writing is not that of detective-avenger but that of willing victim, the romantic heroine who refuses to let go the illusions that lead, over and over again, to the threat of seduction and betrayal.

Food writing as Harlequin romance—it is in such terms, I think, that we should read her indiscriminate eagerness to justify fast food, her hymns of praise to those who make it, and, especially, her vilification of the writers who attempt to undermine its emotional solace. We should take it, that is, as defending not a belief so much as a dream.

If you go by the commercials, the Big Mac, the diet Pepsi, the Lay's potato chip are all you need to transform a family meal or a gathering of friends into a joyous event; they are sold, that is, as Energizer batteries for human beings. Food, perhaps, should not be put to this purpose. But it is, and it works—at least for a time. *Better Cookery Cookbook*—the title is without irony, since it is merely mimicking the *Betty Crocker Cookbook* (in case you don't get it, she adds on the next page, "General Thrills Foods")—*because* of its self-illusions, is a compelling, even touching, portrait of the author's, and by extension, many another's, struggles with the junk-food dream.

That unself-conscious honesty is what distances Pitzer from the more publicized mainstream writers on the pleasures of this world. The latter approach it as curious tourists in the land of Big Boys and Chicken in the Rough, tourists who keep their culinary passports in order so that they can get out at the drop of a hat. Gloria Pitzer actually lives there . . . and that makes all the difference.

BOSTON, 1986

Amid the Alien Corn

The Story of Corn, BETTY FUSSELL

The Carolina Rice Kitchen, KAREN HESS

Both these books taste of the academy. Betty Fussell, her book's biographical note announces, holds a doctorate in English literature and "has taught everything from Shakespeare to slapstick comedy [and] has lectured widely on food history." Karen Hess is our country's premier culinary historian (and, though this is less welcomed by some, the food world's most outspoken culinary conscience). Reading these two books together, I found myself unwillingly tumbled back in time to the college classroom and into my accustomed seat at the very back of the hall, notepad open but empty before me on the desk, ballpoint pen dangling slackly from my fingers, my mind boggled by the flood of facts sent pouring through my ears.

The classroom, these two books also reminded me, comes in many flavors. Betty Fussell's is that of Super Course. Even the college's largest amphitheater is too small to hold the overflowing crowd; students sprawl in the aisles and perch on the window ledges. This is what a college education is about—getting the Big Picture. Fussell provides it all: the fragmented wisdom of vanished civilizations woven into ritual and myth; the nobility of the Native American and the savagery of the Ignoble Colonist Invader; the souring wonder of technology and the wholesomeness of arts and crafts.

Furthermore, the lecturer presents her material with the sort of pizazz guaranteed to keep a sophomore audience happily enthralled: jump cutting (Aztec human sacrifice to Arkansas moonshiners to Zuñi Mudhead tricksters to Sioux City corncob palaces to J. J. Kellogg to Hiawatha), freeze framing (Inca peasants drunk on corn brew in a dark and smoky *chicheria* in Cuzco, Peru; Shriner Cooties—motorized minicars—whizzing in and out of the Hoopeston, Illinois, annual National Sweetcorn Festival Parade), and R-rated discourse (mostly revolving around corncob as phallus, but corncob as outhouse wipe is not shorted, either).

"Foodways 431A: The Carolina Rice Kitchen" is being conducted a few flights up in a closet-sized classroom that still manages to feel empty; the few students huddle together before the dais. The professor is known for her erudition, wit, and lack of tolerance for fools. The course is tough, and good grades are hard to get. The lectures explicate a relatively obscure American cooking tome, the *Carolina Rice Cook Book*, published in 1901. Facsimiles of this book lie open on all the desks, turned to page 61 and the recipe for hoppin' John, here genteelized into "Hopping John." The professor, drawing on original research, is explaining the derivation of that name from the Persian *bahatta*, meaning "cooked rice," and the Malay *kachang*, meaning any type of pulse; hence, albeit via a rather circuitous route, "hoppin' John" is another way of saying "rice and peas."

At this moment, however, roars of laughter rise up the stairwell from the amphitheater lecture, and annoyed, the professor looks up from her notes and waves her hand at us to go—and to shut the door behind us. We do, and slip back down the stairs to see what all the commotion is about. We find the lecturer approaching the place of the Zuñi on a New Mexican mesa to watch their celebration of the winter solstice, the night of Shalako. Wandering in the pouring rain, the total darkness illuminated only fitfully by automobiles rushing down Highway 53, she has taken a pratfall, face first, in the sea of mud beneath her feet . . . emerging

> like a mud-volleyball player at Hog Days in Kewanee, or a Mudman in Zuniland.
> I've been lost many times this dark night because there are no maps for this
> territory and this is not my place.

This passage, read in its entirety, conveys what is good and what is finally off-putting about *The Story of Corn*. There were moments when I was spellbound by this book, but there were as many others when I wanted to rush out of the house and toss it after her into that Zuñi mud field. Whatever else there is to say about Betty Fussell, she gets under your skin.

Usually, when we think of corn, we think of it as a foodstuff, embracing a unique category that is part vegetable, part grain. But it is much, much more than that, and Fussell devotes a mere two chapters to corn as food and drink (although these are practically a book unto themselves). When settlers came to this country, corn seized hold of them and never let go. It not only worked its inextricable way into our language, our national mythology, and our history (and not just the history of everyday life) but became a major source of our national wealth. Fortunes were made from it; the farmland of whole states were devoted to it.

The Story of Corn is strongest showing how this is so. Fussell casts a wide net, drawing in mythology, history, agronomy, linguistics, anthropology, genetics, and Native and subsequent American folkways and foodways. The chapters contrasting Native American corn cultures with our own produce ironic refractions of two mutually incompatible myths, neatly dichotomized by the food historian Janice B. Longone as "Mother Maize and King Corn."

All this is fine: the information is freshly imagined and vividly presented. But if Fussell's most striking talent is her ability to pull together and somehow connect an enormous amount of material, her major flaw is her unwillingness to ever linger long with any part of it to listen to what it has to say. When, for instance, she attempts to follow Sarah Rutledge's recipe for baking johnnycake on a slant board before an open fire, the effort exhibits much less interest in colonial hearth baking than in cranking out still more descriptive grist for her eternally turning empathetic mill.

> The first cake slid off whole into the ashes. The next cake stuck to the board in patches, some burned, some gummily raw. Caked with smoke, front red with heat and back blue with cold and stiff from bending, I had new respect for my ancestral grandmothers.

Her ancestral grandmothers would shrug that respect off. Their pride came from doing the task well, and Fussell has no interest in staying around that long. Consequently, her passage tells us no more than "I tried. It was hard. So I quit."

Nothing can weigh more heavily on a reader than such facile empathy spread over three hundred pages of densely worded text, especially when it substitutes incantation for understanding:

> We too had our feasts of new corn, our rites of fertility shaped by husking the corn, loosening the silk, letting the juice run free. These were not just echoes of ceremonies indigenous to the first people of corn. We had formed rites in common, given them . . . our Babel of voices. We made of the cornfields our own heaven and hell, transformed our own pollen words into immutable turquoise and jade, the inner forms "where the gods come and go." Corn was our mutual birthright, corn was our home.

Such passages at first make *The Story of Corn* feel like a vertiginous elevator ride straight down to the bottom floor of the American soul. But they become merely wearisome when, time after time, you emerge from your ride to find that—despite the velocity of the plunge and the wild rattlings of the cage—you don't seem to have descended very far down at all.

To understand the importance of corn to the American experience, you have to patiently dig, down below the images of corn shocks under a harvest moon, the corn-fed beef, cornmash bourbon, and corn-husking bees, down to the depth Wright Morris brings us to in *Home Place*:

> The figure in the carpet, if there is a carpet, is corn. Corn, I guess, is the grass that grows wherever the land is—as Whitman put it—and sometimes it grows whether the water is there or not. No it isn't the carpet. It's under the carpet. Corn is the floor.

What can this mean? As writer after writer has testified, starting with John Lawson in 1709, who wrote in *A New Voyage to Carolina*:

> The Indian corn or Maize proves the most useful Grain in the World; and had it not been for the fruitfulness of this species, it would have proved very difficult to have settled some of the Plantations in America.

Difficult? In many instances, without corn, it would have been hopeless. Corn is the floor because it made America possible.

To understand the full import of this statement, however, you must remember that, for many Native Americans, corn was the great mother goddess, upon whose gift their entire culture and life depended. What did *they* think, then, when this same gift turned against them, by making it possible for the foreign invaders to prosper, grow strong, and ultimately supplant them? There were no outposts of American expansion without the surrounding cornfields, rank after rank of turncoats who had opportunistically abandoned the people who had previously given them their total devotion and care. Take *this* perspective back to those Zuñi Indians and you begin to feel the twitchings of something rather disquieting.

If you do feel this, it is despite Fussell's efforts, not because of them. Corn, to her, is simply a miracle plant, a self-evident good thing. Because of that, her weakest pages attempt to tie corn to her own family's history—weak not only because of the banality of the idea but because of its arbitrariness. She and we would all be just as American—only *different*—if corn had never existed. The question the material in this book raises but its author never really faces is what this difference *is*, and whether—for Native Americans, for us, for humankind—that difference has been for the good.

If this seems a strange statement, it is. But corn is itself a strange thing. It is the one food plant completely unable to replicate itself without man's help. Those tight husks keep the kernels from germinating, even if they fall on the ground; should the husks be ripped open, the seeds are so closely packed that they strangle each other. Corn needs men to plant it . . . and it has been supremely successful over the centuries in making them do this, by making us at least as dependent on it as it is on us.

That "at least" was what increasingly came to haunt me as I read my way through this book. Corn began to take on the visage of an alien creature of human height and of strangely human shape—waving limp arms and stringy yellow hair and sporting a sheath-wrapped phallus, one that arrived bearing the one gift men have never been able to refuse: a promise to take care of them forever.

Corn is nearly a perfect food; more important, it grows in almost any circumstance, not only supporting men generously in fertile places but also allowing them to eke out an existence in places where they could never live before. Also, its "leaves, stalks, husks and cobs were transformed into mats, trays, cushions, hammocks, scrub brushes, moccasins, feather holders, bottle stoppers, comb and back scratchers."

This mysterious visitor, irreversibly become indigenous resident, now starts to absorb men's minds, working its way into the center of their culture, capturing their dreams. Its wealth nurtures a civilization; cities surround huge temples where human sacrifices in its honor are performed. This culture is at once highly wrought and icy cold; it is not only sinisterly inhuman but hollow within. A few strangers arrive from across the sea and the whole thing comes crashing down. About all this, our alien visitor feels neither remorse nor pain. Instead, its limp fronds reach out to these brash newcomers, offering them its same, unrefusable gift.

Soon they, too, begin building corn palaces and holding corn dances. They get drunk on corn liquor and sustain themselves with cornbread. Later, corn, in the form of chemical components broken out of corn-starch, becomes a vital industrial component and food additive. (This is dramatically captured in a painting in the manner of Thomas Hart Benton, used to illustrate Fussell's book, which shows a continuous stream of flatcars, each bearing a giant ear of corn, rolling through a series of processing plants and emerging laden with equally giant cans of Coca-Cola.)

Nature's generous bounty? Maybe—but also maybe something else. Despite Native American myths and our own fond imaginings, nature's role is not that of our handmaiden . . . or, for that matter, our wise guardian. Nature has its own agenda, and humankind is sometimes its beneficiary—but always its pawn. As Lawrence Osborne wrote in *Paris Dreambook*, his disquieting, black-edged tour of the City of Light:

> Food is not an innocent and sweet trifle to be played with, even though it appears to waltz so benignly upon our plates and tables. It is nature herself, stupid, cruel, and ruthless. Everything is food, including yourselves, even if it is only bacteria which eat you now. Nature is . . . no other than the mindless sadist who has commanded all living things to eat all other living things with a perpetual and inane violence . . . and whose supposed capacity to maintain harmonious order is merely the effect of the relentless whip that ensures continual discontinuity, the stick which flagellates every beast on its path to consumption.

This disturbing truth hunkers in the shadows, always just outside the author's ken—or at least her relentless soft focus. In the book's con-cluding passage, the author quotes approvingly from Stanley Kunitz:

> The old myths, the old gods, the old heroes have never died. They are only sleeping at the bottom of our minds, waiting for our call.

The Story of Corn turns out to be just such a summoning, and, as well, an unwitting reminder that what comes out of the darkness isn't always what the beckoner expects.

Karen Hess is the antithesis of Betty Fussell, and the last word to come to mind reading *The Carolina Rice Kitchen* would be "romance." In these pages there are no hikes up the Andes or belly flops into Zuñi mud fields. In fact, although the book is about the rice culture of the Carolinas, focusing on a Charleston cookbook, the author's first visit to that city took place after the work was published.

Initially at least, the reader may wish that Karen Hess had taken from Betty Fussell a little of her imaginative brio. Despite the title, nowhere in these pages is any effort made to bring a particular Carolina rice kitchen to life—that is, to empathetically re-create the smells, sounds, and sights that would greet us if we were allowed in. On the contrary, Karen Hess keeps her—and so the reader's—imagination on a tight rein. There is not only no embroidery, there are none of those quick and vivid sketches of time and place that bring an unfamiliar world to life.

Anyone thinking of tackling these pages must begin by facing the simple truth: this is determinedly *not* a reader-friendly book. The argument can be abstruse and hard for a nonexpert to follow, especially because the author, knowing most readers are unlikely to consult footnotes, crowbars them into the text itself. Those out of practice leaping parenthetical hurdles will quickly find themselves losing wind. Readers for whom a book is an all-or-nothing proposition are faced here with a difficult choice. But those of us who audited courses we'd never dare take for credit will know the strategies. Dig them out. This book is worth the fight.

Let it be said at the start that I rarely read food histories. Life is short and history's midden inexhaustible. Unless you are born with a flea-market sensibility, after one or two books' worth, all piles of culinary oddments begin to look the same. Karen Hess is different. She leaves you, when you put any of her volumes down, not with a handful of trinkets . . . but with an opened, chastened mind.

We, all of us, condescend to those who came before us. We, after all, are the clever ones, the living; they, poor fools, are dead. On one page of *The Story of Corn*, Betty Fussell shows a cross-section of a slave ship, crammed with the bodies of slaves, and blithely writes that it "seems to disclose a giant ear of corn with paired rows of slaves for kernels." The romance writer uses history as an opiate; the serious historian as a purgative.

Hess's method is persuasively simple: she uses primary sources to cut through the accreted barrier reef of evasions, pretensions, misapprehensions, and outright lies of preceding historians and food writers (including me) that has been built around a subject until she breaks through it to the raw historical truth.

For example, it has always been acknowledged that slave labor made rice an American crop, but as Karen Hess reveals in one of the most intellectually satisfying sections of her book, it was these same slaves who also taught Americans how to grow it. Not only did Carolina Gold, the rice that made the Carolinas wealthy (and their name synonymous with fine rice) most probably come from Africa, it was only as the plantation managers "found knowledgeable workers steeped in the lore of cultivating rice, meaning slaves from West African rice lands, [that] things moved apace." When, centuries later, blacks were free to choose their employment elsewhere and did so, the Carolina rice empire collapsed.

Even so, black laborers have been relentlessly portrayed as brutes bought only for their ability to bear the punishing labor that rice cultivation demands. In truth, plantation owners assiduously sought out Africans captured on the Windward Coast (Sierra Leone), a portion of which was then known as the "Rice Coast." These were a people who had mastered the difficult agricultural techniques required for paddy rice growing and successfully transposed them to this country.

Africans also brought their culinary skills to this continent and to Carolina kitchens. They weren't the only influence on Carolina rice cooking—this was a time when Charleston was an urbane and cultured center, enriched by contributions from Huguenot French, Sephardic Jews, and other minorities, and Hess meticulously traces the presence of their various culinary hands in the city's wealth of pilaus.

However, only Africans brought to America an authentic "rice kitchen," which is to say a cuisine where rice was traditionally and unself-consciously central to the eater's sense of identity and well-being. The African-American rice kitchen is a defining feature of Deep South regional cooking—wherever, in fact, hoppin' John holds sway. And to this day, as Hess also points out, only in areas where black cooking is still a dominant influence do Americans know how to cook perfect rice.

The purpose of *The Carolina Rice Kitchen* is to explain to the rest of us what our one native rice culture was all about—where it came from, what its dishes were, and how those who participated in it cooked their rice (this last explained in what may be the most sensitive and instructive chapter on the cooking of plain rice ever written)—and so to serve as an explication of the recipes contained in the facsimile edition reprinted as the second half of this book.

The *Carolina Rice Cook Book* was compiled by Mrs. Samuel G. Stoney as a souvenir to be sold at the South Carolina Interstate and West Indian Exposition, held at the turn of the century. Its 237 recipes were taken from various Southern cookbooks and contributed by interested Carolina

Low Country society ladies, who, no doubt, got them from their cooks. It was a publication issued in the twilight of Carolina rice cooking and, unintentionally, served as its elegy, since Carolina rice culture was to come to an end a decade later. However, the dishes have endured, and in her commentary on the pilaus, on hoppin' John and jambalaya and the various rice breads, Karen Hess makes us understand—and feel— what the mourning might be all about.

Unlike *The Story of Corn*, *The Carolina Rice Kitchen* deals with real mysteries in a real way. It portrays the act of understanding as a struggle against the odds, not a sustained swoon. Karen Hess makes her readers work hard, but those who stay the course receive genuine goods in return. They will learn, or at least begin to understand *how* to learn, to cook rice. They will also come to see that the goal of such an undertaking is not to root about until one finally uncovers the flawless amphora but instead to try to make out what one can from the random potsherds that lie everywhere underfoot. People often fail to record the things that ultimately matter; when they do, the records can be lost, altered, intentionally destroyed, or, as often, persistently misread.

We are all human, yes, but cultures are no more interchangeable than consciousnesses. The past is not a place where our imagination can roam at will, helping itself to whatever it finds. Those who treat it that way can do irrevocable damage to its fragile ecology. As this difficult book makes clear, authentic knowledge of the past is the same as authentic knowledge of oneself: hard-won and fraught with risk.

STEUBEN, 1993

Walking the Wild Side

A recent story in *The Ellsworth American*, our local "big-city" newspaper, recorded the death of Reggie Sherman, a lobsterman. He encountered something that happens to lobstermen more than they want to admit: they pull up a trap, clean it, bait it, and toss it back, not noticing that this one time they've stepped over a coil of the rope. A trap, especially one of the old, wooden sort, is heavy enough to drag a man overboard. Even if it doesn't pull him underwater, if he can't get at the rope or back into the boat, he drowns. Some lobstermen carry a knife in their boot for just this eventuality. Reggie Sherman either didn't or couldn't get to it quickly enough.

One distinction to be made between country and city life is that people who work in the country run the risk of getting seriously hurt and even dying on the job. Lumbermen, fishermen, linemen, farmers— almost all of them know someone this has happened to, and many know several. Those who struggle to understand why men hunt, as many of these men do, might start with this sense of the casual closeness of death. It is something you tend to take personally, and one way of arguing out the experience is with a fly rod, a shotgun, or a .30–.30 deer rifle.

This casual intimacy with death and its disquieting effect on one's perceptions of everyday life can be felt as a powerful undertow in much of Jim Harrison's fiction—*Sundog, Dalva, The Woman Lit by Fireflies*— and poetry—*The Theory and Practice of Rivers*. In *Just Before Dark*, a highly personal collection of essays, several of them on cooking and eating and many more on hunting (for Harrison, all closely related activities), it bursts up to the surface and all but sweeps the reader away.

Harrison lives on a farm in Michigan and comes "from many generations of unprosperous farmers." His father got out by becoming a government agricultural agent; he himself has taken another big step away. But the land still has a hold on him and so do the people who work it.

> Another short event: our Labor Day beef roast with a whole side of rare beef, plus two roasts, a barrel of sweet corn, beans, kegs of cider, cases of whiskey . . . To say it was a hog show is to give the finger improperly to the pigs. People danced, sometimes rolling on the ground. There was a fistfight over the twin questions of cherry farming and deer hunting. So much brave irreverence, and hormones, spilling over wantonly.

In these pages you feel how the physicality of things bears down hard on the spirit as well as the body of those who have to wrest their living from the land. People deal with this in different ways, and otherwise unconnected essays in *Just Before Dark* cohere into a long, brooding look at what some of those ways are.

Harrison's writing has about it too much of a midnight conversation in a bus station with a slightly nervous-making stranger to be long confused with ordinary nature writing. Even so, the pull of the land is there, not only in the subject matter, but also in his hypersensitivity to landscape and his prodigality with the kind of small observations a writer can never make up because they're at once too out of nowhere and too perfect—a bird squeezing its eyes shut as it lays an egg.

In his food writing Harrison is an unapologetic, no-holds-barred, old-fashioned gourmand. My surprise at that, however, only caught out my own suburban soul. A keenly attentive gluttony has always been closely connected—at least outside of food writing—with this same personal quarrel with death.

> At the hotel's Sunday brunch, I got a "tsk-tsk" from the waitress when I failed to polish off the plate of fruit and basket of breads, the platter of eggs, bacon, ham, real beef hash, and chicken livers, which was followed by an assortment of desserts, including a whipped-cream-stuffed pastry swan. My error was reading during the meal—Bernd Heinrich's *Ravens in Winter*, from which I learned that in the late forties in Illinois, 100,000 crows were destroyed in a single night by hand grenades. This was the American version of Cortés burning the aviaries of Montezuma, and it put me off my feed.

If you think this sentiment is pretty rich, coming from an unrepentant duck hunter, you don't understand that the aesthetics of hunting are built out of intimacy, and that there's none of either in blowing up thousands of crows. This sort of slaughter leaches out the meaning of a hunter's act with a virulence akin to, say, what prejudice does to the fabric of human connection.

The phrase "country cooking" has such knee-jerk, platitudinous associations with trestle tables laden with smothered pork chops and fresh-baked, lard-crust pies that it discourages us from immediately connecting the product and the pig. Real country appetites know that link. "No animal's cries were more anguished in my forty-year-old barn-yard memories," Harrison writes, than "the unearthly screams of the butchered piglet." Serious shooting/serious gourmandizing: the flip sides of an orgy of death.

> A few years back when we were quite poor, lower-class by all the charts, we had a game dinner at our house. There were about twelve people contributing food, and with a check for a long poem I bought two cases of a white Bordeaux. We ate, fixed in a number of ways, venison, duck, trout, woodcock, snipe, grouse, rabbit, and drank both cases of wine.

Accept this and it seems to me no subtle understanding is needed to trace the appetite of the boy who hungered for his first .22 rifle to that of the successful writer who sits down to a meal in a Normandy *auberge* of

> saddle of wild boar, a 1928 Anjou with fresh pâté de foie gras in slabs, trout laced with truffles, *côtelettes* of loin from a small forest deer called a *chevreuil*, pheasant baked under clay with wild mushrooms.

Killing, eating, and writing: these not necessarily harmonious obsessions have brought him to stranger places than the table of a French country inn.

There are some, I know, who will not accept this. For them, Harrison's gastronomic excesses are nothing more than drinking sprees, with food replacing part of the booze. Certainly they produce a similar uneasiness—half-boastful, half-remorseful—at the other side. But even if this is so, I may not be wrong in finding something more interesting going on as well—just as others do in the writing of Charles Bukowski. I feel a powerful and poignant moral illumination in Harrison's refusal, on the one hand, to accept limits and, on the other, to close his eyes to the consequences. I feel the same tidal pull, but I don't have the character to knowingly pay the price that comes of yielding to it—and just enough to know what happens when you pretend that there is no price, or that it can be perpetually deferred.

In any case, there is much more to Harrison than this. Recently I came across an essay by him in *Antaeus*, a fierce and fine defense of poetry in general and Native American poetry in particular. In the weavy way of his prose, he pauses at one point to remember himself

> as a young bohemian discovering garlic in New York City in 1957 when a Barnard girl made me listen to Richard Tucker sing something from Jewish liturgy. I was swept away by beauty, also jealousy, as the music was so powerful and unlike the sodden Protestant hymns of my youth. I felt the same thing in St. Basil's Cathedral in Leningrad, where I was told that in the Russian Orthodox Church, one does not talk to God, one sings.

A sensibility that steps without pause from garlic to the glory of listening to Richard Tucker singing from the Jewish liturgy has the ability to take food writing where it has never gone before—and on the sunny as well as the dark side of the street.

Only the first fifty pages of *Just Before Dark* are specifically about eating, but death and food are an inextricable part of much of Jim Harrison's *oeuvre*. His writing never manages to get far from images of disturbing violence—some absorbed from observation, others from the ruptures of the heart—and the solace of fighting, feeding, and, sometimes, flight. Read him not for moral uplift but for the scouring of reckless honesty, the obsessive urgency of hunger and fear, and the abrasively beautiful poetry of a wounded psyche in a wounded land.

STEUBEN, 1991

Italian-American

Although Edward Giobbi's *Italian Family Cooking* was first published by Random House in 1971, I didn't get hold of a copy until the paperback was released in 1978. There are many reasons why, at the time, this book should have been my culinary lifeline. I had started to think about building a personal cuisine out of patient devotion to a few well-chosen, well-loved ingredients, and that was just what Giobbi himself had done. His book proposed a way of cooking that sprang from food he had raised himself and bread he had baked himself, and from simple recipes resonant with family memory. Why, then, did I *resist* the book so much? Why instead of embracing it as a friend, did I find myself keeping it at arm's length?

Well, to start with a little unflattering honesty, I was extremely jealous of Ed Giobbi. This was not so much because of his cooking but because, unlike me, he came from a family that openly, even aggressively, celebrated its ethnic roots.

If I didn't realize this at the time, I know it now. When I sat down in 1982 to write my own first, never-finished cookbook, I began it with a preface in which I imagined such an ethnic family gathering around the table for a special feast. I wrote ironically, my point being that most of us are born into families that don't possess anything like this open sensual awareness of the pleasures of the table. But the irony melted away somewhere in the first few paragraphs; the rest was pure longing.

No reader can spend time with *Italian Family Cooking* without soon coming to realize the equal importance of each of the three words in its title: it is as much about family and ethnic identity as it is about food. The illustrations for the book were done by Giobbi's children; the recipes were gathered from his parents, grandparents, uncles, and aunts.

These people are all palpably present in his pages: his father, walking with him past the cages of small North American mammals in the Central Park Zoo and telling him how he would cook them; his grandfather, at seventy-five, still climbing his favorite fig tree to pick its fruit for his breakfast; and his Aunt Ada, at her farm in Centobuchi, teaching him how to make a wonderful pasta sauce out of a beef bone, chicken feet, a chicken head, and a piece of salt pork.

Last but not least was his godfather, Tommaso, a former coal miner who ate two pounds of pasta at every meal without ever getting fat. A bachelor, he made a superb meat sauce that none of the Italian women in the neighborhood could duplicate. (Giobbi's mother admitted this, but she also added that this was because he didn't clean his pots as thoroughly as the women cleaned theirs.)

This enchanted me. It also conveyed a life from which I was entirely excluded. I could have imitated Ed Giobbi, yes, but that wasn't the same as *being* him. All the Italian cooking in the world wouldn't give me an aunt in Centobuchi. More to the point, in my particular instance, it couldn't connect me to the relations of my great-grandfather Matteo Ciravegna, from Fossano, in the Piedmont . . . a place which for the first time in my life I have now actually located on a map.

Unlike Achille Giobbi, Giobbi's father, my great-grandfather turned his back on his origins, adopting an entirely new (and entirely Anglicized) name on his arrival at Ellis Island in 1887. As best as I can understand it, his reason for this was that the Piedmont had become part of Italy only in the year of his birth, 1860. An artisan with no fixed abode, he lived in France before he came to the United States, and would move again to Kiel, in Germany, before settling down for good near Boston, then a hotbed of anti-Italian prejudice.

Consequently, he invested his need for fraternal bonding in Freemasonry, not church or family. When in Kiel, he had married a German, and his son, my grandfather (all this on my mother's side), although possessing the profile of a Renaissance cardinal, considered himself, if anything, German. Grampa married Nana, a woman of Irish descent whose sense of self-pride came more from gentility than from ethnicity. So, although my mother grew up in an Irish-Italian neighborhood, her identity was one of lace-curtain apartness. In that place and time, any benefits ethnic identity possessed seemed retrograde: it made you either a victim of or a self-conscious reveler in parochial prejudice.

A generation later, my own lack of ethnic identity at first seemed a liberation from familial claims, an affirmation that I could make my life as I wished. What I hadn't expected was the force with which this freedom, in certain circumstances, could invert itself into an absence, a feeling that something vital was missing. Whatever name you choose to give this lack, it is obvious that something more than hunger was being assuaged in my appetite for ethnic cookbooks . . . or, rather, by the way that their authors made a point of wrapping an arm around me, introducing me to everyone, and pulling out a chair for me at the family repast.

I'm not, I think, the only one to discover in myself an almost Pavlovian response to this kind of genial embrace, nor is it necessarily a criticism to point out the measure of calculation in its effect. One way ethnic minorities have won over the sympathy of exclusive majorities has been to play the big-hearted clown. Food writers who stress their ethnicity have gotten much useful mileage from the ploy, sometimes blatantly—as witness Dom DeLuise in what is actually a first-rate Italian-American cookbook, *Eat This . . . It'll Make You Feel Better*— and sometimes slyly—in the manner of Angelo Pellegrini, *paisano*-philosopher of the kitchen garden and wine cellar. It not only disarms an outsider's uneasy sense of exclusion, but wards off any jealousy. Ethnicity is made to appear as warm and comforting as a hot bowl of soup, soothing a heartache that, before, one hardly realized was there.

The problem is that the comfort these books offer is only an illusion. After we shake Angelo's proferred hand or gratefully kiss that of Vincenza DeLuise (Dom's mother and that family's culinary genius) and go out the door, we become our normal de-ethnicized selves again, no longer any kin to the merriment that still pours from the window. This, and no more, is what it means to be, for an evening, an "honorary Italian."

These books at once reinforce and benefit from our emotional—and hence uncritical—association of ethnicity with warm family ties. Giobbi also utilizes this connection, but in a subtler and consequently more persuasive way.

In the *Pleasures of the Good Earth*, Giobbi continues the tale of *Italian Family Cooking*, explaining what he has done with his patrimony. As he reveals how he grows his own vegetables, raises his ducks and chickens, vinifies grapes into wine, ferments vinegar, and cures prosciutto, he is also making a case for the father not only as breadwinner but as bread *maker*, the literal provider of food for his family.

These two books are replete with the physical acts of provisioning—

tasks handed down from grandfather to father to son—providing both a experientially rich and an emotionally compelling case for the primal role of the father.

This vision is so pervasive that I suspect few of his readers are conscious—at least at first—of the extent to which *men* dominate his pages: Giobbi himself, his father, his grandfather, and his godfather, surely something unusual in an ethnic family cookbook. It is a beneficent patriarchy, but a patriarchy nonetheless.

> In 1966 my father died, and when the wine-making season arrived, I was faced with a dilemma. I did not think I would be able to make wine. Furthermore, it was much easier to buy it. But what about the wine-making tradition that had existed in our family for centuries? God only knows how many centuries! The thought of this tradition dying out because of me gave me pause. Finally I decided that I didn't have the right to deprive my children of that tradition, that it was up to me to carry it on and pass it along to them.

Although this passage occurs at the very end of *Pleasures of the Good Earth*, it captures the wealth of sentiment that fills Giobbi's father-dominated universe. This and his ability to capture its physical tangibility return to the word "husband" its primary meaning: the grower and preserver of that from which the family takes its sustenance.

Husbandry: even though the word is never used, Giobbi's desire to give back to that word both sensual reality and moral urgency can be heard from the very first sentence:

> I think that no matter how old or infirm I may become, I will always plant a large garden in the spring . . . It is one of the most natural human instincts to want to make things grow, to nourish our own bodies and those of the ones we love.

This almost mystical union of obligation and pleasure adds luster to all the pages that follow, a luster made deeper by the accompanying sense of assimilated heritage. When he writes:

> Like other Italians, I rarely use ripe tomatoes in salads. We prefer tomatoes that are half-green, with just a blush of red—unripe-looking ones, in fact . . .

he is speaking for himself, his father and grandfather, all avid tomato growers, harvesters, eaters.

Unlike most cookbooks, which take on authority from the strength of their recipes, in this one it is Giobbi's imaginative adaptability in the role of gardener-cook that makes us pay attention to his food. His dishes have a homespun Italian rusticity to them that can belie their actual sophistication. Giobbi is the child of his parents, but he is also his own cook.

This is one of the few garden cookbooks that manage to convey—and, in doing so, risk a certain sense of sameness to the recipes—how it feels to produce meals from what has been brought in from the garden, the herb patch, and the chicken coop. Giobbi teaches us to read the profusion of his vegetable medleys as a strategy for dealing with a burgeoning garden and finally to see the river of tomato sauce that flows through these pages as the resourcefulness of a stubborn peasant with a cupboard stacked with quart-sized jars of the stuff.

In fact, reading these books together offers a unique opportunity to observe the evolution of the sensibility of an extremely gifted cook, especially since, while the first book emphasizes the traditional dishes of his family, the new one shows what he has done with them—dishes and tradition both.*

The author, however, is less interested in describing his culinary development than in laying out the case for something altogether different: a personal ethos, which, for lack of a better phrase, might be described as a kind of Catholicism minus the religion. These two books are about a life committed to family and good works, which to him means living out the role of husband and father. It is this subtext that depends so heavily on our positive associations of ethnicity and family. By persuading us to value what he does and need what he has, he also convinces us to uncritically assent to who he is.

Ed Giobbi, like all of us, no matter our individual faith or lack of it, lives in a culture driven by the Protestant-work-ethic dread of wasting time. Despite lip service to leisure (the Protestant heaven minus God), this ethic, by making time precious, makes everything that costs time a luxury . . . even things as basic as cooking a meal from scratch.

All of us block off certain areas of experience and exempt them from this moral cost accounting; otherwise novels would never get read or

---

* This narrative becomes even more complex if one includes Giobbi's *second* cookbook, *Eat Right, Eat Well—The Italian Way* (1985), a tour-de-force collection of low-cholesterol recipes which has left its trace on his everyday cooking. In the new book, for instance, a recipe for duck with lentils is taken almost word for word from *Italian Family Cooking*, but it omits half a cup of minced salt pork. Similarly, in a recipe for asparagus with shrimp, the cooking fat in the first book, half butter and half olive oil, becomes all olive oil in the new one. This latter dish is also simplified and made stronger: Giobbi eliminates tomato, celery, and fresh mint, transforming it into a more sharply focused, garlicky sauté of asparagus and shrimp.

gardens planted. But a whole life paced to the slowness of the earth is more than a luxury; it is stubbornness enlarged into rebellion. Giobbi's vision of an ethnic patriarchy is a subversive, liberating act of defiance. The values of his *contadino* ancestors have provided him with an identity which serves as a sea anchor against the constant drag of modernity and its erosion of personal time, allowing him the freedom to paint pictures, raise a family, grow his vegetables, hunt mushrooms in the woods.

Our culture, of course, is highly censorious of those who elect this path, which is why, attractive as it is, most of us are dissuaded from following it. Giobbi's response is to claim the moral high ground (as, in a more polemical way, the writer-farmer Wendell Berry has done in books like *Standing on Earth*). Unfortunately, this moral positioning means that Giobbi sometimes writes as if from some distant place, miles away from the world of supermarkets and the compromises—about food and other things—that most of us face in our own daily lives.

Here is precisely where my original sense of unease, of exclusion, returns. At least part of the persuasive power of this book is accomplished by omission. Since Giobbi raises no cows, such contemporary commonplaces as sterilized milk and ultrapasteurized cream are simply not discussed. He deals in the same way with the flaws of the ethnocentric, patriarchal universe: if there are no trips to the IGA in *Pleasures of the Good Earth*, neither are there disaffected children or incredulous wives or lives crippled by insularity and close-mindedness.

Insularity is present here, but the reader comes to notice it only obliquely. The radiant heat that suffuses the charmed world of these pages is kept entirely within them. Giobbi is willing enough to take us into his garden and show us his kitchen, but he stops short of inviting us to sit down at the family table. In the true Old World tradition, strangers and family are kept firmly, if unobtrusively, apart.

Thus, as in other ethnic cookbook narratives, the reader retains the role of outsider looking into a closely knit familial universe . . . only this time is left to feel like a prodigal son who, standing indecisively at the gate, suddenly realizes that no one here is going to embrace him and welcome him home.

This sense of exclusion may not be intentional, but that of a paternal barrier certainly is. The father is not only the family provider in patriarchal societies, he is also the family protector, the guardian at the threshold. This is the reason that, as much as I admire this book, I also feel that it means to keep me at a certain distance. Childless, suspicious of fathers, unable to get a firm handhold on my family roots—I find no place at this table set for me.

Other readers—men, especially—may seize hold of Giobbi's image of the providing, nurturing father/husband as an inspiration to re-imagining their own parental and marital roles. But they may also discover that, without a strong ethnic identity of their own to use as a fulcrum, this vision of the good life, despite its concreteness, is disappointingly ephemeral—that, for all their genuine virtues, these two books portray a utopia that offers everything . . . except the way in.

STEUBEN, 1992

Road Food

New England/Mid-Atlantic Roadside Delights, WILL ANDERSON

American Diner: Then and Now, RICHARD J.S. GUTMAN

Diners, JOHN BAEDER

Diners: People, and Places, GERD KITTEL

I grew up in the back seat of the family Buick. For one reason or another, we were always on the road . . . en route to the next army base that would be our new home, returning to New England each summer to see the folks, or just heading out of town for one of the long drives that filled our Sunday afternoons. When my mother told me to stop poring over the pile of comic books in my lap and look at the view, I would lift my eyes to find Kansas plains, Texas deserts, New Mexico mountains, Hawaiian sugarcane fields rolling past outside.

Big thrill. But when we came to a town, I stared and stared. To a child, roadside architecture and billboards are as much a part of the landscape as redwood forests or rolling farmland—and, more often than not, a lot more interesting. I learned to read in Japan, and I can still remember how ravished with pleasure I was when, on coming back to the States, I discovered that that knack, hitherto useful only with books, now let me decipher an entire world. For years, I never passed a sign I didn't want to read, usually out loud. I was a kid to get out of any city as fast as possible.

All this returned to me perusing two self-published books by Will Anderson, *New England* and *Mid-Atlantic Roadside Delights*. Each is a colorful collection of matchbook covers, postcards, advertising throwaways, and photographs of and from filling stations; motor lodges, cabins, and motels; billboards; drive-in theaters; and, naturally, every kind of eatery—diners, clam shacks, ice-cream and root-beer stands, hot-dog and hamburger joints, pancake palaces—you name it. Leafing through them, I found myself transported back into the old Buick Super's rear seat. *This* is my U.S.A.

I was just in time. The heyday of roadside vernacular signage and architecture occurred between the Depression and the arrival of post–Korean War prosperity. The Eisenhower years inaugurated corporate-chain-inspired "good taste" (a combination of money and professional design) that would bring about the demise of the cheaper but more playful—and often more inspired—individualist creations.

I don't mean by this the particularly outrageous examples—ice-cream stands built to resemble a milk bottle or an ice-cream carton with a spoon stuck in the top—but the innocent, comic-book stylizing common to them all: the gaudy neon sign, the snappy name (the Koffee Kottage, the Bon Ton Café), the unwittingly humble boast ("New England's most modern dining car," "Hi-Test Ice Cream") emblazoned on the giveaway paper-wrapped toothpicks or matchbook covers.

Some of these places are still around—and when they are, Anderson gives all the particulars to help you find them—but for the most part they are gone, gone, gone. Certainly they are gone in the sense that in my own childhood they were the rule, and today they are, at best, the rare exception. As Richard Ford writes in his novel *Independence Day*:

> Everybody over forty (unless they were born in the Bronx) has pristine and un-complicated memories of such places: low, orange-painted wooden bunker boxes with sliding-screen customers' windows, strings of yellow bulbs outside, white-washed tree trunks and trash barrels, white car tires designating proper parking etiquette, plenty of instructional signs on the trees and big frozen mugs of too-cold root beer you could enjoy on picnic tables by a brook or else drink off metal trays with your squeeze in the dark, radio-lit sanctity of your '57 Ford.

This theater of the road is what animates both Will Anderson's imagination and his books, which are built up out of a fascinating mélange of artifacts—in fact, almost everything along the roadside that would capture the attention of a child. I know this because Will himself several times drove past, without noticing, a great big green fiberglass dinosaur (Sinclair gasoline's mascot, "Dino") perched on the roof of Conroy's

Garage in Pine Point, Maine. However, his eight-year-old friend, Austin Ward, spotted it on every trip.

In the past several years here in Maine, I've watched the doughnut shop fade into near-extinction, leaving only the roadside ice-cream stand, the sandwich shop, the hot-dog vendor, and the meal truck as the last vigorous examples of the vernacular specialized eatery. However, the one that generates the most interest, here and everywhere, is the diner—even though the number of surviving specimens in most areas of this or any state can be counted on one hand.

The diner, in other words, is much more successful at generating nostalgia than business, except for the ones—and their number is not inconsiderable—where that same nostalgia has been turned into very profitable business. As often as not, however, once the owners of such places step onto the slippery slope of kitsch—posters of James Dean and Marilyn Monroe on the walls, cute neon signs cluttering the windows, a pink Cadillac perched on the roof—they discover too late that, whatever their original intentions, they are no longer running a diner but a diner-shaped toy.

This isn't an activity restricted to fifties-crazed entrepreneurs with Elvis or Roy Orbison on the brain. Young American chefs, having reconceptualized the grill, the roadhouse, and the BBQ joint to their own tastes, have taken on the diner, too. A notable example of this sort of thematization is San Francisco's trendy, upscale Fog City Diner. As one of its co-owners, Bill Higgins, revealingly states in his introduction to *The Fog City Diner Cookbook*:

> Everybody loves a diner. Why? It's comfortable, and it's affordable. It's unintimidating. It's accommodating. It's American. It's colorful. It's shiny. And it's fun. We just added . . . what's happening today.

For Higgins, what's happening today includes an oyster bar, a serious bar bar (sixteen single malt whiskies, no blender drinks), and reservations—not the usual diner accouterments. The Fog City Diner is not in any real sense a diner at all; it's a place where *everybody*—customers and staff alike—can play diner in a lightheartedly funky atmosphere where DON'T WORRY is spelled out on the illuminated wall clock and NO CRYBABIES on the front door.

Which is only to say that diner play is one thing and diner reality another. The diner started out as a horse-drawn cart, direct kin to the meal trucks that today tour the parking lots of perimeter businesses, dispensing java and Danishes at coffee break and short-order meals at all hours. Then, as now, it was mobile because its customers weren't— but unlike today's motor-driven meal trucks, it wasn't all *that* mobile (in this regard, it's analogous to its first cousin, the "mobile" home). If it found a good corner, it preferred to remain there, eventually blocking up its wheels for good.

For most people, it is the diner's emblematic if idiosyncratic, railroad-car shape that makes it a "diner," a shape that, as it happens, evolved only out of pure necessity into intentional design. Because diners were manufactured elsewhere and delivered by rail, their cartlike shape could be elongated but only slightly widened. As they were drawn out, they came to more and more resemble the similarly shaped (and for the same reasons) railroad dining car. Soon diner makers were going out of their way to emphasize this connection—a railway car, after all, was more prestigious than a cart. Eventually, function vanishing into form, the immobile diner became more streamlined than the real thing.*

And so we arrive at that eatery's golden age in the late 1930s, when diner makers—O'Mahony, Paramount, Silk City, Sterling, DeRaffele— like car manufacturers would in the 1950s, attempted to differentiate what was essentially the same product with increasingly exaggerated statements of style. Step into a 1940s Paramount and you encounter a dizzyingly Art Deco interior with fluted stool columns, octagonal seats, "tumbling blocks" floor tiles, elaborately patterned stainless-steel wall panels, and the counters and tabletops a symphony of Formica.

All this is spelled out in loving detail in Richard J.S. Gutman's *American Diner: Then and Now, the* book to turn to if you're interested in diner-spotting. Gutman's particular interest is the history of diner construction and design and the continual challenge of operating them. He has collected an astonishing amount of information—including a treasure trove of photographs ranging from the original "Night Owl" lunch carts to diner-factory assembly lines to single menus—from which he has fashioned an illuminating narrative history of the diner from its humble lunch-cart beginnings to its extremely depressing end as a mansard-roofed mall clone.

This is the book to tell you whether your local diner is a Paramount

---

* One imaginative owner had his diner—a Sterling Streamliner—set on actual railroad tracks and emerging from a tunnel (which, in fact, was the kitchen). The effect is so realistic that, in a photograph at least, you have the impression that you're catching a glimpse of some 1930s version of the New York–Washington, D.C., Metroliner whipping along at full throttle.

or an O'Mahony and when it was built (indeed, odds are it will be listed in the book's state-by-state directory). However, because of this emphasis, the *people* who enter his text do so in direct proportion to their relevance to his concerns: diner builders are there aplenty, diner owners to a somewhat lesser extent, the customers not at all. His book, then, is like one of those illustrated atlases of the human body—completely engrossing but also eternally abstract. This is a book full of photographs of pristine diner interiors—for the design or architecture buff, a diner touches perfection at the moment just before its owner first throws open the door. For the rest of us, however, it is only when we, the customer, step through it that the diner begins to take on life.

One interesting fact that Gutman uncovered in his research is that, almost from the moment of its inception, the diner was recognized by temperance societies as an ideal medium through which to battle demon drink, and especially to combat that insidious corrupter, the barroom's universal come-on, the free meal.

> At the time, a man could go into a saloon, buy a couple of beers for a dime, and partake of a free lunch that included pig's feet, ham and beans, bread, and other tidbits. The Church Temperance Society proceeded to serve meat, vegetables, and coffee [in their own chain of diners] for that same thin dime.

Direct temperance involvement in the diner business was, of course, short: Prohibition arrived to do its business for it. But by the time the Depression came, the diner, with its cheap eats, was an established part of the American landscape. The New York newspaperman Ed Wallace once claimed, apropos of chili parlors, that during that time "the five cent bowl of chili saved more lives than the Red Cross." I expect it did, but the diner, serving two doughnuts and a cup of coffee for a dime in the morning and a chopped ham sandwich, a bowl of chicken soup, or a hamburger for a dime the rest of the day, pulled its fair share of weight.

Also like the chili parlor, the diner was in essence a saloon without the liquor (the Fog City and its sixteen single malts to the contrary, it's rare to find a diner today that serves anything more alcoholic than beer—and many don't even offer that), with a clientele to match. The diner has always been essentially a blue-collar institution, and as the fortunes of that class rose, so at first did its.

However, as its customers moved out of their tightly knit urban neighborhoods and into the suburbs, they left the diner behind. Despite its aura of motion, the diner has always had an ambivalent relationship with the automobile. For every diner set along a highway, there were twenty others put up in the farther reaches of urban sprawl, in a landscape of linoleum-shingled triple-decker houses, battered brick factories, weed-strewn backlots, and, of course, endless stretches of railway sidings dotted with the occasional solitary boxcar. In the heart of the city you have plenty of late-night eateries; in the suburbs you first had the roadhouse, then the drive-in, and now, everywhere, fast-food emporiums of every ilk.

Affluence killed off the diner, not by offering us a better culinary deal, but by destroying its native habitat. What could look more out of place than a derailed railroad car in a landscape of malls and miracle miles? The fast-food place of today is intimately associated with automobiles—if carhops proved a short-lived fad, the same cannot be said of the drive-up window.

What has kept the diner—the real diner—alive in the face of all this is the simple fact that fast-food places are almost entirely manned by high-school kids. If you're a forty-eight-year-old driver of a fuel delivery truck, you want your food cooked and served by someone more companionable and in better synch with your own particular wavelength. Diners are still here because salesmen, UPS drivers, line workers are also still here—and feel most at home in a place where they can slide into a booth and trade wisecracks with the counterman or a world-weary waitress with a cigarette hanging out of the corner of her mouth.

You don't come close to what diners are all about unless you can work some of the atmosphere, the attitude, in—which means, at least for me, that nothing apart from parking myself in the booth of one better captures the diner experience than the work of two artists—John Baeder and Gerd Kittel—one a painter and the other a photographer. Each evokes diner truth in a way diametrically opposed to each other, but each does it so powerfully that you have to hold the work of the one next to that of the other to experience how two entirely separate visions can cohere into a still larger whole.

Baeder first. I find painting a hard thing to write about, but like everybody else, I know what I like, and John Baeder is a painter who takes my breath away. Although he is described as a "photo-realist," this phrase does him a disservice. He doesn't mimic photographs, he blows them out of the water. There are a few photographers—I think of Atget—who can give you a plain brick wall and make it wring your heart, but I think even Atget would throw up his hands before porcelain-enameled steel or linoleum siding. Baeder makes them sing.

Open the collection of his paintings, *Diners* and turn to his portrait of Scott's Bridge Diner in Mount Vernon, New York. It stands there so radiant in the crisp morning light that you don't notice at first the sheets of plywood blocking its door, or the entire window frame, wrenched from its socket and laid against the wall. Scott's has been abandoned by its owners, but not by its painter, who is as alert to the modulations of tone inherent in dirty asphalt and painted tin roofing as he is to the unbesmirchable glint of chrome or the sheen of a bright-blue-painted oil-drum trash receptacle.

Baeder can tease character out of the most nondescript working-class neighborhoods, partly by his unprejudiced receptiveness to their shy but genuine beauty, and partly because he keeps their human population entirely out of sight. It's a sad truth but, as with nature, we connect better to cityscapes with no one else around. Human absence draws out the majesty and pathos of architecture, which is why there's no better time to swim in the mood of a place than at the crack of Sunday dawn, when its inhabitants are all tucked safely away in bed.

The artist situates each of his approximately one hundred diner portraits (sixty-nine are reproduced in full color) with an affectionate narrative of how and where the artist found it and why he decided to paint it. But his feeling for them is most powerfully conveyed in the sustained painterly attention he gives to each—and the places in which they find their home. *Diners*, as it turns out, was first published in 1977. This is a revised, updated, and expanded edition. If, as I did, you missed it the first time around, be sure not to let it slip by now; this is an important and wonderful book.

Baeder is essentially a portraitist of exteriors (his book contains only one painting of an interior). Gerd Kittel's collection of photographs, *Diners: People, and Places*, also has plenty of exterior shots, but in these he has to drag in the tricks of the trade—expert framing, a judicious application of atmosphere (sunsets, stormy weather, or, best of all, the dark of night)—to hold our eye.

When he steps inside, however, something miraculous happens. Diners came in with, and help define, the meal eaten on the run; one reason the place looked speedy is that the decor suggested the reassuring fiction that, even as its customers sat and ate, the place was whisking them toward their next destination. And if, in truth, the diner wasn't going anywhere, neither were a lot of people who ate there. For them that sense of hustle shaped a different fiction—that, after eating, they actually had someplace to go.

So, at the counter you found deliverymen hurrying through the blue-plate special, while many of the booths were held by a solitary diner nursing a cup of coffee through yet another quarter hour, bemusedly considering whether the cards fate dealt him could ever be worked into a winning hand.

Kittel gets all of this. Check out the gang of loners at the Miss Portland Diner; the moody tableau glimpsed through the windows of the Teamster's Diner in Fairfield, New Jersey; the old-timer lost in his newspaper in Casey's Diner in Natick, Massachusetts. In one shot after another, Kittel reaches beyond the moment to touch the vulnerability that frames it all. The diner . . . so small in size, so limited in menu, so bogus in its chrome-plated pretense of luxury, so much like home.

CASTINE, 1991 / STEUBEN, 1995

ROADSIDE MAGAZINE

The subtitle reads "The journal devoted to the appreciation and preservation of a truly unique American institution, the Diner." This, while an accurate enough statement of its mission, completely misrepresents in its sobersidedness the lively and adventurous spirit of what is a really amazing zine. Publisher Randy Garbin, a New England School of Art and Design graduate and born-again diner enthusiast, brings to his publication both passion and a spiffy sense of design. *Roadside* speaks to and for diner customer and owner alike, and does so in so many different voices that opening an issue is like stepping into Buddy's Diner in Somerville, Massachusetts, during the breakfast rush.

Even so, there's no doubt that it's Garbin who sets the journal's tone. Somehow, he manages to pull off the unlikely dual roles of Diner Man —striking fear in the hearts of fake diners, fast-food chains, and ill-conceived remodeling efforts (*Roadside* bestows a special prize for the worst of these)—and of the diner world's Jewish mother. He pleads with diner owners to throw out their stale coffee, coaxes them into sharing their recipes for meat loaf, fried onion rings, and peach-raspberry pie . . . and endlessly frets about their bottom line.

The result is a publication you can turn to for diner reviews, rambles down diner-dotted blue highways, diner owner profiles, state diner maps, and the like. And it is *the* place to keep abreast of diner gossip (who's opening, who's closing, who's doing something new, and—perhaps the biggest spur to reader fantasy—who's just put their mint Silk City up for sale).

Like any enthusiast publication, *Roadside* is a gold mine of minutiae. The front-page story of the Spring 1994 issue was a blow-by-blow account of how Victor coffee mugs are made (the method is based on a process originally developed for producing porcelain electric insulators); an earlier issue featured an explanation of wall-box music systems. But it also manages to devote an impressive amount of space to debating the big issues as well.

The *big* big issue, of course, is what you might expect:

> As far as *Roadside* is concerned, a diner is this: a prefabricated structure, with counter service, hauled out to a distant site. A diner is also a free-standing structure built to conform to classic diner proportions . . . and operating with the singular intention of providing good meals at reasonable prices.
>
> If your diner is a storefront, or built into a shopping mall, or into a strip plaza, it is *not* a diner. If it sits anywhere within the boundaries of an amusement park, it is *not* a diner. If it serves $8.95 cheeseburgers and requires reservations, it is *not* a diner.

However, *Roadside* also ponders the kinds of towns in which diners flourish (another feature story, this one in the Fall 1994 issue, was titled "A Walk Through Wellsboro" and offered a guided tour of and meditation on the homey Pennsylvania town that hosts the Wellsboro Diner), and the kind of people who make such places—towns *and* diners—work.

Roadside, then, is about something more than diners—at heart it's a proselytizing effort for the sort of good life in which such unpretentious eateries might play a feature part. As Randy Garbin puts it:

> Eat in diners; take trains; shop on Main Street; put a porch on your house; and live where you can walk to stuff.

At the time of writing, a four-issue subscription to *Roadside* is $14 a year from Coffee Cup Publications, P.O. Box 652, West Side Station, Worcester, MA 01602. Or connect up with them on the Internet's World Wide Web: http://www1.usa1.com/~roadside/RoadsideWebPage.html

Shaker Your Plate

1

No Dutch town has a neater aspect, no Moravian hamlet a softer hush. The streets are quiet, for here you have no grog-shop, no beer house, no lock-up, no pound; of the dozen edifices rising about you . . . not one is either foul or noisy; and every building . . . has something of the air of a chapel.

—WILLIAM HEPWORTH DIXON, *New America* (1867)

Like that of many people, my romance with the Shakers began with a visit to one of their communities. At the time, I was teaching at a small private school in western Massachusetts, a short drive away from the Hancock Shaker Village. Now a museum, it had been an active Shaker community as late as 1950, and twenty of its original buildings were still standing, including the famous round barn. Annual food festivals were held there where Shaker-style meals were served, but my original interest had nothing to do with food.

I arrived on a quiet day in October, and found that the serenity and amplitude of the architecture immediately seized hold of my imagination—especially the expansive, six-story, brick-walled and slate-roofed family dwelling. The first floor was really the basement, containing storage rooms and the kitchen; the second floor held the public rooms, dining rooms, and family meeting room. Above this were two floors of bedrooms—or, as they were then called, retiring rooms—topped by a two-story attic.

The gracefully proportioned rooms with their spare but aesthetically pleasing furnishings, the sweetness of the light, the stillness of the place—all so directly offered a simple spiritual nourishment that the visitor was gradually made aware of a previously unnoticed hunger for that very thing. I wanted to stand there forever, drinking it in.

I was then freshly out of college—a college also located in rural Massachusetts, with buildings of a similar age and distinction—and I now imagine I conflated the two in my mind: the sheltered scholastic life and the sheltered spiritual one. I would have no more made a good Shaker than a good scholar, but that wasn't important. It wasn't the task that drew me; it was the life.

This nostalgia for a homespun, communal existence is part of our shared sense of being American. This is something that is not all that easy to convey to foreigners, as E. M. Forster perplexedly noted in *Two Cheers for Democracy*, during a visit with some *New Yorker* writers to just such a community.

> Life had shrunk into one enormous house, a huge wooden box measuring a hundred and eighty feet long and fifty feet thick, and it was five or six stories high . . . My friends were in a great excitement. The experience was more romantic for them than it was for me, and the idea of home-made chairs hanging from pegs on a wall filled them with nostalgia. It was part of the "dream that got bogged," the dream of an America which should be in direct touch with the elemental and the simple. America has chosen the power that comes through machinery but she never forgets her dream . . .
>
> While the New Yorker questioned them, I went out and looked at the five or six other houses which completed the original Mount Lebanon colony (Shaker houses are always in little colonies). They were empty except for ponderous wooden machinery . . . The simplicity of the buildings was impressive but not interesting.

For many Americans, however, the response is very different. For some, the appeal of the Shakers lies in their social, sexual, and racial egalitarianism (not perfect, but far ahead of its time); others find it in the sect's radical communalism and sense of social responsibility; still others respond to the Shakers' commitment to ecological balance, to giving back to the earth at least as much as they took from it. And there is the Shakers' belief in the sacred quality of honest manual labor.

Their work ethic—"hands to work, heart to God"—was expressed in a refusal to invest more labor in some objects than in others. Shaker craftsmen devoted as much effort and care to laying the floor of a cellar as an entrance hall, and as much ingenuity was devoted to making some task easier long before this knack began to turn the community a profit.

Collectors still eagerly seek out the homeliest of Shaker objects— sieves, ladles, brooms, seed boxes, medicine bottles—because the sect's craftspeople imbued such things with what might be called self-respect.

Although the Shakers claimed to have no use for beauty, their belief that "every force evolves a form" formed an aesthetic that is very much with us today in modernism's distrust of superfluous ornamentation. The Shakers remind us that skilled craftsmen who turn for their design inspiration to the *use* of the object often thereby make that object beautiful.

Unlike the Amish and Mennonite communities, whose moral authority is firmly attached in our imagination to their categorical rejection of modernity—their determination, that is, to remain several steps behind us—the Shakers, for all their strange ways, their enforced celibacy and ritual dancing, have always seemed somehow several steps ahead.

For example, the sect embraced both capitalism and the American worship of practical ingenuity, managing successful businesses selling seeds, patent medicines, and, eventually, furniture and—as Jeffrey S. Paige details in *The Shaker Kitchen*—inventing the hand-cranked dough-kneading machine and later the motor-powered ice-cream freezer; the mechanical cream separator, corn sheller, and apple peeler, corer, and slicer; and an implement so perfect in its simplicity that it remains in use today: the flat corn broom.

If the engine that drove them was a millennial vision of heaven established on earth, that vision was cloaked in the practical utopianism of self-sufficient communalism. It is a vision that still resonates in the American imagination because it offers a compelling alternative to our notion of ourselves as rugged, self-sufficient individualists—proposing, instead, the rugged, self-sufficient community.

Whatever the reason, the hours I spent at the Hancock Shaker Village clung to me in a way that visits to other historical shrines—Pilgrim villages, colonial mansions, forts, and battlefields—have not. As time passed, however, this yearning for a connection to Shaker life condensed into a desire to possess some Shaker artifact; most particularly, a Shaker chair. Each time I encountered the photograph of the kit-made version that still appears, year after year, in certain magazines, I conceived the notion that, if I ever escaped from the ragtag mob of junk that followed me from one apartment to the next, I would make myself an entire set, spindle backs, cloth-taped seats, and all.

This fantasy, like many seemingly original dreams of youth, was, of course, a cliché. Most people, if they are familiar with any Shaker creation, are familiar with and admire the Shaker chair. As it happens, there is no such thing as *a* Shaker chair—only many different Shaker chairs. In addition to side chairs, the Shakers made armchairs, stools, special low-backed dining chairs, wheelchairs, and their famous rockers.

Some had five slats in back and others four or three; some seats were made of ash splints and others of latticed cloth tape. Some were straight-backed; others had their back posts steamed and bent back, to provide more comfort. Others had a Shaker-invented ball-and-socket gadget fitted to the rear legs, allowing the sitter to lean the chair back without doing damage to a pine-board floor. And otherwise similar chairs might have so-called shawl racks fastened to the top of their posts, while others ended in finials.*

Even so, I was absolutely sure I knew what I meant by "Shaker chair." The thing is visible, almost, in the mind's eye, perhaps hanging upside down (so that dust didn't gather on the seat to ruin clothes) on that Shaker peg: something spare, tautly glued, well-knit, and shapely —displaying, as the judges at the 1876 Centennial Exhibition put it, "strength, sprightliness, and modest beauty."

Initially, when this chair was built by Shakers for other Shakers to sit in, it was simply a chair. The making of it was an act of love—love of God, love of neighbor, and love of the wood itself. As for the love of God, there was in the Shaker dogma no line drawn between craftsman and believer—if there was no vanity in the making, a well-wrought chair could only example a well-wrought faith. The Shakers believed that angels walked among them—and sat among them, too, on the same chairs.

Love of wood, because Shaker craftsmen took it from trees they personally knew, with an eye for the special qualities that it would bring to their purpose. The chairs were usually made of maple, chosen for its straight grain (although sometimes an attractive burr or bird's-eye would catch the chairmaker's eye), but cherry, birch, and butternut were also used.

It was, in part, love of neighbor that caused Shaker craft to bend form to function. With any new chair the wood of the slats, posts, and splints might be shaped to a slightly different purpose. Even a chair as seemingly basic and standardized as the Shaker side chair shows a

* At least one commentator has identified the function of this "shawl rack"—a bar that runs across the top of the chair—as a place not to drape a shawl but to tie a cushion (which would then provide additional comfort to the sitter's back). Because this use went against our notions of Shaker design, the rod was assigned a fictional but appropriate use. If true, this is a good example of how the preconceived ideas we bring to history affect the way we perceive its artifacts. It is we, not the Shakers, who created the "Shaker aesthetic," which demands of their furnishings a spartan purity.

continuing—if subtle—evolution. Because, at least at first, these chairs were often carried from place to place (dining room, meeting room, etc.), they had to be both strong and light. So the Shaker chairmaker selected seasoned maple for its durability and resilience, fined each part down as much as he dared (some side chairs weighed as little as five and a half pounds), then fitted it together and glued it tight. As with the masts and rigging of a Yankee clipper, the chair's strength came from carefully calculated stresses; it was less made than strung.

All this was an expression of the chairmaker's love for the Believers who would sit in the chair and find comfort there. Each of the chair's components was considered from this perspective, from the height of the seat (higher for weavers) to the removal of the arms from rockers (so that Sisters could rock while they sewed a fine seam).

In other words, the Shaker chair originated as a *gift*, and it is an object that embodies a complex awareness of giving. The chairmaker saw the wood as a gift from the tree and the craft as a gift from and an opportunity to give back to his Maker. Although chairs were sometimes fitted to a single individual, the Shaker ideal was that everyone gave to everyone, and Shaker chairs expressed this. They are not personalized; they are themselves. In this regard, as furniture, they are unique.

However, when the Shakers discovered they had a ready market in the World for their chairs, this artisanal ethos began to erode. Soon, rockers and side chairs were pouring out of the Shaker furniture factories that had sprung into existence by the second half of the nineteenth century. Produced by power-driven iron lathes, boring machines, planers, and dressing machines, these chairs—one expert came up with the astonishing figure of fifty-two different models—were both "Shaker" and well made. Even so, the individuality of the original hand-crafted chairs was gone.

The Shaker chair continued to evolve. It no longer followed the forceful logic of its use, however, but, instead, the changing tastes in furniture fashion. Later versions, with Victorian fancy moldings, are not often shown in books on Shaker "art"; they are considered something of a lapse of taste. It was not taste that had lapsed, it was the community of the gift. When William Dean Howells visited the Shakers in Shirley, Massachusetts, in 1876, he observed:

The Shakers used to spin and weave all the stuff they wore, but to do this now would be a waste of time; they buy the alpaca and linen which both sexes wear in summer, and their substantial woolens for the winter.

There are no longer carpenters, blacksmiths, and shoemakers among the Shakers at Shirley, because their work can be more cheaply performed by the world-outside, and the shops once devoted to these trades now stand empty.

By 1908, the community at Shirley was empty of Shakers as well.

This was not the final stage in the evolution of the Shaker chair. That came with its eventual replication by companies that have no connection whatever with the sect—such as the ones sold today in kit form by a company called Shaker Workshops. It is an instructive exercise to compare a photograph of one of their reproductions with a photograph of an actual Shaker chair.* This is especially so because the Shaker Workshops catalogue expresses such persuasive piety regarding the Shakers themselves and these reproductions of their furniture—"produced by our own skilled craftspeople to rigid specifications, based on specific Shaker pieces in museums and private collections"—that we begin to believe that we see what we are told we see.

The truth is more complex. These reproductions may resemble Shaker furniture, but only, as it were, at a distance—the exact distance that the hushed atmosphere of the catalogue manages to establish. Seen in each other's company, these chairs look quite fine. But compare them to the Shaker originals and it is immediately apparent that something has gone wrong. Never mind the coarseness of proportion that, if small enough in any particular post or slat or rung, adds up to an overwhelming feeling of crudeness. The real problem with these reproduction chairs is that they are *dead.*

A genuine Shaker chair in repose exhibits a muscular tension; it visibly expects to receive weight. In the kit chair, this tautness has fled. This is so in the catalogue photographs themselves. These chairs were obviously assembled by those well practiced in the business, and yet the result still has a flaccid look. When some friends of mine bought these kits and assembled them, the result—despite the fact that one is a carpenter and both are professional home renovators—left one feeling that they had assembled less a chair than a *model* of a chair, albeit a model that could be—somewhat gingerly—sat on.

Doesn't respect for craftsmanship demand that we pay the money to have a craftsman make us the chair or spend the necessary time to

* The reader can easily do this by ordering a copy of the Shaker Workshops catalogue (P.O. Box 8001, Ashburnham, MA 01430 • 800–840–9121), which contains color photographs of their chairs, and then obtaining from the library a book on Shaker crafts, such as Michael Horsham's *The Art of the Shakers* or June Sprigg and David Larkin's *Shaker Life, Work, and Art.*

master the craft ourselves? Maine is a state in which chairmakers live and work; their price for a finished chair is approximately what Shaker Workshops charges for one of their kit chairs finished by themselves. The craftsman, however, doesn't assemble a kit for you—he makes you a chair. My friends knew all this, so why didn't they elect to do it?

I can't answer for them—they have since left our lives, and even if they hadn't, this would be a delicate subject to broach. But I can answer for myself, because I have actually called one of these chairmakers to ask him about his prices. What I discovered was, apart from what I have already said above, that I was incredibly *anxious* . . . and he was incredibly *defensive.*

Why was this? Because I was having to justify to myself spending $250 for an ordinary chair . . . and he was having to justify charging me that amount. In fact, I did think the chairs were worth the money. What frightened me was that their presence in my house might make me uneasy about the provenance of the rest of our furniture . . . make me wonder what it would be like if everything we owned came directly from someone else's hand. A major appeal of four wobbly, aesthetically distressing kit chairs was that they would never prompt me to ask this question. They possess no intimacy; they are fakes. Nothing about them would ever make me wonder if I deserved to own them: they are all promise and no gift. Pondering this, I also began to wonder whether there might be something threatening—even to the Shakers—about a *real* Shaker chair.

2

If talent, genius, and skill are looking for a good missionary field, the kitchen is the great uncivilized realm. We want the coming generation of girls to be taught how to cook intelligently . . . What to eat, how to cook it and when and how to eat it, are certainly subjects of study, quite as practical and beneficial as the conjugation of Greek verbs.   —*The Shaker Manifesto* (1883)

Anyone interested in the history of American cooking will know that here, too, the Shakers are often accorded a place all their own. "Long ago, Shaker sisters helped bring art to American cooking," writes the food historian Evan Jones in his foreword to *The Best of Shaker Cooking*, a collection of recipes assembled by Amy Bess Miller and Persis Miller, and he goes on to note that it has begun "to receive the same kind of admiration that Shaker furniture gets."

Certainly, no one would deny that, at least on first encounter, Shaker cooks do seem to speak directly to us today, with their emphasis on natural ingredients and the importance of vegetables, their appreciation of herbs, and, especially, their appetizing but unfussy recipes.

Over the years, I had absorbed all this and completely believed it to be true. After all, the sect's cooking, as it is presented in Shaker cookbooks, not only melded easily with my already existing fantasies about them, it was also a refraction of the plain-style Yankee tradition under whose lingering shadows I grew up; their recipes had a homey familiarity.

Consequently, when at last I turned to these cookbooks—by now I had acquired several—for some practical guidance in altering my cooking to reflect something of those tenets to which I was tentatively beginning to subscribe, I was dismayed to discover, on closer examination, how much like Shaker kit furniture were the books themselves—as lifeless as any other museum copy.

At least part of the reason for this was that the compilers of these books seemed depressingly ignorant of our shared culinary heritage. If they had only set aside the Shaker manuscripts they were editing to spend a little time with other cookbooks and culinary writings of the period, they might have realized that much of what they pronounce as special to the Shakers was the common property of many other good nineteenth-century cooks.

Shaker women were indefatigable recipe clippers, and much so-called Shaker fare was originally copied from Worldly cookbooks and publications. Among these is such classic "Shaker" fare as "Shaker Fish and Egg," the recipe for which the Shakers originally clipped from *The Chicago Times*, and "Shaker Lemon Pie" and "Shaker Apple Pie with Rose Water," both of which had earlier appeared in Worldly cookbooks.

Contemporary writers on Shaker cooking also seem ignorant of the fact that most Americans in the last century depended on medicinal plants—and the concoctions, syrups, elixirs, and the like distilled from them—for the treatment of many ills and complaints. The "simpler," or itinerant herb gatherer, was a common character in rural areas—as indeed he or she continued to be in slowly changing parts of the country well into this century. The Shakers may, for a time, have dominated this trade, but most of their herbal beverages and remedies were variants of familiar vernacular receipts.

However, ignorance slides into evasion when these authors discuss —"romanticize" is more the word—the Shaker use of herbs. Discount the herbal switchels, shrubs, and other nonalcoholic beverages, universally popular forerunners of today's soda pop, and the medicinal use of what we now consider culinary herbs, and what remains is not especially impressive.

The nineteenth-century Shakers sold a very small number of herbs for culinary use—sweet marjoram, sage, summer savory, and thyme—and mostly did not use them all that much themselves. Instead, they spent a disproportionate amount of their talent and mechanical ingenuity producing and flogging a frightening variety of patent medicines, all equally promiscuous in their promises. The label of just one of these, "Alternative Syrup, a Compound Concentrated Decoction of Rumex," prescribed its contents for a long list of ailments, including acne, leprosy, cancerous tumors, tuberculosis, chronic diseases of the liver, rheumatism, gout, scurvy, and dropsy.

From this perspective, the Shakers' much publicized remonstrances regarding the unhealthiness of modern foodstuffs have more than a touch of the old-fashioned health-food store . . . where the proprietor would fix you in the eye, terrorize you with a jeremiad on the destructive effects of white bread, and send you out the door clutching a jar of zinc tablets and another of brewer's yeast. Indeed, the first Shaker cookbook, *Mary Witcher's Shaker House-Keeper*, was a promotional pamphlet produced to help sell Shaker medicinals, and it is unclear what hand—if any—Mary Witcher (or any Shaker cook) had in its production, since many of its recipes were taken from newspapers.

These books do contain "authentic" Shaker recipes, in the sense that they record dishes that Believers actually made, ate, and enjoyed. But few of these recipes possess the radiant clarity of Shaker handicraft. Unlike Shaker kitchen implements, Shaker recipes have a dated quality that makes them complicated for us in a way they never were for the Shaker Sisters. They, working in harmony in their big, airy kitchens, turned out a continuous stream of pies, breads, cakes, muffins, and similar baked stuff, just as they put up a phenomenal number of jars of pickles, relishes, and jams.

This is the kind of cooking you learn by doing it every day. If, for example, Shaker pies were astonishing, it is because of the deft hands that made them, not because of anything that can be conveyed in a recipe. Nor are we likely to set on the table many of the other makable but antiquated dishes like chicken and spinach pudding with bread lid; chipped beef pie with mushrooms; beef liver, sausage, and carrot hash; ham croquettes with raisin sauce; or orange-marmalade pudding.

As with the Shaker kit chair, these Shaker cookbooks are not quite as substantial as they first appear. *The Best of Shaker Cooking*, with its

900 recipes, is a hefty volume, but as I looked through it for something like an enabling spirit that might encourage me toward a simpler, more direct style—a Shaker style—of cooking, I felt it wobble and creak, as if it was not made to bear that kind of weight.

This is because that spirit had nothing to do with recipes, and no recipe, however authentic, can put us in touch with it. The Shakers took their members not from the clerical/intellectual class but from farmers and craftspeople, artisans who found in this utopian community a place where their talents could bloom. It's not surprising that Shakers possess an enduring culinary reputation: the Brothers were skilled and loving in their husbandry; the Sisters spent a lifetime sharpening—among many other skills—their kitchen craft.

The Shakers gave this artisanal focus a further refinement—as well as their own particular twist. Everyone in the community was expected to share in the general work, including the drudgery, and it was not uncommon to find the head Eldress washing dishes after a meal or the head Elder lugging firewood or emptying chamber pots. For the individual member, this kind of participation meant an unusually rich sense of shared life.

Eleven-year-old Benjamin Gates, although officially a tailor's apprentice in the New Lebanon community, recorded in his diary for the year 1828 a wide range of other activities, described by Priscilla J. Brewer in *Shaker Communities, Shaker Lives*:

> During the winter . . . he also attended school, and helped with daily tasks such as filling woodboxes. In the spring, he helped with the general cleaning of dooryards, tagged sheep, weeded the onions, grafted apple trees, and worked in the medicinal garden. The summer months were occupied with berrying, washing sheep, haying, pulling flax, and helping in the blacksmith and wood shops. In the fall, he was employed in harvesting wild herbs, gathering butternuts and chestnuts, digging potatoes, picking apples, and butchering hogs.

Notice how much of this everyday activity affected the communal table and how much of what was eaten at that table reflected the spirit and interest of those who sat down to eat it. Young Benjamin, when he bit into a pocket-sized pork-and-sage pie ("to go along with a picnic party," advises the Shaker receipt), may never have specifically considered that he had helped weed the onions, butcher the pig, dig the potatoes, pick the sage, and gather the apples that went into it. Even so, there is an awareness of things that is all the sweeter for not having to be thought upon. The food the Shakers ate radiated fellowship, the intensity of which we can barely imagine today.

How does one eat in heaven, with an angel sitting beside you at the table? In modest silence and without undue appreciation of the food. If you wonder what the Shakers would think about our curiosity regarding their cooking, imagine breaking bread with Mother Teresa and then having a friend wanting to talk to you only about the food ("Sounds delicious! Did you have seconds?"). It is one thing to express your worship of God by baking a perfect pie, a very different thing indeed to then sit down to eat it.

3

NOTICE: RULES FOR VISITORS

FIFTH. At the Table we wish all to be as free as at home, but we dislike the wasteful habit of leaving food on the plate. No vice is with us the less ridiculous for being in fashion.

The Shakers fed strangers often but did not invite them to their own tables, preferring to serve them in a separate place. Shaker meals followed a strictly disciplined ritual. When the dinner bell summoned them, they filed in, men to the right and women to the left, gathering at their separate tables. They knelt to pray, then sat, and platters of food were set on the table. They immediately began to eat, fiercely and fast, the platters being repeatedly refilled. Course followed course with no sound in the room except the noise of determined chewing. As soon as they were done, they prayed again, rose silently, and left.

This is not eating without pleasure, maybe, but it is a kind of eating that denies its pleasure. Fun, the Shakers often said, had its place in their scheme of things, but they never allowed themselves to forget that the reason they were placed on earth was not to enjoy themselves but to set a good example. And just as this meant not sleeping on their sides but flat on their backs as if already fitted to their coffins, it also meant (apart from the occasional picnic) no cheerful buzz of conversation during the meal or enjoyment of that comfortable moment after it, when, chair pushed back, you linger over the coffee, still savoring what has just transpired.

Rose bushes were planted along the sides of the road which ran through our village and were greatly admired by the passersby, but it was strongly impressed upon us that a rose was useful, not ornamental. It was not intended to please us by its color or its odor, its mission was to be made into rose water, and if we

thought of it in any other way we were making an idol of it and thereby imperiling
our souls.

Yes, and what was the purpose of the rose water? Not to please its
users by its smell and taste? The moment that purpose became pleasure,
it also became dangerous. In Shaker pleasures, purpose is always somehow there, chugging away. The Shakers' adoration of the rocking chair
can be explained by its ability to allow the sitter to be simultaneously
busy and comforted. Eating, as long as you were chewing, was fine; it
was pausing to relish what was in your mouth that was the sin.

Again and again in the literature that narrates Shaker life, a particularity governing their eating habits appears: their obsession with cleaning their plates. They wrote poems about it, they stressed it in their
instructions to visitors, and they mentioned it constantly in their writings
to and about themselves.

Shaker apologists see this as an admirable frugality, at once generous
and never wasteful. I disagree. I think it stabs generosity in the heart.
Imagine taking a child to a bookstore and telling it to choose any book
it wants—it just has to read every word of every book it takes. No
quicker way to kill a gift. I know this. I remain ensnared by a Puritan-
tinged Yankee upbringing which insisted that, if you didn't like something, it was your moral duty to eat every bit; if you did like it, you
were to understand that your having it was always somehow an exception. "Clean your plate" is the nagging sort of homily that is next of kin
to "Enough is as good as a feast" and "Remember the starving children
in India."

The Shakers, of course, said this not only to the orphans and abandoned children they took it upon themselves to rear (most of whom,
despite the great care lavished on them, left as soon as they could) but
to each other, constantly. It grimly floats above their spotless, cleverly
managed (condiment trays hanging from the ceiling, eating cloths that
served both as tablecloths and napkins, short-backed chairs that could
be slid under the table to speed its clearing) dining halls, the Banquo
at every Shaker feast.

The Shakers saw it not as a ghost but as a reminder of their spiritual
yoke. Theirs was a life of persuasion by example, and this persuasion
was mostly directed at each other. The Shakers were a democratic society in all things but one: individuality had no place. Indeed, they did
all they could to stamp it out. Contact with the outside world was strictly
limited and friendships within the community discouraged. Praise was
dispensed, if at all, in tiny pinches.

Theirs was a world of endless petty rules, with cleaning your plate the least of them. It was "contrary to order" for Believers to have nicknames, possess pets, sleep curled in bed, have left and right shoes, own watches, yawn or blink in public, step with the left foot first onto a flight of stairs, etc., etc.—prohibitions meant for no other purpose than to create a state of perpetual spiritual rebuke.

As I read about the Shakers, I continually found myself thinking about the word "good." It is a strangely ambiguous word; its different meanings seem less to complement each other than to live in a condition of anxious, mutual denial. Hepworth Dixon wrote at length and with great admiration of the goodness of the Shakers in his book *New America* (1867), a personal investigation into various revolutionary attempts to reimagine and perfect American life. At one point, he describes his conversation with one of the Elders while they strolled together through a Shaker apple orchard:

> "A tree has its wants and wishes," said the Elder; "and a man should study them as a teacher watches a child, to see what he can do. If you love the plant, and take heed of what it likes, you will be well repaid by it. I don't know if a tree ever comes to know you; and I think it may; but I am sure it feels when you care for it and tend it; as a child does, as a woman does. Now, when we planted this orchard . . . we built a house for every plant to live in, that is to say, we dug a deep hole for each; we drained it well; we laid down tiles and rubble, and then filled in a bed of suitable manure and mould; we put the plant into its nest gently, and pressed up the earth about it, and protected the infant tree by this metal fence." "You take a world of pains," I said. "Ah, Brother Hepworth," he rejoined, "thee sees we love our garden."

It is a lovely, moving passage, but to read it correctly is also to know that, at the time, the Shakers were famous for their wonderful apple orchards and for the superlative hard cider they produced from them. But when they decided that cider drinking was contrary to good Shaker ways, they cut their orchards down. What did that Elder say then about his lovingly cared-for trees? Or, more important, *to* them?

A gift embodies two kinds of goodness: the goodheartedness of the giver and the pleasure-giving nature of the gift. In the true gift, these two goodnesses merge, which is why, if one is missing, the whole becomes suspect, even devastating, as when a child finds a pair of socks wrapped up in Christmas paper. The Shakers were expert in this kind of manipulation. They had a very particular meaning for the word "gift"—for them it meant something received via direct contact with heaven.

Their dancing, or "shaking," was a ritual of opening themselves to the reception of such transmissions, and these could arrive in a variety of forms, most often as an intense sense of embodiment of spirit. But they could and did express themselves in other ways, specifically in setting out missions and laying down rules. Believers vied among themselves to be the "instruments" of such gifts and, to abet this, shunned all others. Eventually, the source of the other gifts dried up. The community of the gift degenerated into the community of the Gift.

As the last century progressed, the Shakers found themselves fast losing the ability to attract believers, in part because their fundamental tenet had been secularized out from under them. America itself became the place where heaven was to be made on earth. The abolitionist, temperance, and suffrage movements, not to mention those against cruelty to animals and children, each took another bite out of the Shaker conception of the perfectly lived life.

None of these movements more shook the Shakers' confidence in their vision or proved more divisive than the meatless, whole-grain diet crusade headed by former Presbyterian minister Sylvester Graham.* The younger Shakers argued that a sect so conspicuously busy digging their grave with their teeth could hardly be seen as a paragon of virtue. Their Elders found something impious in this picking and choosing among the good foods God had seen fit to set before them. Worse, embracing *this* Worldly fad would only make Believers that much more vulnerable to the next. They correctly saw that the cumulative message of these fads was that goodness could be found outside of godliness . . . and, in fact, as susceptible Shakers began to listen to it, more and more of them did start edging for the door.

In ironic contrast to this exodus, crowds of sightseers began to visit, enchanted with this surviving remnant of historic, small-town America, the "Shaker Village." The stop has been an enduring attraction on the tourist map for much longer than you might expect. As early as 1850, Shaker Elder Freegift Wells was railing against the establishment of a

---

* Although this is not much mentioned today, one of the main purposes of Graham's regimen was to control the sexual impulses of young men, a matter of much anguish and concern to the younger Shaker males. As Harriet Martineau observed in 1837: "Their thoughts are full of the one subject of celibacy: with what effect, may be easily imagined. Their religious exercises are disgustingly full of it. It cannot be otherwise: for they have no interesting subject of thought beyond their daily routine of business; no objects in life; no wants, no hopes, no novelty to experience whatever."

souvenir shop for this flood of casual visitors, decrying it as even more harmful to young members than the 1841 "Gift" that had banned the eating of pork:

> This fancy Store is a lure, hung out to draw the gentry, who come by Coach loads . . . They will go into the Store and purchase a few articles, and then will seem to feel they have purchased a right and we ought to let them go round wherever they please . . . The frequent exhibitions on our walks, in our gardens and about among our buildings of groups of young men and women, gaily dressed, and their arms locked together, talking, tittering and laughing has a powerful tendency to fill the minds of young people with lustful sensations, and cause them to hunger and thirst after the vanities and gratifications of the world.

He was more right than he knew. Where there is a gift shop, can the museum be far behind? Indeed, before they knew it, the curators were edging through the door, eager to mark out the locations for the display cases. And the remaining Shakers, unable to defeat them, instead joined forces, embracing a kind of self-reflexive antiquarianism—bonnets, guided tours, and all. Why not? By then, Shaker communities had more in common with the Shaker museums that replaced them than with anything approaching authentic Shaker life.

The Shakers failed, and in failure became tame. At the height of their powers they caused disruption and dismay; they tore apart families, even broke up communities. They were attacked by pamphlets and by fists. Do we understand them any better now? We write paeans to their meat-less ways, indifferent to the divisiveness of that decision to the Shaker community, and we laud their labor-saving ingenuity—their mechanical pea podders and apple corers and rotating bread ovens, their concoctions that evolved into Bisquick and Carnation evaporated milk—despite the fact that this proclivity, when the outside world became more ingenious still, led the Shakers straight into its arms.

Likewise, it is failure that gives Shaker cooking its special character. That self-conscious herbalism is a cuisine of the museum. If Shakers had continued into this century as a vital sect, their cooking today would have no special character. Listen to Sister Frances Carr, the cook for the Sabbathday Lake Shaker Community, who wrote in 1985:

> Early Shaker cooks . . . were not privileged to have many of the convenience ingredients which we take so much for granted . . . (I am sure they would have loved using such ingredients.)

The eponymous tuna casserole of Eldress Bertha Lindsay, author of another contemporary Shaker cookbook, contains "1 large can of tuna, 1 large can of shrimp, 1 10-oz. can of cream of chicken soup, 1 10-oz. can of cream of mushroom soup," and not much else.

About the same time I visited the Hancock Shaker Village, I discovered an old brick power-generating plant beside the Housatonic River. I didn't think of this then, but it had something in common with that six-story Shaker dwelling. The massive electric turbines had long since been sold for scrap; here, as well, everything was sun-dappled, peaceful space. In the Shaker dwelling I thought that peace was the property of its former inhabitants, when, in fact, among them, too, powerful engines of another order had once filled that space with electrically charged currents.

It is this force that still radiates—even out of faded photographs—from the authentic Shaker chair. For a brief moment that piece of furniture resolved an inherently unstable equation, bringing into harmony two volatile and seemingly irreconcilable meanings of goodness, two equally potent but conflicting human needs. However, you can make excellent things and simultaneously forbid yourself the enjoyment of them for only so long. The life-enhancing Shaker chair on one side, its rule-racked makers on the other . . . it was only a matter of time before one or the other would have to go.

What haunts me is how much we have in common with the Shakers and how little with the chair. Surely, if there is anything for us to find in Shaker foodways, it is evidence of a shared confusion about eating. How much of our current fear of food relates to genuine health concerns and how much to an increasing inability to resolve this conflicting nature of goodness. Does it taste good? Is it good for me? When one of these meanings of the word pushes to the fore, the other recedes in confusion . . . or, worse, is suborned to lie.

Today, with "good for you" allowed full rein, talk about food has become a language riddled with denial. More and more we say, the real thing isn't worth the time, the money, or the risk, but we still can't let it go. We cling to what gives us pleasure and is not yet quite condemned, and find ourselves running ahead of bad news we already know. We mouth mealy platitudes of our own—"No pain, no gain," "A minute in the mouth, a lifetime in the belly"—all current equivalents to Shakering our plates.

Recently, bearing away two fresh chickens from the Ellsworth farmers' market, I was stopped by a man who said, "You must really love chicken to spend two dollars a pound for it." His tone implied that it was outrageous to lay out that kind of money on *chicken*, no matter how good it tasted. I simply nodded to him as I put them in the car. Here —unlike my earlier, nervous-making exchange with the Maine chairmaker—I found myself on solid ground. The truth is that I couldn't begin to pay Bob Bowen for what he gives us, raising these chickens. He has, in effect, put his livelihood at risk to give me pleasure, and I find myself wanting to give him something more than money in return. Yes, his free-range chickens taste better than any store-bought bird, but it isn't just this that lifts the transaction between us out of commerce and/or charity into something else. It is a kind of mutual nurturing . . . in the best possible sense, a gift.

SOME SHAKER RECIPES

BLUE FLOWER OMELET
(SERVES 2)

Variously attributed to Eldress Clymena and Sister Abigail of the Shaker community in North Union, Ohio, this dish represents authentic Shaker herb cooking. Although Shaker cookbooks say this omelet feeds four, we think two would find it more of a meal.

4 eggs
4 tablespoons milk or water
½ teaspoon salt
Pinch of black pepper
1 tablespoon minced parsley
1 teaspoon minced chives
2 tablespoons best butter
12 chive blossoms

This delicious omelet can be made only when the chives are in full bloom. Take the eggs and beat them just enough to blend whites and yolks well. Add milk or water, seasonings, and the minced parsley and chives. Melt butter in a heavy iron skillet; pour in the mixture. When the edges of the omelet begin to set, reduce the heat. With a pancake shovel [i.e., a spatula], slash uncooked parts until bottom is well browned. Then sprinkle the washed blooms over the omelet and fold. Serve immediately on a hot platter. The blue blossoms add a delicious flavor and interest to the dish.

DANDELION GREENS ON TOAST
(SERVES 2)

"One of the first signs of spring is the tiny sawlike leaf of the dandelion sticking its leaves above the thawing earth. Before they have a chance to burst into bloom, have the children gather these succulent plants. This furnishes you with a tasty dish and at the same time rids your dooryard of weeds."
                                                                    —The Shaker Manifesto

2 cups dandelion leaves
2 egg yolks
½ cup cream
Salt and pepper to taste
2 slices stale bread
1 tablespoon butter or drippings
Oil and vinegar to dress
2 hard-boiled eggs, chopped
Fresh parsley, minced

Wash young dandelion leaves thoroughly and simmer in salted water until tender. Drain and press to extract all moisture. Place in a saucepan with egg yolks, cream, and salt and pepper. Heat through, spread the mixture on slices of stale bread, and fry quickly in hot butter or drippings. Sprinkle with oil and vinegar, then heap with the hard-boiled eggs and garnish with the parsley.

COOK'S NOTE. We suggest a few drops of fresh lemon juice in place of the oil and vinegar. This recipe, from the Shaker community in Shirley, Massachusetts, is best when only the tiniest, tenderest dandelion leaves are used.

MELTED CHEESE ON TOAST
(SERVES 1)

Scrape or thinly pare some country cheese—Cheddar- or Cheshire-type—into a cup until it is three-fourths full. Fill up with boiling water to the rim of the cup and cover with a saucer. Stand in a warm place for ten minutes. Pour off water, and pour the cheese, which will be like thick cream, upon hot toast. Sprinkle with salt and pepper and serve. If the cheese is packed fairly compactly, this amount will be enough for two slices of toast.

SHAKER BOILED APPLES

Shaker cooks turned to advantage the flavor and pectin in apple pie parings (the peels and cores) by saving them to make jelly. "A tumblerful of the richest sort can thus be obtained from the dozen [pie] apples. Boil the skins, etc., a few minutes and strain. Add a little sugar to the liquid and boil until right to turn into the tumbler." This simple dessert makes its own jelly the same way.

About the nicest morsel that ever tickled the palate is a boiled apple. Not boiled like a potato nor steamed like a pudding, but as follows. Place a layer of fair-skinned Baldwins, or any nice variety [of red cooking apple], in a large stew pan, with about a quarter of an inch of water. Throw on about half a cup of sugar to 6 good-sized apples and boil until the apples are thoroughly cooked and the syrup nearly thick enough for jelly.

COOK'S NOTE. Modern cooks may want to core the apples. Gently boil them for about 20 minutes, turning them carefully several times. The syrup will gel slightly. Delicious served with heavy cream.

LEMONADE

Lemonade is one of the healthiest and most refreshing of all drinks; suitable for almost all stomach and bowel disorders and excellent in most sicknesses. —The Shaker Manifesto (1881)

6 lemons
1 cup sugar
1 cup boiling water
8 cups very cold water

Roll the lemons well; cut in half and squeeze out juice. Strain and add sugar. Pour the boiling water over the lemon rinds and let stand until cold. Strain and add cold water to juice. The hot water extracts the oil from the rinds and thus adds greatly to the flavor. Add a little ice to each mug. Very refreshing for the sick and aged.

COOK'S NOTE. This is the recipe of Sister Amelia of the Shaker community in North Union, Ohio. To roll a lemon, place it on a table, set your palm on it, and vigorously roll it back and forth. This breaks down the connective tissue, so the lemon yields more juice.

STEUBEN, 1994

Just Another Bowl of Texas Red

Chili, chili con carne, Texas red—whatever you call that savory concoction of meat, grease, and fire—is the natural child of the arguing state of mind. There's no recipe for it, only disputation, and almost anyone's first thought after a taste of somebody else's version, no matter how easily it slides down the throat, is that they themselves could make it better.

Chili brings out that attitude. There's something contentious about Texas red, something so jittery, even just plumb wild, that you never come to terms with it for long. Even your own chili—however good it is—keeps you wrangling. That's because it can truly be Texas red only if it walks the thin line just this side of indigestibility: daring the mouth to eat it and defying the stomach to digest it, the ingredients hardly willing to lie in the same pot together.

Chili's restless, ornery nature is why men have made a special effort to claim it as their own. Until recently, it was men who wrote about it and mostly men who made it—or argued their women into fixing it for them. The word itself calls to mind army camps and cowboying and oil-town chili joints. This isn't to say that women don't like chili or that they can't make it as good as any man—only that there is something about chili that draws men to it, especially men who otherwise don't have much interest in cooking at all.

Chili making is not the culinary art that, say, good barbecuing is—anyone can put together a passable bowl of red by following the recipe on a chili-powder can. But no one learns anything about *making* chili until they pick an argument with that recipe. And they have to go on arguing, first with themselves, then—long and persistently—with other chili makers, until they get to their own true bowl of red.

This is why Texans insist that no one else but they can put up a decent bowl of it. Because—at least in their opinion—only the Texas chili maker has been forced to fight his way to his version over every inch of chili-making territory, honing it to perfection through constant disputation.

Anyone familiar with this kind of Texas talk—a cagey verbal tussle devised to nurse a long-neck or two through the hotter part of an afternoon—will know that while it may be amiable enough, each discussant is still watching to outmaneuver his opponent—preferably before an appreciative audience—head over heels into a mesquite patch. Chili has this same quality. It is social food edged with a suspicious rejection of mere socializing. Almost anyone is welcome to pull up and have a bowl—if they can take the heat. Otherwise, the good ol' boys are going to get a laugh.

Nowadays we do not immediately warm to this kind of rancorous individualism and its sheer cussed refusal to go along. But chili was fathered by the sort of person who, if he didn't populate the West as much as myth would have it, certainly came to popularize it: the tough and silent solitary. Sometimes he really did ride alone—as mountain man, sheepherder, or outlaw. However, even when he traveled with companions—as ranch hand or dog soldier—he was still a loner at heart. He had to be. His life was in his hands alone—and sometimes not even there.

Survival. If that was only a matter of skill, those who rode the range would have been sober and God-fearing to a man. But the West was a place without doctors, spare parts, or second chances. One moment of bad luck could claim the chips of a lifetime's worth of cautious behavior. Even a strong man tired of those odds, and a weak man got restless in mind. Such as these constantly justified to themselves why they should not be claimed—or, if they were, how they might escape at someone else's expense. It might or might not be good to be shifty in a new country, as a popular fictional character declared, but it was sometimes absolutely necessary.

So, whatever the reasons that brought a man into this life, survival put the same brand on him. That's why his social life was punctuated by braggery, quarrel, and sudden death, and why the rituals evolved to contain this violence still had their tense and solitary edge. Unlike civilized men, who competed with each other for a living, these men had to pick a fight with the whole universe simply to survive.

Argumentation, you might therefore say, is the main form of socialization of the naturally solitary. That this is the case with chili can be seen by the chili cook-off: a congregation of disputants, each anxiously tending his solitary pot. To enjoy chili, we need only spoon it up and fire the mouth with its powerful pungency. But to touch the passion men feel for it, we have to do more than taste it; we have to stare deep into its restless, lonely heart.

BUFFALO HUNTER

Mountain men, a well-defined class of backwoodsmen . . . versed in everything pertaining to life upon the plains and in the mountains.
—FRANCIS PARKMAN, *The Oregon Trail* (1849)

The hunters came in with a fat [buffalo] cow; and . . . we enjoyed a supper of roasted ribs and boudins, the *chef d'oeuvre* of a prairie cook.
—JOHN C. FRÉMONT (1845)

The great-grandpappy of the chili bowl was the buffalo roast, a great, greasy orgy that was—apart from the yearly drunken sprees at the trader forts when he sold his pelts and restocked his supplies—the mountain man's premier social event and his only contribution to American cuisine. To throw one, you first had to kill your buffalo (accurately speaking, of course, a bison). Later, when larger groups crossed the Great Plains—wagon trains, railroad workers, army troops—official buffalo hunters were appointed. But among the earlier trapper parties, no man cared to yield this honor to another. When a herd of buffalo was spotted (or, rather, when the herd spotted them and stampeded to the safety of broken country), every man broke into pursuit.

Whooping and hollering, spurring their horses to their limit, they charged into the thundering herd. Each man picked his beast and rode right up next to it, since his rifle had almost to be shoved into the buffalo's side to get off a good shot—and even a well-placed shot into a vital organ was not guaranteed to slow it. A buffalo could weigh in at close to a ton and stood six feet high at the hump; it took a lot of killing. And in the days before the bullet and the repeating rifle, any subsequent shot had to be muzzle-loaded and primed . . . no mean feat on horseback in a stampeding buffalo herd.

In truth, it was a foolhardy stunt and, for anyone who calculated his risks, often unnecessary, since one or two hunters could bring down enough animals to feed everyone. However, once the herd was spotted, all caution was swept away. Everyone wanted to try his hand. Even missionaries were carried away by the fever of the kill; among men, at least, it was the nonparticipant who was rare.

The reason for this was simple. Every prairie crossing was a dreary, exhausting tale of accumulated disaster—broken axles, violent storms, bouts of fever, attacks on livestock by predatory animals, and constant harassment by Indians. The plunge into the buffalo herd was an electric discharge of days of constant tension and fear, a cathartic outburst of maniacal violence. The hunters took heart-stopping risks with heedless abandon, killed wantonly as long as there were buffalo to chase, and emerged from this frenzy of slaughter gasping wildly, soaked with sweat, and ravenously hungry, eager to begin butchering the giant, steaming corpses strewn across the suddenly silent prairie.

The animals were too heavy to move; they were cut up where they fell. The mountain man's hunting knife was a simple butcher's blade whetted razor-sharp. The first piece to be cut away was the tongue, a traditional trophy, taken even if the rest of the animal was too tough (or too redundant) to eat. Then the beast was propped on its belly, legs folded under or extended as necessary, and the butcher's blade was run along the spine, freeing a flap of hide that could be peeled down to provide a protective apron from the dirt underneath.

The cuts of meat taken depended entirely on the number of beasts killed and the size of the party to be fed. Joints would certainly be set aside to supply the group for the next several days or until they were completely rotten, but the feasting itself had a certain logical progression. Experienced mountain men would quench the thirst of the hunt with a long draught of warm blood, which they claimed tasted sweet as milk. Then they would devour the raw liver, seasoning it with the contents of the animal's gall bladder or perhaps a pinch of gunpowder.

The intestines, a favored savory that was quick to spoil, were ripped out, squeezed free of their contents, and set to roast on a fire of buffalo chips until seared and sizzling and all puffed up from their own steam. These *boudins* were wolfed down as is, the appetite stimulated as well by a pint or so of melted kidney fat or a "soup" made of marrow and blood, which disgusted the greenhorn "pork-eater" but made the faces of the mountain men, as an observer succinctly put it, "shine with grease and gladness."

All this, of course, was mere preliminary to the main course, which, if the hunting had been good, was a giant portion of hump ribs for each man, roasted to his own taste over his own fire. Each rib steak was cut from the roast as it reached perfection and was enjoyed without benefit of plate, silverware, or napkin, save the trapper's knife and sleeve. Eight pounds of meat a day was considered a reasonable ration by these men, but at a feast like this they put that amount down at one sitting. They would then most likely pass out, that much greasy meat as intoxicating to the system as alcohol. When they came to, they might well start in all over again.

This gluttonous gorging sprang from more than simple hunger: the mountain man saw it as his due. In civilization, only the royal and the wealthy could eat all the meat they wanted. These men saw themselves as the royalty of the prairie; they claimed their meat to be the best there ever was. Like those who played this same role after them—the cowboys—the trappers rarely had any money. Fur profits went to the Astors just as the cattle wealth went to the range barons. The emblems of pride for these men were their free ways and free meat, a diet due half to craft and half to the sheer boldness of the taking—that same mix of craft and craziness that made them such a different breed from the sober, responsible homesteaders.

Far from suffering from this meat-glutted diet, the mountain man was amazingly healthy. Apart from acts of violence, he suffered few ailments—and credited this to "buffler." Buffalo meat, one of them claimed, could "cure dyspepsy, prevent consumption, amend a broken constitution, put flesh on the bones of a *skeleton*, and restore a *dead man* to life."

The sun sinks and the horizon is suffused with brilliant reds and scarlets, the dark sky above it an ever-deepening, star-flecked royal blue. A touch of chill floats in the fresh air, sweet with the scent of prairie grass and smoldering buffalo chips. The plain around is dotted with tiny fires, each sending up a pencil trace of smoke that abruptly vanishes when it touches the night sky. The men themselves are barely visible, each wrapped in his sleeping robe, staring into the dying embers, alone with his thoughts, ears alert to every quiet murmur that breaks the great prairie silence—the clump of hooves as his tethered horse grazes its small plot, the scurry and bark of the coyotes pulled close to camp by the intoxicating scent of raw meat.

If you can imagine this scene—the contented, fat-smeared visages of exhausted men, the stunning vista littered with the now-reeking corpses of partially butchered beasts—and feel, even despite yourself, the tug of nostalgia, and the stirrings of some primal appetite, you understand more about the origins of chili than you will from any number of visits to the Indian/Mexican kitchen in which it was most likely first concocted.

Here in this prairie scene we find almost everything important about that dish except its contents: the sense of solitary possessiveness, the great and greasy glut of meat, the poignant beauty of the landscape rubbed hard by the coarse-bearded face of violence, with its afterwash of melancholy. The mountain man was the original solitary; crowded out by settlers, ranchers, and townsfolk, he was soon to vanish into the landscape. But his appetite for grease and gladness was taken up by the men who trod in his footsteps and appropriated his myth: the American cowboy.

S.O.B.

Texans claim chili as a Texas dish; cowboys as a cowboy one. Both these claims have their truth; neither is true. There's nothing obscure or mysterious about the origins of chili, for while it may or may not be a "Mexican" dish, it is certainly a Southwest Indian one. Called *chile con carne*, it was a simple stew of fresh chiles seasoned with herbs and flavored with meat, usually chicken or pork but also sometimes beef. This is the way it is still made among the people who call the dish *chile*, not chili, and who describe our adaptation of it—with more accurate emphasis—as *carne con chile*.

Mexicans, at least poor Mexicans, are mostly of Indian, not Spanish, descent, and while the missionaries may have converted them to Christianity and a form of Latin culture, their own poverty and that of their land have kept their diet close to their origins. They adopted some Spanish dishes and gave Spanish names to some Indian ones, but their food has far more in common with the Indian cuisine from which it sprang than with that of their peasant Iberian counterparts across the Atlantic.

As proof that chili did originate in the Lone Star State, Texans often point out that the earliest recorded description of the dish came from J. C. Clopper, a Texan who visited San Antonio in 1827. What Clopper actually described, however, was the cooking of the Mexican-Indian—

or mestizo—poor, who, he noted, could afford only meager portions of the cheapest cuts of meat "cut into a kind of hash with nearly as many peppers as there are pieces of meat—this is all stewed together."

No historical chronicle of the last century mentions this dish of chiles stewed with meat—sometimes called *chile con carne* and sometimes *chile colorado*—as anything other than indigenous to the Mexican-Indian inhabitants of the Southwest, encountered as often in New Mexico as in Spanish-speaking parts of Texas. The real question is not who "invented" chili con carne—the Aztecs were cooking meat with chiles before the arrival of the Conquistadors—but when and how Anglo eaters came to start thinking of it as their own.

This is a matter that has been greatly obfuscated in recent decades by the growing popularity of Tex-Mex cooking and the more recent fad for chiles themselves. Today, no one would ever suspect that well into the second half of this century, Texans were content to write books about their state and its cooking without ever once mentioning chili and that Texas cookbooks could be found with no recipe for it at all.

The truth is that, historically speaking, most Texans never ate chili or any other so-called Tex-Mex cooking with regularity, or certainly with any sense of personal identity. Popular misconceptions to the contrary, Texas cooking is Southern cooking. Texas is a big state, with parts closer to Kansas than to Mexico, and—more to the point—with an Anglo populace that generally feels itself a lot more kith and kin to folk in Baton Rouge or Jackson than to those in Tampico or Monterey. Historically, Texans have never been especially fond of Mexicans; when they condescended to eat their food they did so at the local greasy spoon, not at home—except when they ate it out of a can.

Texas lavished its culinary passion on barbecue, hush puppies, and pecan pie, relegating its "Mexican" dishes to the back of the cookbook. Most Texans thought of chili as not so much theirs as their kind of Mexican food—on a par with tacos and enchiladas, if a tad more familiar. But there was an impudence in chili that set it apart from its more modest siblings, the knowing look of a street child wise beyond his years, who knows who his daddy really is.

This urchin impudence is our single clue to chili's connection to the Texas cowboy, a linkage that otherwise does not seem to want to be made at all. None of the earliest authentic cowboy narratives mentions the dish, and it is unlikely that this omission was accidental. Chuck-wagon cuisine was so strictly codified that every food the cowboy ate can be itemized in a single exhale: chicken-fried steak, beans cooked with fat pork and lick (the cowboy tag for molasses or corn syrup), sourdough biscuits, and, if they were lucky, vinegar pie or a sourdough cobbler of stewed dried fruit for dessert. With this came all the coffee they could drink, brewed strong enough to chew. There might be bacon in the beans and some barbecue now and then, but all variations were on the same theme: frontier Anglo (and especially Southern) cooking pared to the bare bones. As Roberta Campbell wrote:

> In talking to a long-retired XIT hand, he told me the cooks only prepared beef four ways: fried, boiled, son-of-a-gun, and, if the wagon remained in one place long enough, barbecued. He said the first chili he ever ate was in a restaurant.

This isn't to say that the early cowboy never ate chili, but when he did, he may well have felt mistreated. Ramon F. Adams set this out plainly in *Come an' Get It: The Story of the Old Cowboy Cook.*

> Most bosses preferred a native white cook, both at the ranch and at the wagon. Some Negroes were good cooks, but . . . white cowboys refused to take orders from them. The Mexicans wanted to flavor all the food with chile peppers—a diet which became monotonous to the white man.

Anglo cowboys thought Mexican seasoning low-class and an insult to good chuck-wagon cooking—their derogatory epithet for Mexicans was "chili-chompers" (or just plain "chilies").* Chile pepper was a flavor they tolerated only in their beans.

Also, chili con carne is made with tough, cheap cuts, and cowboys, like the mountain men before them, claimed all the fresh, choice meat they could eat as their natural due. And, except on the poorest ranches, they got it. On the free range, beef cattle multiplied in numbers large enough for the cowboy to have his fill, since beef gained its value only at the end of the long drive to the railhead.

Unlike the mountain man, however, each cowboy could not claim his own cow. The closest he came to the conspicuous consumption of the buffalo feast was in the chuck-wagon specialty that provides the evolutionary link between buffalo hump and the chili pot—son-of-a-bitch stew. While every chuck-wagon cook had his secret fine-tuning for this delicacy, the basic dish was composed of the meat and offal of a freshly killed calf: the brains, liver, heart, fry (testicles), sweetbreads, and especially the marrow gut, a rich and succulent substance that fills the

---

* Adams, this time in his *Western Words: A Dictionary of the Range, Cow Camp, and Trail,* offers the following illustrative definition: "Chili eater—another nickname for the Mexican. Commonly used to mean low-caste or low-brow."

tube connecting the animal's two stomachs while it is still suckling its mother.

Just as the mountain men loved their *boudins* of seared fresh buffalo gut and bone flagons of melted kidney fat all the more for the greenhorn's horrified gaggings, so did the tenderfoot's revulsion season the cowboy's tin plate of son-of-a-bitch. This was not because he ate it and the new hand refused, but because the true cowboy actually craved it. Son-of-a-bitch was not only delicious but chockful of nutrients his body wanted after a winter without a vitamin. And it contained that same edge of raw violence—the death of an innocent nursing animal—that lay at the bottom of the cowboy's ethos of survival . . . and resonated in the name of the dish itself.

If chili is conspicuously absent from early cowboy narratives, son-of-a-bitch is ubiquitously present. Euphemized as son-of-a-gun or "that gentleman from Texas," cowboys reminisced about it with genuine relish long after they had savored their last bite. It and not chili would have been the cowboy's symbolic dish right to today, if civilization—or, at least, the railroad—hadn't caught up with them first. For the closer it got to the ranch, the more the value of the cattle appreciated even as they stood. The range was fenced in, each calf branded and accounted for, and the dish suddenly too expensive to make.

More important, as ranching modernized, the smaller ones were driven out of business and the larger ones needed less manpower. A lot of men who still thought of themselves as "cowboys" were cowboying less and less, some not at all. If they remained cowboys, it was because that had always been less a reality than a state of mind.

Even in the heyday of the open range, cowboying was seasonal work. Only a few hands were hired permanently; most were let go at the start of winter when the bulk of the herd had been sold off. Once a cowboy was laid off, he wasn't a cowboy anymore to anyone but himself. To his employers and the world at large, he was now a drifter—that is, a vagrant—and no longer welcome. He had no choice but to head for town, and the bigger the town the better. In Texas, one of those towns was San Antonio—where the cowboy was to discover chili and eventually make it his own special brand of grease and gladness.

THE URBAN COWBOY—1896

[If] the cowboy had been depicted as he actually was—a mostly drab, hard-working, hard-drinking, illiterate, shabbily dressed, over-sexed, and unambitious drifter—there would have been little audience for [cowboy] movies.
    —BUCK RAINEY, *The Cowboy: Six-Shooters, Songs, and Sex*

So far as anyone can make out for sure, Anglo eaters first began casually consuming chili con carne in San Antonio, Texas, sometime in the second half of the last century. By the 1880s, chili began to appear regularly in contemporary accounts, both fact and fiction, of San Antonio life. Seemingly out of nowhere, chili con carne became a cultural commonplace.

At that time, San Antonio was a wide-open town: a cattle town, a railroad town, and an army town. It was the natural focus for sundowners, drifters, loungers, and hangers-on, a significant segment of the population and one always on the lookout for entertainment. Their hangout was the Military Plaza, just then the liveliest spot in Texas. By day it was San Antonio's municipal food market; by night, as Frank Bushick, an eyewitness, described it, it was

an open air bazaar for fakers, peddlers, and every variety of Bedouins of the night . . . The houses and saloon bars in the adobe buildings on the four sides of the square were concealed by thirsty humanity bellied up two rows deep.

The Military Plaza was also the home of San Antonio's fabled "chili queens." Some writers have misunderstood this title, since while these ladies did sell chili con carne (still a stew of meat, fresh chiles, and herbs), they did not specialize in it. In those days, the word "chili" referred strictly to the pepper, and their bill of fare was a collation of simple, chile-spiked, mestizo delicacies: tamales, tortillas, chili con carne, and enchiladas, served with coffee or *atole* (a cinnamon-flavored hot-milk drink, thickened with *masa harina*, the same corn flour used to make tortillas), and a stack of tortillas to serve as spoon, fork, and napkin. The food was cooked over a wood fire and served on trestle tables covered with oilcloth.

Diners sat elbow to elbow, eating a meal that could cost as little as a nickel and rarely more than a dime. Rich ate with poor, black with white, Mexican with Anglo in unique if sometimes uneasy harmony, lingering over their coffee to listen to the strolling guitar players and shrugging off buskers hawking tooled leather belts and holsters, cheap perfume, fake jewelry, and marijuana.

Young, attractive mestizo women using their flirtatious charm to coax some chili into the suspicious mouths of Anglo cowboys, who then find that they have acquired a taste for it—an appealing scene and one that might seem to reveal at last that momentous point in history when chili made its great cross-cultural leap. But neat an explanation as it is, it doesn't resolve the perplexing mystery as to why—of all the dishes the chili queens sold—*chili* would be the one most fiercely favored by Anglos. Nothing in the early accounts shows the faintest suspicion that this special love affair had already started to bloom.

What is notably curious about the accounts, however, is their emphasis on the moral rectitude of the situation. Flirtatious, yes, even vulgar-mouthed, these young women might have been, but this was only talk, for they were always fiercely duennaed by their mothers (who also did the actual cooking). No doubt this was true, but even so, not every mother has such control over her daughters—nor is virtue always so neatly apportioned between young and old.

In fact, I believe that this reportage is convention's way of asserting one thing to avoid having to notice another. Why, after all, did anyone *care* about the morals of these women? No special emphasis is put on the virtue of the *Anglo* chili queens. Although not often written about, they also existed. In Frank Bushick's nice phrase: "Anglo-Saxon aggressiveness asserted itself even in this limited field of conquest." In the late 1880s, the "queen of the queens" was a blond Anglo woman named Sadie. No mention is made of *her* mother, or of that of her nearest competitor, Martha, who later joined a "Wild West aggregation and dog and pony show" as a "genuine Indian princess, performing in a gaudy spangled dress."

Of course, none of this necessarily imputes accommodating morals. But given the demimonde atmosphere, it would have surprised no one, even at the time, if these women made themselves—at least on a casual basis—available. What titillated the contemporary readers of these accounts—and what we ourselves may hardly notice—was something else. The reason that writers insisted on the virtue of the mestizo chili queens was because their flirtation with their Anglo cowboy customers hinted at a far darker scandal than simple promiscuity—racial miscegenation.

Much is made of the cowboy's shyness before women, but it was a shyness reserved for Anglo women, or at least for those of good breeding.

As one knowing hand put it, "The old-time cowboy was most respectful of women as long as they kept their place. If they let down the bars, one of those boys would go the limit."

Of course, there were women who did let down the bars. These were rarely the ladies of Western fiction, the demure Eastern schoolmarm or the painted dance-hall harlot. To the cowboy, the respectable Anglo woman represented all that he had fled from—especially familial responsibilities—the settled life that ran counter to his restless, rootless ways. In truth, he rarely was able to marry even should he be inclined to, because cowboying provided him with neither decent income nor steady employment. He would have to make foreman or become a rancher in his own right before he could afford anything like respectability and a wife.

For the same reason—that he was chronically broke—a cowboy could enjoy the company of real, card-carrying prostitutes only on those rare, bust-out occasions when he rode into town with a pocketful of pay. Once that was gone—and it went quickly—the best he could hope for was to enter into a temporary alliance with a woman who—given her alternatives—would find him an acceptable companion. With her he found shelter, food, and as much company as he cared for until the ranches were hiring again. That woman, at least in the early years of cowboy life, was most likely not Anglo but mestizo.

This sort of alliance was a tradition that dated back to the time of the mountain man. Early explorers of the American West wrote with glowing astonishment of the beauty of Indian women, especially the younger ones, who—if the artists who drew them can be trusted—displayed their charms with an easy abandon.

The mountain men did more than contemplate. According to Bernard De Voto, not only was it "hospitable to sleep with a white man, of one's own initiative or at a husband's or father's suggestion . . . [but] prostitution was an integral part of Indian economy." Mountain men took Indian women on as "wives," not only for company over the long winters, but also because their skills and family connections proved highly useful. And these women prepared for their Anglo "husbands" their own Indian foods.

As common as all this was, it is a subject even today only obliquely alluded to. At that time, the Southwest was no less prejudiced about racial mixing than the South or, for that matter, the nation generally. But it happened . . . and surely it was in households such as these where the original Tex-Mex cuisine came to be, and where stews of fresh chiles and chicken or pork evolved into the dish that, this side of the border, it now is. The woman adapted her cooking to the pleasure of her man, who himself was just prosperous enough—especially in a cattle town—to afford the cheap cuts of meat the dish required and who had little tolerance for the inexpensive but foreign dishes his woman would otherwise be inclined to make . . . always discounting beans, which were already familiar cowboy fare.

Texas red, then, began its life as the natural child of a cowboy father and a mestizo mother, and this scandal is why the families of both parents kept the child at arm's length for so long. On the one side, there is the infamous repudiation by the *Diccionario de Mejicanismos*, which defines chili as a *"detestable comida que con el falso título de mejicana"* ("a detestable dish falsely described as Mexican"). On the other hand, we have the common insistence, even in Texas, that the dish is "Mexican" (even Gebhardt's of San Antonio, the first commercial maker of chili powder, still describes their recipe as "genuine Mexican Chili con Carne").

Most telling of all, however, is the common suspicion that there is something unrepentantly *vulgar* about chili, something stubbornly low-class. Its parentage was too clearly displayed to be missed and too scandalous to be admitted. Chili has always been the one Tex-Mex dish that refused to know its place. It wouldn't pretend to be Mexican nor would it adopt good Anglo manners. It was what it was, and when it grew up and found no welcome on either side of its heritage, it headed straight for the honky-tonk side of town.

THE JOINT

Chili joint—a small cheap restaurant, particularly one that serves poor quality food.   —*The Dictionary of American Regional English*

The chili joint appeared in Texas sometime before the turn of the century and gradually spread across the nation. By the 1920s, it was a familiar if seedy sight just about anywhere west of the Mississippi. It gave the nation a taste for chili and at the same time gave chili the status of ordinary American chow. Nobody eating a bowl of red in a chili joint ever had the illusion he was eating Mexican food. Here at last is chili as we know it: the chile peppers and herbs nothing more than seasoning; the meat, everything.

The chili joint itself was no more than a shed or room with some

minimal improvement: a counter put up and some stools knocked together, a blanket hung up to privatize the kitchen, which was often
nothing more than a woodstove. Kitchen sinks required plumbing, still,
in those days, in these kinds of places, an unheard-of luxury. Apart
from the food, the only necessary supplies were bowls, cups, and spoons.
No need even to hang a sign outside: CHILI 5¢, hand-lettered on a piece
of cardboard and propped in the window, would bring the custom drift-
ing in.

In other words, it was nothing much as an eatery. Let the Texas poet
Carlos Ashley, Sr., set the scene:

> Now it wasn't much to look at,
> Just a hole there in the wall;
>   No sign above the entrance,
> No fancy front at all.
>
> A stranger couldn't find it
> 'Less the wind was blowin' right;
>   Then he couldn't hardly miss it,
> Even on the darkest night.

A chili joint rarely sold anything but what the name claimed; the cook
had little in the way of cooking credentials. But a bowl of red didn't
require much culinary expertise, and the one produced in the chili joints
is still fondly remembered by those who ate there. The bad-mouthing
of these places was an attack on them as a *class* of eating place. It rarely
sprang from any kind of disinterested taste-testing (which is why it's
surprising—even depressing—to find the canard repeated unexamined
in a modern, scholarly dictionary of our native tongue).

Social critics at the time already thought chili a no-account food.
Even if they bothered to taste it, they were determined to dislike it . . .
and to damn the place that served it. What they truly objected to was
the clientele—and, for that matter, the owner himself, who was pretty
much the same cut as the drifters he was feeding.

Most likely, he was also a cowboy who at one point or another in his
career had turned to trail cooking. Chuck-wagon cooks didn't start out
in life with that as their ambition. They were cowboys who, through
injury, age, or just permanent stiffness of the joints, couldn't do their
regular work anymore. Somewhere along the line, a skillet was shoved
into their hands, and when it stuck, they had a new trade.

Unlike the regular ranch cook, a trail cook's position was temporary.
He was laid off with the rest of the boys when the year's work was done.

By that time he was glad to see the job go, even though the pay was good. He was up from before dawn to after dark, cooking in what were at best primitive conditions and at worst impossible ones, trying to feed a bunch of rowdy adolescents with tremendous and ungrateful appetites. The only whiskey allowed on the trail drives belonged to the cook, but it wasn't enough to cure his famous bad temper—or his tendency to suddenly walk away from the job.

For a trail cook fed up with his chuck wagon, the only trade he was qualified for—apart from washing dishes—was running a chili joint. Since he ate in them himself when he was at loose ends, he knew what was required and—perhaps even more important—how to handle the clientele.

Reputable restaurants didn't serve chili in those days any more than did respectable homes. The men who frequented chili parlors went there not only because they were hungry but because they felt comfortable in such a joint's other-side-of-the-tracks atmosphere. A chili joint was a man's place, like a pool hall or a saloon, and so eaters could consider themselves "sports" for going to one, and not the almost-paupers they mostly were.

Especially after Prohibition, there weren't a lot of places that welcomed a lounger with time to kill. In a chili parlor he could spend a nickel (later a dime) and nurse a bowl of red the same distance he used to work a beer. And later, when the Depression hit, there were a lot of men who turned that practice into habit.

But even if he was just hungry, a man with a nickel would rather go to a chili parlor than a soup kitchen, because it saved him his self-respect. Likewise, he preferred it to a restaurant, because at the joint the cheapest thing on the menu was the *only* thing on it, and so there was no slur in always having to order it. For his five cents, he got a bowl of red, with or without beans, a double handful of crackers to crumble over it, and a cup of hot coffee.

He also got companionship. Not necessarily company . . . that depended on the circumstances. Some chili parlors may have been convivial places, but most were like any other location where strangers congregate—barbershop, lunch counter, bus station—the majority sitting quiet, looking into the middle distance, and slowly picking through their thoughts.

No, they found companionship in the chili. Unlike the usual stew, half-decent chili holds its own kept hot on the stove all day; it relishes abuse. Because of that, there was no constant reminder in it that the best you could do was second-best. On the contrary. Unlike the usual lunch-counter item, chili had the stamp of individuality. Each bowl was different and worth contemplation. Finally, the stuff had some fire to it. A man could mutter to himself that he might take it twice as hot as this, and that gave him a good feeling. It reminded him that he was a cowboy. And if that was the best feeling he was going to get that day —it would do.

Chili joint: a small, cheap eatery that once upon a time served up bowls of grease and gladness to all who entered.

It's now gone, of course. Changing times and sanitation laws ran it out of town. It hitchhiked north and found work in places like Cincinnati. It endured. The rest is only history.

THE MAKINGS

There is no recipe for Texas red. The compelling logic of the dish is enough. Meat, fat, fire . . . merely to name them spurs the imagination on. This is true whether our appetite shares the mountain man's and cowboy's hunger or rejects it. Chili has the power to force us to come to terms with it. In doing so, our own bowl of red takes shape in our mind—whether it yields to its mestizo heritage, yearning for fresh chiles and fragrant herbs, or pulls us with it in that Anglo lusting after the searing grace of meat.

This quarrel is in chili's blood. The split between Anglo and mestizo visions of the dish is the tension that defines it, and neither side can hope to win . . . despite the penchant of Anglo chili writers to drag in spurious genealogies claiming the dish as Hungarian or Russian or German, to build whole theories around the presence of cumin, or to insinuate into the dish such exotica as olives or fresh coriander, lime marmalade or cocoa.

Well, let them. As we've said from the start, disputation is the heart of chili. Everything is at issue—how it is made, how it is served, how it is eaten. Nor is the argument only about parentage. Chili quarrels with the chili parlor for adding beans and—worse—as much liquid as it could get away with. (Chili recipes that call for more liquid than is necessary to merely moisten the meat—sometimes quarts of it—but are otherwise strictly to the old Anglo code—no onions, no tomatoes—most likely originated in some chili joint.)

Chili rails against us today because our guts just can't take the real thing anymore—even if we could find it somewhere. Texas red was originally made from the cheapest cuts of longhorn cattle, which, at the end of the cattle trail, were lean and notoriously tough (which is why the nation then preferred pork). This was beef that required lots of fat and long cooking to tenderize it. Now even cheap cuts of beef are tender but not nearly as juicy as the range-fed product. So chili is cooked less, and rather than suet, some kind of cooking liquid is mixed in.

All these changes are sensible, too, except to those who insist on keeping chili an antiquarian specialty. The important thing is to remain true, not to the ingredients, but to the argument—to be willing to listen and respond. Almost no one gets interested in chili by seeing a recipe for it somewhere. Instead, at one point or another, the dish stirs awake the cowpoke deep inside them, and the cowpoke's powerful nostalgia for free country and free meat. If they turn to a recipe, it is because they don't know what to do next.

But no cowboy ever made chili from a recipe. Most likely, he wouldn't have been able to read one even if he had a mind to. Instead, he would just trust his instincts and go after the thing. You don't need to know much about cooking to make chili—if you've eaten the dish, it pretty much explains itself. What you want instead is a plan of action.

Pick a nice cheap cut of beef or other lean meat. Trim away the fat, gristle, and bone. Cut it or grind it to a coarsely textured mass. Heat some suet or olive oil in an deep old iron pot and sear the meat. The moment it turns brown, lower the heat and stir in the seasonings, tasting all the while: chile for fire and flavor, garlic for pungency, Mexican oregano and cumin seed for zest. Salt to taste. Then moisten all this with a little meat stock or beer or well water, and set it simmering. Every hour or so, taste for flavor and texture, adding more liquid if it is going dry or stirring in a pinch or two of masa harina *if it needs thickening. The result should be powerfully scented and darkly red, tempting to the mouth, vibrant to the eye. The meat should have bite but be moist and succulent; the sauce should cling rich and thick as molten chocolate. Such is the perfect bowl of Texas red.*

Beyond this, all is argument; nothing is given. Each cook will be pulled by appetite and passion to a different course. They will vary amounts, substitute ingredients, devise personal strategies of making, swear by a particular battered pot and their grandpappy's wooden stirring spoon. In chili making, every cook tends his or her own pot. Even so, some pots of chili are better than others, and more often than not, the bad ones are concoctions of overachievers. "Keep things as simple as possible," Frank X. Tolbert said wisely in *A Bowl of Red*, adding, "Above all, remember that it's not the heat but the taste that counts."

Good chili is attained by the cook who has some sense of the character of the dish, and great chili when this sense is substantiated with knowledge about the ingredients themselves and how they balance off against each other. The essence of chile is meat, grease, and chile pepper—and it need go no further. Witness the testimony of Woody Barron, an old Waco, Texas, chili maker, who once

> tried cooking chopped beef in tallow [beef suet], adding only ground chilies and salt and found even this simple recipe a taste treat.

This means that no other ingredient should ever be added without the cook having some good reason for doing so. What follows is a list of common chili makings—the three mandatory items and then some optional ones, with the gist of why—or why not—they might belong in your pot.

MEAT. Beef, of course, and some others . . . venison makes a superb chili, pork a passable and lamb a controversial one. The treatment is what's important. Hamburger wasn't standard issue in the Old West; it was too prone to spoilage. Even so, in parts of Texas, butchers now offer a coarse "chili" grind that is generally popular. Ordinary ground meat turns to mush when subjected to long cooking. It also reminds some cooks of spaghetti sauce, with disastrous results. Better to take a weighty piece of fresh brisket or round, or a nice thick slab of chuck, and cut it down as small as you have patience for: half-inch cubes are the norm. Then, if you wish, add a portion of hamburger to serve as a thickener.

GREASE. See previous comments; if you still ride the range you've earned all you can eat. The rest of us should honor it more in the breach. There will be enough in the meat; sear that in just a little fat or olive oil and moisten with a little liquid (which see) instead.

CHILE. If it is meat that gives a bowl of red its substance, it is chile that gives it its soul, its prickly balance of fire and flavor. This is why access to a good selection of dried whole chile peppers offers an opportunity to advance the average bowl of red a giant step toward perfection. Ordinary "chili powder" is a predetermined mixture of powdered chile and seasoning; its familiar stale flavor and musty odor summons nostalgia and indigestion in equal portion. Use it only as a last resort.

Powdered chile, sold in packages marked "hot" or "mild," is a move in the right direction. However, while usually fresher-tasting than chili powder, it is made from standard commercial chiles and offers little variety in flavor. This is also true of "chile caribe"—a coarsely crushed version of the powdered "hot" chile, though hotter, since it still contains the seeds, which the powdered version does not.

The best powdered chile is made at home from a blend of different dried chiles, especially the milder ones. For while the fiery pods give chili myth and heat, the sweeter ones give it depth of flavor. An ideal blend would start with a base of some mild but rich-tasting New Mexican ground chile powder (Chimayo is our favorite). Then mix in some dark and wrinkled ground *ancho* chiles for their deep, earthy flavor, and perhaps some ground *pasilla* for a hint of smoky chocolate.

Once this flavor base is established, it's time to start adding the heat. The proportion of mild to hot powder in your own blend will depend on your tolerance of and liking for heat: start cautiously, expecting to use about one tablespoon of powdered chile for every pound of meat. Choices run from the two-alarm *guajillo* and *de arbol* to the three-alarm *pequín* and cayenne to the mouth-torturing *habanero* and African birdseye. These are the ones to use to take your chili to the limit.

Some sources (see page 486) offer these hotter chile peppers in powdered form, but they are more widely available in the pod. If you're using a few tiny *pequíns* for that extra heat, these can be simply crushed into small bits in the fist. But if you intend to use larger-sized, fiery-type dried chiles to augment or replace powdered chile entirely, their capsaicin-containing pithy centers, cross walls (veins), and seeds must be removed, or else the chile pulp will be too hot to use in the quantity needed to provide that rich chile flavor.

To turn dried chiles to powder, they must first be parched for a minute or two in a hot, ungreased skillet, to make the skin brittle and easy to crush. Shake the pan constantly to keep them from burning; as soon as the skins are crisp, remove the peppers from the pan and let cool.

Then crack the peppers open and discard the stem, core and connecting side walls, and seeds, along with any discolored bits of flesh. Break the remaining flesh into pieces and pulverize these with a mortar and pestle or in a food processor to a coarse powder, being careful not to inhale the dust. Sealed in a jar or plastic bag, the resulting powdered chile will keep indefinitely in a freezer or for months on a cool shelf.

Some enthusiasts prefer to use only fresh chile peppers, red or green, for their sweeter, fresher taste, though most makers find that chili without the harsh rasp of dried chile is no true bowl of red at all. But one or two fresh chiles can give your chili a distinctive taste. Prepare them thusly: wearing plastic gloves, pull them open, discarding stems, seeds, veins, and the central core. Break the flesh into pieces and mince it, with a very sharp knife, to a coarse paste. Stir this into the chili, one minced hot pepper equaling a tablespoon of chile powder.

LIQUID. Chili makers argue about both type and amount. Beer is a common choice, but shouldn't be an automatic one. Texans took Prohibition seriously and some still argue the only liquid that should come close to chili—in it or served with it—is strong black coffee. Others push for water, meat stock, or the abhorred tomato. Always remember, though, whichever you choose: like Missouri River water, chili should be too thick to pour.

THICKENER. This blends liquid and fat into a rich, clinging gravy. The two favorites are flour and *masa harina*. The advantage of the latter is that it adds a hint of sweet corn flavor to the chili and can also be sprinkled in pinch by pinch during the cooking without fear of lumps. Since the finer the meat is diced the more liquid it will absorb, some cooks grind about a third of their beef to use as a thickener. Others use cracker meal or—as the U.S. Army does—ground cooked beans.

Chili writer Bill Bridges once confided to me that a secret of cowboy chili was the addition of some ground pork skin. This works not as a thickener exactly but as a texturizer—giving the mouth something to chew. The cracklings from rendered suet are another excellent option.

GARLIC. Garlic sweetens and deepens the pungent flavor of chili without adding liquid (as do onions). It is a necessary part of the true bowl of Texas red.

MEXICAN OREGANO (*Lippia graveolens*). The authenticity of this herb in chili is evidenced by its presence in the earliest published recipes. Like cumin, it provides an unmistakable Tex-Mex flavor note. Mexican oregano—sometimes called Mexican marjoram or Mexican wild sage— is related to the verbena family, not (as the European one is) to mint, and their flavors have nothing in common. Mexican oregano is brassy-tasting and deeply herbaceous; like *epazote*, the flavor takes some getting used to, but—also like *epazote*—when you do get used to it, you'll find that nothing else will do.

CUMIN. If you note a vaguely sweaty aftertaste to your bowl of red, someone had an overeager hand with the cumin. It is undeniably popular with Texas chili makers, who sometimes use more of it than they do chile itself. Cumin has a crisper, fresher taste if the whole seeds are toasted before they are ground. To do this, toss or stir them continuously in a hot, ungreased skillet for a minute or two until they release their scent. Let them cool and then grind them to a coarse powder in a coffee mill or mortar.

SODA CRACKERS. A true chilihead considers soda crackers (or at least tortillas) as essential an ingredient of a bowl of red as the meat itself. Chili served on (or with) steamed rice is strictly family food. The crackers, by the way, should be large enough to give each eater the pleasure of crumbling them into the bowl. Saltines are both authentic and acceptable, but my own favorite chili cracker is the O.T.C. (see page 179).

FRIJOLES. Just because *frijoles* (beans; specifically, pinto beans) taste good with chili—and indeed they do—doesn't mean that they should be put *in* it. People who add them usually argue that chili otherwise tastes too rich or is too expensive (two ways of saying "all that *meat*"). This is the wrong solution to a simple problem. Better to use lean, cheap cuts of beef and trim away all visible fat. Chili made with beans can't be reheated, since the beans get sour and turn to mush. But real (no bean) chili requires reheating to attain its final patina of perfection. By all means, serve *frijoles* on the side. And if someone should serve you chili with beans, show forbearance—just pick them out and quietly slip them under the table to the dog.

TOMATOES/ONIONS. Tomatoes and onions worked their way into chili from a familiar Southwestern dish called *chile colorado* (or "red chile"). This phrase at one time referred to both a sauce of fresh red chile peppers and a stew made from red chiles, tomatoes, and onion, usually containing chicken. The two names, *chile colorado* and *chile con carne*, were then interchangeable, since early chile con carne recipes (such as *chili con cana* [sic] in *Mrs. Rorer's New Cook Book* [1902] or *chili con carni* [sic] in *The Boston Cooking-School Cook Book* [1914] were often simple chicken and chile stews. Since then, chili makers who interpret chili as a bowl of grease and gladness eschew them, while those more in sympathy with the dish's indigenous heritage embrace them.

AND SO ON. No doubt about it, a properly made chili is a *meat* dish. Greasy or not, it gives the palate pause. A meal this meat-heavy has an alkalyzing effect on our digestive system: we crave a little acid to balance things. This is why chile is added in the first place, but chile burns more than it bites. To give our digestive system that needed zing, some add vinegar, others lime juice, others tomato. Commercial chili powder can have a bitter aftertaste, tempting cooks to stir in some sugar to smooth the flavor out. Better to use powdered chile and let the long cooking do the sweetening.

Other things are added to the dish, some justified by their presence in Southwestern cooking in general, others merely to flaunt the perversity of the cook. In California, toppings are set out separately—grated cheese, chili beans, sour cream, chopped black olives, raw onion, pickled chile peppers, *ad infinitum* (thus, I suppose, the taco was born). However, none of these items plays any part in our story, since not one of them belongs in a bowl of true Texas red.

THE POT. Ideally, of course, this should be a big old cast-iron Dutch oven, heavy enough to break a weakling's wrist and blackened by years of campfire smoke. Most of us will have to make do with a solid, thick-bottomed pot that can sit on a low flame for hours, evenly spreading the heat throughout the contents within. No chili has ever been improved by the taste of scorched meat. Dutch oven or no, cast iron is the chili pot norm, and many chili cooks think chili just isn't chili without the metallic tang that leaches out the sides. Those who don't care for it can turn to enameled cast iron—it has the heft, the capacity, and the comfortable feeling of having been around awhile.

THE BOWL. These should not be purchased as a set from a fancy kitchenware emporium with a matching serving bowl, all colored fire-engine red. Chili should be eaten out of mismatched, off-white, chipped chinaware, typical restaurant issue. J. O. Mahaffrey spelled it all out years ago in the *Texarkana Gazette*:

> Chili must be served in a very thick bowl, the kind usually found in joints . . .
> The utility of the bowl is in direct ratio to its thickness. One must be able to
> grasp the bowl with assurance.

BENCHMARK CHILI

Every chili maker has a few recipes, written down or just remembered, that have helped define his or her own special bowl of red: read over, thought about, argued with, and then put aside. The following more-or-less historical collection serves this purpose for the reader, as indeed it has for the author. Since—with the exception of the last recipe, my own—these are meant to be meditated on, not cooked from, no attempt has been made to bring the older ones up to modern cookbook usage or to shrink army quantities to manageable size; that would only have destroyed their unique voice.

Listen to that voice—there are valuable lessons to be gleaned from it, many of them purely practical. Note, for example, how the later U.S. Army recipes use ground beans as a thickener or how Erna Fergusson softens the coarse edge of chile powder by first heating it in sizzling fat. But more than that, reading them through, notice how no recipe will stay in focus long. This is chili's stubborn refusal to hold still and let the shutter snap. Ain't nobody taken that boy's picture yet.

Mrs. Owen's Cook Book (1880)

This may be the earliest printed recipe for chili con carne, and it is surprisingly authentic, save for the suspect addition of "espagnole"— white sauce seasoned with ham, carrot, onion, celery, and clove.

Chili con Carne

This might be called the national dish of Mexico. Literally, it means "pepper with meat" and, when prepared to suit the taste of the average Mexican, is not mis-named. Take lean beef and cut in small dice, put to cook with a little oil. When well braised, add some onions and a clove of garlic chopped fine and one table-spoon flour. Mix and cover with water or stock and two tablespoons espagnole, 1 teaspoon each of ground oregano, camino, and coriande. The latter can be purchased at any drug store. Take dried whole peppers and remove the seeds, cover with water and put to boil and when thoroughly cooked pass through a fine strainer. Add sufficient puree to the stew to make it good and hot, and salt to taste. To be served with a border of Mexican beans (frijoles), well cooked in salted water.

Frijoles or Mexican Brown Beans

Boil beans in an earthen vessel until soft (four to eight hours). Mash and put them into a frying pan of very hot lard and fry until comparatively dry and light brown. Sometimes chopped onions are put into the lard before the beans are added and sometimes pods of red pepper or grated cheese.

U.S. Army (1896–1944)

Soldiers of the U.S. Army on the Western frontier had been eating chili since the war with Mexico (1846), but not necessarily in their messes. The first army publication to give a recipe for chili was *The Manual for Army Cooks* (War Department Document #18), issued in 1896. By World War I, the army had added beans; by World War II, garlic and tomatoes. This was a national pattern—Fannie Farmer's *Boston Cooking-School Cook Book* did exactly the same (see the editions for 1914, 1930, and 1941).

Chili con Carne 1896
(per soldier)

1 beefsteak (round)
1 tablespoon hot drippings
2 tablespoons rice
1 cup boiling water
2 large dried red chile pods
1 cup boiling water
Flour
Salt
Onion, chopped (optional)

Cut steak in small pieces. Put in frying pan with hot drippings, cup of hot water, and rice. Cover closely and cook slowly until tender. Remove seeds and parts of veins from chile pods. Cover with second cup of boiling water and let stand until cool. Then squeeze them in the hand until the water is thick and red. If not thick enough, add a little flour. Season with salt and a little onion, if desired. Pour sauce over meat-rice mixture and serve very hot.

Chili con Carne 1910
(for 50 men)

15 pounds meat scraps, trimmed of all fat
Rendered fat or oil
3½ ounces chile pods, ground
Chile powder to taste
Salt to taste
Beef stock
3 quarts small red beans, cooked

Chop meat into ½-inch cubes. Fry in the same manner as beefsteak but use a smaller amount of fat. Cover fried meat with about one inch of beef stock. Add ground chiles and chile powder, and salt to taste. Run two-thirds of boiled beans through a meat chopper and stir into meat mixture. Add remaining third of beans whole. When cooking, it may be necessary to add more beef stock to replace that lost by evaporation. Simmer for one hour or more until meat is tender and mixture is of proper consistency. When ready to serve, there should be just sufficient liquid to cover the preparation.

CHILI CON CARNE 1944
(FOR 100 MEN)

8 pounds chili beans, cooked
35 pounds meat carcass or 25 pounds ground meat
4 cloves garlic, crushed
1 pound fat
6 ounces ground chile pepper
2 ounces chili powder
2 gallons meat stock
6 ounces salt
1 no. 10 can tomatoes

The beans should be cooked until tender, but not split or mushy. Run two-thirds of the beans through food chopper, leaving the rest whole. Cut the meat into ½-inch cubes or run through meat grinder fitted with a coarse blade. Cook crushed garlic in fat until brown; add meat and cook until brown. Add chile pepper, chili powder, salt, and enough meat stock to cover. Cover tightly and heat to boiling; reduce heat and simmer until meat is tender. Add remainder of stock as needed. Mix ground beans, whole beans, and tomatoes with meat. Serve very hot.

One Hundred & One Mexican Dishes (1906)

This early California cookbook by May E. Southworth presents a chile con carne with pure Mexican antecedents. The use of pork immediately captures the attention, but note also the use of clove and a roasted tomato.

CHILE CON CARNE
(SERVES 4 TO 6)

5 dry red chiles
Black pepper, garlic, and salt to taste
2 cloves
1 tomato, roasted
1 pound fresh pork shoulder
Lard
Salt

Soak the chiles in hot water. Remove the stems, seeds, and veins. Put the cleaned chiles in a mortar and pound to a pulp, adding the black pepper, garlic, cloves, and grilled tomato. Cut the pork into chunks and parboil. Fry the chile sauce in hot lard. Then add the meat with some of its cooking liquor. Add a little salt, cover, and cook down until rather thick.

Walker's Red Hot Chile Con Carne (1918)

In 1918, Walker Austex was producing 45,000 cans of Walker's Red Hot Chile Con Carne (with beans) and 15,000 cans of Mexene Chili Powder a day in their new factory in Austin, Texas. But Walker had already been selling canned Mexican foods for over a quarter century and may have been the first to can chili. (Gebhardt's didn't start canning chili—as opposed to making chili powder—until 1911.) Walker's 1918 recipe booklet had recipes for "chile huevos" and "chili mac," plus something called "combination chili con carne"—one can chili minced with one can tomatoes. Et tu, Mexene.

GENUINE MEXICAN CHILE CON CARNE
(MAKES 1 QUART)

1 pound of beef cut in small pieces
1 pound beef suet or lard, ground fine
2 tablespoons of Walker's Mexene Chili Powder
1 medium sized onion, minced

Put the beef and suet or lard in a large skillet and heat, stirring until the meat is seared brown. Stir in Walker's Mexene Chili Powder and the onion and cook until the onion is soft. Then add water to cover and simmer until the meat is tender.

The gravy from this chile con carne is fine for macaroni, spaghetti and vegetables. If beans are wanted, use any good red bean. For instance—California Bayous, California Pinks or Pinto Beans. When these are not convenient, use French Red Kidney Beans. Boil the beans separately and add beans when serving.

Sometime in the 1940s, Walker's updated this rather fat-intensive recipe as follows:

(MAKES 1 QUART)

1 pound chopped beef
1 pound chopped pork or another pound chopped beef
¼ cup shortening
1 clove garlic, crushed
1 onion, chopped fine
2 tablespoons chili powder
2 tablespoons flour
Salt to taste

Fry the onions, garlic, and meat in the melted shortening until the meat browns. Stir in the flour, add 1 pint water and chili powder. Add 2 cans red beans or chili beans after 15 minutes of chili simmering. (It may be necessary to add more water while cooking.)

Ramona's Spanish-American Cookery (1929)

This California-based cookbook, edited and "modernized" in 1929 by Pauline Wiley-Kleeman, has three chili recipes. The one labeled "Texas style" contains onions, beans, and tomatoes, plus a whole cup of extra fat, half suet and half lard. The "California" version is also made with beans, but without tomatoes or onions. The first—and best—recipe has none of those things.

CHILE CON CARNE WITHOUT BEANS
(SERVES 6 TO 8)

2 pounds lean beef
¼ pound beef fat
12 large dried red chile peppers or 2 tablespoons chile powder
1 tablespoon paprika
2 pods garlic
2 teaspoons chopped oregano
½ cup olive oil
1 cup minced onion
Beef stock as needed
Salt and pepper to taste

Remove the seeds and veins from the chile peppers, place in sufficient hot water to cover, bring to the boiling point and then remove from the heat. Cool in the water, drain, and remove the pulp with a spoon. Cut the meat and suet in ¾-inch cubes. Heat the oil and fry the meat and suet to a light brown, then add onions and garlic and continue to cook, stirring continuously. Before the onions start to brown add the chile pulp and paprika, stir a few minutes, then add oregano, salt and pepper and sufficient stock to continue cooking till the meat is tender. Serve with beans or Spanish rice.

The Mexican Cookbook (1934)

Erna Fergusson's recipe has enraged Texas commentators ever since this book was published—especially the pint of ripe olives. (Chili with *mutton* was something they couldn't even bring themselves to speak about.) Made with the pork alone, it is a simple, tasty guisado of chile colorado. With the added beef or mutton, it becomes an already extravagant New Mexican dish pushed even further to satisfy the Anglo appetite for meat. It was in just this way that Texas red was born.

CHILE CON CARNE
(SERVES 8)

2 pounds mutton or beef
1 pound fresh pork
4 cloves garlic, minced
2 tablespoons lard or drippings
3 bay leaves
1 onion, chopped
1 quart ripe tomatoes or 1 large can tomatoes
1 cup chile pulp or 6 tablespoons ground hot chile
1 tablespoon Mexican oregano
1 tablespoon salt
2 cups pitted ripe olives

Cut the meat into small cubes. Brown the onion and garlic in the fat, then add the meat. Cover and steam thoroughly. Rub tomatoes through colander, add to meat, stir in chile pulp, and cook for 20 minutes. Add Mexican oregano and salt and cook slowly for 2 hours. Add the olives and cook for another half hour. Serve with *frijoles*. (If ground hot chile is used, mix with 1 tablespoon flour, stir into fat in which onions and garlic were browned, and continue stirring until smooth. Then add meat and proceed as above.)

Early California Hospitality (1934)

The author of this cookbook, Ana Bégué de Packman, was of Spanish-Californian descent, and her authentic recipe for *carne con chile*, which Californio cooks have always insisted should not be confused with chili con carne, suggests why Mexicans have disowned the latter dish entirely. In some versions of *carne con chile*, minced fresh cilantro is stirred in just before serving.

CARNE CON CHILE
(SERVES 8)

The meat being the main ingredient of the pot, and the chile only the sauce, it is insisted by the Californians that the carne (meat) be given the place of honor. The dish was called carne con chile and not chile con carne.

FOR THE STEW
2 pounds beef chuck
1 teaspoon salt
1 dash black pepper
2 tablespoons fat

Cut the beef chuck into small inch pieces and season with salt and pepper. Heat the fat in a stew kettle and add cut meat. Simmer until meat is tender.

FOR THE SAUCE
¼ pound dry red chiles
2 tablespoons fat
1 tablespoon flour or 2 tablespoons toasted breadcrumbs
1 clove garlic
1 tablespoon vinegar
1 cup ripe pitted black olives

Remove stems and cut open the chiles. Wipe clean. Place in stew kettle and pour 1 quart boiling water over them. Cook until pulp easily separates from hulls. Rub through sieve. This should make about 1½ pints of thick, red purée. Heat 2 tablespoons fat in iron skillet. Add flour or toasted breadcrumbs and the garlic well mashed in salt. Stir continuously until a light golden color. Pour in chile purée and vinegar. Simmer

15 minutes. Then add meat. Cook ten minutes longer. It is now ready to serve; garnish with luscious ripe black olives.

Texas Jail Chili (circa 1950)

Texas prison chili got its good reputation from Sheriff Smoot Schmid's truly fine recipe for the Dallas County Jail. Recently, however, a Texas prison chili contest was won by the Huntsville Penitentiary with a god-awful recipe that called for twice as much cumin as chili powder and "2 handfuls" of monosodium glutamate. In Texas, this is called crime deterrence.

DALLAS COUNTY JAIL CHILI
(SERVES 6)

½ pound beef suet, ground
2 pounds coarsely ground beef
3 garlic cloves, minced
1½ tablespoons paprika
3 tablespoons chili powder
1 tablespoon cumin seeds
1 tablespoon salt
1 teaspoon black pepper
1½ teaspoons ground dried sweet chili
3 cups of water

Try suet out in a heavy kettle. Add meat, finely diced garlic, and seasonings. Cover and cook slowly for 4 hours, stirring occasionally. Add the water and continue cooking until the chili has thickened slightly, about 1 hour. Serve plain or mixed with equal portion of cooked pink or red beans.

Houston Fire Station #1 Chili (circa 1970)

This is about as close to a good, standard, modern chili recipe as you could hope to get.

CHILI CON CARNE
(SERVES 8)

4 pounds beef brisket
3 garlic cloves, minced
1 cup chopped onion
4 cups boiling water
1 cup tomato sauce
3 tablespoons chili powder
1½ teaspoons crushed cumin
1 teaspoon salt
Hot red pepper sauce to taste

Cut 3 pounds of the brisket into ½-inch dice and coarsely grind the rest. In small batches, brown this meat in its own fat in a large heavy skillet over high heat, stirring frequently to prevent sticking. As each batch is browned, transfer it to a cooking pot. After browning the last batch, add the garlic and onion to the remaining hot fat and sauté until softened but not browned. Add to the meat. Lower the cooking flame and put on the pot. Stir in the boiling water, tomato sauce, chili powder, and cumin, and cook uncovered until the meat is thickened and "rich in flavor"—about 4 hours. Remove from the heat; season with salt and hot red pepper sauce. Serve at once.

OLD BUFFALO BREATH (1985)
(SERVES 8)

This writer's own. On the Texas range, firewood meant mesquite. Not only did the trail cook use it for his open pit cooking, but the ranch cook used it to fire his woodstove. Until it was replaced by gas and electricity, mesquite flavored rural Texas cooking with its distinctive sweet savor. The meat for this chili is seared over charcoal where mesquite chips have been set to flame (the taste of mesquite charcoal is indistinguishable from that of any other charcoal), which gives the resulting chili a haunting hint of smoke—without it tasting a bit like barbecue, since there is no onion or tomato in it, none at all.

FOR THE FIRE
Mesquite wood chips and hardwood charcoal
FOR THE RUB
2 or 3 cloves of garlic
1 teaspoon salt
Ground hot red chile

TO MAKE THE CHILI
5 pounds shoulder chuck
8 cloves garlic, minced
Salt
2 tablespoons ground hot red chile (see page 468)
2 tablespoons ground mild red chile (see page 468)
¼ cup olive oil
Beef broth
Juice of 1 lime
2 teaspoons Mexican oregano
1 tablespoon cumin seeds, toasted and ground
Small whole dried *pequín* peppers
Salt to taste
Masa harina

The chuck should be as lean as possible and cut at least 3 inches thick. Two or 3 hours before you plan to make the chili, rub the meat all over with a mash of crushed garlic and salt, then sprinkle it with the ground chile to lightly coat. Loosely cover it with plastic and set it aside.

In an outdoor grill, preferably one with a cover, fire up enough hard-wood charcoal to sear the meat. At the same time, soak a few handfuls of the mesquite chips in water. When the coals are covered with gray ash, spread them out evenly and scatter the damp mesquite chips over them. Then immediately set the meat over the smoke, about an inch from the coals. Cover the grill and adjust the dampers to maintain slow, steady heat. Let the meat sear for about 12 minutes (this process is meant to flavor, not cook, the meat) and turn it over to sear the other side for the same amount of time. Remove it from the heat, saving any juices on its surface, and transfer it, unwrapped, to the refrigerator. Let it cool thoroughly (about 1 hour).

When the meat has cooled, trim away any surface fat. With a sharp knife, cube the meat into the smallest pieces you have the patience for, saving all juices. Heat the olive oil in a large, heavy pot over moderate heat. Stir in the garlic and sauté until it turns translucent. Turn in the meat and all reserved meat juices, adding just enough beef broth to cover, or about 1 cup. Pour in the lime juice and sprinkle in the rest of the seasonings, stirring and tasting as you do. Crumble in a few whole *pequíns* or other fiery chile peppers to bring the heat up to taste. (But don't try to perfectly adjust the seasoning. It's easy to ruin a chili by correcting this too soon—the long cooking will smooth and sweeten it.)

Turn the heat as low as possible. Long cooking toughens, not tenderizes, if the pot is let boil. Every half hour or so, taste for seasoning, adjusting and thickening (with the *masa harina*—a teaspoonful at a time) after the first hour. The chili should be ready to eat in 3 hours, although it will benefit from a night's aging in the refrigerator.

Serve it steaming hot in large, heavy bowls, with an ample supply of soda crackers and a side of beans, but not much else except, maybe, hot black coffee or quart-sized glasses of iced tea or a few frosty bottles of Lone Star beer. And after a good long while, we'll push things aside, lean back in our chairs, and start arguing.

> "She must be pretty good."
> Frank looked over again as he took the water off the fire. "Buddy, it's all good. Like chili, when you're in the mood. Even when it's bad it's good."
> —ELMORE LEONARD, *Swag*

THE SEARED & THE STEWED

Why are chiliheads so insistent that onions, tomatoes, and beans have no place in the chili pot? Beans were familiar cowboy fare, and every chuck-wagon cook had his special *frijoles* recipe. The cowboy relished his can of tomatoes as the pause that refreshed long before he ever swigged a Coke, and he packed a couple of cans in his saddlebag to quench his thirst on the trail in preference to the stale, flat liquid from the chuck wagon's water barrel or the alkali-drenched sludge of the waterhole.* And onions would certainly have been familiar to him and without the "foreign" stigma of chile and garlic.

Despairing of finding any strictly economic or historical answer to this question, I dropped in on my old professor of contemporary mythology, Dr. Claudia Lévi-Strauss, an expert on such matters, and an ardent feminist and woman of Latino descent besides. Not unexpectedly, she had decided opinions about chili con carne.

"Disgusting stuff," she said, "the pure embodiment of rampant male chauvinism. It's only because you refuse to look yourself in the face that you can't see the whole ritual of chili making for what it is—a

---

* This was so much the cowboy practice that, as early as 1902, the novelist Owen Wister could observe in *The Virginian* that discarded tomato cans and sardine tins "were the first of her trophies that Civilization dropped upon Wyoming's virgin soil. The cowboy is now gone to worlds invisible; the wind has blown away the white ashes of his campfires; but [the empty tin can] lies rusting over the face of the Western earth."

species of culinary magic meant solely to banish women from the little boys' clubhouse."

She rose from her desk and went to the blackboard, where she drew a simple diagram, a pair of interlocking triangles, with a few slashes of chalk. Above the top one she wrote THE MALE; below the bottom one, THE FEMALE.

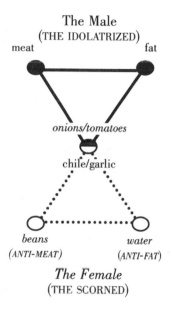

The Male
(THE IDOLATRIZED)

meat   fat

onions/tomatoes

chile/garlic

beans   water
(ANTI-MEAT)   (ANTI-FAT)

The Female
(THE SCORNED)

"It isn't by accident," she said, "that what is approved in your 'cowboy' chili—meat, chile, fat—and what is forbidden—beans, onions, tomatoes—come in units of three, since the triad or trinity is the basic structure of any myth. And *this* myth, the chili myth, we'll call 'the seared and the stewed,' since so-called real chili, man's chili, must be fried, not boiled. Men claim frying and grilling (which naturally require the best cuts) as their own province, leaving women with the tedious work of making pot roasts, stews, and soups.

"Water, of course," she went on, "is generally designated a feminine element, because it is soft and yielding. Following the same sort of logic, the chile is the embodiment of fire, which is a masculine element. Fat feeds fire, while water extinguishes it.

"Your mountain men, by the way, loved to drink melted fat because it was a conspicuous consumption of richness. Remember, at that time meat was lean and tough—so tender and fatty meat had a special premium. And since fat is also a symbol of wealth, men have always claimed it for themselves. When women were owned by men, it was good that they were fat; now that they have gained freedom, fat is denied them—to be desired, they must stay thin.

"That is why water is connected with everything forbidden in the making of chili—no water says 'No women allowed.' Beans are forbidden in chili not only because they are a kind of anti-meat—a cheap protein substitute—but because they are first cooked in water. They are accepted on the side—after all, they are the potato of the West—but not in the dish itself, because (as potatoes also would!) their presence signifies a stew."

"But," I interrupted, "almost all chili recipes call for some kind of liquid besides fat."

"True," she rejoined, "but men rationalize this by saying that it is for making gravy—an acceptable accompaniment to fat-cooked meat. And garlic and chile are used to give that gravy an especially masculine character. But when you start adding onions and tomatoes you can no longer hide the fact that chili con carne is really no more than an especially tedious kind of stew."

I ignored this bit of pique and pointed to where the two triads intersected, with chile/garlic lumped together as male seasonings and onions/tomatoes as female ones. "Why," I asked, "and why *there*, do the two triangles meet?"

"Ah, yes," she said. "A delicate topic. But it will make you understand how myth gains its power over our collective unconscious. Because we are all human, it is impossible to completely separate the male and the female. This is the point where, in this myth, the two commingle—the area of the 'seasoning.' This merging, of course, is highly sexual."

"Of course," I murmured.

She shot me a suspicious glance. "In my schema, the chile pepper symbolizes the main element of male sexuality—not only because of its pungent strength, which, naturally, the male seizes as a personal attribute, but also because of its color and shape. Are you familiar with the variant chile grown in Texas and politely called the 'Peter pepper'?"

I shook my head.

"Well," she said, "I can't say that you've researched your subject very thoroughly. Go look at one—it will entirely prove my point. In any case . . ." Here she paused, reached over to one of many crowded bookshelves, extracted a volume by Frederick Turner called *Of Chiles, Cacti, and Fighting Cocks*, and began flipping through its pages.

"Ah!" she said, "here it is. Listen to this." And she read:

According to a myth of the Cora Indians of Mexico's west coast, chiles were introduced into the world when the First Man shook them from his testicles onto the plates of food at a primordial feast. When the other animals had recovered somewhat from the crudeness of this action, they tasted the chile-seasoned food and blessed First Man.

She made a scornful noise. "Garlic is also masculine—*el chile, el ajo*—and is a symbol, if you like, of the secondary male sexual parts. Like the chile, the garlic does not lose its potency when heated and it is a flavoring that goes especially well with fats and oils—but not so much with water, which sours it."

"Onions can be fried, too," I objected.

"So they can," she replied, "but when they are, they let off liquid and lose their potency. No, the onion, with its hollow center and powerful but elusive and delicate fragrance is definitely feminine—*la cibolla, la tomate . . .*"

"The tomato," I said, "not only because of its liquidity, but also its warm, globular shape, at once tender and firm . . ." I held up my hands, cupping them as if supporting two large, round, soft objects.

"Don't get carried away," she interrupted tartly. "But I see you have the idea. Now, I will show you one last thing before I throw you out." She covered "chile/garlic" with her hand. "Replace the male with the female seasonings in the male mythic triad, and what do you have?"

"Uh . . . meat, fat, and onions and tomatoes," I said.

"Exactly. An ordinary Mexican stew . . . and just the sort of thing that a male chili maker would regard as sissy food, even effeminate, but hardly anything to fear.

"But now let's do the reverse. Look what happens when I cover 'onions/tomatoes' and thus allow the female mythic triad to appropriate the male sexual element . . ."

I said, reading around the triad, "Beans . . . water . . . garlic . . . chile . . ." I looked at her in horror.

She smiled sweetly back. "Yes. The most terrible of threats to the male chili maker, the total repudiation of his masculinity—and so the feminist's ideal culinary riposte—*vegetarian chili!*"

BOSTON, 1985 / STEUBEN, 1995

RESOURCES

OLD SOUTHWEST TRADING COMPANY (P.O. Box 7545, Albuquerque, NM 87194 • 505–836–0168). Nancy and Jeffrey Gerlach specialize in chile: fresh New Mexican green and red chiles during the harvest season (August and September), chile seeds for the gardener (over 30 varieties), and, especially, a wide assortment of premium quality dried chiles, crushed, ground, and whole—*chiltepin, habanero,* wild *pequín,* etc. They also carry a limited supply of such other Southwestern ingredients as *bolita* and Anasazi beans, *posole,* and dried herbs (including *epazote* and Mexican oregano). Price list is free.

THE CHILE SHOP (109 East Water Street, Santa Fe, NM 87501 • 800–983–6080). This Santa Fe firm sends out an appealing, hand-illustrated catalogue that offers assorted New Mexican dried chiles, red and green, including whole or powdered *anchos* and super-hot *habaneros,* and whole dried *pasillas, negros, guajillos, tepins, pequíns, cascabels,* and *jalapeños,* plus Dixon and Hatch red chile powders. You will also find chile-laden holiday wreaths, tin picture frames, Kokopeli gourd vases, and reproductions of the china, decorated with Mimbreño Indian designs, originally produced for the Santa Fe Railroad's Super Chief, as well as locally produced salsas, a hot pepper vinegar, and blue cornmeal.

THE GREAT SOUTHWEST CUISINE CATALOG (1364 Rufina Circle, Suite #4, Santa Fe, NM 87501 • 800–869–9218). While this shop offers a collection of hot sauces and other fiery foods from around the world, its most distinctive items are regional: fresh-frozen *posole* (shipped UPS air); Mexican vanilla; *tomatillo,* cactus, and *chipotle* salsas; *bizcochitos* (locally baked traditional anise-flavored cookies); red corn flour; Indian fry-bread mix; and, of course, whole dried chiles— including *chipotles* (smoked *jalapeños*), *pasillas, japones,* and others. Catalogue $2.

PENDERY'S (1221 Manufacturing, Dallas, TX 75207 • 800–533–1870). In 1890, DeWitt Clinton Pendery began packaging his own unique blend of powdered chile pods, cumin, oregano, and other spices, under the trade name "Chiltomaline"—the first "chili powder" ever marketed in the United States. Five generations later, his family continues the tradition, offering herbs, seasonings, Tex-Mex cooking equipment, bottled hot sauces, and, of course, an impressive range of powdered chiles, dried chile pods, and chile-spice blends, including "Pendery's Original." Catalogue $2.00.

The Great American Chili Book* Bill Bridges is unique among chili book authors in his generosity of spirit; he is truly interested in *everybody's* chili. And while he offers some sure-footed guidance of his own in the intricacies of the making of chili and to the tangled tale that is its history, these pages really spring to life when he ambles into someone's kitchen and crumbles crackers into yet another bowl of red. Bridges talks chili not only in all the expected joints but also in such unlikely ones as the home of Margaret Manning, book reviewer for *The Boston Globe*, and on Foggy Island in Alaska's Beaufort Sea, where Red Skinner makes chili with slab bacon and caribou meat for the oil men drilling on the North Slope.

Tag along and you'll begin to recognize chili as a resonantly American art form; a solitary passion that its practitioners can't help but make public . . . since few can eat all the chili they concoct and fewer still can bear not to show at least one other person how good their version is. Some of the recipes are terrific (Sam Huddleston's Texas chili, Casados Farms' *carne adovada*), others terrifying (mountain oyster chili) —but all are edifying, not least in demonstrating *ad absurdum* that universal American culinary rule: Never leave a good thing alone. Frank X. Tolbert and Joe Cooper, step aside. The original title got it right: *this* is the great American chili book.

---

* The book's original title. When it was reissued in 1992, the new publishers, Lyons & Burford, for mysterious reasons of their own, retitled it *The Great Chili Book*.

BIBLIOGRAPHY

H. Pearl Adam. *Kitchen Ranging.* New York: Jonathan Cape and Harrison Smith, 1929.

Mitford M. Adams, ed. *A Dictionary of Americanisms on Historical Principles.* Chicago: University of Chicago, 1956.

Ramon F. Adams. *Come an' Get It: The Story of the Old Cowboy Cook.* Norman: University of Oklahoma Press, 1952.

———. *Western Words: A Dictionary of the Range, Cow Camp, and Trail.* Norman: University of Oklahoma Press, 1944.

Africa News Service. *The Africa News Cookbook.* New York: Viking Penguin, 1985.

The American Heritage Cookbook. New York: Simon & Schuster, 1964.

Jean Anderson. *The Grass Roots Cookbook.* New York: Times Books, 1977.

Will Anderson. *Mid-Atlantic Roadside Delights.* 7 Bramhall Terrace, Portland, ME 04102, 1991.

———. *New England Roadside Delights.* 7 Bramhall Terrace, Portland, ME 04102, 1989.

Margarette de Andrade. *Brazilian Cookery, Traditional and Modern.* Rio de Janeiro: Libro Eldorado, 1982.

Jean Andrews. *Peppers: The Domesticated Capsicums.* Austin: University of Texas Press, 1984.

Trent Angers and Sue McDonough. *Acadia Profile's Cajun Cooking.* Lafayette, LA: Angers, 1980.

Sam Arnold. *Fryingpans West.* Denver: The Fur Press, 1969.

David Arora. *Mushrooms Demystified.* Berkeley, CA: Ten Speed, 1986.

Jim Auchmutey and Susan Puckett. *The Ultimate Barbecue Sauce Cookbook.* Atlanta: Longstreet, 1995.

John Baeder. *Diners* (revised and expanded edition). New York: Abrams, 1995.

A. L. Tommie Bass, Herbalist. *Plain Southern Eating.* Durham, NC: Duke University Press, 1988.

Balen Beale and Mary Rose Boswell. *The Earth Shall Blossom: Shaker Herbs and Gardening.* Woodstock, VT: The Countryman Press, 1991.

Edward Behr. "The Coast of Maine," *The Art of Eating.* Summer 1994.

———. "Potatoes," *The Art of Eating.* Summer 1991.

Ewald Bultman Bethany. "A True and Delectable History of Creole Cooking," *American Heritage.* December 1986.

Ray A. Billington. *America's Frontier Culture.* College Station, TX: Texas A & M University Press, 1977.

Mark Bittman. *Fish: The Complete Guide to Buying and Cooking.* New York: Macmillan, 1994.

Pierre Blot. *Hand-Book of Practical Cookery.* New York: Appleton, 1869.

Mia Boynton. "A Gift of Native Knowledge: The History of Russell's Motor Camps in Rangeley, Maine," *Motor Camps and Maine Guides: Two Studies.* Northeast Folklore, 1989.

Priscilla J. Brewer. *Shaker Communities, Shaker Lives.* Hanover, NH: University Press of New England, 1986.

Bill Bridges. *The Great American Chili Book.* New York: Rawson, Wade, 1981. Reissued as *The Great Chili Book.* New York: Lyons & Burford, 1992.

Cora, Rose, and Bob Brown. *America Cooks: Practical Recipes from 48 States.* New York: Norton, 1940.

Mike Brown. *The Great Lobster Chase: The Real Story of Maine Lobsters and the Men Who Chase Them.* Camden, ME: International Marine, 1985.

Fearing Burr. *Field and Garden Vegetables of America* (1865). Chillicothe, IL: The American Botanist, 1988.

Frank H. Bushick. *Glamorous Days.* San Antonio, TX: Naylor, 1934.

Jane Butel. *Finger Licken' Rib Stickin' Great Tastin' Hot & Spicy Barbecue.* New York: Workman, 1982.

Camden Connection Cookbook. Camden, ME: Cricketfield, 1989.

Frances A. Carr. *Shaker Your Plate: Of Shaker Cooks and Cooking.* Hanover, NH: University Press of New England, 1987.

Frederic G. Cassidy, ed. *Dictionary of American Regional English*, Vol. 1. Cambridge, MA: Belnap/Harvard University Press, 1985.

Sarah Leah Chase and Jonathan Chase. *Saltwater Seasonings: Good Food from Coastal Maine.* New York: Little, Brown, 1992.

Lydia Maria Child. *The American Frugal Housewife. Dedicated to Those Who Are Not Ashamed of Economy.* Boston: Carter, Hendee, 1832.

Rex Clements. *A Gipsy of the Horn.* Boston: Houghton Mifflin, 1925.

Sophie D. Coe. *America's First Cuisines.* Austin: University of Texas Press, 1994.

Robert P. Tristram Coffin. *Mainstays of Maine.* New York: Macmillan, 1944.

Arthur Coleman. *The Texas Cookbook.* New York: A. A. Wyne, 1949.

Rima and Richard Collin. *The New Orleans Cookbook.* New York: Knopf, 1984.

Harriet Ross Colquitt. *The Savannah Cook Book.* Charleston, SC: Walker, Evans & Cogswell, 1933.

Joe Cooper. *With or Without Beans.* Dallas. W. S. Henson, 1952.

Marion Cunningham. *The Breakfast Book.* New York: Knopf, 1987.

——, ed. *The Fannie Farmer Cookbook.* 12th edition. New York: Knopf, 1979.

Elizabeth David. *Summer Cooking.* Harmondsworth: Penguin, 1965.

Alan Davidson. *North Atlantic Seafood.* New York: Viking, 1980.

Sydney Dean. *Cooking American,* revised edition. New York: Noonday, 1975.

Dom DeLuise. *Eat This . . . It'll Make You Feel Better!* New York: Simon & Schuster, 1988.

Huntley Dent. *The Feast of Santa Fe.* New York: Simon & Schuster, 1985.

Jacqueline Denuzière and Charles Henri Brandt. *Cuisine de Louisiane: Histoire et recettes.* Paris: Editions Denoël, 1989.

Thomas F. De Voe. *The Market Assistant, Containing a Brief Description of Every Article of Human Food Sold in the Public Markets of the Cities of New York, Boston, Philadelphia, and Brooklyn.* New York: Hurd and Houghton, 1867. Facsimile edition, Detroit: Gale Research, 1975.

Bernard De Voto. *Across the Wide Missouri.* Boston: Houghton Mifflin, 1947.

William Hepworth Dixon. *New America.* Philadelphia: Lippincott, 1867.

J. Frank Dobie. *Cow People.* Boston: Little Brown, 1964.

Marshall J. Dodge, with Walter Howe. *"Frost, You Say?" A Yankee Monologue.* Camden, ME: Down East, 1982.

Eleanor Early. *New England Cookbook.* New York: Random House, 1954.

———. *A New England Sampler.* Boston: Waverly House, 1940.

Louis Woodbury Eaton. *Pork, Molasses, and Timber: Stories of Bygone Days in the Logging Camps of Maine.* New York: Exposition Press, 1954.

Linda West Eckhardt. *The Only Texas Cookbook.* Austin: Texas Monthly Press, 1981.

John Egerton. *Southern Food.* New York: Knopf, 1987.

Lolis Eric Elie. *Smokestack Lightning.* New York: Noonday, 1996.

Célestine Eustis. *Cooking in Old Créole Days* (1904). Reprint edition, Toronto: Coles, 1980.

Donald Everette. *San Antonio: The Flavor of Its Past, 1845–1898.* San Antonio, TX: Trinity University Press, 1975.

Fannie Merritt Farmer. *The Boston Cooking-School Cook Book.* New York: Weathervane, 1973. Facsimile of the 1896 (first) edition.

———. *The Boston Cooking-School Cookbook,* revised edition. Boston: Little, Brown, 1914.

Peter S. Feibleman and the Editors of Time-Life Books. *American Cooking: Creole and Acadian.* New York: Time-Life Books, 1971.

Debbie Fields and the Editors of Time-Life Books. *Mrs. Fields Cookie Book.* Alexandria, VA: Time-Life, 1992.

M. F. K. Fisher. *The Art of Eating.* New York: World, 1954.

William H. Forbes and the Editors of Time/Life Books. *The Cowboys.* New York: Time-Life, 1973.

Richard Ford. *Independence Day.* New York: Knopf, 1995.

E. M. Forster. *Two Cheers for Democracy.* New York: Harcourt Brace, 1951.

Betty Fussell. *The Story of Corn.* New York: Knopf, 1992.

Gebhardt's Mexican Cookery for Americans (circa 1965).

Nancy Moody Genthner. *What's Cooking at Moody's Diner.* West Rockport, ME: Dancing Bear, 1989.

Euell Gibbons. *Stalking the Blue-Eyed Scallop.* New York: David McKay, 1964.

———. *Stalking the Healthful Herbs.* New York: David McKay, 1966.

———. *Stalking the Wild Asparagus.* New York: David McKay, 1962.

Edward Giobbi. *Eat Right, Eat Well—The Italian Way.* New York: Knopf, 1985.

———. *Italian Family Cooking.* New York: Knopf, 1971.

———. *Pleasures of the Good Earth.* New York: Knopf, 1991.

Camille Glenn. *The Heritage of Southern Cooking.* New York: Workman, 1986.

John Gould. *Dispatches from Maine: 1942–1992.* New York: Norton, 1994.

———. *The House That Jacob Built.* New York: Morrow, 1948.

———. *Maine Lingo: Boiled Owls, Billdads, & Wazzats, or How Maine People Talk.* Camden, ME: Down East, 1975.

R. E. Gould. *Yankee Storekeeper.* New York: Whittlesey House, 1946.

"Grace Before Corn Meal," *Gourmet.* November 1957.

Josiah Gregg. *Commerce of the Prairies.* Reprint of the 1844 edition, unabridged. New York: Lippincott, 1962.

Jane Grigson. *English Food.* Harmondsworth: Penguin, 1977.

———. *The Mushroom Feast.* New York: Knopf, 1975.

Eugene H. Grubb. *The Potato: A Compilation from Every Available Source.* New York: Doubleday, Page, 1912.

Keith J. Guenther, Jr. "The Development of the Mexican-American Cuisine," *National & Regional Styles of Cookery: Oxford Symposium 1981.* Proceedings, Part 1. London: Prospect, 1981.

Rufus Gunn. *Something for Sergio.* London: Gay Men's Press, 1985.

C. Paige Gutierrez. *Cajun Foodways.* Jackson: University Press of Mississippi, 1991.

Richard J. S. Gutman. *American Diner: Then and Now.* New York: Harper Perennial, 1993.

Hazel V. Hall. *No, We Weren't Poor, We Just Didn't Have Any Money.* New York: Carlton Press, 1970.

Helen Hamlin. *Pine, Potatoes, and People: The Story of Aroostook.* New York: Norton, 1948.

Charles W. Harris and Buck Rainey, eds. *The Cowboy: Six-Shooters, Songs, and Sex.* Norman: University of Oklahoma Press, 1976.

Jim Harrison. *Just Before Dark.* Livingston, MT: Clark City, 1991.

———. "Poetry as Survival," *Antæus.* Spring–Autumn 1990.

Lafcadio Hearn. *Creole Sketches.* Boston: Houghton Mifflin, 1924.

———. *Gombo Zhèbes.* New York: Will. H. Coleman, 1885.

———. *Lafcadio Hearn's Creole Cookbook.* Gretna, LA: Pelican, 1990. A reprint of *La Cuisine Créole* (1885).

Maida Heatter. *Maida Heatter's Book of Great Desserts.* New York: Knopf, 1974.

Ulysses P. Hedrick. *The Land of the Crooked Tree.* New York: Oxford University Press, 1948.

John Hendrix. *If I Can Do It Horseback.* Austin: University of Texas Press, 1964.

L. Francis Herreshoff. *The Compleat Cruiser.* New York: Sheridan, 1953.

Karen Hess. *The Carolina Rice Kitchen: The African Connection.* Columbia: University of South Carolina Press, 1992 (contains a facsimile edition of the 1901 edition of *Carolina Rice Cook Book*).

Sheila Hibben. *American Regional Cookery.* Boston: Little, Brown, 1946.

Stan Hoig. *The Humor of the American Cowboy.* Lincoln: University of Nebraska Press, 1958.

Buster Holmes. *The Buster Holmes Restaurant Cookbook.* Gretna, LA: Pelican, 1983.

Roy Holt. "Frijoles: Texan Stomping Ground," *Hereford Journal.* January 1, 1946.

Richard J. Hooker. *The Book of Chowder.* Boston: Harvard Common, 1978.

Sue Hubbell. "A Reporter at Large: The Great American Pie Expedition," *The New Yorker.* March 27, 1989.

Cheryl Alters Jamison and Bill Jamison. *Smoke & Spice.* Boston: Harvard Common, 1994.

Ivan F. Jesperson. *Fat-Back and Molasses: A Collection of Favourite Old Recipes from Newfoundland & Labrador.* St. John's, Newfoundland: 1974.

Walter Jetton, with Arthur Whitman. *The LBJ Barbecue Book.* New York: Pocket Books, 1965.

Sarah Orne Jewett. *Novels and Stories.* New York: The Library of America, 1994.

Greg Johnson and Vince Staten. *Real Barbecue.* New York: Harper & Row, 1988.

Evan Jones. *American Food: The Gastronomic Story.* New York: Dutton, 1975.

Evan and Judith Jones. *The L. L. Bean Book of New New England Cookery.* New York: Random House, 1987.

Barbara Karoff. *South American Cooking.* New York: Aris/Addison Wesley, 1989.

W. Park Kerr, with Michael McLaughlin. *The El Paso Chile Company's Burning Desires: Salsa, Smoke & Sizzle from Down by the Rio Grande.* New York: Morrow, 1994.

Augustus M. Kelley. "Appendix on Chowder" (*Dwarf Conifer Notes*, Supplement VI), *Dwarf Conifer Notes.* November 1985.

Edward King. *The Great South.* Facsimile reprint of the 1875 edition. New York: Benjamin Franklin, 1969.

Louise Tate King and Jean Stewart Wexler. *The Martha's Vineyard Cookbook.* Chester, CT: Globe Pequot, 1971.

Gerd Kittel. *Diners: People and Places.* New York: Thames & Hudson, 1990.

Kathleen Olsen LaCombe. *It's Edible: My Maine Recipes.* Blue Hill, ME: 1988.

Elmore Leonard. *Swag.* New York: Dell, 1984.

Mary Lincoln. *Mrs. Lincoln's Boston Cook Book.* Boston: Roberts Brothers, 1893.

Eldress Bertha Lindsay. *Seasoned with Grace: My Generation of Shaker Cooking.* Woodstock, VT: The Countryman Press, 1987.

Allan Lockyer. *Clamdiggers and Downeast Country Stores.* Orono, ME: Northern Lights, 1993.

Sheryl and Mel London. *A Seafood Celebration.* New York: Simon & Schuster, 1993.

Janice B. Longone. *Mother Maize and King Corn: The Persistence of Corn in the American Ethos.* Ann Arbor, MI: 1986.

Nathan S. Lowrey. "Tales of the Northern Maine Woods: The History and Traditions of the Maine Guide," *Motor Camps and Maine Guides: Two Studies.* Northeast Folklore, 1989.

Pino Luongo. *A Tuscan in the Kitchen.* New York: Clarkson Potter, 1988.

Della T. Lutes. *The Country Kitchen.* Boston: Little, Brown, 1936.

Johnrae Earl and James McCormick. *The Chili Cookbook.* Los Angeles: Price/Stern/Sloan, 1973.

Bart McDowell. *The American Cowboy in Life and Legend.* Washington, DC: National Geographic Society, 1972.

Gwen McKee and Barbara Moseley. *Best of the Best from Louisiana.* Brandon, MS: Quail Ridge, 1986.

Gretchen McMullen, ed. *Foods That Made New England Famous.* Charleston, MA: H. P. Hood & Sons, 1946.

Blanche and E. V. McNeil. *First Foods of America.* Los Angeles: Sutton House, 1936.

The Maine Rebekahs Cookbook. Auburn, ME: 1946.

Len Margaret. *fish & brewis, toutens & tales.* Canada's Atlantic Folklore–Folklife Series # 7. St. John's, Newfoundland: Breakwater, 1980.

Matinicus Island Ladies Aid Society. *More Favorite Recipes from Matinicus Island, Maine.* 1982.

Robert F.W. Meader. *Illustrated Guide to Shaker Furniture.* New York: Dover, 1972.

Marguerite Melcher. *The Shaker Adventure.* Princeton: Princeton University Press, 1941.

Merrymeeting, Merry Eating: A Collection of Recipes Gathered in Maine. Brunswick, ME: Regional Memorial Hospital Auxiliary, 1988.

Ernest Matthew Mickler. *White Trash Cooking.* Winston-Salem, NC: The Jargon Society, 1986.

Amy Bess Miller and Persis Miller. *The Best of Shaker Cooking.* New York: Collier Books, 1993.

Joni Miller. *True Grits: The Southern Mail-Order Catalog.* New York: Workman, 1992.

Daniel G. Moore. *Shoot Me a Biscuit.* Tucson: University of Arizona Press, 1974.

Flo Morse. *The Shakers and the World's People.* New York: Dodd, Mead, 1980.

Marjorie Mosser, with introduction and notes by Kenneth Roberts. *Good Maine Food.* New York: Doubleday Doran, 1939.

Joan Nathan. *An American Folklife Cookbook.* New York: Schocken, 1984.

The New England Cook Book. Boston: Chas. E. Brown, 1905.

Lewis Nordyke. *Cattle Empire: The Fabulous Story of the 3,000,000 Acre XIT.* New York, Morrow, 1949.

Patrick O'Brian. *Joseph Banks: A Life.* Boston: Godine, 1993.

Sandra L. Oliver. *Saltwater Foodways.* Mystic, CT: Mystic Seaport Museum, 1995.

Frederick Law Olmsted. *A Journey in the Seaboard Slave States, with Remarks on Their Economy.* New York: Dix & Edwards, 1856.

———. *Journeys and Explorations in the Cotton Kingdom.* London: Samson Low, Son & Co., 1861.

Frank Oppel, ed. *Tales of the West.* New York: Castle Books, 1984.

Elisabeth Lambert Ortiz. *Caribbean Cooking.* New York: Penguin, 1977.

Lawrence Osborne. *Paris Dreambook: An Unconventional Guide to the Splendor and Squalor of the City.* New York: Pantheon, 1990.

Ana Bégué de Packman. *Early California Hospitality: The Cookery Customs of Spanish California, with authentic recipes and menus of the period.* Glendale, CA: Arthur H. Clark, 1938.

Clementine Paddleford. *How America Eats.* New York: Scribner's, 1960.

Linda Garland Page and Eliot Wigginton. *The Foxfire Book of Appalachian Cookery.* Chapel Hill: University of North Carolina Press, 1992.

Jeffrey S. Paige. *The Shaker Kitchen.* New York: Clarkson Potter, 1994.

Maria Parloa. *The Appledore Cook Book.* Boston: Andrew F. Graves, 1872.

———. *First Principles of Household Management and Cookery.* Boston: Houghton Mifflin, 1884.

Cindy Pawlcyn. *Fog City Diner Cookbook.* San Francisco: Ten Speed, 1993.

Haydn S. Pearson. *The Countryman's Cookbook.* New York: Whittlesey House, 1946.

———. *Memories of a Country Boyhood.* New York: Norton, 1961.

Angelo Pellegrini. *The Unprejudiced Palate.* New York: Macmillan, 1948.

Wilma Lord Perkins, ed. *The All New Fannie Farmer Boston Cooking School Cookbook*, 10th edition. Boston: Little, Brown, 1959.

Noel Perrin. *Third Person Rural: Further Essays of a Sometime Farmer.* Boston: Godine, 1983.

Lee Allen Peterson. *A Field Guide to Edible Wild Plants of Eastern and Central North America.* Boston: Houghton, Mifflin, 1977.

Green Peyton. *San Antonio: City in the Sun.* New York: McGraw-Hill, 1946.

The Picayune's Creole Cook Book, second edition (1901). New York: Dover, 1971.

Robert E. Pike. *Tall Trees, Tough Men.* New York: Norton, 1967.

Glen Pitre. *The Crawfish Book.* Jackson: University Press of Mississippi, 1993.

Gloria Pitzer. *Gloria Pitzer's Better Cookery Cookbook: Secret Recipes for Famous Foods from Famous Places.* Box 237, Marysville, MI 48040: Secret Recipes, 1984.

June Platt. *June Platt's New England Cook Book.* New York: Atheneum, 1971.

Sydney Poitier. *This Life.* New York: Knopf, 1980.

Jean Ann Pollard. *The New Maine Cooking.* Augusta, ME: Tapley, 1987.

E. Annie Proulx. "North Woods Provender," *Gourmet*. November 1979.

―――. *The Shipping News*. New York: Scribner's, 1993.

Paul Prudhomme. *The Prudhomme Family Cookbook*. New York: Morrow, 1987.

Barbara Pullen. *New England Recipes from Nana's Kitchen*. Augusta, ME: American Institute for Creative Education, 1982.

John J. Pullen. *The Transcendental Boiled Dinner*. Philadelphia: Lippincott, 1972.

Charles Ramsdell. *San Antonio: A Historical and Pictorial Guide*. Austin: University of Texas Press, 1976.

Mary Randolph. *The Virginia House-Wife*. (Facsimile of the first edition, 1824, with additional material from the editions of 1825 and 1826 to present a complete text, with historical notes and commentaries by Karen Hess.) Columbia: University of South Carolina Press, 1984.

Louise Dickinson Rich. *The Peninsula*. Philadelphia: Lippincott, 1958.

Don Rickey. *Forty Miles a Day on Beans and Hay*. Norman: University of Oklahoma Press, 1963.

Kenneth Roberts. *Trending into Maine*. Boston: Little, Brown, 1938.

Charles Roeder. "Notes on Food and Drink in Lancashire and Other Northern Counties." *The Journal of the Lancashire and Cheshire Antiquarian Society*. 1904. Reprinted in *Petits Propos Culinaires*, 1992.

Dora Romanzo. *Rice and Beans and Tasty Things: A Puerto Rican Cookbook*. Hato Rey, PR: 1986.

Sarah Tyson Rorer. *Mrs. Rorer's New Cook Book*. Philadelphia: Arnold, 1902.

John J. Rowlands. *Cache Lake Country: Life in the North Woods*. New York: Norton, 1947.

Lyle Saxton, Edward Dreyer, and Robert Tallant. Gumbo Ya-Ya. Boston: Houghton Mifflin, 1945.

Richard Schweid. *Hot Peppers: Cajuns and Capsicum in New Iberia, Louisiana*. Berkeley, CA: Ten Speed, 1989.

Natalie V. Scott. *Mandy's Favorite Louisiana Recipes*. Reprint edition of *Mirations and Miracles of Mandy* (1929). Gretna, LA: Pelican, 1988.

Natalie V. Scott and Caroline Merrick Jones. *Gourmet's Guide to New Orleans*. New Orleans: Scott & Jones, 1951.

Loana Shibles and Annie Rogers. *Maine's Jubilee Cookbook*. Rockland, ME: *Courier-Gazette*, 1969.

John Shields. *The Chesapeake Bay Crab Cookbook*. New York: Aris/Addison Wesley, 1992.

Amelia Simmons. *American Cookery*. (Facsimile edition of *American Cookery, or the art of dressing viands, fish, poultry and vegetables, and the best modes of making pastes, puffs, pies, tarts, puddings, custards and preserves, and all kinds of cakes, from the imperial plumb to plain cake. Adapted to this country, and all grades of life. By Amelia Simmons, an American orphan*. Hartford: Hudson & Goodwin, 1796.) New York: Oxford University Press, 1958.

Suellen Simpson and Margaret Welch. "Bean-Hole Beans," *Salt*. December 1975.

Alexander H. Smith. *The Mushroom Hunter's Field Guide*. Ann Arbor: University of Michigan Press, 1963.

Andrew F. Smith. *The Tomato in America*. Columbia: University of South Carolina Press, 1994.

H. Allen Smith. *The Great Chili Confrontation*. New York: Trident Press, 1968.

Raymond Sokolov. *Fading Feast.* New York: Farrar, Straus & Giroux, 1981.

————. *Why We Eat What We Eat.* New York: Simon & Schuster/Touchstone, 1993.

Leon E. Soniat, Jr. *La Bouche Créole.* Gretna, LA: Pelican, 1987.

May E. Southworth. *One Hundred & One Mexican Dishes.* San Francisco: Paul Elder, 1906.

June Sprigg and David Larkin. *Shaker Life, Work, and Art.* New York: Stewart, Tabori & Chang, 1987.

Jeffrey Steingarten. "Going Whole Hog," *Vogue.* September 1993.

Jane and Michael Stern. *Real American Food.* New York: Knopf, 1986.

————. *Roadfood* (revised edition). New York: Harper Perennial, 1992.

Tom Stobart. *The Cook's Encyclopedia.* New York: Harper & Row, 1981.

Bill Surface. *Roundup at the Double Diamond: The American Cowboy Today.* Boston: Houghton Mifflin, 1974.

John Taylor. *Hoppin' John's Lowcountry Cooking.* New York: Bantam, 1992.

James Tazelaar. *The Articulate Sailor.* Tuckahoe, NY: John de Graff, 1973.

Carroll F. Terrell. *Growing Up Kennebec: A Downeast Boyhood.* Orono, ME: Northern Lights, 1993.

Jude W. Theriot. *La Cuisine Cajun.* Gretna, LA: Pelican, 1986.

Sylvia Thompson. *The Kitchen Garden Cookbook.* New York: Bantam, 1995.

Terry Thompson. *Cajun-Creole Cooking.* Tucson, AZ: HP Books, 1986.

Henry David Thoreau. *A Week on the Concord and Merrimack Rivers; Walden; The Maine Woods; Cape Cod.* Ed. by Robert F. Sayre. New York: The Library of America, 1985.

John Thorne. *Simple Cooking.* New York: Viking, 1987.

Howard Jack Thorp, as told to Neil M. Clark. *Pardner to the Wind.* Caldwell, ID: Caxton, 1945.

Lon Tinkle and Adam Maxwell. *The Cowboy Reader.* New York: David McKay, 1959.

Frank X. Tolbert. *A Bowl of Red.* New York: Doubleday, 1972.

Calvin Trillin. *American Fried.* New York: Penguin, 1975.

Frederick Turner. *Of Chiles, Cacti, and Fighting Cocks: Notes on the American West.* San Francisco: North Point, 1990.

Tomi Ungerer. *Far Out Isn't Far Enough.* New York: Grove Press, 1984.

James Villas. *American Taste.* New York: Arbor House, 1982.

Mary L. Wade. *The Book of Corn Cookery.* Chicago: A. C. McClurg, 1917.

Waggoner, Glen. "34 Billion Baked Beans," *Yankee.* December 1994.

Wakefield, Ruth Graves. *Ruth Wakefield's Toll House Tried and True Recipes.* New York: M. Barrows, 1938.

Walker's Red Hot Chili Con Carne Recipe Booklet. Austin, TX: Walker's Properties, 1918.

Allie Patricia Wall and Ron L. Layne. *Hog Heaven.* Orangeburg, SC: Sandlapper, 1979.

James Walvin. *Black Ivory: A History of British Slavery.* Washington, DC: Howard University Press, 1992.

Julia Nott Waugh. *The Silver Cradle.* Austin: University of Texas Press, 1955.

Jack Weatherford. *Indian Givers: How the Indians of the Americas Transformed the World.* New York: Crown, 1988.

Jasper White. *Jasper White's Cooking from New England.* New York: Harper & Row, 1989.

Jessup Whitehead. *Hotel Meat Cooking,* seventh edition. Chicago: Jessup Whitehead, 1921.

Ruth Wiggin and Gertrude Hupper, eds. *Maine Coastal Cooking*. Rockland, ME: *Courier-Gazette*, 1963.

———— and Loana Shibles, eds. *All Maine Cooking*. Rockland, ME: *Courier-Gazette*, 1967.

William D. Williamson. *History of the State of Maine: From Its First Discovery*, A.D. *1602, to The Separation*, A.D. *1820*. Hallowell, ME: Glazier, Masters & Co., 1832.

Charles Morrow Wilson. *Aroostook: Our Last Frontier*. Brattleboro, VT: Stephen Daye Press, 1937.

Owen Wister. *The Virginian*. New York: Grosset & Dunlap, 1902.

Helen Witty. *Mrs. Witty's Home-Style Menu Cookbook*. New York: Workman, 1990.

———— and Elizabeth Schneider Colchie. *Better Than Store-Bought*. New York: Harper & Row, 1979.

Imogene Wolcott. *The New England Yankee Cookbook*. New York: Coward-McCann, 1939.

Works Project Administration, Writers' Program. *New Orleans City Guide*. Boston: Houghton Mifflin, 1938.

Yankee Magazine's Great New England Recipes and the Cooks Who Made Them Famous. Dublin, NH: Yankee Books, 1983.

Hugo Ziemann and Mrs. F. L. Gillette. *The White House Cook Book*. New York: Saalfield, 1915.

INDEX